Lecture Notes in Computer Science 4301

Commenced Publication in 1973
Founding and Former Series Editors:
Gerhard Goos, Juris Hartmanis, and Jan van Leeuwen

David Pointcheval   Yi Mu
Kefei Chen (Eds.)

Cryptology and Network Security

5th International Conference, CANS 2006
Suzhou, China, December 8-10, 2006
Proceedings

 Springer

Volume Editors

David Pointcheval
CNRS, École Normale Supérieure
Paris, France
E-mail: David.Pointcheval@ens.fr

Yi Mu
Center for Information Security Research
SITACS, University of Wollongong
Wollongong NSW 2522, Australia
E-mail: ymu@uow.edu.au

Kefei Chen
Dept. of Computer Science and Engineering
Shanghai Jiaotong University
Shanghai 200240, P.R., China
E-mail: kfchen@sjtu.edu.cn

Library of Congress Control Number: 2006937156

CR Subject Classification (1998): E.3, D.4.6, F.2.1, C.2, J.1, K.4.4, K.6.5

LNCS Sublibrary: SL 4 – Security and Cryptology

ISSN	0302-9743
ISBN-10	3-540-49462-6 Springer Berlin Heidelberg New York
ISBN-13	978-3-540-49462-1 Springer Berlin Heidelberg New York

Springer is a part of Springer Science+Business Media

springer.com

© Springer-Verlag Berlin Heidelberg 2006
Printed in Germany

Typesetting: Camera-ready by author, data conversion by Scientific Publishing Services, Chennai, India
Printed on acid-free paper   SPIN: 11935070   06/3142   5 4 3 2 1 0

Preface

The fifth International Conference on Cryptology and Network Security (CANS 2006) was held in Suzhou, Jiangsu, China, December 8–10, 2006. The conference was organized in cooperation with the International Association for Cryptologic Research (IACR) and the National Nature Science Foundation of China (NSFC).

The 1st International Workshop on Cryptology and Network Security was held in Taipei, Taiwan, 2001. The second one was in San Francisco, California, USA, September 26-28, 2002, the third in Miami, Florida, USA, September 24-26, 2003, and the fourth in Xiamen, Fujian Province, China, December 14-16, 2005. CANS 2005 was the first CANS with proceedings published in the *Lecture Notes in Computer Science* series by Springer and granted the success of last year and this year, CANS 2006 was also published in the same series. The Program Committee received 148 submissions, and accepted 26 papers, all included in the proceedings.

The reviewing process, which took eight weeks, was run using the iChair software, written by Thomas Baignères and Matthieu Finiasz (EPFL, Switzerland). Each paper was carefully evaluated by at least three members from the Program Committee. We appreciate the hard work of the members of the Program Committee and external referees who gave many hours of their valuable time.

Note that these proceedings contain the revised versions of the selected papers. Since the revisions were not checked again before publication, the authors (and not the committee) bear full responsibility of the contents of their papers.

In addition to the contributed papers, there were two invited talks: Moni Naor and Xiaoyun Wang.

We would like to thank all the people involved in organizing this conference. In particular we would like to thank the General Chair, Kefei Chen, the Co-chairs of the Organizing Committee Dong Zheng and Weidong Qiu, and people from the Shanghai Jaotong University for their time and efforts.

Finally, we wish to thank all the authors who submitted papers, and the authors of accepted papers for sending their final versions on time.

December 2006
David Pointcheval
Yi Mu
Kefei Chen

Fifth International Conference on Cryptology and Network Security (CANS 2005)

In Cooperation with
The International Association for Cryptologic Research (IACR)

Sponsored by
Shanghai Jiao Tong University (SJTU), China
National Nature Science Foundation of China (NSFC)

General Chair

Kefei Chen .... Shanghai Jaotong University, China

Program Chairs

Yi Mu .... University of Wollongong, Australia
David Pointcheval .... CNRS and ENS, France

Program Committee

Farooq Anjum .... Telcordia, USA
Feng Bao .... Institute for Infocomm Research, Singapore
Christophe Bidan .... Supélec, France
John Black .... University of Colorado, USA
Carlo Blundo .... Università di Salerno, Italy
Colin Boyd .... QUT, Australia
Xavier Boyen .... Voltage, USA
Laurent Bussard .... EMIC, Germany
Liqun Chen .... HP Laboratories, UK
Anand Desai .... NTT MCL, USA
Cunsheng Ding .... Hong Kong Univ. Sci. Tech., China
Steven Galbraith .... Royal Holloway Univ. of London, UK
Marc Girault .... France Telecom, France
Nick Howgrave-Graham .... NTRU Cryptosystems, USA
Marc Joye .... Thomson R&D, France
Kwangjo Kim .... ICU, South Korea
Kaoru Kurosawa .... Ibaraki University, Japan
Xuejia Lai .... Shanghai Jiao Tong University, China
Dong Hoon Lee .... Korea University, South Korea
Arjen Lenstra .... EPFL, Switzerland

Javier Lopez .... University of Malaga, Spain
Atsuko Miyaji .... JAIST, Japan
David Naccache .... ENS and University of Paris II, France
Kaisa Nyberg .... TU of Helsinki and Nokia, Finland
Giuseppe Persiano .... Università di Salerno, Italy
Josef Pieprzyk .... Macquarie University, Australia
C.-Pandu Rangan .... Indian Institute of Technology, India
Kazue Sako .... NEC, Japan
Berry Schoenmakers .... TU Eindhoven, Netherlands
Willy Susilo .... University of Wollongong, Australia
Vijay Varadharajan .... Macquarie University, Australia
Xiaofeng Wang .... Indiana University, USA
Duncan Wong .... City University of Hong Kong, China
Chaoping Xing .... National Univ. of Singapore, Singapore
Shouhuai Xu .... University of Texas, USA
Sung-Ming Yen .... National Central Univ., Taiwan

Organizing Committee

Dong Zheng (Chair) .... Shanghai Jiaotong University, China
Weidong Qiu (Chair) .... Shanghai Jiaotong University, China
Zheng Huang .... Shanghai Jiaotong University, China
Shengli Liu .... Shanghai Jiaotong University, China
Jie Guo .... Shanghai Jiaotong University, China

External Referees

Patrick Amon
Toshinori Araki
Roberto Avanzi
Pedro Bados Aguilar
Chris Charnes
Jing Chen
Xiaofeng Chen
Benoît Chevallier-Mames
Bessie C. Hu
Carlos Cid
Yang Cui
Paolo D'Arco
Alex Dent
Hiroshi Doi
Gerardo Fernandez
Jun Furukawa

Clemente Galdi
Changzhe Gao
Juan Gonzalez
Vanessa Gratzer
Gaurav Gupta
Goichiro Hanaoka
Matt Henricksen
Guillaume Hiet
Paul Hoffman
Chao-Chih Hsu
Xinyi Huang
Toshiyuki Isshiki
Erhan Kartaltepe
Hiroaki Kikuchi
Mehmet Kiraz
Yuichi Komano

Jérôme Lebègue
Tieyan Li
Zhuowei Li
Benoît Libert
Wei-Chih Lien
Hsi-Chung Lin
Liang Lu
Ludovic Mé
Miao Ma
Frédéric Majorczyk
Toshihiko Matsuo
Krystian Matusiewicz
Kengo Mori
Benjamin Morin
Sean Murphy
Satoshi Obana

Tatsuaki Okamoto
Dag Arne Osvik
Dan Page
Pascal Paillier
Kenny Paterson
Rodrigo Roman
Nicholas Sheppard
Martijn Stam
Ye Tang

Christophe Tartary
Isamu Teranishi
Xiaojian Tian
Rafael Timóteo de Sousa
Júnior
Eric Totel
Udaya Kiran Tupakula
Lionel Victor
Jos Villegas

Ivan Visconti
Kumar Viswanath
Huaxiong Wang
William Whyte
Robert W. Zhu
Shidi Xu
Guomin Yang
Dennis Y. W. Liu
Bo Zhu

Table of Contents

Cryptanalysis

Implementation

Steganalysis and Watermarking

Boolean Functions and Stream Ciphers

Intrusion Detection

Disponibility and Reliability

Concrete Chosen-Ciphertext Secure Encryption from Subgroup Membership Problems

Jaimee Brown, Juan Manuel González Nieto, and Colin Boyd

Information Security Institute
Queensland University of Technology
Brisbane, Australia
{j2.brown, j.gonzaleznieto, c.boyd}@qut.edu.au

Abstract. Using three previously studied subgroup membership problems, we obtain new concrete encryption schemes secure against adaptive chosen-ciphertext attack in the standard model, from the Cramer-Shoup and Kurosawa-Desmedt constructions. The schemes obtained are quite efficient. In fact, the Cramer-Shoup derived schemes are more efficient than the previous schemes from this construction, including the Cramer-Shoup cryptosystem, when long messages are considered. The hybrid variants are even more efficient, with a smaller number of exponentiations and a shorter ciphertext than the Kurosawa-Desmedt Decisional Diffie-Hellman based scheme.

Keywords: public key encryption, chosen ciphertext security, Cramer-Shoup framework, subgroup membership problems, hybrid encryption.

1 Introduction

The underlying security goal for a public key encryption scheme is to guarantee that no partial information about a plaintext message is revealed from its ciphertext, a notion often called indistinguishability of encryptions. Indistinguishability against adaptive chosen ciphertext attack (IND-CCA), where an adversary is given the capability to decrypt ciphertexts of his choice, with the exception of a target ciphertext, is considered to be the correct notion of security for general-purpose public key encryption schemes. We shall refer to schemes that achieve this level of security as CCA-secure schemes.

We present several practical, concrete encryption schemes that are proven CCA-secure in the standard model each based on the difficulty of a particular subgroup membership problem. Several of these schemes are more efficient than previous CCA-secure schemes, and all schemes rely on different problems than have previously been used for CCA-schemes. We have used three subgroup membership problems previously studied in the literature: the subgroup membership problem discussed by González-Nieto, Boyd and Dawson [6], the r-th residue problem [8], and Okamoto and Uchiyama's [9] p-subgroup problem.

Cramer and Shoup [1] proposed the first encryption scheme that was simultaneously practical and CCA-secure under standard intractability assumptions. Cramer and Shoup [3] later generalised their encryption scheme to give a

D. Pointcheval, Y. Mu, and K. Chen (Eds.): CANS 2006, LNCS 4301, pp. 1–18, 2006.

framework for constructing CCA-secure encryption schemes from general subgroup membership problems and *hash proof systems* (HPS). Accompanying their framework, Cramer and Shoup also described three instantiations of the framework using three subgroup membership problems, namely Decisional Diffie-Hellman, Decisional Composite Residuosity [10] and the classical Quadratic Residuosity problem. Kurosawa and Desmedt [7] later presented an efficient hybrid encryption scheme based on the Cramer-Shoup cryptosystem, as well as a generalised construction of CCA-secure hybrid encryption schemes from the HPS primitive introduced by Cramer and Shoup.

Motivation and Contribution. The Cramer-Shoup construction is an important development in the area of chosen-ciphertext security for public key encryption. However, their general construction is quite complicated, and developing schemes requires a strong understanding of how the construction works, and the steps involved applying it concretely. We believe that understanding in this case is best achieved through example, and our hope is that by applying the construction to a number of different subgroup membership problems, and detailing the steps taken, the process of deriving new schemes will become clearer.

Of independent interest are the actual schemes obtained by applying both the Cramer-Shoup and Kurosawa-Desmedt to the three previously proposed subgroup membership problems. For the Cramer-Shoup construction, the resulting encryption schemes are in fact more efficient than the schemes presented by Cramer and Shoup, including the Cramer-Shoup cryptosystem, when the encryption of long messages is considered. The hybrid schemes obtained by applying the Kurosawa-Desmedt construction to the same subgroup membership problems, are even more efficient. In fact, the number of exponentiations and the size of the ciphertexts are smaller than the previous DDH-based hybrid scheme.

Related Work. Gjøsteen [5] discussed symmetric subgroup membership (SSM) problems and described an instantiation of the Cramer-Shoup framework specific for such problems. A symmetric subgroup membership problem considers a group X and non-trivial subgroups L and $\tilde{L}$ such that $X = L\tilde{L}$, $L \cap \tilde{L} = \{1\}$. It is said to be hard if distinguishing elements of L from elements of $X \backslash L$, and elements of $\tilde{L}$ from elements of $X \backslash \tilde{L}$ are both hard problems. Gjøsteen also showed that the decisional Diffie-Hellman (DDH) problem and the symmetric subgroup membership problem are related such that SSM is not harder than DDH. In other words, the difficulty of SSM implies the difficulty of DDH. Although Gjøsteen showed the general encryption scheme for SSMs, we analyse instances of subgroup membership problems and the resulting concrete schemes obtained.

2   Preliminaries

If x is an integer, we denote the bit length of x as $|x|$. For a set S, we denote the order of S as $|S|$. We denote by $x \in_R S$ the act of sampling x from S uniformly at random. The notation G_α is used to denote a group of order α.

We say that two distributions X and Y on a set S are β-close if the distance between them is at most β. The distance between distributions X and Y is defined as

$$Dist(X,Y) = \frac{1}{2} \sum_{s \in S} |Pr[X = s] - Pr[Y = s]|.$$

3   Chosen-Ciphertext Security

3.1   The Cramer-Shoup Construction

Cramer and Shoup introduced the notions of universal projective hash families and universal hash proof systems. Let us now summarise the main notions and definitions from Cramer and Shoup's work. For further details, we refer the reader to the full version of their paper [2].

A hash proof system relies on a finite set X, or more formally a distribution on sets, a subset $L \subset X$ with an associated witness set W and a relation $R \subset X \times W$. A pair $(x, w) \in R$ allows one to show that an element $x \in X$ is also in L. We say that $w \in W$ is a witness for $x \in L$. The underlying assumption is that it is infeasible to distinguish between a random element in L and a random element in $X \backslash L$. This is called the *subset membership problem*.

The hash proof system associates an instance of a subset membership problem with a family of keyed hash functions H that operate on X, called a *projective hash family*. It is required that given a hash key k and an element $x \in X$, the value of the function $H_k(x)$ can be computed. It is also required that this family of functions be *projective*, that is, given only an additional key $\alpha(k)$ and a subgroup element $x \in L$, the value $H_k(x)$ is uniquely determined. Moreover, it is a requirement that given $\alpha(k)$ and a pair $(x, w) \in R$, that $H_k(x)$ can be computed efficiently (without k). The hash proof system also requires that hash keys and witness elements can be efficiently sampled uniformly (or close to uniformly) from the hash key set K and the witness set W, respectively.

Let $\mathbf{H} = (H, K, X, L, \Pi, S, \alpha)$ be such a projective hash family, where K, Π and S are finite sets, and X and L are also finite sets as defined above. The functions H and α are defined such that $H_{k \in K} : X \to \Pi$ and $\alpha : K \to S$.

A projective hash family is ϵ-*universal* if given the projection key $s = \alpha(k)$, even though $H_k(x)$ is completely determined for $x \in L$, for any $x \in X \backslash L$, one can guess $H_k(x)$ with probability at most ϵ (without knowledge of k).

A projective hash family is ϵ-*universal$_2$* if given $s = \alpha(k)$ and $H_k(x^*)$ for some $x^* \in X \backslash L$, even though $H_k(x)$ is completely determined for $x \in L$, for any $x \in X \backslash L$, one can guess $H_k(x)$ with probability at most ϵ (without knowledge of k).

A projective hash family is ϵ-*smooth* if the distributions $U = (x, s, \pi')$, $V = (x, s, \pi)$, where $x \in_R X \backslash L$, $s = \alpha(k)$ for $k \in_R K, \pi' \in_R \Pi, \pi = H_k(x)$, are ϵ-close.

It is also useful to describe an *extended* hash proof system, which associates the subset membership problem with a projective hash family $\hat{\mathbf{H}} = (H, K, X \times E, L \times E, \Pi, S, \alpha)$ for a finite set E.

A hash proof system is *strongly* universal (respectively, universal$_2$, smooth) if the associated projective hash family is also ϵ-universal (respectively, ϵ-universal$_2$, ϵ-smooth) for negligible ϵ, or more formally $\epsilon(\ell)$ is a negligible function in security parameter ℓ.

The Cramer-Shoup framework constructs a CCA-secure encryption scheme given a ϵ-smooth hash proof system $\mathbf{P}$ with associated projective hash family $\mathbf{H} = (H, K, X, L, \Pi, S, \alpha)$, and a $\hat{e}$-universal$_2$ extended hash proof system $\hat{\mathbf{P}}$ with associated projective hash family $\hat{\mathbf{H}} = (\hat{H}, \hat{K}, X \times \Pi, L \times \Pi, \hat{\Pi}, \hat{S}, \hat{\alpha})$ for the subset membership problem (X, L, W, R), where ϵ and $\hat{e}$ are negligible (or more formally, negligible functions of the security parameter). The construction requires that Π is an abelian group, which we will notate additively in the encryption scheme below. Note also that the message space is Π.

Key Generation

1. $k \in_R K, \hat{k} \in_R \hat{K}$
2. $s = \alpha(k) \in S$
3. $\hat{s} = \hat{\alpha}(\hat{k}) \in S$
4. pk $= (s, \hat{s})$.
5. sk $= (k, \hat{k})$.

Encryption of $m \in \Pi$

1. $(x, w) \in_R R$
2. $\pi = H_k(x) \in \Pi$ given (s, x, w)
3. $e = m + \pi \in \Pi$.
4. $\hat{\pi} = \hat{H}_{\hat{k}}(x, e) \in \hat{\Pi}$ given (s, x, e)
5. ciphertext is $(x, e, \hat{\pi})$

Decryption of $(x, e, \hat{\pi})$

1. $\hat{\pi}' = \hat{H}_{\hat{k}}(x, e) \in \hat{\Pi}$ given (x, e, k)
2. if $\hat{\pi} \neq \hat{\pi}'$ then halt
3. $\pi = H_k(x) \in \Pi$ given (x, k)
4. $m = e - \pi \in \Pi$

Cramer and Shoup show that if there exists an adversary that has non-negligible advantage in an adaptive chosen ciphertext attack, then a distinguisher for L that has non-negligible advantage can be constructed. In other words, they show that the above scheme is secure against adaptive chosen ciphertext attack provided that the underlying subset membership problem is hard.

3.2 The Kurosawa-Desmedt Hybrid Construction

Kurosawa and Desmedt [7] showed that a hash proof system that associates a subset membership problem with a strongly universal$_2$ projective hash family can be used to construct efficient hybrid encryption schemes. Let $\mathbf{P}$ be a hash proof system that associates the strongly universal$_2$ projective hash family $\mathbf{H} = (H, K, X, L, \Pi, S, \alpha)$ with the subset membership problem (X, L, W, R). Let $SKE = (E, D)$ be a semantically secure symmetric-key encryption scheme, let MAC be a one-time secure message authentication code, and KDF a key derivation function (whose output is hard to distinguish from random). Kurosawa and Desmedt prove that the following hybrid encryption schemes is CCA-secure.

Key Generation

1. $k \in_R K$
2. $s = \alpha(k) \in S$
3. pk $= s$.
4. sk $= k$.

Encryption of $m \in \Pi$

1. $(x, w) \in_R R$
2. $\pi = H_k(x) \in \Pi$ given (s, x, w)
3. $(K', K) = KDF(\pi)$
4. $\chi = E_K(m)$
5. $t = MAC_{K'}(\chi)$
6. ciphertext is (x, χ, t)

Decryption of (x, χ, t)

1. $\pi = H_k(x)$ given (x, k)
2. $(K', K) = KDF(\pi)$
3. If $t \neq MAC_{K'}(\chi)$ then halt
4. $m = D_K(\chi)$

A concrete hybrid encryption scheme based on the HPS used to construct the Cramer-Shoup cryptosystem was proposed and proven secure under the Decisional Diffie-Hellman assumption when used with information theoretic KDF and MAC. Gennaro and Shoup [4] later showed that relying on these information theoretic tools eliminates the efficiency gain of the hybrid scheme versus the original Cramer-Shoup scheme, and gave a different proof that instead relies on any computationally secure KDF and MAC.

4 Concrete CCA-Secure Schemes from Subgroup Membership Problems

We describe concrete encryption schemes obtained by applying the Cramer-Shoup and the Kurosawa-Desmedt constructions to three particular subgroup membership problems which have been studied previously in the literature.

4.1 The GBD Subgroup Membership Problem

The GBD cryptosystem [6] is semantically secure based on the difficulty of the following subgroup membership problem. Consider primes p,q_0,q_1 such that $p = 2N + 1$ where $N = q_0 q_1$ and $|q_0| = |q_1| = \lambda$. The set of quadratic residues modulo p is a cyclic subgroup of order N of the multiplicative group $\mathbb{Z}_p^*$. Let this group be X, and let L be the subgroup of X with order q_0. The GBD subgroup membership problem is to distinguish elements of L from elements of $X \backslash L$. We can also view these groups by considering that $\mathbb{Z}_p^*$ can be viewed as an internal direct product of subgroups:

$$\mathbb{Z}_p^* = G_{q_0} \cdot G_{q_1} \cdot T$$

where T is the subgroup $\{-1, 1\}$. Then $X = G_{q_0} \cdot G_{q_1}$ and $L = G_{q_0}$. Indeed this is an instance of the symmetric subgroup membership problem as discussed by Gjøsteen [5].

Constructing a CCA-secure Encryption Scheme. We now apply the Cramer-Shoup construction to this subgroup membership problem, which is also the application of the Gjøsteen's construction [5]. To find a generator g for L, one can select μ at random from $\mathbb{Z}_p^*$ and compute $g = \mu^{2q_1}$. It will be a generator with overwhelming probability. Let $W_* = \{0, ..., q_0 - 1\}$. One can sample an element x from L with a corresponding witness $w \in W$ by choosing w at random in W and computing $x = g^w$. However, in practice q_0 is kept private and w must instead be selected from $W = \{0, ..., N - 1\}$.

Now, let $K = \{0, ..., N - 1\}$ and define $H_{k \in K}(x) = x^k$ and $\alpha(k) = H_k(g)$. Hence $\Pi = X$ and $S = L$. It is easy to see that $\mathbf{H} = (H, K, X, L, X, L, \alpha)$ is projective since given $s = \alpha(k) = g^k$ and $x = g^w$, $H_k(x) = x^k = s^w$ is uniquely determined. By Lemma 1 in [5], $\mathbf{H}$ is $1/q_1$-smooth. Since K can be sampled uniformly, and the required algorithms for computing H_k are available, we have a strongly smooth hash proof system $\mathbf{P}$ that associates the GBD subgroup membership problem with $\mathbf{H}$ when q_1 is large.

To obtain a strongly universal$_2$ hash proof system $\hat{\mathbf{P}}$, let us first suppose that for some sufficiently large n, there is an available injective function $\Gamma : X \times X \to R^n$ for $R = \{0, ..., 2^\lambda - 1\}$. Consider the extended projective hash family $\hat{\mathbf{H}} = (\hat{H}, K^{n+1}, X \times X, L \times X, X, L^{n+1}, \hat{\alpha})$ where for $(\tilde{k}, \hat{k}_1, ..., \hat{k}_n) \in K^{n+1}$ and $(\gamma_1, ..., \gamma_n) = \Gamma(x, e)$, where we define

- $\hat{H}_{\tilde{k}, \hat{k}_1, ..., \hat{k}_n}(x, e) = H_{\tilde{k}}(x) \prod_{i=1}^n H_{\hat{k}_i}(x)^{\gamma_i} = x^{\tilde{k} + \sum_{i=1}^n \hat{k}_i \gamma_i}$
- $\hat{\alpha}(\tilde{k}, \hat{k}_1, ..., \hat{k}_n) = (\alpha(\tilde{k}), \alpha(\hat{k}_1), ..., \alpha(\hat{k}_n)) = (g^{\tilde{k}}, g^{\hat{k}_1}, ..., g^{\hat{k}_n})$

By theorem 3 in [3], $\hat{\mathbf{H}}$ is $1/q_1$-universal$_2$. It is easy to show that the required algorithms are available for the resulting strongly universal$_2$ hash proof system $\hat{\mathbf{P}}$ for $\hat{\mathbf{H}}$. We now have what is necessary to build a CCA-secure encryption scheme based on this problem.

Since we now have a strongly smooth HPS $\mathbf{P}$, and a strong universal$_2$ HPS $\hat{\mathbf{P}}$, applying the Cramer-Shoup construction will give us a CCA-secure encryption scheme. However, to improve efficiency, we can replace the injective function $\Gamma : X \times X \to R^n$ by a collision resistant hash function $h : X \times X \to \{0, 1\}^m$ (such as SHA-1 where $m = 160$) so that the n can be much smaller. Indeed, we can choose $n = 1$ and the resulting scheme will still be secure against chosen-ciphertext attack. The resulting encryption scheme is as follows:

The CS-GBD encryption scheme. For the description below, $p = 2N + 1$ is prime where $N = q_0 q_1$ for primes q_0, q_1 of bit length λ. Let h be a collision resistant hash function.

Key Generation

1. Choose $p = 2q_0 q_1 + 1$
2. $\mu \in_R \mathbb{Z}_p$
3. $g = \mu^{2q_1}$
4. $k, \tilde{k}, \hat{k} \in_R \mathbb{Z}_N$
5. $s = g^k, \tilde{s} = g^{\tilde{k}}, \hat{s} = g^{\hat{k}}$
6. $pk = (p, g, s, \tilde{s}, \hat{s})$
7. $sk = (q_0, k, \tilde{k}, \hat{k})$

Encryption of $m \in X$

1. $w \in_R \{0, ..., N - 1\}$
2. $x = g^w$
3. $\pi = s^w$
4. $e = m\pi$
5. $\hat{\pi} = \tilde{s}^w \hat{s}^{h(x,e)w}$
6. Ciphertext is $(x, e, \hat{\pi})$

Decryption of $(x, e, \hat{\pi})$

1. $\hat{\pi}' = x^{\tilde{k} + h(x,e)\hat{k}}$
2. If $\hat{\pi} \neq \hat{\pi}'$, then halt
3. $\pi = x^k$
4. $m = e/\pi$

Note that we are implicitly assuming that $(x, e, \hat{\pi}) \in X^3$, so the decryption algorithm should check that $\left(\frac{x}{p}\right) = \left(\frac{e}{p}\right) = 1$ and reject otherwise. This check can be performed at low cost using an efficient algorithm for computing Jacobi symbols.

Security of CS-GBD. For a probabilistic polynomial-time adversaries A, A', let $Adv_{A,CS-GBD}^{CCA}$ be A's advantage in an adaptive chosen ciphertext attack, and let $Adv_{A'}^{GBD}$ be the advantage of A' in distinguishing subgroup elements from non-subgroup elements. Let Q be the number of decryption queries allowed by A. Also, let δ_{tcr} be the probability of finding a collision for the hash function h for input (x, e).

Theorem 1. *If the GBD subgroup membership problem is hard, and the hash function h is a collision resistant hash function, the CS-GBD is secure against adaptive chosen ciphertext attack. In particular, for all adversaries A, there exists a probabilistic polynomial-time algorithm A′ such that*

$$Adv^{CCA}_{A,CS-GBD} \leq Adv^{GBD}_{A'} + (Q+1)/q_1 + \delta_{tcr} \qquad (1)$$

Proof. We consider a simulator A' that interacts with a chosen-ciphertext adversary A against CS-GBD in the following way.

1. Given input (p, g) and target element $x^* \in X$.
2. Run the Key Generation algorithm to get (pk, sk) and gives the pk to A
3. Answer A's decryption queries $(x, e, \hat{\pi})$ by running decryption algorithm
4. When A outputs messages m_0, m_1:

   (a) Flip coin $b \in_R \{0, 1\}$
   (b) Compute $\pi^* = H_k(x^*)$
   (c) Compute $e^* = \pi^* m_b$
   (d) Compute $\hat{\pi}^* = \hat{H}_k(x^*, e^*)$
   (e) Give A challenge ciphertext $(x^*, e^*, \hat{\pi}^*)$

5. Answer A's decryption queries $(x, e, \hat{\pi}) \neq (x^*, e^*, \hat{\pi}^*)$ by running decryption algorithm
6. When A output guess bit b', output 1 if $b = b'$. Otherwise output 0.

We want to consider the behaviour this simulator in two different cases: when $x^* \in L$ and when $x^* \notin L$. Let T' be the event that the simulator outputs 1 in the former case, and let T' be the event that it outputs 1 in the latter case. The advantage that A' has in distinguishing the subgroup membership of x^* is

$$Adv^{GBD}_{A'} = |\Pr[T] - \Pr[T']| \qquad (2)$$

Let $Adv^{CCA}_{A,CS-GBD}$ be the adversary's advantage in an adaptive chosen ciphertext attack against CS-GBD. Our goal is to show that if $Adv^{GBD}_{A'}$ is negligible, then $Adv^{CCA}_{A,CS-GBD}$ will also be negligible.

When $x^* \in L$, the simulation provided by the simulator to the adversary is perfect. Therefore, we have

$$Adv^{CCA}_{A,CS-GBD} \leq |\Pr[T'] - 1/2| \qquad (3)$$

When $x^* \notin L$, we must analyse the behaviour more closely. To do so, we describe a sequence of simulators that contain modifications of the previous simulators. In the following analysis, we denote T_i as the event that the simulator i outputs a 1.

Simulator 1. We change the simulator such that when answering decryption queries, it rejects ciphertexts $(x, e, \hat{\pi})$ where $(x, e) \neq (x^*, e^*)$ but $h(x, e) = h(x^*, e^*)$. Of course, this can only happen in decryption queries performed after the challenge ciphertext has been given. The probability that this happens is bounded by the probability that the adversary can find a collision for $h(x, e)$, which we denote δ_{tcr}. This simulator and the previous simulator proceed identically until this occurs, so we have

$$|\Pr[T_1] - \Pr[T]| \leq \delta_{tcr} \qquad (4)$$

Simulator 2. We now alter the simulator such that it rejects decryption queries where $x \notin L$. This is exactly the simulation provided to the adversary as in the previous simulator, except in the event that a ciphertext of this form is rejected where $\hat{H}_{\hat{k}}(x) = \hat{\pi}$. By the $1/q_1$-universal$_2$ property of the projective hash family $\hat{\mathbf{H}}$, we have that

$$|\Pr[T_2] - \Pr[T_1]| \leq Q/q_1 \qquad (5)$$

where Q is the number of total decryption queries the adversary is allowed to make.

Simulator 3. Simulator 3 is exactly the simulator 2 except with the following modification. Step 4b sets $\pi^* = \pi'$, where $\pi' \in_R X$, instead of $\pi^* = H_k(x^*)$. It then follows from the $1/q_1$-smoothness of $\mathbf{H}$ that

$$|\Pr[T_3] - \Pr[T_2]| \leq 1/q_1 \qquad (6)$$

Now from this simulator, it is evident that the adversary's output b' is independent of the bit b. So,

$$\Pr[T_3] = 1/2 \qquad (7)$$

Combining equations (2)-(7), the result in equation (1) is obtained. This completes the proof. □

4.2   The r-th Residuosity Problem

Kurosawa *et al.* [8] described how the r-th residue problem can be used for constructing a public key cryptosystem. We will use this problem as the underlying problem for a CCA-secure scheme. Consider primes p, q of bit length, where e_1, e_2 are odd integers dividing $p - 1$ and $q - 1$ respectively such that e_1 is prime to $q - 1$ and e_2 is prime to $p - 1$. Set $N = pq$ and $r = e_1 e_2$. Let G be the multiplicative group $\mathbb{Z}_N^*$ and H be subgroup of r-th residues of G. That is,

$$H = \{y^r \mod N \text{ for } y \in G\}$$

The r-th residuosity problem is to distinguish elements of H from elements of $G \backslash H$ given only N. This is the definition given by Yamamura and Saito [12].

However, the groups G and H described are not cyclic, so we describe the following subgroup membership problem. Let $r = e_1 e_2$ be an integer such that e_1, e_2 are primes of bit length λ'. Let p, q, p', q' be primes such that $p = 2e_1 p' + 1$ and $q = 2e_2 q' + 1$ where p', q' are of bit length λ, $N = pq$ and $N' = p'q'$. Without loss of generality, let us assume $e_1 < e_2$. Also, let us assume that $\lambda' \leq \lambda$. Let X be the group of elements modulo N that have a Jacobi symbol of 1. Let L be the subgroup of elements of X that are r-th residues modulo N. That is, $L = \{y^r \bmod N \text{ for } y \in X\}$. Now X is a cyclic group of order $2rN'$ and L is a cyclic subgroup of order $2N'$. The subgroup membership problem is to distinguish random elements of L from random elements of $X \backslash L$. Note that this is also the symmetric subgroup membership problem described by Gjøsteen [5]. We can also view these groups by considering that $\mathbb{Z}_N^*$ can be viewed as an internal direct product of subgroups:

$$\mathbb{Z}_N^* = G_r \cdot G_{N'} \cdot G_2 \cdot T$$

where T is the subgroup $\{-1, 1\}$. Then $X = G_r \cdot G_{N'} \cdot T$ and $L = G_{N'} \cdot T$.

We now argue that the r-th residue assumption implies that this subgroup membership problem is hard. Firstly, note that the description of r-th residue problem does not restrict p and q to the form described for our subset membership problem. However, it can be easily seen that the r-th residue assumption without this restriction implies the r-th residue assumption with this restriction, assuming that primes of these special forms are sufficiently dense, which seems a reasonable assumption. Secondly, given a random element x of G, if we then choose a random $b \in \{0, 1\}$, then $x^{2r}(-1)^b$ is uniformly distributed over X. Similarly, given a random element y of H, if we then choose a random $b \in \{0, 1\}$, then $y^{2r}(-1)^b$ is uniformly distributed over L. This implies that it is at least as hard to distinguish X from L as it is to distinguish G from H.

Constructing a CCA-secure encryption scheme. We now apply the Cramer-Shoup construction, which is roughly also the application of the Gjøsteen's construction [5]. To produce a random generator g for L, one can select a random $\alpha \in \mathbb{Z}_N^*$ and compute $g = -\alpha^{2r}$. Let us define the witness set $W = \{0, ..., \lfloor N/2 \rfloor\}$. To sample an $x \in L$ at random together with a witness for x, generate a $w \in W$ at random and compute $x = g^w$. The output distribution of this algorithm will be $O(2^{-\lambda})$-close to the uniform distribution over L.

Now, let $K = \{0, ..., 2N'r - 1\}$ and define $H_{k \in K}(x) = x^k$ for $x \in X$, and $\alpha(k) = H_k(g)$. Hence $\Pi = X$ and $S = L$. By Theorem 2 in [3], the projective hash family $\mathbf{H} = (H, K, X, L, X, L, \alpha)$ is $1/e_1$-universal.

When $\lambda'(= |e_1|)$ is sufficiently large, from Lemma 1 in [5], $\mathbf{H}$ is a strongly smooth. Indeed making λ' as large as possible whilst keeping λ (and consequently $|L|$) sufficiently large will allow for faster operations in the subgroup. It is easy to see that the algorithms required for a hash proof system for $\mathbf{H}$ are available. Then to obtain a universal$_2$ extended has proof system, we suppose there is an available injective function $\Gamma : X \times X \to \mathbb{Z}_{e_1}^n$ for sufficiently large n, then consider the extended projective hash family $\hat{\mathbf{H}} = (\hat{H}, K^{n+1}, X \times X, L \times X, X, L^{n+1}, \hat{\alpha})$ where for $(\tilde{k}, \hat{k}_1, ..., \hat{k}_n) \in K^{n+1}$ and $(\gamma_1, ..., \gamma_n) = \Gamma(x, e)$, we define

$- \hat{H}_{\tilde{k},\hat{k}_1,...,\hat{k}_n}(x,e) = H_{\tilde{k}}(x) \prod_{i=1}^{n} H_{\hat{k}_i}(x)^{\gamma_i} = x^{\tilde{k}+\sum_{i=1}^{n} \hat{k}_i \gamma_i}$

$- \hat{\alpha}(\tilde{k}, \hat{k}_1, ..., \hat{k}_n) = (\alpha(\tilde{k}), \alpha(\hat{k}_1), ..., \alpha(\hat{k}_n)) = (g^{\tilde{k}}, g^{\hat{k}_1}, ..., g^{\hat{k}_n})$

By theorem 3 in [3], $\hat{H}$ is $1/e_1$-universal$_2$. It is easy to show that the required algorithms are available for the resulting strongly universal$_2$ hash proof system $\hat{P}$ for $\hat{H}$. We can now apply the Cramer-Shoup construction. To improve efficiency of both the resulting scheme, we can replace the injective function Γ by a collision resistant hash function h (such as SHA-1 where output length is 160 bits) so that we can set $n = 1$. The resulting scheme is follows:

The CS-RR encryption scheme. For the description below, $N = pq$ where $p = 2e_1p' + 1, q = 2e_2q' + 1$, for primes p', q', p, q where bit length of p', q' is λ, and primes e_1, e_2 of bit length λ' where $e_1 < e_2$. Let $r = e_1e_2$, and $N' = p'q'$. Let h be a collision resistant hash function.

Key generation:

1. Choose $N = pq$
2. $\mu \in_R \mathbb{Z}_N^*; g = -\mu^{2N'}$
3. $k, \tilde{k}, \hat{k} \in_R \{0, ., 2N'r-1\}$
4. $s = g^k, \tilde{s} = g^{\tilde{k}}, \hat{s} = g^{\hat{k}}$
5. $pk = (N, g, s, \tilde{s}, \hat{s})$
6. $sk = (p, q, k, \tilde{k}, \hat{k})$

Encryption of $m \in X$

1. $w \in_R \{0, ..., \lfloor N/2 \rfloor\}$
2. $x = g^w$
3. $\pi = s^w$
4. $e = m\pi \in X$
5. $\hat{\pi} = \tilde{s}^w \hat{s}^{h(x,e)w}$
6. Ciphertext is $(x, e, \hat{\pi})$

Decryption of $(x, e, \hat{\pi})$

1. $\hat{\pi}' = x^{\tilde{k}+h(x,e)\hat{k}}$
2. If $\hat{\pi} \neq \hat{\pi}'$, then halt
3. $\pi = x^k$
4. $m = e/\pi$

Again, the decryption assumes that $(x, e, \hat{\pi}) \in X^3$, which suggests that it should only proceed if $(\frac{x}{N}) = (\frac{e}{N}) = 1$.

Theorem 2. *If the r-th residuosity subgroup membership problem is hard, and h is a collision resistant hash function, then CS-RR is secure against adaptive chosen ciphertext attack. In particular, for all adversaries A, there exists a probabilistic polynomial-time algorithm A' such that*

$$Adv_{A,CS-RR}^{CCA} \leq Adv_{A'}^{RR} + Q/e_1 + O(2^{-\lambda'}) + \delta_{tcr} + O(2^{-(\lambda'+\lambda)})$$

The proof for this theorem follows the same argument as for CS-GBD. The difference comes from the fact that elements of L are sampled from distributions $O(2^{-(\lambda'+\lambda)})$-close to uniform on L. The other differences in the reductions lie in the smoothness and universal$_2$ probabilities related to the projective hash families.

We should note that the scheme can be used such that the modulus is a fixed public parameter rather than chosen during key generation, and the key generation algorithm chooses the private keys without knowledge of the factorisation of the modulus. We would then need to choose keys $k, \tilde{k}, \hat{k}$ from a key space statistically close to K. The uniform distribution on $\{0, ..., \lfloor N/2 \rfloor\}$ is $O(2^{-(\lambda'+\lambda)})$-close to uniform on K, so this would result in an extra term in theorem 2.

4.3   The p-Subgroup Problem

Okamoto and Uchiyama [9] described a semantically secure encryption scheme based on the intractability of the following problem. Let p, q be primes and set $N = p^2 q$. Let g be a random element of $\mathbb{Z}_N^*$ such that the order of $g^{(p-1)} \mod p^2$ is p. Consider the groups G and H:

$$G = \{x = g^m y^N \mod N \text{ for } m \in \mathbb{Z}_p \text{ and } y \in \mathbb{Z}_N^*\}$$
$$H = \{x = y^N \mod N \text{ for } y \in G\}$$

The p-subgroup problem is to distinguish elements of H from elements of $G \backslash H$ given only N and g.

Let p, q, p', q' be primes such that $p = 2p' + 1, q = 2q' + 1$ where p', q' have bit lengths of λ. Set $N = p^2 q$ and $N' = p'q'$. Let X be the group of elements modulo N that have a Jacobi symbol of 1, and let $L = \{y^N \mod N \text{ for } y \in X\}$. Now X is a cyclic group of order $2N'p$ and L is a cyclic subgroup of order $2N'$. The subset membership problem is to distinguish random elements of L from random elements of $X \backslash L$. We can also view these groups by considering that $\mathbb{Z}_N^*$ can be viewed as an internal direct product of subgroups:

$$\mathbb{Z}_N^* = G_p \cdot G_{N'} \cdot G_2 \cdot T$$

where T is the subgroup $\{-1,1\}$. Then $X = G_p \cdot G_{N'} \cdot T$ and $L = G_{N'} \cdot T$.

Now we argue that the hardness of the p-subgroup assumption implies that the above subset membership problem is hard. Firstly, the assumption without the restriction of p and q to strong primes implies that the assumption holds with the restriction, as long as strong primes are sufficiently dense. Secondly, consider a random element x of $\mathbb{Z}_N^*$, if we choose a random $b \in \{0,1\}$, then $x^2(-1)^b$ is uniformly distributed over X. Similarly, given a random element y of H, if we choose a random $b \in \{0,1\}$, then $y^2(-1)^b$ is uniformly distributed over L. This implies that it is at least as hard to distinguish X from L as it is to distinguish G from H.

Constructing a CCA-secure encryption scheme. To produce a random generator g for L, one can select a random $\alpha \in \mathbb{Z}_N^*$ and compute $g = -\alpha^p$. This g will generate L with overwhelming probability. Let us define the witness set $W = \{0, ..., \lfloor N/2 \rfloor\}$. To generate an $x \in L$ at random together with a witness for x, generate a $w \in W$ at random and compute $x = g^w$. The output distribution of this algorithm will be $O(2^{-\lambda})$-close to the uniform distribution over L.

Now, let $K = \{0, ..., 2N' - 1\}$ and define $H_{k \in K}(x) = x^k$ for $x \in X$, and $\alpha(k) = H_k(g)$. Hence $\Pi = X$ and $S = L$. By Theorem 2 in [3], the projective hash family $\mathbf{H} = (H, K, X, L, X, L, \alpha)$ is $1/p$-universal and by Lemma 1 in [5] is $1/p$-smooth. It is then easy to verify that the required algorithms for evaluating H are available, so we can obtain a strongly smooth hash proof system, since p will be large.

To obtain a strongly universal$_2$ hash proof system $\hat{\mathbf{P}}$, let us first suppose that for some sufficiently large n, there is an available injective function Γ :

$X \times X \to R^n$ for $R = \{0, ..., 2^\lambda - 1\}$. Consider the extended projective hash family $\hat{\mathbf{H}} = (\hat{H}, K^{n+1}, X \times X, L \times X, X, L^{n+1}, \hat{\alpha})$ where for $(\tilde{k}, \hat{k}_1, ..., \hat{k}_n) \in K^{n+1}$ and $(\gamma_1, ..., \gamma_n) = \Gamma(x, e)$, where we define

- $\hat{H}_{\tilde{k}, \hat{k}_1, ..., \hat{k}_n}(x, e) = H_{\tilde{k}}(x) \prod_{i=1}^{n} H_{\hat{k}_i}(x)^{\gamma_i} = x^{\tilde{k} + \sum_{i=1}^{n} \hat{k}_i \gamma_i}$
- $\hat{\alpha}(\tilde{k}, \hat{k}_1, ..., \hat{k}_n) = (\alpha(\tilde{k}), \alpha(\hat{k}_1), ..., \alpha(\hat{k}_n)) = (g^{\tilde{k}}, g^{\hat{k}_1}, ..., g^{\hat{k}_n})$

By theorem 3 in [3], $\hat{\mathbf{H}}$ is $1/p$-universal$_2$. By verifying that the required algorithms for evaluating $\hat{H}$ are available, we can build a strongly universal$_2$ hash proof system from $\hat{\mathbf{H}}$.

Since we now have a strongly smooth HPS $\mathbf{P}$ an a strong universal$_2$ HPS $\hat{\mathbf{P}}$, applying the Cramer-Shoup construction will give us a CCA-secure encryption scheme. However, to improve efficiency, we can replace the injective function $\Gamma : X \times X \to R^n$ by a collision resistant hash function $h : X \times X \to \{0,1\}^m$ (such as SHA-1 where $m = 160$) so that the n can be much smaller. Again, we can choose $n = 1$ and the resulting scheme will still be secure against chosen-ciphertext attack. The resulting encryption scheme is as follows:

The CS-PSUB encryption scheme. For the description below, $N = p^2 q$ where p, q, p', q' are primes such that $p = 2p' + 1, q = 2q' + 1$ where p', q' have bit lengths of λ. Let h be a collision resistant hash function.

Key generation

1. Choose $N = p^2 q$
2. $\mu \in_R \mathbb{Z}_N^*; g = -\mu^p$
3. $k, \tilde{k}, \hat{k} \in_R \{0, .., 2N'p - 1\}$
4. $s = g^k, \tilde{s} = g^{\tilde{k}}, \hat{s} = g^{\hat{k}}$
5. $pk = (N, g, s, \tilde{s}, \hat{s})$
6. $sk = (p, q, k, \tilde{k}, \hat{k})$

Encryption of $m \in X$

1. $w \in_R \{0, ..., \lfloor N/2 \rfloor\}$
2. $x = g^w$
3. $\pi = s^w$
4. $e = m\pi$
5. $\hat{\pi} = \tilde{s}^w \hat{s}^{h(x,e)w}$
6. Ciphertext is $(x, e, \hat{\pi})$

Decryption of $(x, e, \hat{\pi})$

1. $\hat{\pi}' = x^{\tilde{k} + h(x,e)\hat{k}}$
2. If $\hat{\pi} \neq \hat{\pi}'$, then halt
3. $\pi = x^k$
4. $m = e/\pi$

Again, the decryption algorithm should check that $x, e \in X$, and reject if this is not the case.

Theorem 3. *If the p-subgroup membership problem is hard, and h is a collision resistant hash function, then CS-PSUB is secure against adaptive chosen ciphertext attack. In particular, for all adversaries A, there exists a probabilistic polynomial-time algorithm A' such that*

$$Adv_{A,CS-PSUB}^{CCA} \leq Adv_{A'}^{PSUB} + (Q+1)/p + \delta_{tcr} + O(2^{-\lambda}) \qquad (8)$$

The proof for this theorem follows the same argument as for CS-GBD. The differences comes from the fact that elements of L are sampled from a distribution $O(2^{-\lambda})$-close to uniform on L, and in the smoothness and universal$_2$ probabilities related to the projective hash families.

We should again note that the scheme can be used such that the modulus is a fixed public parameter rather than chosen during key generation, and the key generation algorithm chooses the private keys without knowledge of the factorisation of the modulus. We would then need to choose keys $k, \tilde{k}, \hat{k}$ from a key space statistically close to K. The uniform distribution on $\{0, ..., \lfloor N/2 \rfloor\}$ is $O(2^{-(\lambda)})$-close to uniform on K, so this approximation will result in an extra term in Theorem 3.

4.4 Avoiding Message Embedding for Short Messages

In each of the above encryption schemes, the message space is the group X. This means that messages will need to be embedded into the group prior to encryption, and then again recovered after decryption. Alternatively, if the message lengths are sufficiently shorter than the approximately $|X|$-bits offered by the above schemes, we can use the Leftover Hash Lemma construction in [3] and avoid the message embedding needed in our schemes. Additionally, the ciphertexts will be shorter. To do this, let $A = \{0,1\}^a$ be this message space, choose $f : X \to \{0,1\}^a$ from a family of universal hash functions F, and let $\bar{H}_k(x) = f_i(H_k(x))$. By the Leftover Hash Lemma, the projective hash family $\bar{\mathbf{H}} = (\bar{H}, K, X, L, A, L, \bar{\alpha})$ is $2^{-(b+1)}$-smooth for $a + 2b \leq \log_2(1/\tilde{p})$, where $\tilde{p}$ is the smallest prime dividing $|X \backslash L|$. Then for the the extended universal$_2$ projective hash family we use $\hat{\mathbf{H}} = (\hat{H}, K^{n+1}, X \times A, L \times A, X, L^{n+1}, \hat{\alpha})$. The resulting scheme based on the GBD subgroup membership problem is similar to CS-GBD except that $\pi = f(s^w)$, and $e = m \oplus \pi$. Alternative schemes for the r-th residue problem and the p-sub problem can also be constructed in a similar way.

5   Concrete CCA-Secure Hybrid Variants

To apply the Kurosawa-Desmedt hybrid construction to each of the discussed subgroup membership problems, we use the strongly universal$_2$ hash proof systems $\hat{\mathbf{P}}$ obtained previously, but without the extension on the projective hash family. More precisely, instead of $\hat{\mathbf{H}}$, we consider the projective hash family $\hat{\mathbf{H}}' = (\hat{H}', K^{n+1}, X, L, X, L, \bar{\alpha})$ where for $(\tilde{k}, \hat{k}_1, ..., \hat{k}_n) \in K^{n+1}$ and $(\gamma_1, ..., \gamma_n) = \Gamma'(x)$, we define

- $\hat{H}'_{\tilde{k}, \hat{k}_1, ..., \hat{k}_n}(x) = H_{\tilde{k}}(x) \prod_{i=1}^n H_{\hat{k}_i}(x)^{\gamma_i} = x^{\tilde{k} + \sum_{i=1}^n \hat{k}_i \gamma_i}$
- $\hat{\alpha}(\tilde{k}, \hat{k}_1, ..., \hat{k}_n) = (\alpha(\tilde{k}), \alpha(\hat{k}_1), ..., \alpha(\hat{k}_n)) = (g^{\tilde{k}}, g^{\hat{k}_1}, ..., g^{\hat{k}_n})$

Note that the injective function in this projective hash family only acts on $x \in X$. By theorem 3 in [3], $\hat{\mathbf{H}}'$ is $1/\tilde{p}$-universal$_2$, where $\tilde{p}$ is the smallest prime dividing $|X \backslash L|$, which is q_1, e_1 and p for the respective problems. It is easy to show that the required algorithms are available for the resulting strongly universal$_2$ hash proof system $\hat{\mathbf{P}}$ for $\hat{\mathbf{H}}$.

To improve efficiency of the resulting scheme, we can replace the injective function Γ' with a collision resistant hash function h and can set $n = 1$. In each of the resulting schemes that follow, we implicitly assume that the decryption algorithm also tests that ciphertext element x is in the group X.

The KD-GBD encryption scheme. For the description below, $p = 2N+1$ is prime where $N = q_0 q_1$ for primes q_0, q_1 of bit length λ. Let h be a collision resistant hash function. Let $SKE = (E, D)$ be a symmetric-key encryption scheme, let MAC be a one-time secure message authentication code, and KDF a key derivation function.

Key Generation

1. Pick $p = 2q_0q_1 + 1$
2. $\mu \in_R \mathbb{Z}_p$
3. $g = \mu^{2q_1}$
4. $k, \hat{k} \in_R \mathbb{Z}_N$
5. $\tilde{s} = g^{\tilde{k}}, \hat{s} = g^{\hat{k}}$
6. $pk = (p, g, \tilde{s}, \hat{s})$
7. $sk = (q_0, q_1, \tilde{k}, \hat{k})$

Encryption of m

1. $w \in_R \{0, ..., N-1\}$
2. $x = g^w$
3. $\hat{\pi} = \tilde{s}^w \hat{s}^{h(x)w}$
4. $(K', K) = KDF(\hat{\pi})$
5. $\chi = E_K(m)$
6. $t = MAC_{K'}(\chi)$
7. ciphertext is (x, χ, t)

Decryption of (x, χ, t)

1. $\hat{\pi} = x^{\tilde{k}+h(x)\hat{k}}$
2. $(K', K) = KDF(\hat{\pi})$
3. If $t \neq MAC_{K'}(\chi)$
   then $halt$
4. $m = D_K(\chi)$

For a probabilistic polynomial-time adversaries A, A', let $Adv_{A,KD-GBD}^{CCA}$ be A's advantage in an adaptive chosen ciphertext attack, and let $Adv_{A'}^{GBD}$ be the advantage of A' in distinguishing subgroup elements from non-subgroup elements. Let δ_{tcr} be the probability that an adversary can find a collision for $h(x)$, let δ_{mac} be the probability that it breaks the message authentication code, and let δ_{enc} be the probability that it breaks the semantic security of SKE. Let Q be the number of decryption queries allowed by an adversary.

Theorem 4. *The proposed encryption scheme KD-GBD is secure against chosen-ciphertext attack under the difficulty of GBD subgroup membership problem if SKE is semantically secure, h is a collision resistant hash function, KDF is a secure key derivation function and MAC is a one-time secure message authentication code. In particular, for all adversaries A, there exists a probabilistic polynomial-time algorithm A' such that*

$$Adv_{A,KD-GBD}^{CCA} \leq Adv_{A'}^{GBD} + \delta_{tcr} + 2Q\delta_{mac} + \delta_{enc} \tag{9}$$

The proof follows the argument of the proof for the Kurosawa-Desmedt DDH-based hybrid scheme (KD-DDH), and will be featured in the full version. Roughly speaking, when the challenge ciphertext (x^*, χ, t) is constructed correctly by applying a projective hash function to an element $x^* \in L$, then the attack works as in the real case. However, if $x^* \notin L$, the symmetric key K^* which is derived from $H_k(x^*)$ will be uniformly distributed and totally secret from the adversary due to the strongly universal$_2$ property of the projective hash family, which comes from the hardness of the subgroup membership problem and the collision intractability of the CRHF. As the attack progresses, K^* remains secret from the adversary because the MAC ensures that invalid   queries are rejected and the adversary wins with negligible advantage. The proof requires that the KDF and MAC are information theoretically secure functions which are typically implemented using universal hashing techniques. In particular, for random $\hat{\pi} \in X$ we require that (at least) the first component K' of the output be (statistically close to) uniform. This will be achieved since X will be sufficiently large, unlike the case of KD-DDH where $|X|$ will typically be chosen to be 160. The alternative proof [4] of KD-DDH, does not require the KDF and MAC to be information theoretically secure, but rather any (computationally) secure KDF and MAC. This proof is also adaptable to KD-GBD. The drawback is the additional computational assumptions required for the security of particular choices of KDF and MAC.

The KD-RR scheme. For the description below, $N = pq$ where $p = 2e_1 p' + 1, q = 2e_2 q' + 1$, for primes p', q', p, q where bit length of p', q' is λ, and primes e_1, e_2 of bit length λ' where $e_1 < e_2$. Let $N' = p'q'$. Let h be a collision resistant hash function, let $SKE = (E, D)$ be a symmetric-key encryption scheme, let MAC be a one-time secure message authentication code, and KDF a key derivation function.

Key Generation

1. Pick $N = pq$
2. $\mu \in_R \mathbb{Z}_N^*$
3. $g = -\mu^{2N'}$
4. $\tilde{k}, \hat{k} \in_R \{0, ..., \lfloor N/2 \rfloor\}$
5. $\tilde{s} = g^{\tilde{k}}, \hat{s} = g^{\hat{k}}$
6. $pk = (N, g, \tilde{s}, \hat{s})$
7. $sk = (p, q, \tilde{k}, \hat{k})$

Encryption of m

1. $w \in_R \{0, ..., \lfloor N/2 \rfloor\}$
2. $x = g^w$
3. $\hat{\pi} = \tilde{s}^w \hat{s}^{h(x)w}$
4. $(K', K) = KDF(\hat{\pi})$
5. $\chi = E_K(m)$
6. $t = MAC_{K'}(\chi)$
7. ciphertext is (x, χ, t)

Decryption of (x, χ, t)

1. $\hat{\pi} = x^{\tilde{k} + h(x)\hat{k}}$
2. $(K', K) = KDF(\hat{\pi})$
3. If $t \neq MAC_{K'}(\chi)$ then *halt*
4. $m = D_K(\chi)$

Note: Gjøsteen [5] presented a hybrid scheme similar to KD-RR. The subgroup membership problem is of a similar construction, and the resulting scheme is slightly different to the one presented above. The problem in [5] considers X to be the quadratic residues in $\mathbb{Z}_N^*$. This results in extra squarings in the encryption and decryption algorithms to ensure that ciphertext element x is a quadratic residue, and consequently in a "benign malleability" property of the ciphertexts. Using X as the group of elements with the Jacobi symbol 1 allows these issues to be avoided. Gjøsteen also proposes that the additional assumption that is needed when using a typical CRHF such as SHA-1 can be avoided by using the simple hash function $h(x) = x$. The cost of this is a much larger exponent, and consequently slower encryption and decryption.

The KD-PSUB encryption scheme For the description below, $N = p^2 q$ where p, q, p', q' are primes such that $p = 2p' + 1, q = 2q' + 1$ and where p', q' have bit lengths of λ. Let h be a collision resistant hash function. Let $SKE = (E, D)$ be a symmetric-key encryption scheme, let MAC be a one-time secure message authentication code, and KDF a key derivation function.

Key Generation	**Encryption** of m	**Decryption** of (x, χ, t)
1. Pick $N = p^2 q$	1. $w \in_R \{0, ..., \lfloor N/2 \rfloor\}$	1. $\hat{\pi} = x^{\tilde{k} + h(x)\hat{k}}$
2. $\mu \in_R \mathbb{Z}_N^*$	2. $x = g^w$	2. $(K', K) = KDF(\hat{\pi})$
3. $g = -\mu^p$	3. $\hat{\pi} = \tilde{s}^w \hat{s}^{h(x)w}$	3. If $t \neq MAC_{K'}(\chi)$
4. $\tilde{k}, \hat{k} \in_R \{0, ..., \lfloor N/2 \rfloor\}$	4. $(K', K) = KDF(\hat{\pi})$	then *halt*
5. $\tilde{s} = g^{\tilde{k}}, \hat{s} = g^{\hat{k}}$	5. $\chi = E_K(m)$	4. $m = D_K(\chi)$
6. $pk = (N, g, \tilde{s}, \hat{s})$	6. $t = MAC_{K'}(\chi)$	
7. $sk = (p, q, \tilde{k}, \hat{k})$	7. ciphertext is (x, χ, t)	

The proofs of security for KD-RR and KD-PSUB follow the argument of KD-GBD and KD-DDH, but have been omitted due to space constraints.

6   Comments on Efficiency

In all the schemes we have described, we have included the choice of modulus as part of key generation, and included the factorisation as part of the private key. Knowledge of the factorisation will allow for faster decryption, however, the schemes will work without it. Also, in all of the schemes described we have specified that the witness w be chosen from a set of (about) the size of the group X. Ideally, w should be chosen from the set $\{0, ..., |L| - 1\}$, however $|L|$ will not be available to an encrypter. In practice, we can choose w from $\{0, ..., m\}$ where m is sufficiently larger than $|L|$.

We firstly compare in terms of efficiency our three schemes constructed from the Cramer-Shoup framework with previous similarly constructed encryption schemes based on Decisional Diffie-Hellman, Decisional Composite Residuosity and Quadratic Residuosity in [3]. In the following discussion, we shall refer to these schemes as CS-DDH, CS-DCR and CS-QR respectively. Table 1 compares the schemes in terms of number of exponentiations in encryption and decryption, and ciphertext length. Note that to make a fair comparison, we compare the schemes in terms of encryption of long messages (where possible), and consider equal modulus lengths for each scheme. For CS-DDH, the modulus is a prime $p = 2q + 1$ and the group G is the quadratic residues in $\mathbb{Z}_p^*$. The CS-QR scheme has only been discussed for short messages, so we will include these in our comparisons. Using a larger message space will be more costly than the already expensive short message scheme. Note that for CS-DCR, exponentiations are modulo N^2. From this table it can be seen that the three schemes described in this paper achieves encryption and decryption in less exponentiations than the three previous schemes. Additionally, for long messages, the ciphertexts are shorter for the new schemes also.

Table 2 compares the schemes obtained using the Kurosawa-Desmedt hybrid construction from section 5 with the original DDH-based Kurosawa-Desmedt scheme (KD-DDH) in terms of exponentiations in encryption and decryption, as well as ciphertext overhead (ciphertext length minus the message length).

Interestingly, each of the new schemes has shorter ciphertexts and less exponentiations than KD-DDH. However, for KD-DDH the subgroup can be chosen

Table 1. CS schemes. A multi-exponentiation is counted as 1.5 exponentiations.

	CS-DDH	CS-DCR	CS-QR	CS-GBD	CS-RR	CS-PSUB
Enc.	4.5	3.5	543	3.5	3.5	3.5
Dec.	3	2	256	2	2	2
Msg len	$\approx |p| - 1$	$\approx |N| - 1$	128	$\approx |p| - 1$	$\approx |N| - 2$	$\approx |N| - 2$
Ciphertext length	$4|p|$	$4|N|$	$2|N| + 256$	$3|p|$	$3|N|$	$3|N|$

Table 2. KD schemes. A multi-exponentiation is counted as 1.5 exps.

	KD-DDH	KD-GBD	KD-RR	KD-PSUB
Enc.	3.5	2.5	2.5	2.5
Dec.	1.5	1	1	1
Ciph overhead	$2|p| + $ mac	$|p| + $ mac	$|N| + $ mac	$|N| + $ mac

as small as order 160, making exponentiation in this subgroup much faster than the proposed schemes. Between the three proposed schemes, the KD-RR has the most amount of flexibility in its choice of subgroup size, and can have advantage in encryption. For KD-GBD, the subgroup size is fixed at $|p|/2$, and for KD-PSUB, approximately $2|N|/3$. However, it may be possible to improve efficiency by restricting the random exponents in encryption to lengths much shorter than the subgroup size, while still maintaining chosen ciphertext security of the scheme. This would require an additional assumption, the Short Exponent Discrete Log Assumption [11] (DLSE), but if the exponents could be shortened to the commonly used 160-bits of the KD-DDH, the resulting schemes would surpass the efficiency of the KD-DDH in encryption. In decryption, the KD-DDH private key exponents will be quite shorter than for the three proposed schemes. However, it should not be overlooked that, like our schemes, KD-DDH decryption implicitly assumes that ciphertext elements are in the group G. While for our schemes, this means two fast Jacobi symbol computations, when G is the subgroup of $\mathbb{Z}_p^*$ of prime order q for $p = 2rq + 1$, checking that an element $x \in G$ means computing $x^q \equiv 1 \pmod{p}$. Thus two additional 160-bit exponentiations are necessary on top of the 1.5 decryption exponentiations. Between the three proposed schemes, if the private key holder doesn't know the size of L, then KD-GBD has slight advantage over the other two, since the order of G is known.

7   Conclusion and Future Work

We constructed CCA-secure encryption schemes using the Cramer-Shoup construction that are more efficient, in terms of exponentiations and ciphertext length, than other schemes from this construction. When we use the same hash proof systems to construct hybrid encryption schemes via the Kurosawa-Desmedt construction, we obtain efficient schemes with only 2.5 exponentiations in encryption, and one in decryption, as well as shorter ciphertexts than previous schemes. The advantage of the Kurosawa-Desmedt DDH-based scheme over our schemes its ability to choose a small subgroup, thereby speeding up the encryption and decryption processes. However, using an additional assumption about using exponents much shorter than the size of the subgroup, it may be possible to obtain better efficiency than the DDH-based scheme. An interesting open question is whether one could find another subgroup membership problem such that when the construction is applied, the number of exponentiations and ciphertext length remains as small as for our schemes, but where the size of the subgroup can be as small as for the DDH problem. The resulting scheme would be the most efficient integer-based scheme yet, without requiring any additional assumptions about the use of short exponents.

References

1. R. Cramer and V. Shoup. A Practical Public Key Cryptosystem Provably Secure Against Adaptive Chosen Ciphertext Attack. In *CRYPTO '98*, volume 1462 of *LNCS*, pages 13–25. Springer-Verlag, 1998.
2. R. Cramer and V. Shoup. Universal Hash Proofs and a Paradigm for Adaptive Chosen Ciphertext Secure Public-Key Encryption. http://shoup.net/papers/uhp.pdf, December 2001.
3. R. Cramer and V. Shoup. Universal Hash Proofs and a Paradigm for Adaptive Chosen Ciphertext Secure Public-Key Encryption. In *EUROCRYPT '02*, volume 2332 of *LNCS*, pages 45–64. Springer-Verlag, 2002.
4. R. Gennaro and V. Shoup. A Note on The Encryption Scheme of Kurosawa and Desmedt. Cryptology ePrint Archive, Report 2004/194, 2004. http://eprint.iacr.org/.
5. K. Gjøsteen. Symmetric Subgroup Membership Problems. In S. Vaudenay, editor, *PKC '05*, volume 3386 of *LNCS*, pages 104–119. Springer-Verlag, 2005.
6. J. M. González-Nieto, C. Boyd, and E. Dawson. A Public Key Cryptosystem Based On A Subgroup Membership Problem. *Design, Codes and Cryptography*, 36(3):301–316, 2005.
7. K. Kurosawa and Y. Desmedt. A New Paradigm of Hybrid Encryption Scheme. In *CRYPTO '04*, volume 3152 of *LNCS*, pages 426–442. Springer-Verlag, 2004.
8. K. Kurosawa, Y. Katayama, W. Ogata, and S. Tsujii. General public key residue cryptosystems and mental poker protocols. In *EUROCRYPT '90*, volume 473 of *LNCS*, pages 374–388. Springer-Verlag, 1990.
9. T. Okamoto and S. Uchiyama. A New Public-Key Cryptosystem as Secure as Factoring. In *EUROCRYPT '98*, volume 1403 of *LNCS*, pages 308–318. Springer-Verlag, 1998.
10. P. Paillier. Public-Key Cryptosystems Based on Composite Degree Residuosity Classes. In *EUROCRYPT '99*, volume 1592 of *LNCS*, pages 223–238. Springer-Verlag, 1999.
11. P. C. van Oorschot and M. J. Wiener. On Diffie-Hellman Key Agreement with Short Exponents. In *EUROCRYPT '96*, volume 1070 of *LNCS*, pages 332–343. Springer-Verlag, 1996.
12. A. Yamamura and T. Saito. Private Information Retrieval based on the Subgroup Membership Problem. In *ACISP '01*, volume 2119 of *LNCS*, pages 206–220. Springer-Verlag, 2001.

Efficient Identity-Based Encryption with Tight Security Reduction

Nuttapong Attrapadung[1], Jun Furukawa[1,2], Takeshi Gomi[1],
Goichiro Hanaoka[3], Hideki Imai[3], and Rui Zhang[3]

[1] Institute of Industrial Science, University of Tokyo, Japan
{nuts, takego}@imailab.iis.u-tokyo.ac.jp
[2] NEC Corporation, Japan
j-furukawa@ay.jp.nec.com
[3] Research Center for Information Security, AIST, Japan
{hanaoka-goichiro, h-imai, r-zhang}@aist.go.jp

Abstract. In a famous paper at CRYPTO'01, Boneh and Franklin proposed the first fully functional identity-based encryption scheme (IBE), around fifteen years after the concept was introduced by Shamir. Their scheme achieves chosen-ciphertext security (*i.e.*, secure in the sense of IND-ID-CCA); however, the security reduction is far from being tight.

In this paper, we present an efficient variant of the Boneh-Franklin scheme that achieves a tight security reduction. Our scheme is basically an IBE scheme under two keys, one of which is randomly chosen and given to the user. It can be viewed as a continuation of an idea introduced by Katz and Wang; however, unlike the Katz-Wang variant, our scheme is quite efficient, as its ciphertext size is roughly comparable to that of the original full Boneh-Franklin scheme. The security of our scheme can be based on either the gap bilinear Diffie-Hellman (GBDH) or the decisional bilinear Diffie-Hellman (DBDH) assumptions.

1 Introduction

Identity Based Encryption (IBE) provides a public key encryption mechanism where an arbitrary string, such as recipient's identity, can be served as a public key. The ability to use identities as public keys avoids the need to distribute public key certificates. Such a scheme is largely motivated by many applications such as to encrypt emails using recipient's email address or to encrypt messages for users that have not their proper key at that moment.

Although the concept of identity based encryption was proposed two decades ago [21], it is only recently that the first fully functional schemes were proposed. Boneh and Franklin [5,6] defined a security model namely IND-ID-CCA and gave the first efficient construction provably secure in the random oracle model based on the bilinear Diffie-Hellman (BDH) assumption. A few years after, new schemes were proposed and shown to be secure without random oracles, but in a weaker model of security known as "Selective-ID" model [8,2]. Such schemes in this weaker model are known to be secure also in the sense of IND-ID-CCA, but the

D. Pointcheval, Y. Mu, and K. Chen (Eds.): CANS 2006, LNCS 4301, pp. 19–36, 2006.
© Springer-Verlag Berlin Heidelberg 2006

proofs use an inefficient security reduction [2], which degrades reduction costs by a factor of the size of identities' space, which is indeed not polynomial in the security parameter. Boneh and Boyen [3] subsequently proposed the first scheme which is provably secure in the sense of IND-ID-CCA with a polynomial time reduction in the absence of random oracles, which was then improved by Waters [23].

However, for each of the above schemes, the security as in the sense of IND-ID-CCA is reduced only *loosely* to its underlying intractability assumption. An inefficient security reduction would imply either a lower security level or the requirement of larger key and ciphertext sizes to obtain the same security level.

It had been an open problem (as posed in [23,12]) whether efficient IBE systems can exist with their security in the sense of IND-ID-CCA being reduced *tightly* (*i.e.*, the factor between the difficulty of the underlying problem and the security of the scheme being only a constant term, as close to 1 as possible) to some reasonable intractability assumption. In the standard model, this problem was partially solved recently by Gentry [13], which we will discuss below.

In the random oracle model, however, essentially it has been solved using a technique by Katz and Wang [16]. However, they only introduced the key technique at the end of their paper [16], of which main topic was regarding a different subject, namely, signature schemes; hence, some thoughts were left to the reader.

Towards Achieving Tightly IND-ID-CCA-secure IBE. As a prologue to our result, we will explain that by applying the Katz-Wang technique (in order to achieve tight reduction) and the generic Fujisaki-Okamoto [10,11] transforms (in order to achieve ID-CCA security) to the basic Boneh-Franklin scheme, one would already get such a tightly IND-ID-CCA-secure scheme (or to be more precise, tightly reduced to the Gap BDH problem). We note that the only thing that we have to take into account is that we should apply the Katz-Wang technique first and then apply the Fujisaki-Okamoto transform over it. Applying in the reverse order will yield an insecure scheme (*cf.* §3).

Unfortunately, it turns out that the ciphertexts in this scheme are roughly twice as much as in the *full* Boneh-Franklin scheme and the encryption time is twice long. Recall that efficiency is one of the important motivations for designing schemes with tight security reduction. Hence the above scheme is not really a desirable result. Therefore, an important problem left to solve is to construct a tightly IND-ID-CCA-secure IBE scheme of which efficiency does not degrade much, in particular, degrades only less than twice, from the original full Boneh-Franklin scheme.

Our Contribution. Our result is a new efficient IBE scheme with a tight reduction to either the gap bilinear Diffie-Hellman (GBDH) problem or the decisional bilinear Diffie-Hellman (DBDH) problem. This is done by first (tightly) reducing the security of our scheme to the list bilinear Diffie-Hellman (LBDH) problem, which itself can be shown to be tightly reduced to the GBDH or DBDH problem.

Our scheme is quite efficient in term of ciphertext size: it is comparable to that of the full Boneh-Franklin IBE. Moreover, it also outperforms the tightly secure IBE scheme mentioned above (whose ciphertexts are roughly twice longer). Furthermore, one can precompute most of the quantities during the encryption process, before knowing the message.

Related Work. As mentioned above, Gentry [13] recently proposed a fully-secure IBE scheme proven secure in the standard model with a tight security reduction under a new assumption called q'-Decision Augmented BDH Exponent (q'-DABDHE), where $q' - 2$ is the number of private key extraction queries. However, this is not a very satisfying solution to the open problem, as already mentioned by Gentry [13] himself, since (1) the q'-DABDHE assumption is seemingly stronger than the DBDH assumption and (2) it is not clear what it means to have a tight reduction to the q'-DABDHE assumption, since this assumption varies as q' varies. Typically, it is preferable to obtain a tight reduction under a "mild assumption" (*cf.* see the precise definition in [7]), such as the DBDH assumption. In contrast, our scheme is based on the DBDH or GBDH assumptions, albeit proven secure in the random oracle model. Moreover, due to a recent attack over this DABDHE assumption by Cheon [9], to achieve a satisfactory security level for the Gentry IBE, one has to choose larger bilinear groups, which then result in longer ciphertexts.

Roadmap. We begin in §2 with some definitions. Then, in §3, we recall the idea of Katz and Wang, and show how it allows a tight reduction from IND-ID-CPA attackers. We then explain secure and insecure applications of the Fujisaki-Okamoto transformations to the Katz-Wang variant of the Boneh-Franklin IBE. In §4, we introduce our new IBE scheme, and show how it achieves IND-ID-CCA security, with tight reduction. In §4.3, we compare our scheme with existing ones.

2 Preliminaries

2.1 Identity-Based Encryption

Formally, an IBE scheme consists of four polynomial-time algorithms:

Setup: takes a security parameter k and returns params (system parameters) and master-key. Intuitively, params will be publicly known, while the master-key will be known only to the private key generator.

Extract: takes as input params, master-key, and an arbitrary ID $\in \{0, 1\}^*$, and returns a private key sk. Here ID is an arbitrary string that will be used as a public key, and sk is the corresponding private decryption key.

Encrypt: takes as input params, ID, and $M \in \mathcal{M}$. It returns a ciphertext $C \in \mathcal{C}$.

Decrypt: takes as input params, $C \in \mathcal{C}$, and a private key sk. It returns $M \in \mathcal{M}$ or *"reject"*, which is a special symbol not in $\mathcal{M}$.

These algorithms must satisfy the standard consistency constraint; that is, if (params, master-key, $\mathcal{M}, \mathcal{C}$) $\leftarrow$ **Setup**(1^k), then for all ID and all $M \in \mathcal{M}$, $M =$ **Decrypt**(params, **Encrypt**(params, ID, M), **Extract**(params, master-key, ID)).

Security Notion. We review the strongest security definition for IBE, namely, semantic security under chosen ciphertext and chosen identity attacks (IND-ID-CCA) [5,6]. The IND-ID-CCA game takes place between the challenger and the adversary $\mathcal{A}$:

Setup: The challenger takes a security parameter k and runs the **Setup** algorithm. It gives the adversary $\mathcal{A}$ the resulting system parameters params. It keeps the master-key to itself.

Phase 1: $\mathcal{A}$ issues queries $q_1, \cdots, q_m$ adaptively where query q_i is one of:
- EXTRACTION query $\langle ID_i \rangle$: The challenger responds by running algorithm **Extract** to generate the private key sk_i corresponding to the public key $\langle ID_i \rangle$. It sends sk_i to $\mathcal{A}$.
- DECRYPTION query $\langle ID_i, C_i \rangle$: The challenger responds by running algorithm **Extract** to generate the private key sk_i corresponding to ID_i. It then runs algorithm **Decrypt** to decrypt the ciphertext C_i using the private key sk_i. It sends the result to $\mathcal{A}$.

Challenge: Once the adversary decides that Phase 1 is over it outputs two equal length plaintexts $M_0, M_1 \in \mathcal{M}$ and an identity ID^* on which it wishes to be challenged. The only constraint is that ID^* did not appear in any Extraction query in Phase 1. The challenger picks a random bit $\beta \in \{0, 1\}$, sets $C^* = \mathbf{Encrypt}(\mathsf{Params}, ID^*, M_\beta)$, and sends C^* to $\mathcal{A}$.

Phase 2: $\mathcal{A}$ issues more queries $q_{m+1}, \ldots, q_{max}$ where each is one of:
- EXTRACTION query $\langle ID_i \rangle$ where $ID_i \neq ID^*$: challenger responds as before.
- DECRYPTION query $\langle ID_i, C_i \rangle \neq \langle ID^*, C^* \rangle$: challenger responds as before.

Guess: The adversary outputs a guess $\beta' \in \{0, 1\}$ and wins the game if $\beta = \beta'$.

We define adversary $\mathcal{A}$'s advantage in attacking the scheme $\mathcal{E}$ as $\mathsf{AdvIBE}_{\mathcal{E}}(\mathcal{A}) = |\Pr[\beta = \beta'] - 1/2|$. We say that $\mathcal{A}$ is an (ϵ, t)-IND-ID-CCA adversary if $\mathsf{AdvIBE}_{\mathcal{E}}(\mathcal{A}) \geq \epsilon$ and its running time is at most t. We say that an IBE scheme $\mathcal{E}$ is (ϵ, t)-IND-ID-CCA secure if there exists no (ϵ, t)-IND-ID-CCA adversary.

2.2   Bilinear Maps

We briefly review several facts about bilinear maps. Throughout this paper, we let $\mathbb{G}_1$ and $\mathbb{G}_2$ be two multiplicative cyclic groups of prime order q and g be a generator of $\mathbb{G}_1$. A *bilinear map* $e : \mathbb{G}_1 \times \mathbb{G}_1 \to \mathbb{G}_2$ satisfies the following properties: (i) *Bilinearity*: For all $u, v \in \mathbb{G}_1$ and $a, b \in \mathbb{Z}$, $e(u^a, v^b) = e(u, v)^{ab}$. (ii) *Non-degeneracy*: $e(g, g) \neq 1$. (iii) *Computability*: There is an efficient algorithm to compute $e(u, v)$ for any $u, v \in \mathbb{G}_1$.

2.3   Underlying Hard Problems

We review hard problems related to bilinear maps which are those variants of *bilinear Diffie-Hellman* (BDH) problems: the *computational BDH* (CBDH) [5], the *list BDH* (LBDH), the *decisional BDH* (DBDH) [8], and the *gap BDH* (GBDH) [20] problems.

CBDH and LBDH Problems. The ℓ-*LBDH problem* is defined as follows: given a tuple $(g, g^a, g^b, g^c) \in (\mathbb{G}_1)^4$ as input, output a list $\mathcal{L}$ of length at most

ℓ $(\ell \geq 1)$ which contains $T \in \mathbb{G}_2$ such that $T = e(g,g)^{abc}$. Especially, 1-LBDH problem is referred to as the *CBDH problem*. We say that $\mathcal{A}$ is a (ϵ, t)-ℓ-LBDH algorithm if it runs with time at most t and outputs a list $\mathcal{L}$ of length at most ℓ which contains $T = e(g,g)^{abc}$ with probability at least ϵ, that is,

$$\Pr[\mathcal{A}(g, g^a, g^b, g^c) = \mathcal{L} \wedge e(g,g)^{abc} \in \mathcal{L} \wedge |\mathcal{L}| \leq \ell] \geq \epsilon,$$

where $|\mathcal{L}|$ denotes the number of elements of $\mathcal{L}$ and the probability is taken over the random choice of generator $g \in \mathbb{G}_1^*$, the random choice of $a, b, c \in \mathbb{Z}_q$, and random coins consumed by $\mathcal{A}$.

DBDH Problem. The *DBDH problem* is defined as follows: given a tuple $(g, g^a, g^b, g^c, T) \in (\mathbb{G}_1)^4 \times \mathbb{G}_2$ as input, outputs a bit $\beta \in \{0,1\}$. We say that $\mathcal{A}$ is a (ϵ, t)-DBDH algorithm if it runs with time at most t, and distinguishes the BDH-tuple with advantage at least ϵ, that is,

$$\left| \Pr[\mathcal{A}(g, g^a, g^b, g^c, e(g,g)^{abc}) = 0] - \Pr[\mathcal{A}(g, g^a, g^b, g^c, T) = 0] \right| \geq \epsilon,$$

where the probability is taken over the random choice of generator $g \in \mathbb{G}_1^*$, the random choice of $a, b, c \in \mathbb{Z}_q$, the random choice of T in $\mathbb{G}_2$, and the random coins consumed by $\mathcal{A}$.

GBDH Problem. The *GBDH problem* is defined as follows: given a tuple $(g, g^a, g^b, g^c) \in (\mathbb{G}_1)^4$ as input, output $e(g,g)^{abc} \in \mathbb{G}_2$ with the help of a DBDH oracle $\mathcal{O}$ which for given $(g, g^a, g^b, g^c, T) \in (\mathbb{G}_1)^4 \times \mathbb{G}_2$, answers *"true"* if $T = e(g,g)^{abc}$, or *"false"* otherwise [20]. We say that $\mathcal{A}$ is a (ϵ, t)-GBDH algorithm if it runs with time at most t and succeeds in outputting $e(g,g)^{abc}$ with probability at least ϵ, that is,

$$\Pr[\mathcal{A}^{\mathcal{O}}(g, g^a, g^b, g^c) = e(g,g)^{abc}] \geq \epsilon,$$

where the probability is taken over the random choice of generator $g \in \mathbb{G}_1^*$, the random choice of $a, b, c \in \mathbb{Z}_q$, and random coins consumed by $\mathcal{A}$.

2.4   IND-CCA Length Preserving Symmetric Key Encryption

A (deterministic) symmetric key encryption (SKE) scheme $\mathcal{E} = (\text{Enc}, \text{Dec})$ contains two algorithms: an encryption algorithm $\text{Enc} : \mathcal{K} \times \mathcal{M} \to \mathcal{C}$ and a decryption algorithm $\text{Dec} : \mathcal{K} \times \mathcal{C} \to \mathcal{M}$, where $\mathcal{K}$, $\mathcal{M}$ and $\mathcal{C}$ are the spaces of keys, plaintexts and ciphertexts, respectively. Two algorithms are conform to the standard consistency constraint: for all $K \in \mathcal{K}, M \in \mathcal{M}$, $M = \text{Dec}(K, \text{Enc}(K, M))$. Moreover, if for all $K \in \mathcal{K}, M \in \mathcal{M}$, $|\text{Enc}(K, M)| = |M|$ then we say that $\mathcal{E}$ is *length preserving*. We often let $\text{Enc}_K(\cdot)$ denote $\text{Enc}(K, \cdot)$.

Security Notion. A challenger plays the following game with an adversary $\mathcal{A}$: The challenger randomly chooses a key $K \in \mathcal{K}$ and a bit γ. $\mathcal{A}$ is given access to two oracles $\text{Enc}_K(\cdot)$ and $\text{Dec}_K(\cdot)$. $\mathcal{A}$ chooses a pair (M_0, M_1) in M of the same length that were not submitted to $\text{Enc}_K(\cdot)$ or obtained from $\text{Dec}_K(\cdot)$, submits to $\text{Enc}_K(\cdot)$ and gets $C^* = \text{Enc}_K(M_\gamma)$. $\mathcal{A}$ can further query the oracles as before but is not allowed to ask $\text{Dec}_K(C^*)$, $\text{Enc}_K(M_0)$ or $\text{Enc}_K(M_1)$. Finally, $\mathcal{A}$ outputs a bit γ'. The advantage of $\mathcal{A}$ is defined by $\text{AdvSKE}_{\mathcal{E}}(\mathcal{A}) = |\Pr[\gamma = \gamma'] - 1/2|$. We say that $\mathcal{A}$ is an (ϵ, t)-IND-CCA adversary if $\text{AdvSKE}_{\mathcal{E}}(\mathcal{A}) \geq \epsilon$ and it runs in time at most t. We say that a SKE scheme $\mathcal{E}$ is (ϵ, t)-IND-CCA secure if there exists no (ϵ, t)-IND-CCA adversary.

We will use a length preserving IND-CCA-secure SKE in our construction.[1] Such a scheme can be built, for example, by applying CMC [14] or EME [15] mode of operation to a block cipher, if the underlying block cipher is modeled as (strong) pseudorandom permutation, e.g. AES. Though the above formulation of IND-CCA security differs from that of [14], one can show by some standard arguments that it is implied by the definition given in [14].

3   Boneh-Franklin IBE and Its Katz-Wang Variants

3.1   Boneh-Franklin Identity Based Encryption

The Boneh-Franklin [5,6] IBE scheme (more precisely, its basic variant) is defined in Table 1. In Tables 1 and 2, $M \in \{0,1\}^n$ denotes a plaintext, $G : \mathbb{G}_2 \to \{0,1\}^n$ and $H : \{0,1\}^* \to \mathbb{G}_1$ denote random oracles. We refer to [5,6] for a more precise study of its security. In this subsection, we just recall that the basic version of the Boneh-Franklin IBE is IND-ID-CPA secure, while using Fujisaki-Okamoto [11] transform, one gets the full version of the Boneh-Franklin IBE, which is IND-ID-CCA secure. All these reductions are in the random oracle model.

Table 1. The Boneh-Franklin Identity Based Encryption

The Boneh-Franklin Identity Based Encryption: BF	
Setup (1^k): $\quad s \leftarrow \mathbb{Z}_q^*; \ g_{pub} := g^s$ $\quad \text{params} := \langle q, \mathbb{G}_1, \mathbb{G}_2, e, n, g, g_{pub}, G, H \rangle$ $\quad \text{master-key} := s$ $\quad return \ (\text{params}, \text{master-key})$	**Extract** (ID, params, master-key): $\quad h_{\text{ID}} := H(\text{ID})$ $\quad d_{\text{ID}} := (h_{\text{ID}})^s$ $\quad return \ d_{\text{ID}}$
Encrypt (ID, params, M): $\quad h_{\text{ID}} := H(\text{ID}); \quad r \leftarrow \mathbb{Z}_q^*$ $\quad w := e(g_{pub}, h_{\text{ID}})^r$ $\quad C := \langle g^r, \ G(w) \oplus M \rangle$ $\quad return \ C$	**Decrypt** $(C, \text{params}, d_{\text{ID}})$: $\quad \text{parse } C = \langle u, V \rangle$ $\quad w' := e(u, d_{\text{ID}})$ $\quad M := V \oplus G(w')$ $\quad return \ M$

Unfortunately, the security reduction for the Boneh-Franklin IBE scheme is very loose, as there is a factor equal to the number of extract queries that an

---

[1] Indeed our scheme does not need the full power of the IND-CCA-secure SKE. More precisely, as it will become clear, we do not need the encryption oracles at all.

attacker can make, between the difficulty of the underlying problem (*i.e.*, the CBDH) and the security of the scheme. Roughly, this factor is due to the fact that the reduction must *guess* which of the identity will be used in the challenge, as for this special identity, it must return a special H output, while for other identities, it must return another type of H output, to be able to answer extract queries.

3.2   Katz and Wang's Variants of Boneh-Franklin IBE

A technique to solve the tightness problem of IBE has been presented by Katz and Wang at the end of a paper [16] whose subject was quite different. Hence, these authors only gave few points of their ideas, and left the rest to the reader. In this subsection, we explain what we believe that Katz and Wang meant.

Katz and Wang proposed that, for each identity, there should be two corresponding public keys: instead of using $H(\mathsf{ID})$ as in the Boneh-Franklin, they proposed to use both $H(\mathsf{ID}, 0)$ and $H(\mathsf{ID}, 1)$. However, only one of the corresponding private key is known to the user. With this trick, the reduction does not need to guess which of the identity will be used in the challenge: for each identity, one of the two hash output (let say the one with bit b_{ID}) is controlled in order the simulator to be able to answer to extract queries, while the other is let to be used in case the identity is the one that appears in the challenge. Hence, for the identity $\mathsf{ID}^\star$ of the challenge, if the bit $b_{\mathsf{ID}^\star}$ is absolutely indistinguishable to the attacker, with a chance of one half, $H(\mathsf{ID}^\star, \bar{b}_{\mathsf{ID}^\star})$ will be used by the attacker and the simulator will succeed in solving the underlying problem. More precisely, the idea of Katz and Wang is depicted in the Table 2.

From [16], the security of this scheme against IND-ID-CPA can be *tightly* reduced to the Gap Bilinear Diffie-Hellman problem. However, Katz and Wang did not explain how to achieve a tight IND-ID-CCA security with their scheme.

One approach to obtain such a tightly IND-ID-CCA-secure scheme is by applying both the Katz-Wang technique (to achieve tight reduction) and the generic Fujisaki-Okamoto [10,11] transforms (to achieve ID-CCA security) to the basic Boneh-Franklin scheme. Indeed, (at least) two schemes can be obtained, depending on the order of applications of the two techniques as follows.

KW(FO(BF)): Fujisaki-Okamoto then Katz-Wang. This scheme is depicted in Table C in Appendix C. We will prove a more general result: for all Σ that is an IND-ID-CCA-secure IBE, we have that the scheme $\mathsf{KW}(\Sigma)$, which is obtained from applying the Katz-Wang technique to Σ, is *not* IND-ID-CCA-secure. Let E be the encryption function of Σ. We construct the adversary $\mathcal{A}$ as follows. After setup phase, $\mathcal{A}$ asks the decryption oracle for $(\mathsf{E}_{H(\mathsf{ID}^\star, 0)}(M_0), \mathsf{E}_{H(\mathsf{ID}^\star, 1)}(M_1))$ for some $M_0 \neq M_1$. If the result is M_α then we know that $b_{\mathsf{ID}^\star} = \alpha$. Now $\mathcal{A}$ submits $M_0^\star, M_1^\star, \mathsf{ID}^\star$ to the challenge encryption oracle and gets back $(C_0^\star, C_1^\star) = (\mathsf{E}_{H(\mathsf{ID}^\star, 0)}(M_\beta^\star), \mathsf{E}_{H(\mathsf{ID}^\star, 1)}(M_\beta^\star))$ and will try to guess β. Then $\mathcal{A}$ asks the decryption oracle for $(C_0^\star, \mathsf{E}_{H(\mathsf{ID}^\star, 1)}(M'))$ if $b_{\mathsf{ID}^\star} = 0$ or $(\mathsf{E}_{H(\mathsf{ID}^\star, 0)}(M'), C_1^\star)$ if $b_{\mathsf{ID}^\star} = 1$

Table 2. The Katz-Wang Identity Based Encryption

The Katz-Wang Identity Based Encryption: KW(BF)	
Setup (1^k): $\quad s \leftarrow \mathbb{Z}_q^*; \ g_{pub} := g^s$ $\quad$ params $:= \langle q, \mathbb{G}_1, \mathbb{G}_2, e, n, g, g_{pub}, G, H \rangle$ $\quad$ master-key $:= s$ $\quad return$ (params, master-key)	**Extract**[†] (ID, params, master-key): $\quad b_{ID} \leftarrow \{0, 1\}$ $\quad h_{ID} := H(ID, b_{ID})$ $\quad d_{ID} := (h_{ID})^s$ $\quad sk_{ID} := (d_{ID}, b_{ID})$ $\quad return \ sk_{ID}$
Encrypt (ID, params, M): $\quad h_{ID,0} := H(ID, 0)$ $\quad h_{ID,1} := H(ID, 1)$ $\quad r_0 \leftarrow \mathbb{Z}_q^*$ $\quad r_1 \leftarrow \mathbb{Z}_q^*$ $\quad w_0 := e(g_{pub}, h_{ID,0})^{r_0}$ $\quad w_1 := e(g_{pub}, h_{ID,1})^{r_1}$ $\quad C := \langle g^{r_0}, \ G(w_0) \oplus M, g^{r_1}, \ G(w_1) \oplus M \rangle$ $\quad return \ C$	**Decrypt** $(C, \text{params}, b_{ID}, d_{ID})$: $\quad$ parse $C = \langle u_0, V_0, u_1, V_1 \rangle$ $\quad w' := e(u_{b_{ID}}, d_{ID})$ $\quad M := V_{b_{ID}} \oplus G(w')$ $\quad return \ M$

[†] **Extract** first checks to see if sk_{ID} has been generated before. If it has, the previously-generated sk_{ID} is output.

for some $M' \neq M_0^*, M_1^*$. The oracle will return M_β^* with probability 1. $\mathcal{A}$ then outputs β and wins the game.

FO(KW(BF)): Katz-Wang then Fujisaki-Okamoto. This scheme is depicted in Table C in Appendix C. To analyze its security, we first remind the theorem which states that the Fujisaki-Okamoto transforms [10,11] convert any IND-ID-CPA-secure scheme to a IND-ID-CCA-secure scheme with tight security reduction in the random oracle model.[2] Hence, due to the fact that KW(BF) is IND-ID-CPA-secure with a tight reduction to the GBDH problem, we have that FO(KW(BF)) is IND-ID-CCA-secure with a tight reduction to the same problem.

A disadvantage of this latter scheme is its cost: roughly, the FO(KW(BF)) IBE ciphertexts are twice as much as in the full Boneh-Franklin IBE, and the encryption process is twice longer (*i.e.*, two exponentiations and two pairing computations).

4   Our IBE Scheme

4.1   Proposed Scheme (TightIBE)

In this section, we give the description of our proposed construction. Let k be a given security parameter. Let $\mathbb{G}_1$ and $\mathbb{G}_2$ be two groups of order q (which is a k-bit prime number) and g be a generator of $\mathbb{G}_1$. Let $e : \mathbb{G}_1 \times \mathbb{G}_1 \rightarrow \mathbb{G}_2$ be a bilinear

---

[2] Indeed, this fact was not clear in the first place, since the Fujisaki-Okamoto transform was originally designed and proved to be secure for the case of normal PKE; therefore, it was not known whether it can apply to IBE generically. However, the recent work of [17] has proved that this fact also holds for the case of IBE.

map. Let $\mathcal{E} = (\text{Enc}, \text{Dec})$ be a SKE that the key space is $\mathcal{K}$ and the message space is $\mathcal{M}$. Let $G, H, \hat{H}$ be cryptographic hash functions $G : \{0,1\}^* \to \{0,1\}^{k_1}$ for some k_1, $H : \{0,1\}^* \to \mathbb{G}_1$, $\hat{H} : \{0,1\}^* \to \mathbb{Z}_q \times \mathcal{K}$ respectively. The TightIBE scheme consists of the four algorithms which are shown in Table 3.

The initial intuition of our scheme for saving the ciphertext size is that (1) we reuse the randomness for both ciphertexts of the Katz-Wang twin encryption and (2) we encrypt the message M once via the symmetric encryption, not twice as in the FO(KW(BF)) scheme. We emphasize that, however, it was *not* clear in the first place that the security from Katz-Wang scheme will still hold when the randomness is reused. Our scheme is constructed in such a way that it achieves both above intuitive goals while preserving security, as we will show the proof in the next subsection.

Table 3. The TightIBE scheme

TightIBE	
Setup (1^k): $\quad s \leftarrow \mathbb{Z}_q^*; \; g_{pub} := g^s$ $\quad$ params $:= \langle q, \mathbb{G}_1, \mathbb{G}_2, e, g, g_{pub}, G, H, \hat{H} \rangle$ $\quad$ master-key $:= s$ $\quad return$ (params, master-key)	**Extract**[†] (ID, params, master-key): $\quad b_{\text{ID}} \leftarrow \{0,1\}$ $\quad h_{\text{ID}, b_{\text{ID}}} := H(\text{ID}, b_{\text{ID}});$ $\quad d_{\text{ID}} := (h_{\text{ID}, b_{\text{ID}}})^s$ $\quad sk_{\text{ID}} := (d_{\text{ID}}, b_{\text{ID}})$ $\quad return \; sk_{\text{ID}}$
Encrypt (ID, params, M): $\quad h_{\text{ID},0} := H(\text{ID}, 0)$ $\quad h_{\text{ID},1} := H(\text{ID}, 1)$ $\quad R \leftarrow \{0,1\}^{k_1}$ $\quad r\|K := \hat{H}(R, \text{ID})$ $\quad w_0 := e(g_{pub}, h_{\text{ID},0})^r$ $\quad w_1 := e(g_{pub}, h_{\text{ID},1})^r$ $\quad u := g^r$ $\quad V_0 := G(w_0, \text{ID}, 0) \oplus R$ $\quad V_1 := G(w_1, \text{ID}, 1) \oplus R$ $\quad \alpha := \text{Enc}_K(M)$ $\quad C := \langle u, V_0, V_1, \alpha \rangle$ $\quad return \; C$	**Decrypt** $(C, \text{params}, sk_{\text{ID}})$: $\quad$ parse $C = \langle u, V_0, V_1, \alpha \rangle$ $\quad w'_{b_{\text{ID}}} := e(u, d_{\text{ID}})$ $\quad R_{b_{\text{ID}}} := V_{b_{\text{ID}}} \oplus G(w'_{b_{\text{ID}}}, \text{ID}, b_{\text{ID}})$ $\quad r'\|K := \hat{H}(R_{b_{\text{ID}}}, \text{ID})$ $\quad w'_{\bar{b}_{\text{ID}}} := e(g_{pub}, h_{\text{ID}, \bar{b}_{\text{ID}}})^{r'}$ $\quad R_{\bar{b}_{\text{ID}}} := V_{\bar{b}_{\text{ID}}} \oplus G(w'_{\bar{b}_{\text{ID}}}, \text{ID}, \bar{b}_{\text{ID}})$ $\quad$ if $R_{b_{\text{ID}}} \neq R_{\bar{b}_{\text{ID}}} \vee u \neq g^{r'}$ $\quad\quad return$ "reject" $\quad$ else $\quad\quad M := \text{Dec}_K(\alpha)$ $\quad\quad return \; M$

[†] **Extract** first checks to see if sk_{ID} has been generated before. If it has, the previously-generated sk_{ID} is output.

4.2 Security Results

We first state the reduction of the security of our scheme to the LBDH problem.

Theorem 1. *Suppose that the hash functions $G, H, \hat{H}$ are random oracles. Suppose there exists an $(\epsilon_{ibe}, t_{ibe})$-IND-ID-CCA adversary $\mathcal{A}$ against TightIBE. Suppose $\mathcal{A}$ makes at most q_G G-queries, q_H H-queries, $q_{\hat{H}}$ $\hat{H}$-queries, q_D decryption queries, and q_E extraction queries. Suppose that $\mathcal{E}$ is an $(\epsilon_{sym}, t_{sym})$-IND-CCA secure SKE. Then there exists an $(\epsilon_{lbdh}, t_{lbdh})$-$(q_G + q_D)$-LBDH algorithm where*

$$\epsilon_{lbdh} \geq \frac{1}{2}\epsilon_{ibe} - \epsilon_{sym} - \frac{q_{\hat{H}}}{2^{k_1+1}},$$

$$t_{lbdh} \leq t_{ibe} + (3q_H + q_G + 3q_E + 10q_D)\tau + q_{\hat{H}}\tau' + q_D t_{sym},$$

where, τ is the maximum time among times for computing an exponentiation in $\mathbb{G}_1, \mathbb{G}_2$ and pairing e, and τ' is the time for responding to an $\hat{H}$-query.

Before going to the proof, we now state the reduction of the security of our scheme to the DBDH, GBDH and CBDH problems as follows. This result is immediate from the reductions from the LBDH problem to these three problems, which we describe as Lemma 3 in Appendix A.

Theorem 2. *Given the same hypothesis as in Theorem 1, we have that there exists an $(\epsilon_{dbdh}, t_{dbdh})$-DBDH algorithm $\mathcal{D}$, an $(\epsilon_{gbdh}, t_{gbdh})$-GBDH algorithm $\mathcal{G}$, and an $(\epsilon_{cbdh}, t_{cbdh})$-CBDH algorithm $\mathcal{C}$ such that*

$$\left.\begin{array}{l} \epsilon_{dbdh} \geq \frac{1}{2}\epsilon_{ibe} - \epsilon_{sym} - \frac{q_{\hat{H}}}{2^{k_1+1}} - \frac{q_G + q_D}{|\mathbb{G}_2|}, \\[2mm] t_{dbdh} \leq t_{ibe} + (3q_H + q_G + 3q_E + 10q_D)\tau + q_{\hat{H}}\tau' + q_D t_{sym} + (q_G + q_D)\tau_1, \end{array}\right\} DBDH$$

$$\left.\begin{array}{l} \epsilon_{gbdh} \geq \frac{1}{2}\epsilon_{ibe} - \epsilon_{sym} - \frac{q_{\hat{H}}}{2^{k_1+1}}, \\[2mm] t_{gbdh} \leq t_{ibe} + (3q_H + q_G + 3q_E + 10q_D)\tau + q_{\hat{H}}\tau' + q_D t_{sym} + (q_G + q_D)\tau_2, \end{array}\right\} GBDH$$

$$\left.\begin{array}{l} \epsilon_{cbdh} \geq \frac{1}{q_G + q_D}\left(\frac{1}{2}\epsilon_{ibe} - \epsilon_{sym} - \frac{q_{\hat{H}}}{2^{k_1+1}}\right), \\[2mm] t_{cbdh} \leq t_{ibe} + (3q_H + q_G + 3q_E + 10q_D)\tau + q_{\hat{H}}\tau' + q_D t_{sym} + \tau_3, \end{array}\right\} CBDH$$

where τ, τ' are defined as in Theorem 1 and τ_1, τ_2, τ_3 are defined as in Lemma 3, namely, where τ_1 is the time required to check an equality of two elements in $\mathbb{G}_2$, τ_2 is the time required to access the DBDH oracle (as provide for $\mathcal{G}$), and τ_3 is the time required to randomly choose one element from a list of size ℓ.

Now we present the proof of Theorem 1 as follows.

Proof. The proof is provided by a sequence of games. Let $(g, g_1 = g^a, g_2 = g^b, g_3 = g^c)$ be a random instance of the LBDH problem, for which we do not know a, b, c.

GAME $\mathbf{G}_0$: This is the real IND-ID-CCA game. We denote by S_0 the event that $\beta' = \beta$ and use a similar notation S_i in any $\mathbf{G}_i$ below. By definition, we have $\Pr[\mathsf{S}_0] = \frac{1}{2} + \epsilon_{ibe}$.

GAME $\mathbf{G}_1$: In this game, one makes classical simulation of the random oracles, with random answers for any new query, as shown in Figure 1. Moreover, it maintains the evaluation of b_{ID} for each ID by randomly choosing from $\{0, 1\}$ for the first-time evaluation and using the same value after that. This game is clearly identical to the previous one, hence $\Pr[\mathsf{S}_0] = \Pr[\mathsf{S}_1]$.

Simulation

G, H, $\hat{H}$ oracles

Query $G(w, \mathsf{ID}, b)$: if a record (w, ID, b, g) appears in the G-list, the answer is g. Otherwise g is chosen randomly in $\{0, 1\}^{k_1}$ and the record (w, ID, b, g) is added in the G-list.

Query $H(\mathsf{ID}, b)$: if a record $(\mathsf{ID}, b, *, h)$ appears in the H-list, the answer is h. Otherwise do the following.

▶ **Rule H$^{(1)}$**

  The answer h is chosen randomly in $\mathcal{G}_1$ and the record $(\mathsf{ID}, b, *, h)$ is added in the H-list.

Query $\hat{H}(R, \mathsf{ID})$: if a record (R, ID, r, K) appears in the $\hat{H}$-list, the answer is $r \| K$. Otherwise the answer (r, K) is chosen randomly in $\mathbb{Z}_q \times \mathcal{K}$ and the record (R, ID, r, K) is added in the $\hat{H}$-list.

Ext-Oracle

Query $\mathrm{EXTRACT}(\mathsf{ID})$: the answer $(b_{\mathsf{ID}}, d_{\mathsf{ID}})$ is defined by the following rules.

▶ **Rule Extract$^{(1)}$**

  Compute $d_{\mathsf{ID}} = H(\mathsf{ID}, b_{\mathsf{ID}})^s$.

Decryption-Oracle

Query $\mathrm{DECRYPT}(\mathsf{ID}, u, V_0, V_1, \alpha)$: the answer M is defined by the following rules. First get the secret key d_{ID} by using **Extract** rule.

▶ **Rule Decrypt–Exception$^{(1)}$**

  Do nothing.

Then compute:
(D1) $w'_{b_{\mathsf{ID}}} = e(u, d_{\mathsf{ID}})$, $R_{b_{\mathsf{ID}}} = V_{b_{\mathsf{ID}}} \oplus G(w'_{b_{\mathsf{ID}}}, \mathsf{ID}, b_{\mathsf{ID}})$,
(D2) $r' \| K = \hat{H}(R_{b_{\mathsf{ID}}}, \mathsf{ID})$,
(D3) $w'_{\bar{b}_{\mathsf{ID}}} = e(g_{pub}, H(\mathsf{ID}, \bar{b}_{\mathsf{ID}}))^{r'}$, $R_{\bar{b}_{\mathsf{ID}}} = V_{\bar{b}_{\mathsf{ID}}} \oplus G(w'_{\bar{b}_{\mathsf{ID}}}, \mathsf{ID}, \bar{b}_{\mathsf{ID}})$,
(D4) if $R_{b_{\mathsf{ID}}} \neq R_{\bar{b}_{\mathsf{ID}}}$ or $u \neq g^{r'}$, then return *"reject"*
    else compute $M = D_K(\alpha)$ and return M.

Challenge

For two messages (M_0, M_1) and identity $\mathsf{ID}^\star$, flip a coin β and set $M^\star = M_\beta$, choose randomly $R^\star \in \{0, 1\}^{k_1}$, and then answer $(u^\star, V_0^\star, V_1^\star, \alpha^\star)$ where

▶ **Rule Chal–DEM–Key$^{(1)}$**

  Compute $r^\star \| K^\star := \hat{H}(R^\star, \mathsf{ID}^\star)$, then let $K^\ddagger = K^\star$.

▶ **Rule Chal–KEM$^{(1)}$**

  $u^\star = g^{r^\star}$,
  $w_0^\star = e(g_{pub}, H(\mathsf{ID}^\star, 0))^{r^\star}$, $V_0^\star = G(w_0^\star, \mathsf{ID}^\star, 0) \oplus R^\star$,
  $w_1^\star = e(g_{pub}, H(\mathsf{ID}^\star, 1))^{r^\star}$, $V_1^\star = G(w_1^\star, \mathsf{ID}^\star, 1) \oplus R^\star$.

▶ **Rule Chal–DEM–Enc$^{(1)}$**

  Let $\alpha^\star = \mathrm{Enc}_{K^\ddagger}(M^\star)$.

Fig. 1. The formal simulation of the IND–ID–CCA game

GAME $\mathbf{G_2}$: In this game, we change the simulation of the H-oracle:

▶ **Rule** $\mathsf{H}^{(2)}$

  - If $b = b_{\mathsf{ID}}$, then randomly choose $\pi_{\mathsf{ID}} \in_R \mathbb{Z}_q$ and set $h = g^{\pi_{\mathsf{ID}}}$. Record $(\mathsf{ID}, b_{\mathsf{ID}}, \pi_{\mathsf{ID}}, h)$ in the H-list;
  - Else, randomly choose $\pi_{\mathsf{ID}} \in_R \mathbb{Z}_q$ and set $h = g_2^{\pi_{\mathsf{ID}}}$. Record $(\mathsf{ID}, \bar{b}_{\mathsf{ID}}, \pi_{\mathsf{ID}}, h)$ in the H-list.

The two games $\mathbf{G_1}$ and $\mathbf{G_2}$ are perfectly indistinguishable: $\Pr[\mathsf{S_1}] = \Pr[\mathsf{S_2}]$.

GAME $\mathbf{G_3}$: From now, we change the setup, as well as Extract rule. Instead of using $g_{pub} = g^s$, for a chosen $s \in \mathbb{Z}_q$, we use $g_{pub} = g_1$ (for which we do not know the value a such that $g_1 = g^a$). Furthermore our Extract rule becomes:

▶ **Rule** $\mathsf{Extract}^{(3)}$

  Ask $H(\mathsf{ID}, b_{\mathsf{ID}})$ to the H-oracle. Find $(\mathsf{ID}, b_{\mathsf{ID}}, \pi_{\mathsf{ID}}, h)$ in the H-list and let $d_{\mathsf{ID}} = g_1^{\pi_{\mathsf{ID}}}$.

One can see that d_{ID} is valid: $d_{\mathsf{ID}} = H(\mathsf{ID}, b_{\mathsf{ID}})^a$. This is since $H(\mathsf{ID}, b_{\mathsf{ID}}) = g^{\pi_{\mathsf{ID}}}$. The two games $\mathbf{G_2}$ and $\mathbf{G_3}$ are perfectly indistinguishable: $\Pr[\mathsf{S_2}] = \Pr[\mathsf{S_3}]$.

GAME $\mathbf{G_4}$: In this game, we make a conceptual modification for the decryption oracle. This modification will be useful in game $\mathbf{G_6}$ below.

▶ **Rule** $\mathsf{Decrypt\text{--}Exception}^{(4)}$

  - If $(\mathsf{ID}, u, V_0, V_1) = (\mathsf{ID}^\star, u^\star, V_0^\star, V_1^\star)$ but $\alpha \neq \alpha^*$, then return $\mathsf{Dec}_{K^\ddagger}(\alpha)$.
  - If $u \neq u^\star$ and $V_{b_{\mathsf{ID}^\star}} \oplus G(e(u, d_{\mathsf{ID}^\star}), \mathsf{ID}^\star, b_{\mathsf{ID}^\star}) = R^\star$, return "reject".

The two games $\mathbf{G_3}$ and $\mathbf{G_4}$ are perfectly indistinguishable since the change is only conceptual. The first one is verified by observing that from $u = u^\star$ we have $r = r^*$ which then leads to $R = R^\star$ due to (D1) and the above condition. Hence $K = K^\star = K^\ddagger$ due to (D2) and the Chal–DEM–Key rule. The second one is verified by first assuming that such a query is valid. Since $u \neq u^\star$, then $r \neq r^\star$. From the above constraint we must have $r\|K = \hat{H}(R^\star, \mathsf{ID}^\star) = r^\star\|*$ hence a contradiction. Thus such a query must be invalid. Therefore $\Pr[\mathsf{S_3}] = \Pr[\mathsf{S_4}]$.

GAME $\mathbf{G_5}$: In this game, we modify the challenge rule, by simplifying its KEM component to:

▶ **Rule** $\mathsf{Chal\text{--}KEM}^{(5)}$

  $u^\star = g_3,$
  $G_0^\dagger \leftarrow \{0,1\}^{k_1}, \qquad V_0^\star = G_0^\dagger \oplus R^\star,$
  $G_1^\dagger \leftarrow \{0,1\}^{k_1}, \qquad V_1^\star = G_1^\dagger \oplus R^\star.$

The two games $\mathbf{G_4}$ and $\mathbf{G_5}$ are perfectly indistinguishable unless at least one of the following events occurs:

  $\mathsf{AskGoodG} : (e(g, g)^{abc\pi_{\mathsf{ID}^\star}}, \mathsf{ID}^*, \bar{b}_{\mathsf{ID}^\star})$ is asked to G-oracle;
  $\mathsf{AskBadG} \;\; : (e(g_1, g_3)^{\pi_{\mathsf{ID}^\star}}, \mathsf{ID}^*, b_{\mathsf{ID}^\star})$ is asked to G-oracle

either by the adversary or the decryption oracle. We first claim the following.

Lemma 1. $\Pr[\mathsf{AskGoodG}] = \Pr[\mathsf{AskBadG}]$. (The proof is given in Appendix B.1).

By the difference lemma (see [22]), we thus have

$$|\Pr[\mathsf{S}_4] - \Pr[\mathsf{S}_5]| \leq \Pr[\mathsf{AskGoodG}] + \Pr[\mathsf{AskBadG}] \leq 2\Pr[\mathsf{AskGoodG}],$$

where the last inequality is due to Lemma 1. Before proving the claim, we will conclude the result from this game by constructing an algorithm $\mathcal{B}$ for solving the LBDH problem. Assume that $\mathsf{AskGoodG}$ occurs. Let L be a list which is empty at first. From each record $(w, \mathsf{ID}^\star, \bar{b}_{\mathsf{ID}^\star}, g)$ in the G-list, algorithm $\mathcal{B}$ adds $g^{1/\tau_{\mathsf{ID}^\star}}$ to the L list and output this list. Since $\mathsf{AskGoodG}$ occurs, L contains $e(g, g)^{abc}$. This implies $\Pr[\mathsf{AskGoodG}] \leq \epsilon_{lbdh}$. Hence, $|\Pr[\mathsf{S}_4] - \Pr[\mathsf{S}_5]| \leq 2\epsilon_{lbdh}$.

$\underline{\text{GAME } \mathbf{G}_6:}$ In this game, we modify the challenge rule, by simplifying its DEM component to:

▶ **Rule** Chal–DEM–Key$^{(6)}$
| Randomly choose $K^\dagger \in_R \mathcal{K}$, then let $K^\ddagger = K^\dagger$.

The two games $\mathbf{G}_5$ and $\mathbf{G}_6$ are perfectly indistinguishable unless the query $(R^\star, \mathsf{ID}^\star)$ is asked to the $\hat{H}$-oracle, by either the adversary or the decryption oracle. But the latter case is not possible. This is since such a decryption query must be $(\mathsf{ID}^\star, u, V_0, V_1, \alpha)$ such that $R^\star = V_{b_{\mathsf{ID}^\star}} \oplus G(e(u, d_{\mathsf{ID}^\star}), \mathsf{ID}^\star, b_{\mathsf{ID}^\star})$ in order to force the decryption oracle to ask $(R^\star, \mathsf{ID}^\star)$ to the $\hat{H}$-oracle. If $u = u^\star$, then this leads to $(\mathsf{ID}, u, V_0, V_1) = (\mathsf{ID}^\star, u^\star, V_0^\star, V_1^\star)$. Hence in this case the decryption query is either the challenge ciphertext itself (so it will be rejected) or its process for decryption falls into the first Decrypt–Exception rule (so the decryption oracle will not ask such a $\hat{H}$-oracle query). If $u \neq u^\star$, then such a query will be rejected due to the second Decrypt–Exception rule (and so in particular, the decryption oracle will not ask such a $\hat{H}$-oracle query). Therefore, from the difference lemma, we have

$$|\Pr[\mathsf{S}_5] - \Pr[\mathsf{S}_6]| \leq \frac{q_{\hat{H}}}{2^{k_1}}$$

which is the probability that the adversary correctly guesses $R^\star$ in one of $q_{\hat{H}}$ times. The adversary is forced to simply guess since the other information about $R^\star$ is perfectly hiding thanks to the independent random values $G_0^\dagger$ and $G_1^\dagger$.

$\underline{\text{GAME } \mathbf{G}_7:}$ In this game, we further modify the challenge rule, by replacing the challenge message by another fixed message with the same length:

▶ **Rule** Chal–DEM–Enc$^{(7)}$
| Let $\alpha^\star = \mathsf{Enc}_{K^\ddagger}(0^{|M^\star|})$.

The output of the adversary follows from a distribution that does not depend on β. Accordingly, $\Pr[\mathsf{S}_7] = 1/2$. We also claim the following lemma.

Lemma 2. $|\Pr[\mathsf{S}_6] - \Pr[\mathsf{S}_7]| \leq 2\epsilon_{sym}$. (The proof is given in Appendix B.2)

From all the results above, we now can conclude that $\epsilon_{ibe} \leq 2\epsilon_{lbdh} + 2\epsilon_{sym} + \frac{q_{\hat{H}}}{2^{k_1}}$, which completes the proof. The running time can be easily verified. $\square$

Table 4. Comparison among various IBE schemes provably secure in the random oracle model. q_H, q_E, q_D are the numbers of hash, extraction, decryption queries resp., where we assume the same number of hash queries for all random oracles in a scheme, if there are more than one. $|M|$ is the message length. t is the bit length of the representation of an element in $\mathbb{G}_1$. k_1 is the bit length of the randomness in the scheme such that $1/2^{k_1}$ must be made negligible in the security parameter (typically, $k_1 = 80$). Times (for Encryption and Decryption procedures) are expressed as triples consisting of the numbers of pairing applications, exponentiations in $\mathbb{G}_1$, and exponentiations in $\mathbb{G}_2$ resp. Reduction cost refers to the multiplicative ratio between the advantage of the adversary attacking the IBE scheme and of the algorithm solving the underling problem.

Scheme	Security			Size	Time‡	
	Assumptn.	Notn.	Reduction cost	Ciphertext	Enc	Dec
FullBF01† [5,6]	CBDH	CCA	$O(\frac{1}{(q_E+q_D)\cdot q_H^2})$ [6] $O(1/q_H^3)$ [12] $O(1/(q_E q_H))$ [24]	$|M| + t + k_1$	1, 1, 1	1, 1, 0
	GBDH	CCA	$O(1/q_E)$			
	DBDH	CCA	$O(1/q_E)$			
G05 [12]	CBDH	CCA	$O(1/q_H^2)$	$|M| + t + k_1$	1, 1, 1	1, 1, 0
LQ05 [18]	GBDH	CCA	$O(1/q_E)$	$|M| + t$	1, 1, 1	1, 0, 0
KW(BF)	GBDH	CPA	$O(1)$	$2|M| + 2t$	2, 2, 2	1, 0, 0
KW(FO(BF))	GBDH	CPA	$O(1)$	$2|M| + 2t + 2k_1$	2, 2, 2	1, 1, 0
FO(KW(BF))	GBDH	CCA	$O(1)$	$2|M| + 2t + 2k_1$	2, 2, 2	2, 2, 1
TightIBE	DBDH	CCA	$O(1)$	$|M| + t + 2k_1$	2, 1, 2	2, 1, 1
	GBDH	CCA	$O(1)$			
	CBDH	CCA	$O(1/q_H)$			

† The first reduction cost is from the original paper [6]; however, a flaw in the proof was pointed out and fixed in [12], where a new reduction cost was shown. This was then improved in [24]. The reduction to GBDH or DBDH can be done straightforwardly.

‡ We remind that for the LQ05 and TightIBE scheme, there is also the computational cost due to symmetric encryption, but this can be done quite relatively efficiently.

4.3 Competitive Performances

We now draw comparisons among our scheme and previous IBE schemes proven secure in the random oracle model by wrapping up in Table 4. It can be argued that for those schemes without tight security reductions, the security parameters have to be chosen larger in order to compensate such a security loss. Put in other words, we conclude that our scheme achieves the shortest ciphertext among those CCA-secure schemes when considering the same security level.

5   Conclusion

We have presented an efficient identity based encryption scheme whose security can be tightly reduced to a reasonable complexity assumption in the random oracle model. Although our scheme is a continuation of an idea introduced by

Katz and Wang, this is the first explicitly presented scheme with a formal security proof that appear in literatures.

It is still an open problem to build chosen ciphertext secure IBE that obtain tight security reductions under reasonable mild assumptions, which does not depend on the number of queries, in the standard model.

Acknowledgement. The preliminary version of this paper [1] is available at the IACR ePrint server. We would like to thank Benoit Chevallier-Mames for many fruitful discussions. We also thanks to anonymous reviewers for useful comments.

References

1. N. Attrapadung, B. Chevallier-Mames, J. Furukawa, T. Gomi, G. Hanaoka, H. Imai, R. Zhang, "Efficient Identity-Based Encryption with Tight Security Reduction," IACR ePrint Report 2005/320.
2. D. Boneh and X. Boyen, "Efficient Selective-ID Secure Identity-Based Encryption Without Random Oracles," In Advances in Cryptology–Eurocrypt'04, LNCS 3027, pp.223-238, 2004. The full version is available as IACR ePrint Report 2004/172.
3. D. Boneh and X. Boyen, "Secure Identity Based Encryption Without Random Oracles," In Advances in Cryptology–Crypto'04, LNCS 3152, pp.443-459, 2004.
4. D. Boneh, B. Lynn, and H. Shacham, "Short signatures from the Weil pairing," In Advances in Cryptology– Asiacrypt'01, LNCS 2248, pp. 514-532, 2001.
5. D. Boneh and M. Franklin, "Identity Based Encryption from the Weil Pairing," In Advances in Cryptology–Crypto'01, LNCS 2139, pp.213-229, 2001.
6. D. Boneh and M. Franklin, "Identity Based Encryption from the Weil Pairing," SIAM Journal of Computing, 32(3), pp.586-615, 2003, full version of [5].
7. X. Boyen and B. Waters. "Anonymous Hierarchical Identity-Based Encryption (Without Random Oracles)," In Advances in Cryptology–Crypto'06, LNCS 4117, pp. 290-307, 2006.
8. R. Canetti, S. Halevi and J. Katz, "A Forward-Secure Public-Key Encryption Scheme," In Advances in Cryptology–Eurocrypt'03, LNCS 2656, pp.255-271, 2003.
9. J. H. Cheon. "Security Analysis of the Strong Diffie-Hellman Problem," In Advances in Cryptology–Eurocrypt'06, LNCS 4004, pp. 1-11, 2006.
10. E. Fujisaki and T. Okamoto, "How to Enhance the Security of Public-Key Encryption at Minimum Cost," In PKC'99, LNCS 1560, pp.53-68, 1999.
11. E. Fujisaki and T. Okamoto, "Secure Integration of Asymmetric and Symmetric Encryption Schemes," In Advances in Cryptology–Crypto'99, LNCS 1666, pp.537-554, 1999.
12. D. Galindo, "Boneh-Franklin Identity Based Encryption Revisited," In ICALP'05, LNCS 3580, pp.791-802, 2005.
13. C. Gentry. "Practical Identity-Based Encryption Without Random Oracles," In Advances in Cryptology–Eurocrypt'06, LNCS 4004, pp. 445-464, 2006.
14. S. Halevi and P. Rogaway, "A Tweakable Enciphering Mode" In Advances in Cryptology–Crypto'03, LNCS 2729, pp.482-499, 2003.
15. S. Halevi and P. Rogaway, "A Parallelizable Enciphering Mode." In CT-RSA'04, LNCS 2964, pp.292-304, 2004.
16. J. Katz and N. Wang, "Efficiency Improvements for Signature Schemes with Tight Security Reductions," In ACM-CCS'03, pp.155-164, 2003.

17. K. Kitagawa, P. Yang, G. Hanaoka, R. Zhang, K. Matsuura and H. Imai. "Generic Transforms to Acquire CCA-Security for Identity Based Encryption: the Case of FOpkc and REACT." In ACISP'06, pp. 348-359, 2006.
18. B. Libert and J. Quisquater, "Identity Based Encryption Without Redundancy," In ACNS'05, pp.285-300, 2005.
19. A. Miyaji, M. Nakabayashi, S. Takano. "New explicit conditions of elliptic curve traces for FR-reduction," IEICE Trans. Fundamentals, E84-A(5):1234-43, 2001.
20. T. Okamoto, D. Pointcheval, "The Gap-Problems: a New Class of Problems for the Security of Cryptographic Schemes," In PKC'01, LNCS 1992, pp.104-118, 2001.
21. A. Shamir, "Identity-Based Cryptosystems and Signature Schemes," In Advances in Cryptology–Crypto'84, LNCS 293, pp.341-349, 1984.
22. V. Shoup, "Sequences of Games: A Tool for Taming Complexity in Security Proofs," IACR ePrint Report 2004/332.
23. B. Waters,"Efficient Identity-Based Encryption Without Random Oracles," In Advances in Cryptology–Eurocrypt'05, LNCS 1666, pp.114-127, 2005. The full version is available as IACR ePrint Report 2004/180.
24. R. Zhang and H. Imai,"Improvements on Security Proofs of Some Identity Based Encryption Schemes," In CISC'05, LNCS 3822, pp. 28-41, 2005.

A   Reductions from LBDH to DBDH, GBDH, CBDH

In this section, we describe quite straightforward reductions from the ℓ-LBDH problem to the DBDH, GBDH, CBDH problems, which are postponed from §4.2. The first two are tight, while the last one is degraded by factor ℓ.

Lemma 3. *Suppose that there exists an $(\epsilon_{lbdh}, t_{lbdh})$-$\ell$-LBDH algorithm $\mathcal{L}$. Then there exists an $(\epsilon_{dbdh}, t_{dbdh})$-DBDH algorithm $\mathcal{D}$, $(\epsilon_{gbdh}, t_{gbdh})$-GBDH algorithm $\mathcal{G}$, and $(\epsilon_{cbdh}, t_{cbdh})$-CBDH algorithm $\mathcal{C}$ such that*

$$
\begin{aligned}
\epsilon_{dbdh} &\geq \epsilon_{lbdh} - \ell/|\mathbb{G}_2|, & t_{dbdh} &\leq t_{lbdh} + \ell\tau_1, \\
\epsilon_{gbdh} &\geq \epsilon_{lbdh}, & t_{gbdh} &\leq t_{lbdh} + \ell\tau_2, \\
\epsilon_{cbdh} &\geq \epsilon_{lbdh}/\ell, & t_{cbdh} &\leq t_{lbdh} + \tau_3,
\end{aligned}
$$

where τ_1 is the time required to check an equality of two elements in $\mathbb{G}_2$, τ_2 is the time required to access the DBDH oracle (as provide for $\mathcal{G}$), and τ_3 is the time required to randomly choose one element from a list of size ℓ.

Proof. The description of the algorithms $\mathcal{D}, \mathcal{G}, \mathcal{C}$ are as follows. Given these descriptions, the relations can be easily verified.

- The algorithm $\mathcal{D}$, upon input (g, g_1, g_2, g_3, T), runs $\mathcal{L}$ on the input (g, g_1, g_2, g_3) and, in response, obtains a list, which contains $e(g_1, g_2)^{\log_g g_3}$ with probability ϵ_{lbdh}. Then $\mathcal{D}$ outputs 1 if the list contains T, and 0 otherwise.
- The algorithm $\mathcal{G}$ forwards its input to $\mathcal{L}$ and get a list. Then it tests all the elements in the list by calling the DBDH oracle $\mathcal{O}$. If the oracle returns 1 for some query, then $\mathcal{G}$ outputs that query.
- The algorithm $\mathcal{C}$ forwards its input to $\mathcal{L}$ and get a list. Then it randomly chooses one element in the list and outputs it.

This completes the proof.   □

B   Proofs of Lemmas

B.1   Proof of Lemma 1

Proof. It is sufficient to prove that the adversary's view is independent of the variable $b_{\mathsf{ID}^\star}$. Moreover, since the only variables that are possibly dependent on $b_{\mathsf{ID}^\star}$ are those responses from the decryption oracle, it is sufficient to prove that there exists no ciphertext such that its decryption result may become different values according to the value of b_{ID}. We assume for the sake of contradiction that there exists $C = \langle u, V_0, V_1, \alpha \rangle$ such that $\mathrm{DECRYPT}_{b_{\mathsf{ID}^\star}=0}(\mathsf{ID}^\star, C) \neq \mathrm{DECRYPT}_{b_{\mathsf{ID}^\star}=1}(\mathsf{ID}^\star, C)$, where the subscripts denote the conditional events. Without loss of generality, we assume that the value on the left is M which is not *"reject"*. Let $r = \log_g u$. As in (D1) (when $b_{\mathsf{ID}^\star} = 0$), we let $\bar{R} := V_0 \oplus G(e(g_{pub}, H(\mathsf{ID}^\star, 0))^r, \mathsf{ID}^\star, 0)$ and as in (D2) we let $r' \| K := \hat{H}(\bar{R}, \mathsf{ID})$. Then we have $\alpha = E_K(M)$ from (D4).

Since M is not *"reject"*, we have $\bar{R} = V_1 \oplus G(e(g_{pub}, H(\mathsf{ID}^\star, 1))^{r'}, \mathsf{ID}^\star, 1)$ and $r = r'$ due to (D3) and (D4). Thus

$$V_1 = G(e(g_{pub}, H(\mathsf{ID}^\star, 1))^r, \mathsf{ID}^\star, 1) \oplus \bar{R}. \tag{1}$$

Now the decryption oracle conditioned on $b_{\mathsf{ID}^\star} = 1$ will decrypt C by executing (D1) (when $b_{\mathsf{ID}^\star} = 1$) and obtaining $\bar{R}$ due to Eq.(1). From (D2), we thus obtain the same K as above. The condition in (D4) is true by the definition of $\bar{R}$. Thus the oracle will return M, a contradiction. This completes the proof.   □

B.2   Proof of Lemma 2

Proof. We prove this by constructing an algorithm $\mathcal{S}$ which has an IND-CCA advantage for the symmetric encryption scheme of exactly $(\Pr[\mathsf{S_6}] - \Pr[\mathsf{S_7}])/2$. Algorithm $\mathcal{S}$ first asks $(0^{|M^\star|}, M^\star)$ to obtain the challenge ciphertext ψ^+, and will try to guess the bit γ. Algorithm $\mathcal{S}$ runs the IBE adversary by providing the simulation in exactly the same way as done by the challenger in game $\mathbf{G}_6$ except only for the rules which produce or use $K^\ddagger$, which are (1) the Chal–DEM–Key rule (producing $K^\ddagger$), (2) the Chal–DEM–Enc rule (using $\mathrm{Enc}_{K^\ddagger}(\cdot)$), and (3) the first Decrypt–Exception rule (using $\mathrm{Dec}_{K^\ddagger}(\cdot)$). For those exceptions, $\mathcal{S}$ does nothing for (1), let $\alpha^\star = \psi^+$ for (2), and queries to its decryption oracle for (3). Finally if $\beta' = \beta$, then $\mathcal{S}$ output 1; else 0. It is clear that $\Pr[\gamma' = 1 | \gamma = 1] = \Pr[\mathsf{S_6}]$ and $\Pr[\gamma' = 1 | \gamma = 0] = \Pr[\mathsf{S_7}]$. Hence $\Pr[\gamma' = \gamma] - 1/2 = (\Pr[\mathsf{S_6}] - \Pr[\mathsf{S_7}])/2$ as claimed.   □

C   Variants of Katz-Wang Application

We describe the KW(FO(BF)) and FO(KW(BF)) IBE, postponed from §3.2. Let $G : \mathbb{G}_2 \to \{0,1\}^{n+k_1}$, $\tilde{H} : \{0,1\}^n \times \{0,1\}^{k_1} \to \mathbb{Z}_q$, $\check{H} : \{0,1\}^n \times \{0,1\}^{k_1} \to \mathbb{Z}_q^2$.

Table 5. The KW(FO(BF)) and FO(KW(BF)) Identity Based Encryption

The KW(FO(BF)) Identity Based Encryption	
Setup (1^k): $\quad s \leftarrow \mathbb{Z}_q^*; \, g_{pub} := g^s$ $\quad$params $:= \langle q, \mathbb{G}_1, \mathbb{G}_2, e, n, g, g_{pub}, G, H \rangle$ $\quad$master-key $:= s$ $\quad return \,$ (params, master-key)	**Extract**[†] (ID, params, master-key): $\quad b_{\mathsf{ID}} \leftarrow \{0,1\}$ $\quad h_{\mathsf{ID}} := H(\mathsf{ID}, b_{\mathsf{ID}})$ $\quad d_{\mathsf{ID}} := (h_{\mathsf{ID}})^s$ $\quad sk_{\mathsf{ID}} := (d_{\mathsf{ID}}, b_{\mathsf{ID}})$ $\quad return \, sk_{\mathsf{ID}}$
Encrypt (ID, params, M): $\quad h_{\mathsf{ID},0} := H(\mathsf{ID},0), \quad h_{\mathsf{ID},1} := H(\mathsf{ID},1)$ $\quad R_0, R_1 \leftarrow \{0,1\}^{k_1}$ $\quad r_0 := \tilde{H}_0(M, R_0), \quad r_1 := \tilde{H}_1(M, R_1)$ $\quad w_0 := e(g_{pub}, h_{\mathsf{ID},0})^{r_0}$ $\quad w_1 := e(g_{pub}, h_{\mathsf{ID},1})^{r_1}$ $\quad C := \langle g^{r_0}, \, G(w_0) \oplus (M \| R_0),$ $\qquad\qquad g^{r_1}, \, G(w_1) \oplus (M \| R_1) \rangle$ $\quad return \, C$	**Decrypt** $(C,$ params, $b_{\mathsf{ID}}, d_{\mathsf{ID}})$: $\quad$parse $C = \langle u_0, V_0, u_1, V_1 \rangle$ $\quad w'_{b_{\mathsf{ID}}} := e(u_{b_{\mathsf{ID}}}, d_{\mathsf{ID}})$ $\quad M' \| R'_{b_{\mathsf{ID}}} := V_{b_{\mathsf{ID}}} \oplus G(w'_{b_{\mathsf{ID}}})$ $\quad r'_{b_{\mathsf{ID}}} := \tilde{H}_{b_{\mathsf{ID}}}(M', R'_{b_{\mathsf{ID}}})$ $\quad$if $u_{b_{\mathsf{ID}}} \neq g^{r'_{b_{\mathsf{ID}}}}$ then $\qquad\qquad return \,$ "reject" $\quad$else $return \, M'$
The FO(KW(BF)) Identity Based Encryption	
Setup (1^k): $\quad s \leftarrow \mathbb{Z}_q^*; \, g_{pub} := g^s$ $\quad$params $:= \langle q, \mathbb{G}_1, \mathbb{G}_2, e, n, g, g_{pub}, G, H \rangle$ $\quad$master-key $:= s$ $\quad return \,$ (params, master-key)	**Extract**[†] (ID, params, master-key): $\quad b_{\mathsf{ID}} \leftarrow \{0,1\}$ $\quad h_{\mathsf{ID}} := H(\mathsf{ID}, b_{\mathsf{ID}})$ $\quad d_{\mathsf{ID}} := (h_{\mathsf{ID}})^s$ $\quad sk_{\mathsf{ID}} := (d_{\mathsf{ID}}, b_{\mathsf{ID}})$ $\quad return \, sk_{\mathsf{ID}}$
Encrypt (ID, params, M): $\quad h_{\mathsf{ID},0} := H(\mathsf{ID},0), \quad h_{\mathsf{ID},1} := H(\mathsf{ID},1)$ $\quad R \leftarrow \{0,1\}^{k_1}$ $\quad r_0 \| r_1 := \check{H}(M, R)$ $\quad w_0 := e(g_{pub}, h_{\mathsf{ID},0})^{r_0}$ $\quad w_1 := e(g_{pub}, h_{\mathsf{ID},1})^{r_1}$ $\quad C := \langle g^{r_0}, \, G(w_0) \oplus (M \| R),$ $\qquad\qquad g^{r_1}, \, G(w_1) \oplus (M \| R) \rangle$ $\quad return \, C$	**Decrypt** $(C,$ params, $b_{\mathsf{ID}}, d_{\mathsf{ID}})$: $\quad$parse $C = \langle u_0, V_0, u_1, V_1 \rangle$ $\quad w'_{b_{\mathsf{ID}}} := e(u_{b_{\mathsf{ID}}}, d_{\mathsf{ID}})$ $\quad M' \| R' := V_{b_{\mathsf{ID}}} \oplus G(w'_{b_{\mathsf{ID}}})$ $\quad r'_0 \| r'_1 := \check{H}(M', R')$ $\quad w'_{\bar{b}_{\mathsf{ID}}} := e(g_{pub}, h_{\mathsf{ID}, \bar{b}_{\mathsf{ID}}})^{r'_{\bar{b}_{\mathsf{ID}}}}$ $\quad$if $u_0 \neq g^{r'_0} \vee u_1 \neq g^{r'_1} \vee$ $\qquad V_{\bar{b}_{\mathsf{ID}}} \neq G(w'_{\bar{b}_{\mathsf{ID}}}) \oplus (M' \| R')$ then $\qquad\qquad return \,$ "reject" $\quad$else $return \, M'$

[†] **Extract** first checks to see if sk_{ID} has been generated before. If it has, the previously-generated sk_{ID} is output.

A Diffie-Hellman Key Exchange Protocol Without Random Oracles

Ik Rae Jeong[1], Jeong Ok Kwon[2,*], and Dong Hoon Lee[2,*]

[1] Electronics and Telecommunications Research Institute (ETRI), Daejeon, Korea
jir@etri.re.kr
[2] Center for Information Security Technologies (CIST), Korea University,
Seoul, Korea
{pitapat, dhlee}@korea.ac.kr

Abstract. The MQV protocol of Law, Menezes, Qu, Slinas and Vanstone has been regarded as the most efficient authenticated Diffie-Hellman key exchange protocol, and standardized by many organizations including the US NSA. In Crypto 2005, Hugo Krawczyk showed vulnerabilities of MQV to several attacks and suggested a hashed variant of MQV, called HMQV, which provides the same superb performance of MQV and provable security in the random oracle model. In this paper we suggest an efficient authenticated Diffie-Hellman key exchange protocol providing the same functionalities and security of HMQV *without* random oracles. There exist some provably secure key exchange schemes using signatures in the standard model, but all of the schemes do not provide the same level of security of HMQV. So far there are no authenticated Diffie-Hellman protocols which are proven secure in the standard model and achieve the same level of security goals of HMQV efficiently yet. Dispensing of random oracles in our protocol does not require any expensive signature and encryption schemes.

Keywords: Key exchange; Diffie-Hellman protocol; Strong forward secrecy; Key compromise impersonation; Unknown key share.

1 Introduction

One of the most basic cryptographic primitives is a key exchange protocol. A two-party key exchange protocol makes it possible that two parties establish a common *session key* securely. The original Diffie-Hellman key exchange protocol [24] is a fundamental technique in designing key exchange protocols, which is considered to be secure against passive eavesdroppers, but not against active attacks; indeed, that protocol provides no authentication at all. To resist active attacks, huge number of *authenticated* Diffie-Hellman protocols have been suggested [39,27,17,11,46,22].

* This work was supported by the MIC (Ministry of Information and Communication), Korea, under the ITRC (Information Technology Research Center) support program supervised by the IITA (Institute of Information Technology Assessment).

D. Pointcheval, Y. Mu, and K. Chen (Eds.): CANS 2006, LNCS 4301, pp. 37–54, 2006.

At the most basic level, an authenticated key exchange protocol must provide secrecy of a shared session key. Yet to completely define the notions of security, we must consider adversarial behaviors which should be tolerated by a protocol. *Implicit authentication* simply means secrecy of session keys against an adversary who passively eavesdrops on protocol executions and may also send messages of its choice to the various parties. A stronger notion of security (and the one that is perhaps most often considered in the cryptographic literature) is *key indepen-dence (known key security)*, which means that session keys are computationally in-dependent from each other. A bit more formally, key independence protects against "Denning-Sacco" attacks [26] involving compromise of multiple session keys (for sessions other than the one whose secrecy must be guaranteed). Protocols achiev-ing *weak forward secrecy* (w-FS) maintain secrecy of session keys which are shared through honest executions of the protocol without any interference by an adversary, even if the adversary is able to obtain long-term secret keys of parties. Protocols achieving *strong forward secrecy* (s-FS) maintain secrecy of session keys which have been established with interference of an adversary, even if the adversary is able to obtain long-term secret keys of parties after the session keys was established.

The above notions are most widely used in key exchange protocols. Besides above three security notions, there are various security notions such as key com-promise impersonation and unknown key share [15,39,41]. If an adversary obtains a long-term secret key of a party, the adversary can trivially impersonate the party to the other parties. But the adversary may not impersonate other parties to the party. A protocol is secure against *key compromise impersonation* (KCI) attacks, if an adversary can not impersonate other parties (whose long-term secret keys are not revealed) to the parties (whose long-term secret keys are revealed). The security against *session state reveal* (SSR) is formally considered in [21,36]. This security is originated from the consideration that the random values of the ses-sions may be more easily leaked than the secret keys of the public keys. A proto-col is secure against *unknown key share* (UKS) attacks, if the following holds: If two parties *Alice* and *Bob* compute the same session key, *Alice* should consider that she is establishing the session key with *Bob* and *Bob* should consider that he is establishing the session key with *Alice*. In our security model in Section 3, key independence implies the security against unknown key share attacks.

In many common applications parties can actually transmit messages simulta-neously. It may be possible to design protocols with improved round complexity by fully exploiting the communication characteristics of the underlying network, and in particular the possibility of simultaneous message transmission. Recently, the possibility of simultaneous message transmission for two-party key exchange was exploited in [34]. They designed one-round two-party key exchange proto-cols assuming a (bidirectional) *duplex* channel and proved their securities. Our protocol is constructed based on the duplex channels.

1.1   Our Work in Relation to Prior Work

In [41,39], Menezes et al. suggested a two-party key exchange scheme, MQV, which was considered as the most efficient one of authenticated Diffie-Hellman protocols. MQV has been standardized, and chosen by the US NSA as the key exchange mechanism underlying "the next generation cryptography to protect US government information" [3,4,31,33,42,43]. But the scheme has not been formally proved.

In [36], Hugo Krawczyk pointed out the weaknesses of MQV and suggested HMQV, a (1-round) 2-message hashed variant of MQV. HMQV provides the same superb performance and functionalities of MQV, and was proved to satisfy all the MQV's security goals in the random oracle model, including w-FS, security against KCI and SSR attacks. To provide s-FS additionally, the author proposed HMQV-C which is a (3-round) 3-message protocol.

The idealized random oracle methodology may enable the design and security proof of cryptographic schemes more easy and efficient. But a secure scheme in the random oracle model may be not secure in the real world if an idealized random function is instantiated with real functions [20,30,8]. In the standard model (i.e., without random oracles), Shoup [44] and Jeong et al [34] proposed provably secure authenticated 1-round Diffie-Hellman protocols. There also exist 3-round Diffie-Hellman protocols using signatures such as STS [25], Σ_0 [23], and SIG-DH [21]. However in all of these protocols a session key is calculated using only ephemeral values, and hence the schemes are not secure against SSR attacks. It seems that there are no authenticated Diffie-Hellman protocols which are proven secure in the standard model and achieve the same level of security goals of HMQV efficiently yet.

In the paper we propose an authenticated Diffie-Hellman key exchange protocol, KAM, which provide the same functionalities and security of HMQV. The security of KAM is proven based on the hash Diffie-Hellman (HDH) assumption and the oracle Diffie-Hellman (ODH) assumption [1,2] without random oracles in the Bellare-Rogaway (BR) model [17]. The BR model in the paper is extended to capture KCI and SSR attacks, and to refine the notions of w-FS and s-FS. Note that the security of HMQV is analyzed in the extended Canetti-Krawczyk (CK) model [21] and 1-round (2-message) HMQV provides only w-FS. The relation between the BR model and CK model is analyzed in [19]. Dispensing of random oracles usually needs to use the expensive signature and encryption schemes that do not rely on random oracles [36]. But our 2-round protocol KAM does not need to use the expensive signature or encryption schemes. KAM requires 2-rounds and provides s-FS.

The proposed protocol KAM achieves the above security goals without degrading performance seriously. We compare the performance of the provably secure schemes providing w/s-FS, security against KCI and SSR attacks in Table 1.

2 Preliminaries

We use a strongly unforgeable MAC scheme to design our key exchange scheme.

A message authentication code (MAC) consists of $\mathsf{M} = (\mathsf{Mac}, \mathsf{Vrfy})$. Given a random key sk, Mac computes a tag τ for a message M; we write this as $\tau \leftarrow \mathsf{Mac}_{sk}(M)$. Vrfy verifies the message-tag pair using the (shared) key, and

Table 1. The detailed comparison among provably secure schemes providing FS, KCI, and SSR

	Security			Computation	Model
	FS	KCI	SSR		
2-message HMQV (1-round) [36]	w-FS	KCI	SSR*	3.5 exp.[†]	random oracle
3-message HMQV-C (3-round) [36]	s-FS	KCI	SSR*	3.5 exp.[†]	random oracle
KAM (2-round)	s-FS	KCI	SSR	6 exp.	standard

* The security proof in [36] requires somewhat non-standard assumption so called "knowledge of exponent assumption".
† The basic HMQV requires 2.5 exponentiations. But the group membership tests of (static and ephemeral) Diffie-Hellman messages are required for SSR security as noted in [37,40]. We assume that the group membership tests of static Diffie-Hellman messages are done by the trusted center which issues a certificate of a public key.

returns 1 if the tag is valid or 0 otherwise. We require that for all keys sk, for all M, and for all τ output by $\mathsf{Mac}_{sk}(M)$ we have $\mathsf{Vrfy}_{sk}(M, \tau) = 1$. For formal definitions, see Appendix. We use notation $[a, b]$ for a set of integers from a to b. We use notation $c \leftarrow S$, if c is randomly selected from a set S. We denote an exclusive-or of two strings a and b (having same length) as $a \oplus b$. We denote a concatenation of two strings a and b as $a \| b$. If evt is an event, $\Pr[\mathsf{evt}]$ is a probability that evt occurs.

3   A Key Exchange Model

The BR model considers implicit authentication, key independence, and forward secrecy in the half-duplex channel [17]. The variant of the model is considered in the duplex channel [34]. We bring the definitions and extend the model in [17,34] such that w/s-FS, KCI, and SSR are also considered. We assume that each party's identity is denoted as P_i, and each party P_i holds a pair of private and public keys. We consider key exchange protocols in which two parties want to exchange a session key using their public keys to provide authentication. Π_i^k represents the k-th instance of player P_i. If a key exchange protocol terminates, then Π_i^k generates a session key sk_i^k.

A *session identifier* of an instance in the duplex channel, denoted sid_i^k, is a string different from those of all other sessions in the system (with high probability). Without loss of generality, we assume that sid_i^k is simply the concatenation of all messages sent and received by a particular instance Π_i^k, where the order of these messages is determined *by the lexicographic ordering of the two parties' identities*. (Note that ordering messages according to the time they were sent cannot be used in the duplex channel, because the two parties may send their messages simultaneously.)

Consider instance Π_i^k of player P_i. The *partner* of this instance is the player $P_j (\neq P_i)$ with whom P_i believes it is interacting. We say that two instances Π_i^k and $\Pi_j^{k'}$ are *partnered*, if the following conditions are true:

1. $\text{sid}_i^k = \text{sid}_j^{k'}$,
2. P_j is the partner of Π_i^k,
3. P_i is the partner of $\Pi_j^{k'}$.

Any protocol should satisfy the following correctness condition: Two partnered instances compute the same session key.

To define a notion of security, we define the capabilities of an adversary. We allow the adversary to potentially control all communications in the network via access to a set of oracles as defined below. We consider an *experiment* in which the adversary asks queries to oracles, and the oracles answer back to the adversary. Oracle queries model attacks which an adversary may use in the real system. We consider the following types of queries in this paper.

- The query $\text{Initiate}(i, j)$ is used to "prompt" party P_i to initiate execution of the protocol with partner P_j. This query will result in P_i sending a message, which is given to the adversary.
- A query $\text{Send}(i, k, M)$ is used to send a message M to instance Π_i^k (this models active attacks on the part of the adversary). When Π_i^k receives M, it responds according to the key exchange protocol.
- A query $\text{Reveal}(i, k)$ models *known key* attacks (or Denning-Sacco attacks) in the real system. The adversary is given the session key sk_i^k for the specified instance Π_i^k.
- A query $\text{Corrupt}(i)$ models exposure of the secret key of the public key held by player P_i. The adversary is assumed to be able to obtain secret keys of players, but cannot control the behavior of these players directly (of course, once the adversary has asked a query $\text{Corrupt}(i)$, the adversary may impersonate P_i in subsequent Send queries.)
- A query $\text{State}(i, k)$ models exposure of the internal state of Π_i^k. The adversary is given the intermediate random values used in making sk_i^k.
- A query $\text{Test}(i, k)$ is used to define the advantage of an adversary. When an adversary $\mathcal{A}$ asks a Test query to an instance Π_i^k, a coin b is flipped. If b is 1, then the session key sk_i^k of Π_i^k is returned. Otherwise, a random string chosen uniformly from the space of θ-bit strings is returned, where θ is a security parameter. The adversary is allowed to make a single Test query to a *fresh* instance (see below), at any time during the experiment.

To define a meaningful notion of security, we must first define *freshness*:

Definition 1. An instance Π_i^k is *fresh* if the following conditions are true at the conclusion of the experiment described above:

(a) The adversary has not queried $\text{Reveal}(i, k)$.

(b) The adversary has not queried $\mathsf{Reveal}(j, k')$, if Π_i^k is partnered with instance $\Pi_j^{k'}$.

(c) The adversary does not control P_j, if P_j is the partner of Π_i^k. That is, P_j is not an *insider*[1] attacker generated by the adversary.

In all the notions of security considered below, the adversary $\mathcal{A}$ outputs a bit b' at the end of the experiment above. The advantage of $\mathcal{A}$, denoted $\mathsf{Adv}_{\mathcal{A}}(\theta)$, is defined as $2 \cdot \Pr[b' = b] - 1$, where θ is a security parameter. Generically speaking, a protocol is called "secure" if the advantage of any probabilistic polynomial-time (PPT) adversary is negligible. The following notions of security may then be considered, depending on the types of queries the adversary is allowed to ask:

- IA (Implicit Authentication): The most basic level of security does not allow adversary $\mathcal{A}$ to make any Reveal, Corrupt, or State queries.
- KI (Key Independence): An adversary $\mathcal{A}$ can ask Reveal queries, but can not ask Corrupt or State queries.
- w-FS (Weak Forward Secrecy): An adversary $\mathcal{A}$ can ask Corrupt and Reveal queries, but can not ask State queries. To define this notion, the freshness requires the following additional condition:

   (d) If the adversary has queried $\mathsf{Corrupt}(i)$, then there exists instance $\Pi_j^{k'}$ which is partnered with Π_i^k.

- s-FS (Strong Forward Secrecy): An adversary $\mathcal{A}$ can ask Corrupt and Reveal queries, but can not ask State queries. To define this notion, the freshness requires the following additional condition:

   (d) If the adversary has queried $\mathsf{Corrupt}(i)$ and $\mathsf{Send}(i, k, *)$, then the adversary has queried $\mathsf{Corrupt}(i)$ and/or $\mathsf{Corrupt}(j)$ *after* all $\mathsf{Send}(i, k, *)$ queries, where P_j is a partner of Π_i^k.

- KCI (Key Compromise Impersonation): An adversary $\mathcal{A}$ can ask Corrupt and Reveal queries, but can not ask State queries. To define this notion, the freshness requires the following additional condition:

   (d) If the adversary has queried $\mathsf{Corrupt}(i)$ and $\mathsf{Send}(i, k, *)$, then the adversary has queried all $\mathsf{Send}(i, k, *)$ queries *after* $\mathsf{Corrupt}(i)$ query and partner P_j has not corrupted.

- SSR (ephemeral Diffie-Hellman): An adversary $\mathcal{A}$ can ask State queries, but can not ask Reveal and Corrupt queries[2]. To define this notion, the freshness requires the following additional condition:

---

[1] Insider attackers and their public keys are generated from the information gathered by the adversary. All of the information of insider attackers are completely known to the adversary, and the behaviors of insider attackers are completely controlled by the adversary.

[2] Note that if some session keys and ephemeral random values are revealed, HMQV is not secure.

(d) If the adversary has queried $\mathsf{State}(i, k)$ and $\mathsf{Send}(i, k, *)$, then the adversary has queried $\mathsf{State}(i, k)$ *after* all $\mathsf{Send}(i, k, *)$ queries.

Note that s-FS implies w-FS. w-FS and KCI imply KI. KI and SSR imply IA. For an adversary $\mathcal{A}$ attacking a scheme in the sense of XX (where XX is either IA, KI, w-FS, s-FS, KCI, or SSR), we denote the advantage of this adversary by $\mathsf{Adv}_{\mathcal{A}}^{XX}(\theta)$, where θ is a security parameter. For a protocol P, we define its security as:

$$\mathsf{Adv}_P^{XX}(\theta, t) = \max_{\mathcal{A}}\{\mathsf{Adv}_{\mathcal{A}}^{XX}(\theta)\},$$

where the maximum is taken over all adversaries running in time t. A scheme P is said to be XX–secure if $\mathsf{Adv}_P^{XX}(\theta, t)$ is negligible (in θ) for any $t = \mathrm{poly}(\theta)$.

Proposition 1. KI implies UKS.

Proof of Proposition 1. Let Π_i^k and $\Pi_j^{k'}$ compute the same session key sk. If P_j is not a partner of Π_i^k or P_i is not a partner of $\Pi_j^{k'}$, an adversary first makes $\mathsf{Reveal}(j, k')$ query and gets a session key sk. Then the adversary can correctly guess a session key of the test oracle Π_i^k. This strategy is valid, because in this case Π_i^k is not partnered with $\Pi_j^{k'}$, and thus Π_i^k is a fresh oracle. □

4   A Key Exchange Protocol

Achieving authentication is only possible if some out-of-band initialization phase is assumed prior to execution of the protocol. One common assumption is that each communicating party has an associated public-/private-key pair. We assume that a certificate of a public key is issued by the trusted center which checks the validity of the public key. We do not describe procedures related to certificates such as validity check of certificates before using public keys.

For the protocol we present, we assume that parties can be ordered by their names (e.g., lexicographically) and write $P_i < P_j$ to denote this ordering. Let θ be a security parameter, and let G be a group of prime order q (where $|q| = \theta$) with generator g. (We assume that G, q and g are fixed in advance and known to the entire network.) We assume that each party P_i has a public-/private-key pair $(y_i = g^{x_i}, x_i)$. We also assume that the group membership test of y_i is done by the trusted center which issues a certificate of a public key. Let M be an unforgeable MAC scheme. Let H be a hash function such that $H : \{0, 1\}^* \to \{0, 1\}^\theta$, where θ is a security parameter.

4.1   KAM

The two-round key exchange protocol KAM is as follows and its execution is illustrated in Fig. 1.

KAM

Setup: P_i is going to establish a session key with $P_j(\neq P_i)$, and $P_i < P_j$. P_j behaves as similarly as P_i, so we describe the protocol on behalf of P_i.

Round 1: P_i selects a random number $\alpha_i \leftarrow Z_q$, calculates $Z_i = g^{\alpha_i}$, and sends Z_i.

Round 2: P_i executes a group membership test of Z_j. If the test is successful, P_i calculates $k_{i,j} = H(Z_j^{x_i}) = H(g^{x_i\alpha_j})$ and sends $\tau_i \leftarrow \mathsf{Mac}_{k_{i,j}}(i||j||g^{\alpha_i})$.

Computation of session keys: P_i calculates $k_{j,i} = H(y_j^{\alpha_i}) = H(g^{x_j\alpha_i})$ and verifies $\mathsf{Vrfy}_{k_{j,i}}(\tau_j, j||i||g^{\alpha_j}) = 1$. Note that $k_{i,j} \neq k_{j,i}$. If the MAC from the communicating party is not valid, P_i stops. P_i makes a session key $\mathsf{sk}_i^k = H(y_j^{x_i}) \oplus H(Z_j^{\alpha_i}) = H(g^{x_ix_j}) \oplus H(g^{\alpha_i\alpha_j})$.

	P_1's message	P_2's message
Round 1	g^{α_1}	g^{α_2}
Round 2	τ_1	τ_2

$$k_{1,2} = H(g^{\alpha_2 x_1}); k_{2,1} = H(g^{\alpha_1 x_2}) \text{ (Note that } k_{1,2} \neq k_{2,1})$$
$$\tau_1 \leftarrow \mathsf{Mac}_{k_{1,2}}(1||2||g^{\alpha_1}); \tau_2 \leftarrow \mathsf{Mac}_{k_{2,1}}(2||1||g^{\alpha_2})$$
$$\mathsf{sk} = H(g^{x_1x_2}) \oplus H(g^{\alpha_1\alpha_2})$$

Fig. 1. An example of an execution of KAM

Theorem 1. If a secure MAC scheme exists, KAM is an s-FS/KCI/SSR[3]–secure key exchange scheme under the ODH and HDH assumptions.

Proof of Theorem 1. We prove Theorem 1 by the following three lemmas. We prove s-FS security in Lemma 1, KCI security in Lemma 2, and SSR security in Lemma 3. □

Lemma 1. If M is a secure MAC scheme, KAM is an s-FS–secure key exchange scheme under the ODH and HDH assumptions. More formally,

$$\mathsf{Adv}_{\mathsf{KAM}}^{\text{s-FS}}(\theta, t) \leq \frac{2q_s^2}{q} + 2N^2q_s \cdot \mathsf{Adv}_{\mathsf{M}}^{\text{SUF}}(\theta, t) + 2N^2q_s \cdot \mathsf{Adv}_{H,\mathcal{GG}}^{\text{ODH}}(\theta, t) + (Nq_s)^2 \cdot \mathsf{Adv}_{H,\mathcal{GG}}^{\text{HDH}}(\theta, t),$$

where θ is a security parameter and t is the maximum total experiment time including an adversary's execution time. Here, N is an upper bound on the number of honest[4] parties, and q_s is an upper bound on the number of the sessions an adversary makes.

---

[3] For SSR security of KAM, State query returns α of the ephemeral Diffie-Hellman message g^α.

[4] We call the parties which are not insider attackers as honest parties.

Proof of Lemma 1. The intuition is as follows: For an adversary to get a non-negligible advantage, the adversary has to break the underlying MAC scheme, the ODH assumption, or the HDH assumption. Details follow.

Consider an adversary $\mathcal{A}$ attacking KAM in the sense of s-FS. Let col be the event that a value g^{α_i} is used twice (possibly by different parties). Let forge be the event that there exists at least one forged MAC. We have

$$\Pr_{\mathcal{A}}[b = b'] \le \Pr_{\mathcal{A}}[\text{col}] + \Pr_{\mathcal{A}}[\text{forge}] + \Pr_{\mathcal{A}}[b = b' \wedge \overline{\text{col}} \wedge \overline{\text{forge}}].$$

We bound the probability of the terms of the above equation in the following claims.

Claim 1. $\Pr_{\mathcal{A}}[\text{col}] \le \frac{q_s^2}{q}$.

Claim 2. $\Pr_{\mathcal{A}}[\text{forge}] \le N^2 q_s \cdot (\text{Adv}_{H,\mathcal{GG}}^{\text{ODH}} + \text{Adv}_M^{\text{SUF}})$.

Claim 3. $\Pr_{\mathcal{A}}[b = b' \wedge \overline{\text{col}} \wedge \overline{\text{forge}}] \le \frac{(Nq_s)^2 \cdot \text{Adv}_{H,\mathcal{GG}}^{\text{HDH}} + 1}{2}$.

From Claim 1, Claim 2, and Claim 3, we get $\Pr_{\mathcal{A}}[b = b'] \le \frac{q_s^2}{q} + N^2 q_s \cdot (\text{Adv}_{H,\mathcal{GG}}^{\text{ODH}} + \text{Adv}_M^{\text{SUF}}) + \frac{(Nq_s)^2 \cdot \text{Adv}_{H,\mathcal{GG}}^{\text{HDH}} + 1}{2}$. From $\text{Adv}_{\text{KAM},\mathcal{A}}^{\text{s-FS}} = 2\Pr_{\mathcal{A}}[b = b'] - 1$, the theorem follows.   □

Now we proceed to prove the claims.

Proof of Claim 1. The probability of col is upper bounded by $\frac{q_s^2}{q}$ by "birthday paradox", where q is the order of group G.   †

Proof of Claim 2. We define a series of games
(Game_0,
$\text{Game}_{1,1,2}, \text{Game}_{1,1,3}, ..., \text{Game}_{1,1,N}$,
$\text{Game}_{1,2,2}, \text{Game}_{1,2,3}, ..., \text{Game}_{1,2,N}, ...$,
$\text{Game}_{1,q_s,2}, \text{Game}_{1,q_s,3}, ..., \text{Game}_{1,q_s,N}$,
$\text{Game}_{2,1,1}, \text{Game}_{2,1,3}, ..., \text{Game}_{2,1,N}, ...$,
$\text{Game}_{2,q_s,1}, \text{Game}_{2,q_s,3}, ..., \text{Game}_{2,q_s,N}, ...$,
$\text{Game}_{N,q_s,1}, \text{Game}_{N,q_s,2}, ..., \text{Game}_{N,q_s,N-1})^5$ as follows :

- Game_0 is same with the experiment.
- In $\text{Game}_{1,1,2}$, we replace $k_{2,1}$ with $k'_{2,1} \leftarrow \{0,1\}^\theta$ for the MAC key used in Π_1^1, if Π_1^1's partner is P_2.
- $\text{Game}_{i,\ell,j}$ is same with the previous game except that in $\text{Game}_{i,\ell,j}$ we additionally replace $k_{j,i}$ with $k'_{j,i} \leftarrow \{0,1\}^\theta$ for the MAC key used in Π_i^ℓ, if Π_i^ℓ's partner is P_j.

Claim 2.1. $\Pr[\text{forge in Game}_0] - \Pr[\text{forge in Game}_{N,q_s,N-1}] \le N^2 q_s \cdot \text{Adv}_{H,\mathcal{GG}}^{\text{ODH}}$.

---

[5] Note that $\text{Game}_{i,*,i}$ is not defined.

Claim 2.2. $\Pr[\text{forge in Game}_{N,q_s,N-1}] \leq N^2 q_s \cdot \mathsf{Adv}_M^{\text{SUF}}$.

From Claim 2.1 and Claim 2.2, Claim 2 follows.   †

Proof of Claim 2.1. Let $\mathsf{Game}_{i',\ell',j'}$ and $\mathsf{Game}_{i^*,\ell^*,j^*}$ be two adjacent games. If $\Pr[\text{forge}]$ between the two games is non-negligibly different, we can construct distinguisher $\mathcal{D}$ which breaks the ODH assumption with non-negligible probability. Note that

$$\Pr[\text{forge}] = \Pr[\text{forge}|\Pi_{i^*}^{\ell^*}\text{'s partner is } P_{j^*}] + \Pr[\text{forge}|\Pi_{i^*}^{\ell^*}\text{'s partner is not } P_{j^*}].$$

If $\Pi_{i^*}^{\ell^*}$'s partner is not P_{j^*}, $\mathsf{Game}_{i',\ell',j'}$ and $\mathsf{Game}_{i^*,\ell^*,j^*}$ are same experimental games. So $\Pr[\text{forge}|\Pi_{i^*}^{\ell^*}\text{'s partner is not } P_{j^*}]$ is same in the two adjacent games. From this observation, we know that if $\Pr[\text{forge}]$ between the two games is non-negligibly different, $\Pr[\text{forge}|\Pi_{i^*}^{\ell^*}\text{'s partner is } P_{j^*}]$ is non-negligibly different in two adjacent games.

Consider the following algorithm $\mathcal{D}$ which tries to break the ODH assumption using the difference of $\Pr[\text{forge}|\Pi_{i^*}^{\ell^*}\text{'s partner is } P_{j^*}]$ in two adjacent games. $\mathcal{D}$ is given an oracle $\mathcal{H}_{u_2}$ and an input (G, q, g, U_1, U_2, W) in the experiment of the ODH problem, and inserts them as the protocol messages. The more concrete description of $\mathcal{D}^{\mathcal{H}_{u_2}}(G, q, g, U_1, U_2, W)$ is as follows:

1. $\mathcal{D}$ is given (G, q, g, U_1, U_2, W). $\mathcal{D}$ uses U_2 as the public key of P_{j^*}. $\mathcal{D}$ chooses public keys for all other parties normally (i.e., choosing a random x_i and letting $y_i = g^{x_i}$ for $1 \leq i(\neq j^*) \leq N$).
2. For each oracle query of $\mathcal{A}$, $\mathcal{D}$ answers it as in the $\mathsf{Game}_{i',\ell',j'}$ except the followings:

   - For Initiate and Send:
     - Use U_1 as the ephemeral Diffie-Hellman message of $\Pi_{i^*}^{\ell^*}$.
     - If P_{j^*} is communicating with $\Pi_{i^*}^{\ell^*}$, $\mathcal{D}$ uses W for the MAC key k_{j^*,i^*} and $H(y_{i^*}^{\alpha_{j^*}})$ for the MAC key k_{i^*,j^*}.
     - If P_{j^*} is communicating with other than $\Pi_{i^*}^{\ell^*}$, $\mathcal{D}$ uses $\mathcal{H}_{u_2}(Z_i)$ for the MAC key $k_{j^*,i}$ and $H(y_i^{\alpha_{j^*}})$ for the MAC key k_{i,j^*}.
   - For Reveal(i,k) and Test(i,k):
     - If P_{j^*} is communicating with $\Pi_{i^*}^{\ell^*}$, $\mathcal{D}$ makes a session key $\mathsf{sk}_{i^*,j^*} = H(U_2^{x_{i^*}}) \oplus H(U_1^{\alpha_{j^*}})$.
     - If P_{j^*} is communicating with other than $\Pi_{i^*}^{\ell^*}$, $\mathcal{D}$ makes a session key $\mathsf{sk}_{i,j^*} = \mathcal{H}_{u_2}(y_i) \oplus H(Z_i^{\alpha_{j^*}})$.
   - For Corrupt(i): If $i = j^*$, HALT.

3. If an event forge occurs, $\mathcal{D}$ outputs 1, and quits. If $\mathcal{A}$ quits (and forge does not occur), $\mathcal{D}$ outputs 0, and quits.

$\mathcal{D}$ simulates $\mathsf{Game}_{i',\ell',j'}$ or $\mathsf{Game}_{i^*,\ell^*,j^*}$ depending on whether $W = H(g^{u_1 u_2})$ or not, where $U_1 = g^{u_1}$ and $U_2 = g^{u_2}$. So the following inequality holds:

$$\mathsf{Adv}_{\mathcal{D}}^{\mathrm{HDH}} \geq \Pr[\mathcal{D}^{\mathcal{H}_{u_2}}(U_1, U_2, W) = 1 | U_1 = g^{u_1}, U_2 = g^{u_2}, W = H(g^{u_1 u_2})]$$

$$-\Pr[\mathcal{D}^{\mathcal{H}_{u_2}}(U_1, U_2, W) = 1 | U_1 = g^{u_1}, U_2 = g^{u_2}, W = \{0, 1\}^\theta]$$

$$= \Pr[\text{forge in Game}_{i', \ell', j'} \wedge \Pi_{i*}^{\ell*}\text{'s partner is } P_{j*}]$$

$$-\Pr[\text{forge in Game}_{i*, \ell*, j*} \wedge \Pi_{i*}^{\ell*}\text{'s partner is } P_{j*}]$$

$$= \Pr[\text{forge in Game}_{i', \ell', j'}] - \Pr[\text{forge in Game}_{i*, \ell*, j*}].$$

So by the hybrid arguments, Claim 2.1 follows. †

Proof of Claim 2.2. If $\Pr[\text{forge}]$ is non-negligible in $\text{Game}_{N, q_s, N-1}$, we can construct forger $\mathcal{F}$ which breaks the unforgeability of the underlying MAC scheme.

Consider the following algorithm $\mathcal{F}$ which breaks the unforgeability of the underlying MAC scheme using $\mathcal{A}$ in $\text{Game}_{N, q_s, N-1}$. $\mathcal{F}$ is given an oracle Mac_{sk} in the experiment of the MAC scheme, and uses the oracle to make a MAC which is supposed to be generated with $k'_{j,i}$ in randomly selected Π_i^k. The more concrete description of $\mathcal{F}$ is as follows:

1. $\mathcal{F}$ is given an oracle Mac_{sk}. $\mathcal{F}$ chooses public keys for all parties normally (i.e., choosing a random x_i and letting $y_i = g^{x_i}$ for $1 \leq i \leq N$). $\mathcal{F}$ selects $i^*, j^* \leftarrow [1, N]$ and $\ell^* \leftarrow [1, q_s]$.
2. For each oracle query of $\mathcal{A}$, $\mathcal{D}$ answers it as in $\text{Game}_{N, q_s, N-1}$ except the followings:
   - For Send: We use an oracle Mac_{sk} for a MAC which is supposed to be generated with $k'_{j*, i*}$ in $\Pi_{i*}^{\ell*}$, if $\Pi_{i*}^{\ell*}$'s partner is P_{j*}.
3. If an event forge occurs with respect to $k'_{j*, i*}$ in $\Pi_{i*}^{\ell*}$ with partner P_{j*}, $\mathcal{F}$ outputs the forged MAC and message pair and quits. Otherwise, $\mathcal{F}$ stops.

If $\mathcal{F}$ correctly selects i^*, j^*, ℓ^*, $\mathcal{F}$ does not fail. So the following inequality holds:

$$\mathsf{Adv}_{\mathcal{F}}^{\mathrm{SUF}} \geq \frac{1}{N^2 q_s} \Pr[\text{forge in Game}_{N, q_s, N-1}].$$

So Claim 2.2 follows. †

Proof of Claim 3. The intuition is as follows: Without col and forge, the only way $\mathcal{A}$ gets the information of the session key of the test oracle seems to have to calculate $H(g^{\alpha_i \alpha_j})$ of the test oracle, where g^{α_i} and g^{α_j} are ephemeral Diffie-Hellman messages. Note that $\mathcal{A}$ may get secret keys x_i and x_j, but the secret keys are of no use in calculating $H(g^{\alpha_i \alpha_j})$.

Consider the following algorithm $\mathcal{D}$ which tries to break the HDH assumption using $\mathcal{A}$. $\mathcal{D}$ is given (G, q, g, U_1, U_2, W) in the experiment of the hash Diffie-Hellman problem, and inserts them as the protocol messages. The more concrete description of $\mathcal{D}$ is as follows:

1. $\mathcal{D}$ is given (G, q, g, U_1, U_2, W). $\mathcal{D}$ begins by choosing public keys for all parties normally (i.e., choosing a random x_i and letting $y_i = g^{x_i}$). $\mathcal{D}$ selects i' and j' from $[1, N]$, and chooses random t_1 and t_2 from $[1, q_s]$.

2. For each oracle query of $\mathcal{A}$, $\mathcal{D}$ answers it as in the protocol except the followings:

  - For Initiate: Use U_1 as the t_1-th ephemeral Diffie-Hellman message of $P_{i'}$, and U_2 as the t_2-th ephemeral Diffie-Hellman message of $P_{j'}$.
  - For Reveal(i, k): If Π_i^k uses U_1 or U_2 as the ephemeral Diffie-Hellman message, HALT.
  - For Test(i, k): If Π_i^k does not see (U_1, U_2) as the ephemeral Diffie-Hellman messages, HALT. Otherwise, return sk $= H(g^{x_{i'}x_{j'}}) \oplus W$ to $\mathcal{A}$.

3. Assume that $\mathcal{A}$ outputs b', and quits. Then $\mathcal{D}$ outputs b', and quits.

If $\mathcal{A}$ makes Test query for Π_i^k which sees (U_1, U_2) as the ephemeral Diffie-Hellman messages, $\mathcal{D}$ does not fail. That is, $\mathcal{D}$ simulates $\mathbf{Exp}_{\mathcal{A}_{\mathsf{HDH}}}^{\mathsf{HDH\text{-}1}}$ or $\mathbf{Exp}_{\mathcal{A}_{\mathsf{HDH}}}^{\mathsf{HDH\text{-}0}}$ depending on whether $W = H(g^{u_1 u_2})$ or not, where $U_1 = g^{u_1}$ and $U_2 = g^{u_2}$. Note if W is a random value, then $H(g^{x_{i'}x_{j'}}) \oplus W$ is a random value. So the probability of success of $\mathcal{D}$ depends on whether or not $\mathcal{D}$ guesses correctly i', j', t_1 and t_2. If these guesses are correct, $\mathcal{D}$ provides exactly the same view as in $\mathbf{Exp}_{\mathcal{A}_{\mathsf{HDH}}}^{\mathsf{HDH\text{-}1}}$ or $\mathbf{Exp}_{\mathcal{A}_{\mathsf{HDH}}}^{\mathsf{HDH\text{-}0}}$ to $\mathcal{A}$. So the following inequality holds:

$$
\begin{aligned}
\mathsf{Adv}_{\mathcal{D}}^{\mathsf{HDH}} &= \Pr[\mathcal{D}(U_1, U_2, W) = 1 | U_1 = g^{u_1}, U_2 = g^{u_2}, W = H(g^{u_1 u_2})] \\
&\quad - \Pr[\mathcal{D}(U_1, U_2, W) = 1 | U_1 = g^{u_1}, U_2 = g^{u_2}, W = \{0,1\}^{\theta}] \\
&\geq \frac{1}{(Nq_s)^2} \cdot (\Pr[\mathcal{A}() = 1 | \text{sk is real in Test query}] \\
&\quad - \Pr[\mathcal{A}() = 1 | \text{sk is random in Test query}]) \\
&= \frac{1}{(Nq_s)^2} \cdot (2\Pr_{\mathcal{A}}[b = b' \wedge \overline{\mathsf{col}} \wedge \overline{\mathsf{forge}}] - 1).
\end{aligned}
$$

So the claim follows.   †

Lemma 2. If M is a secure MAC scheme, KAM is a KCI–secure key exchange scheme under the ODH and HDH assumptions. More formally,

$$
\mathsf{Adv}_{\mathsf{KAM}}^{\mathsf{KCI}}(\theta, t) \leq \frac{2q_s^2}{q} + 2N^2 q_s \cdot \mathsf{Adv}_{\mathsf{M}}^{\mathsf{SUF}}(\theta, t) + 2N^2 q_s \cdot \mathsf{Adv}_{H,\mathcal{G}\mathcal{G}}^{\mathsf{ODH}}(\theta, t) + (Nq_s)^2 \cdot \mathsf{Adv}_{H,\mathcal{G}\mathcal{G}}^{\mathsf{HDH}}(\theta, t),
$$

where t is the maximum total experiment time including an adversary's execution time. Here, N is an upper bound on the number of honest parties, and q_s is an upper bound on the number of the sessions an adversary makes.

Proof of Lemma 2. (sketch) Consider an adversary $\mathcal{A}$ attacking KAM in the sense of KCI. Let col and forge be the events as in the proof of Lemma 1. $\mathcal{A}$ may get the advantage from the events col or forge. If so, we can break the ODH assumption or the underlying MAC scheme using $\mathcal{A}$. If $\mathcal{A}$ breaks KCI without col and forge, we can break the HDH assumption using $\mathcal{A}$. Because without col and forge $\mathcal{A}$ seems to have to calculate $H(g^{\alpha_i \alpha_j})$ of the test oracle Π_i^{ℓ}, where

g^{α_i} and g^{α_j} are ephemeral Diffie-Hellman messages. Note that $\mathcal{A}$ may get secret key x_i of P_i, but the secret key is of no use in calculating $H(g^{\alpha_i \alpha_j})$.

The detailed proof is almost same with the proof of Lemma 1, so we omit it.   □

Lemma 3. If KAM is an SSR–secure key exchange scheme under the HDH assumption. More formally,

$$\mathsf{Adv}_{\mathsf{KAM}}^{\mathsf{SSR}}(\theta, t) \leq \frac{q_s^2}{q} + N^2 \cdot \mathsf{Adv}_{H,\mathcal{GG}}^{\mathsf{HDH}}(\theta, t),$$

where t is the maximum total experiment time including an adversary's execution time. Here, N is an upper bound on the number of honest parties, and q_s is an upper bound on the number of the sessions an adversary makes.

Proof of Lemma 3. Consider the following algorithm $\mathcal{D}$ which tries to break the hash Diffie-Hellman assumption using $\mathcal{A}$. $\mathcal{D}$ is given (G, q, g, U_1, U_2, W) in the experiment of the hash Diffie-Hellman problem, and inserts them as the protocol messages. The more concrete description of $\mathcal{D}$ is as follows:

1. $\mathcal{D}$ is given (G, q, g, U_1, U_2, W). $\mathcal{D}$ randomly selects i' and j' from $[1, N]$, and uses U_1 as public key $y_{i'}$ of $P_{i'}$ and U_2 as $y_{j'}$ of $P_{j'}$. $\mathcal{D}$ chooses all other public keys normally.
2. For each oracle query of $\mathcal{A}$, $\mathcal{D}$ answers it as in the protocol except the followings:
   - For Test(i, k): Let P_j be a partner of Π_i^k. If $\{P_i, P_j\} \neq \{P_{i'}, P_{j'}\}$, HALT. $\mathcal{D}$ gives $W \oplus H(g^{\alpha_{i'} \alpha_{j'}})$ to $\mathcal{A}$.
3. Assume that $\mathcal{A}$ outputs b' and quits. Then $\mathcal{D}$ outputs b' and quits.

If $\mathcal{A}$ makes Test query for oracles in $P_{i'}$ whose partner is $P_{j'}$, $\mathcal{D}$ does not fail. That is, $\mathcal{D}$ simulates $\mathbf{Exp}_{\mathcal{A}_{\mathsf{HDH}}}^{\mathsf{HDH\text{-}1}}$ or $\mathbf{Exp}_{\mathcal{A}_{\mathsf{HDH}}}^{\mathsf{HDH\text{-}0}}$ depending on whether $W = H(g^{u_1 u_2})$ or not, where $U_1 = g^{u_1}$ and $U_2 = g^{u_2}$. Note if W is a random value, then $W \oplus H(g^{\alpha_{i'} \alpha_{j'}})$ is a random value. So the probability of success of $\mathcal{D}$ depends on whether or not $\mathcal{D}$ guesses correctly i' and j'. If these guesses are correct, $\mathcal{D}$ provides exactly the same view as in $\mathbf{Exp}_{\mathcal{A}_{\mathsf{HDH}}}^{\mathsf{HDH\text{-}1}}$ or $\mathbf{Exp}_{\mathcal{A}_{\mathsf{HDH}}}^{\mathsf{HDH\text{-}0}}$ to $\mathcal{A}$. So the following inequality holds:

$$\mathsf{Adv}_{\mathcal{D}}^{\mathsf{HDH}} = \Pr[\mathcal{D}(U_1, U_2, W) = 1 | U_1 = g^{u_1}, U_2 = g^{u_2}, W = H(g^{u_1 u_2})]$$
$$-\Pr[\mathcal{D}(U_1, U_2, W) = 1 | U_1 = g^{u_1}, U_2 = g^{u_2}, W = \{0, 1\}^\theta]$$
$$= \frac{1}{N^2} \cdot (\Pr[\mathcal{A}() = 1 | \mathsf{sk} \text{ is real in Test query}]$$
$$-\Pr[\mathcal{A}() = 1 | \mathsf{sk} \text{ is random in Test query}])$$
$$= \frac{1}{N^2} \cdot \mathsf{Adv}_{\mathcal{A}}^{\mathsf{SSR}}.$$

So the lemma follows.   □

References

1. M. Abdalla, M. Bellare and P. Rogaway, DHAES: an encryption scheme based on the Diffie-Hellman problem. Submission to IEEE P1363, 1998.
2. M. Abdalla, M. Bellare and P. Rogaway, The oracle Diffie-Hellman assumption and an analysis of DHIES, CT-RSA01, pp. 143-158, 2001.
3. American National Standard (ANSI) X9.42-2001, Public Key Cryptography for the Financial Services Industry: Agreement of Symmetric Keys Using Discrete Logarithm Cryptography.
4. American National Standard (ANSI) X9.63: Public Key Cryptography for the Financial Services Industry: Key Agreement and Key Transport using Elliptic Curve Cryptography.
5. R. Ankney, D. Johnson, and M. Matyas, The Unified Model, Contribution to ANSI X9F1, 1995.
6. G. Ateniese, M. Steiner, and G. Tsudik, New Multi-Party Authentication Services and Key Agreement Protocols, IEEE Journal of Selected Areas in Communications 18 (4) (2000) 628-639.
7. C. Boyd, On Key Agreement and Conference Key Agreement, in: Proceedings of ACISP'97, 1997, pp. 294-302.
8. Mihir Bellare, Alexandra Boldyreva, Adriana Palacio, An Uninstantiable Random-Oracle-Model Scheme for a Hybrid-Encryption Problem, in: EUROCRYPT 2004: 171-188.
9. M. Bellare, A. Boldyreva, and J. Staddon, Randomness Re-use in Multi-recipient Encryption Schemes, in: Proceedings of PKC'03, 2003, pp. 85-99.
10. E. Bresson, O. Chevassut, A. Essiari and D. Pointcheval, Mutual Authentication and Group Key Agreement for Low-Power Mobile Devices, in: Proceedings of MWCN'03, 2003, pp. 59-62.
11. M. Bellare, R. Canetti, and H. Krawczyk, A Modular Approach to the Design and Analysis of Authentication and Key Exchange Protocols, in: Proceedings of 30th Annual Symposium on the Theory of Computing, 1998, pp. 419-428.
12. E. Bresson, O. Chevassut, and D. Pointcheval, Provably Authenticated Group Diffie-Hellman Key Exchange — The Dynamic Case, in: Proceedings of ASIACRYPT'01, 2001, pp. 290-309.
13. M. Burmester and Y. Desmedt, A Secure and Efficient Conference Key Distribution System, in: Proceedings of EUROCRYPT'94, 1994, pp. 275-286.
14. Mihir Bellare, Marc Fischlin, Shafi Goldwasser, and Silvio Micali, Identification Protocols Secure against Reset Attacks, in: EUROCRYPT 2001, pp. 495-511.
15. S. Blake-Wilson and A. Menezes, Authenticated Diffie-Hellman Key Agreement Protocols, in: SAC 98, 1998, pp. 339-361.
16. C. Boyd and J.M.G. Nieto, Round-Optimal Contributory Conference Key Agreement, in: Proceedings of PKC'03, 2003, pp. 161-174.
17. M. Bellare and P. Rogaway, Entity Authentication and Key Distribution, in: Proceedings of CRYPTO'93, 1993, pp. 232-249.
18. Mihir Bellare, Phillip Rogaway, Random Oracles are Practical: A Paradigm for Designing Efficient Protocols, in: ACM Conference on Computer and Communications Security 1993, pp. 62-73.
19. Kim-Kwang Raymond Choo, Colin Boyd, Yvonne Hitchcock, Examining Indistinguishability-Based Proof Models for Key Establishment Protocols, in: ASIACRYPT 2005, pp. 585-604.

20. R. Canetti, O. Goldreich, and S. Halevi. The random oracle methodology, revisited. STOC 98.
21. Ran Canetti and Hugo Krawczyk. Analysis of Key-Exchange Protocols and Their Use for Building Secure Channels. in: Advances in Cryptology-EUROCRYPT 2001, pp. 453-474, Springer Verlag, 2001.
22. R. Canetti and H. Krawczyk, Universally Composable Notions of Key Exchange and Secure Channels, in: Proceedings of EUROCRYPT'02, 2002, pp. 337-351.
23. Ran Canetti and Hugo Krawczyk, Security Analysis of IKE's Signature-Based Key-Exchange Protocol, in: Proceedings of CRYPTO'02, 2002, pp. 143-161.
24. W. Diffie and M. Hellman, New Directions in Cryptography, IEEE Transactions on Information Theory 22 (6) (1976), 644-654.
25. Whitfield Diffie, Paul C. van Oorschot, Michael J. Wiener, Authentication and Authenticated Key Exchanges, Designs, Codes and Cryptography, 2, pp. 107-125, 1992.
26. D. Denning and G. M. Sacco, Timestamps in Key Distribution Protocols, Comm. ACM 24 (8) (1981) 533-536.
27. W. Diffie, P. van Oorschot, and M. Wiener, Authentication and Authenticated Key Exchanges, in: Designs, Codes, and Cryptography 2 (2), 1992, pp. 107-125.
28. O. Goldreich, S. Goldwasser and S. Micali, How to construct random functions, in: Journal of the ACM, Vol. 33, No. 4, 1986, pp. 210-217.
29. Shafi Goldwasser, Silvio Micali, Ronald L. Rivest, A Digital Signature Scheme Secure Against Adaptive Chosen-Message Attacks, in: SIAM J. Comput. 17(2): 281-308 (1988).
30. Shafi Goldwasser and Yael Tauman. On the (In)security of the Fiat-Shamir Paradigm. FOCS03, pages 102-115, IEEE Computer Society, 2003.
31. IEEE 1363-2000: Standard Speci.cations for Public Key Cryptography.
32. I. Ingemarasson, D.T. Tang, and C.K. Wong, A Conference Key Distribution System, IEEE Transactions on Information Theory 28 (5) (1982) 714-720.
33. ISO/IEC IS 15946-3 Information technology - Security techniques Cryptographic techniques based on elliptic curves - Part 3: Key establishment, 2002.
34. I. Jeong, J. Katz, and D. Lee, One-Round Protocols for Two-Party Authenticated Key Exchange, in: ACNS'04, 2004.
35. Kaoru Kurosawa, Multi-recipient Public-Key Encryption with Shortened Ciphertext, in: Proceedings of PKC'02, 2002, pp. 48-63.
36. Hugo Krawczyk, HMQV: A High-Performance Secure Diffie-Hellman Protocol, in: Proceedings of CRYPTO'05, 2005, pp. 546-566.
37. Hugo Krawczyk, HMQV: A High-Performance Secure Diffie-Hellman Protocol, Full version of [36], in: eprint.iacr.org/2005/176, 2005.
38. J. Katz and M. Yung, Scalable Protocols for Authenticated Group Key Exchange, in: Proceedings of CRYPTO'03, 2003, pp. 110-125.
39. L. Law, A. Menezes, M. Qu, J. Solinas, and S. Vanstone, An Efficient Protocol for Authenticated Key Agreement, in: Designs, Codes and Cryptography, 28, 2003, pp. 119-134.
40. A. Menezes, Another Look at HMQV, in: http://eprint.iacr.org/2005/205, 2005.
41. A. Menezes, M. Qu, and S. Vanstone, Some new key agreement protocols providing mutual implicit authentication, in: SAC 95, 1995.
42. NIST Special Publication 800-56 (DRAFT): Recommendation on Key Establishment Schemes. Draft 2, Jan. 2003.
43. NSAs Elliptic Curve Licensing Agreement, presentation by Mr. John Stasak (Cryptography Office, National Security Agency) to the IETF's Security Area Advisory Group, Nov 2004. http://www.machshav.com/ smb/saag-11-2004/NSA-EC-License.pdf

44. V. Shoup, On Formal Models for Secure Key Exchange, Available at http://eprint.iacr.org.
45. Secure hash standard. National Institute of Standards and Technology, NIST FIPS PUB 180-1, U.S. Department of Commerce, Apr. 1995.
46. S. Blake-Wilson, D. Johnson, and A. Menezes, Key Agreement Protocols and their Security Analysis, in: Proceedings of Sixth IMA International Conference on Cryptography and Coding, 1997, pp. 30-45.

A   Hash Diffie-Hellman Problem [24]

Let $\theta \in N$ be a security parameter. Let H be a hash function such that $H : \{0,1\}^* \to \{0,1\}^\theta$. Let $\mathcal{GG}$ be a group generator which generates a group G whose prime order is q and a generator is g. Consider the following experiment:

$\mathbf{Exp}_{H,\mathcal{GG},\mathcal{A}_{\mathrm{HDH}}}^{\mathrm{HDH-1}}(\theta)$	$\mathbf{Exp}_{H,\mathcal{GG},\mathcal{A}_{\mathrm{HDH}}}^{\mathrm{HDH-0}}(\theta)$
$(G,q,g) \leftarrow \mathcal{GG}(1^\theta)$	$(G,q,g) \leftarrow \mathcal{GG}(1^\theta)$
$u_1, u_2 \leftarrow [1,q]$	$u_1, u_2 \leftarrow [1,q]$
$U_1 \leftarrow g^{u_1}; U_2 \leftarrow g^{u_2}$	$U_1 \leftarrow g^{u_1}; U_2 \leftarrow g^{u_2}$
$W \leftarrow H(g^{u_1 u_2})$	$W \leftarrow \{0,1\}^\theta$
$d \leftarrow \mathcal{A}_{\mathrm{HDH}}(G,q,g,U_1,U_2,W)$	$d \leftarrow \mathcal{A}_{\mathrm{HDH}}(G,q,g,U_1,U_2,W)$
return d	return d

The advantage of an adversary $\mathcal{A}_{\mathrm{HDH}}(\theta)$ is defined as follows:

$$\mathsf{Adv}_{\mathcal{A}_{\mathrm{HDH}}}^{\mathrm{HDH}}(\theta) = \Pr[\mathbf{Exp}_{H,\mathcal{GG},\mathcal{A}_{\mathrm{HDH}}}^{\mathrm{HDH-1}}(\theta) = 1] - \Pr[\mathbf{Exp}_{H,\mathcal{GG},\mathcal{A}_{\mathrm{HDH}}}^{\mathrm{HDH-0}}(\theta) = 1].$$

The advantage function is defined as follows:

$$\mathsf{Adv}_{H,\mathcal{GG}}^{\mathrm{HDH}}(\theta, t) = \max_{\mathcal{A}} \{\mathsf{Adv}_{\mathcal{A}_{\mathrm{HDH}}}^{\mathrm{HDH}}(\theta)\},$$

where $\mathcal{A}_{\mathrm{HDH}}$ is any adversary with time complexity t. The HDH assumption is that the advantage of any adversary $\mathcal{A}_{\mathrm{HDH}}$ with time complexity polynomial in θ is negligible.

If hash function H is derived from some cryptographic hash function like SHA-1 [45], the HDH assumption seems to hold. The hash function should provide one-wayness. For more detailed discussion about selection of a hash function, refer to [1,2].

B   Oracle Diffie-Hellman Problem [1,2]

Let $\mathcal{GG}$ be a group generator which generates a group G whose prime order is q and a generator is g. Let $k \in N$ be a security parameter. Consider the following experiment:

$\mathbf{Exp}_{H,\mathcal{GG},\mathcal{A}_{\mathrm{ODH}}}^{\mathrm{ODH\text{-}1}}(\theta)$	$\mathbf{Exp}_{H,\mathcal{GG},\mathcal{A}_{\mathrm{ODH}}}^{\mathrm{ODH\text{-}0}}(\theta)$
$(G,q,g) \leftarrow \mathcal{GG}(1^\theta)$	$(G,q,g) \leftarrow \mathcal{GG}(1^\theta)$
$u_1, u_2 \leftarrow [1,q]$	$u_1, u_2 \leftarrow [1,q]$
$U_1 \leftarrow g^{u_1}; U_2 \leftarrow g^{u_2}$	$U_1 \leftarrow g^{u_1}; U_2 \leftarrow g^{u_2}$
$W \leftarrow H(g^{u_1 u_2})$	$W \leftarrow \{0,1\}^\theta$
$\mathcal{H}_{u_2}(X) \overset{def}{=} H(X^{u_2})$	$\mathcal{H}_{u_2}(X) \overset{def}{=} H(X^{u_2})$
$d \leftarrow \mathcal{A}_{\mathrm{ODH}}^{\mathcal{H}_{u_2}(\cdot)}(G,q,g,U_1,U_2,W)$	$d \leftarrow \mathcal{A}_{\mathrm{ODH}}^{\mathcal{H}_{u_2}(\cdot)}(G,q,g,U_1,U_2,W)$
return d	return d

In the above experiment $\mathcal{A}$ can query any string to the oracle $\mathcal{H}_{u_2}(\cdot)$ except U_1. The advantage of an adversary $\mathcal{A}_{\mathrm{ODH}}(\theta)$ is defined as follows:

$$\mathsf{Adv}_{\mathcal{A}_{\mathrm{ODH}}}^{\mathrm{ODH}}(\theta) = \Pr[\mathbf{Exp}_{H,\mathcal{GG},\mathcal{A}_{\mathrm{ODH}}}^{\mathrm{ODH\text{-}1}}(\theta) = 1] - \Pr[\mathbf{Exp}_{H,\mathcal{GG},\mathcal{A}_{\mathrm{ODH}}}^{\mathrm{ODH\text{-}0}}(\theta) = 1].$$

The advantage function is defined as follows:

$$\mathsf{Adv}_{H,\mathcal{GG}}^{\mathrm{ODH}}(\theta, t) = \overset{\max}{_{\mathcal{A}}}\{\mathsf{Adv}_{\mathcal{A}_{\mathrm{ODH}}}^{\mathrm{ODH}}(\theta)\},$$

where $\mathcal{A}_{\mathrm{ODH}}$ is any adversary with time complexity t. The ODH assumption is that the advantage of any adversary $\mathcal{A}_{\mathrm{ODH}}$ with time complexity polynomial in θ is negligible.

If hash function H is derived from some cryptographic hash function like SHA-1, the ODH assumption seems to hold. The hash function should provide one-wayness. For more detailed discussion about selection of a hash function, refer to [1,2].

C Strong Unforgeability (SUF) of Message Authentication Codes

In defining the security of a MAC we use the standard definition of strong unforgeability under adaptive chosen-message attack. Namely, let M be a MAC scheme and $\mathcal{A}$ be an adversary, and consider the following experiment:

$\mathbf{Exp}_{\mathcal{A},M}^{\mathrm{SUF}}(\theta)$
$sk \leftarrow \{0,1\}^\theta$
$(M,\tau) \leftarrow \mathcal{A}^{\mathsf{Mac}_{sk}(\cdot),\mathsf{Vrfy}_{sk}(\cdot,\cdot)}(1^\theta)$
if $\mathsf{Vrfy}_{sk}(M,\tau) = 1$ and oracle $\mathsf{Mac}_{sk}(\cdot)$
$\quad$ never returned τ on input M then return 1
else return 0

The advantage of an adversary $\mathcal{A}_{\mathrm{SUF}}(\theta)$ is defined as follows:

$$\mathsf{Adv}_{M,\mathcal{A}_{\mathrm{SUF}}}^{\mathrm{SUF}}(\theta) = \Pr[\mathbf{Exp}_{M,\mathcal{A}_{\mathrm{SUF}}}^{\mathrm{SUF}}(\theta) = 1].$$

The advantage function of the scheme is defined as follows:

$$\mathsf{Adv}_{M}^{\mathrm{SUF}}(\theta, t, q_m, q_v) = \overset{\max}{_{\mathcal{A}}}\{\mathsf{Adv}_{M,\mathcal{A}_{\mathrm{SUF}}}^{\mathrm{SUF}}(\theta)\},$$

where $\mathcal{A}_{\text{SUF}}$ is any adversary with time complexity t making at most q_m MAC generation queries and q_v MAC verification queries. The scheme M is SUF–secure if the advantage of any adversary $\mathcal{A}_{\text{SUF}}$ with time complexity polynomial in θ is negligible.

Authenticated Group Key Agreement for Multicast

Liming Wang[1,2] and Chuan-Kun Wu[1]

[1] State Key Laboratory of Information Security, Institute of Software,
Chinese Academy of Sciences, Beijing 100080, P.R. China
[2] Graduate School of Chinese Academy of Sciences, Beijing 100039, P.R. China
{limingwang, ckwu}@is.iscas.ac.cn

Abstract. Secure multicast communication provides an efficient way to deliver data to a large group of recipients. Scalability, efficiency and authenticity are the key challenges for secure multicast. In this paper, we propose a novel group key agreement scheme called logical identity hierarchy(LIH) for multicast to support secure communications for large and dynamic groups, which is based on bilinear pairing. Compared with the previous tree-based schemes, LIH provides dual authentication between group controller(GC) and group members and hierarchical authentication among group members. GC and all the users do not need to execute any encryption/decryption process during the rekeying operation. Moreover, in LIH, the group members can be stateless receivers, who do not need to update their state during the protocol execution. Using a public board, GC does not need to multicast any rekeying message when a user joins/leaves the communication group. Security analysis shows that LIH satisfies both backward secrecy and forward secrecy.

1 Introduction

Many web and multimedia applications such as audio and video conference, pay-TV systems, secure distribution of copyright-protected material, require a secure and reliable group communication. Multicast is the core component of the group communications, which greatly reduces the server's communication overhead and network bandwidth usage by sending one multicast message instead of n messages to n destinations.

However, IP multicast [1, 2, 3] by itself does not provide any security services. Anyone can join a multicast group to receive data or to send data to the group. Therefore, security is crucial for the multicast communications. Basic security services needed in multicast communication are largely the same as in the unicast communications: data secrecy, integrity and entity authentication. But often the cryptography mechanisms used in the unicast environment may not be directly deployed into multicast environment. In the most basic form, the first step towards securing traffic within a multicast group is to provide a cryptographic key that is shared by the group members [4, 5, 6, 7, 8, 9, 10, 11, 12, 13, 14, 15, 16, 17]. Having such a key allows group members to decode the messages, while the entities outside the group cannot decode them. The group key is updated on every

D. Pointcheval, Y. Mu, and K. Chen (Eds.): CANS 2006, LNCS 4301, pp. 55–72, 2006.
© Springer-Verlag Berlin Heidelberg 2006

membership change for forward and backward secrecy. Because the group rekeying is very consumptive and frequently performed due to the dynamic nature of multicast communication, the way to update it in a scalable and secure fashion is required.

1.1 Related Work

The logical key hierarchy(LKH) method was proposed by Wallner et al. [11] and Wong et al. [12] independently. In this approach, the group controller(GC) maintains a logical key tree where each node represents a key encryption key(KEK). The root of the key tree is the group key used for encrypting data in group communications and it is shared by all users. The leaf node of the key tree is associated with a user in the communication group. Each user secretly maintains the keys related to the nodes in the path from its leaf node to the root. As a result, in an addition or eviction of a user, the rekeying communication cost is equivalent to $2 \log_2 n - 1$ keys. In a balanced binary tree, each user stores $\log_2 n + 1$ keys, where n is the number of users. The joining operation in LKH can be improved to run in constant time as suggested by Waldvoggel et al. [18]. The new group key can be computed by applying a one-way function to the keys affected by the membership change. Hence, each member that already knew the old key can compute the new one.

Another optimization of the logical key hierarchy approach is one-way function tree(OFT) proposed by McGrew and Sherman [13,19]. Their scheme reduces the size of rekeying messages from $2 \log_2 n$ to $\log_2 n$. Canetti et al. [5] proposed a slightly different method that achieves the same communication overhead using a pseudo-random generator tree. This algorithm is known as the one-way function chain tree(OFCT) and it is applied only on users removal.

Kim et al. proposed a tree-based key agreement protocol(TGDH) [14, 16]. TGDH is a contributive tree key management protocol which is a combination of key tree and Diffie-Hellman key exchange to generate and maintain the group key. It is similar to OFT but each member can act as a sponsor according to its position in the tree. The sponsor is responsible for the communication and the broadcasting of intermediate node keys to other members of the group.

Chang et al. [6] used boolean function minimization technique to binary trees to minimize the cost of communication. Although the size of rekeying messages and the storage of GC are reduced, their scheme is not secure against the attack by colluding or compromised members who can cooperate to determine all the keys of the system.

1.2 Our Contribution

We present a novel group key agreement scheme called logical identity hierarchy(LIH) for multicast, which uses a bilinear pairing based cryptography [20, 21, 22, 23, 24, 25, 26, 27, 28, 29]. LIH is an identity tree where each node in the tree is associated with an identity and a key generation key(KGK). The leaf node's identity is corresponding to the user's identity and the interior node's identity is generated by its children's identities. So in LIH, an interior node represents a set of users in the subtree rooted at this node. Thus, LIH provides a hierarchical authentication among group members. Moreover, LIH also provides dual authentication between GC and group members.

LKH method and its variants require the group users to update their state whenever users join or leave the group. In this case, if a legitimate receiver is not capable of recording the past history of rekeying materials and change its state accordingly, it may not be able to decipher the messages from a future rekeying instance. In LIH, the users can be stateless. In such a scenario, there is no dependency between the previous group key and the current group key, i.e., for any legitimate users, the current group key can be deduced from the current rekeying messages. The statelessness property is very desirable for multicast applications in which group members go off-line frequently. In LIH, even though a member has not participated in multicast communication for a long time, it can easily decrypt the messages with the initial private key without keeping track of the history of rekeying materials.

Furthermore, GC and all the users do not need to execute any encryption/decryption process during the rekeying operation in LIH. However, we point out that the public information size in LIH is linear in the number of group members. This is not a large problem in applications. The members can access to a public board where the public information can be stored. Using a public board, all members can compute the current group key without any rekeying messages. This is a desirable feature since it greatly reduces the network bandwidth requirements and user's storeage. Thus, in LIH, a legitimate user just need to store a private key. Note that the public board is not necessary in LIH and it can be used combined with the other rekeying methods.

The rest of paper is organized as follows. Section 2 gives the background definitions associated with LIH. Section 3 presents the logical identity hierarchy scheme. Section 4 gives security analysis of LIH. Section 5 compares LIH with the previously published schemes for multicast. Section 6 concludes the paper.

2 Preliminaries

2.1 Bilinear Groups

Let $\mathbb{G}_1$ be a cyclic additive group, whose order is a prime q and $\mathbb{G}_2$ be a multiplicative group of the same order. A bilinear map $\hat{e} : \mathbb{G}_1 \times \mathbb{G}_1 \to \mathbb{G}_2$ must satisfy the following properties:

1. *Bilinear:* for all $P, Q \in \mathbb{G}_1$ and $a, b \in \mathbb{Z}$, we have $\hat{e}(aP, bQ) = \hat{e}(P, Q)^{ab}$
2. *Non-degenerate:* $\hat{e}(P, P) \neq 1_{\mathbb{G}_2}$, if P is a generator of $\mathbb{G}_1$.
3. The map $\hat{e}$ is efficiently computable.

Typically the admissible map $\hat{e}$ can be derived from the Weil or Tate pairings on an elliptic curve over a finite field. For a more comprehensive description of how these pairings should be constructed in practice in terms of efficiency and security, please refer to [30, 31, 32, 33].

2.2 Complexity Assumptions

Definition 1. *Elliptic Curve Discrete Logarithm Problem(ECDLP): Given $\mathbb{G}_1$ as above, choose P a generator from $\mathbb{G}_1$, given xP, the ECDLP is to find x, where x is an random element of $\mathbb{Z}_q^*$.*

Definition 2. *ComputationalDiffie-HellmanProblem(CDHP):thecomputational DH problem is to compute abP when given a generator P of $\mathbb{G}$ and aP, bP for some $a, b \in \mathbb{Z}_q^*$.*

Definition 3. *Bilinear Diffie-Hellman Problem (BDHP): Let $\mathbb{G}_1$, $\mathbb{G}_2$, P and $\hat{e}$ be as above. The BDHP in $\langle \mathbb{G}_1, \mathbb{G}_2, \hat{e} \rangle$ is as follows: Given (P, aP, bP, cP) with uniformly random choices of $a, b, c \in \mathbb{Z}_q^*$, compute $\hat{e}(P, P)^{abc} \in \mathbb{G}_2$. An algorithm $\mathcal{A}$ has advantage ϵ in solving the BDHP in $\langle \mathbb{G}_1, \mathbb{G}_2, \hat{e} \rangle$ if*

$$Pr[\mathcal{A}(P, aP, bP, cP) = \hat{e}(P, P)^{abc}] \geq \epsilon$$

Similarly, we say that an algorithm $\mathcal{B}$ that outputs $b \in \{0, 1\}$ has advantage ϵ in solving decision BDH problem(DBDHP) in $\mathbb{G}_1$ if

$$|Pr[\mathcal{B}(P, aP, bP, cP, \hat{e}(P, P)^{abc}) = 0] - Pr[\mathcal{B}(P, aP, bP, cP, r) = 0]| \geq \epsilon$$

where the probability is over the random choice of $a, b, c \in \mathbb{Z}_q^*$, the random choice of $r \in \mathbb{G}_2$ and the random bits of $\mathcal{B}$.

Assumptions: We assume that ECDLP, CDHP, BDHP, DBDHP are hard, which means that there is no polynomial time algorithm to solve any of them with non-negligible probability.

2.3 Security Requirements for Multicast

The goal of multicast security is to ensure that the source of the multicast stream and the group of multicast recipients communication securely. We consider the dynamic group where users may join or leave the group at any time. The main security properties of a multicast system are secrecy and authenticity. We define the following security properties:

1. Group Key Secrecy guarantees that it is computationally infeasible for a passive adversary to discover any group key.
2. Backward Secrecy is used to prevent a new member from being able to decode messages exchanged before it joins the group. This property guarantees that a passive adversary who knows a subset of group keys cannot discover the previous group keys.
3. Forward Secrecy is used to prevent a leaving user or expelled group member to continue accessing the group communication. This property guarantees that a passive adversary who knows a subset of old group keys cannot discover the subsequent group keys.
4. Source authentication ensures that the data originated from the claimed source.
5. Group authentication ensures that the data is sent to the legitimate users only.

3   Logical Identity Hierarchy

In this section we present a novel key agreement scheme for multicast called logical identity hierarchy(LIH). The basic technique of LIH is the usage of a bilinear map $\hat{e} : \mathbb{G}_1 \times \mathbb{G}_1 \to \mathbb{G}_2$, where $\mathbb{G}_1$ denotes an additive group of order q and $\mathbb{G}_2$ is a multiplicative group of the same order.

There are two parties in the system, the group controller(GC) and a set $\mathcal{U} = \{U_1, U_2, \cdots, U_n\}$ of n users. GC is responsible for n authenticated members. To start a new session, GC will rekey the group. In LIH, the GC maintains a logical tree of identities. Every node in the tree is associated with an identity and a key generation key(KGK)which is used to generate a parent key. The leaf node's identity corresponds to the user's identity and the interior node's identity can be generated from its two children's identities by using a cryptographic one-way hash function. The KGK on the leaf node is also called *individual key* which can be computed only by the user and GC. The root key is used as the group key. Figure 1 shows an example of an identity tree.

3.1   System Setup

Given security parameter 1^k, GC generates two groups $\mathbb{G}_1$, $\mathbb{G}_2$ of order q, and an admissible bilinear map $\hat{e} : \mathbb{G}_1 \times \mathbb{G}_1 \longrightarrow \mathbb{G}_2$. GC chooses a random element $s \in \mathbb{Z}_q^*$ and a generator P of $\mathbb{G}_1$. Then GC keeps s as the *master key* and sets $P_{pub} = sP$. Suppose the user's identity is denoted by the string ID_i and GC's identity is given by the string ID_s. Then the public key for the user i is: $Q_i = H_1(ID_i)$ and the public key for the GC is: $Q_s = H_1(ID_s)$. GC publishes the system parameters **params** $= \{\mathbb{G}_1, \mathbb{G}_2, \hat{e}, g, P_{pub}, Q_i, Q_s, H_1, H_2, H_3\}$, here $H_1 : \{0,1\}^* \to \mathbb{G}_1, H_2 : \mathbb{G}_2 \to \mathbb{Z}_q^*, H_3 : \mathbb{G}_1 \times \mathbb{G}_1 \to \mathbb{G}_1$ are cryptographic hash functions. In security analysis, H_1, H_2, H_3 can be viewed as random oracles.

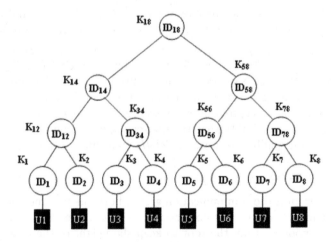

Fig. 1. An example of identity tree

GC constructs a rooted binary tree that has at least n leaf nodes and each interior node of the tree has exactly two children. Then GC computes key $P_i = sQ_i$ called *private key* for U_i and securely unicast the key P_i to U_i. Using the private key, a user can compute its *individual key* $K_i = H_2(\hat{e}(P_i, Q_s))$ in the identity tree. During the computation of the individual key, LIH achieves authentication between GC and group members. Each interior node's identity is generated from its two children's identities, $Q_j = H_3(Q_{L(j)}, Q_{R(j)})$. Computation of KGK on a interior node key is as follows.

$$K_j = H_2(\hat{e}(K_{L(j)}Q_{L(j)} + K_{L(j)}Q_{R(j)}, K_{R(j)}Q_j))$$
$$= H_2(\hat{e}(K_{R(j)}Q_{R(j)} + K_{R(j)}Q_{L(j)}, K_{L(j)}Q_j))$$
$$= H_2(\hat{e}(Q_{L(j)} + Q_{R(j)}, Q_j)^{K_{L(j)}K_{R(j)}})$$

Where $L(j)$ and $R(j)$ denote the left and right child of the node n_j respectively. We define $K_{L(j)}Q_j$ and $K_{R(j)}Q_j$ as a pair of blinded factor of K_j and $K_{L(j)}Q_j(K_{R(j)}Q_j)$ is the blinded key of $K_{R(j)}(K_{L(j)})$. After GC publishes the identity tree with $(n-1)$ pairs of blinded factors$(K_{L(j)}Q_j, K_{R(j)}Q_j)$ on a public board, each group user can compute KGKs in the path from the corresponding leaf to the root by using its private key and each blinded key of KGKs. For example, as shown in Figure 1, U_1 can compute K_{12}, K_{14} and K_{18} as follows:

First U_1 computes the individual key $K_1 = H_2(\hat{e}(P_1, Q_s))$ for the leaf node. Then U_1 computes

$$K_{12} = H_2(\hat{e}(K_1Q_1 + K_1Q_2, K_2Q_{12}) = H_2(\hat{e}(Q_1 + Q_2, Q_{12})^{K_1K_2})$$
$$K_{14} = H_2(\hat{e}(K_{12}Q_{12} + K_{12}Q_{34}, K_{34}Q_{14})) = H_2(\hat{e}(Q_{12} + Q_{34}, Q_{14})^{K_{12}K_{34}})$$
$$K_{18} = H_2(\hat{e}(K_{14}Q_{14} + K_{14}Q_{58}, K_{58}Q_{18})) = H_2(\hat{e}(Q_{14} + Q_{58}, Q_{18})^{K_{14}K_{58}})$$

But for a passive eavesdropper, who has access to all the public information cannot compute the KGKs in the identity tree. For example, the eavesdropper who knows $Q_{L(j)}, Q_{R(j)}, Q_j, K_{L(j)}Q_j$ and $K_{R(j)}Q_j$, and wishes to determine $\hat{e}(Q_{L(j)} + Q_{R(j)}, Q_j)^{K_{L(j)}K_{R(j)}}$. Even if he can obtain $\hat{e}(Q_{L(j)} + Q_{R(j)}, Q_j)^{K_{L(j)}}$ and $\hat{e}(Q_{L(j)} + Q_{R(j)}, Q_j)^{K_{R(j)}}$ from the tuple $(Q_{L(j)}, Q_{R(j)}, Q_j, K_{L(j)}Q_j, K_{R(j)}Q_j)$, he would still have to compute $\hat{e}(Q_{L(j)} + Q_{R(j)}, Q_j)^{K_{L(j)}K_{R(j)}}$ from $\hat{e}(Q_{L(j)} + Q_{R(j)}, Q_j)^{K_{L(j)}}$ and $\hat{e}(Q_{L(j)} + Q_{R(j)}, Q_j)^{K_{R(j)}}$, thus effectively solving the CDHP in $\mathbb{G}_2$.

Furthermore, LIH is also secure against collusion attack. We note that the group members cannot generate another valid group key. In LIH, the group key is derived by applying a cryptographically secure hash function to the root key, i.e. $H_2(key)$. So the probability that the groups members can generate another valid group key is negligible since we model H_2 as a random oracle.

3.2   Join Operation

When a new user joins the communication group, both the new member and the prior group members receive this notification. In a join operation, GC searches the nearest leaf node n_j from the root to keep the height of the tree as low as possible. Then GC creates a new intermediate node n_p, and promotes the new intermediate node to be the parent of both the node n_j and the new user node.

GC rearranges the levels of the affected nodes and keys in the updated identity tree T', and recomputes the identities and blinded keys of the affected nodes. Then GC publishes T' in a bulletin board. Figure 2 shows an example of new user U_3 joining the group. A new node n_{34} is generated by GC and becomes the parent of leaves n_3 and n_4.

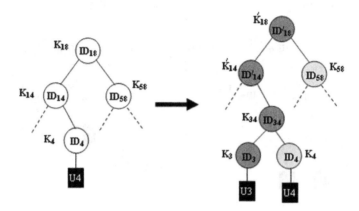

Fig. 2. U_3 is added to the group

To provide the backward secrecy, GC has to update the identity of affected nodes and all the blinded keys from leaf node (n_3) to the root. The GC recomputes the identities $Q_{34} = H_3(Q_3, Q_4), Q'_{14} = H_3(Q_{12}, Q_{34})$, $Q'_{18} = H_3(Q'_{14}, Q_{58})$ and the blinded keys $K_4Q_{34}, K_3Q_{34}, K_{12}Q'_{14}, K_{34}Q'_{14}, K_{58}Q'_{18}, K'_{14}Q'_{18}$. Next, GC sends the private key $P_3 = sQ_3$ to U_3 securely. Then GC publishes the new identity tree T' with all blinded keys on a public board. U_3 computes the new group key as follows:

$$K_3 = H_2(\hat{e}(P_3, Q_s))$$

$$K_{34} = H_2(\hat{e}(K_3Q_3 + K_3Q_4, K_4Q_{34}))$$

$$K'_{14} = H_2(\hat{e}(K_{34}Q_{34} + K_{34}Q_{12}, K_{12}Q'_{14}))$$

$$K'_{18} = H_2(\hat{e}(K'_{14}Q'_{14} + K'_{14}Q_{58}, K_{58}Q'_{18}))$$

Note that the blinded keys $K_4Q_{34}, K_3Q_{34}, K_{12}Q'_{14}, K_{34}Q'_{14}, K_{58}Q'_{18}, K'_{14}Q'_{18}$ were generated by GC and can be obtained from the public board, thus GC does not need to multicast any rekeying messages.

3.3 Leave Operation

When a user U_j leaves the group, GC updates the tree by deleting the leaf node n_j corresponding to the user. The member assigned to the sibling of n_j

is reassigned to the parent n_p of n_j. As a result, GC removes redundant nodes from the tree and rearranges the levels of affected nodes in the updated identity tree T'. Figure 3 shows an example of user U_6 being deleted from the group.

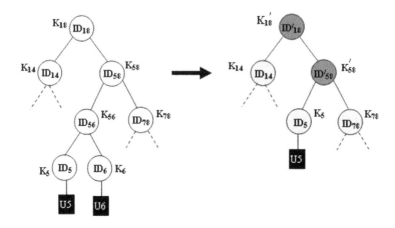

Fig. 3. U_6 is deleted from the group

Since U_6 is deleted from the identity tree, the GC must recompute the affected nodes' identities and blinded keys. Nodes n_6 and n_{56} are removed from the tree and the node n_5 is prompted to its parent's place. The GC computes $Q'_{58} = H_3(Q_5, Q_{78})$, $Q'_{18} = H_3(Q_{14}, Q'_{58})$ for the intermediate node n_{58} and n_{18}. Then GC computes K'_{58} and K'_{18} as follows:

$$K'_{58} = H_2(\hat{e}(K_5 Q_5 + K_5 Q_{78}, K_{78} Q'_{58}))$$

$$K'_{18} = H_2(\hat{e}(K_{14} Q_{14} + K_{14} Q'_{58}, K'_{58} Q'_{18}))$$

GC publishes the updated identity tree T' and all the blinded keys $K_{78} Q'_{58}$, $K_5 Q'_{58}, K_{14} Q'_{18}, K'_{58} Q'_{18}$ on a public board and gives a notification to all users.

3.4   Mass Join Operation and Mass Leave Operation

The multiple member join event (or multiple member eviction event) can be handled similarly to the single member join event (or single member eviction event). For example, as shown in Figure 4, when member U_4 and U_5 leaves the communication group, GC removes the node n_4 and n_5 from the identity tree and promotes the leaf node n_3 and n_6 to their respective parents' places. Then GC recomputes the affected nodes' identities and blinded keys.

GC computes:

$$Q'_{13} = H_3(Q_{12}, Q_3)$$
$$K'_{13} = H_2(\hat{e}(Q_{12} + Q_3, Q_{13})^{K_{12} K_3})$$

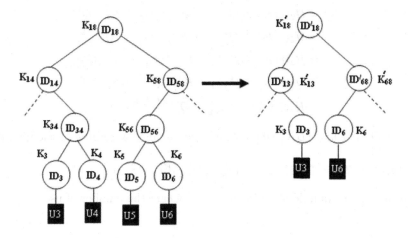

Fig. 4. U_4 and U_5 are deleted from the group

$$Q'_{68} = H_3(Q_6, Q_{78})$$
$$K'_{68} = H_2(\hat{e}(Q_6 + Q_{78}, Q_{68})^{K_6 K_{78}})$$
$$Q'_{18} = H_3(Q'_{13}, Q'_{68})$$
$$K'_{18} = H_2(\hat{e}(Q'_{13} + Q'_{68}, Q'_{18})^{K'_{13} K'_{68}})$$

Finally, GC publishes the updated identity tree T' with all blinded keys on a public board. Then each member in the current communication group can compute the current group key. In LIH, the addition operation and the deletion operation do not need any encryption/decryption process for both GC and all users. Moreover, GC does not need to multicast any rekeying messages. This feature greatly reduces the network bandwidth requirements.

4 Security Analysis

In this section, we present security proofs of LIH.

For $(q, \mathbb{G}_1, \mathbb{G}_2, \hat{e}) \leftarrow g(1^k)$, $Q = (I_1, I_2, \ldots, I_n)$ and $X = (S_1, S_2, \ldots, S_n)$ where $I_i \in \mathbb{G}_1$ and $S_i \in \mathbb{Z}_q^*$ and a binary identity tree T, we define the following random variables:

- Q_s: GC's identity.
- Q_j^i: i-th level j-th node's identity. If the node is a leaf node, Q_j^i is the identity of the user j. If the node is an internal node, Q_j^i is recursively defined as following: $Q_j^i = H_3(Q_{2j-1}^{i-1}, Q_{2j}^{i-1})$.
- BK_j^i: i-th level j-th blinded key(public information).
- K_j^i: i-th level j-th key. If the node is a leaf node, $K_j^i = H_2(\hat{e}(P_j, Q_s))$. If the node is a internal node, K_j^i is recursively defined as follows:

$$K_j^i = H_2(\hat{e}(K_{2j-1}^{i-1}Q_{2j-1}^{i-1} + K_{2j-1}^{i-1}Q_{2j}^{i-1}, K_{2j}^{i-1}Q_j^i))$$
$$= H_2(\hat{e}(K_{2j-1}^{i-1}Q_{2j-1}^{i-1} + K_{2j-1}^{i-1}Q_{2j}^{i-1}, BK_{2j-1}^{i-1}))$$
$$= H_2(\hat{e}(K_{2j}^{i-1}Q_{2j-1}^{i-1} + K_{2j}^{i-1}Q_{2j}^{i-1}, K_{2j-1}^{i-1}Q_j^i))$$
$$= H_2(\hat{e}(K_{2j}^{i-1}Q_{2j-1}^{i-1} + K_{2j}^{i-1}Q_{2j}^{i-1}, BK_{2j}^{i-1}))$$
$$= H_2(\hat{e}(Q_{2j-1}^{i-1} + Q_{2j}^{i-1}, Q_j^i)^{K_{2j-1}^{i-1}K_{2j}^{i-1}})$$

- $vw(h,Q,X,T) := \{BK_j^i$ where i and j are defined according to the identity tree $T \}$
- $K(h,Q,X,T) := H_2(\hat{e}(Q_L^{h-1} + Q_R^{h-1}, Q_{LR}^h)^{K_L^{h-1}K_R^{h-1}})$

Figure 5 is an example of an identity tree where the number of users is 8.

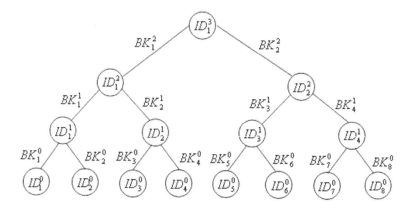

Fig. 5. Notions for the identity tree in LIH

Note that $vw(h,Q,X,T)$ is exactly the view of the adversary in the identity tree T where the final key is $K(h,Q,X,T)$. Our goal is to show that the final key $K(h,Q,X,T)$ cannot be distinguished by a polynomial time algorithm from a random number. We assume that all the blinded keys, public parameters and identity tree T in the protocol are known. We define two random variables as follows:

- $A_k := (vw(h,Q,X,T),y), y \in_R \mathbb{Z}_q^*$
- $F_k := (vw(h,Q,X,T),K(h,Q,X,T))$

Definition 4. Let $(q,\mathbb{G}_1,\mathbb{G}_2,\hat{e}) \leftarrow g(1^k)$, $n \geq 2$ be a positive integer, $Q = (I_1,I_2,\ldots,I_n)$, $X = (S_1,S_2,\ldots S_n)$ for $I_i \in \mathbb{G}_1$ and $S_i \in \mathbb{Z}_q^*$ and an identity tree T with n leaf nodes. A_k and F_k are defined as above. An algorithm $\mathcal{F}$ for $(q,\mathbb{G}_1,\mathbb{G}_2,\hat{e})$ is a probabilistic polynomial time algorithm satisfying, for some fixed l and sufficiently large m:

$$|Prob[F(A_k) = 1] - Prob[\mathcal{F}(F_k) = 1]| > \frac{1}{m^l}$$

We call $\mathcal{F}$ a polynomial time distinguisher that distinguishes A_k and F_k.

Let adversary $\mathcal{A}$ be a (polynomial time) probabilistic Turing machine. First, we will prove that the individual key and 2-party key in LIH are indistinguishable from a random value respectively. Then we will show that the n-party case is reducible to the 2-party case. To aid the adversary we allow it to query the following random oracles:

- Identity Hash Oracle: For any given identity $ID \in \{0,1\}^*$ this oracle will produce the corresponding hash value $H_1(ID)$.
- Key Generation Oracle: the adversary submits any $ID \in \{0,1\}^*$, and is told the corresponding private key.
- Individual Key Oracle: the adversary submits any $ID \in \{0,1\}^*$ and is told the corresponding individual key.
- Parent Identity Hash Oracle: the adversary submits two identity hash values $Q_i = H_1(ID_i), Q_j = H_1(ID_j)$, where $ID_i, ID_j \in \{0,1\}^*$, and is told the corresponding hash value $H_3(Q_i, Q_j)$.
- Blinded Key Oracle: the adversary submits any two identity hash values $Q_i = H_1(ID_i), Q_j = H_1(ID_j)$, and is told the corresponding blinded keys.
- Group Key Oracle: the adversary submits any elements $g \in \mathbb{G}_2$, and is told the corresponding hash value $H_2(g)$.

Theorem 1. Suppose $\mathcal{A}$ is a polynomially bounded attacker that can distinguish a user's individual key from a random number with advantage ϵ and makes at most n_1 of H_1 queries of the identity hash oracle and at most n_2 group key oracle queries. Then there exists a polynomially bounded algorithm $\mathcal{B}$ that solves the BDH problem with advantage at least $\epsilon/n_1^2 n_2$

Proof. Given input of $(\mathbb{G}_1, \mathbb{G}_2, \hat{e})$, a generator of P of $\mathbb{G}_1$, and a triple of elements aP, bP, cP with a, b, c be randomly chosen from $\mathbb{Z}_q^*$, $\mathcal{B}$'s task is to output the value $\hat{e}(P, P)^{abc}$. $\mathcal{B}$ simulates the Setup algorithm and sets P_{pub} to be aP and the GC's identity Q_s to be bP. Then $\mathcal{B}$ starts $\mathcal{A}$ and gives it the system parameters P, aP. To respond to $\mathcal{A}$'s queries, $\mathcal{B}$ maintains a list H_1^{list} that stores the information on H_1 queries, and a list H_2^{list} for H_2 queries. All the lists are initially empty. Then $\mathcal{B}$ starts A and answers all $\mathcal{A}$'s queries as follows.

- Identity queries: $\mathcal{B}$ chooses a random number i between 1 and n_1. when $\mathcal{A}$ makes queries on H_1 oracles, $\mathcal{B}$ responds as follows: if it is the i-th H_1 query, then $\mathcal{B}$ responds with cP, we call $\mathcal{A}$ a guessed ID. Otherwise, $\mathcal{B}$ chooses a random γ from $\mathbb{Z}_q^*$ and inserts $(\mathcal{A}, \gamma)$ into H_1^{list}.
- Private key queries: suppose $\mathcal{A}$ issues a private key query for an ID $\mathcal{A}$. If $\mathcal{A}$ is the guessed ID, then $\mathcal{B}$ aborts. Otherwise the H_1^{list} must contain the entry $(\mathcal{A}, \gamma)$ for some γ and $\mathcal{B}$ outputs γaP.

Now, $\mathcal{B}$ picks a random value l from $\{1, \ldots, n_2\}$, guessing that l-th distinct query made to H_2 oracle will be on the guessed ID. If $\mathcal{A}$ has not made at least l queries to the H_2 oracle, then $\mathcal{B}$ aborts. Otherwise $\mathcal{B}$ picks $\mathcal{A}$'s l-th query (on some value s) to the H_2 oracle, which $\mathcal{B}$ guesses to be the value $\hat{e}(P, P)^{abc}$.

We know that $\mathcal{B}$ fails if $\mathcal{A}$ asks the private key associated with the guessed ID during the simulation. Then the probability that $\mathcal{A}$ never issues private key query on the guessed ID is at least $1/n_1$. Further, the probability that $\mathcal{A}$'s challenge ID is the guessed ID is also at least $1/n_1$. If $\mathcal{A}$ has never queried the group key oracle, then A's view is independent of the identity, because we model H_2 as a random oracle. In this case, $\mathcal{A}$ has no advantage, thus the probability that $\mathcal{A}$ queries H_2 oracle is at least ϵ. If $\mathcal{A}$ has queried H_2 oracle, then it may be able to distinguish the simulation from the real attack. However, this implies that $s = \hat{e}(P,P)^{abc}$ has been recorded on the H_2^{list}. $\mathcal{B}$ wins if it guesses the correct element to output. But the size of H_2^{list} is bounded by n_2. Therefore $Adv(\mathcal{B}) \geq \epsilon/n_1^2 n_2$. $\square$

Theorem 2. Suppose $\mathcal{A}$ is a polynomially bounded attacker that can distinguish 2-party key in LIH from a random number with advantage ϵ and makes at most n_1 of H_1 queries of the identity hash oracle and at most n_2 group key oracle queries. Then there exists a polynomially bounded algorithm $\mathcal{B}$ that solves the BDH problem with advantage at least $\epsilon/\binom{n_1}{2}^2 n_2$.

Proof. The algorithm $\mathcal{B}$ is given aP, bP, cP. In order to output $\hat{e}(P,P)^{abc}$ with $\mathcal{A}$'s assistance, $\mathcal{B}$ has control over the hash functions H_1 and H_2. There is a list H_1^{list} that stores information on identity hash oracle queries, a list H_2^{list} for group key oracle queries and a list H_p^{list} stores information on parent identity hash oracle queries.

$\mathcal{B}$ chooses distinct random values I and J from $\{1, \ldots, n_1\}$. Without loss of generality, we may assume that all H_1 queries are distinct.

- Identity queries: When H_1 oracle is queried with an ID_i, $\mathcal{B}$ responds as follows. If it is the I-th query, $\mathcal{B}$ chooses a random r_I from $\mathbb{Z}_q^*$ and responds with $r_I P$. We call ID_i a guessed ID. If it is the J-th H_1 query, then $\mathcal{B}$ responds with aP, we call ID_i a guessed ID. Otherwise, $\mathcal{B}$ chooses a random r_i from $\mathbb{Z}_q^*$ and inserts (ID_i, r_i) into H_1^{list}, then $\mathcal{B}$ outputs $r_i P$.
- Individual key queries: suppose $\mathcal{A}$ issues an individual key query for an ID A. If A is a guessed ID, then $\mathcal{B}$ aborts. Otherwise $\mathcal{B}$ picks a random value K_A from $\mathbb{Z}_q^*$ and outputs K_A. By Theorem 1, we know that an adversary cannot distinguish an individual key from a random value. Hence, $\mathcal{A}$ cannot tell it is in simulation or in a real attack.
- Parent identity queries: suppose adversary $\mathcal{A}$ issues a parent identity query for ID_i and ID_j. $\mathcal{B}$ picks a random value $M_{i,j}$ from $\mathbb{Z}_q^*$ and inserts the entry $(ID_i, ID_j, M_{i,j})$ into the H_p^{list}. Then $\mathcal{B}$ responds with $M_{i,j}P$.
- Blinded key queries: suppose $\mathcal{A}$ issues a blinded key query between $\mathcal{I}$ and $\mathcal{J}$. $\mathcal{B}$ examines the H_p^{list} for the entry with the form $(\mathcal{I}, \mathcal{J}, M_{\mathcal{I},\mathcal{J}})$. If such an entry is not present, then $\mathcal{B}$ picks a random value $M_{\mathcal{I},\mathcal{J}}$ from $\mathbb{Z}_q^*$ and inserts the entry $(\mathcal{I}, \mathcal{J}, M_{\mathcal{I},\mathcal{J}})$ into the H_p^{list}. If $\mathcal{I}$ and $\mathcal{J}$ are the guessed IDs, then $\mathcal{B}$ respond with $M_{\mathcal{I},\mathcal{J}}bP$ and $M_{\mathcal{I},\mathcal{J}}cP$. Otherwise, $\mathcal{B}$ picks two

random values $K_{\mathcal{I}}$ and $K_{\mathcal{J}}$ from $\mathbb{Z}_q^*$, then $\mathcal{B}$ responds with $K_{\mathcal{I}}M_{\mathcal{I},\mathcal{J}}P$ and $K_{\mathcal{J}}M_{\mathcal{I},\mathcal{J}}P$.

Finally, $\mathcal{A}$ terminates. Now if H_2^{list} is empty, then $\mathcal{B}$ fails. Otherwise, $\mathcal{B}$ picks a random element of H_2^{list} as its guess to the value $h = \hat{e}(aP + r_{\mathcal{I}}P, M_{\mathcal{I},\mathcal{J}}P)^{bc} = \hat{e}(P,P)^{abcM_{\mathcal{I},\mathcal{J}}}\hat{e}(r_{\mathcal{I}}bP, M_{\mathcal{I},\mathcal{J}}cP) = \delta\hat{e}(P,P)^{abcM_{\mathcal{I},\mathcal{J}}}$. $\mathcal{B}$ outputs $(h/\delta)^{1/M_{\mathcal{I},\mathcal{J}}}$ as its guess for the value $\hat{e}(P,P)^{abc}$.

The probability that $\mathcal{A}$ never issues a individual key query on one of the guessed IDs is at least $1/\binom{n_1}{2}$ (there are at least two IDs it cannot query the individual keys). Further, the probability that $\mathcal{A}$'s challenge IDs are the guessed identity pair $(ID_{\mathcal{I}}, ID_{\mathcal{J}})$ is also at least $1/\binom{n_1}{2}$. If $\mathcal{A}$ never make H_2 queries, then $\mathcal{A}$'s view is independent of identity. If this happens, $\mathcal{A}$ cannot tell it is in a simulation, and has no advantage, since we model H_2 as a random oracle. Hence, the probability that $\mathcal{A}$ make queries to H_2 oracle is at least ϵ. If $\mathcal{A}$ has issued a H_2 query, then it may be able to distinguish the simulation from the real life. However, this implies that $h = \delta\hat{e}(P,P)^{abcM_{\mathcal{I},\mathcal{J}}}$ has been recorded on H_2^{list}. In the other words, $\mathcal{A}$ can realize that it is in a simulation only after $\mathcal{B}$ has deposited h on H_2^{list}. $\mathcal{B}$ wins if it guesses the correct element to output, but the size of H_2^{list} is bounded by n_2. Therefore, $Adv(\mathcal{B}) \geq \epsilon/\binom{n_1}{2}^2 n_2$. $\square$

Theorem 3. If 2-party key in LIH is indistinguishable from a random value, the same is for the n-party key.

Proof. We prove the theorem by induction and contradiction. Note that 2-party key in LIH is secure. We assume that A_{k-1} and F_{k-1} can be distinguished in polynomial time as the induction hypothesis. We will show that the ability to distinguish A_k and F_k implies either can be used to distinguish 2-party key from a random value or to distinguish A_{k-1} and F_{k-1}.

Let T_L, T_R respectively be the left and right subtree of height at most $k - 1$ of the identity tree T. Let $Q_L = (I_1, I_2, \ldots, I_l)$, $Q_R = (I_{l+1}, I_{l+2}, \ldots, I_n)$, $X_L = (S_1, S_2, \ldots, S_l)$, and $X_R = (S_{l+1}, S_{l+2}, \ldots, S_n)$ where I_1 through I_l and S_1 through S_l are associated with T_L, I_{l+1} through I_n and S_{l+1} through S_n are associated with T_R.

We consider the following random variables:

$$A_k := (vw(k-1, X_L, Q_L, T_L), vw(k-1, X_R, Q_R, T_R), Q_{LR}, K_L^{k-1}Q_{LR}, K_R^{k-1}Q_{LR}, y)$$

$$B_k := (vw(k-1, X_L, Q_L, T_L), vw(k-1, X_R, Q_R, T_R), Q_{LR}, r_1 Q_{LR}, K_R^{k-1}Q_{LR}, y)$$

$$C_k := (vw(k-1, X_L, Q_L, T_L), vw(k-1, X_R, Q_R, T_R), Q_{LR}, r_1 Q_{LR}, r_2 Q_{LR}, y)$$

$$D_k := (vw(k-1, X_L, Q_L, T_L), vw(k-1, X_R, Q_R, T_R), Q_{LR}, r_1 Q_{LR}, r_2 Q_{LR}, K_1)$$

$$E_k := (vw(k-1, X_L, Q_L, T_L), vw(k-1, X_R, Q_R, T_R), Q_{LR}, r_1 Q_{LR}, K_R^{k-1}Q_{LR}, K_2)$$

$$F_k := (vw(k-1, X_L, Q_L, T_L), vw(k-1, X_R, Q_R, T_R), Q_{LR}, K_L^{k-1}Q_{LR}, K_R^{k-1}Q_{LR}, K)$$

where r_1, r_2, y are random numbers in $\mathbb{Z}_q^*$, $Q_{LR} = H_3(Q_L, Q_R)$, $K_1 = H_2(\hat{e}(Q_L + Q_R, Q_{LR})^{r_1 r_2})$, $K_2 = H_2(\hat{e}(Q_L + Q_R, Q_{LR})^{r_1 K_R^{k-1}})$ and $K = H_2(\hat{e}(Q_L + Q_R, Q_{LR})^{K_L^{k-1} K_R^{k-1}})$.

If we can distinguish A_k and F_k in a polynomial time, then we can distinguish at least one of the following: $(A_k, B_k), (B_k, C_k), (C_k, D_k), (D_k, E_k), (E_k, F_k)$.

- $(A_k$ and $B_k)$: Suppose A_k and B_k can be distinguished in polynomial time by a distinguisher $\mathcal{D}_{AB_k}$. We will show that $\mathcal{D}_{AB_k}$ can be used to distinguish A_{k-1} and F_{k-1}. Let $V_{k-1}^* = (vw(k-1, X^*, Q^*, T^*), r^*)$. We want to decide V_{k-1}^* is an instance of LIH or r^* is a random value. First, we construct another identity tree T' of height $k-1$ with leaf level secrete key distribution X'. Then we construct an identity tree of height k with T^* and T' as the left and right subtree respectively. We consider the distribution:

$$V_k^* = (vw(k-1, X^*, Q^*, T^*), vw(k-1, X', Q', T'), Q^{*'}, r^* Q^{*'}, K' Q^{*'}, y)$$

where y is a random element in $\mathbb{G}_1$, $Q^{*'} = H_3(Q^*, Q')$ and $K' = K(k-1, Q', X', T')$. Now, we put V_k^* as input $\mathcal{D}_{AB_k}$. Let us first consider the case that V_k^* is an instance of A_k. In this case, it implies that V_{k-1}^* is an instance of F_{k-1}. Hence, we have

$$Prob[\mathcal{D}_{AB_k}(A_k = V_k^*) = 1] = Prob[\mathcal{D}_{AF_{k-1}}(F_{k-1} = V_{k-1}^*) = 1]$$

If V_k^* is an instance of B_k, it implies that V_{k-1}^* is an instance of A_{k-1}. We have

$$Prob[\mathcal{D}_{AB_k}(B_k = V_k^*) = 1] = Prob[\mathcal{D}_{AF_{k-1}}(A_{k-1} = V_{k-1}^*) = 1]$$

Consequently,

$$|Prob[\mathcal{D}_{AB_k}(A_k = V_k^*) = 1] - Prob[\mathcal{D}_{AB_k}(B_k = V_k^*) = 1]| =$$
$$|Prob[\mathcal{D}_{AF_{k-1}}(F_{k-1} = V_{k-1}^*) = 1] - Prob[\mathcal{D}_{AF_{k-1}}(A_{k-1} = V_{k-1}^*) = 1]|$$

Hence, if $\mathcal{D}_{AB_k}$ can distinguish A_k and B_k, then $\mathcal{D}_{AF_{k-1}}$ can distinguish A_{k-1} and F_{k-1}.

- In the case of $(B_k$ and $C_k)$, $(D_k$ and $E_k)$ and $(E_k$ and $F_k)$, we can use the similar method as used in $(A_k$ and $B_k)$. If one of the pairs can be distinguished in polynomial time by a distinguisher $\mathcal{D}_k$, then we can construct a distinguisher $\mathcal{D}_{AF_{k-1}}$ that can distinguish A_{k-1} and F_{k-1} in polynomial time.

- $(C_k$ and $D_k)$: If C_k and D_k can be distinguished by $\mathcal{D}_{CD_k}$ in polynomial time. Then $\mathcal{D}_{CD_k}$ can be used to distinguish 2-party key from a random value in LIH. Let $u = r_1 Q_{LR}$, $v = r_2 Q_{LR}$, $w = H_2(\hat{e}(Q_L + Q_R, Q_{LR})^{r_1 r_2})$ (or a randomly chosen from $\mathbb{Z}_q^*$). If (u, v, w) is an instance of $C_k(D_k)$, then it is an instance of $A_2(F_2)$. $\quad\square$

Theorem 4. LIH satisfies backward secrecy and forward secrecy.

Proof (sketch). In order to show that LIH satisfies backward secrecy and forward secrecy, we only need to show that the view of the former(prospective) member to the current identity tree is exactly the same as the view of a passive adversary respectively.

We first consider forward secrecy. When a user J leaves the communication group, the GC erases the leaf node n_j corresponding to the user J from the identity tree and updates the identity tree as described in section 3.2. Consequently, all the keys known to J is changed accordingly. Therefore, the view of J is exactly the same as the view of the passive adversary.

Now we consider the backward secrecy. When a new user J is added to the communication group, GC refreshes the identity tree as described in section 3.1, and consequently, the previous group key is changed. Therefore, the new user J's view is exactly same as the view of an passive adversary. This shows that the new user has exactly the same advantage of the old group key as an outsider. □

5   Performance Evaluation

In this section, we compared LIH with LKH, OFT and OFCT introduced in Section 1. We have divided comparison into two tables. Table 1 summarizes our comparisons focusing on the size of rekeying messages for a membership change, storage requirements for both GC and users and authentication feature. Table 2 shows the computation cost of these protocols. The notations used in Tables 1,2 are described as follows.

n	number of user in the group
K	size of a key in bits
d	height of an identity tree(for a balanced binary tree $d = log_2 n$)
P	pairing computation
E	encryption operation
D	decryption operation
H	one-way hash function execution
X	xor operation
R	operations needed in one key generation
M	point scalar multiplication

In LIH, the pairings computation is a critical operation which still requires considerable computational resources now. According to the recent advances in efficient pairings implementation [30, 31, 32, 34, 35, 36], the complexity of a pairing computation is now of a similar order to that of elliptic curve point multiplication. However, the research of pairings implementation continuously have been studied, so the computation costs are decreasing day by day.

A public board is needed during the rekeying operation in LIH. GC just publishes the identity tree with all the blinded keys on it. Then the legitimate user can compute the current group key using this public board. Even

Table 1. Size of Rekeying Messages,Storage and Security Feature Comparison

Scheme	join		leave	Storage		Authentication	
	multicast	unicast		GC	User	Group Member	Source
LKH	$(2d-1)K$	$(d+1)K$	$2dK$	$(2n-1)K$	$(d+1)K$	N	N
OFT	$(d+1)K$	$(d+1)K$	$(d+1)K$	$(2n-1)K$	$(d+1)K$	N	N
OFCT	$(d+1)K$	$(d+1)K$	$(d+1)K$	$(2n-1)K$	$(d+1)K$	N	N
LIH	0	K	0	$2nK$	K	Y	Y

Table 2. Computation Cost Comparison

Scheme	Adding a user		Evicting a user	
	GC	user	GC	User
LKH	$(d+1)R+(2d+1)E$	$(d+1)D$	$dR+2dE$	dD
OFT	$R+d(H+X)+(2d+1)E$	$(d+1)D+d(H+X)$	$R+d(H+X+E)$	$D+d(H+X)$
OFCT	$R+dH+(d+1)E$	$(d+1)D$	$R+d(PRG+E)$	$D+dPRG$
LIH	$R+2d(P+H+M)$	$d(P+H)$	$2d(P+H)$	$d(P+H)$

though the public board is not available, GC only needs to multicast the log_2n blinded keys as well as log_2n nodes' identities without any encryption/decryption operation.

6 Conclusion

We have proposed an efficient, authenticated, scalable key agreement(LIH) for multicast communications which uses pairing-based cryptography. LIH provides advantages over the previous solution for multicast. LIH achieves dual authentication between group controller(GC) and group members and hierarchical authentication among group members. From the performance analysis it can be see that, using a public board, every legitimate member can compute the group key using its private key and the GC does not need to mulitcast any rekeying messages. The only thing for GC is to give a membership chage notification to all users. This is a desirable feature especially in the environment where the packet-loss rate is high and the users are low-memory devices.

Furthermore, the user in LIH can be stateless who might not be constantly on-line to record the past history. The private key for the user does not have to be updated through the lifetime of the system. Each user can compute the current group key with its private key and current blinded keys no matter how many times group rekeying operations it has missed. GC and all the users do not need to execute any encryption/decryption process during the rekeying operation. Security analysis shows that LIH satisfies both forward secrecy and backward secrecy. LIH also has key independent property.

Acknowledgements

This work was supported by the National Natural Science Foundation of China No.90304007 and China National 973 Project No.2004CB318004.

References

1. Deering, S. E.: Multicast Routing in Internetworks and Extended LANs. In Proceedings of the ACM SIGCOMM '88, Stanford, California, (1988) 55-64.
2. Deering, S. E.: Host Extensions for IP Multicasting. RFC **1112**, August 1989.
3. Deering, S. E., Estrin, D., Farinacci,D., Jacosen, V.: An Architecture for Wide-Area Multicasting. In Proceedings of the ACM SIGCOMM '94, London, (1994) 126-135.
4. Lu, H.: A Novel High-Order Tree for Secure Multicast Key Management. IEEE Trans.Computers, **54(2)** (2005) 214-224.
5. Canetti, R., Garay, J., Itkis, G.: Multicast Security: A Taxonomy and Some Efficient constructions. In Proc, of INFOCOM 99, (1999) 708-716.
6. Chang, I., Engel, R., Pendarakis, D., Saha, D.: Key management for Secure Internet Multicast Using Boolean Function Minimization Techniques. Proceedings of INFOCOM '99, (1999) 689-698.
7. Canetti, R., Malkin, T., Nissim, K.: Efficient Communication Storage Tradeoffs for Multicast Encryption. Advances in Cryptology, EUROCRYPT 1999, LNCS **1592** (1999) 459-474.
8. Hardjono, T., Tsudik, G.: Ip Multicast Security: Issues and Directions. Annales de Telecom,(2000) 324-340.
9. Micciancio, D., Panjwani, S.: Optimal communication complexity of generic multicast key distribution. In proceedings of Eurocrypt 2004, LNCS **3027** (2004) 153-170.
10. Steiner, M., Tsudik, G., Waidner, M.: Cliques: A new approach to group key agreement. IEEE Transactions on Distributed and Computing Systems. (1998) 380-387.
11. Wallner, D., Harder, E., Agee, R.: Key management for multicast: Issues and architectures. RFC **2627**, Internet Engineering Task Force, June 1999.
12. Wong, C. K., Lam, S.: Secure Group Communications Using Key Graphs. Proceedings of SIGCOMM '98, (1998) 68-79.
13. Sherman, A. T., McGrew, D. A.: Key Establishment in Large Dynamic Groups Using One-Way Function Trees. IEEE Trans. Software Engineering, **29(5)** (2003) 444-458.
14. Kim,Y., Perrig, A., Tsudik, G.: Simple and Fault-Tolerant Key Agreement for Dynamic Collaborative Groups. 7th ACM Conference on Computer and Communications Security, (2000) 235-244.
15. Dutta, R., Barua, R., Sarkar, P.: Provably Scure Authenticated Tree Based Key Agreement. ICICS 2004, LNCS **3269** (2004) 92-104.
16. Kim,Y., Perrig, A., Tsudik, G.: Tree-Based Group Key Agreement. ACM Transactions on Information and System Security, **7(1)** (2004) 60-96.
17. Perrig, A., Song, D., Tygar, J. D.: ELK, a New Protocol for Efficient Large Group Key Distribution. IEEE Symposium on Security and Privacy 2001,(2001) 247-262.
18. Waldvogel, M., Caronni, G., Sun, D., Weiler, N., Plattner, B.: The VersaKey Framework: Versatile Group Key Management. IEEE Journal on Selected Areas in Communications, **17(8)** (1999) 1614-1631.

19. McGrew, D. A., Sherman, A. T.: Key Establishment in large Dynamic Groups Using One-Way Function Trees. Technical Report No.**0755**, TIS Labs at Network Associates, Inc., Glenwood, MD, May 1998.
20. Canetti, R., Halevi, S., Katz, J.: A Forward-Secure Public-Key Encryption Scheme. In Proceedings of Eurocrypt 2003, LNCS **2656** (2003) 255-271.
21. Boneh, D., Katz, J.: Improved Efficiency for CCA-Secure Cryptosystems Built Using Identity-Based Encryption. CT-RSA 2005, LNCS **3376** (2005) 87-103.
22. Canetti, R., Halevi, S., Katz, J.: Chosen-Ciphertext Security from Identity-Based Encryption. In Proceedings of Eurocrypt 2004, LNCS **3027** (2004) 207-222.
23. Boneh, D., Franklin, M.: Identity-Based Encryption from the Weil Pairing. In Advances in Cryptology, CRYPTO 2001, LNCS **2139** (2001) 213-229.
24. Boneh, D., Boyen, X.: Efficient Selective-ID Secure Identity Based Encryption Without Random Oracles. In proceedings of Eurocrypt 2004, LNCS**3027** (2004) 223-238.
25. Hess, F.: Efficient Identity Based Signature Schemes Based on Pairings. SAC 2002, LNCS **2595** (2003) 310-324.
26. Libert, B., Quisquater, J. J.: New Identity Based Signcryption Schemes from Pairing. Cryptology ePrint Archive, Report 2003/023. available at http://eprint.iacr.org/2003/023.
27. Lynn, B.: Authenticated Identity-Based Encryption, Cryptology ePrint Archive, Report 2002/072. available at http://eprint.iacr.org/2003/023.
28. Gentry, C., Silverberg, A.: Hierarchical ID-Based Cryptography. ASIACRYPT 2002, LNCS **2501** 548-566.
29. Boyen, X.: Multipurpose Identity-Based Signcryption: A Swiss Army Knife for Identity-Based Cryptography. CRYPTO 2003, LNCS **2729** (2003) 382-398.
30. Barreto,P.S.L.M., Kim, H.Y., Scott, M.: Efficient Algorithms for Pairing-Based Cryptosystems. CRYPTO 2002, LNCS **2442** (2002) 354-368.
31. Barreto,P. S. L. M., Lynn,B., Scott,M.: On the Selection of Pairing-Friendly Groups. SAC'2003, LNCS **3006**(2004) 17-25.
32. Steven D. G. , Harrison, K., Soldera, D.: Implementing the Tate Pairing. ANTS 2002, LNCS **2369** (2002) 324-337.
33. Blake, I., Seroussi, G., Smart, N.: Elliptic Curves in Cryptography. Cambridge Unversity Press, 2001.
34. Choie, Y.J., Lee, E.: Implementation of Tate Pairing on Hyperelliptic Curves of Genus 2 ICISC 2003, LNCS **2971** (2004) 97-111.
35. Miller,V.S.: The Weil Pairing and Its Efficient Calculation. Journal of Cryptology, **17(4)** (2004) 235-261.
36. Scott, M., Barreto, P. S .L .M .: Compressed Pairings. CRYPTO 2004, LNCS **3152** (2004) 140-156.

Authenticated and Communication Efficient Group Key Agreement for Clustered Ad Hoc Networks*

Hongsong Shi[1,2], Mingxing He[1], and Zhiguang Qin[2]

[1] School of Mathematics & Computer Engineering,
Xihua University, ChengDu, China
[2] School of Computer Science & Engineering,
University of Electronic Science and Technology of China, ChengDu, China
hongsongshi@gmail.com, he_mingxing64@yahoo.com.cn, qinzg@uestc.edu.cn

Abstract. Common group key agreement protocols are not applicable in ad hoc networks because the dynamic and multi-hop nature. Clustering is a method by which nodes are hierarchically organized based on their relative proximity to one another. Driven by this insight, a hierarchical key agreement protocol is proposed to weaken the 1-hop assumption in common group key agreement protocols. We employ Joux's tripartite protocol and a generalized Diffie-Hellman protocol as the basic building block for group key agreement. The protocol can handle efficiently the dynamic events in ad hoc networks. Moreover, in order to authenticate the messages, a provable ID-based signature scheme is presented. The analysis results indicate that the proposed protocol is secure in withstanding many common attacks and is extremely efficient and feasible to ad hoc networks with large size.

Keywords: Ad hoc networks, Group key agreement, Clustering, Hierarchical routing, Bilinear pairings.

1 Introduction

Recently, mobile ad hoc networks have attracted significant attentions for its wide applications in many different fields. An mobile ad hoc network can be seen as a special dynamic and distributed group, so the secure communication is essential in it. Surely, the most common method is to encrypt messages with a group key only shared by the included nodes, so that those outside the group cannot decode the encrypted messages. Thus, the protocol to achieve the group shared key is crucial, which we often name the *key agreement protocol*.

---

* This work is supported by the National Natural Science Foundation of China under Grant No.60473030, No.60473090, No.60573129, the Key Projects Foundation of Ministry of Education of China and the Foundation of Science & Technology Agency of Sichuan Province under Grant No.05JY029-131.

D. Pointcheval, Y. Mu, and K. Chen (Eds.): CANS 2006, LNCS 4301, pp. 73–89, 2006.

Over the years, numerous excellent key agreement protocols for dynamic peer group have been proposed [3], such as the GDH suite [18], TGDH [10] and extended STR (ESTR) [11] protocols. However, not all of them are communication efficient when applied to ad hoc networks. Because all of those protocols hold a common implicit assumption that every two nodes can reach each other within one hop. It is reasonable for nodes within the communication range, however those that are far apart have to rely on some intermediary nodes (routers) to relay messages [13]. Ad hoc network with large size is a kind of random networks to which some researches have indicated that the average path length is approximate to $O(\log n)$ (where n is the node count) [1], so communications with multi-hop are inevitable. If the key agreement model is separated from the actual topology of network, a widening gap about the communication complexity between the result of theoretic analysis and the actual application would occur. We call this issue *the neighbors communication problem*.

Recently, Li, Wang and Frieder [13] firstly proposed a hybrid key agreement protocol to solve this problem. In their protocol, the network is divided into some different subgroups based on locations. Each subgroup selects a leader named dominator. Thereafter, the protocol applies the GDH protocol [18] or some other existed group key agreement protocols (e.g. TGDH, Hypercube protocol [13]) in the set of dominators. As a result, the shared key is generated among the dominators. Once it successes, all the dominators distribute the shared key to their relative group members to ensure all nodes share the same key. This protocol provides an efficient method to reduce the neighbors communication problem, however the protocol is inefficient in handling dynamic events and also not suitable for ad hoc networks where the shared key should be the contributions of all the nodes rather than the dominator set. Yao *et al.* [20] proposed a hierarchical key agreement protocol which is similar to [13], i.e., the protocol also divides the network into different clusters and applies some existed group key agreement protocols to construct the group key. The protocol is communication efficient in handling dynamic events, but it is unauthenticated and lack of security analysis. Apparently, this is insufficient when applying to practical situations. However, to some extent, these protocols have casted a new light in finding approaches to weaken the neighbors communication problem.

In this paper, we also present a key agreement protocol for ad hoc networks based on the hierarchical routing protocol. The protocol can handle some dynamic events as node's movements. In order to reduce further the communication complexity, we employ the generalized Diffie-Hellman protocol [7] for two parties and the Joux's protocol [9] for three parties as the fundamental key agreement protocols and extend them for group key agreement. Moreover, we present an provable ID based signature scheme using bilinear pairings to authenticate communication messages. The security and efficiency of the overall protocol are analyzed, it is enough to show that our protocol is secure in withstanding most common attacks and is also efficient in ad hoc networks with large size.

The rest of the paper is organized as follows. Section 2 gives some preliminaries needed to describe our new protocol. Section 3 describes the new key agreement protocol ACEKA for ad hoc networks. Section 4 analyzes the communication and computation complexity. Section 5 gives the security analysis of the protocol. Lastly, section 6 concludes this paper.

2   Preliminaries

2.1   Clustering Techniques in Ad Hoc Networks

Clustering is a method by which nodes are hierarchically organized based on their relative proximity to one another. Clustering protocols divides nodes into groups, called clusters, and perform hierarchical routing between them. There are a wide variety of clustering protocols [5,15,19]. A hierarchical routing scheme can increase the robustness of routes by providing multiple possibilities for routing between clusters and reduce the size of routing table [5]. Another advantage is that less communication overhead is need for tracking mobile nodes in large multi-hop mobile wireless networks [5,15]. Many clustering protocols establish a cluster leader per cluster and utilize gateway nodes for cluster interconnection; other algorithms take a distributed approach to cluster management. Cluster head is elected by the node connectivity, i.e., the node with the highest connectivity in a given area becomes the cluster head. Generally, all nodes in a cluster are within direct transmission range of the cluster head, i.e., each member of a cluster can reach the cluster head in one hop, and each node pair in the same cluster can communicate in two hops. The overhead involved in clustering techniques includes two phases: the cluster initialization phase and the cluster maintenance phase. Sucec *et al.*[19] provides an overview of many clustering protocols and a theoretical upper bound $\Theta(n)$ (n is the node count) on the communication overhead incurred by a particular clustering algorithm in ad hoc networks. For example, The ad hoc network illustrated by Fig.1 can be divided into six clusters $C_1, C_2, ..., C_6$, where we denote clusters by dashed ellipses, cluster heads by solid roundlets and common nodes by hollow roundlets.

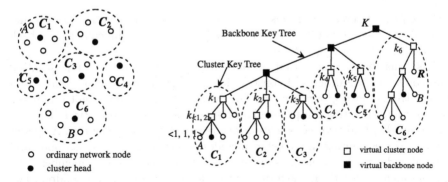

Fig. 1. A clustered ad hoc network

Fig. 2. Group key tree corresponding to the clustered network of Fig.1

2.2   Bilinear Pairings

Over this paper, let G_1, G_2 be two groups of the same prime order q. G_1 is an additive group and G_2 is a multiplicative group.

Definition 1. *Bilinear pairings is a mapping $e : G_1 \times G_1 \to G_2$ satisfying the following three properties :*
(1) Bilinear: $e(aP, bQ) = e(P, Q)^{ab}$ for all $P, Q \in G_1$ and $a, b \in \mathbb{Z}_q^*$.
(2) Non-degenerate: If P is a generator of G_1, then $e(P, P)$ is also a generator of G_2.
(3) Computable: There exists an efficient algorithm to compute $e(P, Q)$.

BDH Assumption. (Bilinear Diffie-Hellman Assumption.) *Given P, aP, $bP, cP \in G_1$, where $a, b, c \in_R \mathbb{Z}_q^*$. To compute $e(P, P)^{abc}$ is hard, which means there is no efficient probabilistic polynomial time algorithm to solve this problem.*
More about the bilinear pairings can be found in [9,6].

3   The Proposed Group Key Agreement Protocol

In this section, we first detail the unauthenticated protocol CEKA (Communication Efficient Key Agreement) and then extend it to the authenticated version ACEKA (Authenticated CEKA). As for our protocol, it is necessary to suppose that the ad hoc network employs hierarchical protocol as routing protocol, and the clustering technique mentioned in section 2.1 is also used. After clustering, all clusters establish their own cluster shared keys in parallel, and finally to establish the group shared key in collaboration. We describe ACEKA protocol in two phases: the Initial Key Agreement (IKA) phase establishes the initial group session key and constructs the group key tree as a byproduct, the Group Key Maintenance (GKM) phase handles all dynamic events, such as member joining and deletion events, and then refreshes the group key.

3.1   Definitions and Notations

We now present some definitions and notations used in this paper. Let G_1 and G_2 be defined as section 2.2 , $H : G_2 \to \mathbb{Z}_q^*$ is a cryptographically secure hash function, and q be a large prime.

It is remarkable to note that, in our protocol, the process of implementing protocol is also the process of constructing a virtual tree, which is similar to a ternary tree, named *group key tree*. For example, Fig.2 is the result group key tree after implementing our protocol for the network described in Fig.1. The tree can be divided into two parts: *cluster key tree* and *backbone key tree*. A cluster key tree, corresponding to a cluster, includes two types of nodes: leaf node and internal node. Each leaf node is associated with a specific group member. The internal nodes are virtual, each of them always has three or two children, i.e., another lower internal node and two (or one) leaf nodes. The backbone key tree, be unique in the group key tree, combines all the cluster key trees to form the group key tree. All the nodes of backbone key tree are virtual and not associated with actual network nodes. We use the notation $< c, l, v >$ to denote a tree node which is the vth node in the lth level of the cth cluster key tree (where $c \in \{0, 1, 2, ...\}$, $l \in \mathbb{N}$ and $v \in \{1, 2, 3\}$). It is remarkable that the l value of the lowest level of every cluster key tree is 1 and increment upwards, and the c value of virtual backbone node is 0. For example, in Fig.2, we use $< 1, 1, 1 >$ to denote the node A, and $< 6, 2, 3 >$ to denote the node B. Notation $< c, l, * >$ represents the set of all the nodes in the lth level of the cth cluster key tree. The node with the largest v value in the lth level is selected as the *l-level sponsor* denoted as $S_{<c,l>}$, which is responsible for updating the *level-shared-key*. Notation $< c, *, * >$ represents the set of all the nodes in the cth cluster key tree. The highest level-sponsor $S_{<c,l>}$ of the cluster C_c act as the *c-cluster sponsor* and is denoted as S_c, which is responsible for updating the *cluster-shared-key*. In Fig.2, for example, R is the sponsor of the cluster C_6 , denoted as S_6. Similarly, the highest cluster sponsor is the *sponsor of the whole network*. For example, R is also the network sponsor. According to the structure of key tree, every $< c, l, 1 > (l > 1)$ node is a virtual node, which is actually the upgrade of $S_{<c,l-1>}$ in higher level. The notation $\#(c, l)$ denotes the node count in the lth level of the cth cluster key tree, including internal nodes. The value of $\#(c, l)$ is 1, 2 or 3. Each leaf node $< c, l, v >$ holds a random value $r_v \in \mathbb{R}$ chosen and kept secretly by the corresponding network node. The blinded version of the secret is $r_v P$ if $\#(c, l) = 3$, or $e(P, P)^{r_v}$ if $\#(c, l) = 2$. Every internal node has an associated secret key $k_{<c,l>}$ and a public blinded key $k_{<c,l>}P$ or $e(P, P)^{k_{<c,l>}}$. The secret key $k_{<c,l>}$, also named *level key*, is the result of agreement among its overall sub nodes. We use k_c to denote the *cluster key* shared by all the nodes in cluster c, and K to denote the *group key* shared by all the nodes in the network. Every node can compute its cluster key and the group key by using its own random value and all the public blinded keys along the simple path from itself to the root node of its cluster key tree or group tree. We call the simple path as *key path* of that node.

Now, take node A (in Fig.2) for example, by using $r_{<1,1,1>}, r_{<1,1,2>}P$ and $r_{<1,1,3>}P$, A can compute the level key

$$k_{<1,2>} = e(r_{<1,1,2>}P, r_{<1,1,3>}P)^{r_{<1,1,1>}} = e(P, P)^{r_{<1,1,1>}r_{<1,1,2>}r_{<1,1,3>}},$$

and by using $k_{<1,2>}, r_{<1,2,2>}P$ and $r_{<1,2,3>}P$, A can compute the cluster key

$$k_1 = e(r_{<1,2,2>}P, r_{<1,2,3>}P)^{k_{<1,2>}} = e(P, P)^{k_{<1,2>}r_{<1,2,2>}r_{<1,2,3>}}.$$

As $e(P, P)$ is an element of group G_2, it is necessary to map it into $\mathbb{Z}_q^*$ by using the hash function H. Thus, by using $k_1, k_2 P, k_3 P, k_4 P, k_5 P$ and $e(P, P)^{k_6}$, A can compute the group key

$$K = H(e(P, P)^{k_6 H(e(P,P)^{k_4 k_5 H(e(P,P)^{k_1 k_2 k_3})})}).$$

In this way, if there are n nodes in the ad hoc network, let $\alpha = e(P, P)$, then the agreed group key will be

$$K = H\left(\alpha^{r_n r_{n-1} H\left(\alpha^{r_{n-2} r_{n-3} H(\alpha^{r_{n-4}} \cdots \cdot H(\alpha^{r_3 r_2 r_1})})\right)}\right).$$

3.2   Basic Key Agreement Protocols

Basic Protocol 1 (BasicPtl3). In the case of three parties A, B, C, we use Joux's protocol [9] as the tripartite key agreement protocol. The protocol runs as: (1) *exchanging messages.* $A \rightarrow B, C: aP; B \rightarrow A, C: bP; C \rightarrow A, B: cP$, here $a, b, c \in_R \mathbb{Z}_q^*$ are respectively and secretly selected by A, B and C. (2) *computing group key.* A computes $K_A = e(bP, cP)^a$, B computes $K_B = e(aP, cP)^b$, C computes $K_C = e(aP, bP)^c$. The final session key is then as $K = K_A = K_B = K_C = e(P, P)^{abc}$.

Basic Protocol 2 (BasicPtl2). In the case of two parties, we generalize the Diffie-Hellman key exchange protocol [7] as follows. (1) *exchanging messages.* $A \rightarrow B: e(P, P)^a$, $B \rightarrow A: e(P, P)^b$, here $a, b \in_R \mathbb{Z}_q^*$ are respectively and secretly selected by A and B . (2) *computing group key.* A compute $K_A = (e(P, P)^b)^a$, B compute $K_B = (e(P, P)^a)^b$. Then the established session key is $K = K_A = K_B = e(P, P)^{ab}$.

3.3   Unauthenticated Group Key Agreement

(1) Initial Key Agreement (IKA) Phase. For easer understanding, we first describe the unauthenticated key agreement protocol CEKA (Communication Efficient Key Agreement) in this subsection. The authenticated version is detailed in section 3.4. Initially, suppose there are $N \geq 2$ nodes in the ad hoc network which can be divided into m clusters $C_i (1 \leq i \leq m)$. Every cluster C_i include n_i nodes and could be divided into $h_i = (n_i - 1)/2$ subgroups $g_j (1 \leq j \leq h_i)$. We denote the node count of the subgroup g_j by $\#(g_j)$. It is easy to know if a cluster includes only 2 nodes then $\#(g_1) = 2$, otherwise, $\#(g_1) = 3$, $\#(g_u) = 2$ $(1 < u < h_i)$, $\#(g_{h_i}) = 2$ or 1.

Based on this division method we can employ the two basic protocols to implement the group key agreement. All the algorithms involved can be found in the foot of this section.

Cluster Key Agreement. All of the clusters implements in parallel their cluster key according to the algorithm *IKA-ClusterKeyAgreement.* The process of establishing cluster session keys is meanwhile the process of constructing cluster key trees. All of the network nodes are regarded as tree nodes. The network nodes in the same subgroup is put on the same level of the cluster key tree. With the help of virtual nodes, the cluster key trees are constructed successfully. In a cluster key tree, the root node represents the cluster key. See also **algorithm1** below.

Group Key Agreement. All cluster sponsors would represent themselves' clusters to implement the group key agreement algorithm *IKA-GroupKeyAgreement.* In this process, every cluster is regarded as a virtual networks node, and the whole network is regarded as a virtual cluster then. After establishing the group key, the group key tree is constructed eventually. See also **algorithm2** below.

(2) Group Key Maintenance (GKM) Phase. The nodes in ad hoc networks possess of strong mobility. In order to ensure the security of session key, it is important and necessary to update the group key. In our protocol, if the nodes' movement does not cause the change of the cluster structures, it is needless to update the group key. Below are some considered events .

Node Joining. Suppose node J moves into the field of cluster C_i, and desires to share a key with all the nodes in the current network. The cluster head of C_i would response the join request event of J, then notify the sponsor S_i of this event. After receiving the notification, S_i would trigger the cluster key updating process in terms of algorithm *GKM-Join* , and update recursively the group session key.

Node Removing. Suppose node R=$< i, l, v >$ has moved out of the range of cluster C_i , The cluster head of C_i would be aware of this variation, then notify the level-sponsor $S_{<i,l>}$ of this event. The sponsor $S_{<i,l>}$ would handle it according to the algorithm *GKM-Remove*. It is remarkable that the cluster should be reconstructed if R is the cluster head of C_i. Cluster reconstruction is the responsibility of hierarchical routing protocols. After reconstructing, a new cluster head would have been chosen, and it is time to implement algorithm *GKM-Remove* again.

   If nodes in ad hoc networks switch clusters frequently, some extreme situations would occur, where the whole network is divided into overmuch small clusters. According to CEKA protocol, the group key would be very high in this situation. As the efficiency of the algorithms *GKM-Join* and *GKM-Remove* are linear to the height of the tree, the efficiency of CEKA protocol would be more and more bad along with the movement of nodes. For solving this problem, the group sponsor can initiate the cluster merging process to merge small clusters into larger clusters and thus reduce the height of group key tree. This process can be handle by the following algorithm. Also, if some exotic clusters want to join or some inner clusters want to leave as a whole, the protocol can also run the following algorithm.

Merging and Partition. Suppose cluster C_i moves into the current network, and desires to share a key with it. In order to handle this event, C_i should have implemented a cluster key agreement protocol before its joining. Then, regard every cluster as a node and the whole network as a cluster, we could implement algorithm *GKM-Join* to finish cluster merging event and update the group session key. A similar method can also be used to handle partition event, i.e. cluster removing event.

Key Updating. It is necessary to update the group key recursively when handling above events. The updating process of group key is often triggered by some sponsor $S_{<i,j>}$ (or S_i). From the view of key trees, $S_{<i,j>}$ (or S_i) need compute all the new level keys $k'_{<c,l>}$ (or cluster keys k'_l) in its key path. Then according to the neighbor node count in the key path is 2 or 1 , the sponsor $S_{<i,j>}$ (or S_i) broadcast $k'_l P$ or $e(P,P)^{k'_i}$. As a result, every network node can compute the new group session key successfully.

Algorithm 1. *IKA-ClusterKeyAgreement*(C_i)
for $j = 1$ to h_i do
    if $j = 1$ then
        if $\#(g_1) = 3$ then $k_{<i,j>} = BasicPtl3(<i,j,*>)$
        else if $\#(g_1) = 2$ then $k_{<i,j>} = BasicPtl2(<i,j,*>)$
            else $k_{<i,j>} = r_{<i,j,1>}$
            end if
        end if
    else   /*if $j > 1$*/
    if $\#(g_j) = 2$ then $k_{<i,j>} = BasicPtl3(S_{<i,j-1>},<i,j,*>)$
    else if $\#(g_j) = 1$ then $k_{<i,j>} = BasicPtl2(S_{<i,j-1>},<i,j,*>)$
    end if
    end if
  end do
  return $k_i = k_{<i,h_i>}$

Algorithm 2. *IKA-GroupKeyAgreement*
1. All the clusters $C_1, ..., C_m$ implement algorithm *IKA-ClusterKeyAgreement* in parallel .
2. Take sponsors $S_1, ..., S_m$ as members of a virtual and special cluster SC.
3. To implement algorithm *IKA-ClusterKeyAgreement* in cluster SC. Eventually, the cluster key K can be agreed, and return it as the group key.

Algorithm 3. *GKM-Join*(J, C_i)
$n = h_i$, J select a random value $r_j \in \mathbb{Z}_q$,
if $\#(g_n) = 2$ then
    J broadcast $r_j P$
    $<i,n,1>$(or $S_{<i,n-1>}$) broadcast $k_{<i,n-1>}P$
    $<i,n,2>$ broadcast $r'_{<i,n,2>}P$
    $k_i = k_{<i,n>} = BasicPtl3(J, <i,n,*>)$
else if $\#(g_n) = 3$ then
    J broadcast $e(P,P)^{r_J}$
    $S_{<i,n>}$ broadcast $e(P,P)^{k_i}, k_i = k_{<i,n+1>} = BasicPtl2(J, S_{<i,n>})$
end if
Lastly, S_i compute and then broadcast all the public blinded keys along its key path for updating group key.

Algorithm 4. *GKM-Remove*(R, C_i)
if $\#(g_l) = 3$ then
    $<i,l,2>$ sever as the sponsor $<i,l>$
    and broadcast $k'_{<i,l>} = BasicPtl2(<i,l,*>)$
else if $\#(g_l) = 2$ then
    if $\#(g_{l-1}) = 3$ then
        $S_{<i,l-1>}$ broadcast $r'_{<i,l-1,3>}P$
        $k'_{<i,l-1>} = BasicPtl3(<i,l-1,*>)$

else if $\#(g_{l-1}) = 2$ then
  $S_{<i,l-1>}$ broadcast $k'_{<i,l-1>} = BasicPtl2(< i, l-1, * >)$
  end if
  end if
end if

Lastly, $S_{<i,l>}$ or $S_{<i,l-1>}$ compute and then broadcast all the public blinded keys along its key path for updating group key.

Remark 1. $k_{<i,j>} = BasicPtl3(< i, j, * >)$ means that all the nodes in the set $< i, j, * >$ implement the basic protocol BasicPtl3 to establish a new level key $k_{<i,j>}$. Furthermore, $k_{<i,j>} = $BasicPtl3 $(S_{<i,j-1>}, < i, j, * >)$ means the sponsor $S_{<i,j-1>}$ and all the nodes in the set $< i, j, * >$ implement the basic protocol BasicPtl3 to establish a new level key $k_{<i,j>}$. It is similar in the case of BasicPtl2.

3.4 Authenticated Key Agreement Protocol

Like the Diffie-Hellman protocol, the two basic protocols, BasicPtl3 and BasicPtl2, also suffer easily from man-in-the-middle attack. Hence it is necessary to provide an authentication service on the source of the protocol messages to make sure that the messages received in a protocol run are indeed from the intended principals. In this paper, we present an ID-based signature scheme to support the authenticity of the protocol.

(1) ID-based Signature Scheme. ID-based public key infrastructure was first proposed by Shamir [17], however, the first practical ID-based public key cryptosystem was proposed by Boneh and Franklin [6] using bilinear pairings on supersingular elliptic curves or Abelian varieties. Their contributions can be applied to design ID-based signature schemes, generally, which include four algorithms. We detail our scheme as follows.

Setup: Let G_1, G_2 and e be defined as section 2.2, P be a generator of G_1. Define two cryptographic hash functions $F : \{0,1\}^* \rightarrow G_1$, $H_2 : \{0,1\}^* \times G_2 \rightarrow \mathbb{Z}_q^*$. The Key Generation Center (KGC) chooses a random number $s \in \mathbb{Z}_q^*$ and sets $P_{pub} = sP$. The center publishes system parameters $params = \{G, q, P, P_{pub}, F, H_2\}$, and keeps s as the *master-key*.

Private Key Extraction: User A submits his identity information ID_A to KGC, KGC computes A's public key as $Q_A = F(ID_A)$, and returns $S_A = sQ_A$ to the user as his private key. A publishes his public key as $\{ID_A, Q_A\}$.

Signing: Support that the message to be signed is $M \in \{0,1\}^*$. Signer A chooses a random number $k \in \mathbb{N}$, and compute $r = kP, u = H_2(M, r), t = uS_A - kP_{pub}$. Then the ID-based signature on message M is the pair (r, t). A sends M and its signature to the receiver B.

Verification: After getting a message M and its corresponding signature (r, t), the verifier B accepts the signature if and only if the following equation holds:

$$e(t, P)e(P_{pub}, r) = e(Q_A, P_{pub})^u, \text{ here } u = H_2(M, r).$$

Our signature scheme is actual a variant of ElGamal signature scheme, and is secure against existent forgery under an adaptively chosen message attack in the random oracle model, which is proved in section 5.

(2) Authenticated CEKA Protocol. In ad hoc networks, every node has its unique identification code, such as IP address or MAC address *etc.*. These unique information can be served as node's identity. Otherwise, we can designate universal unique identities for nodes during producing. Therefore, we can employ the ID-based signature scheme to sign messages before sending. We thus turn the unauthenticated CEKA protocol into an authenticated version, *i.e.*, Authenticated CEKA(ACEKA) protocol.

4   Complexity Analysis of ACEKA Protocol

4.1   Communication Complexity in IKA Phase

In this section, we will analysis the communication complexity of our protocol. In common, the communication overhead of a group key agreement involves communication rounds and messages number needed to implement the protocol. It is meaningless to compare directly our protocol with the proposed protocols in [13] and [20], as the both protocols employ some existed group key agreement protocols. Hence, it is better for us to compare with these fundamental protocols such as GDH suits[18] , TGDH [10] and ESTR [11] protocols. It is remarkable that all of them are based on the two-party Diffie-Hellman key exchange protocol or its some extension version. And as TGDH and ESTR are the most efficient protocols recently and both of them support dynamic membership operations, we thus draw some comparisons with them.

(1) Communication Rounds without Communication Delay. Here we support every node pair can communicate directly without relaying of any others, i.e., the communication delay is least.

For easier analysis, support the whole network with n nodes can be divided averagely into m clusters, with every cluster including $\lceil \frac{n}{m} \rceil$ nodes. It is easy to validate that our protocol requires $c_A(n) \approx \frac{n+m}{2}$ rounds of messages exchange to establish the initial group key in IKA phase. Also, it can be proved that the clustering detail impact little the communication overhead when m is fixed, and the height of group key tree is lowest when $m = \sqrt{n}$. In order to compare impartially, it is necessary to modify the key agreement model of TGDH and ESTR protocol from binary tree to ternary tree. Lee *et al.* [12] has done this work to modify TGDH protocol using bilinear pairings. Therefore, we use their results directly. As for ESTR protocol, it is also not difficult to do this. After that, we have the following results about the communication rounds to establish the initial group key in IKA phase. The TGDH protocol requires $c_T(n) \approx \frac{n-1}{2}$ rounds and the ESTR protocol requires $c_E(n) = \frac{n+1}{2}$ rounds. Obviously, our proposed protocol is the worst one in the comparison when $m > 2$, as it require more communication rounds.

(2) Communication Rounds with Communication Delay. The research on random networks suggests that relaying messages is inevitable in real network environment. Analysis on communication complexity would not reflect the real effect unless considering the communication delay.

Considering a wireless ad hoc network within a $L \times L$ m^2 area. Each node chooses a random direction between 0 and 360 degrees to move, with the largest transmission range below 300m. We design some scenarios shown in Table 1. These areas are chosen so that the node density is approximately constant, and

Table 1. Room sizes for different scenario

Numbers of Nodes(n)	Room Size($L \times L$)	Average Mean Distance(d)
10	750m × 750m	2.3
100	1600m × 1600m	4.6
1000	2930m × 2930m	6.9

hence the impact of network size can be investigated. On average, there are almost $\sqrt{n}$ neighbors per node. The value of *average mean distance d* in Table 1 denotes the average hops every pair of nodes communicate with each other. We set it to $\log n$, which is indicated in the random graph theory [1]. When considering the communication delay, the communication rounds of the three protocol change as $c_A = (n+1) + d \times \frac{m+1}{2}$, $c_E = d \times \frac{n+1}{2}$, $c_T = d \times \frac{n-1}{2}$. Fig.3 illustrates the comparison results of different protocols on communication overhead with different n and d. It is obvious that our protocol ACEKA is better than TGDH and ESTR protocols when considering communication delay. Therefore, in ad hoc network with large size, our protocol is more suitable than TGDH and ESTR protocols.

4.2   Communication Complexity in GKM Phase

In ad hoc networks, dynamic events would occur frequently. After the IKE phase, the ACEKA protocol would evolve into GKM phase to handle dynamic events. We compare the communication overhead of the three protocols of GKM phase in Table 2. The overhead of protocol depends on the tree height, the balance of the key tree, the location of the joining and the leaving nodes. In our analysis, we assume the worst case configuration and list the worst-case overhead for all the protocols. The relevant data of TGDH come from [12], where n and k denote the number of current group members and merging groups respectively. It can be seen from Table 2, our protocol is comparable to ESTR and is better than TGDH

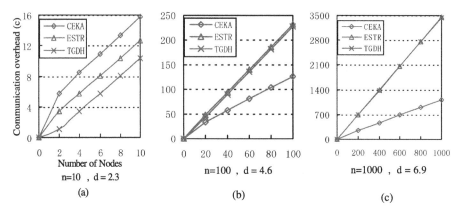

Fig. 3. Comparison of three different protocols on communication overhead with different n and d

protocol with respect to communication overhead. When considering the effect of network delay, the communication overhead of ACEKA is hereby lower than the two others in practice and is more suitable for large size ad hoc networks.

Table 2. Comparison of communication overhead of three protocols in GKM phase

Scheme	Event	Round	Message	Unicast	Broadcast
TGDH	Joining, Merging	2	3	0	3
	Removing	1	1	0	1
	Partition	$\log n$	$2\log n$	0	$2\log n$
ESTR	Joining	2	3	2	1
	Removing, Partition	1	1	0	1
	Merging	2	3	2	1
ACEKA	Joining	2	3	2	1
	Removing, Partition	1	1	0	1
	Merging	2	3	2	1

4.3   Computation Complexity Without Signature

Generally speaking, the computation overhead of cryptosystems based on bilinear pairings involves the arithmetics of scalar multiplications, pairings, modular exponentiations *etc.*. Like the communication overhead, the computation overhead also depends on the tree height, the balance of the key tree and the joining and leaving locations of nodes. As the plain TGDH and ESTR protocols are not authenticated, when drawing comparison, the overhead of signatures can be reduced from ACEKA. So, we just draw the comparisons in computation overhead using CEKA and not ACEKA, and the results are listed in Table 3, where n denotes the node count of the whole network, k denotes the node count of the least group coming to merge, m denotes the cluster count in a clustered network, h_C denotes the height of cluster key tree in CEKA protocol. It is easy to see the

Table 3. Comparison of computation overhead of three protocols in GKM phase

Scheme	Event	Scalar Multiplication	Pairings	Exponentiations
TGDH	Joining, Merging	$\log_3 n + 1$	$\log_3 n - 1$	$\log_3 n - 1$
	Removing	$\log_3 n + 1$	$\log_3 n - 1$	$\log_3 n - 1$
	Partition	$2\log_3 n$	$2\log_3 n$	$2\log_3 n$
ESTR	Joining	2	1	1
	Removing, Partition	$(n-1)/2 + 1$	$(n-1)/2$	$(n-1)/2$
	Merging	$(k-1)/2 + 1$	$(k-1)/2$	$(k-1)/2$
CEKA	Joining, Partition	$(m-1)/2 + 1$	$(m-1)/2$	$(m-1)/2$
	Removing	$h_C + 1$	h_C	h_C
	Merging	2	1	1

average computation cost of TGDH protocol is the lowest, followed by that of CEKA protocol, and then ESTR protocol.

As for ACEKA, the overhead of the ID-based signature should also be considered in practical situation. It can be seen from Section 3.4, the signing step requires 3 Scalar Multiplication operations, and the verification step requires 3 pairings operations and 1 modular exponentiations operation. Pairings computation is a critical and also the most expensive operation in pairings-based cryptosystems. Barreto et al.[4] proposed an efficient algorithm for pairing-based cryptosystems. Still, the fastest algorithms to compute pairings is almost about $1.5 \sim 3$ times slower than the modular exponentiation. However, since involving the pairings computation, our protocol admits of improvement in computational efficiency.

5   Security Analysis of ACEKA Protocol

5.1   Security Analysis of ID-Based Signature Scheme

As the security of the signature scheme is based on an assumption, we describe it as a lemma and then prove it following.

Lemma 1. *Given $P \in E[n]$, $v \in \mu_n$, $e : E[n] \times E[n] \to \mu_n$, where $E[n]$ denotes the subgroup of n-torsion elements in G_1, $\mu_n = \{\alpha | \alpha^n = 1, \alpha \in \overline{G_2}\}$. It is intractable to compute $Q \in E[n]$ such that $e(Q, P) = v$.*

Proof. It can be proven that the problem is a reduction of ECDH problem. Let $u = e(P, P)$, as μ_n is a cycle group with order n, we have $v = u^k, k \leq n$, i.e. $Q = kP$. According to ECDL and ECDH problems, it is hard to compute k. So it is also intractable to compute $w = v^k$. On the other hand, if we have an efficient algorithms $\mathcal{A}$ to compute Q, then we can find an algorithm $\mathcal{A}'$ to compute $e(Q, Q) = e(kP, kP) = e(P, P)^{k^2} = u^{k^2} = v^k = w$. Obviously, it is a contradiction. $\square$

Theorem 1. *The proposed ID-based signature scheme is secure against existent forgery under an adaptively chosen message attack under the assumption of Lemma 1.*

The prove method is similar to that of [8,14]. Now we only give a sketch.

Proof. Suppose there is a polynomial time probabilistic Turing machine $\mathcal{E}$ which takes M and Q_A as input and outputs an existent forgery of a signature from A with a non-negligible probability ε. Here we assume that H_2 is a random oracle. Then we show that there is another polynomial time algorithm $\mathcal{E}'$, which takes advantage of the Turing machine $\mathcal{E}$, solves the hard problem described in Lemma 1. $\mathcal{E}'$ inputs the same random data to $\mathcal{E}$. When $\mathcal{E}$ inquires the hash values of (M, r), $\mathcal{E}'$ returns a random value to $\mathcal{E}$. Suppose that $\mathcal{E}$ is able to forge a valid signature (r, t) for M within time T, by U times of queries of random oracle, and V times of queries of the signer. According to the Forking Lemma of Pointcheval and Stern [16], $\mathcal{E}'$ may be able to get two forgeries of signature from A for the same message of M and r but with different hash values, namely (r, t) and (r, t')(with $H_2(r, t) \neq H_2'(r, t')$), in expected time $T' \leq 120,686UT/\varepsilon$. With the two signature forgeries for M, we have

$$t = uS_A - kP_{pub}$$

and

$$t' = u'S_A - kP_{pub} .$$

It follows that

$$t - t' = (u - u')S_A,$$

hence

$$e(t - t', P) = e(Q_A, P_{pub})^{u-u'}.$$

Let $e(Q_A, P_{pub})^{u-u'} = v$, then $\mathcal{E}'$ can find a solution $Q = t - t'$, such that $e(Q, P) = v$, i.e., we have solved the hard problem of Lemma 1 and the long private key $S_A = (u - u')^{-1}(t - t')$. $\qquad\square$

5.2   Security Analysis of ACEKA Protocol

(1) Security Analysis of Basic Protocol 2. As the building blocks of ACEKA protocol, the security of the basic protocols described in section 3.2 are the base of the security of ACEKA protocol. The security of BasicPtl3 is based on the BDH assumption, which can be found in [9]. As for BasicPtl2, the security of which is based on the following two propositions .

Proposition 1. *Given $P \in G_1, e(P, P)^a \in G_2, a \in_R \mathbb{Z}_q^*$, to compute aP is an intractable problem.*

Proof. By the definition of bilinear pairings, given $P, aP, bP \in G_1; a, b \in_R \mathbb{Z}_q^*$, it is easy to compute $e(P, P)^{ab}$, but the ECDH assumption imply that it is an intractable problem to compute $abP \in G_1$. Go further, if given $e(P, P)^{ab}$, it is intractable to compute abP, let $b = 1$, thus Proposition 1. follows immediately. $\qquad\square$

Proposition 2. *Given $P \in G_1; e(P,P)^a, e(P,P)^b \in G_2; a, b \in_R \mathbb{Z}_q^*$, it is intractable to compute $e(P,P)^{ab}$.*

Proof. As $e(P,P)^a, e(P,P)^b \in G_2$ and G_2 is a cyclic group of prime order q, so the Computational Diffie-Hellman (CDH) assumption is hold in G_2, thus Proposition 2. follows immediately. □

(2) Security of ACEKA Protocol. The security attributes of our protocol are as follows. These security attributes are also listed in [2].

Known session key security: A protocol is called Known session key security if an adversary having obtained some previous session keys cannot get the session keys of the current run of the key agreement protocol. As for our protocol, support a adversary E has learned a session key $e(bP, cP)^a = e(P,P)^{abc}$, previously agreed by A, B and C. To extract a, b, c from this session key is hard if the BDH problems hold. However, without a, b, c, E cannot get a refreshed key of the current run of the key agreement protocol. On the other hand, if E knows k , he can get A's private key $S_A = u^{-1}(t + kP_{pub})$ from the signing algorithm. Then E can impersonate A to broadcast key refreshing messages and get the refreshed session key. However, to compute k is equivalent to solving the Discrete-Log problem in G_1. Therefore, our protocol has Know session key security.

Forward / backward secrecy: A protocol enjoys forward secrecy if, when the long-term private keys of one or more entities are compromised, the secrecy of previous session keys is not affected. As with CEKA protocol, the entities' long-term private keys are not used in the process of key agreement, hence they are not correlative with the group session key. Therefore, our protocol has forward secrecy. The backward secrecy attribute is in the same way.

No key-compromise impersonation: This properties implies that if one entity's static private key is compromised, the adversary may impersonate the compromised entity in subsequent protocols, but he cannot impersonate other entities. As for our protocol, support the adversary E knows principal A's private key S_A, then he can impersonate A to agree session key with B and C. However, as every message should be signed by message source , E cannot impersonate B or C to initial any messages. Therefore, our protocol holds this security property.

No unknown key-share: In an unknown key-share attack, if the adversary convinces a group of entities that they share some session key with the adversary, while in fact the key is shared between the group and another party. To implement such an attack on our protocol, the adversary E is required to learn the private key of some entity. Otherwise, E cannot impersonate other entities to send message with signature, the attack hardly works. Hence, we claim that our protocol has this attribute.

No key control: It should not be possible for any of the participants (or an adversary) to force the session key to a preselected value or predict the value of the session key. Just like the session key obtained from basic Diffie-Hellman protocol, the session keys in basic protocols BasicPtl3 and BasicPtl2 are determined by all the three or two principals, and no one can influence the outcome of the session keys, or enforce them to fall into a pre-determined interval. We employ the two basic protocols to construct the group key agreement protocol ACEKA. Although we introduce the concept of sponsor, the sponsors are only responsible for communication and not dominators. In other words, no key control exists in our protocol.

6   Conclusion

We present an authenticated and communication efficient group key agreement protocol ACEKA for ad hoc networks, using bilinear pairings and hierarchical routing techniques. The logical key model of ACEKA is close to the actual topology of networks and thus the assumption of 1-hop can be weakened. The protocol supports dynamic membership events and enjoys group key secrecy, forward/backward secrecy and other security attributes. The analysis of communication and computation complexity shows that our protocol is better than ESTR and TGDH protocol in many facets, and is more suitable for ad hoc networks with large size.

References

1. R. Albert and A. L. Barabási. Statistical mechanics of complex networks. Reviews of modern physics, 74(1), 47–100, 2002.
2. S. Al-Riyami and K. Paterson. Tripartite authenticated key agreement protocols from pairings. The 9th IMA International Conference on Cryptography and Coding, LNCS 2898, 332–359, Springer-Verlag, 2003.
3. Y. Amir, Y. Kim, C. Nita-Rotaru and G. Tsudik. On the Performance of Group Key Agreement Protocols. ACM Transactions on Information and System Security, 7(3), 457–488, 2004.
4. P.S.L.M. Barreto, H.Y. Kim, B. Lynn and M. Scott. Efficient Algorithms for Pairing-Based Cryptosystems. Advances in Cryptology - Crypto 2002, LNCS 2442, 354–368, Springer-Verlag. 2002.
5. E. M. Belding-Royer. Hierarchical Routing in Ad hoc Mobile Networks. Wireless Communication & Mobile Computing, 2(5), 515–532, 2002.
6. D. Boneh and M. Franklin. Identity-based encryption from the Weil pairing. Advances in Cryptology - Crypto 2001, LNCS 2139, 213–219, Springer-Verlag, 2001.
7. W. Diffie and M. Hellman. New Directions in Cryptography. IEEE Transaction on Information Theory, 22(6), 644–654, 1976.
8. F. Hess. Efficient identity-based signature schemes based on pairings. Selected Areas in Cryptography 2002, LNCS 2595, Springer-Verlag, 310–324, 2002.
9. A. Joux. A One Round Protocol for Tripartite DiffieCHellman. Journal of Cryptology, 17(4), 263–276, Springer New York, 2004.
10. Y. Kim, A. Perrig and G. Tsudik. Simple and Fault-Tolerant Key Agreement For Dynamic Collaborative Groups. The 7th ACM Conference on Computer and Communications Security, 7(1), 235–244, 2000.

11. Y. Kim, A. Perrig and G. Tsudik. Communication-Efficient Group Key Agreement. Proceedings of the 16th International Conference on Information Security 2001, 229–244, 2001.
12. S. Lee, Y. Kim, K. Kim and D.H. Ryu. An Efficient Tree-based Group Key Agreement using Bilinear Map. Applied Cryptography and Network Security 2003, LNCS 2846, 357–371, Springer-Verlag, 2003.
13. X. Li, Y. Wang and O. Frieder. Efficient Hybrid Key Agreement Protocol for Wireless Ad Hoc Networks. IEEE International Conference on Computer Communications and Networks, 404–409, 2002.
14. S. L. Liu, F. G. Zhang and K. F. Chen. Authenticating Tripartite Key Agreement Protocol with Pairings. Joural of Computer Science and Technology, 19(2), 169–176, 2004.
15. G. Pei, M. Gerla, X. Hong and C.C. Chiang. A wireless hierarchical routing protocol with group mobility. Proceedings of IEEE WCNC 1999, 1538–1542, 1999.
16. D. Pointcheval and J. Stern. Security arguments for digital signatures and blind signatures. Journal of Cryptology, 13(3), 361–396, Springer New York, 2000.
17. A. Shamir. Identity-based cryptosystems and signature schemes. Advances in Cryptology - Crypto 1984, LNCS 196, 47–53, Springer-Verlag, 1984.
18. M. Steiner, G. Tsudik and M. Waidner. Key Agreement in Dynamic Peer Groups. IEEE Transactions on Parallel and Distributed Systems, 11(8), 769–780, 2000.
19. J. Sucec and I. Marsic. Clustering Overhead for Hierarchical Routing in Mobile Adhoc Networks. Proceedings of IEEE Infocom 2002, 1698–1706, 2002.
20. G. Yao, K. Ren, F. Bao, et al. Making the Key Agreement Protocol in Mobile Ad Hoc Network More Efficient. Applied Cryptography and Network Security 2003, LNCS 2846, 343–356, Springer-Verlag, 2003.

Efficient Mutual Data Authentication Using Manually Authenticated Strings

Sven Laur[2] and Kaisa Nyberg[1,2]

[1] Nokia Research Center, Finland
kaisa.nyberg@nokia.com
[2] Helsinki University of Technology, Finland
{slaur, knyberg}@tcs.hut.fi

Abstract. Solutions for an easy and secure setup of a wireless connection between two devices are urgently needed for WLAN, Wireless USB, Bluetooth and similar standards for short range wireless communication. All such key exchange protocols employ data authentication as an unavoidable subtask. As a solution, we propose an asymptotically optimal protocol family for data authentication that uses short manually authenticated out-of-band messages. Compared to previous articles by Vaudenay and Pasini the results of this paper are more general and based on weaker security assumptions. In addition to providing security proofs for our protocols, we focus also on implementation details and propose practically secure and efficient sub-primitives for applications.

1 Introduction

In this paper we consider the problem of setting up a shared secret key in an ad hoc manner, that is, in isolation from any key management facility and without pre-shared secrets. Consider two parties Alice and Bob who want to establish a shared secret key over an insecure network without any prior authenticated information. If adversaries are passive, that is, no malicious messages are sent to the network and all messages are delivered unaltered, then exchanging public keys for Diffie-Hellman or similar public key based key exchange protocol is sufficient. However, an active adversary, Charlie, can launch an man-in-the-middle attack. Namely, Charlie can replace a desired secure channel from Alice to Bob by a pair of secure channels, one from Alice to Charlie and one from Charlie to Bob. The attack is transparent to legitimate users without prior authenticated information. Thus secure key exchange is impossible without authenticated channels. The main question is how much information, *authentic out-of-band messages (OOB messages)*, must be sent over the authenticated channel to achieve reasonable security level. We are aiming at an application, where keys are exchanged between various electronic devices and authentic communication is done by an ordinary user who either enters messages into devices or compares output displays. The latter severely limits a plausible size of OOB messages: one could consider 4–6 decimal digits as optimal and 16 hexadecimal characters as an absolute limit. Other possible OOB channels include various visual or audible signals like blinking lights, images, phone calls etc.

Most urgently such a solution is needed for WLAN: the current use of pre-shared keys degrades both practical usability and security. The home users should have a clear

D. Pointcheval, Y. Mu, and K. Chen (Eds.): CANS 2006, LNCS 4301, pp. 90–107, 2006.

and manageable procedure to set up a secure wireless network so that it is easy to add and remove devices from the network. Hence, the WiFi Alliance is working on a better solution. Recently, manual data authentication using short authenticated strings received practical applications in ad hoc key agreement. Phil Zimmermann released a software called Zfone and an Internet draft to offer security to Voice over IP [ZJC06]. A similar protocol (See Protocol 3) was adopted by USB-IF for Wireless USB devices [WUS06] and manual data authentication is going to be incorporated into Bluetooth [BT06].

A formal security model for such protocols consists of three bidirectional asynchronous channels, where messages can be arbitrarily delayed. In-band communication is routed from Alice to Bob via an active adversary Charlie, who can drop, modify or insert messages. The out-of-band channel between Alice and Bob is authentic but has low bandwidth and Charlie can arbitrarily delay[1] OOB messages. The model captures nicely all threats in wireless environment, as malicious adversary with a proper equipment can indeed change the network topology and thus reroute, drop, insert and modify messages. However, security is not the only objective. User-friendliness, low resource consumption and simple setup assumptions are equally important. There should be no public key infrastructure, as it is almost impossible to guarantee authenticity and availability of public keys to the humongous number of electronic devices. Also, protocols should use only symmetric primitives if possible.

All currently known user-aided key exchange and data authentication protocols can be divided into two different groups: protocols with authenticated but public OOB messages [Hoe05, CCH06, Vau05, LAN05, PV06a, PV06b, NSS06] and protocols with confidential passwords. Password-protected key exchange, see [BM92, KOY01] and Mana III in [GMN04], is needed when a user wants to establish a secure connection between devices that have input only, for example, devices with keyboards but no display. The main application for the manual data authentication is also a cryptographically secure but still user-friendly ad hoc key agreement between two or more network devices.

Our contribution. In this paper, we clarify and extend our preliminary results [LAN05]. In particular, we show that the previously presented manual cross authentication protocols [LAN05, PV06b] are indeed instantiations of the same protocol family that uses a commitment scheme to temporarily hide a secret key needed for data authentication. Compared to the results by Pasini and Vaudenay [PV06b], our security proofs (Sec. 4) are more modular and assumptions on used primitives are weaker and geared towards practice. We explicitly consider implementation details, that is, how to choose practical primitives (Sec. 5). Given a data authentication protocol it can be combined with the Diffie-Hellman key agreement in a secure way by taking the Diffie-Hellman key, or the pair of the public keys, as the data to be authenticated. But the designers of the practical protocols from [ZJC06, WUS06] have taken a different approach by using the Diffie-Hellman key shares as the source of randomness. In Sec. 3, we extend our proof of security also for such a case. In App. A, we consider security in any computational context and show that, under reasonable assumptions, security is not abruptly degraded if several protocols are executed in parallel. As an important theoretical result, we show

---

[1] For example, the adversary can distract the user who compares the output of two devices.

that all asymptotically optimal (unilateral) manual data authentication protocols have a certain structure (App. B, Theorem 5) and that there are no asymptotically optimal two round protocols for data authentication (Corollary 1).

2   Cryptographic Preliminaries

Our results are formalised in exact security framework where security reductions are precise and thus reveal quantitative differences between various assumptions. Security goals are formalised through games between a challenger and a t-time adversary[2] A who tries to violate some design property. Advantage of A is a non-trivial success probability $\mathrm{Adv}^{\mathsf{sec}}(A)$ in the game sec. The description of sec is omitted when the shape of $\mathrm{Adv}^{\mathsf{sec}}(A)$ reveals the complete structure of sec. We consider asymptotic complexity only w.r.t. the time-bound t. Let $g(t) = \mathcal{O}(f(t))$ if $\limsup_{t \to \infty} g(t)/f(t) < \infty$. If the working time of adversary can be unbounded, we talk about *statistical security*.

Let $x \leftarrow \mathcal{X}$ denote independent random draws from a set $\mathcal{X}$ and $y \leftarrow A(x_1, \ldots, x_n)$ denote assignment according to a randomised algorithm A with inputs $x_1, \ldots, x_n$.

Keyed hash functions. A keyed hash function $h : \mathcal{M} \times \mathcal{K} \to \mathcal{T}$ has two arguments: the first argument corresponds to a data and the second to a key. In our context an applicable tag space $\mathcal{T}$ is relatively small (may contain as few as 10^4 elements) and we need information theoretic properties. A hash function h is ε_u-*almost universal*, if for any two inputs $x_0 \neq x_1$, $\Pr[k \leftarrow \mathcal{K} : h(x_0, k) = h(x_1, k)] \leq \varepsilon_u$ and ε_u-*almost XOR universal* if for any $x_0 \neq x_1$ and y, $\Pr[k \leftarrow \mathcal{K} : h(x_0, k) \oplus h(x_1, k) = y] \leq \varepsilon_u$.

We need a special notion of almost regular functions when the key is divided into two sub-keys, i.e., $h : \mathcal{M} \times \mathcal{K}_a \times \mathcal{K}_b \to \mathcal{T}$. A hash function h is $(\varepsilon_a, \varepsilon_b)$-*almost regular* w.r.t. the sub-keys if for each data $x \in \mathcal{M}$, tag $y \in \mathcal{T}$ and sub-keys $\widehat{k}_a \in \mathcal{K}$, $\widehat{k}_b \in \mathcal{K}_b$, we have $\Pr[k_a \leftarrow \mathcal{K}_a : h(x, k_a, \widehat{k}_b) = y] \leq \varepsilon_a$ and $\Pr[k_b \leftarrow \mathcal{K}_b : h(x, \widehat{k}_a, k_b) = y] \leq \varepsilon_b$. In particular, $(\varepsilon_a, \varepsilon_b)$-almost regularity implies that the inequalities hold even if y is drawn from a distribution that is independent from k_a and k_b. Finally, a hash function h is ε_u-*almost universal w.r.t. the sub-key* k_a if for any two data $x_0 \neq x_1$ and $k_b, \widehat{k}_b \in \mathcal{K}_b$, we have $\Pr[k_a \leftarrow \mathcal{K} : h(x_0, k_a, k_b) = h(x_1, k_a, \widehat{k}_b)] \leq \varepsilon_u$. We say that h is *strongly* ε_u-*almost universal w.r.t. the sub-key* k_a if for any $(x_0, k_b) \neq (x_1, \widehat{k}_b)$, we have $\Pr[k_a \leftarrow \mathcal{K} : h(x_0, k_a, k_b) = h(x_1, k_a, \widehat{k}_b)] \leq \varepsilon_u$. Note that $\varepsilon_u, \varepsilon_a, \varepsilon_b \geq 1/|\mathcal{T}|$ and the word 'almost' is skipped in the definitions if the latter equality holds.

Commitment schemes. A commitment scheme $\mathcal{C}om$ is specified by a triple of algorithms (Gen, Com, Open). A setup algorithm Gen generates public parameters pk of the commitment scheme. The commitment function $\mathsf{Com}_{\mathsf{pk}} : \mathcal{M} \times \mathcal{R} \to \mathcal{C} \times \mathcal{D}$ transforms data $m \in \mathcal{M}$ into a commitment string c of fixed length and a decommitment value d. Usually $d = (m, r)$, where $r \in \mathcal{R}$ is the used randomness. Finally, correctly formed commitments can be opened, i.e., $\mathsf{Open}_{\mathsf{pk}}(c, d) = m$ for all $(c, d) = \mathsf{Com}_{\mathsf{pk}}(m, r)$. Incorrect decommitment values yield to a special abort value $\perp$. We often use a shorthand $\mathsf{Com}_{\mathsf{pk}}(m)$ to denote $\mathsf{Com}_{\mathsf{pk}}(m, r)$ with $r \leftarrow \mathcal{R}$. Basic properties of commitment

---

[2] We explicitly assume that adversarial code is executed on a universal Turing or RAM machine.

schemes are defined by hiding and binding games. A commitment scheme is (t, ε_1)-hiding if any t-time adversary A achieves advantage

$$\mathsf{Adv}^{\mathsf{hid}}_{Com}(A) = 2 \cdot \left| \Pr \left[\begin{array}{l} \mathsf{pk} \leftarrow \mathsf{Gen}, s \leftarrow \{0,1\}, (x_0, x_1, \sigma) \leftarrow A(\mathsf{pk}) \\ (c_s, d_s) \leftarrow \mathsf{Com}_{\mathsf{pk}}(x_s) : A(\sigma, c_s) = s \end{array} \right] - \frac{1}{2} \right| \leq \varepsilon_1 .$$

A commitment scheme is (t, ε_2)-binding if any t-time adversary A achieves advantage

$$\mathsf{Adv}^{\mathsf{bind}}_{Com}(A) = \Pr \left[\begin{array}{l} \mathsf{pk} \leftarrow \mathsf{Gen}, (c, d_0, d_1) \leftarrow A(\mathsf{pk}) : \\ \bot \neq \mathsf{Open}_{\mathsf{pk}}(c, d_0) \neq \mathsf{Open}_{\mathsf{pk}}(c, d_1) \neq \bot \end{array} \right] \leq \varepsilon_2 .$$

Non-malleable commitment schemes. Many notions of non-malleable commitments have been proposed in cryptographic literature [CIO98, FF00, DG03] starting from the seminal article [DDN91] by Dolev, Dwork and Naor. All these definitions try to capture requirements that are necessary to defeat man-in-the-middle attacks. We adopt the modernised version of [CIO98]—non-malleability w.r.t. opening. The definition is slightly weaker than the definition given in [DG03], as we assume that committed messages are independent from public parameters pk. Such choice allows to define non-malleability without a simulator similarly to the framework of non-malleable encryption [BS99].

Intuitively, a commitment scheme is non-malleable, if given a valid commitment c, it is infeasible to generate related commitments $c_1, \ldots, c_n$ that can be successfully opened after seeing a decommitment value d. Formally, an adversary is a quadruple $A = (A_1, A_2, A_3, A_4)$ of efficient algorithms where (A_1, A_2, A_3) represents an active part of the adversary that creates and afterwards tries to open related commitments and A_4 represents a distinguisher (sometimes referred as a target relation). The adversary succeeds if A_4 can distinguish between two environments World_0 (real world) and World_1 (environment where all adversaries are harmless). In both environments, Challenger computes $\mathsf{pk} \leftarrow \mathsf{Gen}$ and then interacts with adversary A:

1. Challenger sends pk to A_1 that outputs a description of an efficient message sampler MGen and a state σ_1. Then Challenger draws two independent samples $x_0 \leftarrow$ MGen, $x_1 \leftarrow$ MGen and computes a challenge commitment $(c, d) \leftarrow \mathsf{Com}_{\mathsf{pk}}(x_0)$.
2. Challenger sends c, σ_1 to A_2 that computes a state σ_2 and a commitment vector $(c_1, \ldots, c_n)$ with arbitrary length. If some $c_i = c$ then Challenger stops A with $\bot$.
3. Challenger sends d, σ_2 to A_3 that must produce a *valid* decommitment vector $(d_1, \ldots, d_n)$. More precisely, Challenger computes $y_i = \mathsf{Open}_{\mathsf{pk}}(c_i, d_i)$. If some $y_i = \bot$ then Challenger stops A with $\bot$.[3]
4. In World_0 Challenger invokes $A_4(x_0, y_1, \ldots, y_n, \sigma_2)$ with the correct sample x_0 whereas in World_1 Challenger invokes $A_4(x_1, y_1, \ldots, y_n, \sigma_2)$ with the sample x_1.

---

[3] The latter restriction is necessary, as otherwise A_3 can send n bits of information to A_4 by refusing to open some commitments. The same problem has been addressed [DG03] by requiring that behaviour of A_4 should not change if y_i is replaced with $\bot$. The latter is correct but somewhat cumbersome, as static program analysis of A_4 is undecidable in theory. Also, in a real life protocol a honest party always halts when $y_i = \bot$ as in our model.

Fig. 1. Three round manual authentication protocol

The working time of A is the total time taken to run $A_1, \ldots, A_4$ and MGen. A commitment scheme is (t, ε)-non-malleable iff for any t-time adversary A the advantage of distinguishing the two worlds is

$$\mathrm{Adv}^{nm}_{Com}(A) = |\Pr[A_4 = 0|\mathsf{World}_0] - \Pr[A_4 = 0|\mathsf{World}_1]| \leq \varepsilon .$$

The definition given above is natural in the concrete security framework, as it is conceptually clear and easy to apply. Also, the equivalence result between simulation and comparison based definition of non-malleable encryption [BS99] can be directly generalised.[4] Moreover, the definition of non-malleable encryption is stronger and therefore non-malleable encryption schemes (including CCA2 secure encryption schemes) can be used as non-malleable commitments provided that the public parameters pk are generated by the trusted party. See Sec. 5 for more detailed discussion.

3   Manual Data Authentication and Key Exchange Protocols

Formal security model. Consider a three round *manual cross-authentication* protocol for data (depicted in Fig. 1) where messages α, β, γ are routed via an active adversary Charlie who can drop, delay, modify and insert messages. A low bandwidth out-of-band channel between Alice and Bob is bidirectional and authentic, but Charlie can arbitrarily delay OOB messages. As communication is asynchronous, Charlie can arbitrarily reorder in-band messages, e.g., Bob can receive $\widehat{\alpha}$ from Charlie even before Alice has sent α. Throughout the article, the hatted messages are received from Charlie and subscripts a and b denote values Alice and Bob compute locally. In particular, r_a, r_b denote random coins and m_a, m_b input data of Alice and Bob. The desired common output is (m_a, m_b) if both parties reach accepting state.

We assume that Alice and Bob send two OOB messages $\mathrm{oob}_{a \to b}$ and $\mathrm{oob}_{b \to a}$ in a fixed order during the protocol. Additionally, we require that the OOB messages have been specified in such a way that either both Alice and Bob accept the output or neither of them does. Often, the second OOB message just indicates whether the sender reached the accepted state. Charlie succeeds in deception if at the end of the protocol Alice and Bob reach the accepting state but $(m_a, \widehat{m}_b) \neq (\widehat{m}_a, m_b)$. A protocol is *correct* if Alice and Bob always reach the accepting state when Charlie does not intervene.

---

[4] Substitutions in the definitions and proofs of [BS99] are straightforward, except that there is no decommitment oracle and an isolated sub-adversary A_3 has to compute decommitment values.

Let A be an adversarial algorithm used by Charlie. Then the advantage of A against data authentication protocol is defined as

$$\mathrm{Adv}^{\mathrm{forge}}(A) = \max_{m_a, m_b} \Pr\left[\text{Alice and Bob accept } (m_a, \widehat{m}_b) \neq (\widehat{m}_a, m_b)\right]$$

where probability is taken over random coins of A and the honest participants. An authentication protocol is (t, ε)-secure if for any t-time adversary A, $\mathrm{Adv}^{\mathrm{forge}}(A) \leq \varepsilon$. We use the same adversarial model for user-aided key exchange protocols. Here, the number of exchanged messages might be larger than three and the desired common output consists of a fresh key key and a unique session identifier sid. A key exchange protocol is (ε, t)-immune against active attacks if, for any t-time adversary A,

$$\mathrm{Adv}^{\mathrm{forge}}(A) = \Pr\left[\text{Alice and Bob accept } (\mathsf{sid}, \mathsf{key}_a) \neq (\mathsf{sid}, \mathsf{key}_b)\right] \leq \varepsilon \ .$$

A (ε, t)-immune key exchange protocol is secure when it can resist passive attacks: ε quantifies the maximal security drop against active compared to passive attacks.

Clearly, the protocol outcome is determined by the first OOB message. Moreover, for the ℓ-bit message there exists an efficient deception strategy that with $\mathrm{Adv}^{\mathrm{forge}}(A) = 2^{-\ell}$. A protocol family is *asymptotically optimal* if it is possible to choose sub-primitives so that security level reaches asymptotically $2^{-\ell}$, see App. B for further discussion.

Other authors [Vau05, PV06a, PV06b] have used more complex framework [BR93] to define security. Such approach is needed only if consecutive runs of authentication protocols are not statistically independent, i.e., protocols use long-lived authentication keys. In our case, all protocol runs are statistically independent, i.e., given m_a and m_b or sid, a potential adversary can always perfectly simulate all protocol messages. Therefore, our protocols are secure in any computational context, see App. A.

New protocol families. Our new construction for cross-authentication protocols covers all currently known asymptotically optimal protocol families: a construction given by Pasini and Vaudenay [PV06b] and our earlier results [LAN05]. The protocol is depicted in Fig. 2. We explicitly assume that all public parameters are generated correctly by a trusted authority, i.e., we assume the common reference string model. Such assumption is not farfetched, as almost all communication standards provide some public parameters, e.g., descriptions of hash functions.

Protocol

1. Alice computes $(c, d) \leftarrow \mathrm{Com}_{\mathsf{pk}}(k_a)$ for random $k_a \leftarrow \mathcal{K}_a$ and sends (m_a, c) to Bob.
2. Bob chooses random $k_b \leftarrow \mathcal{K}_b$ and sends (m_b, k_b) to Alice.
3. Alice sends d to Bob, who computes $k_a \leftarrow \mathrm{Open}_{\mathsf{pk}}(c, d)$ and halts if $k_a = \bot$.
   Both parties compute a test value $\mathsf{oob} = h(m_a \| m_b, k_a, k_b)$ from the received messages.
4. Both parties accept (m_a, m_b) iff the local ℓ-bit test values oob_a and oob_b coincide.

Specification: h is a keyed hash function with sub-keys k_a, k_b where $\mathcal{K}_a$ is a message space of commitment scheme. The hash function h and the public parameters pk of the commitment scheme are fixed and distributed by a trusted authority.

Fig. 2. Three round cross-authentication protocol Mana IV with ℓ-bit OOB messages

Protocol
1. Alice computes $(c, d) \leftarrow \mathsf{Com}_{\mathsf{pk}}(k_a)$ for $k_a = g^a, a \leftarrow \mathbb{Z}_q$ and sends (id_a, c) to Bob.
2. Bob computes $k_b = g^b$ for random $b \leftarrow \mathbb{Z}_q$ and sends (id_b, k_b) to Alice.
3. Alice sends d to Bob, who computes $k_a \leftarrow \mathsf{Open}_{\mathsf{pk}}(c, d)$ and halts if $k_a = \bot$.
   Both parties compute $\mathsf{sid} = (\mathsf{id}_a, \mathsf{id}_b)$ and $\mathsf{oob} = h(\mathsf{sid}, k_a, k_b)$ from the received messages.
4. Both parties accept $\mathsf{key} = (g^a)^b = (g^b)^a$ iff the ℓ-bit test values oob_a and oob_b coincide.

Specification: h is a keyed hash function with sub-keys $k_a, k_b \in G$ where $G = \langle g \rangle$ is a q element Decisional Diffie-Hellman group; G is a message space of commitment scheme. Public parameters pk and G are fixed and distributed by a trusted authority. Device identifiers id_a and id_b must be unique in time, for example, a device address followed by a session counter.

Fig. 3. Manually authenticated Diffie-Hellman protocol MA–DH with ℓ-bit OOB messages

The Bluetooth authentication mechanisms are undergoing the standardisation phase and the current proposal for the standard [BT06] includes an instantiation of Mana IV (NUMERIC COMPARISON) among other methods. Our security analysis provides the necessary theoretical validation (A more detailed discussion is given in Sec. 5).

One can use the Mana IV protocol to authenticate the transcript of the classical Diffie-Hellman key exchange and thus prevent active attacks. Another reasonable alternative, proposed by Zimmermann and Wireless-USB standard group, is to fuse both protocols into a single one (See Fig. 3). Such solution reduces the number of random bits and computational complexity. Both are scarce resources in small electronic devices. The MA–DH protocol does not directly correspond to these protocols, as it uses commitments to hide g^a whereas these practical protocols use a cryptographic hash function $\mathcal{H}$ instead and set $c = \mathcal{H}(g^a)$. As a result our security proofs do not directly apply for protocols [ZJC06, WUS06]. Still the results give a some insight and provide suggestions how to achieve provable security (See Sec. 5).

Related work. The protocols by Pasini and Vaudenay [PV06b, Fig. 2 and 4] do not directly follow the structure of Mana IV, since in their first message $\alpha = c$ where $(c, d) = \mathsf{Com}_{\mathsf{pk}}(m_a \| r_a)$ and $r_a \leftarrow \mathcal{K}_a$. In our security model, we can always assume that Charlie knows m_a, as m_a can be hardwired into the adversarial code. Therefore, if we send $\alpha = (m_a, c)$, the security level does not drop and sending m_a under the commitment becomes unnecessary. As the authenticated data m_a can be many kilobytes long, it also increases the message space for the commitment scheme. The latter can significantly decrease efficiency, as all currently known provably secure non-malleable commitment schemes are based on asymmetric cryptography.

A modified scheme with $(c, d) \leftarrow \mathsf{Com}_{\mathsf{pk}}(r_a)$ and $\alpha = (m_a, c)$ is a specific instance of Mana IV. We also note that in the security proofs of [Vau05, PV06b] it is assumed that the commitment is either a *simulation sound trapdoor commitment scheme* or a hiding one, even if adversary is allowed to query values for non-challenge commitments $c \neq c_s$. Both of these notions imply non-malleability [MY04], hence our assumptions are weaker. Moreover, in Sec. 4, we show that non-malleability of $\mathcal{C}om$ is also necessary, in a certain sense, to the security of the protocol. Finally, a secure fusion of [PV06b] and Diffie-Hellman key exchange similarly to MA–DH becomes problematic (See Sec. 5).

4   Security Analysis of Mana IV and MA–DH Protocols

The structure of Mana IV and MA–DH protocols forces adversary, Charlie, to fix data $\widehat{m}_a$ and $\widehat{m}_b$ before the complete hash key (k_a, k_b) becomes public. Hence, Charlie must either directly attack the hash function h or some property of commitment scheme to get extra knowledge about the hash key. A good message authentication code h provides security against simple substitution attacks and basic properties of commitment scheme along with non-malleability safeguard against more complex attacks.

Theorem 1 (Statistically binding commitments). *For any t, there exists $\tau = t + \mathcal{O}(1)$ such that if Com is (τ, ε_1)-hiding, ε_2-binding and (τ, ε_3)-non-malleable and h is $(\varepsilon_a, \varepsilon_b)$-almost regular and ε_u-almost universal w.r.t. the sub-key k_a then the Mana IV protocol is $(2\varepsilon_1 + 2\varepsilon_2 + \varepsilon_3 + \max\{\varepsilon_a, \varepsilon_b, \varepsilon_u\}, t)$-secure. If additionally h is also strongly ε_u-almost universal w.r.t. the sub-key k_a, then the MA–DH protocol is $(2\varepsilon_1 + 2\varepsilon_2 + \varepsilon_3 + \max\{\varepsilon_a, \varepsilon_b, \varepsilon_u\}, t)$-immune against active attacks.*

Theorem 2 (Computationally binding commitments). *For any t, there exists $\tau = 2t + \mathcal{O}(1)$ such that if Com is (τ, ε_1)-hiding, (τ, ε_2)-binding and (τ, ε_3)-non-malleable and h is $(\varepsilon_a, \varepsilon_b)$-almost regular and ε_u-almost universal w.r.t. the sub-key k_a then the Mana IV protocol is $(2\varepsilon_1 + \varepsilon_2 + \sqrt{\varepsilon_2} + \varepsilon_3 + \max\{\varepsilon_a, \varepsilon_b, \varepsilon_u\}, t)$-secure. If additionally h is also strongly ε_u-almost universal w.r.t. the sub-key k_a, then the MA–DH protocol is $(2\varepsilon_1 + \varepsilon_2 + \sqrt{\varepsilon_2} + \varepsilon_3 + \max\{\varepsilon_a, \varepsilon_b, \varepsilon_u\}, t)$-immune against active attacks.*

Proof. For clarity, the proof is split into Lemmata 1–5, as all (including passive) attacks can be divided into four disjoint classes. Combining the corresponding upper bounds on success probabilities proves the claims. □

Theorems 1 and 2 have several noteworthy implications. First, the Mana IV and MA–DH protocols are indeed asymptotically optimal, see Def. 1 in App. B, as one can choose h such that $\max\{\varepsilon_a, \varepsilon_b, \varepsilon_u\} = 2^{-\ell}$ and under standard complexity assumptions there exist commitment schemes where $\varepsilon_1, \varepsilon_2, \varepsilon_3$ are negligible w.r.t. the security parameter if allowed working time τ is polynomial. Secondly, statistically binding commitments give better security guarantee than computationally binding ones: ε_2 vs. $\sqrt{\varepsilon_2}$. The latter is caused by the "non-trivial" reduction technique in Lemma 5. Thirdly, the slight difference in security objectives of Mana IV and MA–DH protocol manifests itself as an extra requirement to h. This is quite natural: if $m_a = \widehat{m}_a, m_b = \widehat{m}_b$ but $(k_a, \widehat{k}_b) \neq (\widehat{k}_a, k_b)$, we get a correct output for Mana IV but incorrect output for MA–DH, as $\mathsf{sid}_a = \mathsf{sid}_b$ but $\mathsf{key}_a \neq \mathsf{key}_b$. Finally, if Decisional Diffie-Hellman assumption holds for G, then MA–DH is approximately $2^{-\ell}$ secure key exchange protocol.

We give a formal security proof of Mana IV and MA–DH by constructing black box reductions corresponding to four different attack types. These reductions have the following structure: given an adversary A that is good in deception, we construct an adversary A^* that breaks some property of the commitment scheme. Generic construction of A^* is depicted on Fig. 4: in order to win a security game A^* simulates the original protocol and communicates with Challenger. As the communication is asynchronous, A can reorder protocol messages α, β, γ. Let $\mathsf{msg}_1 \prec \mathsf{msg}_2$ denote that msg_1 was output on a communication channel before msg_2. As Alice and Bob are honest, temporal restrictions $\alpha \prec \widehat{\beta} \prec \gamma$ and $\widehat{\alpha} \prec \beta \prec \widehat{\gamma}$ hold for all executions.

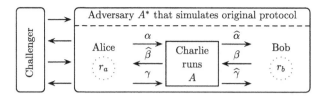

Fig. 4. Generic reduction scheme

An execution path is almost normal (denoted as norm) if the second round is completed before A starts the third round, i.e., $\alpha, \widehat{\alpha}, \beta, \widehat{\beta} \prec \gamma, \widehat{\gamma}$. Otherwise, one of the mutually exclusive events $\gamma \prec \beta$ or $\widehat{\gamma} \prec \widehat{\beta}$ must occur. For brevity, let d-forge denote that Alice and Bob accept $(m_a, \widehat{m}_b) \neq (\widehat{m}_a, m_b)$ in the Mana IV protocol and k-forge denote that Alice and Bob accept $(\mathrm{id}_a, \widehat{\mathrm{id}}_b, \mathrm{key}_a) \neq (\widehat{\mathrm{id}}_a, \mathrm{id}_b, \mathrm{key}_b)$ in the MA–DH protocol. Note that all probabilities in Lemmata 1–5 are taken over random coins of Gen, A and Alice and Bob and for a fixed input data (m_a, m_b) or identifiers $(\mathrm{id}_a, \mathrm{id}_b)$. As all proofs are quite straightforward but tedious, only the proof of Lemma 1 covers all details. All other proofs are more compact: some elementary steps are left to the reader.

Attacks based on almost normal execution paths. In the simplest attack, Charlie attacks directly h by altering only m_a, m_b, k_b and possibly γ. Charlie's aim here is to cleverly choose $\widehat{k}_b$ so that $\mathrm{oob}_a = \mathrm{oob}_b$. An attack where $k_b \neq \widehat{k}_b$ but other messages are unaltered can be successful against MA–DH but not against Mana IV. Strong ε_u-universality w.r.t the sub-key k_a provides appropriate protection against such attacks.

Lemma 1. *For any t, there exists $\tau = t + \mathcal{O}(1)$ such that if Com is (τ, ε_1)-hiding and (τ, ε_2)-binding and h is ε_u-almost universal w.r.t. the sub-key k_a, then for any t-time adversary A and input data (m_a, m_b)*

$$\Pr\left[\text{d-forge} \wedge \text{norm} \wedge c = \widehat{c}\right] \leq \varepsilon_u \cdot \Pr\left[\text{norm} \wedge c = \widehat{c}\right] + \varepsilon_1 + \varepsilon_2 \ . \tag{1}$$

If additionally h is strongly ε_u-almost universal w.r.t. the sub-key k_a, then for any pair of identifiers $(\mathrm{id}_a, \mathrm{id}_b)$

$$\Pr\left[\text{k-forge} \wedge \text{norm} \wedge c = \widehat{c}\right] \leq \varepsilon_u \cdot \Pr\left[\text{norm} \wedge c = \widehat{c}\right] + \varepsilon_1 + \varepsilon_2 \ . \tag{2}$$

Proof. ANALYSIS OF MANA IV. Assume a t-time algorithm A violates (1). Then $\Pr\left[\text{d-forge} \wedge \text{norm} \wedge c = \widehat{c} \wedge k_a = \widehat{k}_a\right] \geq \Pr\left[\text{d-forge} \wedge \text{norm} \wedge c = \widehat{c}\right] - \varepsilon_2$, or otherwise Alice and A together can open the commitment c to two different values $k_a \neq \widehat{k}_a$ with probability more than ε_2. The latter contradicts (τ, ε_2)-binding for $\tau = t + \mathcal{O}(1)$.

Next, we construct A^* that wins the hiding game, i.e., given pk outputs (x_0, x_1, σ) and afterwards given a commitment c_s for $s \leftarrow \{0, 1\}$, can correctly guess the bit s. The adversary A^* acts in the following way:

1. Given pk, chooses $k_a, k_a^* \leftarrow \mathcal{K}_a$ as (x_0, x_1) and sends $(k_a, k_a^*, \mathrm{pk})$ to Challenger.

2. When Challenger replies c_s for $(c_s, d_s) = \mathsf{Com}_{\mathsf{pk}}(x_s)$, A^* simulates a faithful execution of Mana IV with $\alpha = (m_a, c_s)$ until A queries γ. A^* stops the simulation and halts with $\bot$, if there is a protocol failure, $\neg\mathsf{norm}$ or $c \neq \hat{c}$.

3. If $h(m_a \| \widehat{m}_b, k_a, \widehat{k}_b) = h(\widehat{m}_a \| m_b, k_a, k_b)$ and $(m_a, \widehat{m}_b) \neq (\widehat{m}_a, m_b)$ outputs a guess $s = 0$, else outputs a guess $s = 1$.

Now, consider when the simulation diverges from the real run of Mana IV with the same randomness r_a and r_b. If $s = 0$ then $(c_0, d_0) = \mathsf{Com}_{\mathsf{pk}}(k_a)$ and Step 3 does not reflect the protocol outcome in three disjoint cases: (a) abnormal execution or $c \neq \hat{c}$, (b) $\hat{\gamma}$ is not a valid decommitment (d-forge does not happen) and (c) $k_a \neq \widehat{k}_a$. Therefore, we get $\Pr[A^* = 0|s = 0] \geq \Pr[\text{d-forge} \wedge \mathsf{norm} \wedge c = \hat{c} \wedge k_a = \widehat{k}_a]$. For $s = 1$, we get $\Pr[A^* \neq \bot|s = 1] = \Pr[\mathsf{norm} \wedge c = \hat{c}]$, as simulation is perfect until A queries γ. Since c_1 and k_a are statistically independent, all values computed by A are independent from k_a and thus $\Pr[A^* = 0|s = 1, A^* \neq \bot] \leq \varepsilon_u$. We arrive at a contradiction, as these bounds imply $\mathsf{Adv}^{\mathsf{hid}}(A^*) = |\Pr[A^* = 0|s = 0] - \Pr[A^* = 0|s = 1]| > \varepsilon_1$ and A^* runs in time $t + \mathcal{O}(1)$.

ANALYSIS OF MA–DH. Lets update only the forgery test in the last step of A^*:

3. If $h(\mathsf{id}_a \| \widehat{\mathsf{id}}_b, k_a, \widehat{k}_b) = h(\widehat{\mathsf{id}}_a \| \mathsf{id}_b, k_a, k_b)$ and $(\mathsf{id}_a, \widehat{\mathsf{id}}_b, \widehat{k}_b) \neq (\widehat{\mathsf{id}}_a, \mathsf{id}_b, k_b)$ output a guess $s = 0$, else output a guess $s = 1$.

Similarly to Mana IV, $\Pr[A^* = 0|s = 0] \geq \Pr[\text{k-forge} \wedge \mathsf{norm} \wedge c = \hat{c} \wedge k_a = \widehat{k}_a]$ and $\Pr[A^* \neq \bot|s = 1] = \Pr[\mathsf{norm} \wedge c = \hat{c}]$, since the remaining code of A^* is identical. The new forgery test forces a restriction $(x_0, k_b) \neq (x_1, \widehat{k}_b)$ instead of $x_0 \neq x_1$ and we need strongly ε_u-universal h to bound $\Pr[A^* = 0|s = 1, A^* \neq \bot] \leq \varepsilon_u$. $\square$

Note 1. Strong ε_u-universality is necessary for the security of the MA–DH protocol, see Sec. 5 for a concrete counter example.

Another alternative is a direct attack against non-malleability where A tries to create "cleverly" related sub-keys k_a and $\widehat{k}_a$ to bypass the security check.

Lemma 2. *For any t, there exists $\tau = t + \mathcal{O}(1)$ such that if Com is (τ, ε_3)-non-malleable and h is $(\varepsilon_a, \varepsilon_b)$-almost regular, then for any t-time adversary A and inputs (m_a, m_b) or session identifier $(\mathsf{id}_a, \mathsf{id}_b)$*

$$\Pr[\text{d-forge} \wedge \mathsf{norm} \wedge c \neq \hat{c}] \leq \varepsilon_a \cdot \Pr[\mathsf{norm} \wedge c \neq \hat{c}] + \varepsilon_3 , \qquad (3)$$

$$\Pr[\text{k-forge} \wedge \mathsf{norm} \wedge c \neq \hat{c}] \leq \varepsilon_a \cdot \Pr[\mathsf{norm} \wedge c \neq \hat{c}] + \varepsilon_3 . \qquad (4)$$

Proof. Let A be a t-time algorithm that violates (3). Then we can build an adversary $A^* = (A_1^*, A_2^*, A_3^*, A_4^*)$ that can break non-malleability of the commitment scheme:

1. Given pk, A_1^* outputs a uniform sampler over $\mathcal{K}_a$ and a state $\sigma_1 = (\mathsf{pk}, m_a, m_b)$. Challenger computes $x_0, x_1 \leftarrow \mathcal{K}_a$ and $(c, d) \leftarrow \mathsf{Com}_{\mathsf{pk}}(x_0)$.

2. Given c, σ_1, A_2^* simulates the protocol with $k_b \leftarrow \mathcal{K}_b$ and stops before A demands γ. A^* stops the simulation and halts with $\bot$, if there is a protocol failure, $\neg\mathsf{norm}$ or $c = \hat{c}$. Otherwise, A_2^* outputs a commitment $\hat{c}$ and σ_2 containing enough information to resume the simulation including $(m_a, \widehat{m}_a, m_b, \widehat{m}_b, k_b, \widehat{k}_b)$.

3. Given d, σ_2, A_3^* resumes the simulation and outputs $\widehat{d}$ as a decommitment value.
4. If A_3^* was successful in opening $\widehat{c}$ then $A_4^*(x_s, y, \sigma_2)$ sets $k_a \leftarrow x_s$ and $\widehat{k}_a \leftarrow y$ and computes $\mathrm{oob}_a = h(m_a \| \widehat{m}_b, k_a, \widehat{k}_b)$ and $\mathrm{oob}_b = h(\widehat{m}_a \| m_b, \widehat{k}_a, k_b)$. If $\mathrm{oob}_a = \mathrm{oob}_b$ but $(m_a, \widehat{m}_b) \neq (\widehat{m}_a, m_b)$, then A_4^* outputs a guess $s = 0$, else outputs 1.

Again, consider where the simulation can diverge from the real execution of Mana IV. In both worlds, we can have a discrepancy if execution is abnormal or $c = \widehat{c}$. In World_0, Step 4 provides a perfect simulation whereas in World_1 k_a is independent of all variables computed by A. Therefore, using same methodology as before

$$\Pr[A_4^* = 0 | \mathrm{World}_0] = \Pr[\text{d-forge} \wedge \text{norm} \wedge c \neq \widehat{c}] \ ,$$
$$\Pr[A_4^* = 0 | \mathrm{World}_1] \leq \varepsilon_a \cdot \Pr[\text{norm} \wedge c \neq \widehat{c}],$$

as h is $(\varepsilon_a, \varepsilon_b)$-almost regular. A contradiction as $\mathrm{Adv}^{\mathrm{nm}}(A^*) > \varepsilon_3$. For the MA–DH protocol, we have to refine the forgery test in Step 4 similarly to the proof of Lemma 1, but otherwise the analysis is exactly the same.   □

Note 2. Obviously, non-malleability w.r.t. every target relation is not necessary. In particular, if h is fixed then it is necessary and sufficient that *Com* is secure for all adversaries having the same structure as in Lemma 2. The latter requirement is weaker than complete non-malleability, however, one has to reconsider the condition if h is substituted with a different function and technically such condition is not easier to prove.

Attacks based on abnormal execution paths. The remaining two attack patterns are easy to analyse, since they are direct attacks against binding and hiding properties. If $\widehat{\gamma} \prec \widehat{\beta}$ then successful A can predict k_a given only c and thus win the hiding game.

Lemma 3. *For any t there exists $\tau = t + \mathcal{O}(1)$ such that if Com is (τ, ε_1)-hiding, h is $(\varepsilon_a, \varepsilon_b)$-almost regular. Then for any t-time adversary A and input (m_a, m_b) or session identifier $(\mathrm{id}_a, \mathrm{id}_b)$*

$$\Pr[\text{d-forge} \wedge \widehat{\gamma} \prec \widehat{\beta}] \leq \varepsilon_1 + \varepsilon_a \cdot \Pr[\widehat{\gamma} \prec \widehat{\beta}] \ , \tag{5}$$
$$\Pr[\text{k-forge} \wedge \widehat{\gamma} \prec \widehat{\beta}] \leq \varepsilon_1 + \varepsilon_a \cdot \Pr[\widehat{\gamma} \prec \widehat{\beta}] \ . \tag{6}$$

Proof. Let A be a t-time adversary that violates (5). If $\widehat{\gamma} \prec \widehat{\beta}$, the Bob's control value oob_b is fixed before A receives γ. Consider A^* that plays the hiding game:

1. Given pk, chooses $k_a, k_a^* \leftarrow \mathcal{K}_a$ as (x_0, x_1) and sends $(k_a, k_a^*, \mathrm{pk})$ to Challenger.
2. When Challenger replies c_s for $(c_s, d_s) = \mathrm{Com}_{\mathrm{pk}}(x_s)$, A^* simulates a faithful execution of Mana IV with $\alpha = (m_a, c_s)$ until A outputs $\widehat{\beta}$. A^* stops the simulation and halts with $\bot$, if there is a protocol failure, $\widehat{\gamma} \not\prec \widehat{\beta}$ or $\mathrm{Open}_{\mathrm{pk}}(\widehat{c}, \widehat{d}) = \bot$.
3. Next A^* computes $\widehat{k}_a = \mathrm{Open}_{\mathrm{pk}}(\widehat{c}, \widehat{d})$, $\mathrm{oob}_a = h(m_a \| \widehat{m}_b, k_a, \widehat{k}_b)$ and $\mathrm{oob}_b = h(\widehat{m}_a \| m_b, \widehat{k}_a, k_b)$. If $\mathrm{oob}_a = \mathrm{oob}_b$ and $(m_a, \widehat{m}_b) \neq (\widehat{m}_a, m_b)$ outputs 0, else 1.

Again, consider where the simulation can diverge from the real protocol. If $s = 0$ then only $\widehat{\gamma} \not\prec \widehat{\beta}$ can cause the difference. For $s = 1$, simulation is perfect until γ is queried and thus $\Pr[A^* \neq \perp | s = 1] = \Pr[\widehat{\gamma} \prec \widehat{\beta}]$. As k_a is independent from oob_b, $\widehat{m}_b$ and $\widehat{k}_b$, then $\Pr[A^* = 0 | s = 1, A^* \neq \perp] \leq \varepsilon_a$ follows from $(\varepsilon_a, \varepsilon_b)$-almost regularity. A contradiction, as $\text{Adv}^{\text{hid}}(A^*) > \Pr[\text{d-forge} \wedge \widehat{\gamma} \prec \widehat{\beta}] - \varepsilon_a \cdot \Pr[\widehat{\gamma} \prec \widehat{\beta}] > \varepsilon_1$. Same algorithm with a redefined forgery check is suitable for the MA–DH protocol. $\qquad\square$

To win the remaining case $\gamma \prec \beta$, adversary A must double open $\widehat{c}$ to succeed. For statistically binding commitments, the reduction is simple. Analysis of computational binding commitments is more complex.

Lemma 4. *If* Com *is statistically* ε_2-*binding and* h *is* $(\varepsilon_a, \varepsilon_b)$-*almost regular, then for any adversary* A *and input* (m_a, m_b) *or session identifier* $(\text{id}_a, \text{id}_b)$

$$\Pr[\text{d-forge} \wedge \gamma \prec \beta] \leq \varepsilon_2 + \varepsilon_b \cdot \Pr[\gamma \prec \beta] \ , \tag{7}$$

$$\Pr[\text{k-forge} \wedge \gamma \prec \beta] \leq \varepsilon_2 + \varepsilon_b \cdot \Pr[\gamma \prec \beta] \ . \tag{8}$$

Proof. For each commitment $\widehat{c}$, fix a canonical $\widehat{k}_a$ such that $\widehat{k}_a = \text{Open}_{\text{pk}}(\widehat{c}, \widehat{d}_0)$ for some $\widehat{d}_0$. If $\gamma \prec \beta$ then oob_a is fixed before k_b. Now, the probability that different k_b values lead to different valid openings $\widehat{k}_a' \neq \widehat{k}_a$ is at most ε_2. Otherwise, one can find valid double openings $\text{Open}_{\text{pk}}(\widehat{c}, \widehat{d}_0) \neq \text{Open}_{\text{pk}}(\widehat{c}, \widehat{d}_1)$ just by enumerating all possible protocol runs. Now $\Pr[k_b \leftarrow \mathcal{K} : \text{oob}_a = h(\widehat{m}_a || m_b, \widehat{k}_a, k_b)] \leq \varepsilon_b$, as k_b is independent form $\widehat{k}_a$ and oob_a and thus both claims follow. $\qquad\square$

Lemma 5. *For any* t *there exists* $\tau = 2t + \mathcal{O}(1)$ *such that if* Com *is* (τ, ε_2)-*binding and* h *is* $(\varepsilon_a, \varepsilon_b)$-*almost regular, then for any* t-*time adversary* A *and inputs* (m_a, m_b)

$$\Pr[\text{d-forge} \wedge \gamma \prec \beta] \leq \varepsilon_b \cdot \Pr[\gamma \prec \beta] + \sqrt{\varepsilon_2} \ , \tag{9}$$

$$\Pr[\text{k-forge} \wedge \gamma \prec \beta] \leq \varepsilon_b \cdot \Pr[\gamma \prec \beta] + \sqrt{\varepsilon_2} \ . \tag{10}$$

Proof. Let A be a t-time adversary that violates (9). Consider A^* that

1. Simulates protocol run until A queries β and stores $\widehat{c}$. Halts if $\gamma \not\prec \beta$.
2. Provides $k_b^0, k_b^1 \leftarrow \mathcal{K}_b$ and outputs $\widehat{c}$ with the corresponding replies $\widehat{d}_0$ and $\widehat{d}_1$.

For a fixed pk and $\widehat{c}$, let $\varepsilon_{\text{pk},\widehat{c}} = \Pr[\text{d-forge} | \gamma \prec \beta, \text{pk}, \widehat{c}]$ denote the forgery probability w.r.t. a single challenge k_b at Step 2 and

$$\delta_{\text{pk},\widehat{c}} = \Pr[\perp \neq \text{Open}_{\text{pk}}(\widehat{c}, \widehat{d}_0) \neq \text{Open}_{\text{pk}}(\widehat{c}, \widehat{d}_1) \neq \perp | \gamma \prec \beta, \text{pk}, \widehat{c}]$$

the success probability at Step 2. Then $\delta_{\text{pk},\widehat{c}} \geq \varepsilon_{\text{pk},\widehat{c}}(\varepsilon_{\text{pk},\widehat{c}} - \varepsilon_b)$, since h is $(\varepsilon_a, \varepsilon_b)$-almost regular and oob_b^0 is fixed before k_b^1. Using a special case of Jensen's inequality, $\text{E}(X^2) \geq \text{E}(X)^2$ for any distribution of X, we get

$$\Pr[\text{success} | \gamma \prec \beta] = \sum_{\text{pk},\widehat{c}} \Pr[\text{pk} = \text{Gen}, \widehat{c} | \gamma \prec \beta] \, (\varepsilon_{\text{pk},\widehat{c}}^2 - \varepsilon_b \varepsilon_{\text{pk},\widehat{c}})$$

$$\geq \Pr[\text{d-forge} | \gamma \prec \beta]^2 - \varepsilon_b \Pr[\text{d-forge} | \gamma \prec \beta] \ .$$

As $\Pr[\text{d-forge} | \gamma \prec \beta] > \varepsilon_b$, we get $\Pr[\text{success} | \gamma \prec \beta] \geq (\Pr[\text{d-forge} | \gamma \prec \beta] - \varepsilon_b)^2$. Now from $\Pr[\gamma \prec \beta] \geq \Pr[\gamma \prec \beta]^2$, we obtain a contradiction

$$\text{Adv}^{\text{bind}}(A^*) \geq \Pr[\gamma \prec \beta]^2 \, (\Pr[\text{d-forge} | \gamma \prec \beta] - \varepsilon_b)^2 > \varepsilon_2 \ .$$

The same proof is valid also for the MA–DH protocol. $\qquad\square$

Note 3. There are several alternatives to Lemma 5 that offer various tradeoffs between time τ and ε_2 depending how many times A is probed with different values of k_b. As A may totally break the Mana IV protocol on ε_2 fraction public parameters pk and do nothing for other values of pk, we cannot get a better bound than $\Pr\left[\text{d-forge} \wedge \gamma \prec \beta\right] \leq \varepsilon_b \cdot \Pr\left[\gamma \prec \beta\right] + \varepsilon_2$ with black-box reductions. In our earlier work [LAN05], we used knowledge extraction techniques to obtain more complex reductions.

Note 4. Compared to proofs in [Vau05, PV06b] Lemma 5 seems to be inefficient and cumbersome. However, Vaudenay et al uses a different notion of binding—de facto they postulate Lemma 5 for a certain h as a security requirement. In asymptotic sense these notions are equivalent (there are polynomial reduction between them), but the exact security framework reveals that their condition is quantitatively much stronger.

In practical applications, commitments are constructed from cryptographic hash functions like SHA-1 and classical binding is more appropriate notion, since it leads directly to collision resistance. Secondly, Vaudenay's approach does not generalise for more complex constructions of h.

5   Practical Implementation Details

Security constraints. Mana IV and MA–DH protocols are secure in any computational context if (a) random values are never reused, (b) protocol outputs are never used before reaching the accepting state, (c) there are no multiple protocol instances between the *same* device pair at any time. Then a single protocol instance has same security guarantees as in Theorems 1 and 2. See App. A for a formal proof and discussion.

Hash functions. To instantiate Mana IV and MA–DH protocols, we need hash functions $h : \mathcal{M} \times \mathcal{K}_a \times \mathcal{K}_b \to \{0,1\}^\ell$ that are $(\varepsilon_a, \varepsilon_b)$-almost regular and (strongly) ε_u-almost universal w.r.t. the sub-key k_a. In our preliminary work [LAN05], we proposed a construction $h(m, k_a, k_b) = h_0(m, f(k_a, k_b))$ where h_0 is a ε_u-almost universal and ε_a-regular and $f : \mathcal{K}_a \times \mathcal{K}_b \to \{0,1\}^m$ is regular w.r.t. sub-keys k_a, k_b and for any $k_b \neq \widehat{k}_b$ the distribution of pairs $(f(k_a, k_b), f(k_a, \widehat{k}_b))$ for $k_a \leftarrow \mathcal{K}_a$ is statistically δ-close to uniform distribution. Then it is straightforward to verify that h is $(\varepsilon_a, \varepsilon_a)$-almost regular and $\max\{\varepsilon_a + \delta, \varepsilon_u\}$-almost universal, since for $k_b \neq \widehat{k}_b$ keys $f(k_a, k_b)$ are $f(k_a, \widehat{k}_b)$ almost independent.

As a concrete example let $f : \{0,1\}^{2m} \times \{0,1\}^{2m} \to \{0,1\}^m$ be defined as follows: $f(x_0 \| x_1, y) = x_0 y \oplus x_1$ in $\mathrm{GF}(2^m)$ if $x_0 \neq 0$ and $f(0^m \| x_1, y) = x_1 \oplus y$ otherwise. Clearly, f is regular w.r.t. the sub-keys and $f(x_0, x_1, y_1) \oplus f(x_0, x_1, y_2) = x_0(y_1 \oplus y_2)$ covers $\mathrm{GF}(2^m) \setminus \{0\}$ when $y_1 \neq y_2$ and $x_0 \neq 0$. Hence, f is $(\varepsilon_a, \varepsilon_a)$-almost regular and $\max\{2^{-m+1} + \varepsilon_a, \varepsilon_u\}$-secure. Note that for proper choice of m, $2^{-m+1} \ll 2^{-\ell}$.

Pasini et al., [PV06b] proposed a construction $h(m, k_a, k_b) = h_0(m, k_a) \oplus k_b$ where h_0 is ε_u-almost XOR universal and ε_a-almost regular w.r.t. k_a. The latter is $(\varepsilon_a, 2^{-\ell})$-almost regular and strongly ε_u-almost universal. But such construction cannot be used in the MA–DH protocol, as k_b is typically at least 200 bits long. If we compress k_b in some manner, i.e., compute $h(m_a \| m_b, k_a, k_b) = h_0(m_a \| m_b, k_a) \oplus h_1(m_b, k_b)$ then the resulting hash function is only ε_u-almost universal. A malicious adversary can choose

$(m_b, k_b) \neq (m_b, \widehat{k}_b)$ such that $h_1(m_b, k_b) = h_1(m_b, \widehat{k}_b)$. Since ℓ is small in practical protocols, such pair can be found in real time and Charlie can indeed break the MA–DH protocol by choosing $\widehat{k}_b = g^c$ for $c \leftarrow \mathbb{Z}_q$ in this way. As a result Charlie and Alice share a common key. If Bob is a wireless router, then Charlie has successfully completed the attack, as he can transfer Alice's communication to Bob using secure channel between himself and Bob. Hence, the proper choice of h is extremely important.

For practical purposes $\mathcal{M} = \{0, 1\}^{512}$ is sufficiently big, as one can always use a collision resistant hash functions to compress longer messages. And for such parameters many efficient ε_u-almost (XOR) universal and perfect hash functions are known with $\varepsilon_u \leq 2^{-\ell+1}$ (See [Sti91, BJKS93, NGR05] for some concrete examples).

Some practical proposals [BT06, p. 13, 21] propose use cryptographic hash functions to construct h. The latter is a plausible though heuristic choice, as long as statistical tests do not reveal a significant deviation from desired parameters $\varepsilon_a, \varepsilon_b, \varepsilon_u$. Otherwise, the potential adversary can discover and exploit these weaknesses.

Non-malleable commitment schemes. The simplest construction of a non-malleable commitment scheme is based on a CCA2 secure encryption scheme. Let $\mathsf{Enc}_{\mathsf{pk}} : \mathcal{M} \times \mathcal{R} \to \mathcal{C}$ be a deterministic encryption rule where $r \in \mathcal{R}$ denotes randomness used to encrypt a message. Define $(c, d) \leftarrow \mathsf{Com}_{\mathsf{pk}}(x, r)$ as $c = \mathsf{Enc}_{\mathsf{pk}}(x, r)$ and $d = (x, r)$ and $\mathsf{Open}_{\mathsf{pk}}(c, d) = m$ if $\mathsf{Enc}_{\mathsf{pk}}(x, r) = c$ and $\perp$ otherwise. Then the corresponding commitment scheme is non-malleable provided that pk is generated by a trusted party. We suggest Cramer-Shoup or Desmedt-Kurosawa encryption schemes [CS98, KD04], as the public key is a random tuple of group elements and can be easily generated without the secret key. RSA-OAEP is also CCA2 secure in a random oracle model [FOPS01]. Nevertheless, the key pk must be securely distributed, since *a priori* non-malleability w.r.t. pk does not guarantee non-malleability w.r.t. related keys pk_1 and pk_2.

All these constructions are *too inefficient* for small electronic devices and they offer too high levels of security. Recall that $\ell \lesssim 14$ and thus a commitment scheme should be roughly $(2^{80}, 2^{-20})$-non-malleable. Secure distribution of pk is another problem. In principle, it can be managed as there is only single public key, but may still not be well accepted for industrial applications. There are commitment schemes that are non-malleable without commonly shared pk, but these are very inefficient in practice.

In reality, a cryptographic hash functions like SHA-1 are used instead of commitments, as such constructions are hundred times faster and there are no setup assumptions. Let $\mathcal{H}$ be a collision resistant hash function. Then the hash commitment is computed as $(c, d) \leftarrow \mathsf{Com}(x, r)$ with $c = \mathcal{H}(x||r)$ and $d = (x, r)$ or, as in HMAC, $c = \mathcal{H}(r \oplus \mathsf{opad}||\mathcal{H}(r \oplus \mathsf{ipad}||x))$ with $d = r$ (See [BT06, p. 13] as an example). Both constructions are *a priori* not hiding. We would like to have a provably secure construction. In theory, we could use one-wayness of $\mathcal{H}$ and define commitment with hard-core bits but this leads to large commitments. Instead, we use Bellare-Rogaway random oracle design principle to heuristically argue that a hash commitment based on the OAEP padding is a better alternative. Recall that the OAEP padding is $c = \mathcal{H}(s, t), s = (x||0^{k_0}) \oplus g(r), t = r \oplus f(s)$. The corresponding commitment c along with $d = r$ is provably hiding and binding if g is pseudorandom, f is random oracle, and $\mathcal{H}$ is collision resistant. A priori SHA-1 and SHA-512 are not known to be non-malleable, as it has never been a design goal. On the other hand, the security proof of OAEP [FOPS01] shows CCA2 security (non-malleability) provided that $\mathcal{H}$ is a partial-domain one-way permutation. More specifically, it should be infeasible to find s given $h(s, t)$, $s \leftarrow \mathcal{M}_1, t \leftarrow \mathcal{M}_2$. The partial one-wayness follows for $r, t \in \{0, 1\}^{80}$ if we assume that $\mathcal{H}$ is at least $(2^{160}, 2^{-20})$-collision resistant as we can enumerate all possible t values to get a collision. The other assumption that h is a permutation is important in the proof. Therefore, we can only *conjecture* that the proof can be generalised and the OAEP padding provides a non-malleable commitment scheme.

Hence, an important theoretical task is to provide efficient but provably hiding and non-malleable but efficient padding construction for hash commitments. Also, one could reprove Lemma 1 and Lemma 3 without assuming hiding from $\mathcal{C}om$, as in both proofs we do not need hiding of k_a but just Charlie's inability to control Alice's oob_a. Practical implementations [ZJC06, WUS06] of the MA–DH protocol use $c = \mathcal{H}(g^a)$ and such a relaxed security proof would bridge the gap between theory and practice.

Acknowledgements. We would like to thank N. Asokan for joint work on the initial solution and for many useful discussions and comments, and Emilia Käsper for helpful suggestions. The first author was partially supported by the Finnish Academy of Sciences and Estonian Doctoral School in Information and Communication Technologies.

References

[BJKS93] J. Bierbrauer, T. Johansson, G. Kabatianskii, and B. Smeets. On families of hash functions via geometric codes and concatenation. In *Proc. of CRYPTO '93*, LNCS 773. Springer, 1993.

[BM92]   S. Bellovin and M. Merrit. Encrypted Key Exchange: Password-Based Protocols Secure Against Dictionary Attacks. In *Proc. of the IEEE Symposium on Security and Privacy*, pages 72–84, 1992.

[BR93]   Mihir Bellare and Phillip Rogaway. Entity Authentication and Key Distribution. In *Proc. of CRYPTO '93*, LNCS 773, pages 232–249. Springer, 1993.

[BS99]   Mihir Bellare and Amit Sahai. Non-malleable Encryption: Equivalence between Two Notions, and an Indistinguishability-Based Characterization. In *Proc. of CRYPTO '99*, LNCS 1666, pages 519–536. Springer, 1999.

[BT06]   Bluetooth Special Interest Group. Simple Pairing Whitepaper (Revision V10r00). http://www.bluetooth.com/Bluetooth/Apply/Technology/ Research/Simple_Pairing.htm, 2006.

[CCH06]   M. Cagalj, S. Capkun, and J.-P. Hubaux. Key agreement in peer-to-peer wireless networks. *Proc. of the IEEE*, 94(2):467–478, Feb 2006.

[CIO98]   Giovanni Di Crescenzo, Yuval Ishai, and Rafail Ostrovsky. Non-interactive and non-malleable commitment. In *STOC '98*, pages 141–150, 1998.

[CS98]   Ronald Cramer and Victor Shoup. A Practical Public Key Cryptosystem Provably Secure Against Adaptive Chosen Ciphertext Attack. In *Proc. of CRYPTO '98*, LNCS 1462, pages 13–25. Springer, 1998.

[DDN91]   Danny Dolev, Cynthia Dwork, and Moni Naor. Non-malleable cryptography. In *STOC '91*, pages 542–552, New York, NY, USA, 1991. ACM Press.

[DG03]   Ivan Damgård and Jens Groth. Non-interactive and reusable non-malleable commitment schemes. In *STOC 2003*, pages 426–437, 2003.

[FF00]   Marc Fischlin and Roger Fischlin. Efficient Non-malleable Commitment Schemes. In *Proc. of CRYPTO 2000*, LNCS 1880, pages 413–431. Springer, 2000.

[FOPS01]   Eiichiro Fujisaki, Tatsuaki Okamoto, David Pointcheval, and Jacques Stern. RSA-OAEP Is Secure under the RSA Assumption. In *Proc. of CRYPTO 2001*, LNCS 2139, pages 260–274, 2001.

[GMN04]   Christian Gehrmann, Chris J. Mitchell, and Kaisa Nyberg. Manual authentication for wireless devices. *RSA Cryptobytes*, 7(1):29–37, January 2004.

[Hoe05]   Jaap-Henk Hoepman. Ephemeral Pairing on Anonymous Networks. In *Proc. of SPC 2005*, LNCS 3450, pages 101–116. Springer, 2005.

[KD04]   Kaoru Kurosawa and Yvo Desmedt. A New Paradigm of Hybrid Encryption Scheme. In *Proc. of CRYPTO 2004*, LNCS 3152, pages 426–442. Springer, 2004.

[KOY01]   Jonathan Katz, Rafail Ostrovsky, and Moti Yung. Efficient Password-Authenticated Key Exchange Using Human-Memorable Passwords . In *Proc. of EUROCRYPT 2001*, LNCS 2045, pages 475–494. Springer, 2001.

[LAN05]   Sven Laur, N. Asokan, and Kaisa Nyberg. Efficient Mutual Data Authentication Using Manually Authenticated Strings: Preleiminary Version. Cryptology ePrint Archive, Report 2005/424, 2005. http://eprint.iacr.org/.

[LN06]   Sven Laur and Kaisa Nyberg. Efficient Mutual Data Authentication Using Manually Authenticated Strings: Extended Version. Cryptology ePrint Archive, Report 2005/424, 2006. http://eprint.iacr.org/.

[MY04]   Philip D. MacKenzie and Ke Yang. On Simulation-Sound Trapdoor Commitments. In *Proc. of EUROCRYPT*, LNCS 3027, pages 382–400. Springer, 2004.

[NGR05]   Kaisa Nyberg, Henri Gilbert, and Matt Robshaw. Galois MAC with forgery probability close to ideal. General Public Comments on NIST Cryptopage, 2005.

[NSS06]   Moni Naor, Gil Segev, and Adam Smith. Tight Bounds for Unconditional Authentication Protocols in the Manual Channel and Shared Key Models. In *Proc. of CRYPTO 2006*, LNCS 4117, pages 214–231 Springer, 2006.

[PV06a]   Sylvain Pasini and Serge Vaudenay. An Optimal Non-interactive Message Authentication Protocol. In *Proc. of CT-RSA 2006*, LNCS 3860, pages 280–294. Springer, 2006.

[PV06b]   Sylvain Pasini and Serge Vaudenay. SAS-Based Authenticated Key Agreement. In *PKC 2006*, LNCS 3958, pages 395–409. Springer, 2006.

[Sti91]   D. R. Stinson. Universal Hashing and Authentication Codes. In *Proc. of CRYPTO '91*, LNCS 576, pages 74–85. Springer, 1991.

[Vau05]   Serge Vaudenay. Secure Communications over Insecure Channels Based on Short Authenticated Strings. In *Proc. of CRYPTO 2005*, LNCS 3621, pages 309–326. Springer, 2005.

[WUS06]   Association Models Supplement to the Certified Wireless Universal Serial Bus Specification, 2006. http://www.usb.org/developers/wusb/.

[ZJC06]   Philip Zimmermann, Alan Johnston, and Jon Callas. ZRTP: Extensions to RTP for Diffie-Hellman Key Agreement for SRTP draft-zimmermann-avt-zrtp-01, March 2006.

A   Security in Arbitrary Computational Context

Assume that Mana IV and MA–DH protocols are run so that the security constraints presented in Sec. 5 are fullfilled. Then a protocol instance is uniquely determined by the time, origin and destination of the OOB message and a potential adversary cannot interleave OOB messages. This restriction can be trivially fullfilled—there is no need to exchange more than one key at a time and multiple messages can be sent together.

Consider ideal implementations of cross-authentication and Diffie-Hellman key exchange protocols. In ideal world, given m_a and m_b adversary can either deliver them to Alice and Bob or drop messages. Similarly, given g^a, g^b and sid, adversary can either do a passive attack against the key exchange protocol or interrupt it. Now consider a security game sec that defines security of a complex protocol. Next, theorem shows that the security drop compared to the ideal implementation is at most ε.

Theorem 3. *Let t_p be the total computational time needed to complete a complex protocol Π. For any t-time adversary A such that $\mathrm{Adv}_{\mathrm{real}}^{\mathrm{sec}}(A) = \delta$ in the real protocol, there exists a $(t + t_p)$-time adversary A^* that achieves $\mathrm{Adv}_{\mathrm{ideal}}^{\mathrm{sec}}(A^*) \geq \delta - \varepsilon$, if used Mana IV or MA–DH protocol is at least $(t + t_p + \mathcal{O}(1), \varepsilon)$-secure.*

Proof (Sketch). Since the source and destination of OOB messages together with the time uniquely reveal the corresponding Mana IV or MA–DH instance, it is straightforward to verify that honest Alice and Bob accept $m_a \| \widehat{m}_b \neq \widehat{m}_a \| m_b$ or $(\mathrm{sid}_a, \mathrm{key}_a) \neq (\mathrm{sid}_b, \mathrm{key}_b)$ with probability at most ε. Otherwise, we can simulate the surrounding computational context and break a stand-alone Mana IV or MA–DH protocol instance with larger probability than ε. Of course, the preceding history that determines (m_a, m_b) or sid should be fixed in such attack. As all previously used random coins can be hardwired, the corresponding attack still takes $t + t_p + \mathcal{O}(1)$ steps.

Now consider an adversary A^* that tries to win the game sec in the ideal world. It simulates a real protocol run to the adversary A. Essentially, A^* provides A a direct access to the ideal world except for the absent Mana IV or MA–DH protocol instance. Given (m_a, m_b) or $(\mathrm{id}_a, g^a, \mathrm{id}_b, g^b)$, A^* simulates the corresponding protocol to A. If A succeeds in deception, then A^* halts. Otherwise it simulates the end result of the protocol in the ideal world, i.e., delivers all messages unaltered or drops them. Note that when A^* does not halt then there is no discrepancy between the ideal and real protocol run. Since $\Pr[A^* \text{ halts}] \leq \varepsilon$ due to the first part of the proof, the result follows.   □

Note 5. If many protocol instances can be run in parallel between the same device pair, then there are no security guarantees. When more than 2^ℓ protocols run in parallel, then Charlie can certainly swap OOB messages so that at least one attacked protocol reaches accepting state. Of course, such attack is not practical.

B   Theoretical Limitations

In the following, we show that there are no asymptotically optimal two round manual message authentication protocols. In other words, two round protocols are inherently less secure. However, the exact quantification of such security drop is out of our scope.

Here it is advantageous to consider unilateral authentication protocols since unilateral authentication is a special case of cross authentication. In a manual unilateral authentication protocol Sender wants to transfer a authentic message m to Receiver. The restrictions to the protocols are same: protocol must be correct, the order of all messages is fixed ahead and the first OOB message oob determines the protocol outcome.

Let ℓ the maximal length of oob. We explicitly assume that $\ell \leq 30$, since for sufficiently large ℓ (say 160 bits) one can use collision resistant hash functions to protect authenticity, e.g., send oob $= h(m)$. We also assume that the length of inputs m is larger than ℓ or otherwise we can send m as the first OOB message. Note that a simple collision attack where Charlie interacts honestly but uses $2^{\ell+1}$ pre-tabulated values for input and randomness gives a formal proof to the "folklore" bound.

Theorem 4. *Let π be a correct unilateral authentication protocol with fixed message order and let ℓ be the maximal length of the first out-of-band message. Then there exists a strategy A such that $\mathrm{Adv}_\pi^{\mathrm{forge}}(A) \geq 2^{-\ell}$.*

Proof. The proof is omitted due to the lack of space. The complete proof is given in the extended version of the current article [LN06]. □

Such strategy is feasible to follow in real-time for $\ell \leq 30$, as necessary pre-tabulated values can be hardwired into the code of A and then the computational resources needed to construct the actual program code are irrelevant.

Next we show that no two round protocols can achieve security bounds arbitrarily close to $2^{-\ell}$. A practical protocol must be secure against the attacks that take super-linear time w.r.t. the honest protocol run or otherwise the security margin is too small.

Definition 1. *We say that a protocol family $\{\pi_k\}$ with a fixed message ordering is asymptotically optimal when the maximal advantage ε_k with respect to the time-bound t_k approaches $\varepsilon_k \to 2^{-\ell}$ and t_k is at least super-linear in the protocol complexity.*

In principle, unilateral authentication protocols can have arbitrary structure. If we assume asymptotic optimality from the protocol family, then we can show that for large enough k, $\mathrm{oob}(m, r_r, r_s)$ is almost uniform w.r.t. to Receiver's randomness r_r and Sender's randomness r_s, and with high probability only a single value $\mathrm{oob}(m, r_r, r_s)$ leads to acceptance. Formally, we need a concept of uniform convergence to state these properties. A parametrised sequence $x_k(a)$ converges uniformly $x_k(a) \rightrightarrows x$ with respect to the parameter $a \in \{0,1\}^*$, if $\limsup_k \sup_a x_k(a) = \liminf_k \inf_a x_k(a) = x$.

Theorem 5. *Let $\{\pi_k\}$ be an asymptotically optimal and correct protocol family, let probability $\Pr\left[\cdot|\pi_k\right]$ be taken over honest runs of π_k and let two-oob denote the event that more than one value of oob lead to acceptance. Then next statements are true:*

(a) $\Pr\left[\mathrm{oob}|m, r_s, \pi_k\right] \rightrightarrows 2^{-\ell}$ w.r.t. the parameters m, r_s,
(b) $\Pr\left[\mathrm{two\text{-}oob}|m, \pi_k\right] \rightrightarrows 0$ w.r.t. the parameter m,
(c) $\Pr\left[\mathrm{oob}|r_r, m, \pi_k\right] \rightrightarrows 2^{-\ell}$ w.r.t. the parameters r_r and m.

Proof. Follows from an extended analysis of the collision attack, see [LN06]. □

Corollary 1. *There are no asymptotically optimal and correct two round protocol families with a fixed message order for unilateral authentication.*

Proof. Omitted, see the extended version of [LN06]. □

The stated result is rather weak, since it does not quantify how close to the optimal bound the deception probability of two round protocols can go. More accurate analysis is still an open question.

Achieving Multicast Stream Authentication Using MDS Codes

Christophe Tartary and Huaxiong Wang

Centre for Advanced Computing, Algorithms and Cryptography
Department of Computing
Macquarie University
NSW 2109 Australia
{ctartary, hwang}@ics.mq.edu.au

Abstract. We address the multicast stream authentication problem when the communication channel is under the control of an opponent who can drop, re-order or inject data. In such a network model, packet overhead and computing efficiency are important parameters to be taken into account when designing a multicast authentication protocol. Our construction will exhibit three main advantages. First, our packet overhead will only be a few hashes long. Second, we will exhibit a number of signature verifications to be performed by the receivers which will turn to be $O(1)$. Third, every receiver will still be able to recover all the data packets emitted by the sender despite losses and injections occurred during the transmission of information.

Keywords: stream authentication, polynomial reconstruction, erasure codes.

1 Introduction

Broadcast communication is an essential mechanism to disseminate digital media from a single sender to a large audience via a public channel such as the Internet. The applications cover a broad area including digital radio, air traffic control as well as software updates for instance. Unfortunately large-scale multicasts prevent lost content from being redistributed since the loss of any piece of the data stream can cause a flood of retransmission requests at the sender. In addition the network can be under the control of malicious users performing harmful actions on the data stream. Therefore the security of a broadcast protocol relies on two aspects: the network properties and the opponents' computational power. Investigations concerning unconditionally secure protocols have been made in [5, 7, 38]. Unfortunately either these schemes can only be used for a single authentication or they have too large storage requirements for practical applications. In this work, we will consider that the opponents have bounded computational powers.

Applications like digital TV or stock quotes suggest that the data stream can be large and eventually infinite. Nevertheless receivers must be able to authenticate collected information within a short period of delay upon reception. Since many protocols will transfer private or sensitive content, non-repudiation of the sender is required for most

D. Pointcheval, Y. Mu, and K. Chen (Eds.): CANS 2006, LNCS 4301, pp. 108–125, 2006.

of them. Unfortunately signing each packet[1] is impracticable as digital signatures are generally time expensive. In addition bandwidth limitations prevent k-time signatures [36] from being used due to their large size. That is why a general approach is to generate a single signature and to amortize its communication and computation overheads over several packets using hash functions for instance.

By appending the hash of each packet to several followers according to some specific patterns, Perrig et al. [32, 33], Golle and Modadugu [10] and Miner and Staddon [24] designed schemes dealing with packet loss. One signature was generated from time to time and was always assumed to be received. In these contributions, authors modeled the network packet loss by a k-state Markov chain [8, 31, 43] and provided bounds on the packet authentication probability. Gao and Yao [9] proposed to use online/offline signature to speed up signing and verifying time for these schemes. Unfortunately all these protocols rely on reception of signed packets. Since networks like the Internet only provide a best effort delivery, it narrows the range of applications of these schemes.

To overcome this problem one solution is to split the signature into k smaller parts where only ℓ of them ($\ell < k$) are enough for recovery. Along this line, several schemes were developed [1, 27, 28, 29, 30] but none of them tolerates a single packet injection. In 2003, Lysyanskaya et al. [20] designed a technique (called in this paper LTT) resistant to packet loss and data injections using Reed-Solomon codes [35] where the number of signature verifications to be performed per block[2] turns out to be $O(1)$ as a function of the block length n. Unfortunately that approach does not allow lost content to be recovered. This drawback was also present in Tartary and Wang's scheme [41]. This problem was overcome by Karlof et al. in 2004. In [16], they designed a protocol called PRABS using an erasure code (to recover data loss) along with a one-way accumulator [3, 4, 25, 26] based on a Merkle hash tree [23] (to deal with injections). Their approach is similar to Wong and Lam's construction but it has the advantages of allowing recovery of all original data packets with only $O(1)$ signature verifications to compute. Unfortunately PRABS's augmented packets[3] must still carry $\lceil \log_2 n \rceil$ hashes.

In this paper, we propose a scheme having the advantages of the previous two constructions without their drawbacks. Every single original data packet will be recovered by any receiver and, contrary to [20] where only an asymptotic study was performed, we will exhibit an upper bound on the number of signature verifications to be executed per block. This bound will be valid for any block length and will turn to be $O(1)$ as in [16, 20]. Such a bound is valuable for practical applications since the block length is always finite. It allows receivers to get an upper bound on the time spent to verify signatures and therefore on the delay[4] between reception of information and authentication of correct packets. To the best of our knowledge PRABS is the only multicast stream authentication protocol ever designed which exhibits the recovery property and such a complexity value for signature verifications at the same time. As said earlier, this is at the cost of a logarithmic number of hashes appended to each packet. Our

---

[1] Since the stream size is large, it is divided into small fixed-size entities called *packets*.

[2] In order to be processed, packets are gathered into fixed-size sets called *blocks*.

[3] We call *augmented packets* the elements sent into the network. They generally consist of the original data packets with some redundancy used to prove the authenticity of the element.

[4] This delay is called *authentication delay* of the scheme.

recovery capacity will be due to a Maximum Distance Separable (MDS) code construction developed by Lacan and Fimes in 2004. Based on their work [17], we will enlighten that applying their code construction results in a better encoding/decoding complexity than using most other MDS codes. When compared to Reed-Solomon codes (as used in [20]) our technique will generate a slight increase of computing complexity at the sender (which can be compensated by his larger computational power) whereas the complexity at the receivers will be reduced. We will also see that our packet overhead is smaller than in [16] for practical applications. This is a major concern in multicast communication since too large packets may involve irregular throughput of data and sometimes result in congestion of the network information flow.

This paper is organized as follows. In Sect. 2 we will present our network model as well as a few results from [16, 20]. In Sect. 3 we will describe our authentication scheme. Its security and recovery property will be studied in Sect. 4. In Sect. 5, we will compare our scheme to those from [16, 20] as our work can be seen as their extension. Finally we will summarize our contribution to the multicast authentication problem.

2 Preliminaries

We now introduce the terminology and assumptions we will use in this paper. First we need to define our network model. Then we will describe the code construction by Lacan and Fimes. Finally we will recall an algorithm by Guruswami and Sudan achieving polynomial reconstruction. As in [20, 41], it will be used to deal with packet injections.

Network Model. We consider that the communication channel is under control of an opponent $\mathcal{O}$ who can drop and rearrange packets of his choice. He is also allowed to inject bogus data into the network. Since our primary concern is the multicast authentication problem, we can assume that a reasonable number of original augmented packets reaches the receivers and not too many incorrect elements are injected by $\mathcal{O}$. Indeed if too many original packets are dropped then data transmission becomes the main domain of investigation since the small number of received elements would be probably useless even authenticated. On this other hand, if $\mathcal{O}$ injects a large number of forged packets then the main problem to be solved becomes increasing the resistance against denial-of-service attacks. In order to build our signature amortization scheme, we need to split the data stream into blocks of n packets: $P_1, \ldots, P_n$. We define two parameters: $\alpha \, (0 < \alpha \leq 1)$ (the *survival* rate) and $\beta \, (\beta \geq 1)$ (the *flood* rate). It is assumed that at least a fraction α and no more than a multiple β of the number of augmented packets are received. This means that at least $\lceil \alpha n \rceil$ original augmented packets are received amongst a total which does not exceed $\lfloor \beta n \rfloor$ elements.

We also draw the reader's attention to the fact that we are not interested in the cases $(\alpha = 1)$ and $(\beta = 1)$. Indeed in the first case all original data packets are received. Thus we only need to distinguish correct elements from bogus ones. This can be done using Wong and Lam's technique [42]. In the second case there are no packet injections from $\mathcal{O}$. Thus using an erasure code (as in [6] for instance) is enough to recover $P_1, \ldots, P_n$. Therefore in this work we will only study the case: $0 < \alpha < 1 < \beta$.

Code Construction. In this paper we will focus on linear codes. A linear code of length N, dimension K and minimum distance D is denoted $[N, K, D]$. The Singleton bound states that any $[N, K, D]$ code satisfies: $D - 1 \leq N - K$[21]. It is known that any $[N, K, D]$ code can correct up to $D - 1$ erasures [44]. Thus a $[N, K, D]$ code cannot correct more than $N - K$ erasures. In order to maximize the efficiency of our construction, we are interested in codes correcting exactly $N - K$ erasures. These codes are called *Maximum Distance Separable* (MDS) codes [21].

Now we describe the MDS code construction developed in [17]. We will work over the field $\mathbb{F}_{2^q}$. Every element of $\mathbb{F}_{2^q}$ can be represented as a polynomial of degree at most $q - 1$ over $\mathbb{F}_2$ [18]. Operations in $\mathbb{F}_{2^q}$ are performed modulo a polynomial $\mathcal{Q}(X)$ of degree q which is irreducible over $\mathbb{F}_2$. From [17], we have:

Theorem 1. *Let $V(a_1, \ldots, a_K)$ be a non-singular $K \times K$ Vandermonde matrix and let $V(b_1, \ldots, b_{N-K})$ be a $K \times (N - K)$ matrix $(b_i^{j-1})_{i=1,\ldots,N-K}^{j=1,\ldots,K}$ (with convention $0^0 = 1$). Consider the $K \times K$ identity matrix I_K. Then the linear code defined by the generator matrix:*

$$G := [I_K | V(a_1, \ldots, a_K)^{-1} V(b_1, \ldots, b_{N-K})]$$

is MDS if and only if the a_i, b_j are N pairwise distinct elements.

Notice that due to the presence of the identity matrix I_k, each message to be encoded will appear as a part of its corresponding codeword. This means that this MDS code is in a *systematic* form. We now introduce the algorithms EncodeMDS and DecodeMDS which will be used as subroutines in our work. We will encode K symbols $S_1, \ldots, S_K$ into N modified symbols $\hat{S}_1, \ldots, \hat{S}_N$. Each S_i and $\hat{S}_j$ represents r elements of the field $\mathbb{F}_{2^q}$. The choice of the efficiency parameter r will be explained in Sect. 3.

EncodeMDS

Input: The code length and dimension N and K, the polynomial $\mathcal{Q}(X)$ of degree q, the generating matrix G, K symbols $S_1, \ldots, S_K$ and the efficiency parameter r.
1. Parse each symbol S_i into r field elements as: $S_i := S_i^1 \| \cdots \| S_i^r$. Build r messages as: $\forall j \in \{1, \ldots, r\}\, m_j := (S_1^j \cdots S_K^j)$.
2. Encode the r messages into r codewords as: $\forall j \in \{1, \ldots, r\}\, c_j := m_j G$.
3. Write each codeword as: $c_j := (c_1^j \cdots c_N^j)$. Build the N modified symbols as: $\forall j \in \{1, \ldots, N\}\, \hat{S}_j := c_1^j \| \cdots \| c_r^j$.
Output: N modified symbols: $\hat{S}_1, \ldots, \hat{S}_N$.

DecodeMDS

Input: The code length and dimension N and K, the polynomial $\mathcal{Q}(X)$ of degree q, the generating matrix G, $T(\geq K)$ elements $\{(j_i, \hat{S}_{j_i}), 1 \leq i \leq T\}$ and the efficiency parameter r.
1. Reorder the T elements to have $j_1 < \ldots < j_T$ and pick the first K elements. Parse the $\hat{S}_{j_i}$'s as: $\forall i \in \{1, \ldots, K\}\ \hat{S}_{j_i} = c_1^{j_1} \| \cdots \| c_r^{j_i}$ and write: $\forall i \in \{1, \ldots, r\}\, c_i' := (c_i^{j_1} \cdots c_i^{j_K})$.

2. Build G' as the restriction of G to columns $j_1, \ldots, j_K$. Compute r messages as: $\forall i \in \{1, \ldots, r\}\, m_i := c_i'\, G'^{-1}$.

3. Write each message as: $m_j := (m_i^1 \cdots m_i^K)$ where each m_i^j is $deg(\mathcal{Q}(X))$ bits long. Recover the K symbols as: $\forall i \in \{1, \ldots, K\}\, S_i = m_1^i \| \cdots \| m_r^i$.

Output: K symbols: $S_1, \ldots, S_K$.

Notice that the polynomial $\mathcal{Q}(X)$ is used at step 2 of EncodeMDS and DecodeMDS when performing matrix multiplications.

Polynomial Reconstruction Algorithm. In [14], Guruswami and Sudan developed an algorithm to solve the polynomial reconstruction problem. They proved that if T points were given as input then their algorithm Poly-Reconstruct output the list of all polynomials of degree at most K passing through at least N of the T points provided: $T > \sqrt{KN}$. We will use a modified version of Poly-Reconstruct that we call MPR. Denote $\mathbb{F}_{2\tilde{q}}$ the field representing the coefficients of the polynomial. As before we denote $\tilde{\mathcal{Q}}(X)$ the polynomial used to perform operations in that field.

MPR

Input: The maximal degree of the polynomial K, the minimal number of agreeable points N, T points $\{(x_i, y_i), 1 \leq i \leq T\}$ and the polynomial $\tilde{\mathcal{Q}}(X)$ of degree $\tilde{q}$.

1. If there are no more than $\sqrt{KN}$ distinct points then the algorithm stops.

2. Using $\tilde{\mathcal{Q}}(X)$, run Poly-Reconstruct on the T points to get the list of all polynomials of degree at most K over $\mathbb{F}_{2\tilde{q}}$ (where $\tilde{q} = deg(\tilde{\mathcal{Q}}(X))$) passing through at least N of the previous points.

3. Write the list $\{L_1(X), \ldots, L_\mu(X)\}$ and each element: $L_i(X) := \mathcal{L}_{i0} + \ldots + \mathcal{L}_{iK} X^K$ where $\forall i \in \{0, \ldots, K\}\, \mathcal{L}_{ij} \in \mathbb{F}_{2\tilde{q}}$. Form the elements: $\mathcal{L}_i := \mathcal{L}_{i0} \| \cdots \| \mathcal{L}_{iK}$.

Output: $\{\mathcal{L}_1, \ldots, \mathcal{L}_\mu\}$: list of candidates

3 Our Construction

We first give a global overview of our authentication scheme. As in [16, 20], we need a collision-resistant hash function h [34] and a secure signature scheme $(\mathrm{Sign}_{\mathrm{SK}}, \mathrm{Verify}_{\mathrm{PK}})$ [40] the key pair of which (SK,PK) is created by a generator KeyGen.

Informal Scheme Description. From the n data packets $P_1, \ldots, P_n$ we want to generate n augmented packets $\mathrm{AP}_1, \ldots, \mathrm{AP}_n$ such that if at most $n - \lceil \alpha n \rceil$ of them are lost during transmission then the receiver can still recover all the P_i's. Thus we need to encode these n packets using a $[n, \lceil \alpha n \rceil, n - \lceil \alpha n \rceil + 1]$ code. To perform this encoding, the size of elements forming the code's alphabet will be larger than the size of a data packet. In order to provide non-repudiation and to deal with bogus injections, we hash the modified symbols $\hat{S}_1, \ldots, \hat{S}_n$ (generated by the MDS code) and sign the concatenation $h_1 \| \cdots \| h_n$. As in [20], we build a polynomial $A(X)$ of degree at most ρn (for some rational constant ρ), the coefficients of which represent $h_1 \| \cdots \| h_n \| \sigma$ (σ is the signature). We build the augmented packets as: $\forall i \in \{1, \ldots, n\}\, \mathrm{AP}_i := \mathrm{BID} \| i \| \hat{S}_i \| A(i)$ where BID represents the position of the block $P_1, \ldots, P_n$ within the whole data stream.

Upon reception of data, the receiver checks the signature by reconstructing the poly-nomial $A(X)$ using MPR. Once the signature σ is verified, the receiver knows the original hashes $h_1, \ldots, h_n$. Thus he can identify the correct $\hat{S}_i$'s amongst the list of elements he got. According to the definition of α there must be at least $\lceil \alpha n \rceil$ symbols from $\hat{S}_1, \ldots, \hat{S}_n$ in his list. Finally he corrects the erasures using the MDS code and recovers the n data packets $P_1, \ldots, P_n$.

Formal Scheme Construction. For our construction we assume that α and β are ratio-nal numbers (see Sect. 4). Thus we can represent them over a finite number of bits using their numerator and denominator. Denote $\mathcal{P}$ the bit size of the data packets. In order to have $\lceil \alpha n \rceil$ symbols of equal length we must pad $P_1 \| \cdots \| P_n$ with ℓ zeros appropri-ately (see step 1 of Authenticator). Then we can split $P_1 \| \cdots \| P_n \| 0^\ell$ into n symbols $S_1, \cdots, S_{\lceil \alpha n \rceil}$ where each S_i is m bits long with $m := \left\lceil \frac{n\mathcal{P}}{\lceil \alpha n \rceil} \right\rceil$. The efficiency para-meter r is chosen by the sender as a divisor of m such that the receivers can efficiently perform computations over the field $\mathbb{F}_{2^q}$ where $q := \frac{m}{r}$. Notice that the smaller r is, the larger the number of messages to be encoded at step 2 of EncodeMDS is.

In order to run Poly-Reconstruct as a part of MPR, we have to choose $\rho \in (0, \frac{\alpha^2}{\beta})$. Notice that ρ has to be rational since ρn is an integer. Table 1 summarizes the scheme parameters which are assumed to be publicly known.

Table 1. Public Parameters for our Authentication Scheme

n: Block length	$\mathcal{Q}(X)$: Polynomial representing the field for the MDS code
$\mathcal{P}$: Packet size (in bits)	G: Generating matrix of the MDS code
α, β: Network rates	r: Efficiency parameter of the MDS code
ρ: Ratio	$\tilde{\mathcal{Q}}(X)$: Polynomial representing the field for polynomial interpolation

The hash function h as well as Verify and PK are also assumed to be publicly known. We did not include them in Table 1 since they can be considered as general parameters. For instance h can be SHA-256 while the digital signature is RSA-1024. We denote $\mathcal{H}$ the digest bit length and s the bit length of a signature. Since h and the digital signature are publicly known, so are $\mathcal{H}$ and s.

Authenticator

Input: The secret key SK, the block number BID, Table 1 and n data packets $P_1, \ldots, P_n$.

1. Compute: $b = n\mathcal{P} \bmod \lceil \alpha n \rceil$. Denote ℓ as $\ell = (0$ if $b = 0)$ or $(\lceil \alpha n \rceil - b$ otherwise$)$. Write $P_1 \| \cdots \| P_n \| 0^\ell$ as $S_1 \| \cdots \| S_{\lceil \alpha n \rceil}$ where each S_i is $m = \left\lceil \frac{n\mathcal{P}}{\lceil \alpha n \rceil} \right\rceil$ bits long.

2. Compute: $(\hat{S}_1, \cdots, \hat{S}_n) = \text{EncodeMDS}(n, \lceil \alpha n \rceil, \mathcal{Q}(X), G, S_1, \ldots, S_{\lceil \alpha n \rceil}, r)$.

3. Compute: $\forall i \in \{1, \ldots, n\}$ $h_i = h(\hat{S}_i)$ and form the string $h_1 \| \cdots \| h_n \| \sigma$ where $\sigma = \text{Sign}_{\text{SK}}(h(\text{BID} \| \alpha \| \beta \| n \| \mathcal{P} \| h_1 \| \cdots \| h_n))$.

4. Compute: $\tilde{b} = n\mathcal{H} + s \bmod (\rho n + 1)$. Denote $\tilde{\ell}$ as $\tilde{\ell} = (0$ if $\tilde{b} = 0)$ or $(\rho n - 1 - \tilde{b}$ otherwise$)$. Write $h_1 \| \cdots \| h_n \| \sigma \| 0^{\tilde{\ell}}$ as $a_0 \| \cdots \| a_{\rho n}$ where each a_i is $\tilde{m} = \left\lceil \frac{n\mathcal{H}+s}{\rho n+1} \right\rceil$ bits long. Build the polynomial $A(X) = a_0 + a_1 X + \cdots + a_{\rho n} X^{\rho n}$.

5. Using $\tilde{Q}(X)$, evaluate $A(X)$ at the first n elements [5] of $\mathbb{F}_{2^{\tilde{m}}}$. Using the n couples $(i, A(i))$, build the n augmented packets as: $\forall i \in \{1, \ldots, n\}$ $\mathrm{AP}_i = \mathrm{BID}\|i\|\hat{S}_i\|A(i)$.
Output: $\{\mathrm{AP}_1, \ldots, \mathrm{AP}_n\}$: set of augmented packets

We have two remarks which will be important when proving the security of our scheme in Sect. 4. First when assuming that α and β were rational in Sect. 2, we claimed that we could represent them over a finite number of bits. This allows us to include the concatenation $\alpha\|\beta$ as a part of the string to be hashed in step 3. Second it should be pointed out that when $(n, \alpha, \beta, \mathcal{P}, \rho)$ are given, every single step of Authenticator is uniquely determined as soon as $(Q(X), G, r, \tilde{Q}(X))$ are provided. Furthermore since the rational ρ only depends on α, β and n, it is realistic to presume that when (n, α, β) are given, ρ is also uniquely determined. Thus we can assume for our scheme that when $(n, \alpha, \beta, \mathcal{P})$ are given, $(\rho, Q(X), G, r, \tilde{Q}(X))$ are uniquely determined.

Notice that to perform step 5 we must have at least n distinct elements in $\mathbb{F}_{2^{\tilde{m}}}$. It can be shown that this property is verified for n up to 2^{20}. In practical applications however n will be roughly 1000 $(\simeq 2^{10})$ (see [33] for instance). We refer the reader interested in the details of this affirmation to Appendix A.

Decoder

Input: The public key PK, the block number BID, Table 1 and the set of received packets RP.

1. Write the packets as $\mathrm{BID}_i\|j_i\|S'_{j_i}\|A_{j_i}$ and discard those having $\mathrm{BID}_i \neq \mathrm{BID}$ or $j_i \notin \{1, \ldots, n\}$. Denote $\mathcal{N}$ the number of remaining elements. If $(\mathcal{N} < \lceil \alpha n \rceil$ or $\mathcal{N} > \lfloor \beta n \rfloor)$ then the algorithm stops.
2. Rename the remaining elements as $\{\mathrm{AP}'_1, \ldots, \mathrm{AP}'_{\mathcal{N}}\}$ and write each element as: $\mathrm{AP}'_i = \mathrm{BID}\|j_i\|S'_{j_i}\|A_{j_i}$ where $j_i \in \{1, \ldots, n\}$. Run MPR on the set $\{(j_i, A_{j_i}), 1 \leq i \leq \mathcal{N}\}$ to get a list $\{\mathcal{C}_1, \ldots, \mathcal{C}_\mu\}$ of candidates for signature verification. If MPR rejects that set then the algorithm stops.
3. Set $h_k = \emptyset$ for $k \in \{1, \ldots, n\}$. Compute $\tilde{\ell}$ as in step 4 of Authenticator. Set $i = 1$. While $\{\mathcal{C}_1, \ldots, \mathcal{C}_\mu\}$ has not been exhausted, pick $\mathcal{C}_i$. Check if $\mathcal{C}_i$ ends with $\tilde{\ell}$ zeros. If so, write $\mathcal{C}_i$ as: $h_1^i\|\cdots\|h_n^i\|\sigma^i\|0^{\tilde{\ell}}$ where each h_k^i is $\mathcal{H}$ bits long. If $\mathrm{Verify}_{\mathrm{PK}}(h(\mathrm{BID}\|\alpha\|\beta\|n\|\mathcal{P}\|h_1^i\|\cdots\|h_n^i), \sigma^i) = \mathrm{true}$ then set $h_k = h_k^i$ for $k \in \{1, \ldots, n\}$ and break out the loop. In any other cases increment i by 1 and start again the while loop.
4. If $(h_1, \ldots, h_n) = (\emptyset, \ldots, \emptyset)$ then the algorithm stops. Otherwise set $\hat{S}_k = \emptyset$ for all $k \in \{1, \ldots, n\}$. For each AP'_i written as at step 2, if $h(S'_{j_i}) = h_\lambda$ then $\hat{S}_\lambda = S'_{j_i}$.
5. If we have less than $\lceil \alpha n \rceil$ non-empty symbols then the algorithm stops. Otherwise denote $\hat{S}_{p_1}, \ldots, \hat{S}_{p_\gamma}$ the non-empty elements. Decode them as: $(S_1, \ldots, S_{\lceil \alpha n \rceil}) = \mathrm{DecodeMDS}(n, \lceil \alpha n \rceil, Q(X), G, (p_1, \hat{S}_{p_1}), \ldots, (p_\gamma, \hat{S}_{p_\gamma}), r)$.

---

[5] Any element of $\mathbb{F}_{2^{\tilde{m}}}$ can be represented as $\lambda_0 Y^0 + \lambda_1 Y_1 + \ldots + \lambda_{\tilde{m}-1} Y^{\tilde{m}-1}$ where each λ_i belongs to $\mathbb{F}_2$. We define the first n elements as $(0, \ldots, 0)$, $(1, 0, \ldots, 0)$, $(0, 1, 0, \ldots, 0)$, $(1, 1, 0, \ldots, 0)$ and so on until the binary decomposition of n.

6. Set $P'_k = \emptyset$ for $k \in \{1, \ldots, n\}$. Compute ℓ as in step 1 of Authenticator. If the last ℓ bits of $S_1 \| \ldots \| S_{\lceil \alpha n \rceil}$ are not zeros then the algorithm stops. Otherwise write that concatenation as $P'_1 \| \cdots \| P'_n \| 0^\ell$ where each P'_i is $\mathcal{P}$ bits long.

Output: $\{P'_1, \ldots, P'_n\}$: set of authenticated packets.

4 Security and Recovery Analysis

Security of the Scheme. Similarly to [20], we give the following definition:

Definition 1. (KeyGen,Authenticator,Decoder) *is a secure and* (α, β)*-correct multicast authentication scheme if no probabilistic polynomial-time opponent* $\mathcal{O}$ *can win with a non-negligible probability to the following game:*

i) *A key pair* $(\mathrm{SK}, \mathrm{PK})$ *is generated by* KeyGen

ii) $\mathcal{O}$ *is given:* (a) *The public key* PK *and* (b) *Oracle access to* Authenticator *(but* $\mathcal{O}$ *can only issue at most one query with the same block identification tag* BID*)*

iii) $\mathcal{O}$ *outputs* $(\mathrm{BID}, n, \alpha, \beta, \mathcal{P}, \rho, \mathcal{Q}(X), \tilde{\mathcal{Q}}(X), G, r, \mathrm{RP})$

$\mathcal{O}$ *wins if one of the following happens:*

a) *(correctness violation)* $\mathcal{O}$ *succeeds to output* RP *such that even if it contains* $\lceil \alpha n \rceil$ *packets (amongst a total number of elements which does not exceed* $\lfloor \beta n \rfloor$*) for some block identification tag* BID, *Decoder fails at identifying all the correct packets.*

b) *(security violation)* $\mathcal{O}$ *succeeds to output* RP *such that Decoder outputs* $\{P'_1, \ldots, P'_n\}$ *that was never authenticated by* Authenticator *for parameters* $(\mathrm{BID}, n, \alpha, \beta, \mathcal{P}, \rho, \mathcal{Q}(X), \tilde{\mathcal{Q}}(X), G, r,)$.

Lysyanskaya et al. proved that their construction satisfied the previous conditions of security and correctness. We have a similar result for our scheme.

Theorem 2. *Our scheme* (KeyGen,Authenticator,Decoder) *is secure and* (α, β)*-correct.*

Proof (Sketch). If the scheme is neither secure nor (α, β)-correct then $\mathcal{O}$ is able to generate data packets which will be authenticated by the receiver after MDS decoding at step 5 of Decoder. Nevertheless the decoding algorithm of the MDS code is consistent. This means that if only correct elements $\hat{S}_{p_1}, \ldots, \hat{S}_{p_\gamma}$ are given to DecodeMDS then it outputs the corresponding original elements $S_1, \ldots, S_{\lceil \alpha n \rceil}$. This consistency involves that $\mathcal{O}$ can generate (at least) one incorrect symbol S'_i for some $i \in \{1, \ldots, n\}$ such that its hash h'_i is a part of the element $\mathcal{C}'$ which successfully verified the signature at step 3 of Decoder. Since h is collision resistant, we have: $\forall j \in \{1, \ldots, n\}$ $h'_i \neq h_j$. Thus $\mathcal{C}'$ was never signed by the sender and $\mathcal{O}$ is able to forge the signature scheme. Due to space limitations we did not include the complete proof here. It can still be found in the extended version of this paper. It exhibits the necessity of using $\alpha \| \beta \| n \| \mathcal{P}$ as a part of the element to be hashed at step 3 of Authenticator.   □

Recovery Property. We will now demonstrate that our scheme enables any receiver to recover the n data packets (as in [16]) and the number of signature verifications to be performed per block is $O(1)$ (as in [20]). We also provide a non-asymptotic bound on this number of verifications. First we introduce the following definition:

Definition 2. *We say that the survival and flood rates* (α, β) *are accurate to the network for a flow of* n *symbols if:* (1) *data are sent per block of* n *elements through the network and* (2) *for any block of* n *elements* $\{E_1, \cdots, E_n\}$ *emitted by the sender, if we denote* $\{\tilde{E}_1, \ldots, \tilde{E}_\mu\}$ *the set of received packets then* $\mu \leq \lfloor \beta n \rfloor$ *and at least* $\lceil \alpha n \rceil$ *elements of* $\{E_1, \cdots, E_n\}$ *belong to* $\{\tilde{E}_1, \ldots, \tilde{E}_\mu\}$. *Condition* (2) *must be true for each receiver belonging to the communication group.*

Notice that, when n is fixed, (α, β) is not unique since any $(\tilde{\alpha}, \tilde{\beta})$ with $\tilde{\beta} \geq \beta$ and $0 < \tilde{\alpha} \leq \alpha$ is also accurate for the same flow n. That is why we can always choose α, β as rational numbers as claimed in Sect. 3. From now on, we assume that (α, β) is accurate for our network flow n. It should be pointed out that the asymptotic result from [20] was obtained under the same assumption. Despite PRABS can tolerate an unbounded number of injections, it still requires a minimal number of original elements to be received in order to enable recovery of the n data packets $P_1, \ldots, P_n$. Thus assuming the accuracy of (α, β) to compare our scheme to [16] seems to be a realistic hypothesis as well. We now present our main theorem:

Theorem 3. *For any* BID, *each receiver recovers the* n *original data packets* $P_1, \ldots, P_n$. *In addition the number of signature verifications to be performed is upper bounded by* $U(n) := \min(\lfloor U_1(n) \rfloor, \lfloor U_2(n) \rfloor)$ *where:*

$$
\begin{cases}
U_1(n) = \dfrac{1}{\rho n} \left(\dfrac{1}{\sqrt{\alpha^2 - \beta \rho}} - 1 \right) + \dfrac{\beta}{\alpha^2 - \beta \rho} + \dfrac{1}{\rho} \\[3mm]
U_2(n) = \dfrac{\beta}{2(\alpha^2 - \beta \rho)} + \dfrac{1}{\rho} + \dfrac{\sqrt{\dfrac{\beta}{\alpha} + \dfrac{4}{\rho^2 n^2}(1 - \rho \alpha)}}{2(\alpha^2 - \beta \rho)} - \dfrac{1}{\rho n}
\end{cases}
$$

which is $O(1)$ *as a function of the block length* n.

Proof. The proof is given in Appendix B. □

It should be noticed that when n is fixed, the value $U(n)$ increases when ρ gets closer to the threshold value $\frac{\alpha^2}{\beta}$ or to 0. In addition if ρ is too small then the size of the field $\mathbb{F}_{2^{\tilde{m}}}$ gets larger which can result in a prohibitive computational cost for some of the receivers. Therefore the sender must pay attention to the choice of ρ when setting up the scheme in order to have a balanced trade-off between the efficiency of field operations and a reasonable number of signature verifications to perform.

To illustrate this remark we computed $U(n)$ when $n = 1000$ as in [33]. $U(1000)$ was evaluated for values ρ equal to $10\%, 30\%, 50\%, 70\%$ and 90% of the threshold $\frac{\alpha^2}{\beta}$ for each couple (α, β). The reader may notice that some values 1000ρ are not integers (as it should be for our scheme). We committed this abuse because our main goal was to exhibit the behavior of $U(n)$ for a realistic value n. If we had to be consistent with the fact that ρn is an integer then the smallest integer n valid for all couples (α, β) in our table should have been $132,000$ which is not a realistic assumption for the block length n. We also implemented $V(1000)$ where $V(n)$ is the bound provided by Karlof et al.[16] (see Sect. 5 for more details). The results are shown in Table 2.

Table 2. Evaluations of $U(1000)|V(1000)$

	(α, β)							
	$(0.5, 1.1)$	$(0.5, 1.25)$	$(0.5, 1.5)$	$(0.5, 2)$	$(0.75, 1.1)$	$(0.75, 1.25)$	$(0.75, 1.5)$	$(0.75, 2)$
10%	48|3	55|3	66|4	88|5	21|2	24|2	29|3	39|3
30%	20|3	23|3	28|4	38|5	9|2	10|2	12|3	16|3
50%	17|3	20|3	24|4	31|5	7|2	8|2	10|3	13|3
70%	20|3	23|3	28|4	38|5	9|2	10|2	12|3	15|3
90%	48|3	55|3	66|4	88|5	212|	24|2	28|3	36|3
	(α, β)							
	$(0.8, 1.1)$	$(0.8, 1.25)$	$(0.8, 1.5)$	$(0.8, 2)$	$(0.9, 1.1)$	$(0.9, 1.25)$	$(0.9, 1.5)$	$(0.9, 2)$
10%	19|2	21|2	25|2	34|3	15|2	17|2	20|2	27|3
30%	8|2	9|2	11|2	14|3	6|2	7|2	8|2	11|3
50%	6|2	7|2	9|2	11|3	5|2	6|2	7|2	9|3
70%	8|2	9|2	10|2	13|3	6|2	7|2	8|2	10|3
90%	19|2	21|2	25|2	31|3	15|2	16|2	19|2	24|3

5   Efficiency Comparaison

Since our technique is an extension of [16, 20], we will enlighten the benefits our construction provides in this section.

Signature Complexity. We saw in Theorem 3 that the asymptotic behavior of $U(n)$ is identical to the asymptotic result from [20]. According to Theorem 3 from [16] the number of signature verifications for PRABS is upper bounded by $V(n) := \left\lfloor \frac{\beta n}{\lceil \alpha n \rceil} \right\rfloor + 1$. Since $V(n) \leq \frac{\beta}{\alpha} + 1$, it is clear that $V(n)$ is $O(1)$ and $V(n) \leq \lfloor U_1(n) \rfloor$. Table 2 clearly shows that $V(n)$ is much smaller than $U(n)$. Nevertheless this low value of $V(n)$ is precisely due to the fact that each augmented packet carries $\log n$ hashes since the hashes are used to partition the received elements into (at most) $V(n)$ sets. Thus a logarithmic number of hashes per augmented packet is the price paid by Karlof et al. to achieve low number of signature verifications. As said earlier this is impractical since such large packets can cause congestion in the network throughput. Table 2 results suggest that $U(n)$ is minimal when ρ is roughly half the threshold value $\frac{\alpha^2}{\beta}$.

Packet Overhead. Our augmented packets are written as $\text{BID}\|i\|\hat{S}_i\|A(i)$. The element $A(i)$ is $\left\lceil \frac{n\mathcal{H}+s}{n\rho+1} \right\rceil$ bits long (as in [20]) and $\hat{S}_i$ is slightly larger than P_i since it is $\left\lceil \frac{nP}{\lceil \alpha n \rceil} \right\rceil$ bits long. Thus our augmented packet size is slightly larger than those from [20]. We would like to draw the reader's attention to an important fact. When studying the packet overhead of their scheme, Lysyanskaya et al. claimed that it was $\frac{\mathcal{H}}{\rho} + O(1)$ bits long. Unfortunately this is incorrect. Indeed, as in our construction, the field $\mathbb{F}_{2^{\tilde{m}}}$ must contain at least n points for polynomial evaluation. Therefore their construction requires: $n \leq 2^{\tilde{m}}$. Since $2^{\tilde{m}} \in O(1)$, it is clear that the previous inequality is not satisfied for large values of n. Thus it is mathematically impossible to study the asymptotic behavior of packet overhead since LTT is not constructible for large values of n. For practical realizations (i.e. realistic values of n) the previous inequality is satisfied (see Appendix A) and then it makes sense to approximate the overhead bit size to $\frac{\mathcal{H}}{\rho}$.

For the same reason our comparison to PRABS is restricted to practical values of n. In both constructions the n data packets are encoded to recover from a fraction $1 - \alpha$ of erasures. Thus PRABS augmented packets can be written as $\text{BID}\|i\|\tilde{S}_i\|H(i)$ where $H(i)$ is the concatenation of $\lceil \log_2 n \rceil$ hashes and the $\tilde{S}_i$'s are as large as our $\hat{S}_i$'s. Thus our overhead comparison is reduced to a size comparison between $A(i)$ and $H(i)$. The latter only depends on n while the size of $A(i)$ can be tuned according to the rates α and β. This allows us to reduce the overhead per packet which is impossible for PRABS. Consider the same value n as in Table 2. Whatever the rates are, PRABS's overhead is 10 hashes. If we choose ρ as half the threshold $\frac{\alpha^2}{\beta}$ (as suggested above) then when $(\alpha, \beta) = (0.75, 1.25)$ we get $\frac{1}{\rho} \simeq 5$. In that case, our packet overhead is approximately 5 hashes which is twice less than PRABS's. The closer to $(1, 1)$ our rates are, the smaller our packet overhead becomes. Tuning the packet overhead using the network rates can greatly help regulating the information flow within the communication channel.

Coding Efficiency. The field used by the MDS code is $\mathbb{F}_{2^q}$ where q is defined as in Sect. 3. Our results are based on the analysis done in [17]. Encoding a single message m_i requires $O(n \log n)$ field operations. Therefore encoding the r messages needs $O(r \, n \log n)$ field operations. Similarly decoding a single c'_i requires $O(n \log^2 n)$ field operations. Since r of them must be decoded, we get $O(r \, n \log^2 n)$ as total decoding complexity. It is clear that $r \in O(1)$ as a function of n. So the previous two complexities become $O(n \log n)$ and $O(n \log^2 n)$ respectively.

In [16], it was suggested to use Reed-Solomon codes as erasure codes for PRABS. Since Reed-Solomon codes are MDS [21], it is natural to compare their efficiency to our MDS code's one. Karlof et al. refered to the original paper by Reed and Solomon [35] to encode/decode. Based on this consideration the complexity of encoding/decoding a single m_i/c'_j requires $O(n^2)$ field operations. Then it is clear that our complexity for encoding/decoding are better. However Reed-Solomon codes can be processed in a more efficient way than in [35] using the technique developed by Guruswami and Sudan in [14]. This technique which was used in [20] enables any message m_i to be encoded in $O(n \log^2 n)$ field operations and any codeword c'_j to be decoded using $O(n^2)$ field operations. If their technique is to be used to encode/decode data in PRABS then the encoding complexity of our protocol represents an increase by factor $\log n$ (for the whole set of r messages) whereas the decoding complexity is reduced by a factor $\frac{\log^2 n}{n}$ (for the whole set of r codewords). We claim that even in this case, our scheme still gives more benefits than PRABS. Indeed in our network model the sender is assumed to be more computationally powerful than the receivers. Therefore he can cope with the small increasing factor $\log n$ since n will be roughly 1000 in practical applications. At the same time the receivers take advantage of the complexity reduction from quadratic (using Reed-Solomon codes) to sub-quadratic (with our technique).

After treating the case of Reed-Solomon codes, it remains to argue that our MDS code construction gives better complexity for encoding/decoding than other MDS codes used in practical implementations. In [17], Lacan and Fimes pointed out that in computer communication, erasure codes were used in systematic form. They also emphasized that systematic MDS codes employed in practical applications relied on either Cauchy or Vandermonde matrices to generate the redundancy symbols. They proved that their code construction exhibited better complexity for both encoding and decoding than any other systematic MDS code relying on either matrix construction.

Based on these observations we claim that using Lacan and Fimes' codes for our authentication scheme gives us an optimal erasure correcting technique for data streaming over a multicast network.

6   Conclusion

In this paper we introduced a multicast stream authentication scheme which can be considered as an extension of [16, 20]. Our construction ensures non-repudiation of the sender and enables new members to join the communication group at any block boundary. Contrary to [20], our technique allows recovery of all original data packets. In addition only $O(1)$ signature verifications are performed per block. At the same time, our packet overhead is lower than in [16] which reduces the risk of network congestion. When performing video or audio streaming for instance, the recovery property can be used to prevent audio gaps or frozen images when playing the stream content. We also constructed a non-asymptotic upper bound on the number of signature verifications to be performed which can be used in practice to deduce an upper bound on the authentication delay our scheme exhibits. We also showed that our erasure code construction was optimal for two reasons. First MDS codes, by definition, are optimal for correcting erasures. Second the MDS code construction by Lacan and Fimes was proved in [17] to have a better complexity than most MDS codes used in practice. When compared to Reed-Solomon codes (as used in [20]), our erasure code encoding exhibited a slightly larger complexity which can however be compensated by the computational capacities of the sender. At the same time the decoding complexity is much smaller than Reed-Solomon one which benefits to all receivers. We would like to point out that the discovery of faster encoding/decoding codes could improve the performance of our scheme. We are aware of the existence of linear time encoding/decoding (non-linear) codes [2, 12, 13, 15, 37]. We did not use them for our protocol because their construction parameters were not flexible enough to fit our network parameters whereas other linear time codes like [19, 22, 39] only provide recovery of all data packets with some probability. In addition these codes are not MDS which involves extra-generation of symbols to achieve the same capacity of correction.

Acknowledgment

The authors are grateful to the anonymous reviewers for their comments to improve the quality of this paper. This work was supported by the Australian Research Council under ARC Discovery Projects DP0558773 and DP0665035. The first author's work was also funded by an iMURS scholarship supported by Macquarie University.

References

[1] M. Al-Ibrahim and J. Pieprzyk. Authenticating multicast streams in lossy channels using threshold techniques. In *ICN 2001*, volume 2094 of *LNCS*, pages 239 – 249. Springer - Verlag, July 2001.

[2] N. Alon, J. Edmonds, and M. Luby. Linear time erasure codes with nearly optimal recovery (extended abstract). In *36th Annual Symposium on Foundations of Computer Science*, pages 512 – 519, October 1995.

[3] N. Barić and B. Pfitzmann. Collision-free accumulators and fail-stop signature schemes without trees. In *Eurocrypt'97*, volume 1233 of *LNCS*, pages 480 – 494. Springer - Verlag, May 1997.

[4] J. Benaloh and M. de Mare. One-way accumulators: A decentralized alternative to digital signatures. In *Eurocrypt' 93*, volume 765 of *LNCS*, pages 274 – 285. Springer - Verlag, May 1993.

[5] C. Blundo, A. De Santis, A. Herzberg, S. Kutten, U. Vaccaro, and M. Yung. Perfectly-secure key distribution for dynamic conferences. In *Advances in Cryptology - Crypto'92*, volume 740 of *LNCS*, pages 471 – 486. Springer - Verlag, August 1992.

[6] A. F. Dana, R. Gowaikar, R. Palanki, B. Hassibi, and M. Effros. Capacity of wireless erasure networks. *IEEE Transactions on Information Theory*, 52(3):789 – 804, March 2006.

[7] Y. Desmedt, Y. Frankel, and M. Yung. Multi-receiver/multi-sender network security: Efficient authenticated multicast/feedback. In *INFOCOM '92*, volume 3, pages 2045 – 2054, May 1992.

[8] J. C. Fu and W. Y. W. Lou. *Distribution Theory of Runs and Patterns and its Applications*. World Scientific Publishing, 2003.

[9] C. Gao and Z. Yao. How to authenticate real time streams using improved online/offline signatures. In *4th International Conference on Cryptology and Network Security*, volume 3810 of *LNCS*, pages 134 – 146. Springer-Verlag, December 2005.

[10] P. Golle and N. Modadugu. Authenticating streamed data in the presence of random packet loss. In *Proceedings of the Symposium on Network and Distributed Systems Security (NDSS 2001)*, pages 13 – 22. Internet Society, February 2001.

[11] V. Guruswami. *List Decoding of Error-Correcting Codes*. Springer-Verlag, 2004.

[12] V. Guruswami and P. Indyk. Linear-time decoding in error-free settings (extended abstract). In *ICALP*, volume 3142 of *LNCS*, pages 695 – 707. Springer - Verlag, July 2004.

[13] V. Guruswami and A. Rudra. Explicit capacity-achieving list-decodable codes. Technical Report TR05-133, Electronic Colloquium on Computational Complexity, November 2005.

[14] V. Guruswami and M. Sudan. Improved decoding of Reed-Solomon and algebraic-geometric codes. In *IEEE Transactions on Information Theory*, pages 1757 – 1767, May 1999.

[15] P. Indyk. List-decoding in linear time. Technical Report TR02-024, Electronic Colloquium on Computational Complexity, April 2002.

[16] C. Karlof, N. Sastry, Y. Li, A. Perrig, and J. D. Tygar. Distillation codes and applications to DoS resistant multicast authentication. In *11th Network and Distributed Systems Security Symposium (NDSS)*, February 2004.

[17] J. Lacan and J. Fimes. Systematic MDS erasure codes based on Vandermonde matrices. *IEEE Communications Letters*, 8(9):570 – 572, September 2004.

[18] R. Lidl and H. Niederreiter. *Introduction to Finite Fields and their Applications - Revised Edition*. Cambridge University Press, 2000.

[19] M. Luby. LT codes. In *43rd Annual IEEE Symposium on Foundations of Computer Science*. IEEE ComputeR Society, November 2002.

[20] A. Lysyanskaya, R. Tamassia, and N. Triandopoulos. Multicast authentication in fully adversarial networks. In *IEEE Symposium on Security and Privacy*, November 2003.

[21] F. J. MacWilliams and N. J. A. Sloane. *The Theory of Error-Correcting Codes*. North-Holland, 1977.

[22] P. Maymounkov. Online codes. Technical report, New York University, November 2002.

[23] R. Merkle. A certified digital signature. In *Advances in Cryptology - Crypto'89*, pages 218–238. Springer - Verlag, 1989.

[24] S. Miner and J. Staddon. Graph-based authentication of digital streams. In *IEEE Symposium on Security and Privacy*, pages 232 – 246, May 2001.

[25] L. Nguyen. Accumulators from bilinear pairings and applications. In *Topics in Cryptology - CT-RSA 2005*, volume 3376 of *LNCS*, pages 275 – 292. Springer - Verlag, February 2005.

[26] K. Nyberg. Fast accumulated hashing. In *Fast Software encrytion - Third International Workshop*, volume 1039 of *LNCS*, pages 83 – 87. Springer, February 1996.

[27] A. Pannetrat and R. Molva. Authenticating real time packet streams and multicasts. In *7th International Symposium on Computers and Communications*, July 2002.

[28] J. M. Park, E. K. P. Chong, and H. J. Siegel. Efficient multicast packet authentication using signature amortization. In *IEEE Symposium on Security and Privacy*, pages 227 –240, May 2002.

[29] J. M. Park, E. K. P. Chong, and H. J. Siegel. Efficient multicast stream authentication using erasure codes. In *ACM Transactions on Information and System Security*, volume 6, pages 258 – 285, May 2003.

[30] Y. Park and Y. Cho. The eSAIDA stream authentication scheme. In *ICCSA*, pages 799 – 807, April 2004.

[31] V. Paxson. End-to-end Internet packet dynamics. In *IEEE/ACM Transactions on Networking*, pages 277 – 292, June 1999.

[32] A. Perrig, R. Canetti, J.D. Tygar, and D. Song. Efficient authentication and signing of multicast streams over lossy channels. In *IEEE Symposium on Security and Privacy*, pages 56 – 73, May 2000.

[33] A. Perrig and J. D. Tygar. *Secure Broadcast Communication in Wired and Wireless Networks*. Kluwer Academic Publishers, 2003.

[34] J. Pieprzyk, T. Hardjono, and J. Seberry. *Fundamentals of Computer Security*. Springer, 2003.

[35] I. S. Reed and G. Solomon. Polynomial codes over certain finite fields. *Journal of Society for Industrial and Applied Mathematics*, 8(2):300 – 304, June 1960.

[36] P. Rohatgi. A compact and fast hybrid signature scheme for multicast packet authentication. In *6th ACM Conference on Computer and Communications Security*, pages 93 – 100, 1999.

[37] R. M. Roth and V. Skachek. Improved nearly-MDS expander codes. Available online at: http://arxiv.org/PS_cache/cs/pdf/0601/0601090.pdf, January 2005.

[38] R. Safavi-Naini and H. Wang. New results on multi-receiver authentication code. In *Advances in Cryptology - Eurocrypt'98*, volume 1403 of *LNCS*, pages 527 – 541. Springer - Verlag, June 1998.

[39] A. Shokrollahi. Raptor codes. Technical report, Digital Fountain, June 2003.

[40] D. R. Stinson. *Cryptography: Theory and Practice*. CRC Press, 1995.

[41] C. Tartary and H. Wang. Efficient multicast stream authentication for the fully adversarial network. In *6th International Workshop on Information Security Applications*, volume 3786 of *LNCS*, pages 108 – 125. Springer - Verlag, August 2005.

[42] C. K. Wong and S. S. Lam. Digital signatures for flows and multicasts. In *IEEE/ACM Transactions on Networking*, volume 7, August 1999.

[43] M. Yajnik, S. Moon, J. Kurose, and D. Towsley. Measurement and modeling of the temporal dependence in packet loss. In *IEEE Conference on Computer Communications*, pages 345 – 352. IEEE Press, 1999.

[44] J. P. Zanotti. Le code correcteur C.I.R.C. Available online at: http://zanotti.univ-tln.fr/enseignement/divers/chapter3.html.

A   Study of the Cardinality of $\mathbb{F}_{2^{\tilde{m}}}$

In this section we will study the cardinality of the field used to evaluate/interpolate the polynomial $A(X)$. In order to run Authenticator and Decoder, this field must have at least n elements. That is we must have: $2^{\tilde{m}} \geq n$. This condition is verified as soon as:

$$\frac{n\mathcal{H} + s}{n\rho + 1} \geq \log_2 n \tag{1}$$

We have: $\rho n \geq 1$. Therefore $\frac{1}{2\rho n}$ is a lower bound of $\frac{1}{n\rho+1}$. This involves that (1) is verified as soon as we have:

$$\frac{n\mathcal{H} + s}{2\rho n} \geq \log_2 n$$

It is easy to see that the previous inequality is equivalent to:

$$\frac{\mathcal{H}\ln 2}{2\rho} n - n \ln n + \frac{s\ln 2}{2\rho} \geq 0$$

We introduce the function f defined as:

$$f : \mathbb{R}^{+*} \longrightarrow \mathbb{R}$$
$$x \longmapsto \frac{\mathcal{H}\ln 2}{2\rho} x - x \ln x + \frac{s\ln 2}{2\rho}$$

This function is differentiable over $\mathbb{R}^{+*}$ and: $\forall x > 0$ $f'(x) = \frac{\mathcal{H}\ln 2}{2\rho} - \ln x - 1$. We obtain:

$$f'(x) \geq 0 \Longleftrightarrow x \leq \frac{1}{e} 2^{\frac{\mathcal{H}}{2\rho}}$$

Denote $\tilde{x}$ the real defined as: $\tilde{x} := \frac{1}{e} 2^{\frac{\mathcal{H}}{2\rho}}$. From the previous equivalence we deduce that f is increasing over $(0, \tilde{x}]$. In addition we have:

$$\lim_{x \to 0_+} f(x) = \frac{s\ln 2}{2\rho}$$

Since this limit is positive we deduce that f is positive over $(0, \tilde{x}]$. Therefore the restriction of f to $\mathbb{N} \setminus \{0\}$ is positive over $\{1, \ldots, \lfloor \tilde{x} \rfloor\}$. This involves:

$$\forall n \in \{1, \ldots, \lfloor \tilde{x} \rfloor\} \quad 2^{\tilde{m}} \geq n$$

We now have to argue that $\lfloor \tilde{x} \rfloor$ is large enough for real applications. Assume that we have: $\lfloor \tilde{x} \rfloor \leq 2^{20}$. Then we get:

$$\frac{1}{e} 2^{\frac{\mathcal{H}}{2\rho}} \leq 2^{21}$$

Since e is less than 4 we get: $2^{\frac{\mathcal{H}}{2\rho}} \leq 2^{23}$. Therefore $\mathcal{H} \leq 46\,\rho$. Remember that ρ is less than 1. This involves that the length of the digests produced by h does not exceed 46 bits. In this case h cannot be collision resistant since the birthday attack would require about 2^{23} computations to get a collision with probability at least $\frac{1}{2}$. This contradicts our hypothesis concerning the security of h. Therefore we must have: $\lfloor \tilde{x} \rfloor > 2^{20}$. This value is sufficient for practical applications since n will be roughly 1000.

B Proof of Theorem 3

We decompose this proof into three parts. In the first one we will demonstrate the recovery property of our scheme. In the second one we will prove that $U(n)$ is an upper bound on the number of signature verifications to be performed per block. Finally we will show that $U(n)$ is $O(1)$ as a function of the block length n. Since our results have to be valid for any value BID, we start our proof by picking a value BID which will remain fixed throughout this proof.

Packet Recovery. Since (α, β) is accurate, at least $\lceil \alpha n \rceil$ of the original elements $\{AP_1, \ldots, AP_n\}$ are received by the receiver amongst a total of no-more than $\lfloor \beta n \rfloor$ elements. Thus step 1 of Decoder is performed successfully. MPR is run on at most $\lfloor \beta n \rfloor$ elements where at least $\lceil \alpha n \rceil$ of them are correct to get back a polynomial of degree at most ρn. Since $\lceil \alpha n \rceil > \sqrt{(\rho n) \lfloor \beta n \rfloor}$ then Poly-Reconstruct can be run and it successfully outputs the list of all polynomials of degree at most ρn which pass through at least $\lceil \alpha n \rceil$ of the given points. In particular the polynomial $A(X) = a_0 + a_1 X + \cdots + a_{\rho n} X^{\rho n}$ belongs to the list generated at step 2 of MRP. We deduce that $h_1 \| \cdots \| h_n \| \sigma \| 0^\ell$ belongs to the list output by MRP. This means that at least one signature is verified at step 2 of Decoder.

If there is another element C' on this list which verifies the signature then C' must end with $\tilde{\ell}$ zeros due to step 3. It must be written as $C' = h_1' \| \cdots \| h_n' \| \sigma' \| 0^{\tilde{\ell}}$ where each h_i' is $\mathcal{H}$ bits long and we must have $\text{Verify}_{PK}(h(\text{BID}\|\alpha\|\beta\|n\|\mathcal{P}\|h_1'\| \cdots \|h_n'), \sigma') = \text{true}$. The collision resistance property of h involves that the two couples $(h(\text{BID}\|\alpha\|\beta\|n\|\mathcal{P}\|h_1\| \cdots \|h_n), \sigma)$ and $(h(\text{BID}\|\alpha\|\beta\|n\|\mathcal{P}\|h_1'\| \cdots \|h_n'), \sigma')$ are different. Remember that the key SK is only known to the sender. In addition the authentication scheme is designed in such a way that the sender only sign one element per value BID. This means that $(h(\text{BID}\|\alpha\|\beta\|n\|\mathcal{P}\|h_1'\| \cdots \|h_n'), \sigma')$ is a forgery of the digital signature. This is impossible since we assumed in Sect. 3 that it was secure.

Therefore $h_1 \| \cdots \| h_n \| \sigma \| 0^\ell$ is the only element to verify the signature in the list output by MPR. Thus the receiver has recovered the n original hashes $h_1, \ldots, h_n$ at the end of step 3. Since h is collision resistant the only elements to be identified at step 4 are those corresponding to the original received elements. Since (α, β) is accurate there are at least $\lceil \alpha n \rceil$ of them.

Thus the receiver has at least $\lceil \alpha n \rceil$ of the n modified symbols $\hat{S}_1, \ldots, \hat{S}_n$. In addition the input of DecodeMDS at step 5 only contains original symbols since the hash function h sorted out the forgeries at step 4. By construction the MDS code can correct up to $n - \lceil \alpha n \rceil$ erasures. Therefore the receiver recovers $S_1, \ldots, S_{\lceil \alpha n \rceil}$ at the end of step 5.

Since step 6 only consists of removing the pad of length ℓ, we deduce that the receiver has obtained the n original packets $P_1, \ldots, P_n$ as output of Decoder.

Signature Verification. Since at most one signature verification is performed per element of the list output by MPR, it is sufficient to prove that $U(n)$ is an upper bound on the size of that list. Denote N the number of points on which Poly-Reconstruct is run and T the number of original elements in this list. Due to the accuracy of (α, β) we have: $T \geq \lceil \alpha n \rceil$ and $N \leq \lfloor \beta n \rfloor$. As noticed before we have: $T > \sqrt{(\rho n) N}$ which guarantees Poly-Reconstruct to be run successfully. Denote $L(N, T)$ the size of the list output by Poly-Reconstruct. We want to prove: $L(T, N) \leq U(n)$.

According to the proof of Proposition 6.15 in Guruswami's thesis [11], we have: $L(T, N) \leq \lfloor \frac{\ell}{k} \rfloor$ where:

$$\begin{cases} \ell = rT - 1 \\ r = 1 + \left\lfloor \dfrac{kN + \sqrt{k^2 N^2 + 4(T^2 - kN)}}{2(T^2 - kN)} \right\rfloor \end{cases}$$

In our case $k = \rho n$. Therefore we obtain:

$$L(T, N) \leq \frac{T}{\rho n} \left(1 + \frac{(\rho n) N + \sqrt{(\rho n)^2 N^2 + 4(T^2 - (\rho n) N)}}{2(T^2 - (\rho n) N)} \right) - \frac{1}{\rho n} \quad (2)$$

$\underline{1^{\text{st}} \text{ bound}}$: We have: $\forall (a, b) \in \mathbb{R}^+ \times \mathbb{R}^+ \ \sqrt{a + b} \leq \sqrt{a} + \sqrt{b}$. We obtain:

$$L(T, N) \leq \frac{T}{\rho n} \left(1 + \frac{(\rho n) N}{T^2 - (\rho n) N} + \frac{1}{\sqrt{T^2 - (\rho n) N}} \right) - \frac{1}{\rho n}$$

Using $T \geq \lceil \alpha n \rceil$, we deduce that $T^2 - (\rho n) N$ is lower bounded by $n^2 (\alpha^2 - \beta \rho)$. This element is positive since $\rho < \frac{\alpha^2}{\beta}$. Thus:

$$L(T, N) \leq \frac{T}{\rho n} \left(1 + \frac{\rho N}{n (\alpha^2 - \beta \rho)} + \frac{1}{n \sqrt{\alpha^2 - \beta \rho}} \right) - \frac{1}{\rho n}$$

Since $T \leq n$ and $N \leq \lfloor \beta n \rfloor$, $U_1(n)$ is an upper bound of the right hand side of the previous inequality. Since $L(T, N)$ is an integer we get: $L(T, N) \leq \lfloor U_1(n) \rfloor$.

$\underline{2^{\text{nd}} \text{ bound}}$: We start again from (2). Since $T \leq n$ we have: $\frac{T}{\rho n} \leq \frac{1}{\rho}$. The numerator of the fraction is upper bounded by $\beta \rho n + \sqrt{(\beta \rho n^2)^2 + 4(n^2 - \rho \alpha n^2)}$. As before $T^2 - (\rho n) N$ is lower bounded by $n^2 (\alpha^2 - \beta \rho)$. Therefore:

$$L(T, N) \leq \frac{1}{\rho} \left(\frac{\beta \rho + \sqrt{\beta \rho + \frac{4}{n^2}(1 - \rho \alpha)}}{\alpha^2 - \beta \rho} \right) - \frac{1}{\rho n}$$

The right hand side of the previous inequality is equal to $U_2(n)$. Therefore we have: $L(T, N) \leq \lfloor U_2(n) \rfloor$.

Finally we obtain: $L(T, N) \leq \min(\lfloor U_1(n) \rfloor, \lfloor U_2(n) \rfloor)$ which means $L(T, N) \leq U(n)$.

Asymptotic Analysis. As in [20], we consider that ρ is a constant when studying the asymptotic behavior of $U(n)$. Nevertheless ρn must be an integer. Therefore the limit of $U(n)$ can only be studied for values n in $\mathcal{I} := \{n / \rho n \in \mathbb{N}\}$. A necessary and sufficient condition to study the limit in $+\infty$ is to have an infinite number of elements in $\mathcal{I}$ since $\mathcal{I}$ is a subset of $\mathbb{N}$. Remember that ρ is a (positive) rational number. Thus we can write $\rho = \frac{u_\rho}{v_\rho}$ where u_ρ and v_ρ are elements of $\mathbb{N}$. If we consider $\mathbb{N}v_\rho$, the subset of $\mathbb{N}$ representing the multiples of v_ρ, then: $\mathbb{N}v_\rho \subset \mathcal{I}$. Since $\mathbb{N}v_\rho$ is infinite, so is $\mathcal{I}$. Therefore we can study the asymptotic behavior of $U(n)$ as soon as ρ is a rational number. We have:

$$\lim_{\substack{n \to +\infty \\ n \in \mathcal{I}}} \left(\frac{1}{\rho\, n} \right) = 0 \quad \text{and} \quad \lim_{\substack{n \to +\infty \\ n \in \mathcal{I}}} \left(\sqrt{\frac{\beta}{\alpha} + \frac{1}{\rho^2\, n^2}\,(1 - \rho\,\alpha)} \right) = \sqrt{\frac{\beta}{\rho}}$$

These two equations involve that $U_2(n)$ has a finite limit when n tends to $+\infty$ (and $n \in \mathcal{I}$). Thus we get $U_2(n) \in O(1)$ and then $\lfloor U_2(n) \rfloor \in O(1)$.

The left hand side equality involves that $U_1(n)$ has a finite limit when n tends to $+\infty$ (and $n \in \mathcal{I}$). As before we obtain: $\lfloor U_1(n) \rfloor \in O(1)$.

Since $U(n) = \min(\lfloor U_1(n) \rfloor, \lfloor U_2(n) \rfloor)$ we finally deduce: $U(n) \in O(1)$ which achieves to prove our theorem.

Shorter Verifier-Local Revocation Group Signatures from Bilinear Maps*

Sujing Zhou and Dongdai Lin

SKLOIS Lab, Institute of Software,
Chinese Academy of Sciences, Beijing, P.R. China
zhousujing@is.iscas.ac.cn, ddlin@is.iscas.ac.cn

Abstract. We propose a new computational complexity assumption from bilinear map, based on which we construct Verifier-Local Revocation group signatures with shorter lengths than previous ones.

Keywords: LRSW Assumption; Group Signature; Verifier-Local Revocation; Bilinear Map.

1 Introduction

Group signature [1] is motivated by enabling members of a group to sign on behalf of the group without leaking their own identities, and at the same time the signer's identity can be discovered by the group manager (GM) when a dispute occurs.

In brief, a group signature scheme is a signature scheme that has multiple secret keys corresponding to a single public key. A group signature should at least include the following five algorithms: Setup, Join, GSig, GVer and Open. Setup is executed by the group manager (GM); Join is an interactive protocol between a group member and GM or a separate issuing authority (IA); GSig is an algorithm run by any group member; any one can execute GVer to check the validity of a given group signature; Open is used by GM or a separate opening authority (OA) to find the identity of the signer given a group signature.

Various applications have been found for group signature schemes, such as anonymous authentication, internet voting and bidding. But wide implementation of group signatures in the real world has been prevented because of some factors, among which is efficient membership revocation as pointed out in [2].

Nontrivial resolutions to membership revocation have been proposed with regard to specific group signature schemes. The resolutions can be classified into two categories. One is based on *witness* [3,4,5], another is based on revocation list (RL) [6,7]. Resolutions based on witness is advantageous over the latter in that growing revocation lists are not needed to maintain, but in some applications RL based revocations are more suitable because they admit shorter signature size [8].

---

* Supported by 973 Project of China (No.2004CB318004), 863 Project of China (No. 2003AA144030) and NSFC90204016.

D. Pointcheval, Y. Mu, and K. Chen (Eds.): CANS 2006, LNCS 4301, pp. 126–143, 2006.

RL Based Revocation. In this category, a natural resolution is to let GM issue a revocation list of identities (public membership keys) RL, any group member proves in a zero-knowledge way that his identity hidden in the group signature is not equal to any one in RL[6]. The drawback is that signature size is linearly dependent on the size of RL.

[7] improved the above approach resulting in a scheme that signature size and computation are constant while the complexity of GVer is linearly dependent on the size of RL. In this resolution, GM publishes a RL which includes $V_i = f(pcert_i)$, i.e., evaluations of one way function f on partial certificate information $pcert_i$ which is unique to each group member. In signing a message, member i includes a random R, and $T = f'(V_i, R)$ (f' is another one way function which may equal f) in the group signature. Verifiers check if $T = f'(V_i, R)$ by trying every V_i in the current RL.

The idea of [7] is followed by [8,9] etc., and is named *verifier-local revocation* (VLR) and formalized in [8]. Nakanishi et al. [9], however, pointed out previous VLR schemes have a drawback of backward linkability, and proposed another VLR scheme based on [8] with the feature of backward unlinkability (BU), i.e., group signatures generated by the same group member is unlinkable except himself and GM, even after this member has been revoked (his/her revocation token is published).

Contributions. We propose a new computational complexity assumption from bilinear map, and a new standard signature, two new verifier-local revocation group signature, one without backward unlinkability, another with backward unlinkability, based on our assumption. The proposed group signature schemes are more efficient both in signature length and signature generation/verification than previous ones.

Organization. Our new complexity assumption and the new standard signature are described in Section 3. The proposed new group signatures from bilinear map are presented in Section 5, with corresponding security proofs provided in Appendixes.

2   Preliminaries

Suppose that $G_1 = \langle g \rangle$, $G_2 = \langle \tilde{g} \rangle$ and G_3 are multiplicative cyclic groups of prime order p, there exists an efficient non-degenerate bilinear map $e : G_1 \times G_2 \to G_3$, i.e., $e(u^a, v^b) = e(u, v)^{ab}$ for any $u \in G_1$, $v \in G_2$, $a, b \in Z_p$, and $e(g, \tilde{g}) \neq 1$.

Definition 1 (LRSW Assumption [10]). *Suppose G_1, G_2, G_3 are defined as above and generated by a setup algorithm. Let $\widetilde{X} = \tilde{g}^x$, $\widetilde{Y} = \tilde{g}^y$, $O_{x,y}(.)$ be an oracle that, on input a value $m \in Z_p^*$, outputs a triple (a, a^y, a^{x+mxy}) for a randomly chosen $a \in G_1$. Then for any probabilistic polynomial time (PPT) bounded adversary $\mathcal{A}$, the following probability is negligible:*

$$\Pr\{(p, G_1, G_2, G_3, e) \leftarrow Setup(1^k); x \xleftarrow{R} Z_p^*; y \xleftarrow{R} Z_p^*; \widetilde{X} = \tilde{g}^x; \widetilde{Y} = \tilde{g}^y;$$
$$(m, a, b, c) \leftarrow \mathcal{A}^{O_{x,y}}(g, \tilde{g}, e, \widetilde{X}, \widetilde{Y}) : m \in Z_p^* \backslash Q \wedge a \in G_1 \wedge b = a^y \wedge c = a^{x+mxy}\} < \epsilon,$$

where Q is the set of queries that $\mathcal{A}$ has made to $O_{x,y}(.)$.

Definition 2 (DDH). *In the bilinear groups G_1, G_2 defined above, for any PPT bounded probabilistic algorithm $\mathcal{A}$, the following probability is negligible:*
$\Pr\{\mathcal{A}(g^a, g^b, g^{ab}) = 1\} - \Pr\{\mathcal{A}(g^a, g^b, g^c) = 1\} < \epsilon$.
The probability is taken over the coin of $\mathcal{A}$ and random choice of $a, b, c \in Z_p^*$.

Notations. $PK\{(\alpha, \beta, ...) : R(\alpha, \beta, ...)\}$. denotes a proof of knowledge, in which a prover can show that he knows the values of $(\alpha, \beta, ...)$ satisfying the relation $R(\alpha, \beta, ...)$.

$SK\{(\alpha, \beta, ...) : R(\alpha, \beta, ...)\}\{m\}$. denotes a signature of knowledge [11], a non-interactive version of the above proof of knowledge transformed in Fiat-Shamir method [12].

Because the easiness of transformation between PK and SK, they might be mentioned interchangeably in the sequel. We let VSK denote the corresponding verification of SK.

$x \xleftarrow{R} S$ denotes x is chosen uniformly at random from the set S. $x \xleftarrow{\$} A(.,.,.)$ denotes x is generated from executing algorithm A where random variables are chosen uniformly at random. G^k, $(Z_p^*)^k$ denote a k tuple from G and Z_p^* respectively. $|M|$ denotes the binary length of string M, $|S|$ denotes the number of elements in the set S.

3   A New Complexity Assumption

The idea of Assumption 1 comes from an effort to reduce the items in LRSW Assumption from three to two, so that the signature size based on the assumption will be shortened. After an analysis of all possible $(g^r, g^{f(r,x,y,m)})$, where $f(.) = c_0 rx + c_1 ry + c_2 xy$, $c_i \in \{0, 1, m\}$ for $i = 0, 1, 2$, we found it seems unforgeable when $(c_0, c_1, c_2) \in \{(1, m, 1), (m, 1, m)\}$, and actually they are interchangeable to each other.

Assumption 1 (Our New Assumption). *Suppose G_1, G_2, G_3 are defined as in Section 2 and generated by a setup algorithm. Let $X = g^x$, $Y = g^y$, $\tilde{X} = \tilde{g}^x$, $\tilde{Y} = \tilde{g}^y$, $x \neq y$, $O_{x,y}(.)$ be an oracle that, on input a value $m \in Z_p^*$, outputs a pair $(g^r, g^{r(x+my)+xy})$ for a randomly chosen $r \in Z_p^* \setminus \{1\}$. Then for any PPT bounded adversary $\mathcal{A}$, the following probability is negligible:*

$\Pr[(p, G_1, G_2, G_3, e, g, \tilde{g}) \leftarrow Setup(1^k); x \xleftarrow{R} Z_p^*; y \xleftarrow{R} Z_p^*; X = g^x; Y = g^y;$
$\tilde{X} = \tilde{g}^x; \tilde{Y} = \tilde{g}^y; (m, a, b) \leftarrow \mathcal{A}^{O_{x,y}}(p, g, \tilde{g}, e, X, Y, \tilde{X}, \tilde{Y}) : m \in Z_p^* \setminus Q \wedge a = g^r \wedge a \notin \{1_{G_1}, g\} \wedge b = g^{r(x+my)+xy}] < \epsilon$,

where Q is the set of queries that $\mathcal{A}$ has made to $O_{x,y}(.)$, 1_{G_1} is the unit element of G_1.

Assumption 1 is hard in generic groups, i.e.,

Theorem 1. *Let $x \in Z_p^*$, $y \in Z_p^*$ and maps ξ_1, ξ_2, ξ_3 are chosen at random. Let $\mathcal{A}$ be an algorithm that solves the assumption in the generic group model, making a total of polynomial number Q_G queries to the oracles computing the group action in G_1, G_2, G_3, and the oracle computing the bilinear pairing e, and* the oracle $O_{x,y}(.)$ as described in the above definition. Then the probability ε that $\mathcal{A}^{O_{x,y}}(p,\xi_1(1),\xi_2(1),\xi_1(x),\xi_1(y)),\xi_2(x),\xi_2(y)$ outputs $(m,\xi_1(r),\xi_1(r(x+my)+xy))$ is bounded as follows:

$$\varepsilon \leq O(Q_G^2/p).$$

The proof (see Appendix A) follows similar proofs in [13,14]. The relationship among Assumption 1, LRSW, and Strong Diffie-Hellman assumption [14] are still not clear. A new standard signature scheme can be obtained based on this assumption.

Scheme 1. Let G_1, G_2, G_3 and bilinear map e be the same as described in Section 2 and Assumption 1.

- KeyGen. Select $(x,y) \xleftarrow{R} Z_p^* \times Z_p^*$, $x \neq y$, set $X = g^x$, $Y = g^y$, $\widetilde{X} = \tilde{g}^x$, $\widetilde{Y} = \tilde{g}^y$. The secret key is (x,y), public key is $(X,Y,\widetilde{X},\widetilde{Y},g,\tilde{g},e,p)$.
- Sign. Given a message $m \in Z_p^*$, its signature is (U,V), where $U = g^r$, $V = g^{r(x+my)+xy}$, $r \xleftarrow{R} Z_p^* \setminus \{1\}$.
- Verify. Given a signature (U,V) of m, check if $e(V,\tilde{g}) = e(U,\widetilde{X}\widetilde{Y}^m)e(X,\widetilde{Y})$. If the equation holds, then accept (U,V) as a valid signature of m, otherwise reject it as invalid.

Lemma 1. *Signature scheme 1 is existentially unforgeable under Assumption 1.*

For a message $m \in \{0,1\}^*$ other than Z_p^*, apply a hash function $H : \{0,1\}^* \to Z_p^*$ to m, then run Sign and Verify on $H(m)$. Note that in algorithm Sign, Assumption 1 and the proposed VLR group signatures in the sequel, it is required $r > 1$, and further more r should be large enough to foil naive attacks against Discrete Logarithm, e.g., repeatedly multiply g to match a given g^r.

4 Definition of Verifier-Local Revocation Group Signature

We provide a variant definition of VLR group signature from [8,9] as follows.

Definition 3 (VLR Group Signature). A VLR group signature scheme GS is a digital signature scheme comprising the following algorithms:

- Setup: an algorithm to get group public key gpk and group secret key $gsk = (ik)$, where ik is secret key of IA. Each user, for example i, to join in the group has its *user secret key* and *user public key* pair (sk_i, pk_i). A publishable revocation list RL is maintained and initialized empty; a registration table Reg, kept secret to IA and OA, is initialized empty. Let the current time period be j, initialized to 0.
- Join: a probabilistic interactive protocol between IA and a user, in the end, user i obtains its *group signing key* gsk_i. Generally $gsk_i = (msk_i, mpk_i)$, where *member secret key* msk_i is selected jointly by i and IA, and kept secret to i, *member public key* of i or *member certificate* mpk_i is generated by IA. If Join is successful mpk_i is added into Reg.

- Revoke: To revoke member i at time period j, IA generates revocation token $grt_{i,j}$, adds it to RL_j.
- GSig: a probabilistic algorithm on input (gsk_i, j, m), where gsk_i is the group signing key of a member in the group, returns σ as a group signature on m at time period j.
- GVer: a deterministic algorithm on input $(gpk, RL_j, j, m, \sigma)$, where σ is purported to be a group signature on m at time period j when the revocation list is RL_j, returns 1 to accept the group signature as valid or 0 to deny the group signature as invalid.
- Open: on input a message-signature pair (m, j, σ), Reg, returns (i, π) indicating i is the purported identity of the group member who signed the signature when $i > 0$, or none of the members has generated σ when $i = 0$, and π is a proof of this claim.
- Judge: on input of $(gpk, RL_j, j, m, \sigma, i, \pi, pk_i)$, return 1 to accept the claim of π, or 0 to deny the claim.
- If j is constant, GS is a VLR group signature w/o backward unlinkability, otherwise it is a VLR scheme with backward unlinkability.

In the following paragraphs, we investigate a formal adversary model of VLR group signature based on [15,8,9].

Firstly we define the oracles similar to [15]. It is assumed that several global variables are maintained by the oracles: HU, a set of honest users; CU, a set of corrupted users; $GSet$, a set of message signature pairs; and $Chlist$, a list of challenged message signature pairs. Note that not all the oracles will be available to adversaries in defining a certain security feature.

$AddU(i)$: If $i \in HU \cup CU$, the oracle returns $\perp$, else adds i to HU, executes algorithm Join.

$CrptU(i, pk)$: If $i \in HU \cup CU$, the oracle returns $\perp$, else sets $pk_i = pk$, $CU \leftarrow CU \cup \{i\}$, and awaits an oracle query to $SndToI$.

$SndToI(i, M_{in})$: If $i \notin CU$, the oracle returns $\perp$; else it plays the role of IA in algorithm Join replying to M_{in}, a string sent from user i.

$SndToU(i, M_{in})$: If $i \in HU \cup CU$, the oracle returns $\perp$, else it plays the role of user i in algorithm Join, $HU \leftarrow HU \cup \{i\}$.

$USK(i)$: If $i \in HU$, the oracle returns sk_i and gsk_i, $CU \leftarrow CU \cup \{i\}$, $HU \leftarrow HU \setminus \{i\}$; else returns $\perp$.

$RReg(i)$: The oracle returns reg_i, the record in the registration table Reg corresponding to user i.

$WReg(i, s)$: The oracle sets $reg_i = s$ if i has not been added in reg.

$Revoke(i, j)$: The oracle returns revocation token grt_{ij} of member i at time period j.

$GSig(i,j,m)$: If $i \notin HU$, the oracle returns $\perp$, else returns a group signature σ on m by user i at time period j. $GSet \leftarrow GSet \cup \{(i, j, m, \sigma)\}$.

$Ch(b, i_0, i_1, m, j)$: If $i_0 \notin HU \cup CU$ or $i_1 \notin HU \cup CU$, the oracle returns $\perp$, else generates a valid group signature σ with i_b being the signer at time period j. $Chlist \leftarrow Chlist \cup \{(m, j, \sigma)\}$.

Open(m, j, σ): If $(m, j, \sigma) \in Chlist$, the oracle returns $\bot$, else if (m, j, σ) is valid, the oracle returns output of Open(Reg, m, j, σ).
CrptIA: The oracle returns the secret key ik of IA.
CrptOA: The oracle returns the registration table *Reg*.

We say an oracle is over another oracle if availability of the oracle implies functions of another oracle. For example, *WReg* is over *RReg* since the adversary can try to remember everything it has written to *Reg*; *CrptIA* is over *CrptU*, *SndToI* since knowledge of ik enables the adversary to act as the two oracles itself; *CrptIA* is also over *CrptOA*; *CrptOA* is over *Open* and *RReg* since OA has access to *Reg*. Note that we do not let *CrptIA* over *WReg* so as to provide flexibility when accesses to the database *Reg* are granted by an independent DBA (database administrator).

Correctness. For any adversary that is not computationally restricted, a group signature generated by an honest group member is always valid; algorithm Open will always correctly identify the signer given the above group signature; the output of Open will always be accepted by algorithm Judge.

Selfless-anonymity. This concept is named in [8]. Imagine a PPT adversary $\mathcal{A}$, whose goal is to distinguish the signer of a group signature $\sigma \leftarrow Ch(b, i_0, i_1, m, J)$ at time period J between $i_0, i_1 \in HU$, where i_0, i_1, m, J are all chosen by $\mathcal{A}$ itself.
Naturally the adversary $\mathcal{A}$ might want to get the group signing keys of some other honest group members except i_0, i_1 (through oracle *USK*); it might want to obtain some group signatures signed by i_0, i_1 at the time period J(through oracle *GSig*); it might want to see some outputs of OA (through oracle *Open* except (J, m, σ)); it might also try to corrupt some group members by running Join with IA (through oracles *CrptU* and *SndToI*); it might observe the communication of some honest members joining in (through *SndToU* if IA is corrupted, not available otherwise); it might want to write to *Reg* (through oracles *WReg*); it might want to revoke some honest group members except i_0, i_1. Obviously $\mathcal{A}$ should not be allowed to corrupt OA and IA and request to *RReg*, and it is also forbidden from requesting revocation token of i_0, i_1 before the challenged time period J (including J).
A VLR group signature GS is *selfless-anonymous* if the probability for any PPT adversary to win is negligible, i.e., the value of $\text{Adv}_{GS,\mathcal{A}}^{anon}$ defined below is negligible.

$$\text{Adv}_{GS,\mathcal{A}}^{anon}(k) = \Pr[Exp_{GS,\mathcal{A}}^{anon-1}(k) = 1] - \Pr[Exp_{GS,\mathcal{A}}^{anon-0}(k) = 1],$$

where experiments $Exp_{GS,\mathcal{A}}^{anon-b}(k)$ are defined as in Table 1.

Traceability. Imagine a PPT adversary $\mathcal{A}$, whose goal is to produce a valid group signature (m, σ) at time period j and a corresponding revocation list RL_j, the output of Open points to a non-existent and unrevoked member or an existing corrupted member but can not pass Judge.
Naturally the adversary $\mathcal{A}$ might corrupt some group members by running Join with IA (through oracles *CrptU* and *SndToI*); it might want to see some

Table 1. Selfless-anonymity

Experiment $Exp_{GS,A}^{anon-b}(k)$, $b \in \{0,1\}$
$(gpk, ik) \xleftarrow{\$} \text{Setup}(1^k)$; $CU \leftarrow \varnothing$, $HU \leftarrow \varnothing$, $Chlist \leftarrow \varnothing$;
$d \xleftarrow{\$} A(gpk : Open, CrptU, SndToI, USK, Ch(b,.,.,.), GSig, WReg, Revoke)$,
Return d.

outputs of OA (through oracle *Open*); it might want to read from (through oracles *RReg*); or A might corrupt OA directly (through oracle *CrptOA*). Obviously A should not be allowed to corrupt IA and query *WReg*. Note that A might not bother to query about honest group members for they are of little help for it.

A VLR group signature GS is *traceable* if the probability for any PPT adversary to win is negligible, i.e., the value of $\text{Adv}_{GS,A}^{trace}$ defined below is negligible.

$$\text{Adv}_{GS,A}^{trace}(k) = \Pr[Exp_{GS,A}^{trace}(k) = 1],$$

where experiment $Exp_{GS,A}^{trace}(k)$ is defined as in Table 2.

Table 2. Traceability

Experiment $Exp_{GS,A}^{trace}(k)$
$(gpk, ik) \xleftarrow{\$} \text{Setup}(1^k)$; $CU \leftarrow \varnothing$, $HU \leftarrow \varnothing$;
$(m, \sigma, j, RL_j) \xleftarrow{\$} A(gpk : CrptOA, CrptU, SndToI)$.
If $\text{GVer}(gpk, RL_j, j, m, \sigma) = 0$, return 0, else $(i, \pi) \leftarrow \text{Open}(Reg, j, m, \sigma)$.
If $i = 0$ or ($\text{Judge}(gpk, RL_j, j, m, \sigma, i, \pi, pk_i) = 0$ and $i \in CU$) then return 1, else return 0.

Non-frameability. Imagine a PPT adversary A, whose goal is to produce a valid group signature (m, σ) at time period j and a corresponding revocation list RL_j, the output of Open points to an existing unrevoked honest member i_h and the result passes Judge.

Naturally the adversary A might want to get the group signing keys of some group members (through oracle *USK*); it might want to obtain some group signatures signed by some honest group members (through oracle *GSig*); it might want to see some outputs of OA (through oracle *Open*); it might also try to corrupt some group members by running Join with IA (through oracles *CrptU* and *SndToI*); it might observe the communication of some honest members joining in (through *SndToU* if *CrptIA* is queried, not available otherwise); it might wait until more group members has joined in (through *AddU*); it might want to write to or read from *Reg* (through oracles *WReg*, *RReg*); or A might corrupt OA or IA directly (through oracle *CrptOA* and *CrptIA*). Obviously A should not be allowed to query $CrptU(i_h)$, $SndToI(i_h,.)$, $USK(i_h)$.

A VLR group signature GS is *non-frameable* if the probability for any PPT adversary to win is negligible, i.e., the value of $\text{Adv}_{GS,A}^{nf}$ defined below is negligible.

$$\text{Adv}_{GS,A}^{nf}(k) = \Pr[Exp_{GS,A}^{nf}(k) = 1],$$

where experiment $Exp^{nf}_{GS,A}(k)$ is defined as in Table 3 after taking consideration of "over" relationship between oralces.

Table 3. Non-frameability

Experiment $Exp^{nf}_{GS,A}(k)$
$(gpk, ik) \xleftarrow{\$} \text{Setup}(1^k)$; $CU \leftarrow \varnothing$, $HU \leftarrow \varnothing$, $GSet \leftarrow \varnothing$;
$(m, \sigma, j, RL_j, i, \pi) \xleftarrow{\$} A(gpk : CrptIA, CrptOA, SndToU, GSig, USK, WReg)$.
If GVer(gpk, RL_j, j, m, σ) = 0, return 0.
Else if $i \in HU$ and Judge $(gpk, RL_j, j, m, \sigma, i, \pi, pk_i) = 1$
and $(i, j, m, .) \notin GSet$, return 1, else return 0.

Definition 4. *A VLR group signature scheme is secure if it is selfless-anonymous, traceable and non-frameable.*

4.1 VLR Group Signature with Backward Unlinkability

The following model and definitions conform to [9].

Definition 5 (BU-VLR group signature). A BU-VLR group signature, i.e., a group signature scheme with verifier-local revocation and backward unlinkability simultaneously consists of the following algorithms. We suppose the maximum number of group members is n and the total time period is T.

- KGen(n, T): A probabilistic algorithm to generate group public key gpk, secret key gsk_i for each group member $i \in [1, n]$, and revocation tokens grt_{ij} for each member i at time period j.
- GSig(gpk, j, gsk_i, m): A probabilistic algorithm that produces a signature σ on message $m \in \{0, 1\}^*$ at time period j by group member i who possesses the secret key gsk_i.
- Revoke(RL_j, grt_{ij}): If i is to be revoked for the time period j, the group manager adds grt_{ij} to the revocation list of time period j, i.e., $RL_j \leftarrow RL_j \cup \{grt_{ij}\}$.
- GVer(gpk, j, RL_j, σ, m): A deterministic algorithm executable by anyone to generate a one bit b. If $b = 1$, it means σ is a valid group signature on m by some valid member (whose revocation token does not exist in RL_j); if $b = 0$, it means otherwise.

KGen corresponds to algorithms Setup and Join. Open is omitted since GM can run GVer against unpublished revocation tokens to find a group member match.

Definition 6 (Correctness). A BU-VLR group signature is correct if for all $(gpk, gsk, grt) \leftarrow \text{KGen}(n, T)$, all $j \in [1, T]$, all $i \in [1, n]$, and all $m \in \{0, 1\}^*$, GVer($gpk, j, RL_j, \text{GSig}(gpk, j, gsk_i, m), m$) = 1 $\leftrightarrow grt_{ij} \notin RL_j$.

Definition 7 (BU-Anonymity). A BU-VLR group signature has BU-anonymity if any PPT bounded probabilistic adversary A only has probability of $\frac{1}{2} + \epsilon$ (ϵ is negligible), i.e., with advantage of ϵ, to win in the following game.

- Setup: An instance of the BU-VLR group signature is established and gpk, gsk, grt are generated by a challenger, $\mathcal{A}$ is given only gpk.
- Queries:
  - Signing queries: $\mathcal{A}$ is allowed to request a signature on any message m for any group member i at time period j.
  - Corruption: $\mathcal{A}$ is allowed to request the secret key of any group member i, i.e., gsk_i.
  - Revocation: $\mathcal{A}$ is allowed to request the revocation token of any group member i at any time period j, i.e., grt_{ij}.
- Challenge: $\mathcal{A}$ outputs some (m, i_0, i_1, J) on the conditions that group members i_0 and i_1 have not been corrupted, and their revocation tokens have not been requested before time period J (including J). The challenger randomly selects $\phi \in \{0, 1\}$ and responds with a group signature on m by group member i_ϕ at time period J.
- Restricted queries: $\mathcal{A}$ is allowed to continue queries of Signing, Corruption and Revocation, except that i_0 and i_1 are forbidden in Corruption queries, and their Revocation queries are not allowed before time period J and current time period that $\mathcal{A}$ is to generate output (including J and current time)
- Output: $\mathcal{A}$ has to output a one bit value ϕ', and wins if $\phi' = \phi$.

Definition 8 (Traceability). A BU-VLR group signature has traceability if any PPT bounded probabilistic adversary $\mathcal{A}$ only has negligible probability ϵ to win in the following game.

- Setup: An instance of the BU-VLR group signature is established and gpk, gsk, grt are generated by a challenger, $\mathcal{A}$ is given gpk, grt. A set U is initialized empty.
- Queries:
  - Signing queries: $\mathcal{A}$ is allowed to request a signature on any message m for any group member i at time period j.
  - Corruption: $\mathcal{A}$ is allowed to request the secret key of any group member i, i.e., gsk_i, i is added into U.
- Output: $\mathcal{A}$ has to output $(m^*, j^*, RL_{j^*}^*, \sigma^*)$, and it wins if (1) GVer(gpk, j^*, $RL_{j^*}^*$, σ^*, m^*)= 1, and (2) σ^* is traced to a group member outside of $U \setminus RL_{j^*}$ or failure, and (3) $\mathcal{A}$ has not obtained σ^* in signing queries on message m^* for this group member at time period j^*.

5   Proposed VLR Group Signature

Brief Idea. Actually a group signature can be viewed as a proof of knowledge of a standard signature signed by an authority ([11], [16], [17], [18], [19], [4], [10], [20]), so every standard signature can be employed to construct a group signature scheme [21], the point is how to obtain an efficient group signature scheme, and not every standard signature will result in efficient construction.

Scheme 1, however, has two features that make it a suitable candidate for group signature.

- For any signature (U,V) of m, any one can derive a new signature (U',V') of the same message: $U' = Ug^{r'}$, $V' = VX^{r'}Y^{mr'}$, where $r' \xleftarrow{R} Z_p^*$. Every random derivation is independent from each other.
- The generation of (U,V) can be done even when m is not revealed: $U = g^r$, $V = C^r g^{rx+xy}$, where $C = Y^m$.

The brief idea of Scheme 2 is: let group member i choose his secret key s_i, commit it (without information theoretic hiding) to $C_i = Y^{s_i}$. IA, as the signer of Scheme 1, signs blindly on s_i, i.e., outputs (U_i, V_i) as a member certificate of i. Group member i firstly generates a proof of knowledge of (s_i, U_i, V_i), when he is asked to produce a group signature of a message, then randomize his member certificate according to the first feature, now what left is to prove his knowledge of s_i, which has standard and efficient resolution already [22].

The brief idea of Scheme 3 follows the above idea. Additionally a revocation tag $e(g^{s_i}, h_j)^{\delta}$, g^{δ} ($\delta \xleftarrow{R} Z_p^*$) as well as a proof of knowledge of (s_i, δ) is appended to the end of a group signature, where h_j is chosen at the beginning of time period j by the revocation authority (IA or OA), and published along with the revocation list at that time RL_j. The method is the same of [9], but our resulted scheme is about 23% shorter in signature length.

5.1   The Scheme Without Backward Unlinkability

Scheme 2 utilizes a trusted third party TP in case OA might be corrupted. If OA is fully trusted, then the scheme can be simplified by eliminating TP and signature of i on A_i, without invalidating corresponding proofs. Note that we omit the index of time period in the following description because it is a VLR scheme without backward unlinkability.

Scheme 2 (Our Proposal w/o BU). Let G_1, G_2, G_3 and bilinear map e : $G_1 \times G_2 \rightarrow G_3$ be defined as in Section 2.

- Setup: Group secret key is $(x,y) \xleftarrow{R} Z_p^* \times Z_p^*$, $x \neq y$, public key is $(g, \tilde{g}, e, X = g^x, Y = g^y, \tilde{X} = \tilde{g}^x, \tilde{Y} = \tilde{g}^y, p, h \xleftarrow{R} G_2)$. A hash function $H : \{0,1\}^* \rightarrow Z_p^*$. A registration table Reg is maintained and initialized empty. A signature scheme S is selected, which is similar to the scheme in [23]:

S.KeyGen: Select $z \xleftarrow{R} Z_p^*$ as a secret key, set $pk = g^z \in G_1$ as a public key.
   S.Sign: To sign a message $m \in G_2$, calculate $\sigma = m^z$ as the signature.
   S.Verify: To verify a given message-signature pair (m, σ), check if $e(g, \sigma) = e(pk, m)$.

A third trusted party TP is also selected. Each user i has to generate his public key pk_i and secret key $sk_i = z_i$ of S, and register them to TP before joining in the group. TP will publish the users' public key and corresponding identity i.

- Join: A user i interacts with IA to obtain his certificate in a private channel as follows:

> User → IA: User i selects $\tilde{s}_i \xleftarrow{R} Z_p^*$, sends $\widetilde{C}_i = Y^{\tilde{s}_i}$ along with a proof of knowledge of $\tilde{s}_i$ to IA.
>
> User ← IA: IA verifies that the proof of knowledge is correct, then selects $r_1 \xleftarrow{R} Z_p^*$ so that $C_i = \widetilde{C}_i Y^{r_1}$ is different from all values already stored in Reg. It also selects $\alpha_i \xleftarrow{R} Z_p^*$, computes $U_i = g^{\alpha_i}$, $V_i = (XC_i)^{\alpha_i} g^{xy}$ and returns (r_1, U_i, V_i) to i.
>
> User → IA: User i computes $s_i = \tilde{s}_i + r_1$, checks if $e(V_i, \tilde{g}) = e(U_i, \widetilde{X}\widetilde{Y}^{s_i})$ $e(X, \widetilde{Y})$, accepts (U_i, V_i) as his member certificate if the above equation holds. User i also generates a $\mathcal{S}$ signature on $A_i = \widetilde{Y}^{s_i}$, i.e., $\sigma_i = A_i^{z_i}$, and a proof of equality [24,25] of $\log_{\widetilde{Y}} A_i$ and $\log_Y C_i$, sends (A_i, σ_i) to IA.
>
> IA: IA checks if (A_i, σ_i) is valid under pk_i, stores it in Reg if that is the case.

- GSig: Member i (in possession of member certificate (U_i, V_i) and secret key s_i) generates a group signature σ on message m as follows.

> Firstly, calculate $U' = U_i g^{r'}$, $V' = V_i X^{r'} Y^{s_i r'}$, where $r' \xleftarrow{R} Z_p^*$.
> Secondly, generate a signature of knowledge of s_i, i.e.,
> $\tau = SK_1\{s_i: e(U', \widetilde{Y})^{s_i} = e(V', \tilde{g}) e(U'Y, \widetilde{X})^{-1}\}\{m\}$, which is standard, i.e.,
> $\tau = (s, c)$, where $c = H(e(U', \widetilde{Y})^{k_1}, V', X, Y, \widetilde{X}, \widetilde{Y}, m)$, $s = k_1 + cs_i$, $k_1 \xleftarrow{R} Z_p^*$.
> It can be proved sound and of honest verifier zero-knowledge exactly as in [22,20,26] etc.

The group signature of m signed by i is $\sigma = (U', V', \tau)$.
- GVer: A verifier does the following checks, given a group signature $\sigma = (U', V', \tau)$ of m:

> Firstly, check the validity of $\tau = (s, c)$ by running $VSK_1(\tau)$, which is also standard, i.e., verify if $c = H(e(U', \widetilde{Y})^s [e(U'Y, \widetilde{X})^{-1} e(V', \tilde{g})]^{-c}, V', X, Y, \widetilde{X}, \widetilde{Y}, m)$, return 1 if that is the case, 0 otherwise.
> Secondly, check if there is a $A \in RL$ that $e(V', \tilde{g}) = e(U', \widetilde{X}A) e(X, \widetilde{Y})$, return 0 if that is the case, 1 otherwise.
> σ is valid if both checks return 1.

- Open: The identity of the signer of a given group signature (m, U', V', τ) can be opened as follows.

> Check if $e(V', \tilde{g}) = e(U', \widetilde{X}A_i) e(X, \widetilde{Y})$ for some A_i stored in Reg.
> If A_i satisfies the above equation, generates π, a proof of knowledge of (A_i, σ_i), i.e., let $W_\alpha = \sigma_i h^\alpha$, $W_\beta = A_i^\beta$, $(\alpha, \beta) \xleftarrow{R} Z_p^* \times Z_p^*$, $\pi = PK_2\{(\alpha, \beta): [e(V', \tilde{g}) e(U'Y, \widetilde{X})^{-1}]^\beta = e(U', W_\beta) \wedge e(g, W_\alpha)^\beta e(g, h)^{-\alpha\beta} = e(pk_i, W_\beta)\}$.
> If no record in Reg satisfy the above equation, set $i = 0$, $\pi = NULL$.

Here pk_i is the $\mathcal{S}$ public key of the revealed member i, which are bound together with i by TP. The detail of PK_2 is provided in Appendix B. The output of Open is (i, π).

Note that IA can also open a group signature. IA checks if there exists a A_i stored in Reg that $e(U', \widetilde{X}A_i) = e(V'/g^{xy}, \tilde{g})$, it retrieves the matching A_i and generates π, a proof of knowledge of (xy, A_i, σ_i) if that is the case. This method can only be executed by IA knowing x, y, the former method can be done by any opening authority assigned by IA, if only the OA has access to Reg. Thus our scheme has a kind of flexibility.

- Judge: This algorithm judges the correctness of output of Open by checking π.
- Revoke: To revoke a group member i, IA or OA just publishes the corresponding A_i in RL.

The security results of Scheme 2 are as follows.

Theorem 2 (Traceability). *Scheme 2 is traceable in random oracle model under Assumption 1.*

The proof is omitted due to space limit, and available in the full version [1].

Theorem 3 (Non-frameability). *Scheme 2 is non-frameable in random oracle model under Discrete Logarithm assumption in group G_3 which implies Discrete Logarithm is hard in G_1, G_2 too.*

The proof is standard and similar to those of [26] etc., because a valid group signature of Scheme 2 is in fact a zero-knowledge proof of knowledge of s_i that $e(V', \tilde{g}) = e(U', \widetilde{X}\widetilde{Y}^{s_i})e(X, \widetilde{Y})$, and s_i is never exposed to others including IA and OA.

Theorem 4 (Selfless-anonymity). *Scheme 2 is selfless-anonymous in random oracle model under DDH assumption in G_1.*

The theorem is implied by by the following lemma with proof available in the full version of this paper.

Lemma 2. *Suppose an adversary $\mathcal{A}$ breaks the selfless-anonymity of Scheme 2 with advantage ϵ after q_H hash queries, q_{sig} signature queries, then there exists an algorithm $\mathcal{B}$ breaking DDH assumption with advantage $\frac{\epsilon}{2}(\frac{1}{n} - \frac{q_H q_{sig}}{p})$, where n is the total number of group members.*

Open with Complexity $O(1)$. An alternative construction of obtaining Open with complexity independent with size of revocation list is to encrypt Y^{s_i} using the linear encryption scheme based on Linear Diffie-Hellman Assumption [4], i.e., select $(\alpha, \beta) \xleftarrow{R} Z_p^* \times Z_p^*$ and compute $T_1 = u^\alpha$, $T_2 = v^\beta$, $T_3 = Y^{s_i}w^{\alpha+\beta}$, where $u, v, w \in G_1$ are among the group public keys, and OA owns x_1, x_2 that $w = u^{x_1} = v^{x_2}$ as secret keys.

The group signature by member i is $(U_i', V_i'^r, T_1, T_2, T_3)$ plus a proof of knowledge of (α, β, s_i, r) accordingly. The resulted signature length is 1704 bits, equal to [4].

---

[1] Available at http://eprint.iacr.org/2006/286.

5.2 The Scheme with Backward Unlinkability

Our proposal Scheme 2 can be extended to include backward unlinkability in the same method as in [9], see the following description.

Scheme 3 (Our Proposal w/ BU). Let G_1, G_2, G_3 and bilinear map $e : G_1 \times G_2 \to G_3$ be defined as in Section 2.

- Setup: Same as Scheme 2, except that h is missing from the group public key.
- Join: Same as Scheme 2.
- GSig: Member i (in possession of certificate (U_i, V_i) and secret key s_i) generates a group signature σ of message m at time period j as follows.

Calculate $U' = U_i g^{r'}$, $V' = V_i X^{r'} Y^{s_i r'}$, where $r' \xleftarrow{R} Z_p^*$.

Select $\delta \xleftarrow{R} Z_p^*$, calculate $S = e(g^{s_i}, h_j)^{\delta}$, $T = g^{\delta}$.

Generate a signature of knowledge of $(s_i, \delta, s_i \delta)$, i.e.,

$\tau = \text{SK}_2\{\alpha, \beta, \gamma : e(U', \widetilde{Y})^{\alpha} = e(V', \tilde{g})e(U'Y, \widetilde{X})^{-1} \wedge T = g^{\beta} \wedge S = e(g, h_j)^{\gamma} \wedge T^{\alpha} = g^{\gamma}\}\{m\}$,

which is standard, i.e., $\tau = (s_{\alpha}, s_{\beta}, s_{\gamma}, c)$, where

$c = H(e(U', \widetilde{Y})^{k_{\alpha}}, g^{k_{\beta}}, e(g, h_j)^{k_{\gamma}}, T^{k_{\alpha}}/g^{k_{\gamma}}, U', V', S, T, X, Y, \widetilde{X}, \widetilde{Y}, m)$,

$(k_{\alpha}, k_{\beta}, k_{\gamma}) \xleftarrow{R} Z_p^{*3}$, and $s_{\alpha} = k_{\alpha} + cs_i$, $s_{\beta} = k_{\beta} + c\delta$, $s_{\gamma} = k_{\gamma} + cs_i\delta$.

The group signature of m signed by i at time period j is $\sigma = (U', V', S, T, \tau)$.

- GVer: A verifier does the following checks, given a group signature $\sigma = (U', V', S, T, \tau)$ on m at time period j:

Firstly, check the validity of $\tau = (s_{\alpha}, s_{\beta}, s_{\gamma}, c)$ by running $\text{VSK}_2(\tau)$, which is also standard, i.e., verify that if $c = H(e(U', \widetilde{Y})^{s_{\alpha}}[e(U'Y, \widetilde{X})e(V', \tilde{g})^{-1}]^c$, $g^{s_{\beta}}/T^c$, $e(g, h_j)^{s_{\gamma}}/S^c$, $T^{s_{\alpha}}/g^{s_{\gamma}}$, $U', V', S, T, X, Y, \widetilde{X}, \widetilde{Y}, m)$, return 1 if that is the case, 0 otherwise.

Secondly, check if there is a $B \in RL$ that $S = e(T, B)$, return 0 if that is the case, 1 otherwise.

σ is valid if both checks return 1.

- Revoke: To revoke a group member i at time period $j \in [1, t]$, IA or OA selects and publishes a unique $h_j = \widetilde{Y}^{r_j}$ ($r_j \xleftarrow{R} Z_p^*$) for each time period j, and publishes the corresponding $B_{ij} = A_i^{r_j} \triangleq h_j^{s_i}$ in RL, where A_i is obtained from member i during algorithm Join, and stored in Reg.
- Open and Judge: Same as Scheme 2.

The correctness of Scheme 3 is easy to verify. The traceability and non-frameability follow from that of Scheme 2. What remains to analyze is selfless-anonymity in the case of backward unlinkability, i.e., BU-anonymity [9].

Theorem 5. *Scheme 3 is selfless-anonymous in random oracle model under DDH assumption in G_1.*

The theorem is implied by the following lemma (proof available in the full version of this paper).

Lemma 3. *Suppose an adversary $\mathcal{A}$ breaks the selfless-anonymity of Scheme 3 with advantage ϵ, after q_H hash queries, q_S signature queries, then there exists an algorithm $\mathcal{B}$ breaking DDH assumption in G_1 with advantage $\frac{\epsilon}{2}(\frac{1}{n} - \frac{q_H q_S}{p})$.*

Our scheme has the feature of being BU-enabled and non-frameable at the same time. [9] can also be extended to satisfy the two requirements simultaneously just as how the basic scheme is enhanced with strong exculpability in [4], at the cost of longer signature length because knowledge of an extra exponent has to be proved.

5.3 Efficiency Comparison

To implement our schemes, a group where DDH is hard and an efficient bilinear map is defined is required. A natural selection is non-supersingular elliptic curves defined on finite field, with MOV degree, i.e., embedding degree, larger than one, because distortion map which is the only tool solving DDH on an elliptic curve nowadays does not exist in these curves according to [27], and MNT curves happen to satisfy the requirements and can be constructed systematically [28]. So our schemes are realizable on MNT curves. Scheme of [13] has the same requirement as ours, while schemes of [9,8] are also realizable on supersingular elliptic curves besides MNT curves.

The following table is a performance comparison of known VLR schemes in signature size (i.e., length of σ in bits) and computations required in algorithms GSig and GVer, i.e., multi-exponentiations (denoted as ME) number in G_1 and bilinear map (denoted as BM) number, computations that permit preprocessing are not counted.

Table 4. A Comparison of Some VLR Group Signature Schemes

	$|\sigma|$ (bits)	GSig Comp.	GVer Comp.	Back.-Unlink.	Non-Frame.
[9]	2893	11 ME+4 BM	7 ME+1 ME in G_3+$(3 + |RL|)$ BM	**Yes**	No
[13]	2052	8 ME	1 ME+$(9 + 2|RL|)$ BM	No	**Yes**
[8]	1192	8 ME+2 BM	6 ME+$(3 + |RL|)$ BM	No	No
[29]	2215	11 ME+ 2 BM	7 ME+$(3 + |RL|)$ BM	**Yes**	No
Scheme 2	682	3 ME+1 BM	3 ME+$(4 + |RL|)$ BM	No	**Yes**
Scheme 3	2213	8 ME+3 BM	6 ME+1 ME in G_3+$(4 + |RL|)$ BM	**Yes**	**Yes**

The performance evaluations are made according to [8], and the claimed performances of cited schemes (e.g., [8] and [9]) are adjusted accordingly: if a $\prod_i e(a_i, b_i)^{c_i}$ is encountered, a combination is made at first to minimize the number of BM, then the number of ME in G_1 is counted. An alternative evaluation method is to preprocess as more as possible, e.g., to compute $e(g^{s_i}, h_j)^\delta$, $e(g^{s_i}, h_j)$ can be precalculated and stored in advance, that will reduce the number of BM but introducing more ME in the larger group G_3.

Note that the computation estimations are made according to [8], i.e., p is about 170 bits, elements of G_1 are 171 bits, and elements of G_3 are 1020 bits, achieving a security level similar to 1024 bits RSA.

Acknowledgments

The authors would like to show gratitude to Jing Xu, Zhenfeng Zhang for the helpful discussions, and to Lingbo Wei for the final proofreading.

References

1. Chaum and E. van Heyst, "Group signatures," in *EUROCRYPT'91*, LNCS 547, pp. 257–265, Springer-Verlag, 1991.
2. G. Ateniese and G. Tsudik, "Some open issues and new directions in group signature schemes," in *Financial Cryptography'99*, LNCS 1648, Springer-Verlag, 1999.
3. J. Camenisch and A. Lysyanskaya, "Dynamic accumulators and application to efficient revocation of anonymous credentials," in *CRYPTO'02*, LNCS 2442, pp. 61–76, Springer-Verlag, 2002.
4. D. Boneh, X. Boyen, and H. Shacham, "Short group signatures," in *CRYPTO'04*, LNCS 3152, pp. 45–55, Springer-Verlag, 2004.
5. L. Nguyen, "Accumulators from bilinear pairings and applications," in *CT-RSA'05*, LNCS 3376, pp. 275–292, Springer-Verlag, 2005. A modified version is available at Cryptology ePrint Archive: Report 2005/123.
6. E. Bresson and J. Stern, "Efficient revocation in group signatures," in *PKC'01*, LNCS 1992, Springer-Verlag, 2001.
7. G. Ateniese, D. Song, and G. Tsudik, "Quasi-efficient revocation in group signatures," in *Financial Cryptography'02*, LNCS 2357, Springer-Verlag, 2002.
8. D. Boneh and H. Shacham, "Group signatures with verifier-local revocation," in *CCS'04*, LNCS 3108, pp. 168–177, ACM Press, 2004.
9. T. Nakanishi and N. Funabiki, "Verifer-local revocation group signature schemes with backward unlinkability from bilinear maps," in *ASIACRYPT'05*, LNCS 3788, pp. 533–548, Springer-Verlag GmbH, 2005.
10. J. Camenisch and A. Lysyanskaya, "Signature schemes and anonymous credentials from bilinear maps," in *CRYPTO'04*, LNCS 3152, pp. 56–72, Springer-Verlag, 2004.
11. J. Camenisch and M. Stadler, "Efficient group signatures schemes for large groups," in *CRYPTO'97*, LNCS 1296, pp. 410–424, Springer-Verlag, 1997.
12. A. Fiat and A. Shamir, "How to prove yourself: practical solutions to identification and signature problems," in *CRYPTO'86*, LNCS 263, pp. 186–194, Springer, 1987.
13. G. Ateniese, J. Camenisch, B. de Medeiros, and S. Hohenberger, "Practical group signatures without random oracles," in *EUROCRYPT'06*.
14. D. Boneh and X. Boyen, "Short signatures without random oracles," in *EUROCRYPT'04*, LNCS 3027, pp. 56–73, Springer-Verlag, 2004.
15. M. Bellare, H. Shi, and C. Zhang, "Foundations of group signatures: The case of dynamic groups," in *CT-RSA'05*, LNCS 3376, pp. 136–153, Springer-Verlag, 2005. Full Paper at http://www-cse.ucsd.edu/ mihir/papers/dgs.html.
16. J. Camenish and M. Michels, "A group signature scheme with improved efficiency," in *ASIACRYPT'98*, LNCS 1514, pp. 160–174, Springer, 1998.
17. J. Camenisch and M. Michels, "A group signature scheme based on an RSA-variant," in *Technical Report RS-98-27. BRICS, University of Aarhus*, Primary version of this paper appeared at ASIACRYPT'98, Springer-Verlag, November 1998.
18. G. Ateniese, J. Camenisch, M. Joye, and G. Tsudik, "A practical and provably secure coalition-resistant group signature scheme," in *CRYPTO'00*, LNCS 1880, pp. 255–270, Springer-Verlag, 2000.
19. G. Ateniese and B. de Medeiros, "Efficient group signatures without trapdoors," in *ASIACRYPT'03*, LNCS 2894, pp. 246–268, Springer-Verlag, 2003.

20. L. Nguyen and R. Safavi-Naini, "Efficient and provably secure trapdoor-free group signature schemes from bilinear pairings," in *ASIACRYPT'04*, LNCS 3329, pp. 372–386, Springer-Verlag, 2004.

21. H. Peterson, "How to convert any digital signature scheme into a group signature scheme," in *Proc. Security Protocols Workshop, Paris*, LNCS 1361, pp. 177–190, Springer-Verlag, 1997.

22. C. P. Schnorr, "Effcient signature generation by smart cards," in *Journal of Cryptology*, vol. 4, pp. 161–174, 1991.

23. D. Boneh, B. Lynn, and H. Shacha, "Short signatures from the weil pairing," in *ASIACRYPT'01*, LNCS 2248, pp. 514–532, 2001.

24. D. Chaum and T. P. Pedersen, "Wallet database with observers," in *CRYPTO'92*, LNCS 740, pp. 89–105, Springer-Verlag Berlin Heidelberg, 1993.

25. J. Camenisch and M. Michels, "Separability and efficiency for generic group signature schemes," in *CRYPTO'99*, LNCS 1666, pp. 413–430, Springer-Verlag, 1999.

26. A. Kiayias, Y. Tsiounis, and M. Yung, "Traceable signatures," in *EUROCRYPT'04*, LNCS 3027, pp. 571–589, Springer, 2004.

27. E. R. Verheul, "Evidence that xtr is more secure than supersingular elliptic curve cryptosystems," *Journal of Cryptology*, vol. 17, pp. 277–296, 2004.

28. A. Miyaji, M. Nakabayashi, and S. Takano, "New explicit conditions of elliptic curve traces for fr-reduction," *IEICE Trans. Fundamentals*, vol. E84 A, no. 5, 2001.

29. S. Zhou and D. Lin, "A shorter group signature with verifier-location revocation and backward unlinkability." Cryptology ePrint Archive, Report 2006/100, 2006.

A   Proof of Theorem 1

Proof. Consider an algorithm $\mathcal{B}$ that interacts with $\mathcal{A}$ in the following game. $\mathcal{B}$ maintains two lists of pairs $L_1 = \{(F_{1,i}, \xi_{1,i}) : i = 0, ..., \tau_1 - 1\}$, $L_2 = \{(F_{2,i}, \xi_{2,i}) : i = 0, ..., \tau_2 - 1\}$, $L_3 = \{(F_{3,i}, \xi_{3,i}) : i = 0, ..., \tau_3 - 1\}$, such that at step τ in the game, we have $\tau_1 + \tau_2 + \tau_3 = \tau + 6$. The $F_{1,i}$, $F_{2,i}$, $F_{3,i}$ are polynomials in $Z_p[x]$, the $\xi_{1,i}$, $\xi_{2,i}$, $\xi_{3,i}$ are set to unique random strings in $\{0,1\}^*$.

We start the game at step $\tau = 0$ with $\tau_1 = 3$, $\tau_2 = 3$, $\tau_3 = 0$, they corresponds to $F_{1,0} = 1$, $F_{1,1} = x$, $F_{1,2} = y$, $F_{2,0} = 1$, $F_{2,1} = x$, $F_{2,2} = y$, and the random strings $\xi_{1,0}, \xi_{1,1}, \xi_{1,2}, \xi_{2,0}, \xi_{2,1}, \xi_{2,2}$.

$\mathcal{B}$ simulates the following oracles that $\mathcal{A}$ may query. Let τ_v denote the number of queries to oracle $O_{x,y}$ by $\mathcal{A}$, and initialize $\tau_v = 1$.

Group action: $\mathcal{A}$ inputs two group elements $\xi_{1,i}$, $\xi_{1,j}$ where $0 \le i, j \le \tau_1$, and a request to multiply/divide. $\mathcal{B}$ sets $F_{1,\tau_1} \leftarrow F_{1,i} \pm F_{1,j}$ accordingly. If $F_{1,\tau_1} = F_{1,u}$ for some $u \in \{0, ..., \tau_1 - 1\}$, then $\mathcal{B}$ sets $\xi_{1,\tau_1} = \xi_{1,u}$; otherwise it sets ξ_{1,τ_1} to a random string in $\{0,1\}^* \setminus \{\xi_{1,0}, ..., \xi_{1,\tau_1 - 1}\}$. Finally $\mathcal{B}$ returns ξ_{1,τ_1} to $\mathcal{A}$, adds $(F_{1,\tau_1}, \xi_{1,\tau_1})$ to L_1 and increments τ_1. Group actions for G_2, G_3 is handled similarly.

Pairing: $\mathcal{A}$ inputs two group elements $\xi_{1,i}$ and $\xi_{2,j}$, where $0 \le i \le \tau_1, 0 \le j \le \tau_2$. $\mathcal{B}$ sets $F_{3,\tau_3} \leftarrow F_{1,i} \cdot F_{2,j}$. If $F_{3,\tau_3} = F_{3,u}$ for some $u \in \{0, ..., \tau_3 - 1\}$, then $\mathcal{B}$ sets $\xi_{3,\tau_3} = \xi_{3,u}$; otherwise it sets ξ_{3,τ_3} to a random string in $\{0,1\}^* \setminus \{\xi_{3,0}, ..., \xi_{3,\tau_3 - 1}\}$. Finally $\mathcal{B}$ returns ξ_{3,τ_3} to $\mathcal{A}$, adds $(F_{3,\tau_3}, \xi_{3,\tau_3})$ to L_3 and increments τ_3.

Oracle $O_{x,y}$: $\mathcal{A}$ inputs $m_{\tau_v} \in Z_p^*$. $\mathcal{B}$ chooses a new variable v_{τ_v} and sets $F_{1,\tau_1} \leftarrow v_{\tau_v}$, $F_{1,\tau_1+1} \leftarrow v_{\tau_v}(x + m_{\tau_v}y) + xy$. For $t \in \{0,1\}$, if $F_{1,\tau_1+t} = F_{1,u}$ for some $u \in \{0, ..., \tau_1 - 1 + t\}$, then $\mathcal{B}$ sets $\xi_{1,\tau_1+t} = \xi_{1,u}$; otherwise it sets ξ_{1,τ_1+t} to a random string in $\{0,1\}^* \setminus \{\xi_{1,0}, ..., \xi_{1,\tau_1-1+t}\}$. Finally $\mathcal{B}$ returns $(\xi_{1,\tau_1}, \xi_{1,\tau_1+1})$ to $\mathcal{A}$ and adds $(F_{1,\tau_1}, \xi_{1,\tau_1})$, $(F_{1,\tau_1+1}, \xi_{1,\tau_1+1})$ to L_1, τ_1 is incremented 2, τ_v is incremented 1.

Eventually $\mathcal{A}$ stops and outputs $(m, \xi_{1,a}, \xi_{1,b})$, where $m \in Z_p^* \setminus \{m_1, ..., m_{\tau_v}\}$ and $0 \le a, b \le \tau_1$.

Analysis of $\mathcal{A}$'s Output. For $\mathcal{A}$'s output to be always correct, then $F_{1,b} - F_{1,a} \cdot (x + my) - xy = 0$ for any $(x, y, v_1, ..., v_{\tau_v})$, where $F_{1,a}$ ($F_{1,b}$) corresponds to $\xi_{1,a}$ ($\xi_{1,b}$). We now argue that it is impossible for $\mathcal{A}$ to achieve this.

$F_{1,i}$ has the following form according to the description above:

$$F_{1,i} = c_{0,i} + c_{1,i}x + c_{2,i}y + \sum_k f_{k,i}v_k + \sum_k d_{k,i}[v_k(x + m_ky) + xy], \text{ where } \sum_k$$
denotes $\sum_{1 \le k \le \tau_v}$ for simplicity.

It follows that

$$F_{1,b} - F_{1,a} \cdot (x+my) - xy = c_{0,b} + (c_{1,b} - c_{o,a})x + (c_{2,b} - mc_{0,a})y + \sum_k f_{k,b}v_k + \sum_k(d_{k,b} - f_{k,a})v_kx + \sum_k(d_{k,b}m_k - f_{k,a}m)v_ky + (\sum_k d_{k,b} - c_{2,a} - mc_{1,a} - 1)xy - c_{1,a}x^2 - \sum_k d_{k,a}v_kx^2 - \sum_k(m_k - m)d_{k,a}v_kxy - (\sum_k d_{k,a})x^2y - (\sum_k d_{k,a}m)xy^2 - mc_{2,a}y^2 - \sum_k d_{k,a}m_kmv_ky^2.$$

For the above function to be zero for any $(x, y, v_1, ..., v_{\tau_v})$, all the coefficients are to be zero, then

$$d_{k,a} = 0, f_{k,b} = 0, d_{k,b} = f_{k,a}, d_{k,b}m_k = f_{k,a}m \tag{1}$$

$$c_{0,b} = 0, c_{1,b} = c_{0,a}, c_{2,b} = mc_{0,a}, c_{1,a} = 0, c_{2,a} = 0, \sum_k d_{k,b} = c_{2,a} + mc_{1,a} + 1. \tag{2}$$

We have $d_{k,b} = f_{k,a} = 0$ from (1) because $m \ne m_k$ for any k. We also have $\sum_k d_{k,b} = 1$ from (2), which is a contradiction. Thus we conclude that $\mathcal{A}$'s success depends solely on his luck when $(x, y, v_1, ..., v_{\tau_v})$ is instantiated.

Analysis of $\mathcal{B}$'s Simulation. At this point $\mathcal{B}$ chooses random $(x^*, y^*, v_1^*, ..., v_{\tau_v}^*)$. $\mathcal{B}$ now tests if its simulation was perfect by checking (3) and (5), i.e., if the instantiation $(x^*, y^*, v_1^*, ..., v_{\tau_v}^*)$ does not create any equality relation among the polynomials that was not revealed by the random strings provided to $\mathcal{A}$. $\mathcal{B}$ also tests whether or not $\mathcal{A}$'s output was correct by checking (6).

$$F_{1,i}(x^*, y^*, \{v_k^*\}) - F_{1,j}(x^*, y^*, \{v_k^*\}) = 0, \text{ for some } i, j \text{ s.t. } F_{1,i} \ne F_{1,j} \tag{3}$$

$$F_{2,i}(x^*, y^*) - F_{2,j}(x^*, y^*) = 0, \text{ for some } i, j \text{ s.t. } F_{2,i} \ne F_{2,j} \tag{4}$$

$$F_{3,i}(x^*, y^*, \{v_k^*\}) - F_{3,j}(x^*, y^*, \{v_k^*\}) = 0, \text{ for some } i, j \text{ s.t. } F_{3,i} \ne F_{3,j} \tag{5}$$

$$F_{1,b}(x^*, y^*, \{v_k^*\}) - F_{1,a}(x^*, y^*, \{v_k^*\})(x^* + my^*) - x^*y^* = 0 \tag{6}$$

Thus $\mathcal{A}$'s overall success is bounded by the probability that any of the above equation holds.

We observe that $F_{1,i}$ is non-trivial polynomial of degree at most 2, $F_{2,i}$ at most 1, $F_{3,i}$ at most 4, the function of (6) at most 3.

For fixed i, j, the first case occur with probability $\leq 2/p$, the second case $\leq 1/p$, the third case $\leq 4/p$. The fourth case happens with probability $\leq 3/p$. Summing over all (i, j) pairs in each case, we bound $\mathcal{A}$'s overall success probability $\varepsilon \leq \binom{\tau_1}{2}\frac{2}{p} + \binom{\tau_2}{2}\frac{1}{p} + \binom{\tau_3}{2}\frac{4}{p} + \frac{3}{p}$, i.e. $\varepsilon \leq O(Q_G^2/p)$, since $\tau_1 + \tau_2 + \tau_3 \leq Q_G + 6$.

B   Detail of PK$_2$ in Scheme 2

The detail of $\pi = PK_2\{(\alpha, \beta): [e(V', \tilde{g})e(U'Y, \tilde{X})^{-1}]^\beta = e(U', W_\beta) \wedge e(g, W_\alpha)^\beta$ $e(g, h)^{-\alpha\beta} = e(pk_i, W_\beta)\}$:

- Prover selects $(k_1, k_2) \xleftarrow{R} Z_p^* \times Z_p^*$, calculates $R_1 = [e(V', \tilde{g})e(U'Y, \tilde{X})^{-1}]^{k_1}$, $R_2 = e(g, W_\alpha)^{k_1}e(g, h)^{-k_2}$, and sends R_1, R_2 to Challenger. Challenger replies with a random $c \xleftarrow{R} Z_p^*$.
- Prover calculates $s_1 = k_1 + c\beta$, $s_2 = k_2 + c\alpha\beta$, and sends them to Challenger.
- Challenger checks whether the following equations are satisfied:
    $R_1 = [e(V', \tilde{g})e(U'Y, \tilde{X})^{-1}]^{s_1}e(U', W_\beta)^{-c}$,
    $R_2 = e(g, W_\alpha)^{s_1}e(g, h)^{-s_2}e(pk_i, W_\beta)^{-c}$.
Challenger accepts (s_1, s_2) if the above check passes, rejects it otherwise.

The following Lemma can be proved similarly to corresponding Lemmas or Theorems in [10,20,5].

Lemma 4. *The above interactive protocol π is statistical honest verifier zero-knowledge and sound, under Discrete Logarithm assumption in group G_1, G_2 and G_3.*

Proof. Zero-knowledge is easy to see. **Soundness:** By resetting Prover under the same random inputs, an honest verifier can get (s_1, s_2, c) and (s_1', s_2', c') where $s_j' \neq s_j$, $j = 1, 2$, $c' \neq c$.

Let $\Delta s_j = s_j - s_j'$, $j = 1, 2$, $\Delta c = c' - c$, then $[e(V', \tilde{g})e(U'Y, \tilde{X})^{-1}]^{\Delta s_1} = e(U', W_\beta)^{\Delta c}$, $e(g, W_\alpha)^{\Delta s_1}e(g, h)^{-\Delta s_2} = e(pk_i, W_\beta)^{\Delta c}$.

Set $\beta' = \Delta s_1/\Delta c \bmod p$, $\alpha' = \Delta s_2/\Delta s_1 \bmod p$, then $W_\alpha = \sigma_i h^{\alpha'}$, $W_\beta = A_i^{\beta'}$, it follows that (A_i, σ_i) is easy to decide.

Security Model of Proxy-Multi Signature Schemes

Feng Cao and Zhenfu Cao

Department of Computer Science and Engineering, Shanghai Jiao Tong University
800 Dongchuan Road, Shanghai, 200240, P.R. China
cf_1977@163.com, cao-zf@cs.sjtu.edu.cn

Abstract. In a proxy multi-signature scheme, a designated proxy signer can generate the signature on behalf of a group of original signers. Although some work has been done in proxy-multi signature schemes, until now there is no formalized definition and security model for them. In this paper, we will give the formal definition and a security model of proxy-multi signature scheme. We also constructed a proxy-multi signature scheme based on the BLS short signature scheme and proved its security in our security model.

1 Introduction

The concept of a proxy signature was first introduced by Mambo et al. [4] in 1996. In the proxy signature scheme, generally, there are two entities: an original signer and a proxy signer. The original signer can delegate his signing power to a proxy signer. The proxy signer can generate a valid signature on behalf of the original signer. Since then, many proxy signature schemes have been proposed [8,9,10]. Proxy signatures can combine other special signatures to obtain some new types of proxy signatures. Till now, there are various kind of proxy signature schemes have been proposed.

One well-known new type of the proxy signatures is the proxy multi-signature which was first proposed in 2000 by Yi et al. [5]. In a proxy multi-signature scheme, a designated proxy signer can generate the signature on behalf of a group of original signers. It plays an important role in the following scenario: A company releases a document that may involve the financial department, engineering department, and program office, etc. The document must by signed jointly by these entities, or signed by a proxy signer who is trusted by all of these entities. One solution to the later case of this problem is to use a proxy multi-signature scheme [5,6].

In 2003, Boldyreva et al. formalized a notion of security for proxy signature schemes [1], and that was the first work on proxy signature in the provable-security direction. In [2], Wang and Cao identified a security weakness in the model of [1]. But till now, no security notion has been proposed for proxy-multi signature schemes. In this paper, based on the work of [1,2,3], we give a formal definition and security model on the proxy-multi signature schemes.

D. Pointcheval, Y. Mu, and K. Chen (Eds.): CANS 2006, LNCS 4301, pp. 144–152, 2006.

The rest of this paper is organized as follows: In section 2, we introduced some related mathematical problems. In section 3, we given a definition of the proxy-multi signature schemes and then defined a security model of the proxy-multi signature schemes. In section 4, we proposed a new proxy-multi signature scheme and proved its security in our security model. And conclusions are presented in the final section.

2   Preliminaries

In this section, we review some concepts about bilinear maps, and some related mathematic problems.

Let G_1 and G_2 be two groups of order q for some large prime q. A bilinear map is a map $e : G_1 \times G_1 \to G_2$ with the following properties:

1. Bilinear: For all $u, v \in G_1$, and all $a, b \in \mathbb{Z}$, $e(u^a, v^b) = e(u, v)^{ab}$.
2. Non-degenerate: There exist $u, v \in G_1$, such that $e(u, v) \neq 1$.
3. Computability: There is an efficient algorithm to compute $e(u, v)$ for any $u, v \in G_1$.

Let G be a multiplicative group of the prime order q, We consider the following problems in G.

Discrete Logarithm (DL) Problem: Given $y \in G$, find an integer $x \in Z_q^*$ such that $y = g^x$ whenever such integer x exists.

Computational Diffie-Hellman Problem: Given $g, u, v \in G$, to compute $h = g^{\log_g u \cdot \log_g v}$.

Decision Diffie-Hellman Problem: For $a, b, c \in Z_q^*$, given $g, g^a, g^b, g^c, \in G$, decide whether $c \equiv ab \bmod q$.

A group G is a *GDH* group if there exists an efficient algorithm to solve the *DDH* problem in G and there is no polynomial-time algorithm to solve the *CDH* problem.

3   Proxy-Multi Signature Schemes

3.1   Definition of Proxy-Multi Signature Schemes

In a proxy-multi signature scheme, there is a proxy signer and a group of original signers. Let $O_1, \cdots, O_n$ be the original signers and P be the proxy signer designated by $O_1, \cdots, O_n$. For $i \in \{1, \cdots, n\}$, O_i has a public key pk_{o_i} and a secret key sk_{o_i}, P has a public key pk_p and a secret key sk_p.

Definition 1. [Proxy-multi signature scheme] A proxy-multi signature scheme is a tuple $PMS = (KeyGen, Sign, Veri, PMGen, PMsign, PMVeri)$.

KeyGen: On input of a security parameter 1^k, the algorithm produces private/public key pairs as usual. The public and private key pairs for the proxy signer and the original signers are $(pk_p, sk_p), (pk_{o_1}, sk_{o_1}), \cdots, (pk_{o_n}, sk_{o_n})$.

Sign: This is a (possibly) randomized standard signing algorithm. On input of a secret key sk and a message $m \in \{0, 1\}^*$, the algorithm outputs a signature σ.

Veri: This is a deterministic verification algorithm. On input a public key pk, a message m and a candidate signature σ for m, the algorithm outputs 1 if σ is a valid signature for m relative to pk, and outputs 0 otherwise.

PMGen: This is a protocol between the proxy signer and all original signers. All participants input the public keys $pk_p, pk_{o_1}, \cdots, pk_{o_n}$, the original signers also takes as input their secret keys $sk_{o_1}, \cdots, sk_{o_n}$ and the delegation warrant ω which includes the type of the information delegated, the period of delegation, etc. The proxy signer also inputs his secret key sk_p. As a result of the interaction, then outputs a proxy signing key skp that the proxy signer uses it to produce proxy-multi signatures on behalf of the original signers.

PMSign: This is a (possibly) randomized algorithm. It takes input the proxy signing key skp, the warrant ω, and the message $m \in \{0, 1\}$, then outputs a proxy-multi signature $p\sigma$ on the message m on behalf of the original signers.

PMVeri: It is a deterministic algorithm. It takes input the public keys pk_p, $pk_{o_1}, \cdots, pk_{o_n}$, the warrant ω, the message m and a candidate proxy-multi signature $p\sigma$ for m, the algorithm outputs 1 if $p\sigma$ is a valid proxy-multi signature for m by the proxy signer on behalf of the original signers, and outputs 0 otherwise.

3.2 Security Model

In the following discussion, we let pk_i denote the public key of user $i(i \in N)$, and sk_i denote the corresponding secret key.

We model a extreme case in which the adversary is working against a single honest user, say user 1. In this model, there are totally $n + 1$ participants, and the adversary $\mathcal{A}$ is given a single public key pk_1 relative to user 1. We allow the adversary to select and register keys for all other users, but he must to prove knowledge of the associated secret keys.

We emphasize that we do not assume there exists a secure channel. We providing the adversary access to three oracles: a standard signing oracle, a delegation oracle, and a proxy-multi signature oracle. $\mathcal{A}$ can request the user 1 to play the role of the proxy signer or one of the original signers.

The goal of the adversary $\mathcal{A}$ is to produce one of the following forgeries:

(1) A standard signature by user 1 for a message that was not submitted to the standard signature signing oracle.

(2) A proxy-multi signature for a message M by user 1 on behalf of the original signers such that either the original signers never designated user 1, or M was not in a query made to the proxy-multi signing oracle.

(3) A proxy-multi signature for a message M by some user i on behalf of the original signers, such that user i was never designed by the original signers, and user 1 is one of the original signers.

Definition 2. *Let $PMS = (KeyGen, Sign, Veri, PMGen, PMSign, PMVeri)$ be a proxy-multi signature scheme. Consider the following game between the adversary $\mathcal{A}$ and the challenge $\mathcal{C}$:*

1. C runs **KeyGen** on input 1^k to produce public and secret key pair (pk_1, sk_1) relative to user 1, k is a security parameter. A is provided with the public key pk_1, and C keeps sk_1 as secret.

2. A can choose all public keys except the challenged one pk_1, i.e., A can register all other key pairs in the game, $(pk_2, sk_2), \cdots, (pk_{n+1}, sk_{n+1})$.

3. **Signing queries:** Proceeding adaptively, A can query oracle $\mathcal{O}_S(sk_1, \cdot)$ on messages M of his choice, and obtain a standard signature for M by user 1, $\sigma = S(sk_1, M)$. Then the messages are add to a list S_{qu}.

4. Delegation queries:

- A can request to interact with user 1, user 1 playing the role of proxy signer, i.e., the proxy signer is user 1 and the original signers are all user $i (i \in \{2, \cdots, n+1\})$. Challenger C response by running algorithm *PMGen*, taken warrant ω of user 1 is chosen by A as input. Eventually, outputs a proxy signing key skp, then (ω, skp) is added to a list *Warrp*. We emphasize that A does not have access to the element of *Warrp*.
- A can request to interact with user 1, user 1 playing the role of one of the original signers, and A playing the role of proxy signer. Without loss of generality, we assume the proxy signer is user $n+1$, and the original signers are all user $i (i \in \{1, 2, \cdots, n\})$. Challenger C response by running the algorithm *PMGen*, the input of warrant ω is chosen by A. Eventually outputs the corresponding proxy signing key skp, then ω is added to a list *Warro*.

5. **Proxy-multi signature queries:** Proceeding adaptively, A can make a query (ω, m) to the oracle $\mathcal{O}_{PMS}(skp, \cdot)$, where exist a skp such that $(\omega, skp) \in Warrp$ and m satisfies ω. Eventually output a proxy-multi signature σ on message m. Then the query (ω, m) is add to a list PMS_{qu}.

Eventually, A outputs a forge. The adversary A wins the game if any one the following events occurs:

E_1: A forges a standard signature (M, σ), where $Veri(pk_1, M, \sigma) = 1$, and M was not queried to oracle $\mathcal{O}_S(sk_1, \cdot)$, i.e. $M \notin S_{qu}$. [A forges user 1's standard signature]

E_2: A forges a valid proxy-multi signature $(pk_2, \cdots, pk_{n+1}, pk_1, \omega, M, p\sigma)$ on message M under the warrant ω, where $(\omega, M) \notin PMS_{qu}$. The proxy signer is user 1 and the original signers are user $i (i \in \{2, \cdots, n+1\})$. [$A$ forges a valid proxy-multi signature and user 1 plays the role of proxy signer.]

E_3: A forges a valid proxy-multi signature $(pk_1, \cdots, pk_n, pk_{n+1}, \omega, M, p\sigma)$, where $\omega \notin Warro$. The proxy signer is user $n+1$ and the original signers are user $i (i \in \{1, \cdots, n\})$. [$A$ forges a valid proxy-multi signature and user 1 plays the role of one of the original signers.]

The advantage of adversary A, $Adv_{PMS}^{uf}(A)$ is defined to be his probability of success in the above game.

We say that a proxy-multi signature scheme PMS is a secure proxy-multi signature scheme against chosen message attacks and chosen warrant attacks if for any probability polynomial time forger A, the advantage $Adv_{PMS}^{uf}(A)$ is negligible.   □

4   A Secure Proxy-Multi Signature Scheme

In this section, we construct a proxy-multi signature scheme based on a recent short signature due to Boneh, Lynn, and Shacham (BLS) [7]. This signature scheme works in any group where the Decision Diffie-Hellman problem (DDH) is easy, but the Computational Diffie-Hellman problem (CDH) is hard. Then we proved the security of our proxy-multi signature scheme in our security model.

4.1   The Proposed Proxy-Multi Signature Scheme

The system parameter G_1, G_2, g, q, e, H is as following: G_1 is a cyclic multiplicative group generated by g, whose order is a large prime q. G_2 is a cyclic multiplicative group of the same order q. $e : G_1 \times G_1 \rightarrow G_2$ is a bilinear pairing map. $H : \{0,1\}^* \rightarrow G_1$ is a full-domain hash function, viewed as a random oracle.

Let $O_1, \cdots, O_n$ be the original signers, and P be the proxy signer designated by $O_1, \cdots, O_n$.

In the proposed scheme, like [1,3], we concatenate 00 to indicate a designation message, and 01 to indicate a proxy-multi signature message.

The proposed scheme is as follows:

KeyGen: For a particular user, pick a random number $x \in Z_q^*$, and compute $y = g^x$. The user's public key is $y \in G_1$, and the secret key is $x \in Z_q^*$.

Sign: Given a secret key sk, a message $m \in \{0,1\}^*$, the signature of m is $\sigma = H(m)^{sk}$.

Veri: Given a public key pk, a message/signature pair (m, σ) the verifier checks whether $e(g, \sigma) = e(pk, H(m))$ hold.

PMGen:

1.Delegation generation: The original signer $O_i, (i = 1, \cdots, n)$ computes $\sigma_i = H(00||\omega)^{sk_{o_i}}$, where ω is the delegation warrant which includes the type of the information delegated, the period of delegation, etc. O_i sends (ω, σ_i) to the proxy signer P.

2. Delegation verification: After received all $(\omega, \sigma_i), (i = 1, \cdots, n)$, P computes $\sigma_o = \prod_{i=1}^n \sigma_i$, then checks whether $e(g, \sigma_o) = e(PK, H(00||\omega))$ hold, where $PK = \prod_{i=1}^n pk_i$. He accepts the delegation if it is a valid delegation, otherwise, rejects it or terminates this protocol.

PMSign: P signs the message m under ω on behalf original signers $O_1, \cdots, O_n$, he first computes $\sigma = H(01||\omega||m)^{sk_p}$, then computes $p\sigma = \sigma_o \cdot \sigma$. Then $(pk_{o_1}, \cdots, pk_{o_n}, pk_p, \omega, m, p\sigma)$ is a proxy-multi signature.

PMVeri: To verify a proxy-multi signature $(pk_{o_1}, \cdots, pk_{o_n}, pk_p, \omega, m, p\sigma)$ of a message m under a warrant ω, the verifier checks whether
$$e(g, p\sigma) = e(PK, H(00||\omega))e(pk_p, H(01||\omega||m)).$$
If this holds, then accept it, otherwise, reject it.

4.2   Security Proof

Theorem 1. *The above proxy-multi signature scheme is secure if the CDH problem in G_1 is hard.*

Proof. The proof is by reduction. We show that for any adversary $\mathcal{A}$ for the proxy-multi signature scheme with non-negligible advantage $Adv_{PMS}^{uf}(\mathcal{A})$, we can construction an adversary $\mathcal{B}$ for the GS signature scheme [7] with non-negligible advantage $Adv_{GS}^{uf}(\mathcal{B})$. In [7], the authors has proved that if $\mathcal{B}$ has a non-negligible advantage to break the GS signature scheme, then an algorithm $\mathcal{C}$ will have a non-negligible advantage to solve CDH problem in G_1. So if GS is a secure signature scheme, PMS is a secure proxy-multi signature scheme. We consider the following game between $\mathcal{A}$ and $\mathcal{B}$.

The adversary $\mathcal{B}$ is given pk_1 and access to the signing oracle $\mathcal{O}_S(sk_1, \cdot)$. His goal is to forge a signature on some message under the public key pk_1.

$\mathcal{B}$ runs $\mathcal{A}$ on input pk_1, handing all of $\mathcal{A}$'s requests and answering all of $\mathcal{A}$'s queries in any order and any number of times as follows. The lists $Warro, S_{qu}, PMS_{qu}, Warrp$ are all empty at first and maintained by $\mathcal{B}$:

1. If $\mathcal{A}$ requests to register new key pairs $(pk_i, sk_i)(i \in \{2, \cdots, n+1\})$, $\mathcal{B}$ stores these keys and outputs the public keys.

2. **Signing queries:** If $\mathcal{A}$ requests standard signature with pk_1 on a message m, $\mathcal{B}$ queries $\mathcal{O}_S(sk_1, \cdot)$ on message m. Upon receiving an answer σ, $\mathcal{B}$ forwards the response to $\mathcal{A}$. The message m is add to a list S_{qu}.

3. **Delegation queries:**

- If $\mathcal{A}$ requests to interact with user 1, user 1 playing the role of one of the original signers. We assume that user $n+1$ is the proxy signer. $\mathcal{A}$ creates a warrant ω, and requests user 1 to sign the warrant ω. $\mathcal{B}$ queries $00\|\omega$ to its signing oracle $\mathcal{O}_S(sk_1, \cdot)$. Upon receiving an answer σ, it forwards (ω, σ) to $\mathcal{A}$ and add the warrant ω to $Warro$.

- If $\mathcal{A}$ requests to interact with user 1, user 1 playing the role of the proxy signer, the original signers are user $i, (i = 2, \cdots, n+1)$. $\mathcal{A}$ outputs a warrant ω and computes the signature σ_i for warrant ω under secret key $sk_i, (i = 2, \cdots, n+1)$. Then sends $(\omega, \sigma_2, \cdots, \sigma_{n+1})$ to $\mathcal{B}$. After receiving $(\omega, \sigma_2, \cdots, \sigma_{n+1})$, $\mathcal{B}$ computes $\sigma_o = \prod_{i=2}^{n+1} \sigma_i$, and check the validity by $e(g, \sigma_o) = e(PK, H(00\|\omega))$, where $PK = \prod_{i=2}^{n+1} pk_i$. If so, $\mathcal{B}$ adds the warrant ω to list $Warrp$.

4. **Proxy-multi signature queries:** $\mathcal{A}$ requests a proxy-multi signature on (ω, m), where $\omega \in Warrp$, m satisfies ω, and user 1 is the proxy signer. $\mathcal{B}$ submits $01\|\omega\|m$ to the signing oracle $\mathcal{O}_S(sk_1, \cdot)$ and obtains an answer σ. Then forwards σ to $\mathcal{A}$ and add (ω, m) to the list PMS_{qu}. After receiving σ, $\mathcal{A}$ computes $p\sigma = \sigma_o \cdot \sigma$, where $\sigma_o = \prod_{i=2}^{n+1} \sigma_i, \sigma_i = H(00\|\omega)^{sk_i}$.

Eventually, $\mathcal{A}$ outputs a forgery.

- If $\mathcal{A}$ outputs a forgery of the form (M, σ), then the forgery output by $\mathcal{B}$ is (M, σ).

- If $\mathcal{A}$ outputs a forgery of the form $(pk_2, \cdots, pk_{n+1}, pk_1, \omega, M, p\sigma)$, where user 1 is the proxy signer, then $\mathcal{B}$ first computes $\sigma_o = \prod_{i=2}^{n+1} \sigma_i$, where $\sigma_i = H(00\|\omega)^{sk_i}, i = 2, \cdots, n+1$, $\mathcal{B}$ can do it because he has stored $sk_i, i = 2, \cdots, n+1$. Then computes $\sigma = p\sigma \cdot (\sigma_o)^{-1}$. The forgery output by $\mathcal{B}$ is $(01\|\omega\|M, \sigma)$.

– If $\mathcal{A}$ outputs a forgery of the form $(pk_1, \cdots, pk_n, pk_{n+1}, \omega, M, p\sigma)$, where user $n+1$ is the proxy signer, and user 1 is one of the original signers. Then $\mathcal{B}$ computes $\sigma'_o = \prod_{i=2}^{n} \sigma_i$, where $\sigma_i = H(00||\omega)^{sk_i}, i = 2, \cdots, n+1$, and $\sigma' = H(01||\omega||M)^{sk_{n+1}}$, $\mathcal{B}$ can do it because he has stored $sk_i, i = 2, \cdots, n+1$. Then computes $\sigma = p\sigma \cdot (\sigma'_o)^{-1} \cdot (\sigma')^{-1}$. The forgery output by $\mathcal{B}$ is $(00||\omega, \sigma)$.

Since $\mathcal{A}$ has a non-negligible advantage, at least one of the following events will occur with non-negligible probability:

E_1: $\mathcal{A}$ outputs a forgery of the form (M, σ), where $M \notin S_{qu}$, and
$$e(g, \sigma) = e(pk_1, H(M)).$$
E_2: $\mathcal{A}$ outputs a forgery of the form $(pk_2, \cdots, pk_{n+1}, pk_1, \omega, M, p\sigma)$, where user 1 is the proxy signer, $(\omega, M) \notin PMS_{qu}$, and
$$e(g, p\sigma) = e(\textstyle\prod_{i=2}^{n+1} pk_i, H(00||\omega))e(pk_1, H(01||\omega||M)).$$
E_3: $\mathcal{A}$ outputs a forgery of the form $(pk_1, \cdots, pk_n, pk_{n+1}, \omega, M, p\sigma)$, where user $n+1$ is the proxy signer and user 1 plays the role of one of the original signers, $\omega \notin Warro$, and
$$e(g, p\sigma) = e(\textstyle\prod_{i=1}^{n} pk_i, H(00||\omega))e(pk_{n+1}, H(01||\omega||M)).$$

If event E_1 occurs, then (M, σ) are such that $e(g, \sigma) = e(pk_1, H(M))$, and $\mathcal{B}$ outputs (M, σ). Since $\mathcal{A}$ did not query the standard signature on message M under the public key pk_1, $\mathcal{B}$ did not query $11||M$ to its signing oracle $\mathcal{O}_S(sk_1, \cdot)$. Therefore $\mathcal{B}$'s output (M, σ) is a valid forgery.

If event E_2 occurs, then $(pk_2, \cdots, pk_{n+1}, pk_1, \omega, M, p\sigma)$ is a valid proxy-multi signature, where user 1 is the proxy signer. $\mathcal{B}$ outputs $(01||\omega||M, \sigma)$. We have
$$
\begin{aligned}
e(g, \sigma) &= e(g, p\sigma \cdot (\sigma_o)^{-1}) \\
&= e(g, p\sigma)e(g, (\sigma_o)^{-1}) \\
&= e(\textstyle\prod_{i=2}^{n+1} pk_i, H(00||\omega))e(pk_1, H(01||\omega||M)) \cdot e(g, (\sigma_o))^{-1} \\
&= e(\textstyle\prod_{i=2}^{n+1} pk_i, H(00||\omega))e(pk_1, H(01||\omega||M))e(\textstyle\prod_{i=2}^{n+1} pk_i, H(00||\omega))^{-1} \\
&= e(pk_1, H(01||\omega||M))
\end{aligned}
$$
Since $(\omega, M) \notin PMS_{qu}$, $\mathcal{B}$ did not query $01||\omega||M$ to its signing oracle $\mathcal{O}_S(sk_1, \cdot)$. Therefore, σ is a valid signature on message $01||\omega||M$ under the public key pk_1 forged by $\mathcal{B}$. Thus $\mathcal{B}$'s output $(01||\omega||M, \sigma)$ is a valid forgery.

If event E_3 occurs, then $(pk_1, \cdots, pk_n, pk_{n+1}, \omega, M, p\sigma)$ is a valid proxy-multi signature, where user 1 is one of the original signers and user $n+1$ is the proxy signer. $\mathcal{B}$ outputs $(00||\omega, \sigma)$, it satisfies that
$$
\begin{aligned}
e(g, \sigma) &= e(g, p\sigma \cdot (\sigma'_o)^{-1} \cdot (\sigma')^{-1}) \\
&= e(g, p\sigma)e(g, (\sigma'_o)^{-1})e(g, (\sigma')^{-1}) \\
&= e(\textstyle\prod_{i=1}^{n} pk_i, H(00||\omega))e(pk_{n+1}, H(01||\omega||M)) \cdot \\
&\quad e(g, (\sigma'_o))^{-1}e(g, (\sigma')^{-1}) \\
&= e(\textstyle\prod_{i=1}^{n} pk_i, H(00||\omega))e(pk_{n+1}, H(01||\omega||M)) \cdot \\
&\quad e(\textstyle\prod_{i=2}^{n} pk_i, H(00||\omega))^{-1}e(pk_{n+1}, H(01||\omega||M))^{-1}) \\
&= e(pk_1, H(00||\omega))
\end{aligned}
$$
Since $\omega \notin Warro$, $\mathcal{B}$ did not query $00||\omega$ to its signing oracle $\mathcal{O}_S(sk_1, \cdot)$. Therefore, σ is a valid signature on message $00||\omega$ under the public key pk_1 forged by $\mathcal{B}$. Thus $\mathcal{B}$'s output $(00||\omega, \sigma)$ is a valid forgery.

So whenever $\mathcal{A}$ outputs a valid forgery, $\mathcal{B}$ will output a valid BLS signature. Therefore $Adv_{PMS}^{uf}(\mathcal{A}) = Adv_{GS}^{uf}(\mathcal{B})$.

But in [7], it has been proved that if $\mathcal{B}$ has non-negligible probability to break the GS signature scheme, the CDH problem will be solved with a non-negligible probability. This will be contradict the face that G_1 is a GDH group.   □

5   Conclusions

In this paper, we given a formalized definition of the proxy-multi signature scheme, then proposed a security model for the proxy-multi signature scheme. We also built a proxy-multi signature scheme based on the BLS short signature scheme and proved the security of the scheme in our security model.

Acknowledgment

The authors would like to thank anonymous referees of CANS06 for their value comments and suggestions that improve the presentation of this paper.

This work was supported in part by the National Natural Science Foundation of China for Distinguished Young Scholars under Grant No. 60225007 and the National Natural Science Foundation of China under Grant No. 60572155, the Science and Technology Research Project of Shanghai under Grant No. 04DZ07067, and the special research funds of Huawei.

References

1. A. Boldyreva, A. Palacio, B. Warinschi, Secure proxy signature schemes for delegation of signing rights, At:http://eprint.iacr.org/2003/096.
2. Qin Wang, Zhenfu Cao, Security arguments for partial delegation with warrant proxy signature Schemes, At: http://eprint.iacr.org/2004/315.
3. Qin Wang, Zhenfu Cao, Shengbao Wang, Formalized Security Model of Multi-Proxy Signature Schemes. In Proceedings of the 2005 The Fifth International Conference on Computer and Information Technology (CIT'05), IEEE Computer Society, (2005) 668–672.
4. M. Mambo, K. Usuda, E. Okamoto, Proxy signatures: delegation of the power to sign messages, IEICE Transactions on Fundamentals of Electronic Communications and Computer Science E79-A (9) (1996) 1338–1354.
5. L. Yi, G. Bai, G. Xiao, Proxy multi-signature scheme: a new type of proxy signature scheme, Electronics Letters 36(6) (2000) 527–528.
6. Chien-Lung Hsu, Tzong-Son Wu, Wei-HUa He. New proxy multi-signature scheme. Applied Mathematics and Computation 162 (2005) 1201–1206.
7. D. Boneh, B. Lynn and H. Shacham. Short signatures from the Weil pairing. In Proceedings of Asiacrypt 2001, LNCS, Vol. 2248, Springer-Verlag, (2001) 514–532.
8. S. Kim, S. Park, and D. Won. Proxy signatures, revisited. In Y. Han, T. Okamoto, and S. Quing, editors, Proceedings of International Conference on Information and Communications Security (ICICS)'97, LNCS, Vol. 1334, Springer-Verlag, (1997) 223–232.

9. J. Lee, J. Cheon, and S. Kim. An analysis of proxy signatures: Is a secure channel necessary? In M. Joye, editor, Topics in Cryptology-CT-RSA'03, LNCS, Vol. 2612, Spinger-Verlag, (2003) 68–79.

10. B. Lee, H. Kim, and K. Kim. Strong proxy signature and its applications. SCIS2001, Vol. 2/2, pp. 603-608. Jan. 23–26, 2001.

Efficient ID-Based One-Time Proxy Signature and Its Application in E-Cheque

Rongxing Lu, Zhenfu Cao, and Xiaolei Dong

Department of Computer Science and Engineer, Shanghai Jiao Tong University
800 Dongchuan Road, Shanghai 200240, P.R. China
rxlu.cn@gmail.com, {cao-zf, dong-xl}@cs.sjtu.edu.cn
http://tdt.sjtu.edu.cn

Abstract. To put restrictions on signing capability of the proxy signer, the notion of one-time proxy signature was put forth by Kim et al. in 2001. Today, to our best knowledge, although plenty of one-time proxy signature schemes have been proposed, no ID-based one-time proxy signature (IBOTPS) has yet been presented. Therefore, in this paper, to fill this void, we first formalize the security notions for IBOTPS, and propose the first efficient IBOTPS scheme based on the bilinear pairings and provide the formal security proofs in the random oracle model. Also, we consider an application of the proposed scheme in E-cheque scenarios.

1 Introduction

Background and Related Work. With the explosion of electronic business over the Internet in recent years, the proxy signature has been of increasing practical importance, mainly due to its special proxy function. In a proxy signature scheme, an original signer is allowed to delegate his signing capability to a proxy signer, then the proxy signer can sign messages on behalf of the former within a given context. After receiving a proxy signature, any verifier not only can validate its correctness by a given verification procedure, but also be convinced of the original signer's agreement on the signed message. Based on the delegation type [14,15], the proxy signatures can be classified into full delegation, partial delegation, and delegation by warrant schemes. In a full delegation scheme, the original signer's private key is given the proxy signer directly so the latter has the same signing capability as the former. For most of real world settings, such schemes are obviously impractical and insecure. In a partial delegation scheme, the proxy signer holds a proxy secret key which is different from the original signer's private key. So, the proxy signatures are also distinguishable from the original signer's normal signatures. However, in such schemes the range of messages that a proxy signer can sign is not limited. In a delegation by warrant scheme, the above weakness is eliminated by adding a proxy warrant that specifies the identities of the original signer and the proxy signer, the types of message to be delegated, and the delegation period, etc.

D. Pointcheval, Y. Mu, and K. Chen (Eds.): CANS 2006, LNCS 4301, pp. 153–167, 2006.

Following Mambo et al.'s first work in 1996 [14,15], many new constructions and extensions of proxy signature have been proposed, such as threshold proxy signatures [18,20], multi-proxy signature [10], proxy multi-signature [24], proxy blind signatures [21] and so on. In 2001, to put restrictions on signing capability of the proxy signer, Kim et al. [11] introduced the concept of one-time proxy signature. In this paradigm, each proxy key pair can be used to sign only one message. If the proxy signer uses the same proxy key to sign more than once, then his private key will be disclosed. In recent years, several one-time proxy signature schemes have been put forth [8,1,22,13]. Choi et al. [8] proposed a one-time proxy signature to resolve key exposure problem. Al-Ibrahim and Cerny [1] proposed a threshold proxy one-time signature scheme for group-based applications. In Asiacrypt 2003, Wang and Pieprzyk [22] also proposed an efficient one-time proxy signature scheme. More recently, Mehta and Harn [13] have proposed another two efficient one-time proxy signature schemes.

As is known to us, ID-based system introduced by Shamir [17] can simplify key management procedures in certificate-based public key infrastructure, and after the bilinear pairings, namely the Weil pairing and the Tate pairing of algebraic curves, have been found various positive applications in cryptography, many ID-based cryptographic schemes have been proposed [2,7,4,25,23]. However, we observe that no researchers have yet to propose an ID-based one-time proxy signature (IBOTPS) using pairing techniques. Therefore, in this paper, to fill this void, we would like to present the first efficient IBOTPS scheme based on the bilinear pairing.

Our Contributions. We regard the main contributions of this paper to be of two-fold significance:

- We formalize the definition and security notions for IBOTPS at first. Then, we present the *first* efficient IBOTPS scheme based on the bilinear pairings and provide the proofs of security of the scheme in the random oracle model.
- We also discuss the application scenarios of electronic cheque (E-cheque), and show that our proposed IBOTPS scheme will be suitable for such scenarios.

Organization. In the next section, we set up the definition and security notion for IBOTPS. In section 3, we review the bilinear pairings and underlying problems on which we build. Then, we propose our new IBOTPS scheme and provide the proofs of the security in section 4. In section 5, we present an application of the proposed IBOTPS scheme in E-cheque scenarios. Finally, we draw our conclusions in section 6.

2   Definition and Security Model for IBOTPS

2.1   Notations

Let $\mathbb{N} = \{1, 2, 3, \ldots\}$ denote the set of natural numbers. If $k \in \mathbb{N}$, then 1^k is the string of k 1s. If x, y are two strings, then $|x|$ is the length of x and $x\|y$ is the concatenation of x and y. If S is a finite set, $s \xleftarrow{R} S$ denotes sampling an element x uniformly at random from X. And if $\mathcal{A}$ is a randomized algorithm, $y \leftarrow \mathcal{A}(x_1, x_2, \dots)$ means that $\mathcal{A}$ has inputs $x_1, x_2, \dots$ and outputs y.

2.2 Definition

Definition 1 (ID-based One-time Proxy Signature). *Given an integer k, an ID-based one-time proxy signature scheme* IBOTPS $=$(Setup, Extract, PSign, Verify) *with security parameter k is defined by the following:*

- Setup, *run by PKG (Private Key Generator), on input of a security parameter k, generates system parameters **params** and a master secret key **master-key**. The system parameters **params** are publicly known, while the **master-key** will be kept by PKG secretly.*
- Extract, *run by PKG, on input of **params**, **master-key**, and two identities $ID_o, ID_p \in \{0,1\}^*$ of the original signer U_o and the proxy signer U_p respectively, outputs the private keys S_{ID_o} for U_o and S_{ID_p} for U_p.*
- PSign, *run by an original signer U_o and a proxy signer U_p, is an interactive probabilistic algorithm, consists of the following steps.*
    1. *The original signer U_o first chooses and sends a one-time proxy warrant m_w to the proxy signer U_p. There is an explicit description of the delegation relation in warrant m_w, including the identities of original signer and proxy signer, restrictions on the message the proxy signer is allowed to sign.*
    2. *The proxy signer U_p then chooses a pair of matching one-time public and private keys (opk, osk), and sends back opk to the original signer U_o.*
    3. *The original signer U_o makes an ID-based signature σ_o on $opk \| m_w$ and sends σ_o to the proxy signer U_p.*
    4. *The proxy signer U_p later can use his private key S_{ID_p} and the one-time private key osk to sign a signature σ_p on message $m \| m_w$, where m is a given message.*
    5. *In the end, the one-time proxy signature σ is $(\sigma_o, opk, m_w, \sigma_p, m)$.*
- Verify, *run by any verifier, on input a proxy signature $\sigma = (\sigma_o, opk, m_w, \sigma_p, m)$, returns 1 (*accept*) or 0 (*reject*).*

Moreover, an ID-based one-time proxy signature must satisfy the following properties [12]:

1. *Correction: If the original signer U_o and the proxy signer U_p correctly follow the protocol for* IBOTPS, *then any verifier will accept the proxy signature.*
2. *One timeness: The proxy signer U_p can't use a one-time private key to sign more than once.*
3. *Unforgeability: Given the two identities ID_o, ID_p of the original signer U_o and the proxy signer U_p respectively, it is computationally infeasible, without the knowledge of the private key S_{ID_o} or S_{ID_p}, to produce a valid one-time proxy signature.*

4. *Identifiability: Any verifier can determine the identity of the corresponding proxy signer U_p from a given proxy signature.*
5. *Undeniability: Once the proxy signer U_p creates a valid proxy signature on behalf of the original signer U_o, he cannot repudiate the signature creation.*
6. *Prevention of misuse: The proxy signer U_p cannot use the one-time proxy key for any other purposes except to generate a valid proxy signature, i.e., he cannot sign a message that has not been authorized by the original signer U_o.*

2.3 Security Model

In this subsection, we formally define the *unforgeability* of an IBOTPS scheme and emphasize the importance of the one-time proxy warrant m_w.

Security against existential forgery under chosen message attack. For digital signatures, the well-known strongest security notion is *existential forgery against adaptive chosen message attack* (ef-cma) presented by Goldwasser, Micali and Rivest in [9]. In 2003, the security notion for ID-based signatures, *existential forgery against adaptive chosen message and ID attack* (id-ef-cma), was also provided by Cha and Cheon [7]. Therefore, with respect to the *unforgeability* of IBOTPS schemes, we will define it alone the same lines. In the random oracle model [5], given an identity $ID^\star$ of either the original signer or the proxy signer, we consider an adversary $\mathcal{A}$ has access to the extract oracle $\mathcal{O}_E$ on any identities he choices other than the challenging identity $ID^\star$, in addition to the classical access to the proxy signing oracle $\mathcal{O}_S$ (including the original signer signing oracle $\mathcal{O}_{OS}$ and the proxy signer signing oracle $\mathcal{O}_{PS}$) and the random oracle $\mathcal{O}_H$. In the end, $\mathcal{A}$ returns a valid proxy signature $\sigma^\star = (\sigma_o^\star, opk^\star, m_w^\star, \sigma_p^\star, m^\star)$ with respect to the challenge identity $ID^\star$ and another arbitrary extracted identity $ID^\dagger$. As usual, there is a natural restriction on the returned proxy signature $\sigma^\star$:

- If the challenge identity $ID^\star$ is the original signer's identity, then the returned $(\sigma_o^\star, opk^\star \| m_w^\star)$ has not been obtained from the signing oracle $\mathcal{O}_{OS}$;
- While if the challenge identity $ID^\star$ is the proxy signer's identity, then the returned $(\sigma_p^\star, m^\star \| m_w^\star)$ has not been obtained from the signing oracle $\mathcal{O}_{PS}$.

Definition 2 (Unforgeability of IBOTPS). *Let IBOTPS be an ID-based one-time proxy signature scheme, let $\mathcal{A}$ be an id-ef-cma adversary against IBOTPS. We consider the following random experiment, where k is a security parameter, $ID^\star$ is a given identity for either the original signer or the proxy signer, and $ID^\dagger$ is an arbitrary identity in the random experiment:*

Experiment $\mathbf{Exp}_{IBOTPS,\mathcal{A}}^{id\text{-}ef\text{-}cma}(k)$

$(params, master\text{-}key) \leftarrow Setup(k),$
$S_{ID^\star} \leftarrow Extract(params, master\text{-}key, ID^\star),$
$\sigma^\star = (\sigma_o^\star, opk^\star, m_w^\star, \sigma_p^\star, m^\star) \leftarrow \mathcal{A}^{\mathcal{O}_H, \mathcal{O}_E, \mathcal{O}_S[\mathcal{O}_{OS}, \mathcal{O}_{PS}]}(params, ID^\star, ID^\dagger)$
Return $Verify(params, ID^\star, ID^\dagger, \sigma_o^\star, opk^\star, m_w^\star, \sigma_p^\star, m^\star)$

We then define the success probability of $\mathcal{A}$ via

$$\mathbf{Succ}^{id\text{-}ef\text{-}cma}_{IBOTPS,\mathcal{A}}(k) = \Pr\left[\mathbf{Exp}^{id\text{-}ef\text{-}cma}_{IBOTPS,\mathcal{A}}(k) = 1\right]$$

Let $\tau \in \mathbb{N}$ and $\epsilon \in [0,1]$. We say that the IBOTPS is (τ, ϵ)-secure if no id-ef-cma adversary $\mathcal{A}$ running in time τ has a success $\mathbf{Succ}^{id\text{-}ef\text{-}cma}_{IBOTPS,\mathcal{A}}(k) \geq \epsilon$.

Emphasis. We emphasize the importance of the proxy warrant m_w in IBOTPS scheme. Owing to the proxy warrant m_w embedded in the signature (e.g., $opk\|m_w$ and $m\|m_w$), only if the *unforgeability* satisfies, other security requirements, such as *identifiability, undeniability* and *prevention of misuse*, obviously follow.

3 Bilinear Pairings and Underlying Problems

Recently, bilinear pairings have allowed the opening of a new territory in modern cryptography [2]. Because the new IBOTPS scheme will be using bilinear parings in this paper, we thus briefly review the necessary facts in this section.

Let $\mathbb{G}_1, \mathbb{G}_2$ be two cyclic groups of the same prime order q. Let $\hat{e}$ be a computable bilinear map $\hat{e} : \mathbb{G}_1 \times \mathbb{G}_1 \rightarrow \mathbb{G}_2$, which satisfies the following properties:

- *Bilinear*: $\hat{e}(P^a, Q^b) = \hat{e}(P,Q)^{ab}$, where $P, Q \in \mathbb{G}_1$, and $a, b \in \mathbb{Z}_q^*$.
- *Non-degenerate*: There exists $P \in \mathbb{G}_1$ and $Q \in \mathbb{G}_1$ such that $\hat{e}(P,Q) \neq 1_{\mathbb{G}_2}$.
- *Computability*: There exists an efficient algorithm to compute $\hat{e}(P,Q)$ for all $P, Q \in \mathbb{G}_1$.

We call such a bilinear map $\hat{e}$ as an admissible bilinear pairing, and the Weil pairing in elliptic curve can give a good implementation of the admissible bilinear pairing [2]. Next, we define a general bilinear parameter generator $\mathcal{Gen}$.

Definition 3 (Bilinear Parameter Generator). *A bilinear parameter generator $\mathcal{Gen}$ is a probabilistic algorithm that takes a security parameter k as input and outputs a 5-tuple $(q, \mathbb{G}_1, \mathbb{G}_2, \hat{e}, P)$ as the bilinear parameters, including a prime number q with $|q| = k$, two cyclic groups $\mathbb{G}_1, \mathbb{G}_2$ of the same order q, an admissible bilinear map $\hat{e} : \mathbb{G}_1 \times \mathbb{G}_1 \rightarrow \mathbb{G}_2$ and a generator P of $\mathbb{G}_1$.*

Now we review the related underlying problems, namely the Computational Diffie-Hellman Problem and the Decisional Diffie-Hellman Problem.

- **Computational Diffie-Hellman (CDH) Problem.** Given $P, P^a, P^b \in \mathbb{G}_1$, for unknown $a, b \in \mathbb{Z}_q^*$, compute $P^{ab} \in \mathbb{G}_1$.
- **Decisional Diffie-Hellman (DDH) Problem.** Given $P, P^a, P^b, P^c \in \mathbb{G}_1$, for unknown $a, b, c \in \mathbb{Z}_q^*$, decide whether $c = ab \bmod q$. It is known that DDH in $\mathbb{G}_1$ is easy and can be solved in polynomial time.

Definition 4 (CDH assumption). *Let $\mathcal{Gen}$ be a parameter-generator. Let $\mathcal{A}$ be an adversary that takes as input a 5-tuple $(q, \mathbb{G}_1, \mathbb{G}_2, \hat{e}, P)$ generated by $\mathcal{Gen}$ and $(X, Y) \in \mathbb{G}_1^2$. $\mathcal{A}$ returns an element $Z \in \mathbb{G}_1$. We consider the following random experiments, where k is a security parameter.*

$$\boxed{Experiment\ \mathbf{Exp}^{cdh}_{\mathcal{Gen},\mathcal{A}}(k)}$$

$(q, \mathbb{G}_1, \mathbb{G}_2, \hat{e}, P) \leftarrow \mathcal{Gen}(k),$

$x \xleftarrow{R} \mathbb{Z}_q^*, X \leftarrow P^x,$

$y \xleftarrow{R} \mathbb{Z}_q^*, Y \leftarrow P^y,$

$Z \leftarrow \mathcal{A}(q, \mathbb{G}_1, \mathbb{G}_2, \hat{e}, P, X, Y)$

$Return\ 1\ if\ Z = P^{xy},\ 0\ otherwise$

We define the corresponding success probability of $\mathcal{A}$ in solving the CDH problem via

$$\mathbf{Succ}^{cdh}_{\mathcal{Gen},\mathcal{A}}(k) = \Pr\left[\mathbf{Exp}^{cdh}_{\mathcal{Gen},\mathcal{A}}(k) = 1\right]$$

Let $\tau \in \mathbb{N}$ and $\epsilon \in [0, 1]$. We say that the CDH is (τ, ϵ)-secure if no polynomial algorithm $\mathcal{A}$ running in time τ has success $\mathbf{Succ}^{cdh}_{\mathcal{Gen},\mathcal{A}}(k) \geq \epsilon$.

4   The New IBOTPS

In this section we present the new IBOTPS scheme based on the bilinear pairings, and discuss its security properties.

4.1   Description of the New of IBOTPS

Our new scheme IBOTPS is designed as follows. It is derived from Sakai-Ogishi-Kasahara ID-based signature (SOK-IBS) [4] and the online/offline algorithms in [25,23].

Setup: Given a security parameter k, PKG uses the parameter generator $\mathcal{Gen}(k)$ to produce a 5-tuple $(q, \mathbb{G}_1, \mathbb{G}_2, \hat{e}, P)$. Then PKG chooses a random number $s \in \mathbb{Z}_q^*$ and computes $P_{pub} = P^s$. PKG also picks three cryptographic hash functions: H, H_1 and H_2, where $H : \{0,1\}^* \rightarrow \mathbb{G}_1$, $H_1 : \mathbb{G}_1 \times \{0,1\}^* \rightarrow \mathbb{G}_1$ and $H_2 : \mathbb{G}_1 \times \mathbb{G}_1 \times \{0,1\}^* \rightarrow \mathbb{Z}_q^*$. Finally, PKG keeps s as the **master-key** and publishes the system parameters **params**$=(q, \mathbb{G}_1, \mathbb{G}_2, \hat{e}, P, P_{pub}, H, H_1, H_2)$.

Extract: Given two identities $ID_o, ID_p \in \{0,1\}^*$ of the original signer U_o and the proxy signer U_p respectively. PKG computes $Q_{ID_o} = H(ID_o)$, $S_{ID_o} = H(ID_o)^s$ and passes the private key S_{ID_o} to U_o via some secure channel. Similarly, PKG also computes $Q_{ID_p} = H(ID_p)$, $S_{ID_p} = H(ID_p)^s$ and passes the private key S_{ID_p} to U_p.

PSign

1. The original signer U_o first makes a one-time proxy warrant m_w and sends it to the proxy signer U_p.
2. The proxy signer U_p chooses two random numbers $r_1, r_2 \in \mathbb{Z}_q^*$ as his one-time private key $osk = (r_1, r_2)$; then computes the corresponding one-time public key $opk = (R_1, R_2)$, where $R_1 = P^{r_1}$ and $R_2 = S_{ID_p}^{r_2^{-1}}$, and finally sends the one-time public key opk to U_o.

3. The original signer U_o chooses a random number $r_0 \in \mathbb{Z}_q^*$, computes (R_0, S_0), where $R_0 = P^{r_0}$ and $S_0 = S_{ID_o} \cdot H_1(R_0, opk\|m_w)^{r_0}$, and sends $\sigma_o = (R_0, S_0)$ to U_p.

4. To sign a message m, the proxy signer U_p can efficiently compute $\sigma_p = r_2 + r_1 \cdot H_2(R_1, R_2, m\|m_w) \bmod q$. At last, U_p opens the proxy signature $\sigma = (\sigma_o, opk, m_w, \sigma_p, m)$.

Verify: To verify the proxy signature $\sigma = (\sigma_o, opk, m_w, \sigma_p, m)$ with respect to ID_o and ID_p, where $\sigma_o = (R_0, S_0)$ and $opk = (R_1, R_2)$, any verifier can check the following two equations,

$$\hat{e}(P, S_0) \stackrel{?}{=} \hat{e}(P_{pub}, H(ID_o)) \cdot \hat{e}(R_0, H_1(R_0, opk\|m_w))$$

$$\hat{e}(P^{\sigma_p} \cdot R_1^{-H_2(R_1, R_2, m\|m_w)}, R_2) \stackrel{?}{=} \hat{e}(P_{pub}, H(ID_p))$$

If both of them hold, the signature will be accepted; otherwise rejected.

Correctness

$$\begin{aligned}
&\hat{e}(P_{pub}, H(ID_o)) \cdot \hat{e}(R_0, H_1(R_0, opk\|m_w)) \\
&= \hat{e}(P, H(ID_o)^s) \cdot \hat{e}(P, H_1(R_0, opk\|m_w)^{r_0}) \\
&= \hat{e}(P, H(ID_o)^s \cdot H_1(R_0, opk\|m_w)^{r_0}) \\
&= \hat{e}(P, S_{ID_o} \cdot H_1(R_0, opk\|m_w)^{r_0}) \\
&= \hat{e}(P, S_0)
\end{aligned}$$

and

$$\begin{aligned}
&\hat{e}(P^{\sigma_p} \cdot R_1^{-H_2(R_1, R_2, m\|m_w)}, R_2) \\
&= \hat{e}(P^{\sigma_p} \cdot P^{-r_1 H_2(R_1, R_2, m\|m_w)}, R_2) \\
&= \hat{e}(P^{\sigma_p - r_1 H_2(R_1, R_2, m\|m_w)}, S_{ID_p}^{r_2^{-1}}) \\
&= \hat{e}(P^{r_2}, S_{ID_p}^{r_2^{-1}}) = \hat{e}(P, S_{ID_p}) = \hat{e}(P_{pub}, H(ID_p))
\end{aligned}$$

Efficiency. The new IBOTPS scheme is very efficient in terms of the computation complexity, especially in PSign phase. In PSign phase, the original signer U_o doesn't need pairing operations, only requires 1 map-to-point hash, 1 multiplication and 2 exponentiations in $\mathbb{G}_1$; and the proxy signer also doesn't require pairing operations, only needs 2 exponentiations in $\mathbb{G}_1$, 1 cryptographic hash, 1 multiplication, 1 inverse and 1 addition in $\mathbb{Z}_q^*$. In Verify phase, a verifier, however, requires 5 pairing operations, 3 map-to-point hash, 2 exponentiations in $\mathbb{G}_1$ and 1 multiplication in $\mathbb{G}_1$, 1 multiplication in $\mathbb{G}_2$ and 1 cryptographic hash. However, as many computational operations can be pre-computed in off-line phase and the computations of pairings become faster and faster [3], the new IBOTPS scheme remains practical.

4.2   Security Proof

Theorem 1 (One-timeness). *The new IBOTPS scheme satisfies the property of one-timeness.*

Proof. Suppose that the proxy signer U_p want to sign more than one time using his proxy public key $opk = (R_1, R_2)$. Since $opk = (R_1, R_2)$ is chosen by the proxy signer U_p himself, (R_1, R_2) can be chosen differently from their definition in the scheme. Therefore, here we assume that $R_1 = P^a$ and $R_2 = P^b$. Once the proxy signer U_p signs two times on messages m and m', we then get two valid proxy signatures σ_p and σ_p'.

Since σ_p and σ_p' are valid, from the verification equation, we get

$$P^{b(\sigma_p - aH_2(R_1, R_2, m\|m_w))} = S_{ID_p}$$

and

$$P^{b(\sigma_p' - aH_2(R_1, R_2, m'\|m_w))} = S_{ID_p}$$

Then, we will have

$$\sigma_p - aH_2(R_1, R_2, m\|m_w) = \sigma_p' - aH_2(R_1, R_2, m'\|m_w)$$

and

$$a = \frac{\sigma_p - \sigma_p'}{H_2(R_1, R_2, m\|m_w) - H_2(R_1, R_2, m'\|m_w)} \bmod q$$

In the end, we can reveal the proxy signer's private key S_{ID_p} as

$$S_{ID_p} = R_2^{\sigma_p - aH_2(R_1, R_2, m\|m_w)}$$

Therefore, in order to protect his private key S_{ID_p}, the proxy signer U_p would't like to use the same one-time private key to sign more than once. Thus, the new IBOTPS scheme satisfies the one timeness, and the proof is completed.   □

Lemma 1 (Unforgeability of Original Signer). *Let $\mathcal{G}en$ be a bilinear parameter generator, and let $\mathcal{A}$ be an id-ef-cma adversary, in the random oracle model, against the proposed IBOTPS scheme, that produces an existential forgery with provability $\epsilon = \mathbf{Succ}_{IBOTPS, \mathcal{A}}^{id\text{-}ef\text{-}cma}$, within time τ, making q_H and q_{H_1} to the random oracles $\mathcal{O}_H$ and $\mathcal{O}_{H_1}$, q_E queries to extract oracle $\mathcal{O}_E$ and q_S queries to the proxy signing oracle $\mathcal{O}_S$. Then, there exist $\epsilon' \in [0, 1]$ and $\tau' \in \mathbb{N}$ verifying*

$$\epsilon' \geq \frac{\epsilon}{q_H} - \frac{1 + q_S \cdot q_{H_1}}{q}, \quad \tau' \leq \tau + (2q_H + q_{H_1} + 3q_S - 1) \cdot T_{\mathsf{Exp}}.$$

such that CDH problem can be solved with probability ϵ', within time τ', where T_{Exp} denotes the time to perform an exponentiation in $\mathbb{G}_1$.

Proof. Our proof method is inspired by Shoup [19]: we define a sequence of games Game_0, Game_1, Game_2, ..., of modified attacks starting from the actual adversary $\mathcal{A}$, until we reach a final game whose success probability has an upper bound related to solving the CDH problem. All the games operate on the same underlying probability space: the system parameter **params**, the coin tosses of $\mathcal{A}$ and the random oracles. Let $(q, \mathbb{G}_1, \mathbb{G}_2, \hat{e}, P)$ be a 5-tuple generated by $\mathcal{Gen}(k)$, where k is the security parameter. Let $H : \{0,1\}^* \to \mathbb{G}_1$, $H_1 : \mathbb{G}_1 \times \{0,1\}^* \to \mathbb{G}_1$ and $H_2 : \mathbb{G}_1 \times \mathbb{G}_1 \times \{0,1\}^* \to \mathbb{Z}_q^*$ be three cryptographic hash functions, and H, H_1 behave as the random oracles in the simulation. Let $(X^* = P^x, Y^* = P^y)$ be a random instance of CDH problem. We will use an id-ef-cma adversary $\mathcal{A}$ against the IBOTPS scheme to compute P^{xy}.

Game$_0$. This is the real attack game, in the random oracle model. The Setup algorithm chooses $s \in Z_q^*$ as the **master-key** and compute $P_{pub} = P^s$. The Extract algorithm, on inputting q_H user identities $ID_1, ID_2, \cdots, ID_{q_H}$, outputs q_H user public-private key pairs (Q_{ID_1}, S_{ID_1}), (Q_{ID_2}, S_{ID_2}), $\cdots$, $(Q_{ID_{q_H}}, S_{ID_{q_H}})$. We consider the adversary $\mathcal{A}$ is fed with the system parameters **params**$=(q, \mathbb{G}_1, \mathbb{G}_2, \hat{e}, P, P_{pub}, H, H_1, H_2)$, and querying the random oracles $\mathcal{O}_H$, $\mathcal{O}_{H_1}$, the extract oracle $\mathcal{O}_E$ and the proxy signing oracle $\mathcal{O}_S$, outputs a valid proxy signature $\sigma^* = (\sigma_o^*, opk^*, m_w^*, \sigma_p^*, m^*)$ with respect to an unextracted original signer identity ID^* and another arbitrary extracted proxy signer identity ID_p. (Note: we allow the adversary $\mathcal{A}$ to extract any proxy signer's private key in the simulation.) In any Game_j, we denote by Forge_j the event that $\mathsf{Verify}(\sigma_o^*, opk^*, m_w^*, \sigma_p^*, m^*) = 1$. By definition, we have $\Pr[\mathsf{Forge}_0] = \mathsf{Succ}_{\mathsf{IBOTPS}, \mathcal{A}}^{\text{id-ef-cma}}$.

Game$_1$. In this game, we choose randomly an identity ID^* from q_H identities. If the challenging original signer's identity ID^* chosen by $\mathcal{A}$ is not ID^*, we will abort the game. Thus, if the game continues, we will have $\Pr[\mathsf{Forge}_1] = \frac{1}{q_H} \Pr[\mathsf{Forge}_0]$.

Game$_2$. In this game, we modify the simulation by replacing the public key $P_{pub} = P^s$ by $P_{pub} = X^* = P^x$. Since the distribution of P_{pub} is unchanged, we thus will have $\Pr[\mathsf{Forge}_2] = \Pr[\mathsf{Forge}_1]$.

Game$_3$. In this game, we simulate the random oracle $\mathcal{O}_H$. For any fresh query $ID_i \neq ID^*$, we pick up a random number $h_i \in \mathbb{Z}_q^*$ and compute $Q_{ID_i} = P^{h_i}$ and $S_{ID_i} = P_{pub}^{h_i} = P^{xh_i}$. We store $(ID_i, Q_{ID_i}, S_{ID_i})$ in the Λ-list and return $H(ID_i) = Q_{ID_i}$ as the answer to the oracle query. If the fresh query $ID_i = ID^*$, we set $Q_{ID^*} = Y^* = P^y$, store $(ID^*, Q_{ID^*}, \sqcup)$ to the Λ-list, and return $H(ID^*) = Q_{ID^*}$. Clearly, in the random oracle model, this game is identical to the previous one. Hence, $\Pr[\mathsf{Forge}_3] = \Pr[\mathsf{Forge}_2]$.

Game$_4$. In this game, we simulate the Extract oracle $\mathcal{O}_E$. For any fresh query $ID_i \neq ID^*$, we find $(ID_i, Q_{ID_i}, S_{ID_i})$ in the Λ-list and return S_{ID_i} as the answer to the oracle query. If the query is on ID^*, we clearly have to abort the game. However, this case has been excluded in **Game$_1$**. Therefore, we will have $\Pr[\mathsf{Forge}_4] = \Pr[\mathsf{Forge}_3]$.

Game$_5$. In this game, we simulate the random oracle $\mathcal{O}_{H_1}$. From any fresh query $(R_0, opk\|m_w)$, we pick up a random number $u \in \mathbb{Z}_q^*$, compute the hash value

$H_1(R_0, opk\|m_w) = P^u$, store $(R_0, opk\|m_w, P^u, u)$ in the Λ_1-list and return P^u as the answer to the oracle call. In the random oracle model, this game is identical to the previous one. Hence, $\Pr[\mathsf{Forge}_5] = \Pr[\mathsf{Forge}_4]$.

Game$_6$. In this game, we only keep executions that the adversary $\mathcal{A}$ outputs a valid forgery $\sigma^\star = (\sigma_o^\star, opk^\star, m_w^\star, \sigma_p^\star, m^\star)$ with respect to the original signer identity $ID^\star = ID^*$ and another extracted proxy signer identity ID_p, where $\sigma_o^\star = (R_0^\star, S_0^\star)$, and $(R_0^\star, opk^\star\|m_w^\star)$ has been queried from $\mathcal{O}_{H_1}$. This makes a difference only if the signature is valid, while $(R_0^\star, opk^\star\|m_w^\star)$ has not been queried from $\mathcal{O}_{H_1}$. Since $H_1(R_0^\star, opk^\star\|m_w^\star)$ is uniformly distributed, the equality $\hat{e}(P, S_0^\star) = \hat{e}(P_{pub}, H(ID_o)) \cdot \hat{e}(R_0^\star, H_1(R_0^\star, opk^\star\|m_w^\star))$ happen with probability $\frac{1}{q}$. Therefore, we will have $|\Pr[\mathsf{Forge}_6] - \Pr[\mathsf{Forge}_5]| \leq \dfrac{1}{q}$.

Game$_7$. In this game, we simulate the proxy signing oracle $\mathcal{O}_S$. For a new message m, an unextracted original signer's identity $ID_o = ID^*$ and an extracted proxy signer's identity ID_p, we do as follows.

1. Look up the Λ-list and find the extracted entry $(ID_p, Q_{ID_p}, S_{ID_p})$. Choose a one-time proxy warrant m_w and one-time public and private key pairs (opk, osk). Use the private key S_{ID_p} to make the signature σ_p on $m\|m_w$. (Actually, this can be done by the adversary $\mathcal{A}$ himself, owing to knowing the private key S_{ID_p}.)

2. Simulate the original signer's signing oracle $\mathcal{O}_{OS}$. Choose two random numbers $u, v \in \mathbb{Z}_q^*$. Compute $R_0 = P_{pub}^v = P^{xv}$ and $S_0 = P_{pub}^u = P^{xu}$. Set $H_1(R_0, opk\|m_w) = (P^u \cdot H(ID^*)^{-1})^{v^{-1}} = P^{(u-y)v^{-1}}$. If the Λ_1-list includes a tuple $(R_0, opk\|m_w, *, *)$, we abort the simulation, otherwise we store $(R_0, opk\|m_w, P^{(u-y)v^{-1}})$ in the Λ_1-list.

3. In the end, we set $\sigma_o = (R_0, S_0)$ and return $\sigma = (\sigma_o, opk, m_w, \sigma_p, m)$ as a valid proxy signature. If the game doesn't abort, the simulation is perfect in the random oracle. However, since we abort with probability at most $\frac{q_{H_1}}{q}$, then after q_S queries, we will have $|\Pr[\mathsf{Forge}_7] - \Pr[\mathsf{Forge}_6]| \leq \dfrac{q_S \cdot q_{H_1}}{q}$.

At the end of the Game$_7$, $\mathcal{A}$ finally outputs a valid forgery $\sigma^\star = (\sigma_o^\star, opk^\star, m_w^\star, \sigma_p^\star, m^\star)$ with respect to the original signer identity $ID^\star = ID^*$ and another extracted proxy signer identity ID_p, where $\sigma_o^\star = (R_0^\star, S_0^\star)$. Then, we look up the Λ_1-list and find the corresponding entry $(R_0^\star, opk^\star\|m_w^\star, P^{u^\star}, u^\star)$. Since we know that a valid signature will satisfy $R_0^\star = P^{r_0}$, $S_0^\star = S_{ID^*} \cdot H_1(R_0^\star, opk^\star\|m_w^\star)^{r_0}$ and $H_1(R_0^\star, opk^\star\|m_w^\star)^{r_0} = P^{u^\star \cdot r_0} = (R_0^\star)^{u^\star}$, we therefore can output

$$\frac{S_0^\star}{(R_0^\star)^{u^\star}} = \frac{S_{ID^*} \cdot H_1(R_0^\star, opk^\star\|m_w^\star)^{r_0}}{H_1(R_0^\star, opk^\star\|m_w^\star)^{r_0}} = S_{ID^*} = P^{xy}.$$

In the end, we will have $\Pr[\mathsf{Forge}_7] = \mathbf{Succ}_{\mathsf{Game}_7}^{cdh}(k) = \epsilon'$.

From all above, we obtain

$$\epsilon' \geq \frac{\epsilon}{q_H} - \frac{1 + q_S \cdot q_{H_1}}{q}.$$

Also, by a simple computation, (only considering the exponentiation operation in $\mathbb{G}_1$ and neglecting others and the simulation of oracle $\mathcal{O}_{PS}$), we can obtain the claimed bound for $\tau' \leq \tau + (2q_H + q_{H_1} + 3q_S - 1) \cdot T_{\mathsf{Exp}}$. This concludes the proof. $\square$

Remark. Using the similar method of Coron's [6], we may obtain a more tight security reduction.

Lemma 2 (Unforgeability of Proxy Signer). *Let $\mathcal{G}en$ be a bilinear parameter generator, and let $\mathcal{A}$ be an id-ef-cma adversary, in the random oracle model, against the proposed IBOTPS scheme, that produces an existential forgery with provability $\epsilon = \mathbf{Succ}_{IBOTPS,\mathcal{A}}^{id\text{-}ef\text{-}cma}$, within time τ, making q_H and q_{H_2} to the random oracles $\mathcal{O}_H$ and $\mathcal{O}_{H_2}$, q_E queries to extract oracle $\mathcal{O}_E$ and q_S queries to the proxy signing oracle $\mathcal{O}_S$. If $\epsilon \geq 10q_H(q_S+1)(q_S+q_{H_2})/q$, then the CDH problem can be resolved with expected time $\tau' \leq 120686q_H q_{H_2}\tau/\epsilon$.*

Proof. Based on Shoup's sequence of game technique [19], we define a sequence of games Game_0, Game_1, Game_2, ..., of modified attacks starting from the actual adversary $\mathcal{A}$. All the games operate on the same underlying probability space: the system parameter **params**, the coin tosses of $\mathcal{A}$ and the random oracles. Let k be a security parameter and let $(q, \mathbb{G}_1, \mathbb{G}_2, \hat{e}, P)$ be a 5-tuple generated by $\mathcal{G}en(k)$. Let $H : \{0,1\}^* \to \mathbb{G}_1$, $H_1 : \mathbb{G}_1 \times \{0,1\}^* \to \mathbb{G}_1$ and $H_2 : \mathbb{G}_1 \times \mathbb{G}_1 \times \{0,1\}^* \to \mathbb{Z}_q^*$ be three cryptographic hash functions, and H, H_2 behave as the random oracles in the simulation. Let $(X^* = P^x, Y^* = P^y)$ be a random instance of CDH problem, we will use an id-ef-cma adversary $\mathcal{A}$ against the IBOTPS scheme to compute P^{xy}.

Game_0. This is the real attack game, in the random oracle model. The Setup algorithm chooses $s \in Z_q^*$ as the **master-key** and compute $P_{pub} = P^s$. The Extract algorithm, on inputting q_H user identities $ID_1, ID_2, \cdots, ID_{q_H}$, outputs q_H user public-private key pairs (Q_{ID_1}, S_{ID_1}), (Q_{ID_2}, S_{ID_2}), $\cdots$, $(Q_{ID_{q_H}}, S_{ID_{q_H}})$. We consider the adversary $\mathcal{A}$ is fed with the system parameters **params**$=(q, \mathbb{G}_1, \mathbb{G}_2, \hat{e}, P, P_{pub}, H, H_1, H_2)$, and querying the random oracles $\mathcal{O}_H$, $\mathcal{O}_{H_2}$, the extract oracle $\mathcal{O}_E$ and the signing oracle $\mathcal{O}_S$, outputs a valid proxy signature $\sigma^* = (\sigma_o^\star, opk^\star, m_w^\star, \sigma_p^\star, m^\star)$ with respect to an unextracted proxy signer identity $ID^\star$ and another arbitrary extracted original signer identity ID_o. (Note: we allow the adversary $\mathcal{A}$ to extract any original signer's private key in the simulation.) In any Game_j, we denote by Forge_j the event that $\mathsf{Verify}(\sigma_o^\star, opk^\star, m_w^\star, \sigma_p^\star, m^\star) = 1$. By definition, we have $\Pr[\mathsf{Forge}_0] = \mathbf{Succ}_{IBOTPS,\mathcal{A}}^{id\text{-}ef\text{-}cma}$.

Game_1. In this game, we choose randomly an identity ID^* from q_H identities. If the challenging proxy signer's identity $ID^\star$ chosen by $\mathcal{A}$ is not ID^*, we will abort the game. Thus, if the game continues, we will have $\Pr[\mathsf{Forge}_1] = \frac{1}{q_H}\Pr[\mathsf{Forge}_0]$.

Game_2. In this game, we modify the simulation by replacing the public key $P_{pub} = P^s$ by $P_{pub} = X^* = P^x$. Since the distribution of P_{pub} is unchanged, we thus will have $\Pr[\mathsf{Forge}_2] = \Pr[\mathsf{Forge}_1]$.

Game₃. In this game, we simulate the random oracle $\mathcal{O}_H$. For any fresh query $ID_i \neq ID^*$, we pick up a random number $h_i \in \mathbb{Z}_q^*$ and compute $Q_{ID_i} = P^{h_i}$ and $S_{ID_i} = P_{pub}^{h_i} = P^{xh_i}$. We store $(ID_i, Q_{ID_i}, S_{ID_i})$ in the Λ-list and return $H(ID_i) = Q_{ID_i}$ as the answer to the oracle query. If the fresh query $ID_i = ID^*$, we set $Q_{ID^*} = Y^* = P^y$, store $(ID^*, Q_{ID^*}, \sqcup)$ to the Λ-list, and return $H(ID^*) = Q_{ID^*}$. Clearly, in the random oracle model, this game is identical to the previous one. Hence, $\Pr[\mathsf{Forge}_3] = \Pr[\mathsf{Forge}_2]$.

Game₄. In this game, we simulate the Extract oracle $\mathcal{O}_E$. For any fresh query $ID_i \neq ID^*$, we find $(ID_i, Q_{ID_i}, S_{ID_i})$ in the Λ-list and return S_{ID_i} as the answer to the oracle query. If the query is on ID^*, we clearly have to abort the game. However, this case has been excluded in **Game₁**. Therefore, we will have $\Pr[\mathsf{Forge}_4] = \Pr[\mathsf{Forge}_3]$.

Game₅. In this game, we simulate the random oracle $\mathcal{O}_{H_2}$. From any fresh query $(R_1, R_2, m\|m_w)$, we pick up a random number $u \in \mathbb{Z}_q^*$, compute $H_2(R_1, R_2, m\|m_w) = u$, store $(R_1, R_2, m\|m_w, u)$ in the Λ_2-list and return u as the answer to the oracle call. In the random oracle model, this game is identical to the previous one. Hence, $\Pr[\mathsf{Forge}_5] = \Pr[\mathsf{Forge}_4]$.

Game₆. In this game, we simulate the proxy signing oracle $\mathcal{O}_S$. For a new message m, an unextracted proxy signer's identity $ID_p = ID^*$ and an extracted original signer's identity ID_o, we do as follows.

1. Choose three random numbers $u, v, w \in \mathbb{Z}_q^*$. Compute $opk = (R_1, R_2)$, where

$$R_1 = P_{pub}^{-w \cdot u^{-1}} \cdot P^{v \cdot u^{-1}} = P^{u^{-1}(-wx+v)}$$

$$R_2 = H(ID_p)^{w^{-1}} = H(ID^*)^{w^{-1}} = P^{yw^{-1}}$$

2. Simulate the original signer's signing oracle $\mathcal{O}_{OS}$. Look up the Λ-list and find the extracted entry $(ID_o, Q_{ID_o}, S_{ID_o})$. Choose a one-time proxy warrant m_w. Use the private key S_{ID_o} to make the signature σ_o on $opk\|m_w$. (Actually, the signature σ_o can be done by the adversary $\mathcal{A}$ himself, owing to knowing the private key S_{ID_o}.)

3. Simulate the proxy signer's signing oracle $\mathcal{O}_{PS}$. Set $\sigma_p = v$ and the hash value $H_2(R_1, R_2, m\|m_w) = u$. Store $(R_1, R_2, m\|m_w, u)$ in the Λ_2-list. Return $\sigma = (\sigma_o, opk, m_w, \sigma_p, m)$ as a valid proxy signature. In the random oracle model, this simulation is perfect. Therefore, we will have $|\Pr[\mathsf{Forge}_6] = \Pr[\mathsf{Forge}_5]|$.

At the end of the **Game₆**, the adversary $\mathcal{A}$ eventually outputs a new valid proxy signature $\sigma^* = (\sigma_o^*, opk^*, m_w^*, \sigma_p^*, m^*)$. From the *forking lemma* due to Pointcheval and Stern [16], if $\Pr[\mathsf{Forge}_6] \geq 10(q_S + 1)(q_S + q_{H_2})/q$, then $\epsilon = \mathbf{Succ}_{\mathsf{IBOTPS},\mathcal{A}}^{\mathsf{id\text{-}ef\text{-}cma}} \geq 10q_H(q_S + 1)(q_S + q_{H_2})/q$, and then by replaying $\mathcal{A}$ with the same tape but different choices of H_2, $\mathcal{A}$ outputs two valid proxy signature $\sigma^* = (\sigma_o^*, opk^*, m_w^*, \sigma_p^*, m^*)$, $\sigma'^* = (\sigma_o^*, opk^*, m_w^*, \sigma_p'^*, m^*)$ on the same (opk^*, m_w^*, m^*), where $\sigma_p^* = r_2 + r_1 \cdot H_2(R_1^*, R_2^*, m^*\|m_w^*) \bmod q$

and $\sigma_p'^\star = r_2 + r_1 \cdot H_2'(R_1^\star, R_2^\star, m^\star \| m_w^\star) \bmod q$, and $H_2(R_1^\star, R_2^\star, m^\star \| m_w^\star) \neq H_2'(R_1^\star, R_2^\star, m^\star \| m_w^\star)$, we then can compute r_1 and r_2 as

$$r_1 = \frac{\sigma_p^\star - \sigma_p'^\star}{H_2(R_1, R_2, m^\star \| m_w^\star) - H_2'(R_1, R_2, m^\star \| m_w^\star)} \bmod q$$
$$r_2 = \sigma_p^\star - r_1 \cdot H_2(R_1, R_2, m^\star \| m_w^\star) \bmod q$$

Finally, we compute $R_2{}^{r_2} = S_{ID^*}^{r_2^{-1} r_2} = S_{ID^*} = P^{xy}$ and output it. The total running time τ' of solving the CDH problem is roughly equal to the running time of the *forking lemma*, which is bound by $120686 q_{H_2} \tau / \epsilon$, as desired. Thus, this completes the proof. $\qquad\square$

According to the above two lemmas, the proposed IBOTPS scheme is clearly also unforgeable against an adversary who only owns the public keys of the original signer and the proxy signer. Therefore, it is straightforward that the following theorem holds.

Theorem 2. *The proposed IBOTPS scheme is a secure ID-based one-time proxy signature, provided that the CDH assumption is sound in $\mathbb{G}_1$ and the hash functions are modelled as random oracles.* $\qquad\square$

5   Application in E-Cheque Scenarios

In this section, we briefly present an application of the proposed IBOTPS scheme in E-cheque scenarios as follows. As is known to us, an E-cheque is essentially an electronic version of the paper cheque, except it is created on a computer and processed via the Internet. Similarly as the paper cheque, a blank E-cheque is also allowed being signed only *once*. To issue an E-cheque to the merchant, a consumer usually uses an electronic chequebook issued by the bank and sign a blank E-cheque with his digital signature. Here, to guarantee the security and reduce the cost, the following three requirements for issuing an E-cheque should be satisfied:

- The bank should provide the off-line service for every paid E-cheque;
- The consumer should cost the on-line computation as low as possible;
- The E-cheque should be unforgeable, only the consumer can sign a blank E-cheque *once* with the consent of the bank.

Based upon these requirements, when the original signer, the proxy signer and the proxy warrant are regarded as the bank, the consumer and the blank E-cheque respectively, the above proposed IBOTPS scheme is obviously a good candidate to be applied in the E-cheque scenarios. For example, generating the one-time proxy secret key is equal to issuing a blank E-cheque, and signing the one-time proxy signature is also equal to issuing an E-cheque to the merchant.

6   Conclusion

We observed that no IBOTPS scheme has been presented currently, though many one-time proxy signature schemes were put forth. Therefore, in this paper, we formalized the security notion for IBOTPS, and proposed the *first* IBOTPS scheme based on the bilinear pairings and provided the proofs of security in the random oracle model. Moreover, we presented an application of the proposed IBOTPS scheme in E-cheque scenarios. By these analysis, we conclude that the proposed IBOTPS scheme is actually a secure and practical one.

Acknowledgment

The authors would like to thank anonymous referees of CANS06 for their value comments and suggestions that improve the presentation of this paper. This work was supported in part by the National Natural Science Foundation of China for Distinguished Young Scholars under Grant No. 60225007 and the National Natural Science Foundation of China under Grant No. 60572155, the Science and Technology Research Project of Shanghai under Grant No. 04DZ07067, and the special research funds of Huawei.

References

1. M. Al-Ibrahim and A. Cerny, "Proxy and threshold one-time signatures", In *Applied Cryptography and Network Security (ACNS'03)*, Lecture Notes in Computer Science, vol. 2846, Springer-Verlag, pp. 123-136, 2003.
2. D. Boneh, and M. Franklin, "Identity-based Encryption from the Weil pairing", *SIAM. Journal of Computing*, vol. 32 (3), 586-615 (2003). Extended abstract in *Advances in Crptology-Crypto'01*, Lecture Notes in Computer Science, vol. 2139, Springer-Verlag, pp. 213-229, 2001.
3. P. Barreto, H. Kim, B. Lynn, M. Scott, "Efficient algorithms for pairing-based cryptosystems", In *Advances in Cryptology - Crypto 2002*, Lecture Notes in Computer Science, vol. 2442, Springer-Verlag, pp. 354-368, 2002.
4. M. Bellare, C. Namprempre, and G. Neven, "Security proofs for identity-based identification and signature schemes", In *Advances in Cryptology - Eurocrypto 2004*, Lecture Notes in Computer Science, vol. 3027, Springer-Verlag, pp. 268-286, 2002.
5. M. Bellare and P. Rogaway, "Random oracles are practical: a paradigm for designing efficient protocols", In *Proc. of the 1st ACM Conference on Computer and Communication Security*, pp. 62-73, ACM Press, New York, 1993.
6. J. Coron, "On the exact security of full domain hash", In *Advances in Cryptology - Crypto'00*, Lecture Notes in Computer Science, vol. 1880, Springer-Verlag, pp. 229-235, 2000.
7. J. Cha, and J. Choen, "An identity-based signature from gap diffie-hellman groups", In *PKC 2003*, Lecture Notes in Computer Science, vol. 2567, Springer-Verlag, pp. 18-30, 2003.
8. C. Choi, Z. Kim, and K. Kim, "Schnorr signature scheme with restricted signing capability and its application", In *Proc. Computer Security Symp (CSS'03)*, pp.385-390, 2003.

9. S. Goldwasser, S. Micali, R. Rivest, "A digital signature scheme secure against adaptive chosen-message attacks", *SIAM. Journal of Computing*, vol. 17 (2), 281-308 (1988).

10. S.-J. Hwang and C.-H. Shi, "A simple multi-proxy signature scheme", In *Proceedings of the Tenth National Conference on Information Security*, pp. 134-138, 2000.

11. H. Kim, J. Baek, B. Lee, and K. Kim, "Secret computation with secrets for mobile agent using one-time proxy signature", In *Symp. on Cryptography and Information Security (SCIS)*, Oiso, Japan, IEEE press, pp.845-850, 2001.

12. B. Lee, H. Kim, and K. Kim, "Strong proxy signgture and its applications", In *Proceedings of SCIS, 2001*, pp. 603-608, 2001.

13. M. Mehta and L. Harn, "Efficient one-time proxy signatures", *IEE Proc.-Commun.*, vol. 152, no. 2 129-133 (2005).

14. M. Mambo, K. Usuda, E. Okamoto, "Proxy signature: delegation of the power to sign messages", *IEICE Trans. Fundamentals*, vol. E79-A, no. 9, 1338-1353 (1996).

15. M. Mambo, K. Usuda, E. Okamoto, "Proxy signatures for delegating signing operation", In *Proc. 3rd ACM Conference on Computer and Communications Security - CCS'96*, ACM Press, pp. 48-57, 1996.

16. D. Pointcheval and J. Stern, "Security arguments for digital signatures and blind signatures", *J. Cryptology*, vol. 13, no. 3, 361-396 (2000).

17. A. Shamir, "Identity-based cryptosystems and signature schemes", In *Advances in Cryptology - Crypto'84*, Lecture Notes in Computer Science, vol. 196, Springer-Verlag, pp. 47-53, 1984.

18. H.-M. Sun, "An efficient nonrepudiable threshold proxy signatures with known signers", *Computer Communications*, vol. 22, no. 8, 717-722 (1999).

19. V. Shoup, "OAEP reconsidered", *Journal of Cryptography*, vol. 15 (4), 223-249 (2002).

20. H. Sun, N.-Y. Lee, and T. Hwang, "Threshold proxy signatures", *IEE Proceedings-Computes and Digital Technique*, vol. 146, 259-263 (1999).

21. Z.-W. Tan, Z.-J. Liu and C.M. Tang, "Proxy blind signature scheme based on DLP", *Journal of Software*, vol. 14, 1931-1935 (2003).

22. H. Wang, J. Pieprzyk, "Efficient one-time proxy signatures", In *Advance of Cryptology - Asiacrypt'03*, Lecture Notes in Computer Science, vol. 2894, Springer-Verlag, pp. 507-522, 2003.

23. S. Xu, Y. Mu, W. Susilo, "Efficient authentication scheme for routing in mobile ad hoc networks", In *EUC Worshops 2005*, Lecture Notes in Computer Science, vol. 3823, Springer-Verlag, pp. 854-863, 2003.

24. L. Yi, G. Bai and G. Xiao, "Proxy multi-signature scheme: a new type of proxy signature scheme", *Electroinics Letter*, vol. 36, no. 6, 527-528 (2000).

25. F. Zhang, Y. Mu, and W. Susilo, "Reducing security overhead for mobile networks", *Proceedings of The 19th International Conference on Advanced Information Networking and Applications (AINA 2005)*, pp.398-403. IEEE Computer Society, 2005.

Side Channel Attacks and Countermeasures on Pairing Based Cryptosystems over Binary Fields

Tae Hyun Kim[1], Tsuyoshi Takagi[2],
Dong-Guk Han[3], Ho Won Kim[3], and Jongin Lim[1]

[1] Center for Information and Security Technologies(CIST),
Korea University, Seoul, Korea
{thkim, jilim}@cist.korea.ac.kr
[2] FUTURE UNIVERSITY-HAKODATE, Japan
takagi@fun.ac.jp
[3] Electronics and Telecommunications Research Institute(ETRI), Korea
{christa, khw}@etri.re.kr

Abstract. Pairings on elliptic curves have been used as cryptographic primitives for the development of new applications such as identity based schemes. For the practical applications, it is crucial to provide efficient and secure implementations of the pairings. There have been several works on efficient implementations of the pairings. However, the research for secure implementations of the pairings has not been thoroughly investigated. In this paper, we investigate vulnerability of the pairing used in some pairing based protocols against side channel attacks. We propose an efficient algorithm secure against such side channel attacks of the eta pairing using randomized projective coordinate systems for the pairing computation.

Keywords: Pairing based cryptosystems, Side channel attacks, Differential Power Analysis, Randomized projective coordinate systems, Eta pairing.

1 Introduction

Since pairings have new and useful cryptographic properties such as bilinearity and non-degeneracy the interest and active research of them in cryptography is growing. Recently many cryptographic schemes based on the Tate pairing and the Weil pairing have been proposed. For example, identity based encryption schemes [6,28], identity based signature schemes [17,8,26], short signature [7], and identity based authenticated key agreement [31].

To accelerate practical applications of pairing based schemes a lot of work has focused on the development of efficient and easy computations of pairings on elliptic curves. Barreto et al. [2] and Galbraith et al. [13] provided the fast computation of the Tate pairing on supersingular elliptic curves over finite fields of characteristic two and three. Duursma and Lee [11] gave a closed formula in the case of characteristic three, and Kwon [21] extended it to supersingular curves over characteristic two. Barreto et al. [1] proposed a general technique

D. Pointcheval, Y. Mu, and K. Chen (Eds.): CANS 2006, LNCS 4301, pp. 168–181, 2006.

for the efficient computation of pairings on supersingular abelian varieties called *the eta pairing*.

Recently such methods of pairings have been implemented in software and hardware to accelerate constrained devices such as smartcards [5,14,30,4,27]. In the implementation of cryptosystems or protocols on such devices, we should consider not only efficiency but also security. If we don't carefully implement cryptosystems on constrained devices then they can be insecure against side channel attacks (SCAs). Thus it is important to consider the secure implementation of pairing based cryptosystems secure against SCAs. We can divide pairing based schemes into two types by whether or not an input of pairing is secret [10]. For example, identity based signature schemes such as short signature scheme by Boneh et al. require the secret information as an input (i.e., the secret scalar) of the elliptic curve scalar multiplication. Side channel attacks and countermeasures on scalar multiplications have well been studied. However, identity based encryption schemes such as Boneh-Franklin encryption scheme [6] use the secret information as an input of the pairing. In this case, there are only few works of SCAs on the pairings [24,29,33]. In [24], Page and Vercauteren showed side channel attacks against the Duursma-Lee algorithm. In [29], Scott suggested countermeasures to provide resistance to more sophisticated simple power analysis (SPA) and differential power analysis (DPA) attacks. Very recently, Whelan and Scott investigated practical pairing algorithms using correlation power analysis (CPA) [33]. However the form of some multiplication used in the eta pairing on the supersingular curves in characteristic two is different to the case of characteristic three. In this paper, we concretely examine the security of the eta pairing on the supersingular curve over $\mathbb{F}_{2^m}$ against timing attack (TA) or SPA attack and DPA attack.

In general, to speed up elliptic curve point addition and doubling, the projective coordinate systems are used instead of the affine coordinate system because the affine coordinate system requires a modular inversion operation, computationally expensive. In [19], Izu and Takagi showed that the Tate pairing on general elliptic curves over prime fields $\mathbb{F}_{p^m}$ is efficiently computed using the projective coordinate systems. Hess et al. [18] extended the eta pairing over supersingular curves to general curves over prime fields $\mathbb{F}_{p^m}$, and then examined efficiency in the projective coordinate systems. However, for providing protection of SCAs, Coron [9] used the randomized projective coordinate. In this paper, to resist SCAs, we propose an explicit algorithm using randomness of the projective coordinate systems of the eta pairing for a curve over characteristic two.

This paper is organized as follows: In the next section we review several methods for the efficient computation of the Tate pairing. Section 3 describes side channel attacks on the eta pairing over supersingular curves in characteristic two. Section 4 presents a countermeasure to prevent the attack described in Section 3. Section 5 compares the proposed countermeasure with the previous methods. Finally we conclude in Section 6.

2   The Tate Pairing

Let E be an elliptic curve over a finite field $\mathbb{F}_q$. Let l be a positive integer coprime to q, which divides $\#E(\mathbb{F}_q)$, i.e., $l|\#E(\mathbb{F}_q)$. Let k be the smallest positive integer such that the l-th root of unity exists in $\mathbb{F}_{q^k}^*$, i.e., $l|(q^k - 1)$. We call such k the embedding degree or security multiplier. The Tate pairing of P and Q on $E(\mathbb{F}_q)$ of order l is defined as follows:

$$e_l : E(\mathbb{F}_q)[l] \times E(\mathbb{F}_{q^k})[l] \to \mu_l \quad \text{with} \quad e_l(P, Q) = f_{l,P}(\mathcal{D}_Q)^{(q^k - 1)/l}, \qquad (1)$$

where $f_{l,P}$ is a rational function such that $(f_{l,P}) = l(P) - ([l]P) - (l - 1)(\mathcal{O})$ and $\mathcal{D}_Q$ is a zero divisor equivalent to $(Q) - (\mathcal{O})$ such that $\mathcal{D}_Q$ and $(f_{l,P})$ have disjoint supports. Also μ_l is the subgroup of the l-th root of unity in $\mathbb{F}_{q^k}^*$. The first efficient method for computing such a rational function is proposed by Miller [22]. This algorithm is based on the binary method for elliptic curve scalar multiplication combined with an evaluation of the tangent lines used in the elliptic curve addition process. In the original Miller algorithm, a denominator in the step of an evaluation of the tangent lines should be manipulated. Barreto et al. [2] showed the way able to speed up by eliminating the denominator, namely, for supersingular elliptic curves they used a specific endormorphism ψ called a distortion map [32]. Thus the Tate pairing is modified by

$$e_l(P, Q) = f_{l,P}(\psi(Q))^{(q^k - 1)/l}. \qquad (2)$$

To improve the computation speed of the above pairing on curves we can use $N = hl$ to be a multiple of the order of elliptic curve for some integer h instead of l [13]. Since $(f_{N,P}) = h(f_{l,P}) = (f_{l,P}^h)$ the Tate pairing can be computed by $f_{N,P}(\psi(Q))^{(q^k - 1)/N}$, where $N = hl$ and $f_{N,P}$ is a rational function such that $(f_{N,P}) = N(P) - ([N]P) - (N - 1)(\mathcal{O})$. Using this property, Duursma and Lee [11] and Kwon [21] replaced l by $N = hl$ which has low Hamming weight in the case of characteristic three and two, respectively. In characteristic two, the order and the embedding degree of supersingular curves $E : y^2 + y = x^3 + x + b$, where $b \in \mathbb{F}_2$ are $2^m \pm 2^{(m+1)/2} + 1$ and 4, respectively. Thus, we can use $N = 2^{2m} + 1 = (2^m + 2^{(m+1)/2} + 1)(2^m - 2^{(m+1)/2} + 1)$ of Hamming weight 2 in the binary representation and also the final exponentiation by $(2^{4m} - 1)/(2^{2m} + 1) = 2^{2m} - 1$ is very simple, which is computed by applying one Frobenius map and one division [11,21].

The fastest method for computing the Tate pairing is the eta pairing [1], which includes the algorithms by Duursma and Lee [11] and Kwon [21] as special cases. We now present an outline of the eta pairing algorithm. The elliptic curve of our interest is the supersingular curve $E : y^2 + y = x^3 + x + b$ over $\mathbb{F}_{2^m}$ where $m \equiv 3 \mod 8$ and $b \in \mathbb{F}_2$. The extension field $\mathbb{F}_{2^{4m}}$ is represented by the basis $\{1, s, t, st\}$ such that $s^2 + s + 1 = 0$ and $t^2 + t + s = 0$. The distortion map is $\psi(x, y) = (x + s^2, y + sx + t)$. For some integer T the eta pairing η_T is defined to be $\eta_T(P, Q) = f_{T,P}(\psi(Q))$. Then there is the following relation between the eta pairing and the Tate pairing.

$$\left(\eta_T(P, Q)^M\right)^{aT^{a-1}} = \left(e_N(P, Q)\right)^L. \qquad (3)$$

where $T^a + 1 = LN$ for some $a \in \mathbb{N}$ and $L \in \mathbb{Z}$, $T = q + cN$ for some $c \in \mathbb{Z}$, and $M = (q^k - 1)/N$. To reduce of the loop in characteristic two we can choose $T = \mp 2^{(m+1)/2} + 1$, $a = 2$, $c = -1$, and $L = 2$. In this case, we should first compute the rational function corresponding to addition of $2^{(m+1)/2}P$ and $\pm P$. Since $2^{(m+1)/2}P$ is efficiently computed by Frobenius map we can easily deal with it. We have

$$\left(\eta_T(P,Q)^M\right)^{2T} = e_N(P,Q)^2 \Rightarrow \left(\eta_T(P,Q)^M\right)^T = e_N(P,Q). \qquad (4)$$

However, to obtain the same result as the Tate pairing, it must be further exponentiated to the power of T. The concrete algorithm of the eta pairing on supersingular curves in characteristic two with $m \equiv 3 \bmod 8$ is shown in Algorithm 1.

Algorithm 1. $\eta_T(P,Q)$ on the curve E: $y^2 + y = x^3 + x + b$ over $\mathbb{F}_{2^m}$, where $b \in \mathbb{F}_2$ and $m \equiv 3 \bmod 8$ case [1]

Input: $P = (x_P, y_P)$ and $Q = (x_Q, y_Q)$.
Output: $\eta_T(P,Q)$.
1: $u \leftarrow x_P + 1$
2: $f \leftarrow u \cdot (u + x_Q) + y_P + y_Q + b + 1 + (u + x_Q)s + t$
3: **for** $i = 0$ to $(m+1)/2$ **do**
4:     $u \leftarrow x_P$, $x_P \leftarrow \sqrt{x_P}$, $y_P \leftarrow \sqrt{y_P}$
5:     $g \leftarrow u \cdot (x_P + x_Q) + y_P + y_Q + x_P + (u + x_Q)s + t$
6:     $f \leftarrow f \cdot g$
7:     $x_Q \leftarrow x_Q^2$, $y_Q \leftarrow y_Q^2$
8: **end for**
9: **return** $f^{(2^{2m}-1)(2^{2m}-2^{(m+1)/2}+1)}$

Note that we mainly deal with the eta pairing in characteristic two because the algorithm is simpler in characteristic three than characteristic two in the sense of side channel attacks.

3   Side Channel Attacks

Side channel attacks (SCAs) have been recognized as serious menaces to constrained devices such as smartcards. By monitoring computation timing, power consumption, or electromagnetic radiation, etc. during cryptographic operations, it is possible to recover the secret information related to the keys inside the device [20,9]. Timing attack (TA) analyzes the time taken to execute cryptographic algorithms. Simple Power Analysis (SPA) attack directly interprets power consumption measurements collected during cryptographic operations. Differential Power Analysis (DPA) attack analyzes correlation between power consumptions and specific key-dependent intermediate values which appear during computation with the secret by using statistical tools and error correction techniques.

In this section we investigate the eta pairing used in identity based encryption schemes such as Boneh-Franklin encryption scheme [6] and Sakai-Kasahara encryption scheme [28] in the context of side channel attacks such as TA, SPA, and DPA.

3.1 Weak Point in Pairing Computation

In the decryption step of identity based encryption schemes, the critical calculation is $e(S_{ID}, C)$ where S_{ID} is the fixed secret key and C is a part of a ciphertext. In this case, side channel attacks may try to extract the secret key from the pairing computation by repeatedly manipulating C. Recently, Page and Vercauteren [24] presented an SPA attack and a DPA attack on a field multiplication step of the pairing computation with the secret value. They showed that there are such field multiplications in the Duursma-Lee algorithm [24] and the BLKS algorithm [2] of characteristic three, i.e., $y \cdot r$ where y is an unknown and fixed value related with the y-coordinate of the secret point S_{ID} and r is a known and variable value related with the ciphertext C. Since the field multiplication is analogous to exponentiation on a multiplicative group or scalar multiplication on an additive group we can easily apply DPA attacks such as [9].

However, the eta pairing in characteristic two includes the multiplication of the different form $a \cdot (b+r)$ compared with the case of characteristic three, where both a and b are unknown. In this case, since r chosen by an attacker is added by the unknown value b we may not simulate or guess an intermediate value related with secret value. Thus it seems secure against DPA attacks. However, in the next section, we will show that the addition and the multiplication of $a \cdot (b+r)$ can be insecure against TA or SPA attack and DPA attack.

Assumption. From this section assume that the first input $P = (x_P, y_P)$ of the pairing in Algorithm 1 is secret and the second input $Q = (x_Q, y_Q)$ is public. Note however that the description of the attack is similar even if P is public and Q is secret. For the computation of $a \cdot (b+r)$, we also assume that the addition $(b+r)$ is first computed, and the multiplication $a \cdot (b+r)$ is computed.

3.2 Finite Field Arithmetic

Let $f(x)$ be an irreducible polynomial of degree m over $\mathbb{F}_2$. Assume an element a of $\mathbb{F}_{2^m} \simeq \mathbb{F}_2[x]/(f(x))$ is represented by the polynomial basis. Let the bit string $(a_{m-1}a_{m-2} \cdots a_1 a_0)$ where $a_i \in \mathbb{F}_2$ denote an element a of $\mathbb{F}_{2^m}$. Addition and multiplication of $a = (a_{m-1} \cdots a_1 a_0)$ and $b = (b_{m-1} \cdots b_1 b_0)$ in $\mathbb{F}_{2^m}$ are performed as follows:

Addition: $a + b = (c_{m-1} \cdots c_1 c_0)$, where $c_i = (a_i + b_i) \bmod 2$.
Multiplication: $c = a \cdot b = (c_{m-1} \cdots c_1 c_0)$, where c is computed as a multiplication of polynomials $a(x)$ and $b(x)$ of $\mathbb{F}_2[x]$ followed by a reduction by $f(x)$. That is, $c = a(x) \cdot b(x) \bmod f(x)$.

The addition of two elements a and b in $\mathbb{F}_{2^m}$ is easily performed by a bitwise XOR operation. A usual way of multiplying two elements a and b of $\mathbb{F}_{2^m}$ is done by scanning the multiplier b one bit at a time. This method is known as the shift-and-add method based on the following observation

$$a \cdot b = a_{m-1}x^{m-1}b + a_{m-2}x^{m-2}b + \cdots + a_1xb + a_0b.$$

For efficiency reason the irreducible polynomial is selected as a trinomial or a pentanomial. Therefore, we assume that a multiplication of polynomials is first performed, and then the result is reduced by an irreducible polynomial. Note however that the attack is not limited to the above multiplication and the separative computation of multiplication and reduction. we can extend our attack to other multiplication methods and the simultaneous computation of multiplication and reduction. The concrete algorithm of the shift-and-add method is given in Algorithm 2.

Algorithm 2. Shift-and-add(Right-to-left) method for polynomial multiplication

---

Input: $a(x) = (a_{m-1} \cdots a_0)_2$ and $b(x) = (b_{m-1} \cdots b_0)$.
Output: $c(x) = a(x) \cdot b(x)$.
1: $C \leftarrow 0$ and $B \leftarrow b$
2: **for** $i = 0$ to $m - 1$ **do**
3:　　**if** $a_i = 1$ **then**
4:　　　　$C \leftarrow C + B$
5:　　**end if**
6:　　$B \leftarrow B \cdot x$
7: **end for**
8: **return** C

3.3　SPA or Timing Attack on the Eta Pairing in Characteristic Two

We consider the multiplication $a \cdot (b + r)$. If a is multiplier then the addition is performed depending on whether $a_i = 1$ or not. The structure of the shift-and-add method for the multiplication of $a \cdot (b + r)$ is shown in Figure 1.

Page and Vercauteren [24] firstly presented an SPA attack against $a \cdot r$ in $\mathbb{F}_{3^m}$, where a is secret and r is public. It means that this conditional branch is vulnerable to TA or SPA attack [20,9]. Thus, we can also recover u of $u \cdot (x_P + x_Q)$, which is a part of step 5 of Algorithm 1. In this case, u is the x-coordinate of the secret point P. Thus we can obtain the y-coordinate from the x-coordinate.

However, if $b + r$ is multiplier then the conditional branch occurs depending on $b_i + r_i$. So, if we can detect an appearance of the conditional branch by TA or SPA attack then $b_i \neq r_i$. Otherwise, $b_i = r_i$. Thus we can recover x_P by controlling x_Q in $u \cdot (x_P + x_Q)$. Since x_P is the square root of the x-coordinate of the secret point P we can obtain the x-coordinate by squaring x_P, and then the y-coordinate from the x-coordinate of the secret point P.

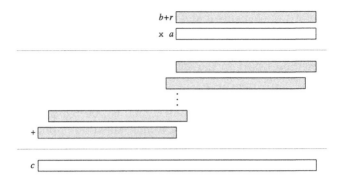

Fig. 1. The shift-and-add multiplication of $a \cdot (b + r)$ in $\mathbb{F}_{2^m}$

3.4 DPA on the Eta Pairing in Characteristic Two

In this section, we investigate DPA attacks against the addition $b + r$ and the multiplication $a \cdot (b + r)$ used in the eta pairing on curves in characteristic two, where a and b are secret and r is public.

To ease the explanation we consider the simplified Hamming weight model for power leakage [23]. In this model, power consumption depends on the Hamming weight of the data being processed. Thus we can express the power consumption $\mathcal{C}$ as follows:

$$\mathcal{C} = \varepsilon \cdot H + n,$$

where H, ε and n represent the Hamming weight of the intermediate data, the incremental amount of power for each extra '1' in the Hamming weight, and the noise, respectively. Note that assume the average of noise n is zero.

Attack on the Addition. The addition of $b + r$ is of the form

$$(b_{m-1} \oplus r_{m-1})x^{m-1} + (b_{m-2} \oplus r_{m-2})x^{m-2} + \cdots + (b_1 \oplus r_1)x + (b_0 \oplus r_0).$$

Let $\mathcal{C}$ be the power consumption associated with the addition operation $b+r$. To recover the i-th bit of b, we guess that $b_i = 1$ and divide power consumptions into two sets by r_i.

$$S_k = \{\mathcal{C}|r_i = k\} \text{ with } k \in \{0, 1\} \tag{5}$$

The averages of S_0 and S_1 are respectively $\varepsilon(M + 1)/2$ and $\varepsilon(M - 1)/2$, where M is the size of the resister. Thus the differential power consumption is

$$\Delta = \langle S_0 - S_1 \rangle. \tag{6}$$

If $\Delta \neq 0$ then $b_i = 1$, otherwise $b_i = 0$.

In conclusion, since the addition operation $(x_P + x_Q)$ of step 5 of Algorithm 1 is vulnerable to the above analysis we can recover x_P. From this value we can obtain the x-coordinate and y-coordinate of the secret point P.

Attack on the Multiplication. Since DPA attacks use correlation between power consumptions and specific key-dependent intermediate values which appear during computation related with the secret it is important to examine the intermediate values for the computation of $a \cdot (b + r)$ by Algorithm 2. We will treat both cases: the first case is that a is multiplier and $b + r$ is multiplicand and the second case is that $b + r$ is multiplier and a is multiplicand.

Theorem 1. *In Algorithm 2, if a is multiplier and $b + r$ is multiplicand then the algorithm is vulnerable to the DPA attack.*

Proof. In this case, the multiplication is performed as follows;

$$a_{m-1}x^{m-1}(b+r) + a_{m-2}x^{m-2}(b+r) + \cdots + a_1 x(b+r) + a_0(b+r). \qquad (7)$$

To describe how to recover a assume the lowest bits $a_{i-1}, \cdots, a_0$ of the secret multiplier a are already recovered. We describe how to find the next bit a_i.

In Algorithm 2, the intermediate value obtained at end of i-th step of the loop is

$$a_i x^i(b+r) + \cdots + a_1 x(b+r) + a_0(b+r). \qquad (8)$$

The i-th bit of (8) is

$$a_i(b_0 + r_0) + a_{i-1}(b_1 + r_1) + \cdots + a_1(b_{i-1} + r_{i-1}) + a_0(b_i + r_i)$$
$$= (a_i b_0 + a_{i-1}b_1 + \cdots + a_0 b_i) + (a_i r_0 + a_{i-1}r_1 + \cdots + a_0 r_i). \qquad (9)$$

In this case, we can not simulate this intermediate value because we don't know the value of $a_i b_0 + a_{i-1}b_1 + \cdots + a_0 b_i$. However, we can accomplish a DPA attack by only controlling the input value r and not the intermediate value.

Let $\mathcal{C}$ be the power consumption associated with computation of $a \cdot (b + r)$. From the formula of (9) we guess the $a_i = 1$ and divide power consumptions into two sets by $a_i r_0 + a_{i-1}r_1 + \cdots + a_0 r_i$, which is derived from the already known $a_{i-1}, \cdots, a_0$ and the random value chosen by ourself.

$$S_k = \{\mathcal{C}| r_0 + a_{i-1}r_1 + \cdots + a_0 r_i = k\} \text{ with } k \in \{0, 1\} \qquad (10)$$

If $a_i b_0 + a_{i-1}b_1 + \cdots + a_0 b_i = 1$ in (9) then the average power consumptions of S_0 and S_1 are respectively $\varepsilon(M+1)/2$ and $\varepsilon(M-1)/2$, where M is the size of the resister. So, we have $\langle S_1 - S_0 \rangle = -\varepsilon$. In the case of $a_i b_0 + a_{i-1}b_1 + \cdots + a_0 b_i = 0$, the averages of S_0 and S_1 are respectively $\varepsilon(M-1)/2$ and $\varepsilon(M+1)/2$. We have $\langle S_1 - S_0 \rangle = \varepsilon$. The difference between two cases is only whether the differential average power consumptions is positive or negative. Thus we will compute the differential power consumption by using absolute value

$$\Delta = \langle |S_1 - S_0| \rangle. \qquad (11)$$

If $\Delta \neq 0$, namely, we can detect an appreciable peak then the guess is right (i.e., $a_i = 1$), otherwise the guess is wrong (i.e., $a_i = 0$). The remaining bits $a_{m-1}, \cdots, a_{i+1}$ are recursively recovered by the same way. Thus we can recover the multiplier of Algorithm 2. $\qquad \square$

Theorem 2. *In Algorithm 2, if $b + r$ is multiplier and a is multiplicand then the algorithm is vulnerable to the DPA attack.*

Proof. The multiplication of $(b + r) \cdot a$ is performed as follows;

$$(b_{m-1} + r_{m-1})x^{m-1}a + (b_{m-2} + r_{m-2})x^{m-2}a + \cdots + (b_1 + r_1)xa + (b_0 + r_0)a.$$

In this case, we also describe how to recover a. Assume the lowest bits $a_{i-1}, \cdots, a_0$ of a are already recovered. The aim is to find the next bit a_i.

In Algorithm 2, the intermediate value obtained at end of i-th step of the loop is

$$(b_i + r_i)x^i a + \cdots + (b_1 + r_1)xa + (b_0 + r_0)a. \tag{12}$$

The i-th bit of (12) is

$$\begin{aligned}
& (b_i + r_i)a_0 + (b_{i-1} + r_{i-1})a_1 + \cdots + (b_1 + r_1)a_{i-1} + (b_0 + r_0)a_i \\
= \ & (b_i a_0 + b_{i-1}a_1 + \cdots + b_0 a_i) + (r_i a_0 + r_{i-1}a_1 + \cdots + r_0 a_i). \tag{13}
\end{aligned}$$

The above equation is equal to (9). Thus, we can recover a_i by the proof of Theorem 1.   □

In conclusion, since the multiplication of $u(x_P + x_Q)$ of step 5 of Algorithm 1 is vulnerable to the proposed attack, we can recover u, the x-coordinate of the secret point P. Finally, we can obtain the y-coordinate from the x-coordinate.

Remark 1. Since the eta pairing over characteristic three also includes the addition $a + r$ and the multiplication $a \cdot r$, where a is secret and r is public (See [1] for detail.) the addition and the multiplication are vulnerable to the above described attack. However, note that Page and Vercauteren [24] also presented DPA attack on the multiplication of $a \cdot r$. Thus the eta pairing over characteristic three is also insecure against side channel attacks.

4   Proposed Countermeasure

The attack described in Section 3 is possible since we can choose and control an input value. To incapacitate such a behavior Coron [9] proposed three methods for securely computing scalar multiplication dP in elliptic curve cryptosystems (ECCs), where d is the secret key and P is public. Let E be an elliptic curve over finite fields $\mathbb{F}_q$. Let $\#E$ be the number of points of the curve. The countermeasures for computing $Q = dP$ are follows:

1. Randomization of the private value, i.e., $dP = (d + r \cdot \#E)P$ for a random number $r \in \mathbb{F}_q$.
2. Blinding the public value, i.e., $dP = d(P + R) - dR$ for a random point R on $E(\mathbb{F}_q)$.
3. Randomized projective coordinate, i.e., $(X; Y; Z) = (\lambda X; \lambda Y; \lambda Z)$ for a random value $\lambda \neq 0$ in $\mathbb{F}_q$.

In the context of the above techniques, Page and Vercauteren [24] and Scott [29] proposed some methods for the pairings. First, they used bilinearity to randomize the private data, i.e., $e(P, Q) = e(sP, tP)^{1/st}$ where s and t are random variables. Furthermore, the exponentiation to the power $1/st$ can be removed by selecting s and t satisfying $s \cdot t = 1 \bmod l$, where l is the order of the underlying elliptic curve for the pairing [24]. Second, they presented the method for blinding the input point by the relation $e(P, Q) = e(P, Q + R) \cdot e(P, R)^{-1}$ [24].

4.1 Projective Coordinate Randomization

In this paper, we propose an explicit algorithm for the eta pairing using the projective coordinate in order to resist DPA attack, which is the fastest method among existing countermeasures, and then we estimate computational efficiency between the proposed method and previous countermeasures. We now describe how to make an algorithm using the randomized projective coordinate technique of the eta pairing in the case of characteristic two. The projective coordinates (X, Y, Z) of a point $P = (x, y)$ are given by

$$x = X/Z, \; y = Y/Z$$

We can randomize the input points by randomly selecting Z-coordinate value before the computation of the pairing $e(P, Q)$. In Algorithm 1, we only randomize Q for efficiency reason. Thus the step 5 of Algorithm 1 for the eta pairing is changed into

$$x_P(\sqrt{x_P} + X_Q/Z_Q) + \sqrt{y_P} + \sqrt{x_P} + Y_Q/Z_Q + (x_P + X_Q/Z_Q)s + t$$
$$= \frac{1}{Z_Q}\left(x_P(Z_Q\sqrt{x_P} + X_Q) + Z_Q(\sqrt{y_P} + \sqrt{x_P}) + Y_Q + (Z_Q x_P + X_Q)s + Z_Q t\right).$$

Since $1/Z_Q$ is in $\mathbb{F}_q$ it becomes one after the final exponentiation. Thus elimination of $1/Z_Q$ does not effect the result. The concrete algorithm is shown in Algorithm 3.

The step 6 of the proposed countermeasure is secure against the attacks described in the previous section because all operands of the addition and the multiplication operations are randomized by the projective coordinate system.

4.2 Randomizing Miller Variables

In [29], Scott introduced a method which multiplies intermediate values appearing during the loop by a random value in $\mathbb{F}_q$. To defend from the DPA attacks described the previous section, all intermediate variables (not only g) in step 2 and the step 5 of Algorithm 1 must be multiplied by a random value. Thus the step 2 and the step 5 should be respectively changed into
$f \leftarrow u \cdot (r \cdot u + r \cdot x_Q) + r \cdot y_P + r \cdot (y_Q + b + 1) + (r \cdot u + r \cdot x_Q)s + t$ and
$g \leftarrow u \cdot (r \cdot x_P + r \cdot x_Q) + r \cdot y_P + r \cdot y_Q + r \cdot x_P + (r \cdot u + r \cdot x_Q)s + rt.$

Algorithm 3. Randomized Projective Coordinate $\eta_T(P,Q)$ on the curve E: $Y^2Z + YZ^2 = X^3 + XZ^2 + bZ^3$ over $\mathbb{F}_{2^m}$, where $b \in \mathbb{F}_2$ and $m \equiv 3 \bmod 8$ case

Input: $P = (x_P, y_P)$ and $Q = (x_Q, y_Q)$.
Output: $\eta_T(P,Q)$.
1: $(X_Q, Y_Q, Z_Q) \leftarrow (\lambda x_Q, \lambda y_Q, \lambda)$, where λ is a random integer.
2: $u \leftarrow x_P + 1$
3: $f \leftarrow u \cdot (Z_Q \cdot u + X_Q) + Z_Q \cdot (y_P + b + 1) + Y_Q + (Z_Q \cdot u + X_Q)s + Z_Qt$
4: **for** $i = 0$ to $(m+1)/2$ **do**
5:   $u \leftarrow x_P,\ x_P \leftarrow \sqrt{x_P},\ y_P \leftarrow \sqrt{y_P}$
6:   $g \leftarrow u \cdot (Z_Q \cdot x_P + X_Q) + Z_Q \cdot (y_P + x_P) + Y_Q + (Z_Q \cdot u + X_Q)s + Z_Qt$
7:   $f \leftarrow f \cdot g$
8:   $X_Q \leftarrow X_Q^2,\ Y_Q \leftarrow Y_Q^2,\ Z_Q \leftarrow Z_Q^2$
9: **end for**
10: **return** $f^{(2^{2m}-1)(2^{2m}-2^{(m+1)/2}+1)}$

5   Efficiency Comparison

We first estimate the computational cost of the proposed algorithm. In the original eta pairing, the initial step requires 1 multiplication in $\mathbb{F}_{2^m}$ and each loop requires 7 multiplications in $\mathbb{F}_{2^m}$, where 1 multiplication to compute g and 6 multiplications at step 6 because of the sparse form of g. However, the initial step of the proposed algorithm requires 5 multiplications in $\mathbb{F}_{2^m}$ where 2 multiplications at step 1 and 3 multiplications at step 3, and each loop requires 13 multiplications in $\mathbb{F}_{2^m}$, where 4 multiplications at step 6 and 9 multiplications at step 7. See Appendix for detail. Since addition and squaring in $\mathbb{F}_{2^m}$ are relatively inexpensive compared to multiplication and inversion we can ignore the cost of field additions and squarings [16]. Moreover, we can ignore the cost of square roots because the method described in [12] for computing square roots in $\mathbb{F}_{2^m}$ is as fast as squaring. Thus the additional cost for the eta pairing including the initial step is $3(m+1) + 4$ multiplications in $\mathbb{F}_{2^m}$.

We now compare computational efficiency of the techniques described in Section 4. First, the method using bilinearity additionally requires 2 scalar multiplications. In supersingular curves, doubling a point is free and adding two distinct points requires two multiplications and one inversion [22]. In general, the ratio of inversion to multiplication is approximately 10 to 1 [16]. If we use the binary method for scalar multiplication then the additional cost of the eta pairing using this method is 12 multiplications in $\mathbb{F}_{2^m}$. Second, the method of $e(P,Q) = e(P, Q+R)e(P,R)^{-1}$ additionally requires 1 pairing computation, 1 extension field multiplication, and 1 extension field inversion. The computational cost of the eta pairing, i.e., Algorithm 1, is approximately $7(m+1)/2$ multiplications in $\mathbb{F}_{2^m}$ plus the final exponentiation required 3 applications of 2^m-Frobenius map, 4 multiplications in the extension field $\mathbb{F}_{2^{4m}}$, and 1 inversion in $\mathbb{F}_{2^{4m}}$ [1]. In the approach randomizing intermediate variables by Scott [29], the additional cost for the eta pairing is $4(m+1) + 4$ multiplications in $\mathbb{F}_{2^m}$

Table 1. Additional Cost for DPA Resistance over the Eta pairing (not over the Tate pairing) on Supersingular Curves on $\mathbb{F}_{2^m}$

Countermeasure	Additional Cost
Page-Vercauteren (randomized private value) [24]	$12mM$
Page-Vercauteren (blinding public value) [24]	$3.5(m+1)M + \alpha$
Scott (randomizing intermediate value) [29]	$4(m+1)M + 4M$
The Proposed Method (Algorithm 3)	$\mathbf{3(m+1)M + 4M}$

as Section 4.2. We give a comparison table of the number of operations among existing techniques in Table 1, where M and α denote the computation time of a multiplication in $\mathbb{F}_{2^m}$ and the final exponentiation plus 1 extension field multiplication in $\mathbb{F}_{2^{4m}}$ and 1 extension field inversion in $\mathbb{F}_{2^{4m}}$, respectively.

6   Conclusion

In this paper, we have investigated the security of pairing based cryptosystems against side channel attacks. Since pairing has different properties from primitives of traditional cryptosystems such as RSA or ECC the application of pairings such as identity based schemes has been interesting for implementing on constrained devices such as smartcards. Although the work for efficient implementation of pairings has been concentrated the secure implementation has not been worked precisely. In this paper, we have investigated security against side channel attacks for implementations of the eta pairing on supersingular curves in characteristic two. To avoid such attacks we have proposed an explicit algorithm of the eta pairing using the projective coordinate and showed that the proposed method is the most efficient countermeasure compared with previous techniques.

Acknowledgments

Tae Hyun Kim and Jongin Lim were supported by the MIC (Ministry of Information and Communication), Korea, under the ITRC (Information Technology Research Center) support program supervised by the IITA (Institute of Information Technology Assessment).

References

1. P.S.L.M. Barreto, S. Galbraith, C. OhEigeartaigh and M. Scott, "Efficient Pairing Computation on Supersingular Abelian Varieties," Preprint 2005, to appear in Designs, Codes and Cryptography.
2. P.S.L.M. Barreto, H.Y. Kim, B. Lynn, and M. Scott, "Efficient algorithms for pairing-based cryptosystems," *CRYPTO 2002*, LNCS 2442, pp.354-368, 2002.
3. P.S.L.M. Barreto, B. Lynn, M. Scott, "Efficient implementation of pairing based cryptosystems," *Journal of Cryptology*, Vol.17, No.4, pp.321-334, 2004.

4. G. Bertoni, L. Breveglieri, P. Fragneto, and G. Pelosi, "Parallel Hardware Architectures for the Cryptographic Tate Pairing," Proceedings of the Third International Conference on Information Technology: New Generations (ITNG'06), pp.186-191, 2006.

5. G.M. Bertoni, L. Chen, P. Fragneto, K.A. Harrison, and G. Pelosi, "Computing tate pairing on smartcards," 2005. http://www.st.com/stonline/products/families/smartcard/ches2005_v4.pdf

6. D. Boneh and M. Franklin, "Identity Based Encryption from the Weil Pairing," SIAM J. of Computing, Vol.32, No.3, pp.586-615, 2003.

7. D. Boneh, B. Lynn, and H. Shacham, "Short signatures from the Weil pairing," Asiacrypt 2001, LNCS 2248, pp.514-532, 2002.

8. J.C. Cha and J.H. Cheon, "An Indentity-Based Signature from Gap Diffie-Hellman Groups," PKC 2003, LNCS 2567, pp.18-30, 2003.

9. J.S. Coron, "Resistance against Differential Power Analysis for Elliptic Curve Cryptosystems," CHES 1999, LNCS 1717, pp.292-302, 1999.

10. R. Dutta, R. Barua, and P. Sarkar, "Pairing-Based Cryptographic Protocols : A Survey," Cryptology ePrint Archive, Report 2004/064, 2006. http://eprint.iacr.org/2004/064.

11. I. Duursma and H.-S. Lee, "Tate pairing implementation for hyperelliptic curves $y^2 = x^p - x + d$," Asiacrypt 2003, LNCS 2894, pp.111-123, 2003.

12. K. Fong, D. Hankerson, Julio López, and A. Menezes, "Field inversion and point halving revisited," Technical Report CORR 2003-18, University of Waterloo, August 2002.

13. S.D. Galbraith, K. Harrison, and D. Soldera, "Implementing the Tate pairing," ANTS V, LNCS 2369, pp.324-337, 2002.

14. Gemplus, "ID based Cryptography and Smartcards," 2005. http://www.gemplus.com/smart/rd/publications/pdf/Joy05iden.pdf.

15. R. Granger, D. Page, and M. Stam, "Hardware and software normal basis arithmetic for pairing based cryptography in characteristic three," IEEE Transactions on Computers, Vol.54, No.7, pp.852-860, July 2005.

16. D. Hankerson, J.L. Hernandez, and A. Menezes, "Software Implementation of Elliptic Curve Cryptography over Binary Fields," CHES 2000, LNCS 1965, pp.1-24, 2000.

17. F. Hess, "Exponent group signature schemes and efficient identity based signature schems based on pairing," SAC 2002, LNCS 2595, pp.310-324, 2002.

18. F. Hess, N. Smart, and F. Vercauteren, "The eta pairing revisited," Cryptology ePrint Archive, Report 2006/110, 2006. http://eprint.iacr.org/2006/110.

19. T. Izu and T. Takagi, "Efficient Computations of the Tate Pairing for the Large MOV Degrees," ICISC 2002, LNCS 2587, pp.283-297, 2003.

20. C. Kocher, J. Jaffe, B. Jun, "Differential Power Analysis," CRYPTO 1999, LNCS 1666, pp.388-397, 1999.

21. S. Kwon, "Efficient Tate Pairing Computation for Elliptic Curves over Binary Fields," ACISP 2005, LNCS 3574, pp.134-145, 2005.

22. A. Menezes, "Elliptic Curve Public Key Cryptosystems," Kluwer Academic Publishers, 1993.

23. T.S. Messerges, "Using Second-Order Power Analysis to Attack DPA Resistant Software," CHES 2000, LNCS 1965, pp.238-251, 2000.

24. D. Page and F. Vercauteren, "Fault and Side-Channel Attacks on Pairing Based Cryptography," Cryptology ePrint Archive, Report 2005/283, 2005. http://eprint.iacr.org/2005/283.

25. D. Page and F. Vercauteren, "A Fault Attack on Pairing Based Cryptography," To appear in IEEE Transactions on Computers 2006.
26. K.G. Paterson, "ID-based signature from pairings on elliptic curves," *Electronics Letters*, Vol.38, No.18, pp.1025-1026, 2002.
27. R. Ronan, C. OhEigeartaigh, C. Murphy, M. Scott, T. Kerins, and W. Marnane, "An Embedded Processor for a Pairing-Based Cryptosystem," Proceedings of the Third International Conference on Information Technology: New Generations (ITNG'06), pp.192-197, 2006.
28. R. Sakai and M. Kasahara, "ID based cryptosystems with pairing on elliptic curve," Cryptography ePrint Archive, Report 2003/054, 2003. http://eprint.iacr.org/2003/054.
29. M. Scott, "Computing the Tate Pairing," *CT-RSA 2005*, LNCS 3376, pp.293-304, 2005.
30. M. Scott, N. Costigan, and W. Abdulwahab, "Implemetation Cryptographic Pairings on Smartcards," Cryptography ePrint Archive, Report 2006/144, 2006. htt://eprint.iacr.org/2006/144.
31. N.P. Smart, "An identity based authentication key agreement protocol based on pairing," *Electronics Letters*, Vol.38, No.13, pp.630-632, 2002.
32. E. Verheul, "Evidence that XTR is more secure than supersingular elliptic curve cryptosystems," *Journal of Cryptology*, Vol.17, No.4, pp.277-296, 2004.
33. C. Whelan and M. Scott, "Side Channel Analysis of Practical Pairing Implementations: Which Path is More Secure?," Cryptography ePrint Archive, Report 2006/237, 2006. htt://eprint.iacr.org/2006/237.

A   Multiplication in $F_{2^{4m}}$

The extension field $\mathbb{F}_{2^{4m}}$ is represented by the basis $\{1, s, t, st\}$ such that $s^2 + s + 1 = 0$ and $t^2 + t + s = 0$. Let $g = (g_0, g_1, g_2, g_3) = g_0 + g_1 s + g_2 t + g_3 st$ and $f = (f_0, f_1, f_2, f_3) = f_0 + f_1 s + f_2 t + f_3 st$. Then we have $h = (h_0, h_1, h_2, h_3) = f \cdot g$ where

$$h_0 = f_0 g_0 + f_1 g_1 + f_3 g_2 + f_2 g_3 + f_3 g_3,$$
$$h_1 = f_1 g_0 + f_0 g_1 + f_1 g_1 + f_2 g_2 + f_3 g_2 + f_2 g_3,$$
$$h_2 = f_2 g_0 + f_3 g_1 + f_0 g_2 + f_2 g_2 + f_1 g_3 + f_3 g_3,$$
$$h_3 = f_3 g_0 + f_2 g_1 + f_3 g_1 + f_1 g_2 + f_3 g_2 + f_0 g_3 + f_1 g_3 + f_2 g_3 + f_3 g_3.$$

In Algorithm 3, since $g_3 = 0$ the above formula is simplified as follows.

$$h_0 = f_0 g_0 + f_1 g_1 + f_3 g_2,$$
$$h_1 = f_1 g_0 + f_0 g_1 + f_1 g_1 + f_2 g_2 + f_3 g_2,$$
$$h_2 = f_2 g_0 + f_3 g_1 + f_0 g_2 + f_2 g_2,$$
$$h_3 = f_3 g_0 + f_2 g_1 + f_3 g_1 + f_1 g_2 + f_3 g_2.$$

Applying the Karatsuba multiplication method we can compute it by 9 multiplications.

Improved Collision Attack on Reduced Round Camellia

Guan Jie and Zhang Zhongya

The Information Engineer University Electronic Technology Institute
Zhengzhou 450004, China

Abstract. Camellia is a 128-bit block cipher which has been selected as an international standard by ISO/IEC and a European encryption standard by the NESSIE project. Wu Wenling presented the collision attack on reduced-round Camellia in 2004, the 128-bit key of 6 rounds Camellia can be recovered with 2^{10} chosen plaintexts and 2^{15} encryptions. The improved collision attack on 6 rounds Camellia which based on four 4-round distinguishers is presented in this paper. This attack requires less than $2^{10.6}$ chosen plaintexts and $2^{11.5}$ encryptions.

Keywords: Block cipher, Camellia, Collision attack.

1 Introduction

Camellia[1] is a 128-bit block cipher which was announced by NTT and Mitsubishi in 2000, it has been selected as an international standard by ISO/IEC , a European encryption standard by the NESSIE(New European Schemes for Signatures,Integrity,and Encryption) project and a secure E-Government standard of Japan. The security of Camellia against higher-order differential cryptanalysis, truncated differential attack, impossible differential cryptanalysis, Square attack, collision attack et.al. are discussed in [2,3,4,5,6,7,8,9]. The collision attack on reduced-round of Camellia by using collision-searching techniques is presented in [2]. The collision attack on 6-round of 128-bit key Camellia is more efficient than know attacks which requires less than 2^{10} chosen plaintexts and 2^{15} encryptions.

   In this paper, we improve the collision attack on 6 rounds Camellia by using the improved collision-searching techniques based on four 4-round distinguishers. The improved collision attack on 6 rounds Camellia requires less than $2^{10.6}$ chosen plaintexts and $2^{11.5}$ encryptions. The time complexity is less than that of collision attack though the data amount is a little more than that of collision attack.

2 Description of the Camellia

Camellia has a 128 bit block size and supports 128, 192 and 256 bit keys. The design of Camellia is based on the Feistel structure. The FL/FL^{-1} function layer is inserted at every 6 rounds. Before the first round and after the last round, there

D. Pointcheval, Y. Mu, and K. Chen (Eds.): CANS 2006, LNCS 4301, pp. 182–190, 2006.

are pre- and post-whitening layers which use bitwise exclusive-or operations with 128 bit subkeys, respectively.

Let L_{r-1} and R_{r-1} be the left and the right halves of the rth round inputs, respectively, and k_r be the rth subkey. Then the Feistel structure of Camellia can be written as

$$L_r = R_{r-1} \oplus F(L_{r-1} \oplus k_r),$$
$$R_r = L_{r-1}.$$

here $F = P \circ S$ is the round function defined below:

$$F : F_2^{64} \times F_2^{64} \rightarrow F_2^{64},$$
$$(X_{64}, k_{64}) \rightarrow Y_{64} = P(S(X_{64} \oplus k_{64})).$$

where S and P are defined as follows:

The substitution $S : F_2^{64} \rightarrow F_2^{64}$ is defined by

$$(x_1, \ldots, x_8) \xrightarrow{s} (s_1(x_1), s_2(x_2), s_3(x_3), s_4(x_4), s_2(x_5), s_3(x_6), s_4(x_7), s_1(x_8)),$$

where s_1, s_2, s_3 and s_4 are four types of S-boxes over $GF(2^8)$, they are permutation.

The permutation function $P : F_2^{64} \rightarrow F_2^{64}$ maps $(z_1, \ldots, z_8)$ to $(z_1', \ldots, z_8')$ defined by

$$\begin{pmatrix} z_8' \\ z_7' \\ z_6' \\ z_5' \\ z_4' \\ z_3' \\ z_2' \\ z_1' \end{pmatrix} = \begin{pmatrix} 0\,1\,1\,1\,1\,0\,0\,1 \\ 1\,0\,1\,1\,1\,1\,0\,0 \\ 1\,1\,0\,1\,0\,1\,1\,0 \\ 1\,1\,1\,0\,0\,0\,1\,1 \\ 0\,1\,1\,1\,1\,1\,1\,0 \\ 1\,0\,1\,1\,0\,1\,1\,1 \\ 1\,1\,0\,1\,1\,0\,1\,1 \\ 1\,1\,1\,0\,1\,1\,0\,1 \end{pmatrix} \begin{pmatrix} z_8 \\ z_7 \\ z_6 \\ z_5 \\ z_4 \\ z_3 \\ z_2 \\ z_1 \end{pmatrix}.$$

The key schedule of Camellia is not described here, details are shown in [1].

3   Improved Collision Attack on 6 Rounds Camellia

The security of reduced Camellia against the collision attack by using collision-searching techniques based on one 4-round distinguisher is presented in [2]. We improve the collision-searching techniques on the foundation of [2], and construct four 4-round distinguishers. The improved collision on the 6 rounds Camellia requires less than $2^{10.6}$ chosen plaintexts and $2^{11.5}$ encryptions.

3.1   4-Round Distinguishers

Firstly, let us review the concept of the active (passive) byte[8].

Let Γ be a collection of state bytes $X = (\chi_1, \chi_2, \ldots, \chi_n)$ where χ_i is the i-th byte of X. If the i-th byte of elements in Γ are different one another, the i-th byte is called an 'active' byte. Likewise, the j-th byte is 'passive'(or fixed), if the j-th bytes of states in Γ have the same value.

By considering the right halve of the input of Camellia-R_0, we know that if the 1-th byte of which is active, the 4-round distinguisher in [2] can be constructed. We can construct another three distinguishers by letting the 2-th, 3-th and 7-th byte of R_0 be active respectively. Then we can use the four 4-round distinguishers to recover the key of Camellia efficiently.

3.1.1   The 1st Distinguisher

The 1st distinguisher is presented in [2].Choose

$$L_0 = (\alpha_1, \alpha_2, \ldots, \alpha_8), R_0 = (\chi, \beta_2, \ldots, \beta_8),$$

where χ take values in F_2^8, it is an active byte, α_i and β_j are constants in F_2^8, they are passive bytes. Thus, the output of 1st round can be written as follows:

$$L_1 = (\chi \oplus \gamma_1, \gamma_2, \ldots, \gamma_8), R_1 = (\alpha_1, \alpha_2, \ldots, \alpha_8),$$

where γ_i are constants when the user key is fixed. In the 2nd round a transformation on L_1 using $F(\circ, k_2)$ is as follows:

$$L_1 = (\chi \oplus \gamma_1, \gamma_2, \ldots, \gamma_8) \xrightarrow{F(\circ, k_2)} (y \oplus \theta_1, y \oplus \theta_2, y \oplus \theta_3, \theta_4, y \oplus \theta_5, \theta_6, \theta_7, y \oplus \theta_8),$$

where $y = s_1(\chi \oplus \gamma_1 \oplus k_{2,1})$, $k_{2,1}$is the first byte of k_2, $\theta_1$are constants when the user key is fixed. Therefore, the output of 2nd round is

$$L_2 = (y \oplus w1, y \oplus w_2, y \oplus w_3, w_4, y \oplus w_5, w_6, w_7, y \oplus w_8), R_2 = (\chi \oplus \gamma_1, \gamma_2, \ldots, \gamma_8),$$

where $w_i = \theta_i \oplus \alpha_i$ are constants. In the 3rd round a transformation on L_2 using $F(\circ, k_3)$ is as follows:

$$L_2 = (y \oplus w1, y \oplus w_2, y \oplus w_3, w_4, y \oplus w_5, w_6, w_7, y \oplus w_8) \xrightarrow{F(\circ, k_3)} (z_1, z_2, \ldots, z_8).$$

Thus, we have the left half of output for the 3rd round:

$$L_3 = (z_1 \oplus \chi \oplus \gamma_1, z_2 \oplus \gamma_2, z_3 \oplus \gamma_3, \ldots, z_8 \oplus \gamma_8).$$

So the right half of output for the 4th round is as follows:

$$R_4 = L_3 = (z_1 \oplus \chi \oplus \gamma_1, z_2 \oplus \gamma_2, z_3 \oplus \gamma_3, \ldots, z_8 \oplus \gamma_8).$$

Now we analyze the relations 8 bytes of R_4.We can get the following 3 equations:

$$z_3 \oplus z_4 \oplus z_5 \oplus z_6 \oplus z_7 = s_4(w_7 \oplus k_{3,7}), \tag{1}$$

$$z_2 \oplus z_3 \oplus z_5 \oplus z_6 \oplus z_8 = s_3(w_6 \oplus k_{3,6}), \tag{2}$$

$$z_1 \oplus z_2 \oplus z_3 \oplus z_5 \oplus z_6 \oplus z_7 = s_4(w_7 \oplus k_{3,7}). \tag{3}$$

The above 3 equations are simpler than which of [2]. Obviously, , $z_3 \oplus z_4 \oplus z_5 \oplus z_6 \oplus z_7$, $z_2 \oplus z_3 \oplus z_5 \oplus z_6 \oplus z_8$ and $z_1 \oplus z_2 \oplus z_3 \oplus z_5 \oplus z_6 \oplus z_7$ are constants. Therefore we get the following conclusions by considering

$$R_4 = L_3 = (z_1 \oplus \chi \oplus \gamma_1, z_2 \oplus \gamma_2, z_3 \oplus \gamma_3, \ldots, z_8 \oplus \gamma_8).$$

Lemma 3.1. *Let $P = (L_0, R_0)$ and $P^* = (L_0^*, R_0^*)$ be two plaintexts of 4-round Camellia, $C = (L_4, R_4)$ and $C^* = (L_4^*, R_4^*)$ be the corresponding ciphertexts. If $L_0 = L_0^*$, $R_{0,1} \neq R_{0,1}^*$, $R_{0,j} = R_{0,j}^* (2 \leq j \leq 8)$, then R_4 and R_4^* satisfy:*

(1) $R_{4,3} \oplus R_{4,4} \oplus R_{4,5} \oplus R_{4,6} \oplus R_{4,7} = R_{4,3}^* \oplus R_{4,4}^* \oplus R_{4,5}^* \oplus R_{4,6}^* \oplus R_{4,7}^*$,
(2) $R_{4,2} \oplus R_{4,3} \oplus R_{4,5} \oplus R_{4,6} \oplus R_{4,8} = R_{4,2}^* \oplus R_{4,3}^* \oplus R_{4,5}^* \oplus R_{4,6}^* \oplus R_{4,8}^*$,
(3) $R_{4,1} \oplus R_{4,2} \oplus R_{4,3} \oplus R_{4,5} \oplus R_{4,6} \oplus R_{4,7} \neq R_{4,1}^* \oplus R_{4,2}^* \oplus R_{4,3}^* \oplus R_{4,5}^* \oplus R_{4,6}^* \oplus R_{4,7}^*$.

We can get the following lemma easily by further researching on the conclusion (3) in lemma 3.1.

Lemma 3.2. *Let $P \oplus P^* = (0,0,0,0,0,0,0,0, \alpha, 0,0,0,0,0,0,0)$, where P and P^* are two different 128-bit plaintexts, $0, \alpha \in F_2^8, \alpha \neq 0$, thus R_4 and R_4^* satisfy*

$$R_{4,1} \oplus R_{4,2} \oplus R_{4,3} \oplus R_{4,5} \oplus R_{4,6} \oplus R_{4,7} \oplus R_{4,1}^* \oplus R_{4,2}^* \oplus R_{4,3}^* \oplus R_{4,5}^* \oplus R_{4,6}^* \oplus R_{4,7}^* = \alpha.$$

Proof. Let

$$P = (L_0, R_0), \ L_0 = (\alpha_1, \alpha_2, \ldots, \alpha_8), \ R_0 = (\chi, \beta_2, \ldots, \beta_8),$$
$$P^* = (L_0^*, R_0^*), \ L_0^* = (\alpha_1, \alpha_2, \ldots, \alpha_8), \ R_0^* = (\chi^*, \beta_2, \ldots, \beta_8),$$

Where χ, χ^* take values in F_2^8, and $\chi \oplus \chi^* = \alpha, \alpha_i$, and β_j are constants in F_2^8. Because

$$R_{4,1} \oplus R_{4,2} \oplus R_{4,3} \oplus R_{4,5} \oplus R_{4,6} \oplus R_{4,7} =$$
$$z_1 \oplus \chi \oplus \gamma_1 \oplus z_2 \oplus \gamma_2 \oplus z_3 \oplus \gamma_3 \oplus z_5 \oplus \gamma_5 \oplus z_6 \oplus \gamma_6 \oplus z_7 \oplus \gamma_7,$$
$$R_{4,1}^* \oplus R_{4,2}^* \oplus R_{4,3}^* \oplus R_{4,5}^* \oplus R_{4,6}^* \oplus R_{4,7}^* =$$
$$z_1^* \oplus \chi^* \oplus \gamma_1 \oplus z_2^* \oplus \gamma_2 \oplus z_3^* \oplus \gamma_3 \oplus z_5^* \oplus \gamma_5 \oplus z_6^* \oplus \gamma_6 \oplus z_7^* \oplus \gamma_7,$$

we can easily get $z_1^* \oplus z_2^* \oplus z_3^* \oplus z_5^* \oplus z_6^* \oplus z_7^* = z_1 \oplus z_2 \oplus z_3 \oplus z_5 \oplus z_6 \oplus z_7$ from (3). So we can get the following equation because of γ_i is constant.

$$R_{4,1} \oplus R_{4,2} \oplus R_{4,3} \oplus R_{4,5} \oplus R_{4,6} \oplus R_{4,7} \oplus R_{4,1}^* \oplus R_{4,2}^* \oplus R_{4,3}^* \oplus R_{4,5}^* \oplus R_{4,6}^* \oplus R_{4,7}^* = \chi \oplus \chi^* = \alpha.$$

over.

3.1.2   The 2nd Distinguisher
The same as the 1st distinguisher, let the 2nd byte be the active byte of R_0, we can obtain the following 3 equations obviously:

$$z_2 \oplus z_3 \oplus z_4 \oplus z_6 \oplus z_7 \oplus z_8 = s_1(\omega_1 \oplus k_{3,1}), \tag{4}$$
$$z_3 \oplus z_4 \oplus z_5 \oplus z_6 \oplus z_7 = s_4(\omega_7 \oplus k_{3,7}), \tag{5}$$
$$z_1 \oplus z_4 \oplus z_6 \oplus z_7 \oplus z_8 = s_1(\omega_8 \oplus k_{3,8}). \tag{6}$$

Likewise we can get the following conclusions easily.

Lemma 3.3. *Let* $P = (L_0, R_0)$ *and* $P^* = (L_0^*, R_0^*)$ *be two plaintexts of 4-round Camellia,* $C = (L_4, R_4)$ *and* $C^* = (L_4^*, R_4^*)$ *be the corresponding ciphertexts. If* $L_0 = L_0^*$, $R_{0,2} \neq R_{0,2}^*$, $R_{0,j} = R_{0,j}^* (1 \leq j \leq 8, j \neq 2)$, *then* R_4 *and* R_4^* *satisfy:*

(1) $R_{4,2} \oplus R_{4,3} \oplus R_{4,4} \oplus R_{4,6} \oplus R_{4,7} \oplus R_{4,8} \neq R_{4,2}^* \oplus R_{4,3}^* \oplus R_{4,4}^* \oplus R_{4,6}^* \oplus R_{4,7}^* \oplus R_{4,8}^*$,
(2) $R_{4,3} \oplus R_{4,4} \oplus R_{4,5} \oplus R_{4,6} \oplus R_{4,7} = R_{4,3}^* \oplus R_{4,4}^* \oplus R_{4,5}^* \oplus R_{4,6}^* \oplus R_{4,7}^*$,
(3) $R_{4,1} \oplus R_{4,4} \oplus R_{4,6} \oplus R_{4,7} \oplus R_{4,8} = R_{4,1}^* \oplus R_{4,4}^* \oplus R_{4,6}^* \oplus R_{4,7}^* \oplus R_{4,8}^*$.

3.1.3   The 3rd Distinguisher

Let the 3rd byte be the active byte of R_0, obviously, we can obtain the following 3 equations:

$$z_1 \oplus z_3 \oplus z_4 \oplus z_5 \oplus z_7 \oplus z_8 = s_2(\omega_2 \oplus k_{3,2}), \tag{7}$$

$$z_1 \oplus z_2 \oplus z_5 \oplus z_7 \oplus z_8 = s_2(\omega_5 \oplus k_{3,5}), \tag{8}$$

$$z_1 \oplus z_4 \oplus z_6 \oplus z_7 \oplus z_8 = s_1(\omega_8 \oplus k_{3,8}). \tag{9}$$

Likewise we can get the following conclusions easily.

Lemma 3.4. *Let* $P = (L_0, R_0)$ *and* $P^* = (L_0^*, R_0^*)$ *be two plaintexts of 4-round Camellia,* $C = (L_4, R_4)$ *and* $C^* = (L_4^*, R_4^*)$ *be the corresponding ciphertexts. If* $L_0 = L_0^*$, $R_{0,3} \neq R_{0,3}^*$, $R_{0,j} = R_{0,j}^* (1 \leq j \leq 8, j \neq 3)$, *then* R_4 *and* R_4^* *satisfy:*

(1) $R_{4,1} \oplus R_{4,3} \oplus R_{4,4} \oplus R_{4,5} \oplus R_{4,7} \oplus R_{4,8} \neq R_{4,1}^* \oplus R_{4,3}^* \oplus R_{4,4}^* \oplus R_{4,5}^* \oplus R_{4,7}^* \oplus R_{4,8}^*$,
(2) $R_{4,1} \oplus R_{4,2} \oplus R_{4,5} \oplus R_{4,7} \oplus R_{4,8} = R_{4,1}^* \oplus R_{4,2}^* \oplus R_{4,5}^* \oplus R_{4,7}^* \oplus R_{4,8}^*$,
(3) $R_{4,1} \oplus R_{4,4} \oplus R_{4,6} \oplus R_{4,7} \oplus R_{4,8} = R_{4,1}^* \oplus R_{4,4}^* \oplus R_{4,6}^* \oplus R_{4,7}^* \oplus R_{4,8}^*$.

3.1.4   The 4th Distinguisher

Let the 7th byte be the active byte of R_0. Obviously, we can obtain the following 3 equations:

$$z_1 \oplus z_2 \oplus z_4 \oplus z_5 \oplus z_6 \oplus z_8 = s_3(\omega_3 \oplus k_{3,3}), \tag{10}$$

$$z_3 \oplus z_4 \oplus z_5 \oplus z_6 \oplus z_7 = s_4(\omega_7 \oplus k_{3,7}). \tag{11}$$

Likewise we can get the following lemma easily.

Lemma 3.5. *Let* $P = (L_0, R_0)$ *and* $P^* = (L_0^*, R_0^*)$ *be two plaintexts of 4-round Camellia,* $C = (L_4, R_4)$ *and* $C^* = (L_4^*, R_4^*)$ *be the corresponding ciphertexts. If* $L_0 = L_0^*$, $R_{0,7} \neq R_{0,7}^*$, $R_{0,j} = R_{0,j}^* (1 \leq j \leq 8, j \neq 7)$, *then* R_4 *and* R_4^* *satisfy:*

(1) $R_{4,1} \oplus R_{4,2} \oplus R_{4,4} \oplus R_{4,5} \oplus R_{4,6} \oplus R_{4,8} = R_{4,1}^* \oplus R_{4,2}^* \oplus R_{4,4}^* \oplus R_{4,5}^* \oplus R_{4,6}^* \oplus R_{4,8}^*$,
(2) $R_{4,3} \oplus R_{4,4} \oplus R_{4,5} \oplus R_{4,6} \oplus R_{4,7} \neq R_{4,3}^* \oplus R_{4,4}^* \oplus R_{4,5}^* \oplus R_{4,6}^* \oplus R_{4,7}^*$.

3.2   Improved Collision Attack on 6-Round Camellia

Wu Wenling used the algorithm 1 and the algorithm 2 which were presented in [2] to recover the subkey k_6. We present a new algorithm-algorithm 2', and use the algorithm 1 and the algorithm 2' to recover the subkey k_6. The improved collision attack on the 6 rounds Camellia requires less than $2^{10.6}$ chosen plaintexts and $2^{11.5}$ encryptions.

From the key schedule of Camellia with 128-bit key, we know that if the subkey k_5 and k_6 are recovered, the user key will be recovered. We also know that the 2-th to the 8-th bits of $k_{6,7}$ are the same as the 1-th to the 7-th bits of $k_{1,1}$ respectively, i.e. $k_{6,7}[2,3,4,5,6,7,8] = k_{1,1}[1,2,3,4,5,6,7]$, so we can use the following the algorithm 1 to recover $(k_{1,1}, k_{6,7})$ as referred in [2].

Algorithm 1[2]

Step 1: For each possible value t of $k_{1,1}$, choose two plaintexts $P0^t = (L0_0^t, R0_0^t)$ and $P1^t = (L1_0^t, R1_0^t)$ as follows:

$$L0_0^t = (i_0, \alpha_2, \ldots, \alpha_8),$$
$$R0_0^t = (s_1(i_0 \oplus k_{1,1}), s_1(i_0 \oplus k_{1,1}), s_1(i_0 \oplus k_{1,1}), \beta_4, s_1(i_0 \oplus k_{1,1}), \beta_6, \beta_7, s_1(i_0 \oplus k_{1,1})),$$
$$L1_0^t = (i_1, \alpha_2, \ldots, \alpha_8),$$
$$R1_0^t = (s_1(i_1 \oplus k_{1,1}), s_1(i_1 \oplus k_{1,1}), s_1(i_1 \oplus k_{1,1}), \beta_4, s_1(i_1 \oplus k_{1,1}), \beta_6, \beta_7, s_1(i_1 \oplus k_{1,1})),$$

where α_i and β_j are constants, $0 \le i_0 \le i_1 \le 255$. The corresponding ciphertexts are $C0^t = (L0_6^t, R0_6^t), C1^t = (L1_6^t, R1_6^t)$.

Step 2: For each possible value of $(t, k_{6,7})$, compute

$$\Delta_0 = s_4(R0_{6,7}^t \oplus k_{6,7}) \oplus (L0_{6,3}^t \oplus L0_{6,4}^t \oplus L0_{6,5}^t \oplus L0_{6,6}^t \oplus L0_{6,7}^t),$$
$$\Delta_1 = s_4(R1_{6,7}^t \oplus k_{6,7}) \oplus (L1_{6,3}^t \oplus L1_{6,4}^t \oplus L1_{6,5}^t \oplus L1_{6,6}^t \oplus L1_{6,7}^t).$$

Check if Δ_0 equals Δ_1. If so, record the corresponding value of $(t, k_{6,7})$. Otherwise, move to next value of $(t, k_{6,7})$.

Step 3: For the recorded value of $(t, k_{6,7})$ in Step2, choose some other plaintexts $P2^t(\ne P1^t, P0^t)$ compute Δ_2, and check if Δ_2 equals Δ_0, if so, record the corresponding value of $(t, k_{6,7})$, otherwise, discard the value of $(t, k_{6,7})$. If there are more than one recorded value, then repeat Step 3 on the newly recorded values.

Thus the number of plaintexts needed for this attack is 3×2^8, the number of encryptions is less than 2^9.

From Lemma 3.2, we know that $k_{6,4}$ can be recovered by using the algorithm 2' described as follows.

Algorithm 2'

Step 1: Choose two plaintexts $P0 = (L0, R0)$ and $P1 = (L1, R1)$ as follows :

$$L0_0 = (i_0, \alpha_2, \ldots, \alpha_8),$$
$$R0_0 = (s_1(i_0 \oplus k_{1,1}), s_1(i_0 \oplus k_{1,1}), s_1(i_0 \oplus k_{1,1}), \beta_4, s_1(i_0 \oplus k_{1,1}), \beta_6, \beta_7, s_1(i_0 \oplus k_{1,1})),$$
$$L1_0 = (i_1, \alpha_2, \ldots, \alpha_8),$$
$$R1_0 = (s_1(i_1 \oplus k_{1,1}), s_1(i_1 \oplus k_{1,1}), s_1(i_1 \oplus k_{1,1}), \beta_4, s_1(i_1 \oplus k_{1,1}), \beta_6, \beta_7, s_1(i_1 \oplus k_{1,1})),$$

where α_i and β_j are constants, $0 \le i_0 \le i_1 \le 255$. The corresponding ciphertexts are $C0 = (L0_6, R0_6), C1 = (L1_6, R1_6)$.

Step 2: For each possible value of $k_{6,4}$, compute

$$\Delta_0 = s_4(R0_{6,4} \oplus k_{6,4}) \oplus (L0_{6,1} \oplus L0_{6,2} \oplus L0_{6,3} \oplus L0_{6,5} \oplus L0_{6,6} \oplus L0_{6,7}),$$
$$\Delta_1 = s_4(R1_{6,4} \oplus k_{6,4}) \oplus (L1_{6,1} \oplus L1_{6,2} \oplus L1_{6,3} \oplus L1_{6,5} \oplus L1_{6,6} \oplus L1_{6,7}).$$

Check if $\Delta_0 \oplus \Delta_1$ equals $i_0 \oplus i_1$. If so, record the corresponding value of $k_{6,4}$. Otherwise, move to next value of $k_{6,4}$.

Step 3: For the recorded value of $k_{6,4}$ in Step2, choose another plaintext $P2$ compute $\Delta_2 \oplus \Delta_1$, and check if $\Delta_2 \oplus \Delta_1$ equals $i_2 \oplus i_1$, if so, record the corresponding value of $k_{6,4}$, otherwise, discard the value of $k_{6,4}$. If there are more than one recorded value, then repeat Step 3 on the newly recorded values.

Invalid subkey will pass step2 with a probability 2^{-8}, and there is about $2^8 \times 2^{-8} = 1$ remaining value after step2. So the attack requires less than 3 chosen plaintexts. The main time complexity of attack is from step2, where the time complexity of computing each Δ is about the same as the 1-round encryption, so the time complexity of attack is less than 2^8 encryptions.

In the algorithm 2', we improve the collision-searching techniques based on Lemma 3.2, so we call it improved collision- searching techniques. Compared with the algorithm 2 presented in[2], the data and compute amount of the algorithm 2' are less.

We have recovered $k_{6,7}$ and $k_{6,4}$ from above, then we will recover the other bytes of k_6 by using the algorithm 1 and the algorithm 2' in the following steps.

Using property (2) and the plaintexts chosen in the algorithm 1 on condition that $k_{1,1}$ is known before, we can recover $k_{6,6}$ by computing Δ from chosen plaintexts above:

$$\Delta = s_3(R_{6,6} \oplus k_{6,6}) \oplus (L_{6,2} \oplus L_{6,3} \oplus L_{6,5} \oplus L_{6,6} \oplus L_{6,8}).$$

Check if Δ is a constant. If so, output the value of $k_{6,6}$, otherwise, discard the value of $k_{6,6}$. Here the attack requires less than 3 chosen plaintexts and 2^8 encryptions.

We can choose plaintexts to let the 2nd byte be the active byte of R_1 if we know $k_{1,2}$. As we know $k_{6,7}$ before, using property (5) and the algorithm 1, we can recover $k_{1,2}$ by computing Δ from chosen plaintexts above:

$$\Delta = s_4(R_{6,7}^t \oplus k_{6,7}) \oplus (L_{6,3}^t \oplus L_{6,4}^t \oplus L_{6,5}^t \oplus L_{6,6}^t \oplus L_{6,7}^t),$$

and the attack requires less than 2^8 chosen plaintexts and 2^8 encryptions.

Using property (4) and the algorithm 2' on condition that $k_{1,2}$ is known before, we can recover $k_{6,1}$ by computing Δ from chosen plaintexts above:

$$\Delta = s_1(R_{6,1} \oplus k_{6,1}) \oplus (L_{6,2} \oplus L_{6,3} \oplus L_{6,4} \oplus L_{6,6} \oplus L_{6,7} \oplus L_{6,8}),$$

and the attack requires less than 3 chosen plaintexts and 2^8 encryptions.

From the key schedule for 128-bit key, we know that $k_{6,8}[1]= k_{1,1}[8]$, $k_{6,8}[2,3,4,5,6,7,8]= k_{1,2} [1,2,3,4,5,6,7]$. Thus we can recover $k_{6,8}$ easily.

We can choose plaintexts to let the 3rd byte be the active byte of R_1 if we know $k_{1,3}$. As we know $k_{6,8}$ before, using property (9) and the algorithm 1, we can recover $k_{1,3}$ by computing Δ from the chosen plaintexts above:

$$\Delta = s_1(R^t_{6,8} \oplus k_{6,8}) \oplus (L^t_{6,1} \oplus L^t_{6,4} \oplus L^t_{6,6} \oplus L^t_{6,7} \oplus L^t_{6,8}),$$

and the attack requires less than 2^8 chosen plaintexts and 2^8 encryptions.

Using property (7) and the algorithm 2' on condition that $k_{1,3}$ is known before, we can recover $k_{6,2}$ by computing Δ from the chosen plaintexts above:

$$\Delta = s_2(R_{6,2} \oplus k_{6,2}) \oplus (L_{6,1} \oplus L_{6,3} \oplus L_{6,4} \oplus L_{6,5} \oplus L_{6,7} \oplus L_{6,8}),$$

and the attack requires less than 3 chosen plaintexts and 2^8 encryptions.

Using property (8) and the algorithm 1 on condition that $k_{1,3}$ is known before, we can recover $k_{6,5}$ by computing Δ from the chosen plaintexts above:

$$\Delta = s_2(R_{6,5} \oplus k_{6,5}) \oplus (L_{6,1} \oplus L_{6,2} \oplus L_{6,5} \oplus L_{6,7} \oplus L_{6,8}),$$

and the attack requires less than 3 chosen plaintexts and 2^8 encryptions.

We can choose plaintexts to let the 7th byte be the active byte of R_1 if we know $k_{1,7}$, As we know $k_{6,7}$ before , using property (11) and the algorithm 2', we can recover $k_{1,7}$ by computing Δ from the chosen plaintexts above:

$$\Delta = s_4(R^t_{6,7} \oplus k_{6,7}) \oplus (L^t_{6,3} \oplus L^t_{6,4} \oplus L^t_{6,5} \oplus L^t_{6,6} \oplus L^t_{6,7}),$$

and the attack requires less than 2^8 chosen plaintexts and 2^8 encryptions.

Using property (10) and the algorithm 1 on condition that $k_{1,7}$ is known before, we can recover $k_{6,3}$ by computing Δ from the chosen plaintexts above:

$$\Delta = s_3(R_{6,3} \oplus k_{6,3}) \oplus (L_{6,1} \oplus L_{6,2} \oplus L_{6,4} \oplus L_{6,5} \oplus L_{6,6} \oplus L_{6,8}),$$

and the attack requires less than 3 chosen plaintexts and 2^8 encryptions.

Now we have recovered $k_{1,1}, k_{1,2}, k_{1,3}, k_{1,7}$ and k_6 , using less than $2^{10.6}$ chosen plaintexts and $9 \times 2^8 + 2^9$ encryptions. However the collision attack requires less than 2^{10} chosen plaintexts and 2^{15} encryptions. Similarly, by decrypting the 6th round, we can recover k_5. Therefore, the attack on the 6-round Camellia requires less than $2^{10.6}$ chosen plaintexts and $2^{11.5}$ encryptions.

4   Conclusion

Wu Wenling presented the collision attack on the reduced round Camellia. The attack on 6-round of 128-bit key Camellia is more efficient than know attacks by using collision-searching techniques and a 4-round distinguisher. In this paper, we improve the collision-searching techniques by using the property of the differences between the different output bytes. In order to make the time complexity of our attack less, we presented a new algorithm- the algorithm 2'based on the improved collision-searching techniques. Then we constructed four distinguishers, so we can use the algorithm 1 and the algorithm 2'to recover the 128-bit key of 6-round Camellia with less than $2^{10.6}$ chosen plaintexts and $2^{11.5}$ encryptions. The improved collision attack of this paper is more effective than the collision attack. How to attack Camellia of more rounds by using the improved collision attack is worthy to study further.

References

1. Aoki, K., Ichikawa, T., Kanda, M.: Specification of Camellia - a 128-bit Block Cipher. Selected Areas in Cryptography-SAC'2000. Berlin: Springer-Verlag (2000) 183-191
2. Wu, W.L., Feng,D.G.:Collision Attack on Reduced-Round Camellia. SCIENCE IN CHINA Ser.E Information Sciences. 34(2004)857-868
3. Hatano, Y., Sekine, H., Kaneko, T.: Higher Order Differential Attack of Camellia(II). Selected Areas in Cryptography-SAC'02. Berlin: Springer-Verlag (2002) 39-56
4. Lee, S., Hong, S., Lim, J. et al.: Truncated Differential Cryptanalysis of Camellia. ICISC2001. Berlin: Springer-Verlag (1993) 32-38
5. Sugita, M., Kobara, K., Imai, H.: Security of reduced version of the block cipher Camellia against truncated and impossible differential cryptanalysis. Asiacrypt'01. Berlin: Springer-Verlag (2001) 193-207
6. Shirai, T., Kanamaru, S., Abe, G.: Improved upper bounds of differential and linear characteristic probability for Camellia. Fast Software Encryption-FSE'02. Berlin: Springer-Verlag (2002) 128-142
7. He,Y.P., Qing, S.H.: Square attack on Reduced Camellia Cipher. ICICS2001. Berlin: Springer-Verlag (2001) 238-245
8. Yeom, Y., Park, S., Kim, I.:On the security of Camellia against the square attack. Fast Software Encryption-FSE'02. Berlin: Springer-Verlag (2002) 89-99
9. Yeom, Y., Park, S., Kim, I. :A study of Integral type cryptanalysis on Camellia. The 2003 Symposium on Cryptography and Security-SCIS'03. Japan: Hamamatsu (2003) 26-29

Stealing Secrets with SSL/TLS and SSH
– Kleptographic Attacks*

Zbigniew Gołębiewski, Mirosław Kutyłowski, and Filip Zagórski**

Institute of Mathematics and Computer Science,
Wrocław University of Technology
{zbyh, mirekk, filipz}@im.pwr.wroc.pl

Abstract. We present very simple kleptographic attacks on SSL/TLS and SSH protocols. They enable a party, which has slightly manipulated the code of a cryptographic library, to steal secrets of the user. According to the scenario of the kleptographic attacks the secrets can be stolen only by a party having a secret key not included in the manipulated code. The attacker needs only to record transmissions. The messages transmitted are indistinguishable from the not manipulated ones (even for somebody that knows the kleptocode inserted). Therefore, detection of infected nodes based on communication analysis is much harder than in the case of classical subliminal channels.

The problems are caused by certain design features of SSL/TLS and SSH protocols that make them vulnerable for a kleptographic attack. We propose changes of these protocols that make them immune against this threat while all previous security features remain preserved.

Keywords: kleptography, SSL, TLS, SSH.

1 Introduction

Security of communication in public networks should be guaranteed by appropriate cryptographic protocols. They have to ensure that a malicious eavesdropper monitoring communication, inserting and deleting packets exchanged between two parties cannot achieve more than interrupting communication. It must be assured that the malicious eavesdropper can neither learn the contents of protected messages nor can change them or insert fake messages. Achieving these goals is absolutely necessary for instance for e-banking, e-voting via Internet, and generally for any legal actions which are performed on electronic way.

The SSL/TLS [] protocol is often claimed to be a universal remedy to all problems mentioned. This is particularly the case, when security system is presented to the consumers. The issues of security of home PC's are neglected. The problem of computer viruses is often discussed only on the level of crushing a PC. The issue of malicious viruses that perform an attack and try to remain hidden in the system is rather underestimated.

---

* Partially supported by Polish Committee for Scientific Research grant 3 T11C 011 26.
** Contact author.

D. Pointcheval, Y. Mu, and K. Chen (Eds.): CANS 2006, LNCS 4301, pp. 191–202, 2006.
© Springer-Verlag Berlin Heidelberg 2006

1.1 Basic Threats

One of the major issues of security is that the system installed may already contain hidden *features* that are used by malicious producer to get information about the user and his activities. The cases of such an attitude have been reported, while probably most of the cases remain unknown to the public. As long as the source codes of an operating system and application programs remain hidden, it is quite easy to hide such features in a compiled code.

There are chances to uncover such activities by monitoring communication by a computer. Contacting remote servers by a computer without ordering such communication by the user might be a trace of malicious activities. The monitoring must be performed by an independent server, for instance by an appropriate gateway. In many cases a user has limited possibilities to perform such an analysis.

But the attacks against the user may be performed in a much subtle way. The critical information like cryptographic keys, seeds to pseudo-random number generators, may be encoded in a perfectly legal messages which are transmitted according to the protocol. Attacks of this kind are known to such basic cryptographic algorithms as Diffie-Hellman [4] key exchange or generation of RSA keys. In this case only a party knowing a secret key used to mount a subliminal channel may view the hidden messages. Note that the subliminal channel, based on steganography are more fragile with this respect. While slight modifications in digital pictures are allowed and may serve as a method of destroying the hidden data, a manipulation of cryptographic data exchanged by a protocol should lead to negative verification.

In the case of subliminal channels disseminating information might be a problem. Once a malicious code is detected it may be used by anybody to get access to information from the subliminal channel.

1.2 Kleptographic Attacks

Young and Yung presented kleptography [11,12,13], which is a technique to attack cryptography using cryptographic methods. Their attack is based on modifications of standard algorithms executed by a device or a software product. Malicious *kleptographic* code inserted into such a system leak the secrets of the user. The data transmitted as in an analogous way as for a subliminal channel. The main difference is that

- encoding for a kleptographic channel requires a public key contained in the kleptographic code,
- decoding information requires a private key that is <u>not present</u> in the kleptographic code.

So, a malicious party needs only to intercept transmission from a contaminated system. Nobody except him can make use of the kleptographic channel, in particular, reverse engineering and detecting kleptographic code does not provide access to the channel. Last not least, as in the case of subliminal channel, the messages are exchanged just like for the original protocol and the change cannot be detected without inspecting the code.

General kleptographic attacks on signature and/or encryption algorithms are introduced in [11,12,13,14]. Detecting and defence techniques were considered in [8,9]. Recently, kleptographic attacks have been mounted against e-voting schemes – profound dangers have been described in [5].

In [7] Goh et. al presented attacks on the SSL/TLS and SSH2 protocols based on the idea of key escrow with asymmetric ciphertexts. These results are closely related to our approach, however the dangers exposed here are not confined to random components transmitted in plaintext.

1.3   Main Results

In this paper we focus our attention on the SSL/TLS (TLS 1.0 [1], TLS 1.1 [3]) and SSH [10](ssh and shh2 as well) protocols. In Sections 3 and 4 we present kleptographic codes which can infect these protocols so that their security is completely broken against a malicious party possessing a certain private key. Even worse, attacks are rather simple and do not demand much skills to be implemented.

The problems are due to the way randomness is used in these protocols. It seems that no countermeasure can be effective against kleptographic attacks using random components of the protocol communication. Since randomness is a source of unpredictability, the situation might seem to be hopeless.

In Section 5 we propose to redesign the protocols like SSL and SSH and eliminate uncontrolled randomness from them (the only thing we need in the protocols is: unpredictability). We propose to use the mechanism due to David Chaum [2]: the role of random numbers will be played by digital signatures for a deterministic scheme. This leaves no room for malicious manipulations of the "random" output and, at the same time provides means for online verification by the remote partner for adherence to the protocol.

2   Basic Techniques

Let us recall basic techniques that will be used in the rest of the paper.

Kleptography for Diffie-Hellman Key Exchange. The following attack was introduced by Young and Yung [11]. Let X be the private key of the malicious manufacturer. Let $Y = \alpha^X \bmod p$ be the public key to be used in a contaminated code. Assume that $H : \mathbb{Z}_p \to \mathbb{Z}_{p-1}$ and let W, a, b be fixed odd integers. A contaminated version of Diffie-Hellman key exchange has the following form:

1. for the first execution of Diffie-Hellman protocol, generate $c_1 \in \mathbb{Z}_{p-1}$ at random,
2. return $m_1 = \alpha^{c_1} \bmod p$,
3. store c_1 in memory for the next execution of Diffie-Hellman protocol;

4. for the second execution of Diffie-Hellman protocol, generate random $t \in \{0,1\}$
5. $z := \alpha^{c_1 - Wt} \cdot Y^{-ac_1 - b} \bmod p$
6. $c_2 := H(z)$
7. return $m_2 = \alpha^{c_2} \bmod p$

So the first execution of Diffie-Hellman protocol is unchanged. The next time instead of a random value, the value m_1 from previous round is used. A "random" value z depends on $\alpha^{c_1} = m_1$ and is blinded by Y^{c_1}.

The following procedure can be applied to recover c_2 by a party that has access to key X:

1. $r := m_1^a \cdot \alpha^b \bmod p$
2. $z_1 := m_1 / r^X \bmod p$
3. if $m_2 := \alpha^{H(z_1)} \bmod p$, then return $H(z_1)$
4. $z_2 := z_1 / \alpha^W \bmod p$
5. if $m_2 := \alpha^{H(z_2)} \bmod p$, then return $H(z_2)$

Having the value of c_2, the attacker can easily calculate the secret key generated in the second key exchange.

The key point in the protocol described is that while it is perfectly legal to show m_1 which is $\alpha^{c_1} \bmod p$, the value $Y^{c_1} \bmod p$ may be used as a shared secret by the contaminated program and by the adversary. Indeed, the program can compute $\alpha^{c_1} \bmod p$ if c_1 is stored for a while, the adversary retrieves $Y^{c_1} \bmod p$ as $m_1^X \bmod p$. In order to hide some algebraic relationship between $\alpha^{c_1} \bmod p$, $Y^{c_1} \bmod p$ and α, Y (for both pairs the discrete logarithms are the same), the "random" parameter used in the next turn is not $Y^{c_1} \bmod p$, but a hash value of it. While an auditor might demand a proof that discrete logarithms are different, it is unfeasible to present a proof that a parameter used is not a hash of a hidden value.

Kleptography with ElGamal Ciphertexts. In this case the attack is equally easy. Recall that an ElGamal ciphertext of a message m for public key β has the form $(m \cdot \beta^k \bmod p, g^k \bmod p)$, where k is chosen at random. In this case a shared secret might be $Y^k \bmod p$, or $H(Y^k \bmod p)$. One can even increase entropy by hashing $Y^k \bmod k$ concatenated with a random string U which is reasonably small to be guessed by an adversary (for instance, $U < 2^{20}$).

Kleptography with RSA Ciphertexts of Random Strings. Certainly, the idea presented above cannot be applied for RSA ciphertexts (provided that the RSA keys are not constructed for a kleptographic channel [14]). So it seems that we are on the safe side and can encode arbitrary values. However, this is not perfectly true if a random value is chosen and encrypted with RSA - we may apply a technique borrowed from [6]. The point is that we assume that the plaintext is random, so a kleptographic program has some room to manipulate the form of the ciphertext by choosing appropriate plaintexts.

The kleptographic code tries to transmit a ciphertext U of some secret to be leaked. Of course, U is obtained with a public key of the adversary, so only the adversary can read it. Each RSA ciphertext contains some information on U, but just a few bits. However, if such RSA ciphertexts are a part of communication protocol, then it is necessary to make many connections and therefore send many such RSA ciphertexts. Assume now that the program has now to send a next such ciphertext. It chooses at random a key r to be encrypted. Let $c = \text{RSA}(r)$. Then the program computes two values with keyed hash functions: $H(K_1, c)$, $H(K, c, 2)$ and truncated them to, say, 7 and respectively 10 bits, obtaining bit strings a and b. (The key K is a secret encoded in the kleptographic program and shared with the adversary.) Then the program inspects 10 bits of U starting at position $a \times 10$. If they agree with b, then the ciphertext c is accepted and used for communication. If not, then the program returns to the point where r is chosen. On average, 2^{10} trials are necessary to find a c that agrees with U and leaks some bits of it. In order to collect all bits of U we perform a process that is called *coupon collector problem*. However, we can speed up leaking U by replacing U by some error correcting code of U. Then we can admit ciphertexts c that make some errors on U, as well we can leave some number of bit positions undetermined.

3 Attack on SLL

3.1 SSL/TLS Protocol Description

The SSL/TLS is client-server protocol to assure reliable and secure communication. It starts with SSL Handshake Protocol. Let us sketch the handshake for the case when a server has a certificate. It consists of the following steps:

ClientHello (plaintext): The client sends the following data: client_version, **random** (we call it *C.rand* for short), client_time (*C.time*), session_id, cipher_suites, compression_methods.

ServerHello (plaintext): The server sends the following data: server_version, **random** (we call it *S.rand*), session_id, cipher_suite (one of *ClientHello.cipher_suite*), compression_method (single compression algorithm selected by the server from the list in *ClientHello.compression_methods*).

ClientKeyExchange (encrypted): There are two possibilities:

RSA: The client generates and sends *preMasterSecret* (*preMS*) encrypted with the public key of the server.

DH: The client and the server execute Diffie-Hellman key exchange protocol, the negotiated key is used as a *preMasterSecret*.

After the SSL Handshake Protocol client and server compute so called masterSecret (*mS*):

$$mS = \text{MD5}(preMS + \text{SHA}('A' + preMS + C.rand + S.rand))$$
$$+ \text{MD5}(preMS + \text{SHA}('BB' + preMS + C.rand + S.rand))$$
$$+ \text{MD5}(preMS + \text{SHA}('CCC' + preMS + C.rand + S.rand))$$

No further communication is necessary for this purpose.

From now on, both sites share the same secret mS and use it to derive appropriate keys for symmetric encryption algorithms which will secure data exchange during this session.

3.2 Simple Non-kleptographic Attack

The first remark is that *preMasterSecret* is the only value needed to compute *masterSecret* that is not transmitted in plaintext. So, the following attack scenarios are possible:

Step 1. option 1: An attacker takes source of the SSL library and modifies a line which is responsible for the pseudo-random generation of the *preMasterSecret*. The modified line can be something of the following form:

$$preMS := H(C.rand + C.time + S.rand +' a')$$

for some hash function H, if the client defines *preMasterSecret*. If Diffie-Hellman protocol is used, then $H(C.rand+C.time+S.rand+'a')$ will be used as the "random" exponent. Then, the attacker distributes compiled versions of programs like Firefox Browser, Mozilla Thunderbird (mail client) etc.

option 2: The attacker prepares a virus which attacks software which uses SSL/TLS protocol. The virus modifies the program so that generation of the *preMasterSecret* is deterministic and depends on $C.rand, S.rand, C.time$ (and/or some other values accessible to the eavesdropper).

Step 2. An attacker creates a virus which is responsible to sniff packets transmitted form/to the infected PC. The virus checks if an infected machine determines *masterSecrets* as described above. If it is so then it sends data transmitted through SSL protocol to the attacker, who can easily decode it.

3.3 Kleptographic Attack

The main reason of troubles are the strings *ClientHello.Random* consisting of 28 bytes, i.e. 224 bits, which are chosen freely by the client's machine. The contaminated machine uses *ClientHello.Random* to leak a secret seed S which is crucial for the following steps of the handshake protocol. For this purpose the contaminated code uses a group G for which the discrete logarithm problem is hard. The choice of G depends on the environment: if elliptic curves are at hand, then one can choose them in order to obtain short bit strings describing the elements of G. In the worst case, we use modular arithmetic. Let g be a generator of G.

First execution. The the client's machine chooses k at random and computes $C = g^k$ in G. If C is too long to fit into a single *ClientHello.Random* string, then the machine splits C it into a few parts and each part is used in a different SSL session.

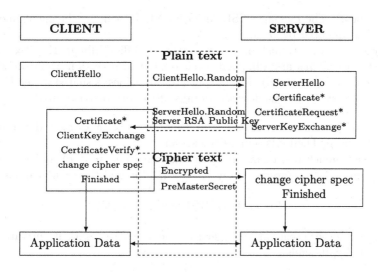

Fig. 1. Communication scheme in SSL v3.0 protocol

Second execution. The seed S used for the following steps is $H(Y^k, i)$, where Y is the public key of the adversary making use of the kleptographic SSL, i is a small sequential number used to ensure that seed S for different sessions used to encode C is different. The next steps depend on the option used:

– *RSA version of ClientKeyExchange.* In this case *preMasterSecret* is determined by the client machine alone, so it might be derived in a pseudorandom way from S. The adversary knows x such that $Y = g^x$, so he may compute $Y^k = C^x$ and therefore S and *preMasterSecret*. Knacking the RSA ciphertext of *preMasterSecret* is unnecessary.
– *Diffie-Hellman version of ClientKeyExchange.* In this case the client's machine uses a "random" exponent which is derived deterministically from S. Since the adversary may decode S as well, he can compute *preMasterSecret* in the same way as the client's machine.

4   Attack on SSH

4.1   SSH Protocol Description

Let us recall shortly the main features of SSH2 protocol according to the RFC 4253 [10].

The client and the server send each other identifiers which will be called V_C and V_S, respectively. Key exchange algorithm begins by each side sending a message called SSH_MSG_KEXINIT. This message contains a 16-byte cookie, lists of preferred algorithms, a few other parameters, and the first message of key exchange algorithm (according to a guess of the preferences of the other side of the protocol). The messages SSH_MSG_KEXINIT sent by the client and the server will be denoted by I_C and I_S.

The next step of establishing a connection is Diffie-Hellman Key Exchange protocol (two versions are admitted, each related to a certain group in which computations are performed). The output are two values: a shared secret K, and an *exchange hash* H. Let us describe details of the protocol executed:

- the client generates a number x at random $(1 < x < q)$ and computes $e = g^x \bmod p$. Then e is sent to the server.
- the server generates a number y at random $(0 < y < q)$ and computes $f = g^y \bmod p$. It computes a key $K = e^y \bmod p$, and the exchange hash

$$H = \mathrm{hash}(V_C||V_S||I_C||I_S||e||f||K) \ .$$

Then the server creates the signature s on H created with its private host key. Finally, it sends

$$(K_S||f||s) \ .$$

to the client, where K_S is the server's public key.
- The client verifies that K_S is really the host key of the server (e. g., using certificates or a local database). Then the client computes K as $f^x \bmod p$, reconstructs H as

$$\mathrm{hash}(V_C||V_S||I_C||I_S||K_S||e||f||K) \ ,$$

and verifies the signature s on H.

After finishing key exchange, the client and the server derive deterministically symmetric keys that will be used for further transmissions. A session_id used for this purpose is the *exchange hash* (if the keys are re-negotiated, then the old session_id remains):

- Initial IV client to server: $\mathrm{HASH}(K||H||'A'||\mathrm{session\_id})$
- Initial IV server to client: $\mathrm{HASH}(K||H||'B'||\mathrm{session\_id})$
- Encryption key client to server: $\mathrm{HASH}(K||H||'C'||\mathrm{session\_id})$
- Encryption key server to client: $\mathrm{HASH}(K||H||'D'||\mathrm{session\_id})$
- Integrity key client to server: $\mathrm{HASH}(K||H||'E'||\mathrm{session\_id})$
- Integrity key server to client: $\mathrm{HASH}(K||H||'F'||\mathrm{session\_id})$

If the output of the function HASH is to short for a key, then the key is generated as follows:

$$K_1 = \mathrm{HASH}(K||H||X||\mathrm{session\_id})$$
$$K_2 = \mathrm{HASH}(K||H||K_1)$$
$$K_3 = \mathrm{HASH}(K||H||K_1||K_2)$$
$$\cdots$$
$$\mathrm{key} = K_1 \text{------} K_2 \text{------} K_3 \text{------} \cdots$$

4.2   Kleptographic Attacks

It is quite easy to implement attacks presented in Section 2 against the SSH protocol. There are two major starting points for such attacks. The first one is making use of Diffie-Hellman key exchange protocol. As it was already described in Section 3, a DH message may transmit a secret random message to the adversary. This secret can be used as an exponent during the second execution of SSH:

- A client sends a DH challenge $e = g^{c_1} \bmod p$, remembers the value c_1, but then closes the connection and starts it again (this is admitted by TCP/IP protocol). During the second run it sends a challenge $e = g^{c_2} \bmod p$, where c_2 depends on c_1 like it was described in Section 2.

Apart from the flaws that come from the usage of Diffie-Hellman key exchange protocol, there are many ways of leaking information kleptographically to the adversary:

- The cookies contained in SSH_MSG_KEXINIT are chosen freely, so they may contain (parts) of a ciphertext of the random seed used by the client, its private keys and similar sensitive data.
- The SSH messages contain padding bytes (at least 4 padding bytes must be contained in any message). The padding bytes are random according to RFC 4253, so they can be replaced by parts of ciphertexts leaking the secrets of the client.
- The client may send a *Ignored Data Message*, which, according to its name, will be ignored by the server. Instead of random values, it may contain a ciphertext of client's secrets. Interestingly, possibility of sending such messages is not considered as a threat, RFC 4253 contains the following passage: "this message [*Ignored Data Message*] can be used as an additional protection measure against advanced traffic analysis techniques".
- Even the list of admitted algorithms contained in SSH_MSG_KEXINIT may carry some information: the permutation of the algorithm names may encode a few bytes.

5   Defence Methods – Redesigning the Protocols

5.1   Chaum's Method

Many cryptographic protocols require that a participant chooses a string r at random and sometimes presents it to the other participant. The main properties are that

- r cannot be predicted in advance,
- if r is long enough, then probability of choosing r for the second time is negligible.

Instead of choosing r at random David Chaum [2] used a deterministic signature scheme, say sig. Let q be a number unique to the current step of the protocol (it might be for instance the current time concatenated with some protocol data). Then $r := \text{sig}_K(q)$, where K is a private signing key. Note that <u>both</u> properties mentioned are fulfilled. However, there are additional ones:

- r cannot be chosen freely, so there is no room for hiding additional information inside r,
- it is possible to check that r has been computed as described.

5.2   Modification of SSH Protocol

There are two main features that allow to attack kleptographically the SSH protocol:

1. freedom of the choice of the random values (randomness that one cannot verify), which are transmitted in plaintext,
2. impossibility of verifying randomness of the exponent used in Diffie-Hellman key exchange, especially, one cannot verify that this value is independent from the previous communication.

The solution to the first problem might be:

- making generation of the cookie dependant on time, client/server version and the signature under that string, say: cookie = $\text{hash}(\text{sig}(C.time, V_C, V_S))$,
- reducing the list of possible encryption and mac algorithms.

Now consider the Diffie-Hellman protocol executed by a (secure) server S and client C. One can solve the problem of generating the random exponent by C in the following way:

- S sends (pseudo)random values (x_1, x_2) to C,
- C computes

$$e_1 = g^{\text{hash}(\text{sig}(x_1, C.time))} , \quad e_2 = g^{\text{hash}(\text{sig}(x_2, C.time))}$$

  and sends $(e_1, e_2, C.time)$ to S,
- S chooses a bit i uniformly at random and sends it to C,
- C replies with $\text{sig}(x_i, C.time)$,
- S verifies, whether e_i was computed properly, if it is so, then e_{1-i} is accepted as a challenge of C.

Let us notice that the exponent used in e_{1-i} is still unknown to the S.

5.3   Modification of SSL/TLS Protocol

The *Client.random* and *Server.random* values should be generated in a way it was suggested concerning cookies of the SSH protocol. But in the SSL/TLS protocol there is an additional problem. One cannot guarantee that a client posses any encryption/signing keys. So, the generation of the *Client.random* is impossible in this way. The second point is that it is hard to send encrypted messages to the client before the session key is agreed. Moreover, it is hard to use Diffie Hellman key exchange protocol (because it seems to be hard to verify the client's choice). We suggest to restrict SSL's key exchange to the RSA case.

For the case of the RSA key exchange we present here a modified, kleptography-immune, version of the SSL protocol. The solution has a nice feature – the communication flow is the same as in the original SSL/TLS. The only change in the protocol is that *Client.Random* value is equal to the hash value of the preMaster-Secret - $Client.Random = hash(preMS)$. So, the "new" clients are compatible with the SSL 3.0 and TLS 1.0 specification. A server sends exactly the same packets as it was specified in the RFC, and the computation of a masterSecret value is exactly the same. But, thanks to the modification, we achieved following: a ("new") server can now verify if a client's version is kleptography-immune by checking if *Client.random* was generated correctly (and that information is transparent to the SSL 3.0/TLS 1.0 version's servers).

6   Conclusions

As we have seen, the SSL/TLS and SSH protocols are quite vulnerable in the sense of kleptographic attacks. On the other hand, for instance security of e-banking depends heavily on security of Internet browsers and so on the SSL/TLS protocol.

Since Internet browsers may contain kleptographic code (the technique is known already for one decade!), the following countermeasures might be considered:

1. *use only Internet browsers for which the source code has been revealed* – access to the source code and legal liability for the trapdoors installed in the code should discourage to install kleptographic code.
2. *use only Internet browsers such that the source code has been revealed only to trustworthy authorities* – in this case malicious parties need to reverse engineer the code of a browser in order to construct a virus infecting the browsers with appropriate kleptographic code.

For the second strategy, one can argue that the institutions like the German BSI are well prepared and trustworthy to achieve the necessary goals. On the other hand, involvement of security agencies awakes distrust in a similar way – this is the case for NSA and a part of the European public oppinion.

It seems that it is absolutely necessary to rethink the fundamental protocols like SSL/TLS and SSH. What we have seen can be classified as severe design faults regarding long known attack strategies.

References

1. C. Allen and T. Dierks. The TLS Protocol. Version 1.0. Informational RFC 2246, IETF, Network Working Group, 1999.
2. David Chaum. Secret-ballot receipts: True voter-verifiable elections. *IEEE Security and Privacy Magazine*, 2(1):38–47, January/February 2004.

3. T. Dierks and E. Rescorla. The Transport Layer Security (TLS) Protocol. Version 1.1. Informational RFC 4346, IETF, Network Working Group, 2006.
4. Whitfield Diffie and Martin E. Hellman. New directions in cryptography. *IEEE Transactions on Information Theory*, 22(6):644–654, November 1976. Available from: http://www.cs.purdue.edu/homes/ninghui/courses/Fall04/lectures/diffie-hellman.pdf.
5. Marcin Gogolewski, Marek Klonowski, Przemysław Kubiak, Mirosław Kutyłowski, Anna Lauks, and Filip Zagórski. Kleptographic attacks on e-voting schemes. In *ET-RICS: Proceedings of the International Conference on Emerging Trends in Information and Communication Security*, Lecture Notes in Computer Science. Springer, 2006. to appear.
6. Marcin Gogolewski, Marek Klonowski, Przemysław Kubiak, Mirosław Kutyłowski, Anna Lauks, and Filip Zagórski. Kleptographic attacks on e-voting schemes. In *Proc. of the Workshop on Electronic Voting and e-Government in the UK*, pages 49–57, e-Science Institute, Edinburgh, 27th–28th February 2006.
7. Eu-Jin Goh, Dan Boneh1, Benny Pinkas, and Philippe Golle. The design and implementation of protocol-based hidden key recovery. In *Information Security: 6th International Conference, ISC 2003*, volume 2851 of *Lecture Notes in Computer Science*, pages 165 – 179, 2003.
8. Daniel Kucner and Mirosław Kutyłowski. Stochastic kleptography detection. In *Public-key Cryptography and Computational Number Theory Proceedings of the International Conference, Stefan Banach International Mathematical Center, 2000*, pages 137–149. Walter de Gruyter & Co, 2001.
9. Daniel Kucner and Mirosław Kutyłowski. How to use un-trusty cryptographic devices. *Tatra Mountains Mathematical Publications.*, 29:57–67, 2004.
10. T. Ylonen. The Secure Shell (SSH) Transport Layer Protocol. Informational RFC 4253, IETF, Network Working Group, 2006.
11. Adam Young and Moti Yung. The dark side of "black-box" cryptography, or: Should we trust capstone? In *CRYPTO*, volume 1109 of *Lecture Notes in Computer Science*, pages 89–103. Springer, 1996.
12. Adam Young and Moti Yung. Kleptography: Using cryptography against cryptography. In *EUROCRYPT*, volume 1109 of *Lecture Notes in Computer Science*, pages 62–74. Springer, 1997.
13. Adam Young and Moti Yung. Bandwidth-optimal kleptographic attacks. In *CHES: International Workshop on Cryptographic Hardware and Embedded Systems, CHES, LNCS*, pages 235–250, 2001.
14. Adam Young and Moti Yung. Malicious cryptography: Kleptographic aspects. In Alfred Menezes, editor, *CT-RSA*, volume 3376 of *Lecture Notes in Computer Science*, pages 7–18. Springer, 2005.

Bitslice Implementation of AES

Chester Rebeiro, David Selvakumar, and A.S.L. Devi

Real Time Systems Group
Centre For Development of Advanced Computing
Bangalore, India
{rebeiro, david}@cdac.in

Abstract. Network applications need to be fast and at the same time provide security. In order to minimize the overhead of the security algorithm on the performance of the application, the speeds of encryption and decryption of the algorithm are critical. To obtain maximum performance from the algorithm, efficient techniques for its implementation must be used and the implementation must be tuned for the specific hardware on which it is running.

Bitslice is a non-conventional but efficient way to implement DES in software. It involves breaking down of DES into logical bit operations so that N parallel encryptions are possible on a single N-bit microprocessor. This results in tremendous throughput. AES is a symmetric block cipher introduced by NIST as a replacement for DES. It is rapidly becoming popular due to its good security features, efficiency, performance and simplicity. In this paper we present an implementation of AES using the bitslice technique. We analyze the impact of the architecture of the microprocessor on the performance of bitslice AES. We consider three processors; the Intel Pentium 4, the AMD Athlon 64 and the Intel Core 2. We optimize the implementation to best utilize the superscalar architecture and SIMD instruction set present in the processors.

1 Introduction

Security is the most important feature of a cryptographic algorithm. An important secondary requirement is an efficient implementation in hardware and software. The most efficient implementations are generally done in dedicated hardware engines such as in FPGAs and ASICs. However, there are several applications such as networking software, operating system modules, etc., which require fast encryptions but do not have these hardware engines. These applications make an efficient software implementation of cryptographic algorithms important.

The bitslice implementation of DES [1][5] is the most efficient software implementation of DES. It involves converting the algorithm into a series of logical bit operations using XOR, AND, OR and NOT logical gates. When implemented on a microprocessor with a N-bit register width, each bit in the register acts as a 1-bit processor doing a different encryption, therefore N encryptions are done in parallel. This results in significant improvements in throughput.

D. Pointcheval, Y. Mu, and K. Chen (Eds.): CANS 2006, LNCS 4301, pp. 203–212, 2006.

Another advantage of a bitslice implementation is that it is immune to cache-timing attacks. Traditional methods of implementing block ciphers make use of several tables to improve performance [4]. The memory access patterns of the implementation make it vulnerable to cryptanalysis [12] [13]. A bitslice implementation on the other hand is based only on logical operations, there are no tables involved, therefore it is free from attacks based on cache timing analysis.

AES is a symmetric key algorithm and offers higher security compared to DES. The simplicity of its design results in efficient implementations on software platforms. In this paper we try to improve its performance by adapting the bitslice techniques used in DES to AES. We first review the AES algorithm. We then present our implementation of AES encryption using the bitslice technique. In the next section we discuss architecture features of the microprocessor which impact the performance of the encryption. We discuss the Intel Pentium 4 (with EM64T), AMD Athlon 64 and the Intel Core 2 microprocessors. All these microprocessors support 64-bit integer operations and 128-bit SIMD operations. The SIMD operations are supported by the Streaming SIMD Extensions (SSE) instructions. The fourth section has the mode of operation of the ciphers, the fifth has the related work followed by the conclusion in the final section.

1.1   The AES Algorithm

The AES algorithm operates on a 4×4 matrix of bytes called *state*. The state undergoes a series of transformations during the encryption process [*Algorithm:1*]. Each iteration in the encryption process is called a *round*. The number of rounds (N_r) is determined by the size of the AES key. $N_r = 10$, 12 or 14 for key sizes of 128, 192 or 256 bits respectively. All operations on the state are in the Galois Field $GF(2^8)$. The *SubstituteByte* function substitutes each byte with a value from a lookup table called *Sbox*. The entries in the Sbox are obtained by taking the inverse of each element in $GF(2^8)$ followed by a linear affine transformation. The *ShiftRow* function shifts each byte in the row by an offset. The *MixColumn*

Algorithm 1. AES Encryption

Input: 4×4 Plaintext bytes
Output: 4×4 Cyphertext bytes

1 AddInitialKey
2 **for** *round* $= 1$ *to* N_r **do**
3   SubstituteByte
4   ShiftRow
5   MixColumn
6   AddRoundKey
7 **end**
8 SubstituteByte
9 ShiftRow
10 AddRoundKey

---

multiplies each column by a constant matrix. The *AddRoundKey* adds the round key which is derived from the initial key by a key expansion algorithm. The final round does not contain the MixColumn operation.

2   Bitslice Implementation

The AES input contains 128 bits. On a N-bit microprocessor, this requires $128/N$ words of memory for storage. With bitslice we work with N inputs at a time which we call a *bundle*. For example, on a 64-bit machine the bundle (*Figure: 1*) would contain 64 consecutive AES input blocks with each block occupying 2 words. The bundle is arranged so that the first bit of each input is present in the first word, the second bit of each input is present in the second word and so on. This is shown in *Figure 2*. The bundle is then encrypted. The N-bit microprocessor acts as a SIMD machine executing N 1-bit instructions in parallel. Therefore a single logical operation operates on N blocks simultaneously. All the AES operations are converted into logical operations. The ShiftRow, MixColumn and AddRoundKey operations are combined into a single function. The Sbox table used in the SubstituteByte operation is replaced with logical equations derived using composite field arithmetic. The final encrypted bundle is rearranged at the end of the encryption.

$b0_{63}$	..	$b0_4$	$b0_3$	$b0_2$	$b0_1$	$b0_0$
$b0_{127}$	..	$b0_{68}$	$b0_{67}$	$b0_{66}$	$b0_{65}$	$b0_{64}$
$b1_{63}$	..	$b1_4$	$b1_3$	$b1_2$	$b1_1$	$b1_0$
$b1_{127}$	..	$b1_{68}$	$b1_{67}$	$b1_{66}$	$b1_{65}$	$b1_{64}$
$b2_{63}$	..	$b2_4$	$b2_3$	$b2_2$	$b2_1$	$b2_0$
$b2_{127}$	..	$b2_{68}$	$b2_{67}$	$b2_{66}$	$b2_{65}$	$b2_{64}$
$b3_{63}$	..	$b3_4$	$b3_3$	$b3_2$	$b3_1$	$b3_0$
$b3_{127}$	..	$b3_{68}$	$b3_{67}$	$b3_{66}$	$b3_{65}$	$b3_{64}$
.	.	.	.	.	.	.
.	.	.	.	.	.	.
.	.	.	.	.	.	.
.	.	.	.	.	.	.
.	.	.	.	.	.	.
$b63_{63}$	..	$b63_4$	$b63_3$	$b63_2$	$b63_1$	$b63_0$
$b63_{127}$	..	$b63_{68}$	$b63_{67}$	$b63_{66}$	$b63_{65}$	$b63_{64}$

Fig. 1. Bundle stored in memory for 64-bit processor

$b63_0$	..	$b4_0$	$b3_0$	$b2_0$	$b1_0$	$b0_0$
$b63_1$	..	$b4_1$	$b3_1$	$b2_1$	$b1_1$	$b0_1$
$b63_2$	..	$b4_2$	$b3_2$	$b2_2$	$b1_2$	$b0_2$
$b63_3$	..	$b4_3$	$b3_3$	$b2_3$	$b1_3$	$b0_3$
$b63_4$	..	$b4_4$	$b3_4$	$b2_4$	$b1_4$	$b0_4$
$b63_5$	..	$b4_5$	$b3_5$	$b2_5$	$b1_5$	$b0_5$
$b63_6$	..	$b4_6$	$b3_6$	$b2_6$	$b1_6$	$b0_6$
$b63_7$	..	$b4_7$	$b3_7$	$b2_7$	$b1_7$	$b0_7$
.	.	.	.	.	.	.
.	.	.	.	.	.	.
.	.	.	.	.	.	.
.	.	.	.	.	.	.
.	.	.	.	.	.	.
$b63_{126}$	..	$b4_{126}$	$b3_{126}$	$b2_{126}$	$b1_{126}$	$b0_{126}$
$b63_{127}$	..	$b4_{127}$	$b3_{127}$	$b2_{127}$	$b1_{127}$	$b0_{127}$

Fig. 2. Rearranged bundle for 64-bit processor

2.1   Arranging the Bundle

On a 128-bit machine the bundle is stored in a 128×128 bit matrix B *[Algorithm: 2]*. To rearrange the bundle, the mth bit from word n is placed in the nth bit of word m. This rearrangement of bits needs to be done for every bundle being encrypted and therefore needs to be efficient. To do the rearrangement, we do an in place transpose of the matrix using the *Algorithm 2*. The algorithm is a slightly modified transpose algorithm from [7] and transposes a $n \times n$ matrix. The complexity of the algorithm is $\Theta(\frac{n}{2} log_2 n)$.

On a 64-bit machine, the bundle is stored in a 128×64 bit matrix (*Figure: 1*). The rearrangement requires that the bit m of an even row n be placed at the position $n/2$ of row m. If n is odd, the mth bit of row n should be placed at the position $(n-1)/2$ of row $(63+m)$. To do the rearrangement, the transpose of all odd rows and even rows are first found using the *Algorithm 2*. Then the rows are rearranged to put the bundle in the required form (*Figure: 2*). The rearrangement of the rows can be done along with the addition of the initial key.

The transpose function is called twice for each encryption of the bundle. The first time on the plaintext before the encryption is started and the second on the ciphertext after the bundle is encrypted. If there are several bundles that need to be encrypted the transpose function could be modified to transpose the ciphertext of one bundle and the plaintext of the next bundle at the same time.

Algorithm 2. Transpose function

Input: Bundle B of dimension $n \times n$
Output: Transposed Bundle B

1 $m_0 \leftarrow (5555555555555555)_{16}$
2 $m_1 \leftarrow (3333333333333333)_{16}$
3 $m_2 \leftarrow (0F0F0F0F0F0F0F0F)_{16}$
4 $\cdots$
5 $m_j \leftarrow (\{0\}^{2^j}\{1\}^{2^j})_2$
6 **for** $j = 0$ *to* $log_2 n$ **do**
7     $k \leftarrow 1 << j$
8     $k2 \leftarrow k * 2$
9     $r \leftarrow k - 1$
10   **for** $i = 0$ *to* $n/2$ **do**
11      $l \leftarrow 2(i - (i \wedge r)) + (i \wedge r)$
12      $temp \leftarrow (B_l \wedge m_j) \oplus ((B_{l+k2} \wedge m_j) << k)$
13      $B_{l+k2} \leftarrow (B_{l+k2} \wedge (\overline{m}_j)) \oplus ((B_l \wedge (\overline{m}_j)) >> k)$
14      $B_l \leftarrow temp$
15   **end**
16 **end**

2.2 AES Round

The SubstituteByte function is called 16 times each round during the encryption process, and is therefore an important factor influencing the performance of the bitslice AES engine. An efficient method of implementing the Sbox using combination logic was introduced in [8] and later enhanced in [6], [9] and [10]. These methods determine the inverse in $GF(2^8)$ by making a transformation to a composite field where the number of gates required for finding the inverse is lesser. We implemented the SubstituteByte function using equations from [10]. Using standard gates, our SubstituteByte function was implemented using 132 gates.

The state of the AES engine after the SubstituteByte operation can be represented as shown in *Figure 3*. Each element S_n consists of 8 words, B_{8n} to B_{8n+7}. Each word is of N bits representing the N encryptions taking place in parallel.

S_{00}	S_{04}	S_{08}	S_{12}
$B_{00} - B_{07}$	$B_{32} - B_{39}$	$B_{64} - B_{71}$	$B_{96} - B_{103}$
S_{01}	S_{05}	S_{09}	S_{13}
$B_{08} - B_{15}$	$B_{40} - B_{47}$	$B_{72} - B_{79}$	$B_{104} - B_{111}$
S_{02}	S_{06}	S_{10}	S_{14}
$B_{16} - B_{23}$	$B_{48} - B_{55}$	$B_{80} - B_{87}$	$B_{112} - B_{119}$
S_{03}	S_{07}	S_{11}	S_{15}
$B_{24} - B_{31}$	$B_{56} - B_{63}$	$B_{88} - B_{95}$	$B_{120} - B_{127}$

Fig. 3. AES State

S_{00}	S_{04}	S_{08}	S_{12}
$B_{00} - B_{07}$	$B_{32} - B_{39}$	$B_{64} - B_{71}$	$B_{96} - B_{103}$
S_{05}	S_{09}	S_{13}	S_{01}
$B_{40} - B_{47}$	$B_{72} - B_{79}$	$B_{104} - B_{111}$	$B_{08} - B_{15}$
S_{10}	S_{14}	S_{02}	S_{06}
$B_{80} - B_{87}$	$B_{112} - B_{119}$	$B_{16} - B_{23}$	$B_{48} - B_{55}$
S_{15}	S_{03}	S_{07}	S_{11}
$B_{120} - B_{127}$	$B_{24} - B_{31}$	$B_{56} - B_{63}$	$B_{88} - B_{95}$

Fig. 4. AES State after ShiftRow

The ShiftRow operation shifts the second row left by eight bits, the third row by sixteen bits and the fourth row by twenty four bits as shown in the *Figure 4*. With bitslice the ShiftRow is implemented using simple move operations.

The MixColumn operation is essentially a multiplication of each column of the matrix with a permutation of $[2 \quad 3 \quad 1 \quad 1]$. For example the MixColumn output for the first byte is given by the equation.

$$S'_{00} = 2S_{00} + 3S_{05} + S_{10} + S_{15}$$

The multiplication by 2 is equivalent to a shift operation. If the most significant bit is one, then this operation will result in an overflow. When an overflow occurs the constant $\{1B\}_{16}$ is added. In bitslice the shift operation is achieved by moving word 0 to word 1, word 1 to word 2, and so on. The overflow bit is added to the words 0, 1, 3 and 4. Multiplication by 3 is a multiplication by 2 followed by a addition with the value.

The AddRoundKey adds each word in the bundle with the corresponding word in the key bundle. The MixColumn, ShiftRow and AddRoundKey can be combined into a single set of equations. The equations for the first byte output is as shown below. The term of handles the overflow. The addition of the round key (kr) is combined with the equations.

$$of = B_{07} + B_{47}$$

$$B'_{00} = B_{40} + B_{80} + B_{120} + kr_{00} + of$$
$$B'_{01} = B_{00} + B_{40} + B_{41} + B_{81} + B_{121} + kr_{01} + of$$
$$B'_{02} = B_{01} + B_{41} + B_{42} + B_{82} + B_{122} + kr_{02}$$
$$B'_{03} = B_{02} + B_{42} + B_{43} + B_{83} + B_{123} + kr_{03} + of$$
$$B'_{04} = B_{03} + B_{43} + B_{44} + B_{84} + B_{124} + kr_{04} + of$$
$$B'_{05} = B_{04} + B_{44} + B_{45} + B_{85} + B_{125} + kr_{05}$$
$$B'_{06} = B_{05} + B_{45} + B_{46} + B_{86} + B_{126} + kr_{06}$$
$$B'_{07} = B_{06} + B_{46} + B_{47} + B_{87} + B_{127} + kr_{07}$$

Table 1. Machines used for testing

Microprocessor	Intel P4 (With EM64T)	AMD Athlon 64	Intel Core 2
Code Name	Prescott 2M	Venice	Woodcrest
Core Speed	3.6GHz	1.8GHz	2.66GHz
Memory	2 GBytes	740 MBytes	4 GBytes
Operating System	Linux	Linux	Linux
Compiler	gcc-4.1.2	gcc-4.1.2	gcc-4.1.0

3   Software Implementation

In this section we see the implications of the microprocessor architecture on the performance of the AES bitslice code, and how best to utilize the architecture to improve performance. We consider three different X86-64 systems as listed in *Table 1*.

The *ShiftRow+MixColumn+AddRoundKey* operation of the AES encryption consists of loading data from memory, performing an XOR operation and writing the results back to memory. The execution of the instructions are architecture specific and the latency and throughput vary between the systems *(Table: 2)*. For our analysis we assume that all code and data is present in the cache. In the SubstituteByte operation, around 60% of the instructions are logical instructions. The remaining are load and store instructions.

The *Table 3* shows the performance for encrypting a single AES input using bitslice code written in C. This clock cycles per encryption was calculated by measuring the time required to encrypt a bundle divided by the number of blocks in the bundle.

Table 2. Instruction Comparison

		Pentium 4	Athlon 64	Core 2
Pipeline stages		31	12	14
Load Instruction	64-bit	2,1	3,2	2,1
(latency,throughput)	128-bit	13,1	2,0.5	2,1
Logical Instructions	64-bit	1,2	1,3	1,3
(latency,throughput)	128-bit	2,1	2,1	1,3
Store Instruction	64-bit	NA,0.5	3,2	3,1
(latency,throughput)	128-bit	NA,0.5	3,0.5	3,1

Table 3. Clock cycles per encryption

Bundle	Clock Cycles		
	Pentium 4	Athlon 64	Core 2
64-bit	540	346	302
128-bit	446	280	135
128-bit+64-bit	410	285	225

Pentium 4: The Pentium 4 (P4) decoder converts instructions to one or more micro operations (μops) at a rate of 1 instruction per clock. The μops are issued to the execute core through 4 issue ports. Although there are 2 ALUs, all logical operations can be dispatched only to ALU 0 through the Port 0. The logical operations are however executed at twice the clock speed. All SSE logical operations are dispatched through Port 1. The Port 2 and Port 3 are used for load and store operations.

Since different ports are used for SSE and integer operations an SSE operation and an integer operation can be executed at the same time. To maximize the utilization of the processor, we encrypt more than one bundle at a time. We start our encryption taking two bundles; one of 128-bit and the other of 64-bit. We interleave the instructions of the 128-bit (SSE instructions) with the 64-bit (integer) instructions so that there is a SSE instruction following every integer instruction. This effectively allows us to do 192 encryptions in parallel.

The Pentium 4 has a deep pipeline of 31 stages. The complexity of each stage is relatively simple, hence Pentium 4 can reach high clock speeds, therefore high encryptions per second. The instruction latencies however are higher, this results in higher number of clock cycles required for encryption.

Athlon 64: The Athlon 64 can decode, execute and retire a maximum of 3 instructions per clock cycle. Most SSE instructions however are split into 2 independent 64 bit operations and are decoded at 1.5 instructions per clock cycle. 128-bit memory access instructions are also split into two independent 64 bit accesses and are handled by the FMISC unit in the core. There are 3 ALUs in the Athlon 64 and all ALUs can execute logical operations. There are also 3 Address Generation Units (AGU) which results in more efficient memory operations.

Core 2: The Core 2 has three SSE execution units. Besides this, the latency in executing an SSE instruction is reduced from 2 in Pentium 4 and Athlon 64 to 1. The Core 2 can decode, issue and retire 4 instructions per cycle. It also uses macro-op and micro-op fusion which allows certain types of instructions to be combined into one data item and sent through the pipeline.

There are 6 execution ports in Core 2. All execution ports support 128 bits. The ports 0, 1 and 2 are used for integer and SSE logical operations therefore interleaving the encryption of two bundles at a time does not have any merits.

4   Operating Modes

There are five modes of operation for block ciphers recommended by NIST in [3]. These are Electronic Codebook (ECB), Cipher Block Chaining (CBC), Cipher Feedback (CFB), Output Feedback (OFB) and Counter (CTR). The bitslice AES can be used in modes that support parallelized encryptions (ECB and CTR) and parallelized decryptions (ECB, CBC, CFB and CTR).

In applications which use modes that do not support parallelized implementations, bitslice techniques cannot be used. However, bitslice can be used for such applications that do a lot of simultaneous independent encryptions or decryptions. For example, a network server application would be communicating simultaneously with several independent clients. For such applications bitslice can be used with each block in the bundle belonging to a different client.

5   Related Work

There have been several efforts [11][14][19][20] to maximize the performance of AES in software. The fastest among them being the assembly code by Brian Gladman[19] which does AES encryptions in 186 clock cycles on a AMD64 machine. There has been only one paper discussing implementation of AES using bitslice. In that paper [6], each input is converted to its equivalent representation in a composite field $GF((2^4)^2)$, and then the AES encryption is done in the new field. The result is converted back into the $GF(2^8)$ field. This works because all arithmetic in the AES algorithm is Galois arithmetic. The ShiftRow and AddRoundKey operations are computationally equivalent in both fields, there is a huge difference in the MixColumn operation. For example, in $GF(2^8)$, multiplication by 2 can be done in one operation, while in a composite field this would require at least 18 operations [10]. On an AMD64 bit system they were able to achieve an encryption rate of 170 clock cycles. In our approach, only the

SubstituteByte operation is done in the composite field. All other operations are done in the standard $GF(2^8)$ field. The conversion to and from the composite field is done at every round. The overhead added by the conversion during each round is lesser than doing all operations in the composite field.

6   Conclusion

This paper presented an implementation of AES using the bitslice technique. The performance was tested, analyzed and optimized for the Pentium 4, Athlon 64 and Core 2 processors. The performance results of bitslice AES differs on each platform due to the different internal architectures. The performance also depends on the type of instructions used.

Among the three processors the Core 2 produces the best results when SSE instructions were used. On Pentium 4, the best results were observed when the SSE instructions were interleaved with the integer instructions. On Athlon 64, the best results were observed when encryption was done with SSE instructions.

The Sbox function, currently written in C, consumes around 75% of the clock cycles of bitslice AES encryption. A more optimized Sbox written in assembly language would produce a high speed AES implementation that could be used for applications requiring high speed encryptions and decryptions.

References

1. E. Biham, *A Fast New DES Implementation in Software*, Fast Software Encryption-4th International Workshop, FSE97, 1997; Proceedings, LNCS, Springer, Vol 1267, pp 260-271.
2. National Institute of Standards and Technology (NIST), Information Technology Laboratory (ITL), *Advanced Encryption Standard (AES)*, Federal Information Processing Standards (FIPS) Publication 197, 2001.
3. National Institute of Standards and Technology (NIST), Computer Security Division, *Recommendation for Block Cipher Modes of Operation: Methods and Techniques*, Special Publication 800-38A, 2001.
4. J. Daemen, V. Rijmen, *AES Proposal: Rijndael*, Version 2, AES submission, 1999, http://csrc.nist.gov/encryption/aes/rijndael/Rijndael.pdf.
5. M. Kwan, *Bitslice implementation of DES*, http://www.darkside.com.au/bitslice.
6. A. Rudra, P.K. Dubey, C.S. Jutla, V. Kumar, J.R.Rao, P.Rohatgi, *Efficient Implementation of Rijndael Encryption with Composite Field Arithmetic*, Workshop on Cryptographic Hardware and Embedded Systems, CHES 2001, 2001.
7. G. Gaubatz, B. Sunar, *Leveraging the Multiprocessing Capabilities of Modern Network Processors for Cryptographic Acceleration*, 4th IEEE International Symposium on Network Computing and Applications (NAC05), Cambridge, Massachusetts, July 2005.
8. V. Rijmen, *Efficient Implementation of the Rijndael SBox*, http://citeseer.ist.psu.edu/rijmen00efficient.html.
9. J. Wolkerstorfer, E. Oswald, M. Lamberger, *An ASIC implementation of the AES Sboxes*, In CT-RSA 2002, LNCS 2271, pages 6778, 2002.

10. D. Canright, *A Very Compact Rijndael S-box*, Workshop on Cryptographic Hardware and Embedded Systems, CHES 2005, 2005.
11. M. Matsui, S. Fukuda, *How to Maximize Software Performance of Symmetric Primitives on Pentium III and 4 Processors*, 12th Fast Software Encryption Workshop, FSE 2005, 2005.
12. D.A.Osvik, A. Shamir, E. Tromer, *Cache Attacks and Countermeasures: the Case of AES*, 2005, http://eprint.iacr.org/2005/271.pdf.
13. D.J. Bernstein, *Cache-timing attacks on AES*, 2005, http://cr.yp.to/antiforgery/cachetiming-20050414.pdf.
14. K. Aoki, H. Lipmaa, *Fast Implementations of AES Candidates*, Proceedings of the 3rd AES Candidate Conference, 2000. Available at http://csrc.nist.gov/encryption/aes/round2/conf3/papers/20-kaoki.pdf.
15. AMD Manual, *Software Optimization Guide for AMD Athlon 64 and AMD Opteron Processors*, http://www.amd.com/us-en/assets/content_type/white_papers_and_tech_docs/25112.PDF.
16. Intel Manual, *IA-32 Intel Architecture Optimization Reference Manual*, http://download.intel.com/design/Pentium4/manuals/24896613.pdf.
17. A. Fog, *Instruction tables: Lists of instruction latencies, throughputs and micro-operation breakdowns for Intel and AMD CPU's*, http://www.agner.org/optimize/instruction_tables.pdf, 2006.
18. *The microarchitecture of Intel and AMD CPUs*, http://www.agner.org/optimize/microarchitecture.pdf, 2006.
19. B. Gladman, AES Code, http://fp.gladman.plus.com/AES.
20. H. Lipmaa *AES/Rijndael : Speed*, http://www.adastral.ucl.ac.uk/~helger/research/aes/rijndael.html.

A Fast Algorithm for Determining the Linear Complexity of Periodic Sequences over $GF(3)^\star$

Jianqin Zhou** and Qiang Zheng

Dept. of Computer Science, Anhui Univ. of Technology, Ma'anshan 243002, China
zhou9@yahoo.com

Abstract. A fast algorithm is derived for determining the linear complexity and the minimal polynomial of periodic sequences over $GF(3)$ with period $3^n p^m$, where p is a prime number, and 3 is a primitive root modulo p^2. The algorithm presented here generalizes the fast algorithm to determine the linear complexity of a sequence over $GF(q)$ with period p^m, where p is a prime, q is a prime and a primitive root modulo p^2.

Keywords: Cryptography; periodic sequence; linear complexity; minimal polynomial.

The concept of linear complexity is very useful in the study of the security of stream ciphers for cryptographic applications. A necessary condition for the security of a key stream generator is that it produces a sequence with large linear complexity. Games-Chan algorithm in [1] was proposed to compute the linear complexity of sequences over $GF(2)$ with period 2^n , and was generalized to the sequences over $GF(p^m)$ with period p^n , where p is a prime, by Ding, Xiao and Shan in [2]. Wei, Xiao and Chen in [4] presented an algorithm to compute the linear complexity of sequences over $GF(q)$ with period p^m , where p is a prime, q is a prime and a primitive root modulo p^2. They in [5] presented an algorithm to compute the linear complexity of sequences over $GF(2)$ with period $2^n p^m$, where 2 is a primitive root modulo p^2.

In this paper, a fast algorithm is derived for determining the linear complexity and the minimal polynomial of periodic sequences over $GF(3)$ with period $3^n p^m$, where p is a prime, 3 is a primitive root modulo p^2. A numerical example is presented to illustrate the new algorithm. The algorithm presented here generalizes both the algorithm in [4] where the period of a sequence over $GF(q)$ is p^m and the algorithm in [5] where the period of a binary sequence is $2^n p^m$. With an approach similar to the case that $q = 3$ as described here, it is easy to derive a fast algorithm for determining the linear complexity and the minimal polynomial of periodic sequences over $GF(q)$ with period $q^n p^m$, where p is a prime, q is a prime and is a primitive root modulo p^2.

* The research is supported by Natural Science Foundation of Anhui Education Bureau (No. 2006KJ238B).
** Corresponding author.

D. Pointcheval, Y. Mu, and K. Chen (Eds.): CANS 2006, LNCS 4301, pp. 213–223, 2006.

1   Preliminaries

For the definitions and lemmas presented here, we refer to [4,5] and the relevant references given in them.

We will consider sequences over $GF(3)$. Let $x = (x_1, x_2, \cdots, x_n)$ and $y = (y_1, y_2, \cdots, y_n)$ be vectors over $GF(3)$. Then define $x + y = (x_1 + y_1, x_2 + y_2, \cdots, x_n + y_n)$.

The generated function of a sequence $s = \{s_0, s_1, s_2, s_3, \cdots, \}$ is defined by

$$s(x) = s_0 + s_1 x + s_2 x^2 + s_3 x^3 + \cdots = \sum_{i=0}^{\infty} s_i x^i.$$

The generated function of a finite sequence $s^N = \{s_0, s_1, s_2, \cdots, s_{N-1}, \}$ is defined by $s^N(x) = s_0 + s_1 x + s_2 x^2 + \cdots + s_{N-1} x^{N-1}$. If s is a periodic sequence with the first period s^N, then,

$$s(x) = s^N(x)(1 + x^N + x^{2N} + \cdots)$$
$$= \frac{s^N(x)}{1 - x^N} = \frac{s^N(x)/gcd(s^N(x), 1 - x^N)}{(1 - x^N)/gcd(s^N(x), 1 - x^N)} = \frac{g(x)}{f_s(x)}$$

where $f_s(x) = (1 - x^N)/gcd(s^N(x), 1 - x^N), g(x) = s^N(x)/gcd(s^N(x), 1 - x^N)$.

Obviously, $gcd(g(x), f_s(x)) = 1, deg(g(x) < deg(f_s(x)))$. $f_s(x)$ is called the minimal polynomial of s, and the degree of $f_s(x)$ is called the linear complexity of s, that is $deg(f_s(x)) = c(s)^{[2]}$.

Let us recall some results in finite field theory[8] and number theory[9].

Definition 1.1. Let n be a positive integer. The polynomial $\Phi_n(x) = \Pi_{0 < j < n, (j,n)=1}(x - \xi_n^j)$, where ξ_n is a n-th primitive unit root, and $(j, n) = 1$ denotes j is relatively prime to n, is called the n-th cyclotomic polynomial.

Lemma 1.1. Let p be a prime. Then $\varphi(p^n) = p^n - p^{n-1}$, where n is a positive integer, φ is the Euler function.

Lemma 1.2. Let $\Phi_n(x)$ be the n-th cyclotomic polynomial. Then $\Phi_n(x)$ is irreducible over $GF(3)$ if and only if that 3 is a primitive root modulo n, that is the order of 3 modulo n is $\varphi(n)$.

Lemma 1.3. Let p be a prime and m a positive integer. Then $\Phi_{p^m}(x) = \Phi_p(x^{p^{m-1}})$.

Lemma 1.4. Let p be a prime, m and n be positive integers. Let $\Phi_{p^m}(x)^{3^n}$ denote $[\Phi_{p^m}(x)]^{3^n}$. Then $\Phi_{p^m}(x)^{3^n} = \Phi_{p^m}(x^{3^n}) = \Phi_p(x^{3^n p^{m-1}})$, where the operation is over $GF(3)$.

Lemma 1.5. Let p be a prime, 3 be a primitive root modulo p^2. Then 3 is a primitive root modulo p^n, $n \geq 1$, so $\Phi_{p^n}(x)$ is irreducible over $GF(3)$.

2   Main Theorems Concerning Algorithms

The following lemma and its proof are from [4].

Lemma 2.1. Let $a = (a_0, a_1, \cdots, a_{N-1})$ be a finite sequence over $GF(3)$, where $N = p^m, p$ is a prime and 3 is a primitive root modulo p^2. Let us denote $a(x)$ as the generated function of the finite sequence $(a_0, a_1, \cdots, a_{N-1})$ and $A_i = (a_{(i-1)p^{m-1}}, a_{(i-1)p^{m-1}+1}, \cdots, a_{ip^{m-1}-1}), i = 1, 2, \cdots, p$. Then $(\Phi_{p^m}(x), a(x)) \neq 1$, that is $\Phi_{p^m}(x)|a(x)$ if and only if $A_1 = A_2 = \cdots = A_p$.

Theorem 2.1. Let $a = (a_0, a_1, \cdots, a_{N-1})$ be a finite sequence over $GF(3)$, where $N = 3^n p^m, p$ is a prime and 3 is a primitive root modulo p^2. Let us denote $a(x)$ as the generated function of the finite sequence $(a_0, a_1, \cdots, a_{N-1})$, $M = 3^{n-1} p^{m-1}$, $A_i = (a_{(i-1)M}, a_{(i-1)M+1}, \cdots, a_{iM-1})$, $A_i(x)$ be the generated function of $A_i, i = 1, 2, \cdots, 3p$. Then,

(i) $\Phi_{p^m}(x)^{3^{n-1}}|a(x)$ if and only if $A_1 + A_{p+1} + A_{2p+1} = A_2 + A_{p+2} + A_{2p+2} = \cdots = A_p + A_{2p} + A_{3p}$;

(ii) If $\Phi_{p^m}(x)^{3^{n-1}}|a(x)$, then $gcd(a(x), \Phi_{p^m}(x)^{3^n}) = \Phi_{p^m}(x)^{3^{n-1}} gcd(A_1'(x) + A_2'(x)x^M + \cdots + A_{3p}'(x)x^{(3p-1)M}, \Phi_{p^m}(x)^{2 \cdot 3^{n-1}})$, where $A_1' = A_1, A_2' = -A_1 + A_2, \cdots, A_{3p}' = -A_{p-1} - A_{2p-1} - A_{3p-1} + A_p + A_{2p} + A_{3p}$;

(iii) If $\Phi_{p^m}(x)^{3^{n-1}} \nmid a(x)$, then

$$gcd(a(x), \Phi_{p^m}(x)^{3^n}) = gcd(a(x), \Phi_{p^m}(x)^{3^{n-1}})$$
$$= gcd(\sum_{i=1}^{p}[A_i(x) + A_{p+i}(x) + A_{2p+i}(x)]x^{(i-1)M}, \Phi_{p^m}(x)^{3^{n-1}});$$

(iv) $gcd(a(x), 1-x^{3M}) = gcd(\sum_{i=1}^{3}[A_i(x)+A_{3+i}(x)+\cdots+A_{3(p-1)+i}(x)]x^{(i-1)M}, 1 - x^{3M})$;

(v) $gcd(a(x), 1 - x^N) = gcd(a(x), 1 - x^{3M})gcd(a(x), \Phi_{p^m}(x)^{3^n})$.

Proof
(i) As 3 is a primitive root modulo p^2, we know that $\Phi_{p^m}(x)$ is irreducible over $GF(3)$.

From lemma 1.4, $\Phi_{p^m}(x)^{3^{n-1}} = 1 + x^M + \cdots + x^{(p-1)M}$. Let b$= \Phi_{p^m}(x)^{3^{n-1}}$. Then,

$$\begin{aligned}
a(x) &= A_1(x) + A_2(x)x^M + \cdots + A_{3p}(x)x^{(3p-1)M} \\
&= A_1'(x)b + A_2'(x)bx^M + \cdots + A_p'(x)bx^{(p-1)M} \\
&+ A_{p+1}'(x)bx^{pM} + A_{p+2}'(x)bx^{(p+1)M} + \cdots + A_{2p}'(x)bx^{(2p-1)M} \\
&+ A_{2p+1}'(x)bx^{2pM} + A_{2p+2}'(x)bx^{(2p+1)M} + \cdots + A_{3p}'(x)bx^{(3p-1)M} \\
&- [A_p(x) + A_{2p}(x) + A_{3p}(x)]bx^{3pM} \\
&+ \{[A_1(x) + A_{p+1}(x) + A_{2p+1}(x)] + [A_2(x) + A_{p+2}(x) + A_{2p+2}(x)]x^M + \cdots \\
&+ [A_p(x) + A_{2p}(x) + A_{3p}(x)]x^{(p-1)M}\}x^{3pM}
\end{aligned}$$

$$\cdots\cdots\cdots\cdots \tag{1}$$

where,

$$A_1' = A_1, A_2' = -A_1 + A_2, \cdots, A_p' = -A_{p-1} + A_p;$$
$$A_{p+1}' = -A_p + A_1 + A_{p+1}, A_{p+2}' = -A_1 - A_{p+1} + A_2 + A_{p+2}, \cdots,$$
$$A_{2p}' = -A_{p-1} - A_{2p-1} + A_p + A_{2p};$$
$$A_{2p+1}' = -A_p - A_{2p} + A_1 + A_{p+1} + A_{2p+1},$$
$$A_{2p+2}' = -A_1 - A_{p+1} - A_{2p+1} + A_2 + A_{p+2} + A_{2p+2}, \cdots,$$
$$A_{3p}' = -A_{p-1} - A_{2p-1} - A_{3p-1} + A_p + A_{2p} + A_{3p}.$$

To understand equality (1), one may add up all the terms of the right hand side concerning every one polynomial $A_i(x)x^{(i-1)M}, 1 \le i \le 3p$.

In the case of $A_2(x)$.

$$x^M A_2(x)(b - bx^M + bx^{pM} - bx^{(p+1)M} + bx^{2pM} - bx^{(2p+1)M} + x^{3pM})$$
$$= x^M A_2(x)[b(1 + x^{pM} + x^{2pM}) - bx^M(1 + x^{pM} + x^{2pM}) + x^{3pM}]$$
$$= x^M A_2(x)[b(1 - x^M)(1 + x^{pM} + x^{2pM}) + x^{3pM}]$$
$$= x^M A_2(x)[(1 - x^{pM})(1 + x^{pM} + x^{2pM}) + x^{3pM}]$$
$$= x^M A_2(x)(1 - x^{3pM} + x^{3pM})$$
$$= A_2(x)x^M$$

In the case of $A_{3p}(x)$.

$$x^{(3p-1)M}(A_{3p}(x)b - A_{3p}(x)bx^M + A_{3p}(x)x^{pM})$$
$$= A_{3p}(x)x^{(3p-1)M}[b(1 - x^M) + x^{pM}]$$
$$= A_{3p}(x)x^{(3p-1)M}$$

By analogy, we may verify other terms of equality (1).

Since $(\Phi_{p^m}(x)^{3^{n-1}}, x^{3pM}) = 1$, we have,

$$\Phi_{p^m}(x)^{3^{n-1}} | a(x) \Longleftrightarrow$$
$$\Phi_{p^m}(x)^{3^{n-1}} | \{[A_1(x) + A_{p+1}(x) + A_{2p+1}(x)] + [A_2(x) + A_{p+2}(x) + A_{2p+2}(x)]x^M$$
$$+ \cdots + [A_p(x) + A_{2p}(x) + A_{3p}(x)]x^{(p-1)M}\}$$

From lemma 2.1, we have,

$$\Phi_{p^m}(x)^{3^{n-1}} | a(x) \Longleftrightarrow$$
$$A_1(x) + A_{p+1}(x) + A_{2p+1}(x) = A_2(x) + A_{p+2}(x) + A_{2p+2}(x)$$
$$= \cdots = A_p(x) + A_{2p}(x) + A_{3p}(x)$$
$$\Longleftrightarrow A_1 + A_{p+1} + A_{2p+1} = A_2 + A_{p+2} + A_{2p+2} = \cdots = A_p + A_{2p} + A_{3p}$$

(ii) If $\Phi_{p^m}(x)^{3^{n-1}} | a(x)$, then $A_1 + A_{p+1} + A_{2p+1} = A_2 + A_{p+2} + A_{2p+2} = \cdots = A_p + A_{2p} + A_{3p}$.

From equality (1), $a(x)/\Phi_{p^m}(x)^{3^{n-1}} = A'_1(x) + A'_2(x)x^M + \cdots + A'_{3p}(x)x^{(3p-1)M}$

Thus, $gcd(a(x), \Phi_{p^m}(x)^{3^n}) =$

$\Phi_{p^m}(x)^{3^{n-1}} gcd(A'_1(x) + A'_2(x)x^M + \cdots + A'_{3p}(x)x^{(3p-1)M}, \Phi_{p^m}(x)^{2 \cdot 3^{n-1}}).$

(iii) If $\Phi_{p^m}(x)^{3^{n-1}} \nmid a(x)$, since $gcd(\Phi_{p^m}(x)^{3^{n-1}}, x^{3pM}) = 1$, and from equality (1), we have,

$$gcd(a(x), \Phi_{p^m}(x)^{3^n}) = gcd(a(x), \Phi_{p^m}(x)^{3^{n-1}})$$

$$= gcd(\sum_{i=1}^{p}[A_i(x) + A_{p+i}(x) + A_{2p+i}(x)]x^{(i-1)M}, \Phi_{p^m}(x)^{3^{n-1}})$$

(iv)

$$\begin{aligned}
a(x) =\ & A_1(x) + A_2(x)x^M + \cdots + A_{3p}(x)x^{(3p-1)M} \\
=\ & \{A_1(x) + [A_1(x) + A_4(x)]x^{3M} + \cdots \\
& + [A_1(x) + A_4(x) + \cdots + A_{3p-5}(x)]x^{(3p-6)M}\}(1 - x^{3M}) \\
& + [A_1(x) + A_4(x) + \cdots + A_{3p-5}(x) + A_{3p-2}(x)]x^{(3p-3)M} \\
& + \{A_2(x) + [A_2(x) + A_5(x)]x^{3M} + \cdots \\
& + [A_2(x) + A_5(x) + \cdots + A_{3p-4}(x)]x^{(3p-6)M}\}x^M(1 - x^{3M}) \\
& + [A_2(x) + A_5(x) + \cdots + A_{3p-4}(x) + A_{3p-1}(x)]x^{(3p-2)M} \\
& + \{A_3(x) + [A_3(x) + A_6(x)]x^{3M} + \cdots \\
& + [A_3(x) + A_6(x) + \cdots + A_{3p-3}(x)]x^{(3p-6)M}\}x^{2M}(1 - x^{3M}) \\
& + [A_3(x) + A_6(x) + \cdots + A_{3p-3}(x) + A_{3p}(x)]x^{(3p-1)M}
\end{aligned}$$

Since $gcd(x^{(3p-3)M}, 1 - x^{3M}) = 1$, we have,

$$\begin{aligned}
& gcd(a(x), 1 - x^{3M}) \\
=\ & gcd([A_1(x) + A_4(x) + \cdots + A_{3p-5}(x) + A_{3p-2}(x)] \\
& + [A_2(x) + A_5(x) + \cdots + A_{3p-4}(x) + A_{3p-1}(x)]x^M \\
& + [A_3(x) + A_6(x) + \cdots + A_{3p-3}(x) + A_{3p}(x)]x^{2M}, 1 - x^{3M}) \\
=\ & gcd(\sum_{i=1}^{3}[A_i(x) + A_{3+i}(x) + \cdots + A_{3(p-1)+i}(x)]x^{(i-1)M}, 1 - x^{3M})
\end{aligned}$$

(v) Since

$$\frac{1 - x^N}{1 - x^{3M}} = 1 + x^{3M} + \cdots + x^{3(p-1)M} = \Phi_{p^m}(x^3)^{3^{n-1}} = \Phi_{p^m}(x)^{3^n},$$

and $gcd(1 - x^{3M}, \Phi_{p^m}(x)^{3^n}) = 1$, we have,

$gcd(a(x), 1 - x^N) = gcd(a(x), 1 - x^{3M})gcd(a(x), \Phi_{p^m}(x)^{3^n}).$ □

Theorem 2.2. Let s be a sequence over $GF(3)$ with period N and $a = (a_0, a_1, \cdots, a_{N-1})$ be the first period, where $N = 3^n p^m$, p is a prime and 3 is a primitive root modulo p^2. Let us denote $a(x)$ as the generated function of the finite sequence $(a_0, a_1, \cdots, a_{N-1}), M = 3^{n-1}p^{m-1}, A_i = (a_{(i-1)M}, a_{(i-1)M+1}, \cdots, a_{iM-1}), A_i(x)$ be the generated function of $A_i, i = 1, 2, \cdots, 3p$. Then,

$$f_s(x) = f_{(b)}(x) \cdot \Phi_{p^m}(x)^z, \quad \text{hence} \quad c(s) = c((b)) + (p-1)p^{m-1}z,$$

where $b = (A_1 + A_4 + \cdots + A_{3p-2}, A_2 + A_5 + \cdots + A_{3p-1}, A_3 + A_6 + \cdots + A_{3p})$, (b) denotes the sequence with the first period b; $deg(\Phi_{p^m}(x)) = \varphi(p^m) = (p-1)p^{m-1}, \Phi_{p^m}(x)^z = \Phi_{p^m}(x)^{3^n}/gcd(\Phi_{p^m}(x)^{3^n}, a(x))$, hence $z = 3^n - t$, where t is the power exponent of $\Phi_{p^m}(x)$ in $gcd(\Phi_{p^m}(x)^{3^n}, a(x))$.

Proof
From (iv) and (v) of theorem 2.1,

$$
\begin{aligned}
f_s(x) &= (1 - x^N)/gcd(a(x), 1 - x^N) \\
&= [(1 - x^{3M})/gcd(a(x), 1 - x^{3M})] \cdot [\Phi_{p^m}(x)^{3^n}/gcd(a(x), \Phi_{p^m}(x)^{3^n})] \\
&= [(1 - x^{3M})/gcd([A_1(x) + A_4(x) + \cdots + A_{3p-2}(x)] \\
&\quad + [A_2(x) + A_5(x) + \cdots + A_{3p-1}(x)]x^M \\
&\quad + [A_3(x) + A_6(x) + \cdots + A_{3p}(x)]x^{2M}, 1 - x^{3M})] \\
&\quad \cdot [\Phi_{p^m}(x)^{3^n}/gcd(a(x), \Phi_{p^m}(x)^{3^n})] \\
&= f_{(b)}(x) \cdot \Phi_{p^m}(x)^z
\end{aligned}
$$

It follows that $c(s) = c((b)) + (p-1)p^{m-1}z$.   □

3   Algorithms to Compute the Linear Complexity of Periodic Sequences over $GF(3)$

The following algorithm was presented in [4] as algorithm 1.

Algorithm 3.1. Let s be a sequence over $GF(3)$ with period $N = p^n$, and the first period be denoted as $a = (a_0, a_1, \cdots, a_{N-1})$, where p is a prime and 3 is a primitive root modulo p^2.

Initial values: $a = (a_0, a_1, \cdots, a_{N-1})$ is the first period of s, $k = p^n, c = 0, f = 1$.
(i) If $a = (0, \cdots, 0)$, then end; if $k=1$, then $c = c + 1, f = (1-x)f$, end;
(ii) $k = k/p$, let $A_i = (a_{(i-1)k}, a_{(i-1)k+1}, \cdots, a_{ik-1}), i = 1, 2, \cdots, p$;
(iii) If $A_1 = A_2 = \cdots = A_p$, then $a = A_1$; if $A_1 = A_2 = \cdots = A_p$ does not hold, then $a = A_1 + A_2 + \cdots + A_p, c = c + (p-1)k, f = f\Phi_{pk}(x)$;
(iv) go to (i)
(v) The final. The linear complexity of $s : c(s) = c$; the minimal polynomial of $s : f_s(x) = f$.
From lemma 2.1, it is easy to show the validity of the algorithm and it computes the minimal polynomial in $n + 1$ loops at most. The reader is referred to [4] for a detailed proof.

Lemma 3.1. Let s be a sequence over $GF(3)$ with period $N = 3^n$ and $a = (a_0, a_1, \cdots, a_{N-1})$ be the first period. Let us denote $a(x)$ as the generated function of the finite sequence $(a_0, a_1, \cdots, a_{N-1})$, $M = 3^{n-1}$, $A_i = (a_{(i-1)M}, a_{(i-1)M+1}, \cdots, a_{iM-1})$, $A_i(x)$ be the generated function of A_i, $i = 1, 2, 3$. Then,

(i) $(1 - x^M)|a(x)$ if and only if $A_1 + A_2 + A_3 = 0$;

(ii) if $(1 - x^M)|a(x)$, then

$$\frac{a(x)}{1 - x^M} = A_1(x) + [A_1(x) + A_2(x)]x^M + [A_1(x) + A_2(x) + A_3(x)]x^{2M};$$

(iii) if $(1 - x^M) \nmid a(x)$, then $gcd(a(x), 1 - x^N) = gcd(A_1(x) + A_2(x) + A_3(x), 1 - x^M)$

(iv) if $(1 - x^M)|a(x)$, then $gcd(a(x), 1 - x^N) = (1 - x^M)gcd(A_1(x) + [A_1(x) + A_2(x)]x^M + [A_1(x) + A_2(x) + A_3(x)]x^{2M}, (1 - x^M)^2)$.

Proof

From the following equality, we have (i) and (ii),

$$a(x) = A_1(x) + A_2(x)x^M + A_3(x)x^{2M}$$
$$= (1 - x^M)\{A_1(x) + [A_1(x) + A_2(x)]x^M + [A_1(x) + A_2(x) + A_3(x)]x^{2M}\}$$
$$+ [A_1(x) + A_2(x) + A_3(x)]x^{3M}$$

Note that the operation is over $GF(3)$, $(1 - x)^3 = 1 - x^3$, thus $(1 - x)^{3^2} = (1 - x^3)^3 = 1 - x^{3^2}$

By analogy, $(1-x)^N = (1-x)^{3^n} = 1-x^{3^n} = 1-x^N$, thus $1-x^N = (1-x^M)^3$. It follows by (iii) and (iv). $\qquad\square$

From lemma 3.1, it is easy to show the validity of the following algorithm.

Algorithm 3.2. Let s be a sequence over $GF(3)$ with period $N = 3^n$ and $a = (a_0, a_1, \cdots, a_{N-1})$ be the first period.

Initial values: $l = 3^n, c = 0, f = 1$.

(i) If $l = 1$, then {If $a = (0)$, then end; else $c = c + 1, f = (1 - x)f$, end.}

(ii) If $l \neq 1$, then $l = l/3$, denote $M = l, A_i = (a_{(i-1)M}, a_{(i-1)M+1}, \cdots, a_{iM-1})$, $i = 1, 2, 3$. Set count=0.

(iii) If $A_1 + A_2 + A_3 = 0$, then {count= count+1, if count<3, then set $A_2 = A_2 + A_1, A_3 = A_3 + A_2$, repeat (iii); if count=3, then end.}

(iv) If $A_1 + A_2 + A_3 \neq 0$, then $a = A_1 + A_2 + A_3$, $c = c + (2 - count)M, f = f(1 - x^M)^{2 - count}$, go to (i).

(v) The final. The linear complexity of $s : c(s) = c$; the minimal polynomial of $s : f_s(x) = f$.

The algorithm computes the minimal polynomial in $2n + 1$ loops at most.

Let s be a sequence over $GF(3)$ with period N and $a = (a_0, a_1, \cdots, a_{N-1})$ be the first period, where $N = 3^n p^m$, p is a prime and 3 is a primitive root modulo p^2. From theorem 2.2, the computation of $f_s(x)$ is equivalent to that of $f_{(b)}(x)$ and $\Phi_{p^m}(x)^z$, where $b = (A_1 + A_4 + \cdots + A_{3p-2}, A_2 + A_5 + \cdots + A_{3p-1}, A_3 + A_6 + \cdots + A_{3p})$. So we first introduce the following algorithm to compute $\Phi_{p^m}(x)^z$.

Algorithm 3.3. Initial values: $a = (a_0, a_1, \cdots, a_{N-1})$ is the first period of s, $l = 3^n$, $c = 0$, $f = 1$, we denote $k = p^{m-1}$.

(i) If $a = (0, \cdots, 0)$, then end ;if $l = 1$, then{let $A_i = (a_{(i-1)k}, a_{(i-1)k+1}, \cdots, a_{ik-1})$, $i = 1, 2, \cdots, p$. If $A_1 = A_2 = \cdots = A_p$, then end; else, $c = c + (p-1)k$, $f = f\Phi_{pk}(x)$, end.}

(ii) If $l \neq 1$, then $l = l/3$, denote $M = lk$, $A_i = (a_{(i-1)M}, a_{(i-1)M+1}, \cdots, a_{iM-1})$, $i = 1, 2, \cdots, 3p$. Set count=0.

(iii) If $A_1 + A_{p+1} + A_{2p+1} = A_2 + A_{p+2} + A_{2p+2} = \cdots = A_p + A_{2p} + A_{3p}$, then{count= count+1, if count<3, set $A_1', A_2', \cdots, A_{3p}'$ according to the definition in theorem 2.1, set $A_1 = A_1', A_2 = A_2', \cdots, A_{3p} = A_{3p}'$, repeat (iii); if count=3, end. }

(iv) If $A_1 + A_{p+1} + A_{2p+1} = A_2 + A_{p+2} + A_{2p+2} = \cdots = A_p + A_{2p} + A_{3p}$ does not hold, then $a = (A_1 + A_{p+1} + A_{2p+1}, A_2 + A_{p+2} + A_{2p+2}, \cdots, A_p + A_{2p} + A_{3p})$, $c = c + (2 - count)(p-1)M$, $f = f\Phi_{pk}(x)^{(2-count)l}$, go to (i)

(v) The final. f is $\Phi_{p^m}(x)^z$, c is $(p-1)p^{m-1}z$.

From theorem 2.1 and theorem 2.2, algorithm 3.3 immediately follows. It computes $\Phi_{p^m}(x)^z$ in $2n + 1$ loops at most.

Now come to our main result, an efficient algorithm for computing the linear complexity and the minimal polynomial of sequences over $GF(3)$.

Algorithm 3.4. Initial values: $a = (a_0, a_1, \cdots, a_{N-1})$ is the first period of s, $l = 3^n$, $k = p^m$, $c = 0$, $f = 1$.

(i) If $a = (0, \cdots, 0)$, then end; if $k > 1$, then $k = k/p$ and go to (iv).

(ii) If $l = 1$, then $c = c + 1$, $f = (1 - x)f$, end; else if $l \neq 1$, then $l = l/3$, denote $M = l$, $A_i = (a_{(i-1)M}, a_{(i-1)M+1}, \cdots, a_{iM-1})$, $i = 1, 2, 3$. Set count=0.

(iii) If $A_1 + A_2 + A_3 = 0$, then {count= count+1, if count<3, then set $A_2 = A_2 + A_1$, $A_3 = A_3 + A_2$, repeat (iii); if count=3, then end.} else if $A_1 + A_2 + A_3 \neq 0$, then $a = A_1 + A_2 + A_3$, $c = c + (2 - count)M$, $f = f(1 - x^M)^{2-count}$, go to (i).

(iv) If $l = 1$, then{let $A_i = (a_{(i-1)k}, a_{(i-1)k+1}, \cdots, a_{ik-1})$, $i = 1, 2, \cdots, p$. If $A_1 = A_2 = \cdots = A_p$, then $a = A_1$,go to (i); else $a = A_1 + A_2 + \cdots + A_p$, $c = c + (p-1)k$, $f = f\Phi_{pk}(x)$, go to (i).}

(v) If $l \neq 1$, then $l = l/3$, denote $M = lk$, $A_i = (a_{(i-1)M}, a_{(i-1)M+1}, \cdots, a_{iM-1})$, $i = 1, 2, \cdots, 3p$. Set $b = (A_1 + A_4 + \cdots + A_{3p-2}, A_2 + A_5 + \cdots + A_{3p-1}, A_3 + A_6 + \cdots + A_{3p})$. Set count=0.

(vi) If $A_1 + A_{p+1} + A_{2p+1} = A_2 + A_{p+2} + A_{2p+2} = \cdots = A_p + A_{2p} + A_{3p}$, then{count= count+1, if count<3, set $A_1', A_2', \cdots, A_{3p}'$ according to the definition in theorem 2.1, set $A_1 = A_1', A_2 = A_2', \cdots, A_{3p} = A_{3p}'$, repeat (vi); if count=3, then $a = b$, $l = 3^n$, go to (i). }

(vii) If $A_1 + A_{p+1} + A_{2p+1} = A_2 + A_{p+2} + A_{2p+2} = \cdots = A_p + A_{2p} + A_{3p}$ does not hold, then $a = (A_1 + A_{p+1} + A_{2p+1}, A_2 + A_{p+2} + A_{2p+2}, \cdots, A_p + A_{2p} + A_{3p})$, $c = c + (2 - count)(p-1)M$, $f = f\Phi_{pk}(x)^{(2-count)l}$.

(viii) If $l = 1$, then{ let $A_i = (a_{(i-1)k}, a_{(i-1)k+1}, \cdots, a_{ik-1})$, $i = 1, 2, \cdots, p$. If $A_1 = A_2 = \cdots = A_p$, then $a = b$, $l = 3^n$, go to (i); else, $c = c + (p-1)k$, $f = f\Phi_{pk}(x)$, $a = b$, $l = 3^n$, go to (i).}

(ix) If $l \neq 1$, then $l = l/3$, denote $M = lk$, $A_i = (a_{(i-1)M}, a_{(i-1)M+1}, \cdots, a_{iM-1})$, $i = 1, 2, \cdots, 3p$. Set count=0, go to (vi).

(x) The final. The linear complexity of s : $c(s) = c$; the minimal polynomial of s : $f_s(x) = f$.

From theorem 2.1, theorem 2.2, algorithm 3.1, algorithm 3.2 and algorithm 3.3, we know that algorithm 3.4 is valid. With a similar argument as that of algorithm 3.2 in [5], it is easy to show that it computes the minimal polynomial in $(2n+1)(m+1)$ loops at most.

4 Numerical Example

To illustrate the algorithm 3.4, we present a numerical example.

Example 4.1. Let s be a sequence over $GF(3)$ with period $N = 3^2 2^3$ and the first period: s^N=100211002201202110202111000012111000 211000112000122211 0110 02200110110201.

From algorithm 3.4, we get the process of computing the minimal polynomial and the linear complexity as follows.

Initial values: $a = s^N, l = 3^2, c = 0, f = 1$.

Step 1. Corresponding to executing algorithm 3.3, where k=4.

(1) $k = 4, l = 3, M = 3 \cdot 2^2$, $A_1 = 100211002201, A_2 = 202110202111$, $A_3 = 000012111000, A_4 = 211000112000, A_5 = 122211011002, A_6 = 200110110201$, $b = (A_1 + A_4, A_2 + A_5, A_3 + A_6)$=011211111201021021210110200122221201. Since $A_1 + A_3 + A_5 \neq A_2 + A_4 + A_6$, we have $a = (A_1 + A_3 + A_5, A_2 + A_4 + A_6)$=222101121200010 220121012, $c = 24, f = \Phi_8(x)^6$.

(2) $k = 4, l = 1, M = 1 \cdot 2^2, A_1 = 2221, A_2 = 0112, A_3 = 1200, A_4 = 0102, A_5 = 2012, A_6$=1012. Since $A_1 + A_3 + A_5 \neq A_2 + A_4 + A_6$, we have $a = 21001220, c = 24 + 8 = 32, f = \Phi_8(x)^8$.

(3) $k = 4, l = 1, A_1 = 2100, A_2$=1220. Since $A_1 \neq A_2$, we have $c = 32 + 4 = 36, f = \Phi_8(x)^9$. Let $l = 3^2, a = b$.

Step 2. Corresponding to executing algorithm 3.3, where k=2.

(1) $k = 2, l = 3, M = 3 \cdot 2, A_1 = 011211, A_2 = 111201, A_3 = 021021, A_4 = 210110, A_5 = 200122, A_6 = 221201, b$=221021011020212222. Since $A_1 + A_3 + A_5 \neq A_2 + A_4 + A_6$, we have $a = 202021212212, c = 36 + 12 = 48, f = \Phi_8(x)^9\Phi_4(x)^6$.

(2) $k = 2, l = 1, M = 1 \cdot 2, A_1 = 20, A_2 = 20, A_3 = 21, A_4 = 21, A_5 = 22, A_6$=12. Since $A_1 + A_3 + A_5 \neq A_2 + A_4 + A_6$, we have $a = 0020, c = 48 + 4 = 52, f = \Phi_8(x)^9\Phi_4(x)^8$.

(3) $k = 2, l = 1, A_1 = 00 A_2$=20. Since $A_1 \neq A_2$, we have $c = 52 + 2 = 54, f = \Phi_8(x)^9\Phi_4(x)^9$. Let $l = 3^2, a = b$.

Step 3. Corresponding to executing algorithm 3.3, where k=1.

(1) $k = 1, l = 3, M = 3 \cdot 1, A_1 = 221, A_2 = 021, A_3 = 011, A_4 = 020, A_5 = 212, A_6 = 222, b$=211200200. Since $A_1 + A_3 + A_5 \neq A_2 + A_4 + A_6$, we have $a = 111200, c = 54 + 6 = 60, f = \Phi_8(x)^9\Phi_4(x)^9\Phi_2(x)^6$.

(2) $k = 1, l = 1, M = 1 \cdot 1, A_1 = 1, A_2 = 1, A_3 = 1, A_4 = 2, A_5 = 0, A_6 = 0$. Since $A_1 + A_3 + A_5 \neq A_2 + A_4 + A_6$, we have $a = 20, c = 60 + 2 = 62, f = \Phi_8(x)^9 \Phi_4(x)^9 \Phi_2(x)^8$.

(3) $k = 1, l = 1, A_1 = 2, A_2 = 0$. Since $A_1 \neq A_2$, we have $c = 62 + 1 = 63, f = \Phi_8(x)^9 \Phi_4(x)^9 Phi_2(x)^9$. Let $l = 3^2, a = b$.

Step 4. Corresponding to executing algorithm 3.2, where $l = 3^2$.

(1) $M = l = 3, A_1 = 211, A_2 = 200, A_3 = 200$. Since $A_1 + A_2 + A_3 = 011 \neq 000$, we have $a = 011, c = 63 + 6 = 69, f = \Phi_8(x)^9 \Phi_4(x)^9 \Phi_2(x)^9 (1 - x^3)^2$.

(2) $M = l = 1, A_1 = 0, A_2 = 1, A_3 = 1$. Since $A_1 + A_2 + A_3 = 2 \neq 0$, we have $a = 2, c = 69 + 2 = 71, f = \Phi_8(x)^9 \Phi_4(x)^9 \Phi_2(x)^9 (1 - x^3)^2 (1 - x)^2$.

(3) $l = 1$. Since $a = 2$, we have $c = 71 + 1 = 72, f = \Phi_8(x)^9 \Phi_4(x)^9 \Phi_2(x)^9 (1 - x^3)^2 (1 - x)^3$.

The final result: $c(s) = 72$ and $f_s(x) = \Phi_8(x)^9 \Phi_4(x)^9 \Phi_2(x)^9 (1 - x)^9$, where $(1 - x)^6 = (1 - x^3)^2$.

5   Conclusion

In this paper, we discussed an efficient algorithm for determining the linear complexity and the minimal polynomial of periodic sequences over $GF(3)$ with period $3^n p^m$, where p is a prime, 3 is a primitive root modulo p^2. A numerical example was presented to illustrate the new algorithm.

We remark that the proposition below can be proved in a similar way to the proof of Theorem 2.1. From Proposition 5.1 and algorithms above, it is straightforward to derive a fast algorithm for determining the linear complexity and the minimal polynomial of periodic sequences over $GF(q)$ with period $q^n p^m$, where p is a prime, q is a prime and is a primitive root modulo p^2.

Proposition 5.1. Let $a = (a_0, a_1, \cdots, a_{N-1})$ be a finite sequence over $GF(q)$, where $N = q^n p^m$, p is a prime, q is a prime and a primitive root modulo p^2. Let us denote $a(x)$ as the generated function of the finite sequence $(a_0, a_1, \cdots, a_{N-1})$, $M = q^{n-1} p^{m-1}, A_i = (a_{(i-1)M}, a_{(i-1)M+1}, \cdots, a_{iM-1}), A_i(x)$ be the generated function of $A_i, i = 1, 2, \cdots, qp$. Then,

(i) $\Phi_{p^m}(x)^{q^{n-1}} | a(x)$ if and only if $A_1 + A_{p+1} + \cdots + A_{(q-1)p+1} = A_2 + A_{p+2} + \cdots + A_{(q-1)p+2} = \cdots = A_p + A_{2p} + \cdots + A_{qp}$;

(ii) If $\Phi_{p^m}(x)^{q^{n-1}} | a(x)$, then $gcd(a(x), \Phi_{p^m}(x)^{q^n}) = \Phi_{p^m}(x)^{q^{n-1}} gcd(A_1'(x) + A_2'(x)x^M + \cdots + A_{qp}'(x)x^{(qp-1)M}, \Phi_{p^m}(x)^{(q-1)q^{n-1}})$, where $A_1' = A_1, A_2' = -A_1 + A_2, \cdots, A_{qp}' = -A_{p-1} - A_{2p-1} - \cdots - A_{qp-1} + A_p + A_{2p} + \cdots + A_{qp}$;

(iii) If $\Phi_{p^m}(x)^{q^{n-1}} \nmid a(x)$, then

$$gcd(a(x), \Phi_{p^m}(x)^{q^n}) = gcd(a(x), \Phi_{p^m}(x)^{q^{n-1}})$$

$$= gcd(\sum_{i=1}^{p} [A_i(x) + A_{p+i}(x) + \cdots + A_{(q-1)p+i}(x)]x^{(i-1)M}, \Phi_{p^m}(x)^{q^{n-1}}).$$

References

1. Games, R.A., Chan, A.H., A fast algorithm for determining the complexity of a binary sequence with period 2^n. IEEE Trans on Information Theory, 1983, **29** (1):144-146.
2. Ding,C. S., Xiao,G..Z., Shan,W.J., The Stability Theory of Stream Ciphers[M]. Berlin/Heidelberg: Springer-Verlag, 1991. 85-88.
3. Blackburn,S.R., A generalization of the discrete Fourier transform: determining the minimal polynomial of a periodic sequence. IEEE Trans on Information Theory, 1994, **40**(5): 1702-1704.
4. Wei,S.M., Xiao,G.Z., Chen,Z., Fast algorithms for determining the linear complexity of periodic sequences. Journal of China Institute of Communications (in Chinese), 2001, **22**(12): 48-54.
5. Wei,S.M., Xiao,G.Z., Chen,Z., A fast algorithm for determining the complexity of a binary sequence with period $2^n p^m$. Science in China (Series F), 2002, **32**(3): 401-408.
6. Wei,S.M., Xiao,G.Z., Chen,Z., A fast algorithm for determining the minimal polynomial of a sequence with period $2p^n$ over $GF(q)$, IEEE Trans on Information Theory, 2002, **48**(10):2754-2758.
7. Massey, J. L., Shift register synthesis and BCH decoding. IEEE Trans on Information Theory, 1969, **15**(1): 122-127.
8. McEliece, R. J., Finite Fields for Computer Scientists and Engineers. Boston: Kluwer Academic Publishers, 1987.
9. Rosen, K. H., Elementary Number Theory and its Applications. Reading: Addison-Wesley, 1988.

Jianqin Zhou received his B.Sc. degree in mathematics from East China Normal University, China, in 1983, and M.Sc. degree in probability and statistics from Fudan University, China. From 1989 to 1999 he was with the Department of Mathematics and Computer Science, Qufu Normal University, China. From 2000 to 2002, he worked for a number of IT companies in Japan. Since 2003 he has been with the Department of Computer Science, Anhui University of Technology, China. His research interests include coding theory, cryptography and combinatorics.

Qiang Zheng received his B.Sc. degree in mathematics from Anqing Teacher College, China, in 2004. Since 2004 he has been a M.E. degree candidate with the Department of Computer Science, Anhui University of Technology, China. His research interests include cryptography and mathematics.

Steganalysis Based on Differential Statistics

Zugen Liu, Lingdi Ping, Jian Chen, Jimin Wang, and Xuezeng Pan

College of Computer Science, Zhejiang University, Hangzhou 310027, China
`lewissy2005@yahoo.com.cn`

Abstract. Differential statistics were proposed in this paper to disclose the existence of hidden data in grayscale raw images. Meanwhile, differential statistics were utilized to improve the algorithm introduced by Fridrich to attack steganographic schemes in grayscale JPEG images. In raw images, to describe the correlation between data and their spatial positions, co-occurrence matrix based on intensities of adjacent pixels was adopted and the use of co-occurrence matrix was extended to high-order differentiations. The *COM*s (center of mass) of *HCF*s (histogram character function) were calculated from these statistics to form a 30-dimensional feature vector for steganalysis. For JPEG files, differential statistics were collected from boundaries of DCT blocks in their decompressed images. The *COM* of *HCF* was computed for each of these differential statistics and statistics from DCT domain so that a 28-dimensional feature vector can be extracted from a JPEG image. Two blindly steganalytic algorithms were constructed based on Support Vector Machine and the two kinds of feature vectors respectively. The presented methods demonstrate higher detecting rates with lower false positives than known schemes.

Keywords: differentiation, co-occurrence matrix, HCF, COM.

1 Introduction

Steganography and digital watermarking have recently emerged as a flourishing research area. Many steganographic software and watermarking algorithms can be downloaded freely from the Internet. People might utilize these tools to communicate secretly with each other. Effective steganalytic techniques are therefore hoped to emerge as means to prevent badmen from covert communicating. Steganalysis aims to expose the presence of hidden messages and, if possible, to extract the hidden messages. Steganalytic techniques can be classified into two categories: targeted and blind. Targeted method is designed to attack specific steganographic algorithm and blind one to conquer various steganographic schemes. Each image is a feature point in the multi-dimensional (M-D) feature space. Blindly steganalytic method has thus become a pattern classification in the M-D feature space.

By using *histogram character function* (HCF) and *center of mass* (COM), Harmsen et al.[1,2] proposed a method to attack cox[3] and piva[4] spread spectrum steganographies in raw images. However, it is found in our experiments that

D. Pointcheval, Y. Mu, and K. Chen (Eds.): CANS 2006, LNCS 4301, pp. 224–240, 2006.

the performance of method in [1] is not good enough for a lot of cover images since it adopts very limited number of features. To attack least significant bit (LSB) matching steganography in grayscale images, Ker[5] introduced two novel ways of applying the HCF: calibrating the output using a down-sampled image and computing the adjacency histogram instead of the usual histogram. In [6], applying HCF and moments of HCF to wavelet sub-bands of gray BMP images, Shi et al. designed a steganalytic method adopting 78-dimensional feature vectors. Compared with [1], its performance has been improved but still not high enough since there are too much relativity among its features calculated using statistical moments of wavelet characteristic function. Lyu et al.[7] proposed to use mean, variance, skewness and kurtosis of coefficients of wavelet sub-bands as features for a general steganalytic method. However, Shi et al.[6] showed the performance of their algorithm outperforms that of Lyu et al.'s method for spread spectrum steganographies in gray BMP images.

Fridrich et al.[8,9] attacked steganographic schemes in gray JPEG files effectively utilizing 21 features from DCT domain and 2 features from sum of differences of intensities distributed at boundaries of DCT blocks. However, Fridrich et al. considered DC coefficients when some features were collected from DCT domain and, the features from spatial domain can not reflect the statistical properties of changes to boundaries of DCT blocks brought by embedded data. Therefore, although Fridrich et al.'s method achieved very good detecting performances for Jsteg[10], F5[11], OutGuess[12] and MB1[13] steganographies, it can not attack MB2[13] and Steghide[14] well. Related researches include Bohme et al.'s work[15] and Lyu et al.'s works[7,16].

In this paper, we introduced differential statistics into steganalysis to attack cox[3] and piva[4] spread spectrum steganographies in raw images and, utilizing differential statistics to improve Fridrich et al.'s methods[8,9] to attack MB2 and Steghide in grayscale JPEG images.

In raw images, the differentiations were computed at pixel-locations in gray BMP image. Firstly, histograms were used to count the frequencies of high order differentiations. Secondly, co-occurrence matrices based on differentiations were calculated at adjacent locations. Finally, *COM* of *HCF* was utilized to calculate features for each of these statistics and, a 30-dimensional feature vector can be obtained from a grayscale raw image.

In JPEG files, firstly, the co-occurrence matrices were used in DCT domain to count the co-occurring state of two AC coefficients at the same locations in original image and its calibrated image. Secondly, in decompressed version of original JPEG image, histogram of intensities distributed at boundaries of DCT blocks were counted. Similarly, histograms of high order differentiations were computed. Finally, *COM*s of *HCF* were utilized to calculate 2 features from each co-occurrence matrix and 1 feature from each histogram. A 28 dimension feature vector can therefore be obtained through these three steps.

Based on the two presented statistical models and Support Vector Machine (SVM), two blindly steganalytic algorithms were constructed. The steganalytic algorithm in grayscale raw images, we call it "***DS***" (*Differential Statistics*) algorithm, was tested on CorelDraw[17] images and Washington[18] images for Cox[3] and Piva[4] steganographies. The steganalytic algorithm in JPEG images, we call it "*MD*" (*Multi-Domain*) algorithm, was tested on CorelDraw[17] images with different qualities for Steghide[14], MB1[13] and MB2[13] Steganographies. The rest of the paper is organized as follows. Section 2 discusses the efficiency of high order differentiations to distinguish stego from its cover version. Section 3 provides the method to extract feature vector in grayscale raw images utilizing differential statistics. Section 4 illustrates how to obtain feature vector in DCT domain and spatial domain from a JPEG file. Section 5 gives details of the experimental scheme. Our work is concluded in Section 6.

2   Efficiency of High Order Differentiations to Distinguish Stego from Its Cover

2.1   High Order Differentiations

Steganography hides data in innocuous covers by embedding bit "0" or "1" in *LSB* (Least Significant Bit) of intensity byte(s) or, changing intensity (adding "1" or subtracting "1" [5]) or DCT coefficients[3,4] tinily. In digital image processing, differential operation is utilized as a high-pass filter for an image. The results of differential processing are just the variable parts, the possible changed parts by steganography[13] in an image. Therefore, high order differentiations can capture the changes brought by steganography in images easily.

To illustrate the formulas of high order differentiations easily, the processed raw files are all supposed to be grayscale images with resolution $M \times N$ and a pixel is represented with 8 bits. Using $b(m, n)$ to denote the intensity at location (m,n) in an image, the first order partial differentiations at location (m,n) can be expressed as $p^{(1,C)}(m, n) = b(m, n+1) - b(m, n)$ in column and $p^{(1,R)}(m, n) = b(m + 1, n) - b(m, n)$ in row respectively. The first order total differentiation at location (m,n) can be written as $d^1(m, n) = |p^{(1,R)}(m, n)| + |p^{(1,C)}(m, n)|$ and second total differentiation be denoted as $d^2(m, n) = p^{(1,R)}(m, n) - p^{(1,R)}(m - 1, n) + p^{(1,C)}(m, n) - p^{(1,C)}(m, n - 1)$. we can therefore get the second order partial differentiation in column as $p^{(2,C)}(m, n) = d^1(m, n + 1) - d^1(m, n)$ and that in row as $p^{(2,R)}(m, n) = d^1(m+1, n) - d^1(m, n)$. The two third order partial differentiations at location (m,n) are $p^{(3,C)}(m, n) = d^2(m, n+1) - d^2(m, n)$ and $p^{(3,R)}(m, n) = d^2(m + 1, n) - d^2(m, n)$ respectively. Without loss of generality, $b(m, n)$ can be looked as the 0-th order differentiation.

2.2   Histograms of High Order Differentiations

Histogram attack is applied in steganalysis widely. From histograms of high order differentiations in a stego and its cover, we can see the efficiency of high order differentiations to differentiate stego from its cover. In Fig. 1, "cover" denotes the histogram of some object for CorelDraw[17] image with serial no. 648000 and "cox" stands related statistic for stego-image produced using Cox[3] method.

The differences between histograms of their high-order differentiations reflect the existence of hidden data.

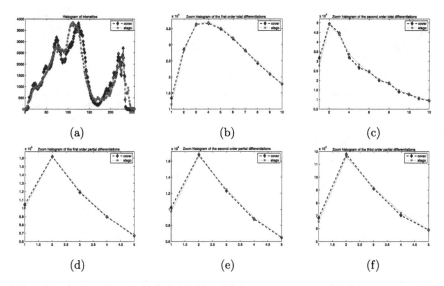

(a)   (b)   (c)

(d)   (e)   (f)

Fig. 1. Histograms of six objects. The six objects are (a)intensity, (b)first and (c)second order total differentiation, (d)first, (e)second and (f)third order partial differentiations.

2.3 *COM* of *HCF* of Histogram

The differences between stego and its cover are not very clear in Fig.1. COM-representations[1,2] of these histograms, points of $(k, COM(H_1[k])), (COM(H_1[k]) = k \cdot H_1[k] / \sum_{k=0}^{\gamma/2-1} H_1[k])$, can make the differences clearer further in sub-figures (a) to (f) of Fig.2. It is very clear that in sub-figure (b) and (c), as frequency increases, the distance between stego and its cover becomes longer. Similar phenomena also occur in other sub-figures. Combining high-order differentiations with co-occurrence matrix, changes caused by hidden data can be more accurately captured. We would utilize such differential statistics to extract more sensitive features which are still not preserved in steganographies.

In JPEG files, as Fridrich concluded, embedded data would make the continual state worse in images. Fridrich et al.'s[8,9] methods attacked MB1 effectively. However, because of considering the DCT block attack[13] and parts of second order statistical properties being preserved, MB2 is more difficult to attack. High order differentiations are introduced to generate much higher order statistics[19] which have not been preserved in embedding operations to attack MB2.

3 Feature Vectors in Grayscale Raw Images

The first and second order partial differentiations reflect the continual property along curves in images. The third order partial differentiation can reveal the

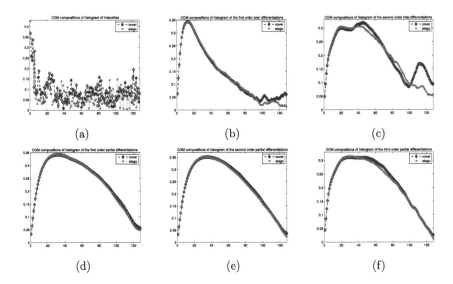

Fig. 2. COM compositions of six histograms in Fig.1

existence of inflexions. The first and second total differentiations are further utilized. The relations between intensities and their spatial locations disclosed in Harmsen et al.'s method remind us that similar statistics can be considered for differentiations. Therefore, co-occurrence matrix is used to denote the relations between higher order differentiations and their locations.

3.1   18 Statistics in Image

Histograms of Intensities, the First and Second Order Total Differentiations. Formula (1) is used to count the frequency of intensity v.

$$h[v] = \sum_{i=0}^{M-1} \sum_{j=0}^{N-1} \varphi[b(i,j), v] \tag{1}$$

where $\varphi[s,t] = 1$ if $s=t$ and 0 otherwise. The histogram of intensities is composed of all the frequencies of all intensities $vs(v \in [0, 255])$. By replacing $b(i,j)$ with $d^1(i,j)$ and modifying the ranges of i, j and v in formula (1), we can get the formula to compute frequency of the first order total differentiation $v(v \in [dMin, dMax]$, $dMin$ denotes the minimal differentiation and $dMax$ the maximum). Similarly, we can calculate frequency of the second order total differentiation v and get histogram of all the second order total differentiations.

Histograms of High Order Partial Differentiations. Formula (2) is utilized to compute frequency of the first order partial differentiation v. Histogram of vs can be attained by iterating v from $dMin$ to $dMax$.

$$h[v] = \sum_{i=0}^{M-1}\sum_{j=0}^{N-2} \varphi[p^{(1,C)}(i,j), v] + \sum_{i=0}^{M-2}\sum_{j=0}^{N-1} \varphi[p^{(1,R)}(i,j), v] \tag{2}$$

Similarly, we can obtain the histograms of the second and third order partial differentiations.

Co-occurrence Matrices of Six Objects at the Adjacent Locations. The six objects are intensity, the first, second and third order partial differentiations, first and second order total differentiations respectively. The adjacent locations can be two neighboring positions in column or in row direction. Using these relations, we can get 12 statistics. Formula (3) is utilized to count frequency of the co-occurring state of two intensities at adjacent locations in column direction. The other formulas can be written out similarly.

$$h[s,t] = \sum_{i=0}^{M-1}\sum_{j=0}^{N-2} \varphi[b(i,j), s] \cdot \varphi[b(i, j+1), t] \tag{3}$$

where, $0 \leq s, t \leq 255$.

3.2 Calculating Features

In Section 3.1, 6 histograms and 12 co-occurrence matrices based on high-order differentiations are computed. Taking 1 dimensional discrete Fourier transform (1-D DFT) of histogram and 2-D DFT of co-occurrence matrix, we define their histogram characteristic functions(HCF), HCF for them are represented as $H_1[k] \triangleq DFT(h[n])$ and $H_2[k] \triangleq DFT_2(h[n])$ respectively. The COM of $H_1[k]$ is thus calculated using formula (4) and (5) is used to get COM of $H_2[k]$.

$$COM(H_1) = (\sum_{k=0}^{\gamma/2-1} k \cdot H_1[k])/\sum_{k=0}^{\gamma/2-1} H_1[k] \tag{4}$$

$$COM(H_2) = \sum_{k_1=0,k_2=0}^{\zeta/2-1,\eta/2-1} (k_1, k_2) \cdot H_2[k_1, k_2]/\sum_{k_1=0,k_2=0}^{\zeta/2-1,\eta/2-1} H_2[k_1, k_2] \tag{5}$$

where γ, ζ and η are maximal indices of frequencies in related dimensions of statistics. Therefore, 30-dimensional feature vector can be collected from a gray image (The number "*30*" is computed as $30 = 6 \times 1 + 12 \times 2$).

4   Feature Vector in JPEG Images

The feature vector is composed of 28 dimension features. The procedure of collecting 28 features from a grayscale JPEG image can be divided into three steps. Firstly, the co-occurring state of two AC coefficients was counted at the same locations in original image and its calibrated image utilizing co-occurrence matrix.

Secondly, in decompressed version of original JPEG image, histograms of intensities and high order differentiations were computed for locations distributed at boundaries of DCT blocks. Finally, HCF was used to calculate the energy distribution of these statistical results in frequency domain and *COM*s of *HCF*s were drawn out as features.

4.1   Statistics in DCT Domain

Fridich[8] et al.'s cropping and recompressing operations were introduced to get calibrated JPEG image from original one so that accurate statistics of DCT coefficients can be obtained. The operations are listed below.

1. Decompress original image J_1 into spatial domain to get B_1.
2. Crop B_1 by 4 pixels in each of horizontal and vertical directions to obtain B_2.
3. Recompress B_2 with the same quantization table as J_1 to generate J_2.

The cropping by 4 pixels is important because the 8×8 grid of recompression "does not see" the previous JPEG compression and thus the obtained DCT coefficients are not influenced by previous quantization (and embedding) in the DCT domain. The calibrated JPEG file obtained by the cropping /recompressing operation can be thought as an approximation to the cover image or a side-information. Using $D_1(i, j)$ to denote the coefficient at location DCT(i,j) in J_1 and $D_2(i, j)$ being corresponding quantity in J_2.

Global Statistics of AC Coefficients. According to [20], in the 8×8 DCT block, the coefficient with zero frequency in both dimensions is called the "DC coefficient" and the remaining 63 coefficients are called the "AC coefficients". After quantization, the DC coefficient is treated separately from the 63 AC coefficients. The DC coefficient is a measure of the average value of the 64 image samples. DC coefficients frequently contain a significant fraction of the total image energy so that a little change to DC coefficients would demolish the quality of the processed image. DCT(0,0) are therefore excluded from embedding. When we calculated statistics of DCT coefficients, DCT(0,0)s were not considered.

Processing images are supposed to be grayscale JPEG files with the resolution $M \times N$. We can calculate co-occurrence distribution of DCT coefficients in original image and its calibrated one exploiting formula (6).

$$G[s,t] = \sum_{r=1}^{R-1}\sum_{c=0}^{C-1}(\sum_{i=0}^{7}\sum_{j=1}^{7}\varphi[D_1(r*8+i, c*8+j), s] * \varphi[D_2(r*8+i, c*8+j), t] +$$

$$\sum_{i=1}^{7}\varphi[D_1(r*8+i, c*8), s] * \varphi[D_2(r*8+i, c*8), t]) \quad (6)$$

where $R = \lfloor M/8 \rfloor$ and $C = \lfloor N/8 \rfloor$. In all DCT coefficients, *dMin* denotes the minimal one and *dMax* is the maximum. The variables s and t satisfy the condition $dMin \le s, t \le dMax$.

Statistics of AC Coefficients at Specific DCT Locations. In the "zigzag" sequence of DCT block, low frequency coefficients (which are more likely to be non-zero) are placed before high frequency coefficients. In JPEG steganographies such as MB1, DCT(0,0) coefficients and zero value coefficients are excluded from embedding. Therefore, steganographies embed secret data in the non-zero and low frequency coefficients. Formula (7) is used to inspect the co-occurrence statistics of coefficients at 8 low frequency locations in a grayscale JPEG file and its calibrated version.

$$g^{(i,j)}[s,t] = \sum_{r=0}^{R-1} \sum_{c=0}^{C-1} (\varphi[D_1(r*8+i, c*8+j), s] * \varphi[D_2(r*8+i, c*8+j), t]) \quad (7)$$

where $ij \in \{10, 20, 01, 11, 02, 12, 22, 21\}$.

Co-occurrence Matrix of Coefficients in Adjacent DCT Blocks. The co-occurrence matrix of coefficients in adjacent DCT blocks describes the probability distribution of pairs of coefficients at same locations in neighboring DCT blocks. Formula (8) is used to collect statistics in original JPEG files for the condition $l=1(l \in \{1,2\})$, otherwise, it does in calibrated images.

$$B_l[s,t] = \sum_{r=0}^{R-1} \sum_{c=0}^{C-2} (\sum_{i=0,j=1}^{7} \varphi[D_l(r*8+i, (c+1)*8+j), s] * \varphi[D_l(r*8+i,$$

$$c*8+j), t] + \sum_{i=1}^{7} \varphi[D_l(r*8+i, (c+1)*8), s] * \varphi[D_l(r*8+i, c*8), t]) \quad (8)$$

4.2   Statistics in Spatial Domain

A grayscale JPEG image J_1 can be decompressed into spatial domain to get a bitmap image B_1. Although JPEG steganographies frequently embed secret data in carriers by modifying their DCT coefficients, these embedding operations would make the boundaries of DCT blocks in the decompressed version more discontinual. High order differential statistics discussed in Section 2 may help to capture the discontinual properties. Formula (9) is utilized to get the histogram of intensities distributed at boundaries of DCT blocks in B_1.

$$h[s] = \sum_{r=0}^{R-2} \sum_{n=0}^{N-1} (\varphi[b(r*8+7, n), s] + \varphi[b((r+1)*8, n), s]) +$$

$$\sum_{m=0}^{M-1} \sum_{c=0}^{C-2} (\varphi[b(m, c*8+7), s] + \varphi[b(m, (c+1)*8), s]) \quad (9)$$

Utilizing the definitions of high order differentiations in Section 2.1, we can easily write out the formulas to calculate histograms of high order differentiations distributed at boundaries of DCT blocks.

4.3 Calculating Features

Using formulas (6), (7) and (8), we calculated 1, 8 and 2 co-occurrence matrices in DCT domain respectively. Utilizing formulas similar to (9), 6 histograms were obtained in spatial domain. From these 17 statistics, a 28 dimensional feature vector can be calculated using methods in Section 3.2.

5   Experimental Results and Discussion

In a raw image, we get a 30-dimensional feature vector and, a 28-dimensional feature vector from a JPEG file. Two proposed blind steganalytic methods were constructed based on SVM and the two kinds of feature vectors respectively. LibSvm[21], the software of SVM, was employed in our experiments. The type of kernel function was set as **RBF**(Radial Basis Function).

5.1 Composition of Experiment

Two Kinds of Original Images and Three Kinds of Covers. CorelDraw[17] and Washington[18] images were used as covers in our experiments. CorelDraw Version 10.0 software CD#3 contains 1096 images in total, including images of leisure, place, animal, food, scenery, architecture and so on. After transforming these images from WI into BMP format using software of Corel Photo Paint 10, we got their gray versions as **CorelDraw cover images** for steganalysis experiments in raw images. Washington image library contains 636 color JPEG files embedded visible watermarks "CREATAS" and 1335 ones without watermarks. We decompress the 1335 JPEG files and get 1324 color BMP images. The gray versions of the 1324 images are **Washington covers** for steganalysis experiments in raw images. The CorelDraw cover images were compressed with qualities 0.7, 0.8 and 0.9 to get covers for steganalysis experiments in JPEG images (**CorelDraw JPEG covers**).

Two Kinds of Spread Spectrum Steganographies for Raw Images and Three Steganographies for JPEG Images. The raw stegos were generated using two types of steganographic methods, i.e., the non-blind spread spectrum (SS) method by Cox et al.[3], the blind spread spectrum method by Piva et al.[4]. The non-blind SS method by Cox et al. is noted for its strong robustness. The hidden data are a random number sequence which complies with Gaussian distribution with zero mean and unit variance. The data are embedded into the 1000 coefficients of global discrete cosine transform (DCT) coefficients of the largest magnitudes. The original cover image is needed for hidden data extraction. The SS method by Piva et al. is blind. That is, it does not need the original cover image for hidden data extraction. It embeds data into 16,000 middle frequency DCT coefficients.

The JPEG stegos were made using MB1, MB2 and Steghide. MB1 algorithm embeds data by modifying the quantized values as most steganographic schemes for JPEG files. This ensures a lossless transmission of all the hidden marginal statistics (histograms) for each individual DCT mode. The MB2 algorithm has the same embedding mechanism as MB1 but reserves one half of the capacity for modifications that bring the blockiness of the stego image to its original value. Steghide uses a graph-theoretic approach to steganography. The embedding algorithm roughly works as follows: at first, the secret data is compressed and encrypted. Then a sequence of positions of pixels in the cover file is created based on a pseudo-random number generator initialized with the passphrase (the secret data will be embedded in the pixels at these positions). Of these positions, those that do not need to be changed (because they already contain the correct value by chance) are sorted out. Then a graph-theoretic matching algorithm finds pairs of positions such that exchanging their values has the effect of embedding the corresponding part of the secret data.

For Steghide, the resolution of embedded image is $n \times n (n \in \{16, 32, 64, 128\})$, a pixel of the image is represented with 8 bits. As to MB1 and MB2, according to [13], the sizes of embedded messages are selected as 10%, 20%, 40%, 60%, 80% and 100% size of maximum embedded capacity for each cover image. The embedding rates can be expressed in bpc (Bits Per non-zero DCT Coefficient). The bpcs of stegos made using MB1 and Steghide schemes are shown in Table 1 and Table 2 respectively. Furthermore, the bpcs of stegos made using MB2 are roughly the halves of those of stegos generated using MB1.

Table 1. BPCs of three kinds of images when MB1 is used to embed messages

Capacity(percent of max.)	10	20	40	60	80	100
Image(0.7)	0.0774	0.1549	0.3097	0.4646	0.6195	0.7739
Image(0.8)	0.0793	0.1586	0.3172	0.4757	0.6343	0.7922
Image(0.9)	0.0833	0.1666	0.3332	0.4998	0.6664	0.8348

Table 2. BPCs of three kinds of images when Steghide is used to embed messages

Capacity(percent of max.)	16×16	32×32	64×64	128×128
Image(0.7)	0.0417	0.0626	0.1183	0.2647
Image(0.8)	0.0331	0.0498	0.0948	0.2145
Image(0.9)	0.0231	0.0348	0.0668	0.1528

Compared Steganalytic Methods. For raw images, schemes in [6,22] were used to extract 78 and 18 dimensional feature vectors respectively and, LibSvm was utilized as classification algorithm. The steganalytic algorithms are named **Shi methods**. For JPEG images, **Fri method** is the compared algorithm with **MD** method. **Fri method** was constructed based on 23 dimensional feature vector[8] and LibSvm.

Train and Test. To evaluate the performance of the proposed steganalysis system, $Y (Y \in \{100, 200, 300, \ldots, K - 10 * X\}$, K is total of some kind of covers and X is the dimension of feature vector) pairs of images are selected as training samples and the others are test samples for each kind of stegos. The Y pairs of images are composed of Y covers and their stegos generated using some steganography. The best results in these multiple groups of open tests are shown in the form of "detecting rate/false positive".

5.2   Experimental Result in Raw Images

It can be observed in Table 3 that DS method outperforms Shi method at a significant advantage. In original Cox scheme, α was set as 0.1. We test the Cox scheme with $\alpha = 0.05$. Meanwhile, we consider the conditions of original value 0.2 and new value 0.1 of α in Piva scheme. It can be found that the given results of Shi method are not so high as those in [6]. In our experiments, when 800 pairs of gray CorlDraw samples were used to train and rest 296 pairs of samples to test, the detecting performance of Shi's method was 96.28%/7.09% for Cox scheme with $\alpha = 0.1$. The detecting result is roughly that in [6]. However, we know it is not practical because the number of test samples must be at least 10 times of the number of features otherwise, we cannot trust the evaluated performance. Furthermore, Piva scheme should be more easily to attack because it hides more bits of secret data in cover than Cox method does in the same cover image. In Table 3, our method shows that stegos made using Piva scheme are more detectable but Shi method draws some reverse conclusions. Similar phenomena also occurred when method in [22] was used to train and test on the same image libraries.

In Table 3, it is obvious that detecting performance of the method in [6] outperforms that of method in [22]. When α is set smaller, Cox scheme and Piva scheme are more difficult to attack for both our steganalytic algorithm and Shi et al.'s methods. Furthermore, the qualities of cover images show much influence to the detecting performances. Compared with Washington covers, CorelDraw

Table 3. Testing results on two kinds of covers

Rates in CorelDraw	Shi[22] method	Shi[6] method	DS method
Cox et al.'s SS($\alpha = 0.05$)	0.8807/0.1925	0.8794/0.1884	0.9564/0.1242
Cox et al.'s SS($\alpha = 0.1$)	0.898/0.0848	0.8516/0.0971	0.9684/0.0503
Piva et al.'s SS($\alpha = 0.1$)	0.8289/0.3926	0.7927/0.2814	0.9468/0.0963
Piva et al.'s SS($\alpha = 0.2$)	0.9358/0.1689	0.8426/0.1261	0.9842/0.0417

Rates in Washington	Shi[22] method	Shi[6] method	DS method
Cox et al.'s SS($\alpha = 0.05$)	0.7222/0.2623	0.8047/0.2012	0.8511/0.1202
Cox et al.'s SS($\alpha = 0.1$)	0.8682/0.3008	0.8823/0.2002	0.9179/0.0821
Piva et al.'s SS($\alpha = 0.1$)	0.7157/0.2198	0.8155/0.1383	0.8125/0.117
Piva et al.'s SS($\alpha = 0.2$)	0.8574/0.1689	0.892/0.1262	0.937/0.0649

Table 4. Contributions of groups of Features in Detecting Performance

Considering Objects	Num. of Fea.	Cox[3] method($\alpha = 0.1$)	Piva[4] method($\alpha = 0.2$)
Intensity	5	0.8794/0.2714	0.9044/0.1359
1-st order partial Diff.	5	0.8277/0.5405	0.9631/0.3473
2-nd order partial Diff.	5	0.848/0.5729	0.8087/0.3641
3-rd order partial Diff.	5	0.6797/0.3554	0.9547/0.3037
1-st order total Diff.	5	0.8406/0.2886	0.9463/0.2064
2-nd order total Diff.	5	0.7567/0.3054	0.9497/0.2584

covers are all cleaner images with higher qualities so that stegos made using CorelDraw covers are more easily to detect and the false positives are smaller.

Contributions of groups of Features in Detecting Performance. In *DS* algorithm, 30-D feature vector is extracted based on 6 objects which are intensity, the first, second and third order partial differentiations, the first and second order total differentiations. To show the contribution of each object for steganalysis, we test performances of the 6 groups of features on CorelDraw images for Cox ($\alpha = 0.1$) and Piva ($\alpha = 0.2$) steganographies. Y ($Y \in \{100, 200, 300, 400, 500\}$) pairs of samples are used to train and, the rest covers and stegos are used as test samples. The best results in these open tests are list in Table 4 in the form of "detecting rate/false positive". It can be observed that the detecting rates of some objects are high. However, the false positive of each object is much larger than that of the whole of 30-D feature vector.

5.3   Experimental Result in JPEG Images

Comparison between two steganalytic methods. In Fig. 3, (a), (b) and (c) are detecting performances of two steganalytic algorithms for MB1, MB2 and Steghide on CorelDraw images respectively. "Fri-fp" and "Fri-dr" are used to denote false positive and detecting rate of *Fri method*. "MD-fp" and "MD-dr" represent false positive and detecting rate of *MD method*. In each sub-figure, performances of each steganalytic method on images with qualities 0.7, 0.8 and 0.9 are plotted respectively. From (a) in Fig. 3, we can find that the false positive of *MD* method is lower 3.69% to 30.2% than that of *Fri method* and detecting rate is higher 3.26% to 16.33% than that of *Fri method* detecting stegos generated using MB1 and covers with quality 0.7. The stegos embedded more message are easier to detect and their false positive become smaller. Meanwhile, from (b) and (c) we can see that similar phenomena occur. It must be noticed that we evaluated the detecting performances of steganalytic algorithms with the practical detecting rates and false positives. However, in [8], detecting performances were represented with "detection reliability $\rho(\rho = 2A - 1)$", where A is the area under the Receiver Operating Characteristic (ROC) curve. Meanwhile, ρ was scaled in order to obtain $\rho = 1$ for a perfect detection and $\rho = 0$ when the ROC coincides with the diagonal line (reliability of detection is 0).

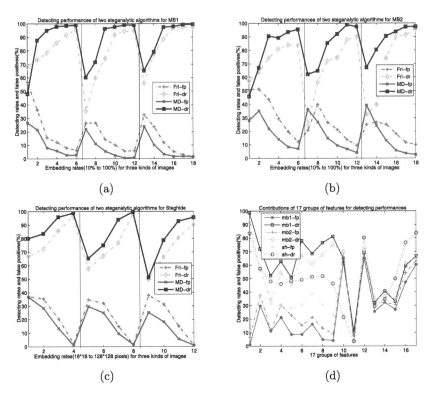

Fig. 3. Detecting performances comparisons between two steganalytic algorithms and contributions of 17 statistics for detecting results

Comparison between images with different qualities. As illuminated in Section 5.1, for MB1 and MB2, because we embedded data in covers according to their capacities, the *bpc*s of stegos become bigger and bigger when quality factor changes from 0.7 to 0.8, and 0.9 eventually. Therefore, in (a) and (b), we can see the detecting performances become better and better when qualities of images are improved. However, embedded messages are certain sizes of images when Steghide was used to generate stegos so that related *bpc*s become smaller when qualities of images are improved. From (c), we can find that stegos become more and more difficult to detect along with ascending of quality factors. When maximum messages are embedded, sometimes the performances of two steganalytic methods get worse because we can only get relatively fewer pairs of training and testing samples from our limited 1096 original covers. From these experiments, we can draw a conclusion that the stegos are more and more easily to be detected with the ascending of *bpc*s.

Contributions of 17 groups of Features in Detecting Performances. To evaluate the contributions of different statistics in detecting performances, we test the detecting performances of the 17 groups of features on covers with quality 0.9 and stegos generated using MB1 and MB2 with 80% of maximal messages. The test of contribution was also done on the same covers and stegos generated using Steghide with 64×64 pixels messages. The detecting results are plotted in (d) of Fig. 3. "mb1-fp" and "mb1-dr" denote the false positives and detecting rates of 13 statistics for stegos made using MB1. The meanings of the rest 4 symbols are similar. In (d), it is clear that false positive of features calculated from each statistic is much higher than that of the whole 28 features. Although each feature is not so efficient to classify covers from their stegos, the integration of 28 features can do.

5.4   Principal Component Analysis to Feature Vectors

We used technique of principal component analysis (PCA) to analyze feature vectors extracted using our method. To plot the feature points in a three-dimensional space, we only selected the maximal three eigenvalues. Therefore, the dimensions of our feature vectors were all decreased to 3. The 3 features of a decreased vector are used as coordinates in x, y and z axis respectively.

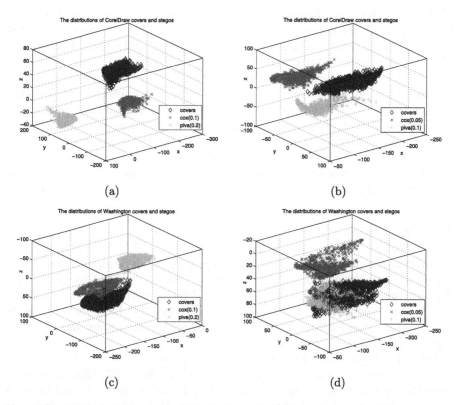

Fig. 4. Distributions of covers and their stegos. In (a), covers are CorelDraw images and stegos were generated using $\cos(\alpha = 0.1)$ and $\text{piva}(\alpha = 0.2)$ schemes. Stegos in (b) were generated using $\cos(\alpha = 0.05)$ and $\text{piva}(\alpha = 0.1)$ schemes. (c) and (d) are the distributions of Washington images and their stegos.

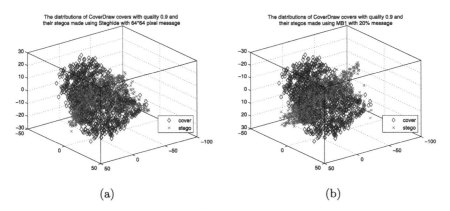

(a)   (b)

Fig. 5. Distributions of covers and their stegos. Covers are CorelDraw images with quality 0.9 and, stegos made using (a)Steghide with 64×64 pixel image, (b)MB1 with 20% of maximal messages.

Therefore, a vector is a feature point in 3-dimension spatial figure. In Fig. 4, (a) and (b) plot the feature points of CorelDraw covers and their stegos generated using cox[3] and piva[4] steganpgraphies. Sub-figure (c) and (d) are distributions of Washington cover images and their stegos. From (a) and (b) in Fig. 4, we observe that covers and their two kinds of stegos can be separated by linear classifier easily. From the comparisons between CorelDraw images and Washington images, we can find the qualities of covers are very important for steganalysis. Of course, we can easily know the influence of α for steganalysis comparing (c) with (d). In Fig.5, (a) plots the feature points of CorelDraw covers and their stegos generated using Steghide scheme embedded with 64×64 pixel image, (b) is distributions of CorelDraw covers and their stegos generated using MB1 scheme embedded with 20% of messages.

6   Conclusion

In this paper, a differential statistics based new steganalytic algorithm was proposed to attack the non-blind spread spectrum (SS) method by Cox et al.[3] and the blind spread spectrum method by Piva et al.[4]. Meanwhile, differential statistics were utilized to improve Fridrich et al.'s[8,9] method. Experimental results show that proposed **DS** and **MD** algorithms achieve significant advancement compared with known schemes.

Differential operations are high-pass filters for images so that tiny changes brought by hidden data can be captured by them. In JPEG files, differential operations can enlarge the discontinuities at boundaries of DCT blocks caused by embedding operations. Our works demonstrate that efficient steganalysis can be obtained based on the consideration of dependencies between covers and embedded messages.

The PCA (*Principal Component Analysis*) processing results show us very impressive visualizing effect. For the future work, we plant to apply PCA technique to select more effective features to construct better steganalytic algorithms.

References

1. Harmsen J J, Pearlman W A. Steganalysis of additive noise modelable information hiding. In Proc. SPIE Electronic Imaging 5022, Santa Clara, CA, January 21-24,(2003), 131-142
2. Harmsen J J, Bowers K D, Pearlman W A. Fast Additive Noise Steganalysis. In Proc. SPIE Symposium on Electronic Imaging, San Jose, CA, January 19-22,(2004), 489-495
3. Cox IJ., Kilian J., Leighton T. , et al. Secure spread spectrum watermarking for multimedia. IEEE Transaction on Image Processing (1997),6(12):1673-1687
4. Piva A., Barni M., Bartolini E, et al. DCT-based watermark recovering without resorting to the uncorrupted original image. In: Proceedings of 4th IEEE International Conference on Image Processing ICIP'97, Atlanta, USA, (1997), 520-523
5. Ker A. Steganalysis of LSB matching in grayscale images. IEEE. Signal Processing Letters, (2005),12(6):441-444
6. Yun Q. Shi, Guorong Xuan, Dekun Zou, Jianjiong Gao, Chengyun Yang, Zhenping Zhang, Peiqi Chai, Wen Chen, Chunhua Chen: Steganalysis Based on Moments of Characteristic Functions Using Wavelet Decomposition, Prediction-Error Image, and Neural Network. In Proc. ICME 2005, Amsterdam, Netherlands, July 6-8,(2005), 269-272
7. Lyu S., Farid H. Detecting hidden messages using higher-order statistics and support vector machines. In Proc. 5th Int. Information Hiding Workshop, Noordwijkerhout, The Netherlands, 2002
8. Fridrich J. Feature-based steganalysis for JPEG images and its implications for future design of steganographic schemes. In Proc. 6th Int. Information Hiding Workshop, Toronto, Ontario, Canada, May 23-25,(2004)67-81
9. Pevny T, Fridrich J. Towards Multi-class Blind Steganalyzer for JPEG Images. In Proc. IWDW 2005, Siena, Italy, September 15-17,(2005)39-53
10. Upham D. Jsteg. ftp.funet.fi.
11. Westfeld A. F5. http://wwwrn.inf.tu-dresden.de/
12. Provos N. http://Outguess. www.outguess.org/
13. Sallee P. Model-based methods for steganography and steganalysis. International Journal of Image and Graphics,(2005),5(1):167-189
14. S. Hetzl. http://steghide.sourceforge.net/
15. Bohme R, Westfeld A. Breaking cauchy model-based. jpeg steganography with first order statistics. In Proc. ESORICS 2004, Sophia Antipolis, France, September 13-15,(2004)125-140
16. Lyu S, Farid H. Steganalysis Using Color Wavelet Statistics and One-Class Support Vector Machines. In Proc. SPIE Symposium on Electronic Imaging, San Jose, CA, January 19-22,(2004)35-45
17. http://www.corel.com/
18. http://www.cs.washington.edu/
19. Chandramouli R., Kharrazi M., Memon N D. Image Steganography and Steganalysis: Concepts and Practice. In Proc. IWDW 2003, Seoul, Korea,October 20-22, (2003), 35-49

20. Wallace G. The JPEG Still Picture Compression Standard. Communications of the ACM, (1991), 34(4):30-44
21. Chih-Chung Chang and Chih-Jen Lin. LIBSVM: a library for support vector machines, (2001). http://www.csie.ntu.edu.tw/~cjlin/libsvm
22. Yun Q. Shi, Guorong Xuan, Chengyun Yang, Jianjiong Gao, Zhenping Zhang, Peiqi Chai, Dekun Zou, Chunhua Chen, Wen Chen. Effective Steganalysis Based on Statistical Moments of Wavelet Characteristic Function. ITCC(1) (2005), 768-773

Watermarking Essential Data Structures for Copyright Protection

Qutaiba Albluwi and Ibrahim Kamel

Department of Computer Engineering
University of Sharjah, UAE
qutaiba@sharjah.ac.ae, kamel@sharjah.ac.ae

Abstract. Software watermarking is a new research area that aims at providing copyright protection for commercial software. It minimizes software piracy by hiding copyright signatures inside the program code or its runtime state. Prior proposals hide the watermarks in dummy data structures, e.g., linked lists and graphs that are created during the execution of the hosting software for this reason. This makes it vulnerable to subtractive attacks, because the attacker can remove the data structure without altering the operation or the semantic of the software program. In this regard, we argue that hiding watermarks in one or more data structures that are used by the program would make the watermark more robust because removing the watermark would alter the semantic and the operations of the underlying software. However, the challenge is that the insertion of the watermark should have a minimal effect on the operations and performance of the data structure.

This paper proposes a novel method for watermarking R-tree data structure and its variants. The proposed watermarking scheme takes advantage of the redundancy in the way the entries within R-tree nodes are ordered. R-trees do not require ordering the entries in a specific way. Node entries are re-ordered in a way to map the watermark. The new order is calculated relative to a "secret" initial order, known only to the software owner, using a technique based on a numbering system that uses variable radix and factorial base. The addition of the watermark in the R-tree data structure neither affects the performance nor increases the size of the R-tree. The paper provides a threat model and analysis to show that the watermarked R-trees are robust and can withstand various types of attacks.

Keywords: Software watermarking, copyright protection, data hiding, indexing, multimedia database.

1 Introduction

Software piracy is one of the main threats targeting software development. A recent study [18] shows that 36% of the software programs used nowadays are pirated. Watermarking is a technique used to provide copyright protection for intellectual properties. Recently there have been a lot of interests in securing and protecting databases [32] [4] [21] [35].

D. Pointcheval, Y. Mu, and K. Chen (Eds.): CANS 2006, LNCS 4301 , pp. 241–258, 2006.

Watermarking means the embedding of digital information into the original work [27]. Watermarks are commonly known in copyright protection of multimedia objects, e.g., images [16] [14], video [20] [23], and audio [11],[29]. In addition to copyright protection, watermarking is used in authentication and privacy protection. Unlike authentication applications, watermarks in copyright protection and privacy applications need to be robust and invisible.

Recently, there has been a lot of interest in applying watermarking techniques to protect the copyrights of the data and the software. Unfortunately, most of the work in this area are trade secrets and are not published.

Technically, most of the software watermarking techniques fall under two categories: *static* watermarking [17] [39] and *dynamic* watermarking [6][30]. In *static* watermarking the watermark is stored in the source code, either in the data section or in the code section. For example, a watermark can be stored in the values of the constants or in debugging information. On the other hand, *dynamic* watermarking stores the watermark in the program's execution state. Static watermarking techniques are considered more fragile as they can be easily attacked by code optimizers or obfuscators [6]. For example, a static watermark that is saved in data strings can be easily attacked by breaking up all strings into substrings scattered over the executable. Unlike static watermarking, in dynamic watermarking the watermarks are generated during the program execution. Usually the watermark is a large integer number[1]. To make the watermark more credible legally, the large integer is chosen to be the multiplication of two large prime numbers [6] [31]. In general, dynamic watermarks are more robust than static ones and can withstand more sophisticated attacks [7]. Our proposed technique falls under the dynamic watermarking category.

Prior techniques in dynamic watermarking hide the watermark in data structures that are built specially for this purpose during the execution of the program. The fact that the data structure is built specifically to house the watermark and it is independent of the application semantic makes the watermark susceptible to subtractive (or removal) attacks. The operation and semantic of the host program will not be affected by removing the data structures that hide the watermark.

We argue that hiding watermarks in data structures, which are used by the program, would make them more robust; because tampering with these data structures would affect the program correctness and/or performance. Software products usually use a number of both memory-based and disk-based data structures e.g., binary trees, linked lists, graphs, B-trees, and R-trees. In general, each data structure requires a watermarking technique that is different from the others. The diversity in the watermarking techniques used in one program will definitely increase the robustness of the whole system and thus, decreases the likelihood of successful attacks.

Notice that disk-based data structures are easier to attack than memory-based data structures because an adversary does not need to execute the application program to attack the watermark. Rather, the adversary can invoke an off-line attack with an independent code. With our proposed algorithm the owner can prove his/her claim by inserting enough records into the data structure to rebuild the watermark.

---

[1] This does not limit the scope of these techniques because any text watermark can be mapped to a numeric watermark.

In this paper, we propose a technique for embedding and extracting watermarks in R-tree and its variants. Our proposed technique has the following desirable features:

- Does not interfere with R-tree functionality and operations
- The watermark does not increase the size of the R-tree
- Robust: it is resilient to various types of attacks
- Simple to implement

The proposed watermarking technique makes use of the redundancy in the order of entries in the R-tree node. It carefully reorders the entries inside the R-tree node to map the watermark.

The next section gives a brief description of the R-tree data structure. Section 3 describes the threat model. In section 0 we discuss some design parameters related to the location and the size of the watermark. Section 0 describes our proposed watermarking scheme and outlines the embedding and extraction algorithms.   In section 0, we provide a threat analysis and evaluation of the proposed techniques. Finally, the related works and the conclusions are presented in sections 0 and 0 respectively.

2   R-Tree

The original R-tree [1] was first suggested by Guttman; it is the extension of the B-tree for multidimensional objects. For simplicity, we describe R-tree data structure in the context of the two dimensional space; however, R-tree and its variants work for any number of dimensions. A geometric object is represented by its minimum bounding rectangle (MBR). Non-leaf nodes contain entries of the form (ptr,R) where ptr is a pointer to a child node in the R-tree; R is the MBR that covers all rectangles in the child node. Leaf nodes contain entries of the form (obj-id, R) where obj-id is a pointer to the object description, and R is the MBR of the object. R-trees allow nodes to overlap. This way, the R-tree can guarantee at least 50% space utilization and at the same time remain balanced.

Figure 1 illustrates data rectangles (in black), organized in an R-tree with fanout 3. Each node in the tree (except the root) contains between m (minimum number of entries per node) and M (maximum number of entries per node) entries, where $m = M/2$. At the same time, each non-leaf node (except the root node) has between m and M child nodes.

R-tree is a balanced data tree; meaning all leaves appear on the same level. The maximum height of the tree can be calculated using the following formula:

$$h = \left| \log {}_m N \right| - 1 \tag{1}$$

Where, N is the number of objects.

Search, insert, delete, split and merge are the popular R-tree operations. The most frequent operation is search. When a node overflows, the split routine is invoked to split the node into two. The split operation is the least frequent operation, but at the same time it is a slow and costly operation. Many techniques have been developed to improve its performance [1]. Contrary to the B-tree, R-trees do not put conditions on the order of entries inside the node. Thus, the search algorithm inspects all entries in the node. Our watermarking algorithm takes advantage of this feature, and hides the watermark by changing the order of entries in the tree.

Our proposed technique works equally on other R-tree variants e.g., packed R-tree [28] [15], the R+-tree [41], and the R*-tree [26].

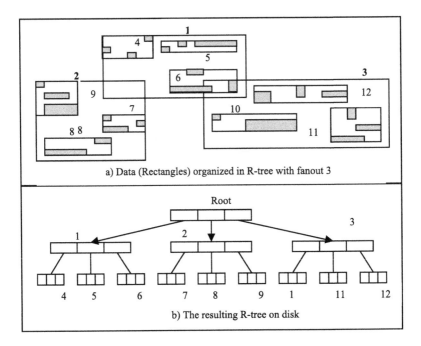

a) Data (Rectangles) organized in R-tree with fanout 3

b) The resulting R-tree on disk

Fig. 1. Example of an R-tree with fan out 3

3 Threat Model

Alice is the owner of the software. She added a watermark to the R-tree. She released only the binary source of her software. Mallory wants to use Alice software without paying intellectual property royalty, thus, he tries to get rid of the watermark that Alice inserted to avoid legal actions.

Before exploring various types of attacks that Mallory can invoke, let us define the following terms:

Robust watermark: Robustness and security are relative measures. There is no system that is 100% secure or a watermark that is 100% robust. However, a system is considered *secure or robust enough*

- if the *cost* of breaking into the system exceeds the cost of the system or benefit from breaking into it, or
- if the *time* required to break into the system exceeds the life time of the data. Let us assume that Mallory wants to remove the watermark from the code

before a certain deadline (like, submission date, inspection or court date). If removing the watermark would take more than the available time window, then the watermark is considered secure or robust.

Code obfuscation: is a set of transformations on a program that preserve the same semantic and specification while making it difficult to reverse-engineer the code. Code obfuscation is very similar to code optimization, except that, obfuscation maximizes obscurity, whereas, optimization minimizes execution time

Reverse engineering: Mallory would use reverse engineering (through de-compilation), to figure out the functionality of the code or identify the watermark and remove it. In [5] it has been argued that the time needed to reverse engineer an obfuscated code is similar to the time needed to rewrite the code from scratch and thus reverse engineering is not a viable attack scenario. If reverse engineering is the only attack that an adversary can invoke on the watermark, then, according to the above definition, the watermark is considered *robust enough*.

Attacks against watermarks fall in three main categories [8][22]:

1) *Subtractive attacks:* In this type of attack, Mallory tries to remove the watermark from the software program inserted by Alice. However, by doing that he might damage parts of the program or some of its functionalities. Thus, the attack is considered successful if the software still retains enough original content to be of value to Mallory.

2) *Distortion attacks:* Mallory might not be able to remove the watermark all together but he might be able to damage or distort the watermark in a way that Alice can not prove the ownership of the code. Mallory should be willing to accept some degradation in quality or the performance of the stolen software.

3) *Additive attacks:* Mallory can insert his own watermark to the software. The new watermark can either replaces the original watermark or is inserted in addition to the original watermark and thus it would be difficult to prove which watermark was inserted first.

4 Design Considerations

Throughout the paper, the notation in Table 1 will be used.

Table 1. Notations

W	Watermark
M	Minimum number of entries per node
M	Maximum number of entries per node
E	A set of entries, where entries ordered as: $E = \{E_1, E_2, E_3 \ldots E_k\}$
E_R	The set of entries E sorted according to the reference order.
E_W	The set of entries E after embedding the watermark.

The proposed watermarking technique makes use of the fact that R-trees do not put requirements on the order of entries inside the R-tree node and hides the watermark W in the order of entries. Thus, the size of watermark (W) that can be hidden depends on the size of the node (number of entries).

4.1 Location of the Watermark

The actual number of entries (fanout) in the R-tree node varies from one node to another depending on the size of the data and the order of insertion. However, R-trees guarantee that nodes are at least half full. To avoid frequent and significant update overhead, the proposed watermarking algorithm uses only the first $M/2$ entries that are guaranteed by R-trees, to hide the watermark. This way the watermark has minimal overhead on the insertion and deletion operations. Typical R-tree node can have couple of hundred entries, so W can be a very large number.   Corollary 2.1 gives a bound on the values of W that can be stored in a given R-tree node.

R-trees have two types of nodes: leaf nodes and non-leaf nodes. However, the structure of the leaf nodes is similar to the structure of the non-leaf node[2]. The proposed watermarking algorithms do not differentiate between leaf and non-leaf nodes and treat them similarly.

There are three possible scenarios for selecting the location of the watermark.

- Store the watermark in a single node
- Store carbon copies of the watermark in a selected subset of nodes or
- Store carbon copies of the watermark in all the nodes.

Contrary to the common practice in image watermarking, hiding the watermark in a single or subset of nodes is easier to detect. Since the code will treat the watermarked node(s) differently, this might alert the adversary that those nodes might be hosting watermarks. Thus, the proposed scheme stores the watermark in all the nodes.

Typical R-tree consists of thousands of nodes. Since we are using all the nodes, one might also hide multiple messages or a large file. This is useful for steganography applications. The file can be divided into small messages. Each message is embedded in one node in the R-tree.

On the other hand, hiding the same watermark (or message) in all nodes offers redundancy that makes the watermarking scheme more robust against possible subtractive attacks. In this paper, we store the same watermark W in all nodes.

4.2 The Effect of R-Tree Operations on the Watermark

The operations that are performed on R-trees can be classified into two main categories: retrieval operations and update operations. Examples of retrieval operations are range queries, nearest neighbor queries and set theoretic queries. Update operations include insertion, split, deletion, and merge. Since the watermark is hidden in the order of entries inside the node, we will investigate the effect of these operations on the entries order.

---

[2] Entries in the leaf nodes point to other R-tree nodes while entries in the leaf nodes point to the object description.

Retrieval Operations: These types of operations do not interfere with the watermark because they do not change the data or the structure of the R-tree. On the other hand, the update operations affect the data and the structure of the R-tree. The problem arises when these operations change the order of the entries inside the node, because these changes might corrupt the watermark.

Split Operations: Splits take place after insertions when nodes overflow. The overflowed node is split into two nodes each with at least $M/2$ entries. The watermarking algorithm should be invoked after split is performed to rebuild the watermark.

Insertion Operation: Insertion adds a new entry to an existing R-tree node. Entries are stored in a sequence. The new entry is inserted in the first available location which will be in the second half of the node[3]. But since the proposed algorithm uses only the first $M/2$ entries for watermarking so inserting a new entry (or object) will not affect the existing watermark. Thus, the watermarking algorithm needs not to be invoked after insertion operations.

Deletion Operations: deletion operations remove entries from anywhere inside the node. Thus, deletion might affect the existing watermark. Moreover, a merge operation might be needed if number of entries fall below the threshold ($M/2$). Thus the watermarking algorithm should be invoked after the deletion and merge operations.

Since the R-tree is stored on the disk, Mallory might try to change the order of the entries and corrupt the watermark even if the program is not running. But since the watermarking algorithm is crafted inside the code, Alice can always prove her claim by inserting enough objects to the database to cause splits and create new nodes that carry the watermark. The following theorem gives the number of objects that one needs to insert to guarantee at least one split in each node.

Theorem 1
For any R-tree of height h, all leaf nodes are going to split at least once if T entries are added, where T is given by:

$$T = M^h - m(M^{h-2} + 1) + 1 \qquad (2)$$

Proof 1
Since each non-leaf node can have a maximum of M entries, then maximum number of leaf nodes $= M^{h-1}$. Similarly, the minimum number of leaf nodes equal to $M^{h-2} + 1$

Therefore, the maximum number of data objects (entries at the leaf level) is given by:

$$E_{max} = M * (M^{h-1}) = M^h$$

Minimum number of leaf entries

$$E_{min} = m (M^{h-2} + 1)$$

The number of insertions that guarantees at least one split is given by $(E_{max} - E_{min} + 1)$. Where

$$E_{max} - E_{min} + 1 = M^h - [m (M^{h-2} + 1)] + 1 \qquad \square$$

---

[3] The first $M/2$ entries are inserted by the split algorithm not the insertion algorithm.

5 Watermarking Algorithm

This section describes the proposed watermarking technique: the watermark embedding algorithm and the watermark extraction algorithm.

5.1 The Basic Idea

The proposed watermarking technique mainly rearranges the entries of the node[4] in such a way to reflect the watermark W that we would like to hide. To achieve that we establish a one to one mapping between all the permutations of the entries at one side and all possible values of W at the other side. Then we use circular shift operator to move entries to their new positions. After fixing the position of the first entry, we apply the circular shift operator on other entries to fix the position of the second entry and so on and so forth.

Basically, there are $k!$ different ways to arrange the entries $E_1, ..., E_k$. If W is an integer decimal number with d digits, then there are 10^d different possible value for W. The first problem we faced is that the number of possible values of W represented in decimal radix format does not match the number of permutation $k!$. Moreover, we realized the need to use a flexible numbering system that can work with variable radix and an alphabet with variable size. Popular numbering systems use fixed radix. For example, decimal systems use radix 10, while binary system uses radix 2.

We worked out the requirement and details of a numbering system that fulfills the previous two requirements. Later, we found an unpopular numbering system that was dated back to 1800s that is similar to ours, called factorial numbering system [13] [12].   Before applying the embedding algorithm we convert W from the decimal system to a factorial system. The following subsection gives a brief description of the factorial number system, and some of its interesting features.

The embedding algorithm first sorts the entries according to the reference order E_R. Then, the entries are shuffled in such a way to reflect the factorial form of W. Starting from the reference order E_R we use circular (left) shift operations to change the order of entries. The number of shift operations depends on the value W. Each node entry E_i moves a number of positions depending on the values of one of the digits of W.

This can be better explained by an example. Let us assume that there are four entries A, B, C, D in the R-tree node and W = "311". The reference order E_R is {A,B,C,D}. Since W has three digits, then the shuffling function will go through three rounds, as illustrated in *Fig.2*.

Since the first digit in W is 3, during the first round, all entries will be shifted to the left three positions as in *Fig.2.a* a resulting in the new order {D,A,B,C}. In the second round, the entries {A, B, C} will be shifted only once, resulting in {D,B,C,A}. The third round shifts the entries {C, A} one time. The final order of the entries would be {D,B,A,C}.

The watermark W can be extracted by comparing the watermarked entries to the reference order E_R. We use a procedure similar to that in *Fig.2*. We use circular shift to align symbols from E_R to E_W. The number of shifts needed to align the first entry (symbol) is the first digit in W. The extraction algorithm is described in Section 0.

---

[4] Calculated relative to some presumed reference sequence E_R of entries.

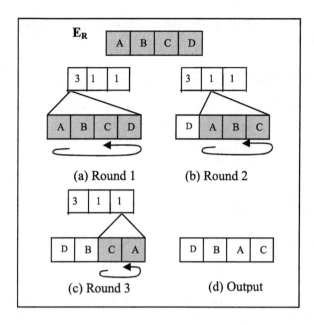

Fig. 2. Example of watermarking embedding

5.2 Factorial Number System

In the factorial system the base of each digit is the factorial of that place index, e.g. place n is of base $n!$. Any integer can be represented in the form:

$$\sum_{k=1}^{n} [a_k * k!] \tag{3}$$

For example, the integer 859 can be represented as
$(1*1!) + (0*2!) + (3*3!) + (0*4!) + (1*5!) + (1*6!)$ which is equivalent to 110301 in the factorial system.

Based on the above, we can define a factorial number (FN) as: *a number where the base of the kth place is $k!$, and the allowed coefficients are between 0 and k.* This condition is important to guarantee one-to-one correspondence between the permutation of the entries and the value of W. For example, a four digits number in the factorial system would have the base and coefficient values presented in Table 3.

Table 2. The relationship between the base and the allowed coefficients in the factorial number system.

Place	Base	Coefficient value
1	$1! = 1$	0,1
2	$2! = 2$	0,1,2
3	$3! = 6$	0,1,2,3
4	$4! = 24$	0,1,2,3,4

The following is an algorithm to convert a number from decimal radix system to factorial radix system:

```
This algorithm converts from decimal to factorial system
Input:
    Decimal number (x)
Output:
    Factorial number (m)
Algorithm:
    1. //Find number of digits n:
    Choose largest L such that: L ! < x
        n = L
        m = int [n]
    2.//Find digits:
        //assume digits are numbered as
        //{ n, n-1, n-2…, 2, 1}
      for (i = n; i>1;i--){
        Find largest k in the range [i, 0] such that
            k* ( i !) < x
        m [i] = k
        x = x - (k*(i !))
      }
    //remainder is put in the least significant digit
        m [i] = x
```

Fig. 3. Conversion from decimal to factorial

To convert from factorial to decimal we use Equation 2. The following theorem and corollary give the largest integer value of W that can be embedded in m entries.

Theorem 2

The decimal value of the largest m-digits factorial number equal to:

$$(m+1)! - 1 \qquad (4)$$

Proof 2

Let x_d be the decimal value of the largest factorial number that can be stored in m places.

From equation (3): $x_d = \sum_{k=1}^{n}[a_k * k!]$ .... (a)

We know from the definition of factorial numbers that a_k can have values in the range $[0, k]$.

Since we want to find the largest number that can fit in m places, we give a_k the maximum possible value which is k. Equation (a) can be rewritten as:

$$x_d = \sum_{k=1}^{n}[k * k!] \quad ... (b)$$

We want to prove that :

$$\sum_{k=1}^{n}[k * k!] = (k+1)! - 1 \quad ... (c)$$

Using induction:

1) for $k = 1$, $x = 1*1! = 1 = (1+1)!-1$
2) assume equation (c) is true, we want to prove that (c) is valid for $k+1$:

$$\sum_{k=1}^{n+1} [k * k!] = (n+2)!-1 \ldots \text{(d)}$$

$$\sum_{k=1}^{n+1} [k * k!] = \sum_{k=1}^{n} [k * k!] + (n+1)(n+1)!$$

From (c) we substitute $\sum_{k=1}^{n} [k * k!]$ with $(n+1)! - 1$:

$$(n+1)! - 1 + (n+1)(n+1)!$$
$$= (n+1)!(n+2)$$
$$= (n+2)! - 1 \qquad \square$$

Corollary 2.1
The permutation of k items equals to the maximum factorial number that can be saved in k-1 places

Proof 2.1
Suppose we have k items.

The permutation of k items $= P_k^k = k!$

Excluding the initial state, $k! -1$ ..... (a)
Let L be a factorial number saved in $k-1$ places.
Using theorem 2: the maximum value of L is:
   $((k-1) + 1)! - 1 = k! - 2$ .... (b)
from (a) and (b) Corollary is proved. $\qquad \square$

The above corollary clarifies the relationship between the size of the node and the size of the watermark W that it can hide. For example, if page size is 8 KBytes, then an R-tree node can store up to 400 entries. Recall that the watermarking algorithm will only use the first half of the entries in the watermarking process. Then if the node maximum capacity $M = 400$, then 200 entries can be used for the watermarking process. Then using Corollary 1, each node can hide a numerical value of W up to:

$$200! = 7.89 * 10^{374}.$$

5.3 Embedding Algorithm

The problem that is addressed in this section can be formulated as follow:
Develop an encoding scheme that takes as an input

1) a numeric value W;
2) a set of entries E; and
3) Reference order E_R.

The encoding scheme should produce a new order E_W such that:

- E_W contains same set of entries in E and E_R
- Given E_W and E_R one can uniquely extracts W
- The calculation of E_W and the extraction of W are efficient and simple

The initialization step converts W from decimal radix system to the factorial radix system. Recall that the order of entries inside the R-tree node is arbitrary and depends on the order of their arrival. To be able to retrieve W from the watermarked node, the entries E should be sorted relative to some default order E_R. This order should be secret and known only to Alice (the owner) to be able to extract W later. E_R can be an arbitrary order or a sort according to some index. For example entries can be sorted on the x-coordinate of the upper left corner of the Minimum Bounding Rectangle (MBR) 28] or sorted according to the Hilbert order [15].

The shuffling algorithm mainly applies circular-left shift on subsets of entries starting with the order E_R. The number of location shifted equal to $W[i]$ where $W[i]$ is the value of the ith digit in factorial radix system. The following is a description of the algorithm.

```
Input:
   E with k entries ,
   Watermark W, number of digits in W is k-1
Output:
   Watermarked set (Ew)
Algorithm:
   For ( i = k-1 ; i > 0 ; i--)
   //Circular-left-shift the subset E [x , y] by the value W [i]
         leftCircularShift (W [i] , E[i+1, k ])
   Where: E[x , y] is a subset of E that contains entries from x to y
   and W[i] is the i^th digit in W
```

Fig. 4. Shuffling function

5.4 Extraction Algorithm

The extraction algorithm is the reverse of the watermarking algorithm. Given a watermarked node and the reference order E_R we need to retrieve the value of W. This is achieved by applying the circular shifts on E_R multiple times in order to make it looks like E_W. The number of applied shifts is used to construct the watermark W. This can be better explained by a counter example. Let us assume E contains four entries A,B,C, and D. The watermarked order is E_W = {D, B, A, C}. Let us also assume that the default order E_R is {A,B,C,D}.

The algorithm mainly tries to align each element from E_R with the corresponding element from E_W. The first element in E_W is "D"; therefore, we need to apply 3 left-circular shifts on E_R in order to achieve this alignment as shown in Figure 5. The value "3" is the most significant digit in W (in factorial radix system). Now E_R = {D,A,B,C}. The entry "D" is in its final position and will not be included in the subsequent circular shift operations. Then apply the same procedure to the next entry "B". Shift the entries {A, B, C} one position to the left. Thus, second digit of W is 1

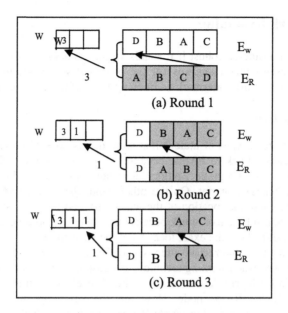

Fig. 5. Example of extracting W from E_R and E_W

and the resulting E_R is {D, B, C, A}. Now "D" and "B" are in their final positions and will not be included in future shift operations. Finally, to align the last two entries in E_R, A and C should be shifted one position. The final result of W would be "311".

The extraction algorithm is described in pseudo-code in Figure 5.

```
Input:
Watermarked node N_W
Reference node N_R
Output:
W_F: watermark in the factorial format.
Algorithm:
Node temp = N_R          //copy reference node
int k = N_W.size
int W [ k-1]             // W has k-1 places

for (i = k-1;  i > 0 ; i--){
//find the distance of the entry E_{i+1} between the subnode N-S_i and temp
    W [i] = CalculateDistance (N_W -S_i ; temp ; N_W [ i + 1] )
    temp = left CircularShift ( temp , W [i] )
    temp = temp-S_{i-1}
}
```

Fig. 6. Extraction Algorithm

In Fig.5 the function *CalculateDistance*() calculates the number of circular shift operations that needed to align an element from E_R with the corresponding element from E_W.

6 Watermark Evaluation

A watermark is considered robust if it stands various attacks and distortion attempts. This section presents threat analysis for the proposed watermarking technique and discusses the effect of the watermark addition on the performance of the R-tree.

6.1 Threat Analysis

From among the three types of attacks that were discussed in *Section 3*, the additive attack is the easiest attack to invoke because it requires zero knowledge about the watermark used in the program. Mallory does not even need to know whether the program is watermarked or not. On the other hand, the subtractive attack requires more knowledge about the location of the watermark and how it is stored. Distortion attack is easier than subtractive attack because the adversary does need to know much accurate information about the exact location of the watermark.

Subtractive attack: Subtractive attacks as defined in *Section 3* can not be invoked against the proposed watermarking technique because the watermark is not occupying physical space in the R-tree data structure; rather, it is encoded in the relative order of the entries inside the R-tree node. However, the adversary might try to invoke subtractive attack by deleting the whole R-tree. In this case, the performance of the code will be affected significantly or it might not work properly. Since R-tree is a secondary storage index structure, Mallory might create a new R-tree that does not contain (Alice) watermark, yet it is similar to Alice R-tree and uses it with Alice's code. The dynamic nature of the proposed watermark provides the solution. Although removing the current R-tree and embedding another one would remove the watermark from pre-watermarked nodes, it can not stop the software from watermarking new nodes. If any split or delete operation is invoked, the watermarking algorithm would be executed. So by inserting enough new objects in the new R-tree, Alice watermark will be created again. Theorem 1 gives the number of objects needed to be inserted to force all the nodes in the R-tree to split at least once.

Distortion attack: If Mallory suspects that there is a watermark hidden in the order of entries, he can access the R-tree, using external code and randomly shuffle all entries in the R-tree node. Again by doing that, the adversary has only corrupted the current watermarks; however, he will not be able to block future watermarks. Therefore, Alice can prove to the judge that she is the owner of the code after inserting T new objects (as defined in Theorem 1) in the R-tree to build the watermark again.

Additive attack: Here Mallory would blindly add his watermark to the software or the R-tree, making it difficult to recognize which watermark is the authentic one. This problem is called the "false claim of ownership". In practice, no watermarking technique is immune to this type of attack 6. One possible solution is to register the watermarks with a third party and time stamp them [30] [38] [37]. In this way the real owner can show that his/her watermark is the original because it has older timestamp.

The above analysis is based on the common assumption that the software is protected and can not be reverse-engineered. Many current software uses obfuscation and other techniques to render the process of reverse-engineering. However, if

Mallory succeeds in obtaining the original code, then applying subtractive and distortion attacks would be much easier. In our algorithm, if Mallory was able to reverse engineer then he can replace the watermarking algorithm with a code that shuffles the R-tree nodes randomly causing meaningless extraction of watermark. However, the accuracy of the current reverse-engineering tools [24], and the size of code would normally make the cost of reverse engineering an obfuscated code more than the cost of building it from scratch [5].

6.2 Effect on the R-Tree Performance

The addition of the watermark to the R-tree has minimal effect on its performance. The most frequent and critical operation in the R-tree is the data retrieval, e.g., range query, nearest neighbor query, join query, etc. Neither the watermark itself nor the watermark embedding algorithms affects R-tree retrieval operations.

The watermarking algorithm is dynamically called after each split/merge or delete request. In practice, split and delete operations are less frequent than insertion and data retrieval operations. Moreover, the watermarking algorithm is a memory-based and it uses simple operations, like, circular shift; therefore, the execution time is negligible.

With respect to the space, the insertion of a watermark in the R-tree does not affect the size of the tree because it is does not occupy physical space on the disk. It is rather encoded in the order of the entries inside the node (relative to a secrete order that is known to the owner only).

7 Related Work

Security research attracted a lot of interest in the research community in areas like databases [35] [32] [4], data mining [9], and Internet transaction [21][3].

The first dynamic software watermark was presented in [6]. The scheme embeds the watermark in the topology of a dummy graph that is built on the heap at runtime. This scheme can be attacked by modifying the pointer topology of the program's fundamental data types, which in turn would change any data structure built at run time. This scheme has been implemented in [19]. The paper provides a detailed discussion on the possible attacks. Khanna and Zane [40] describe a scheme for encoding information in the weights of a graph representing a map so as to preserve shortest paths.

Similar technique was presented in [36], where a watermark is embedded in a control-flow graph that is never executed. Likewise, [2] suggested embedding the watermark in a dummy method that is never executed.

A different approach is presented in [30]. The watermark is embedded in values assigned to designated integer local variables during program execution. The main feature of this scheme is that the watermark can be recovered even if only small part of the code is present. This scheme has been analyzed in [7]. The scheme can be attacked by obfuscating the program such that local variables representing the watermark cannot be located.

Database watermarking technique was introduced in [33] which slightly degrades the data. The main idea is to insert the watermark in the least significant bits in the data values. The authors suggest choosing data that are not sensitive to small changes, e.g., temperature. [25] proposed a technique for data forensics of main memory data structures. The technique is based on a new reduced-randomness construction for non-adaptive combinatorial group testing and it hides information in main memory data structures e.g., arrays, linked list, binary search tree and hash tables to enable them to detect any alteration in the data stored.

Watermarking XML documents was studied by Gross-Amblard [10] and Sion et al. [34]. The idea is to hide the watermark in certain values in a way that preserve the answers to certain queries.

8   Conclusions and Future Work

In this paper we presented a novel technique for hiding watermarks in R-tree data structure. We utilized the fact that R-trees do not put requirements on the order of entries inside the node. The entries are carefully re-ordered according to the value of the watermark. The new order is calculated relative to a secret order E_R using a numbering system with variable radix and factorial base. We presented detailed algorithms for embedding and extraction watermarks and an algorithm that provides a one to one correspondence between a numerical value of the watermark (W) and the permutation of a set of entries. Moreover, the watermark does not increase the size of the R-tree. We provided a threat model for software watermarking and a threat analysis for our proposed method.

Since data structures are essential part of the program logic and their removal would affect manifestly the functionality of the program, we argue that hiding the watermark inside data structures that are used by the software makes the watermark more robust. In the future, we will extend our technique to hide watermarks in other data structures like, B-trees, Binary trees, K-D tree etc.

References

1.   A. Guttman, "R-trees: A dynamic structure for spatial searching", Proc ACM SIGMOD, June 1984, pp. 47-57.
2.   A. Monden, H. Iida, and K. Matusmoto, "A practical method for watermarking java programs," *24th computer software and applications conference* (COMPASAC2000), Taipei, Oct, 2000.
3.   A. Rubin and D. Greer. "A survey of the world wide web security," *IEEE Computer 31 (9)*, September 1998, pp. 34-41.
4.   B. Iyer, S. Mehrotra, E. Mykletun, G. Tsudik and Y. Wu. "A framework for Efficient Storage Security in RDBMS". Proc. EDBT 2004, pp. 147-164.
5.   C. Collberg and C. Thomborson. "Watermarking, tamper-proofing, and obfuscation- tools for software protection," *IEEE transactions on software engineering,* vol.28, no. 8, 2002.
6.   C. Collberg and C. Thomborson., "Software watermarking: models and dynamic Embeddings," *ACM POPL`99*, January 1999, pp.311-324.

7. C. Collberg, E. Carter, S. Debray, A. Huntwork, C. Linn, and M. Stepp, "Dynamic path-based software watermarking," *Proceedings of the ACM SIGPALN '04 conference on programming language design and implementation*, vol. 39, issue 6, June 2004.
8. C. Collberg, J. Nagra, and C. Thomborson, "A functional taxonomy for software watermarking," *Proc. 25th Australian Computer Science Conference 2002*, vol 4, pp. 177-186.
9. D. Barbara, J. Couto and S. Jajodia. " ADAM: A testabed for exploring the use of data mining in intrusion detection,". SIGMOD Record, 30 (4), 2001 pp. 15-24.
10. D. Gross-Amblard. "Query-preserving watermarking of relational databases and XML documents," *ACM Symp on Principles of Database Systems (PODS)*, 2003, pp. 191-201.
11. D. Kirovski, and H. Malvar, "Robust spread-spectrum audio watermarking," *Proceedings of 2001 IEEE International Conference on Acous tics, Speech and Signal Processing*, vol. 3, May 2001, pp. 1345-1348.
12. D.E. Knuth, "The art of computer programming: Volume 2: seminumerical algorithms," *Addison-Wesley*, Third edition, 1998.
13. F. Smarandache, "Definitions, solved and unsolved problems, conjectures, and theorems in number theory and geometry," Edited by: M.L.Perez. *Xiquan publishing house*, 2000, p. 29.
14. F.A. Petitcolas, R.J. Anderson, and M.G. Kuhn, "Information hiding: a survey," *Proceedings of the IEEE, special issue on protection of multimedia content*, vol. 87, issue 7, July 1999, pp.1062-1078.
15. I. Kamel and C. Faloutsos. "On packing R-trees," *Second Int. Conf. on Information and Knowledge Management (CIKM)*, November 1993, pp. 490-499.
16. I.J. Cox and M.L. Miller, "Electronic watermarking: the first 50 years," *EURASIP Journal on Applied Signal Processing*, vol. 2002, issue 2, February 2002, pp. 126-132.
17. I.R. Davidson and N. Myhrvold. "Method and system for generating and auditing a signature for a computer program," *US Patent 5559884*, September 1996, Assignee: Microsoft Corporation.
18. Industrial Design and Construction (IDC) and Business Software Alliance (BSA), "Piracy study," July 2004. http://www.bsaa.com.au/downloads/ PiracyStudy070704.pdf
19. J. Palsberg, S. Krishnaswamy, M. Kwon, D. Ma, Q. Shao, and Y. Zhang. "Experience with software watermarking," *Proceedings of ACSAC'00, 16th Annual Computer security applications conference*, pp. 308-316, 2000.
20. J.A. Bloom, I.J. Cox, T. Kalker, J-P.M. Linnartz, M.L. Miller, and C.B. Traw, "Copy protection for DVD video," *Proceedings of the IEEE* , vol 87, Issue 7, July 1999, pp. 1267 -1276.
21. L. Bouganim and P.Pucheral. "Chip-Secured Data Access: Confidential Data on Untrusted Servers", *Proc. Very Large Databases (VLDB), 2002*, Hong Kong China.
22. M. Razeen, A. Ali and N. Muhammad Sheikh. *"State-of-the-art in software watermarking"*, 2nd International Workshop on Frontiers of Information Technology, December 20-21, 2004, Islamabad, Pakistan
23. M. Wu and B. Liu. "Data hiding in image and video: part I- Fundamental issues and solutions," *IEEE Transactions on image processing*, vol. 12, no. 6, June 2003, p. 685.
24. McAfee Research. "State-of-the-art in decompilation and disassembly (SADD)," http://isso.sparta.com/research/documents/sadd.pdf
25. Michael T. Goodrich, Mikhail J. Atallah and Roberto Tamassia. "Indexing Information for Data Forensics," *ACNS 2005*. pp. 206-221.
26. N. Beckmann, H.-P. Kriegel, R. Schneider, and B. Seeger. "The R*-tree: an efficient and robust access method for points and rectangles," *ACM SIGMOD*, May 1990, pp. 322-331.

27. Neil F. Johnson and Sushil Jajodia, "Exploring Steganography: Seeing the unseen," *IEEE Computer*, vol. 31, No. 2, February 1998, pp 26—34.
28. N. Roussopoulos and D. Leifker. "Direct spatial search on pictorial databases using packed R-trees", *Proc. ACM SIGMOD*, May 1985.
29. P. Bassia, I. Pitas, and N. Nikolaidis, "Robust audio watermarking in the time domain," *Multimedia IEEE transaction*, vol. 3, June 2001, pp. 232-241.
30. P. Cousot and R. Cousot. "An abstract interpretation-based framework for software watermarking", *Proceedings of the 31st ACM SIGPLAN-SIGACT,* 2004, pp. 173,185.
31. P.R. Samson. "Apparatus and method for serializing and validating copies of computer software," *US Patent 5,287,408,* February 1994. Assignee: Autodesk, Inc.
32. R. Agrawal, J. Kieman, R. Srikant and Y.Xu. "Hippocratic Dtabases". *Proc of Very Large Databases (VLDB)*. Hong Kong, China, 2002.
33. R. Agrawal, P.J. Haas and J.Kiernan. "Watermarking relational data: framework, algorithms and analysis" The VLDB journal. vol. 12, issue 2, August 2003, pp. 157-169.
34. R. Sion, M. J. Atallah and S. K Prabhakar. "Resilient information hiding for abstract semistructures,". *In Proc. Of the Workshop on Digital Watermarking (IWDW),* 2003, Seoul.
35. R. Sion, M. J. Atallah and S. K. Prabhakar. "Rights protection for relational data," *ACM International Conference on Management Data (SIGMOD)*, 2003, pp. 98-109.
36. R. Venkatesan, V. Vazirani and S. Sinha, "A graph theoretic approach to software watermarking". *Information Hiding Workshop '01*, vol 2137, April, 2001, pp. 157-168,
37. S. Craver and S. Katzenbeisser. "Security analysis of public-key watermarking schemes," *Proceedings of SPIE Mathematics of Data/Image Coding, Compression and Encryption VI*, vol. 4475, 2001, pp. 172-182.
38. S. Craver, N.Memon, B-L. Yeo, and M.Yeung, "On the invertibility of invisible watermarking techniques," *Proceedings of the '97 Int. Conf. on Image Processing.* vol. 1, 1997, p.540
39. S.A. Moskowitz and M. Cooperman, "Method for stega-cipher protection of computer code," *US Patent 5,745,569,* January 1996. Assignee: The Dice Company.
40. S. Khanna and F. Zane. "Watermarking maps: Hiding information in structured data," *ACM/SIAM Symp on Discrete Algorithms*, 2000, pp. 596-605.
41. T. Sellis, N. Roussopoulos, and C. Faloutsos. "The R+ tree: a dynamic index for multi-dimensional objects," *Proc. 13th Innternational Conference on VLDB*, September 1987, pp. 507-518

A Note of Perfect Nonlinear Functions

Xiyong Zhang[1,2], Hua Guo[3], and Jinjiang Yuan[1]

[1] Department of Mathematics, Zhengzhou University,
450052 Zhengzhou, China
xyzhxy3711@sina.com, yuanjj@zzu.edu.cn
[2] Department of Applied Mathematics, Information Engineering University,
450002 Zhengzhou, China
xyzhxy3711@sina.com
[3] School of Computer Science Engineering, Beihang University,
100083 Beijing, China
hua.g@hotmail.com

Abstract. Perfect nonlinear functions are of importance in cryptography. By using Galois rings and investigating the character values of corresponding relative difference sets, we construct a perfect nonlinear function from $\mathbb{Z}_{p^2}^n$ to $\mathbb{Z}_{p^2}^m$ where $2m$ is possibly larger than the largest divisor of n. Meanwhile we prove that there exists a perfect nonlinear function from $\mathbb{Z}_{2p}^2$ to $\mathbb{Z}_{2p}$ if and only if $p = 2$, and that there doesn't exist a perfect nonlinear function from $\mathbb{Z}_{2^k l}^{2n}$ to $\mathbb{Z}_{2^k l}^m$ if $m > n$ and $l(l$ is odd) is *self-conjugate* modulo $2^k (k \geq 1)$.

1 Introduction

Let n, m, q, k, λ be positive integers, p be prime, and $\mathbb{Z}_q$ be the ring of rediue class modulo q. A perfect nonlinear function(abbr.PNF) $f(x)$ is a map from $\mathbb{Z}_q^n$ to $\mathbb{Z}_q^m$ such that the number of the solutions $x \in \mathbb{Z}_q^n$ of the equation $f(x + w) - f(x) = y$ is exact q^{n-m} for $w \neq 0 \in \mathbb{Z}_q^n, y \in \mathbb{Z}_q^m$. The original motivations for the introduction of the notion [11] were the study of S-boxes for block ciphers and the construction of cryptographic functions. It was also revealed in [14] that perfect nonlinear functions may be used to design word-oriented stream cipher based on S-boxes with high efficiency. Furthermore the notion is also relevant to other topics, such as combinatorics (for example relative difference sets ([12,14])), finite geometries(affine and projective planes) and coding theory([3]).

Assume R is a $k-$element subset of a finite multiplicative group G of order mn with a normal subgroup N of order n, R is called an $(m, n, k, \lambda)-$relative difference set (abbr. RDS) in G relative to N provided that the multiset $r_1 r_2^{-1}(r_1 \neq r_2 \in R)$ replicates each element of $G \setminus N$ exactly λ times and replicates no element of N. If $G \cong G/N \oplus N$, then R is called splitting. If $k = n\lambda$, then R is called semi-regular.

Group ring $\mathbb{Z}[G]$ is the standard setting for studying difference sets. In general, a subset D of a finite group G can be regarded as an element $\sum_{g \in D} g$ in $\mathbb{Z}[G]$.

D. Pointcheval, Y. Mu, and K. Chen (Eds.): CANS 2006, LNCS 4301, pp. 259–269, 2006.

Let G^* be the character group of $G \to \mathbb{C}$, where $\mathbb{C}$ is the complex number field. Suppose $\chi \in G^*, D = \sum_g g \in \mathbb{Z}[G]$, we define $\chi(D) = \sum_{g \in D} \chi(g)$, $D^{(-1)} = \sum_{g \in D} g^{-1}$.

Throughout this paper, χ_0 denotes the principal character of G, ξ_q is a primitive q-th root of unity, and all groups will be limited to be abelian and finite.

In the following, we list a well-known definition and some basic results which will be needed in the further sections.

Definition 1. *Let p be a prime number, m a positive integer and $m = p^a m'$ with $(m', p) = 1$. p is called self-conjugate modulo m if there exists a positive integer i with $p^i \equiv -1 \pmod{m'}$. If every prime divisor p of n is self-conjugate modulo m, then n is called self-conjugate modulo m.*

Lemma 1. *[13] Let m be a positive integer and p a prime number which is self-conjugate modulo m. Let $X \in \mathbb{Z}[\xi_m]$ such that $X\overline{X} \equiv 0 \pmod{p^{2a}}$ where $\overline{X}$ is the complex conjugate of X, then we have*

$$X \equiv 0 \pmod{p^a}.$$

Lemma 1 is frequently used in connection with the following so-called Ma Lemma, which is an important tool in the theory of difference sets.

Lemma 2. *[9] Let A be an element in $\mathbb{Z}[G]$ where G is an abelian group with a cyclic Sylow p-group P. Let P_1 denote the unique subgroup of order p. If $\chi(A) \equiv 0 \pmod{p^a}$ for all nonprincipal characters of G, then*

$$A = P_1 X + p^a Y$$

for suitable X and Y in $\mathbb{Z}[G]$, where the coefficients of X and Y can be chosen to be nonnegative if the coefficients of A are nonnegative.

Lemma 3. *Let G be a finite abelian group of order mn with a subgroup N of order n. Then a k-element subset R of G is an (m, n, k, λ)-RDS in G relative to N if and only if for every nonprincipal character χ of G,*

$$|\chi(R)| = \begin{cases} \sqrt{k - \lambda n} & \text{if } \chi \text{ is principal on } N; \\ \sqrt{k} & \text{if } \chi \text{ is nonprincipal on } N. \end{cases}$$

Lemma 4. *Let R be an (m, n, k, λ)-RDS in G relative to N and let $\rho : G \to G/U$ denote the canonical epimorphism, where U is a subgroup of G and $|U| = u$, then we have*

$$\rho(R)\rho(R^{(-1)}) = k + u\lambda \cdot G/U - |U \cap N|\lambda \cdot N/U.$$

If U is a subgroup of N, then $\rho(R)$ is an $(m, n/u, k, \lambda u)$-RDS in G/U relative to N/U.

The following theorem establishes the equivalent connection between perfect nonlinear functions and a kind of relative difference sets.

Theorem 1. *[12,14] Let $G = \mathbb{Z}_q^n \times N$, where $N \cong \mathbb{Z}_q^m$, then $f(x) : \mathbb{Z}_q^n \to \mathbb{Z}_q^m (x \in \mathbb{Z}_q^n)$ is a perfect nonlinear function if and only if the subset $R = \{ (x, f(x)) \mid x \in \mathbb{Z}_q^n \} \subseteq G$ is a splitting $(q^n, q^m, q^n, q^{n-m})-RDS$ in G relative to N.*

The researches on PNFs focus on their existences, constructions and applications. Let's summarize some recent results. In [11], Nyberg proved that the number of input variables of binary PNFs is at least twice the number of output variables, and constructed two kinds of p−ary perfect nonlinear functions. Bolkhuis et al.[1] proved that if there is a PNF from G_1 of order n to G_2 of the same order, then n is a prime power. Carlet and Dubuc[2] obtained some perfect nonlinear functions from $\mathbb{Z}_4^n$ to $\mathbb{Z}_4$ where $n > 1$ and from $\mathbb{Z}_{p^k}^{2n}$ to $\mathbb{Z}_{p^k}$ where $n \geq k$. Gupta and Sarkar [7] constructed some binary perfect nonlinear S-boxes with some cryptographic properties. Zhang et al.[14] proved that PNFs from $\mathbb{Z}_4^n$ to $\mathbb{Z}_4^m$ exist iff $m \leq \lfloor n/2 \rfloor$, and that the existence of a PNF from $\mathbb{Z}_q^n$ to $\mathbb{Z}_q^m (q = 4t + 2$ for some $t)$ implies $m \leq \lfloor n/2 \rfloor$. Ding and Yuan[6] found a family of new PNF from $GF(3^n)$ to $GF(3^n)$ for odd n. Chen et al.[4] constructed splitting RDS in group $\mathbb{Z}_{p^2}^n \times W$ where W is an arbitrary abelian group of order s, $s|n$. By Theorem 1, Chen's RDS may yield a PNF from $\mathbb{Z}_{p^2}^n$ to $\mathbb{Z}_{p^2}^{\lfloor s/2 \rfloor}$ for some divisor s of n.

It seems interesting to study q−ary PNFs where q is not a prime. In this paper, we present a construction as well as some nonexistence results for PNFs. Firstly, we generalize some results in [14]. We prove that there is a PNF from $\mathbb{Z}_{2p}^2$ to $\mathbb{Z}_{2p}$ iff $p = 2$, there doesn't exist a perfect nonlinear function from $\mathbb{Z}_{2^k l}^{2n}$ to $\mathbb{Z}_{2^k l}^m$ if $m > n$ and l (l is odd) is *self-conjugate* modulo $2^k (k \geq 1)$. We also show the existence of a PNF from $\mathbb{Z}_{p^k(p^k+1)}^2$ to $\mathbb{Z}_{p^k(p^k+1)}$ implies the existence of a PNF from $\mathbb{Z}_{(p^k+1)}^2$ to $\mathbb{Z}_{(p^k+1)}$ ($k \geq 1$). Secondly, by using a result due to Hou [8], we find the condition $s|n$ in the construction [4] of PNF from $\mathbb{Z}_{p^2}^n$ to $\mathbb{Z}_{p^2}^{\lfloor s/2 \rfloor}$ can be improved, and construct a perfect nonlinear function from $\mathbb{Z}_{p^2}^n$ to $\mathbb{Z}_{p^2}^m$ where $2m$ is possibly larger than the largest divisor of n.

This note is arranged as follows. First, we give a short review on Galois rings of character p^2. In section 3, we obtain some nonexistence results. Section 4 gives a construction of perfect nonlinear function on group of exponent p^2.

2   Galois Rings over $\mathbb{Z}_{p^2}$

In order to construct relative difference sets, we need to introduce some basics of Galois rings. Interested readers are referred to [4,8] for some details.

Suppose $\phi(x) \in \mathbb{Z}_{p^2}[X]$ is a monic polynomial of degree $n(\geq 2)$, and $\phi(x)(\bmod p)$ is irreducible in $\mathbb{Z}_p[X]$. If there exists one root g of $\phi(x)$ such that $g^{p^n-1} = 1$, then the finite ring $\mathbb{Z}_{p^2}[X]/(\phi(x))$ is a Galois ring, denoted by $GR(p^2, n)$ (abbr.R in this paper).

The unit group of $GR(p^2, n)$ contains a unique cyclic subgroup T^* of order $p^n - 1$, and the *Teichmüller* system of $GR(p^2, n)$ is $T = T^* \cup \{0\} = \{0, 1, g, \cdots, g^{p^n-2}\}$. It is well known that the finite local ring $GR(p^2, n)$ has a unique maximal ideal $B = pGR(p^2, n) = \{0, p, pg, pg^2, \cdots, pg^{p^n-2}\}$, and the field of residue class $GR(p^2, n)/B = \{\bar{0}, \bar{1}, \bar{g}, \cdots, \bar{g}^{p^n-2}\} \cong \mathbb{F}_{p^n}$, the finite field with p^n elements.

For an arbitrary element $\alpha \in GR(p^2, n)$, we have the unique p-adic representation of α, that is, $\alpha = \xi_0 + p\xi_1, \xi_i \in \mathcal{T}, i = 0, 1$. The Frobenius map σ of $GR(p^2, n)$ is defined by

$$\sigma : \alpha = \xi_0 + p\xi_1 \rightarrow \sigma(\alpha) = \xi_0^p + p\xi_1^p$$

for $\alpha \in GR(p^2, n)$ and we have $Aut(GR(p^2, n)) = <\sigma>$.

The trace $Tr(\alpha)$ of $\alpha \in GR(p^2, n)$ is defined by

$$Tr(\alpha) = \sum_{i=0}^{n-1} \sigma^i(\alpha).$$

Let $l : R \rightarrow \mathbb{Z}_{p^2}$ be a nondegenerate linear map. Note that all linear maps from R to $\mathbb{Z}_{p^2}$ are given by $l_\eta(\alpha) = Tr(\eta\alpha)$ for $\alpha \in R$, where $\eta \in R$.

Define ϕ via $\phi(x) = \xi_{p^2}^{l(x)}$ for $x \in R$. Then all the additive characters of R are of the form

$$\phi_\beta(\cdot) = \xi_{p^2}^{l(\beta \cdot)}, \beta \in R.$$

3   Some Nonexistence Results

In this section we discuss the nonexistence of perfect nonlinear functions by using the technique of relative difference sets.

First let's limit our attention to the simplest case of PNF from $\mathbb{Z}_q^n$ to $\mathbb{Z}_q^m$ where q is not a prime or a prime power. Does a PNF from $\mathbb{Z}_{2p}^2$ to $\mathbb{Z}_{2p}$ exist? We cannot give a direct proof. Instead, we make an analysis of corresponding character sums to reduce the search to the size we can handle with computers.

Theorem 1. *There is a PNF from $\mathbb{Z}_{2p}^2$ to $\mathbb{Z}_{2p}$ if and only if $p = 2$.*

Proof. By Theorem 1 and Lemma 4, a PNF from $\mathbb{Z}_{2p}^2$ to $\mathbb{Z}_{2p}$, i.e. a splitting $(4p^2, 2p, 4p^2, 2p)$-RDS in group $\mathbb{Z}_{2p}^3$, yields a splitting $(4p^2, 2, 4p^2, 2p^2)$-RDS in group $\mathbb{Z}_{2p}^2 \times \mathbb{Z}_2$, which produces a Hadamard difference set in group $\mathbb{Z}_{2p}^2$. A result in [10] implies that $p = 2, 3$ if there is a Hadamard difference set in group $\mathbb{Z}_{2p}^2$.

It is easy to see that there exists a splitting $(16, 4, 16, 4)$-RDS, i.e. a PNF from $\mathbb{Z}_4^2$ to $\mathbb{Z}_4$ (cf.[14]). So it suffices to prove the nonexistence of splitting $(36, 6, 36, 6)$-RDS in $\mathbb{Z}_6^3$.

Suppose that there is a splitting $(36, 6, 36, 6)$-RDS in $G = \mathbb{Z}_6^3$, then there should exist a splitting $(36, 3, 36, 12)$-RDS R_1 in $G_1 = \mathbb{Z}_6^2 \times \mathbb{Z}_3 = G_{11} \times G_{12} \times G_{13}$ and a splitting $(36, 2, 36, 18)$-RDS R_2 in $G_2 = \mathbb{Z}_6^2 \times \mathbb{Z}_2 = G_{11} \times G_{12} \times G_{23}$, where $G_{11} \cong \mathbb{Z}_2^2, G_{12} \cong \mathbb{Z}_3^2, G_{13} \cong \mathbb{Z}_3, G_{23} \cong \mathbb{Z}_2 = \{\bar{0}, \bar{1}\}$.

The existence of R_2 implies the existence of a Hadamard difference set D in group $H = \mathbb{Z}_6^2 = G_{11} \times G_{12}$ such that $R_2 = (D, \bar{0}) \cup (H \setminus D, \bar{1})$. Let $K_i (0 \leq i \leq 3)$ be all the distinct subgroups of order 3 in H. Then D is of the form $\sum_{0 \leq j \leq 3} D_j$, where D_j is the sum of 1 or 2 distinct cosets of K_i in H.

Let $G_{11} = \{1, a, b, ab\}$. Assume $R_1 = B_0 + aB_1 + bB_2 + abB_3$, where $B_0, B_1, B_2, B_3 \subset G_{12} \times G_{13}$.

For any nonprincipal character χ of $G_{12} \times G_{13}$, we can extend it to G_1 in four different ways $\chi_1, \chi_2, \chi_3, \chi_4$, where $\chi_1(a) = \chi_1(b) = 1, \chi_2(a) = 1, \chi_2(b) = -1, \chi_3(a) = -1, \chi_3(b) = 1, \chi_4(a) = \chi_4(b) = -1$. Hence

$$
\begin{cases}
\chi_1(R_1) = \chi(B_0) + \chi(B_1) + \chi(B_2) + \chi(B_3), \\
\chi_2(R_1) = \chi(B_0) + \chi(B_1) - \chi(B_2) - \chi(B_3), \\
\chi_3(R_1) = \chi(B_0) - \chi(B_1) + \chi(B_2) - \chi(B_3), \\
\chi_4(R_1) = \chi(B_0) - \chi(B_1) - \chi(B_2) + \chi(B_3).
\end{cases}
\tag{1}
$$

By adding the four equations in (1), we have

$$
\chi(B_0) = \frac{1}{4} \sum_{1 \leq i \leq 4} \chi_i(R_1). \tag{2}
$$

Since R_1 is a $(36, 3, 36, 12)$-RDS in G_1 and 2 is *self-conjugate* modulo 3, $|\chi_i(R_1)|^2 = 36$ by Lemma 3 and furthermore $\chi_i(R_1) = 6\eta_i$ by Lemma 1, where η_i is a 6-th root of unity. By (2) and the fact that $\chi(B_0)$ is an algebraic integer, we say that $|\chi(B_0)|^2 = 0, 9, 27,$ or 36. Similarly, $|\chi(B_i)|^2 = 0, 9, 27,$ or $36, 1 \leq i \leq 3$.

With the above analysis and the help of computer, we find there are only 672×27 (B_0, B_1, B_2, B_3)s supporting a splitting $(36, 3, 36, 12)$-RDS of the form $R_1 = B_0 + aB_1 + bB_2 + abB_3$ in G_1. However, a little computer search indicates that none of these RDSs combined by R_2 (by using Chinese Remainder Theorem) can yield a splitting $(36, 6, 36, 6)$-RDS in $G = \mathbb{Z}_6^3$, i.e. a PNF from $\mathbb{Z}_6^3$ to $\mathbb{Z}_6$.

In [14], the authors proved that the number of input variables of perfect nonlinear function on group of exponent $2l$ (l is odd) is at least twice the number of output variables. The next theorem is similar.

Theorem 2. *Let* $q = 2^k l$ *where* l *is an odd integer,* $k \geq 1$. *If* l *is self-conjugate modulo* 2^k, *then there doesn't exist a perfect nonlinear function from* $\mathbb{Z}_q^{2n}$ *to* $\mathbb{Z}_q^m$ *when* $m > n$.

Proof. It suffices to prove that there doesn't exist a splitting $(q^{2n}, q^{n+1}, q^{2n}, q^{n-1})$-RDS in group $\mathbb{Z}_q^{2n} \times N$, where $N \cong \mathbb{Z}_q^{n+1}$.

If there exists such a relative difference set, then we can obtain a splitting RDS with parameters $(q^{2n}, 2^{k(n+1)}, q^{2n}, l^{2n} 2^{k(n-1)})$ in $G = \mathbb{Z}_q^{2n} \times N'$ relative to the subgroup $N' \cong \mathbb{Z}_{2^k}^{n+1}$.

Let ρ be the canonical projection epimorphism $G \to G/\mathbb{Z}_q^{2n} \cong \mathbb{Z}_q^{n+1}$, $N_1 = \rho(N') \cong \mathbb{Z}_{2^k}^{n+1}$ and $R_1 = \rho(R)$. According to Lemma 4, $\chi(R_1)\chi(R_1^{(-1)}) = q^{2n}$ for every $\chi \in N_1^* \setminus \{\chi_0\}$. By the assumption that l is *self-conjugate* modulo 2^k, we know $\chi(R_1) = \pm q^n \xi_{2^k}^i$ $(0 \leq i \leq 2^k - 1)$ for every nonprincipal character χ of N_1.

Let

$$A_i = \{\chi \in N_1^* \setminus \{\chi_0\} | \chi(R_1) = q^n \xi_{2^k}^i \}, 0 \le i \le 2^k - 1,$$

we have

$$\sum_{\chi \in N_1^*} \chi(R_1) = q^{2n} + \sum_{\chi \in A_i, 0 \le i \le 2^k - 1} \chi(R_1)$$
$$= q^{2n} + q^n \cdot \sum_{0 \le i \le 2^k - 1} |A_i| \xi_{2^k}^i . \tag{3}$$

Let $R_1 = \sum_{r \in N_1} a_r r$, by the Fourier inversion formula and (3), we get

$$a_1 = \frac{1}{|N_1|} \sum_{\chi \in N_1^*} \chi(R_1) = \frac{1}{2^{k(n+1)}} (q^{2n} + q^n \cdot \sum_{0 \le i \le 2^k - 1} |A_i| \xi_{2^k}^i).$$

Because the cyclotomic polynomial of ξ_{2^k} is $x^{2^{k-1}} + 1$ and $a_1 \in \mathbb{Z}$, we can deduce that $|A_i| = |A_{i+2^{k-1}}|, 1 \le i \le 2^{k-1} - 1$.

By $\sum_{i=0}^{2^k-1} |A_i| = 2^{k(n+1)} - 1$, we have

$$|A_0| + |A_{2^{k-1}}| = 2^{k(n+1)} - 1 - 2 \cdot \sum_{i=1}^{2^{k-1}-1} |A_i|. \tag{4}$$

From (4) we deduce that $|A_0| - |A_{2^{k-1}}|$ is odd. However,

$$a_1 = \frac{1}{2^{k(n+1)}} (q^{2n} + q^n (|A_0| - |A_{2^{k-1}}|)),$$

which indicates that a_1 is not an integer, a contradiction.

Theorem 3. Let p be a prime number , $q = p^k + 1$, and $k \ge 1$. If there exists a perfect nonlinear function from $\mathbb{Z}_{p^k q}^2$ to $\mathbb{Z}_{p^k q}$, then there exists a perfect nonlinear function from $\mathbb{Z}_q^2$ to $\mathbb{Z}_q$.

Proof. If there exists a perfect nonlinear function from $\mathbb{Z}_{p^k q}^2$ to $\mathbb{Z}_{p^k q}$, then by Theorem 1, there exists a splitting $((p^k q)^2, p^k q, (p^k q)^2, p^k q)-$RDS in $\mathbb{Z}_{p^k q}^3$ relative to a subgroup of order $p^k q$. By Lemma 4, there exists a splitting $((p^k q)^2, q, (p^k q)^2, p^{2k} q)-$RDS in $G = \mathbb{Z}_{p^k q}^2 \times N$ relative to $N \cong \mathbb{Z}_q$.

Let $H \cong \mathbb{Z}_q^3$ be the subgroup of G and ρ be the canonical projection epimorphism $G \to H$, and $R_1 = \rho(R), N_1 = \rho(N)$.

Let χ_1 be a nonprincipal character of H. By Lemma 3 and Lemma 4, we have

$$\chi_1(R_1)\chi_1(R_1^{(-1)}) = (p^k q)^2 \text{ or } 0,$$

hence

$$\chi_1(R_1)\chi_1(R_1^{(-1)}) \equiv 0 (\text{mod } p^{2k}). \tag{5}$$

Obviously, p is *self-conjugate* modulo q. By Lemma 1 and (5), we have

$$\chi_1(R_1) \equiv 0 (\text{mod } p^k).$$

By Lemma 2, we obtain

$$R_1 = p^k R_2, \tag{6}$$

where $R_2 \in \mathbb{Z}[H]$, and the coefficients of R_2 are all nonnegative.

By the definition of relative difference sets, we get

$$RR^{(-1)} = (pq)^2 + p^2 q(G - N). \tag{7}$$

By (6) and (7),

$$R_2 R_2^{(-1)} = q^2 + q(p^{2k} H - N_1). \tag{8}$$

Let $R_2 = \sum_{h \in H} a_h h$, $a_h \in \mathbb{Z}$ and $a_h \geq 0$, we have

$$\sum_{h \in H} a_h = (p^k q)^2 / p^k = p^k q^2, \tag{9}$$

$$\sum_{h \in H} a_h^2 = q^2 + q(p^{2k} - 1). \tag{10}$$

Since $q = p^k + 1$, we get $q^2 + q(p^{2k} - 1) = p^k q^2$, thus $\sum_{h \in H} a_h = \sum_{h \in H_2} a_h^2$, which implies $a_h = 0$ or 1. As a result, R_2 is a subset of H.

Let $R_3 = H \setminus R_2$. Note that $|R_3| = q^3 - p^k q^2 = q^2$. By (8) and a little calculation, we get

$$R_3 R_3^{(-1)} = q^2 + qH - qN_1. \tag{11}$$

By (11) and the definition of relative difference set, we have shown that R_3 is a splitting (q^2, q, q^2, q)–RDS in $\mathbb{Z}_q^3$ relative to a subgroup of order q , i.e. a perfect nonlinear function from $\mathbb{Z}_q^2$ to $\mathbb{Z}_q$ by Theorem 1.

4 p^2–ARY Perfect Nonlinear Function

In this section, we will give a construction of perfect nonlinear function on group of exponent p^2. Our aim is to obtain perfect nonlinear functions with larger output dimension .

We follow the notations used in section 2. Let W be a finite group of order p^m, $m \leq n$, h a function from T to W satisfying $|h^{-1}(w)| = p^{n-m}$ for any $w \in W$, and

$$D_h = (B, w_0) \cup \bigcup_{\varepsilon \in T} ((1 + p\varepsilon)T^*, h(\varepsilon)), (w_0 \in W).$$

Let ϕ be the character of R defined in section 2. For any $b \in T$, let $f_{(h,b)}(w)$ be a complex-valued function from W to $\mathbb{C}$, defined by

$$f_{(h,b)}(w) = \sum_{h(\varepsilon)=w, \varepsilon \in T} \phi((1 + pb + p\varepsilon)T^*).$$

Lemma 5. D_h is a $(p^{2n}, p^m, p^{2n}, p^{2n-m})-RDS$ in $G = (GR(p^2, n), +) \bigoplus (W, +)$ relative to W if and only if for any $b \in T$ and any $\chi \in W^* \setminus \{\chi_0\}$,

$$|\sum_{w \in W} \chi(w) f_{(h,b)}(w)| = p^n.$$

Proof. Let ψ be an arbitrary character of G, then $\psi = \lambda \bigotimes \chi$, where λ is an additive character of $(GR(p^2, n), +)$ and χ is a character of group W.

We discuss in two cases.

1) χ is principal on W,

$$\psi(D_h) = \lambda(B) + \sum_{\varepsilon \in T} \lambda((1 + p\varepsilon)T^*).$$

If λ is principal, $\psi(D_h) = |D_h| = p^{2n}$.

If λ is of order p, $\lambda(B) = p^n$, $\lambda(T) = 0$, and $\lambda((1 + p\varepsilon)T^*) = \lambda(T^*) = -1$. Thus

$$\psi(D_h) = p^n + |T| \times (-1) = 0.$$

If λ is of order p^2, say $\lambda = \phi_\beta$ where $\beta = (1 + pb)g^u$, $0 \le u \le p^n - 2$, $b \in T$. In this case $\phi_\beta(B) = 0$.

Since

$$
\begin{aligned}
\sum_{\varepsilon \in T} \phi_\beta((1 + p\varepsilon)T^*) &= \sum_{\varepsilon \in T} \phi((1 + pb + p\varepsilon)T^*) \\
&= \sum_{\eta \in T^*} \phi((1 + pb)\eta) \sum_{\varepsilon \in T} \phi(p\eta\varepsilon) \\
&= \sum_{\eta \in T^*} \phi((1 + pb)\eta)\phi(B) \\
&= 0,
\end{aligned}
$$

we have $\psi(D_h) = 0$.

2) χ is nonprincipal on W. In this case, $\sum_{w \in W} \chi(w) = 0$, and

$$\psi(D_h) = \lambda(B)\chi(w_0) + \sum_{\varepsilon \in T} \lambda((1 + p\varepsilon)T^*)\chi(h(\varepsilon)).$$

If λ is principal on R, $\lambda(B) = p^n$, $\lambda((1 + p\varepsilon)T^*) = |T^*|$, then

$$
\begin{aligned}
|\psi(D_h)| &= |\lambda(B)\chi(w_0) + \sum_{\varepsilon \in T} \lambda((1 + p\varepsilon)T^*)\chi(h(\varepsilon))| \\
&= \left||B|\chi(w_0) + p^{n-m}|T^*| \cdot \sum_{w \in W} \chi(w)\right| \\
&= |B||\chi(w_0)| \\
&= p^n.
\end{aligned}
$$

If λ is of order p, $\lambda(B) = p^n$, and $\lambda((1 + p\varepsilon)T^*) = -1$. So

$$|\psi(D_h)| = |\lambda(B)\chi(w_0) + \sum_{\varepsilon \in T} \lambda((1 + p\varepsilon)T^*)\chi(h(\varepsilon))|$$
$$= |p^n\chi(w_0) - p^{n-m} \sum_{w \in W} \chi(w)|$$
$$= p^n.$$

If λ is of order p^2, let $\lambda = \phi_\beta$, where $\beta = (1 + pb)g^u$, and $0 \le u \le p^n - 2$, $b \in T$. In this case $\phi_\beta(B) = 0$, and

$$|\psi(D_h)| = |\phi_\beta(B)\chi(w_0) + \sum_{\varepsilon \in T} \phi_\beta((1 + p\varepsilon)T^*)\chi(h(\varepsilon))|$$
$$= |\sum_{\varepsilon \in T} \phi((1 + pb + p\varepsilon)T^*)\chi(h(\varepsilon))|$$
$$= |\sum_{w \in W} \chi(w) \sum_{h(\varepsilon)=w, \varepsilon \in T} \phi((1 + pb + p\varepsilon)T^*)|$$
$$= |\sum_{w \in W} \chi(w)f_{(h,b)}(w)|.$$

Summing up the calculations above, and by Lemma 3, we conclude D_h is a $(p^{2n}, p^m, p^{2n}, p^{2n-m})$–RDS in G relative to W iff for any $b \in T$ and any $\chi \in W^* \setminus \{\chi_0\}$,

$$|\sum_{w \in W} \chi(w)f_{(h,b)}(w)| = p^n.$$

Lemma 6. *[8] Let $V \subset R/pR$ be a $\mathbb{Z}_p$-subspace such that $\pi^{-1}(V) \cap T \subset \ker l$, where $\pi : R \to R/pR$ is the projection, and $l : R \to \mathbb{Z}_{p^2}$ is a nondegenerate linear map. Let $pb \in pR$ and*

$$D_{(V,pb)} = T^*(1 + pb + V^\perp),$$

where $V^\perp = \{v \in pR \mid l(v \cdot \eta) = 0 \text{ for every } \eta \in \pi^{-1}(V) \cap T\}$. Then for each $\beta \in R$,

$$|\phi_\beta(D_{(V,pb)})| = \begin{cases} -|V^\perp|, & \text{if } \beta = \xi(1 + p\eta), \ \xi \in T^*, \ \eta \in T, \ p\eta + pb \notin V^\perp, \\ |pR| - |V^\perp|, & \text{if } \beta = \xi(1 + p\eta), \ \xi \in T^*, \ \eta \in T, \ p\eta + pb \in V^\perp. \end{cases}$$

In order for the construction in Lemma 6 to work, we should find the subspace $V \subset R/pR$ such that $\pi^{-1}(V) \cap T \subset \ker l$ for some nondegenerate linear map l from R to $\mathbb{Z}_{p^2}$. In [8], Hou et al. have proved that the maximal dimension of such a V is

$$s(p,n) = max_{k|n} k(\lfloor \frac{n/k - 2}{p} \rfloor + 1).$$

Suppose $V_0 \subset R/pR$ satisfy $\pi^{-1}(V_0) \cap T \subset \ker l_0$ for some nondegenerate linear map l_0 and $|V_0| = p^{s(p,n)}$. Let $V_0^\perp = \{v \in pR \mid l_0(v \cdot \eta) = 0 \text{ for every } \eta \in \pi^{-1}(V_0) \cap T\}$.

Let W_0 be an arbitrary group of order $p^{s(p,n)}$, $\{pb_w \mid w \in W_0\}$ be all the distinct cosets of $V_0^\perp$ in pR, and h_0 be a balanced function from $\mathcal{T}$ to W_0 such that

$$h_0^{-1}(w) = \pi^{-1}(pb_w + V_0^\perp) \cap \mathcal{T}, \quad w \in W_0.$$

Hence by Lemma 6, for each character $\phi_\beta(\cdot)(\beta = \xi(1 + pb) \in \mathcal{T})$, there is a unique w_1, such that $\phi_\beta(D_{(V_0, pb_{w_1})}) = |pR| - |V_0^\perp| = p^n - p^{n-s(p,n)}$, and $\phi_\beta(D_{(V_0, pb_w)}) = -|V^\perp| = -p^{n-s(p,n)}$ when $w \neq w_1$.

So for any character $\chi \in W_0^*$,

$$
\begin{aligned}
&| \sum_{w \in W_0} \chi(w) f_{(h_0, b)}(w)| \\
&= | \sum_{w \in W_0} \chi(w) \cdot \phi_\beta(D_{(V_0, pb_w)})| \\
&= |(p^n - p^{n-s(p,n)})\chi(w_1) + (-p^{n-s(p,n)}) \sum_{w \in W_0, w \neq w_1} \chi(w)| \\
&= p^n.
\end{aligned}
\tag{12}
$$

By Lemma 5 and (12), we have

Theorem 4. D_{h_0} *is a splitting* $(p^{2n}, p^{s(p,n)}, p^{2n}, p^{2n-s(p,n)})-RDS$ *in* $G = (GR(p^2, n), +) \bigoplus (W_0, +)$ *relative to* W_0.

Remark 1. Chen [4] constructed a splitting $(p^{2n}, p^s, p^{2n}, p^{2n-s})-RDS$ in $G = (GR(p^2, n), +) \bigoplus (W, +)$ relative to W. However, the condition $s|n$ is needed in [4]. By Theorem 1 and Theorem 4, we obtain a PNF from $\mathbb{Z}_{p^2}^n$ to $\mathbb{Z}_{p^2}^{\lfloor s(p,n)/2 \rfloor}$, where $s(p,n)$ is possibly larger than the largest divisor of n.

References

1. A.Bolkhuis, D.Jungnickl and B.Schmidt, Proof of the prime power conjecture for projective planes of order n with abelian collineation group of order n^2, *Proc.Amer.Math.Soc.*, 130(2002), 1473-1476.
2. C. Carlet and S. Dubuc, On generalized bent and q-ary perfect nonlinear functions, Proceedings of Fifth International Conference on Finite Fields and Applications, 2000, pp.81-94.
3. C.Carlet, C.Ding and J.Yuan, Linear codes from perfect nonlinear maps and their secret sharing schemes, *IEEE Tran. Inform. Theory*, 61(2005),2089-2102.
4. Y.Q.Chen, D.K.Ray-Chaudhuri, and Q.Xiang, Constructions of partial difference sets and relative difference sets using Galois Rings II, *J.Combin.Theory Ser. A*, 76(1996), 179-196.
5. P.Dembowski and T.G.Ostrom, Planes of order n with collineatiion group of order n^2, *Math.Z.*,193(1968),239-258.
6. C.Ding and J.Yuan, A new family of skew Hadamard difference sets, *J.Comb. Theory(A)*, to appear.
7. K. C. Gupta and P. Sarkar, Construction of Perfect Nonlinear and Maximally Nonlinear Multioutput Boolean Functions Satisfying Higher Order Strict Avalanche Criteria, In *Progress in Cryptology - Indocrypt 2003*, LNCS, 2003, pp.107-120.

8. X.Hou, K.H.Leung and Q.Xiang, New partial difference sets in $\mathbb{Z}_{p^2}^t$ and a related problem about Galois rings. *Finite Fields Appl.*, 7(2000),165-188.

9. S.L.Ma, Polynomial addition sets, Ph.D. thesis, University of Hong Kong, 1985.

10. R.L.McFarland, Difference sets in abelian groups of order $4p^2$, *Mitt. Math. Sem. Giessen*,192(1989),1-70.

11. K.Nyberg, Perfect nonlinear S-boxes, *Advances in Cryptology-EUROCRYPT'91*, Springer-Verlag, 1992, pp.378-386.

12. A.Pott, Nonlinear functions in abelian groups and relative difference sets, *Discrete Applied Mathematics*, 138(2004),177-193.

13. R.J.Turyn, Character sums and difference sets , *Pacific J.Math.*, 15(1965), 319-346.

14. X.Zhang, W.Han and S.Fan, On perfect nonlinear functions, *J. Comb. Designs*, 13(2005),349-362.

Chaotic Keystream Generator Using Coupled NDFs with Parameter Perturbing

Xiaomin Wang[1], Jiashu Zhang[1], and Wenfang Zhang[2]

[1] Sichuan Province Key Lab of Signal and Information Processing,
Southwest Jiaotong University, Chengdu 610031, P.R. China
`hornwong@hotmail.com, jszhang@home.swjtu.edu.cn`
[2] School of Information Science and Technology,
Southwest Jiaotong University, Chengdu 610031, P.R. China
`wfzhang2001@163.com`

Abstract. Chaotic cryptology has been widely investigated recently. This paper analyzes the security pitfalls existing in digital chaotic stream ciphers, which work on the well characterized one-dimensional(1-D) chaotic systems. As a practical solution to these problems caused by 1-D chaotic systems, a chaotic keystream generator using nonlinear digital filters with n-D uniform distribution is proposed. To improve system security further and overcome the effects of finite wordlength, the coupling method with parameter perturbing is considered. Detailed theoretical analyses show that it has perfect cryptographic properties, and can be used to construct stream ciphers with higher security than other 1-D chaotic ciphers. Finally, some numeric experiments are made and the experimental results coincide well with the theoretical analyses.

Keywords: Chaos, Cryptology, Keystream, Nonlinear digital filter.

1 Introduction

In recent years, chaotic cryptography has received considerable attention. Both digital and analog chaotic encryption methods have been proposed and analyzed [13, 12, 14, 5, 1, 16, 36, 15, 33, 4, 17, 30, 27, 3, 2]. The main advantage using chaos lies in the observation that a chaotic signal looks like noise for the unauthorized users. Secondly, some interesting properties, such as mixing and sensitivity to initial conditions, can be connected with those of good ciphers, such as confusion and diffusion [13, 12, 14, 5, 1, 24]. Moreover, generating chaotic signal is often of low cost with simple iterations, which makes it suitable for the construction of stream ciphers.

Generally speaking, chaotic stream ciphers use chaotic systems to generate pseudorandom keystream to encrypt the plaintext one by one. Many different chaotic systems have been utilized to generate such keystreams, 2-D Hénon attractor in [2], generalized logistic map in [1], piecewise linear chaotic map

D. Pointcheval, Y. Mu, and K. Chen (Eds.): CANS 2006, LNCS 4301, pp. 270–285, 2006.
© Springer-Verlag Berlin Heidelberg 2006

(PWLCM) in [30, 3, 4, 31]. In [6] multiple chaotic system are used, and in [14, 11] coupled PWLCMs and coupled map lattices are employed irrespectively. The keystreams are then generated from the outputs of underlying chaotic systems by different post-processing methods, e.g., extracting some bits from chaotic orbits [1, 30, 6], determining by which interval the chaotic orbits reach [3, 2, 32], cascading multiple chaotic systems [8], and coupling chaotic systems [14, 11]. Except the algorithms in [14, 11], unfortunately, several keystream algorithms have been known not secure enough [20, 9, 21, 22].

Why so many chaotic keystream algorithms are not secure? The reasons may lie in at least two aspects. One is bad properties of the underlying chaotic systems, i.e, too small key space to resist brute-force attack; irregular attractor regions with periodic windows to hardly select robust keys. The other factor is the improper construction of the output keystreams. For example, the keystreams directly outputting from the chaotic orbit of a single chaotic system, may suffer from the phase space reconstruction or return map attack [26]; the keystreams coming from the symbols, which have fixed relation with intervals the orbit reaching, will leak some secret information to the opponent, and may be susceptible to the nonlinear forecasting attack [25]; the keys with non-equally strong or the key space not a product but a summation of all the parameters involved, will be compromised under the error function attack (EFA) [28]. Besides the above reasons, other factors such as finite realization precision, parameter sensitivity, ergodicity, etc., have not been considered carefully. For detailed discussions please see [20].

Most digital chaotic stream ciphers and pseudorandom number generators, to our best knowledge, employ the 1-D chaotic maps(e.g. logistic map, tent map, Bernoulli map, PWLCM, etc.) due to their well characterized from a theoretical point of view and simple electronic implementation. These maps, however, only preserve 1-D uniform distribution, which result that any successive points in chaotic orbit are not independent each other. Thus the unpredictability of pseudorandom sequence is decreased. The common and efficient approach is of under-sampling, i.e. only sample one point during every n iterations, to eliminate such correlation. Unfortunately, this way reduces the generator speed inevitably, worst case n times. So signals with not only 1-D but n-D uniform distribution are required for chaotic keystream generators(CKGs).

This paper investigates some fascinating properties of nonlinear digital filter(NDF), such as ergodicity and n-dimensional uniform distribution, and then a NDF-based chaotic keystream generator(NDF-CKG) is presented. Different from the existing CKGs, the proposed scheme works on the chaotic systems with n-dimensional uniform distribution. To overcome the effects of finite computing precision, a coupling method with parameter perturbing is utilized. Theoretical analyses and experiments show that the proposed NDF-CKG has perfect cryptographic properties. Benefiting from the inherent parallel structure of filter, furthermore, the NDF-CKG is suitable for software realization with parallel algorithm or digital circuit implementation.

2   Nonlinear Digital Filter with n-D Uniform Distribution

2.1   Conditions of N-D Uniform Distribution in NDF

The chaotic behavior of digital filter has been firstly noticed by Chua, Lin [16,17], and then utilized for secure communication by Frey [36]. These signals generated by digital filter, however, are only *chaotic* but not *uniform* distribution.

Consider an n-D continue-value discrete-time nonlinear digital filter structure depicted in Fig.1 [19], its state space equations are given by:

$$\begin{cases} z_1(t+1) = h \circ \mathrm{mod}\left(\sum_{i=1}^n c_i z_i(t) + \phi\right), \; z_i \in I, \; \phi \in \Phi = R \\ z_k(t+1) = z_{k-1}(t), \; k = 2,3,\ldots,n \\ \quad y(t) = z_1(t+1) \end{cases} \tag{1}$$

where $\mathbf{z} = (z_1, z_2, \ldots, z_n)^T \in Z = I^n$ denotes the vector of state variables, $\mathbf{c} = (c_1, c_2, \ldots, c_n)$ the vector of feedback parameters, $h(\cdot)$ a piecewise linear map defined by $h : I \to I, h(w) = m_k \cdot w + r_k, w \in W_k \subseteq I, k \in \{1, \ldots, M\}$, and $\mathrm{mod}(\cdot)$ is a modulo map given by

$$\mathrm{mod}(v) = v - 2 \cdot \left\lfloor \frac{v+1}{2} \right\rfloor = v - 2 \cdot l \tag{2}$$

where $v \in [-1 + 2 \cdot l, 1 + 2 \cdot l), \; l \in G$

Without loss of generality, suppose $I = [-1, 1]$, $\Phi = [-1, 1)$, and the eigenvalues of (1) are $\lambda_i, i = 1, \ldots, n$. Kelber [19] has proved that (1) is a ergodic chaotic system and preserves n-D uniform distribution

$$f(\mathbf{z}, t) = f(\mathbf{z}) = \begin{cases} 2^{-n} & \mathbf{z} \in I^n \\ 0 & \mathbf{z} \notin I^n \end{cases}, \quad t \in \mathcal{N} \tag{3}$$

only if the following conditions are satisfied:

(i) $h(\cdot)$ is uniform distribution preserving;

(ii) $c_n \in Z, |c_n| > 1$ and $c_i \neq 0, i \in \{1, \ldots, n-1\}$.

Note that if $|c_n| = 1$, then the linear system (i.e. all nonlinearities are replaced by identities) must be unstable. That is, the characteristic polynomial of linear IIR filter, namely $z^n - c_1 z^{n-1} - \cdots - c_n = 0$, must has at least one solution outside the unit circle ($|\lambda_i| > 1$).

The n-NDF satisfied above conditions (named Kelber conditions) is an chaotic system with n-D uniform distribution. Clearly, such a chaotic system has better cryptographic properties than the ones only with 1-D uniform distribution (e.g. tent-like maps). when the n-NDF is realized in real world, however, it inevitably suffers from the effects of finite wordlength. To overcome such effects, the best effective engineering method is perturbation [18]. In addition, the perturbation method can also improve the strength of system security over the original one. This way then, can the output of perturbed NDF still preserve n-D uniform distribution? The answer is yes, and we will give proofs in following subsection.

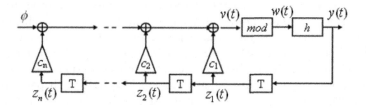

Fig. 1. Block diagram of n-NDF

2.2   Properties of NDF with Parameter Perturbing

In this section, we will prove that the NDF with parameter perturbing is still of ergodicity and n-D uniform distribution. To guarantee $c_n \in Z$, we only perturb the parameters $\{c_1, c_2, \ldots, c_{n-1}\}$. Suppose the perturbing vector at t instance be $\varepsilon_t = (\varepsilon_{t1}, \varepsilon_{t2}, \ldots, \varepsilon_{t(n-1)})$, then the perturbed parameters $\tilde{\mathbf{c}}(t) = (\tilde{c}_1(t), \ldots, \tilde{c}_n(t)) = \mathbf{c} + \varepsilon_t$, are readily given

$$
\begin{cases}
\tilde{c}_1(t) = c_1 + \varepsilon_{t1} \\
\qquad \vdots \\
\tilde{c}_{n-1}(t) = c_{n-1} + \varepsilon_{t(n-1)} \\
\tilde{c}_n(t) = c_n
\end{cases}
\tag{4}
$$

For convenience, let $y_t = F(\mathbf{z}(t), \phi, \mathbf{c})$ be the original NDF, where $t \in \aleph$ the set of discrete time values.

Definition 1. *Assume $I^{n-1}, I \in [-1, 1)$ represent the $(n-1)$th-dimensional perturbing space, $\varepsilon_t \in I^{n-1}$ represent the perturbing point at t instance. Then we call $y_t = F(\mathbf{z}(t), \phi, \tilde{\mathbf{c}}(t))$ the t-th perturbed sub-NDF, and $(F, \tilde{\mathbf{c}}(t), t = T, 2T, \ldots)$ the composite perturbed NDF, where T denotes the unit-time delay.*

For the perturbed NDF, we have following corollaries 1 and 2, and their proofs are given in Appendix.

Corollary 1. *If the t-th perturbed sub-NDF preserves n-D uniform distribution, then the composite perturbed NDF $(F, \tilde{\mathbf{c}}(t), t = T, 2T, \ldots)$ also does.*

Corollary 2. *If the t-th perturbed sub-NDF is ergodic, then the composite perturbed NDF $(F, \tilde{\mathbf{c}}(t), t = T, 2T, \ldots)$ is also ergodic.*

Corollaries 1 and 2 demonstrate that the composite NDF with parameters perturbing is also an ergodic chaotic system with n-D uniform distribution, if and only if the perturbed parameter $\tilde{c}(t)$ satisfies Kelber conditions at any t instance.

3   Chaotic Keystream Generator Using Coupled n-NDFs

As mentioned in Sect.1, the maps used in most CKGs, only preserve 1-D uniform distribution, which result that any two successive points are not independent each other. Thus the randomness of keystream is decreased. In order to enhance the security, many ciphers need multiple iterations to eliminate such correlation. Unfortunately, this way reduces the generator/encryption speed inevitably.

Based on the coupled n-D nonlinear digital filters (n-NDF), a novel chaotic keystream generator (NDF-CKG) is presented in this section. Take advantages of the n-D uniform distribution and the coupled n-NDF with perturbing, the proposed NDF-CKG has very high security. More detailed discussions on security will be given in Sect.4.

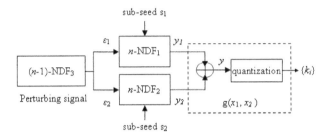

Fig. 2. Architecture of NDF-CKG.
The symbol '$\oplus$' is a modulo operator defined by Eq.(2)

3.1   System Architecture

A keystream generator has a state that evolves in a finite state space Z, according to a recurrence of the form $z(i) = f(z(i-1)), i \geq 1$, where the initial state $z(0) \in Z$ is called the seed, and $f : Z \to Z$ is the transition function. At step i, the generator outputs $k_i = g(z(i))$, where $g : Z \to \{0, 1\}$ is the output function.

In the proposed NDF-CKG(see Fig.2), the transition function consists of two n-dimensional NDFs, namely $n - \text{NDF}_1, n - \text{NDF}_2$, which are given by:

$$y_1(i) = F^{T+i}(s_1) \tag{5a}$$

$$y_2(i) = F^{T+i}(s_2) \tag{5b}$$

where $s = (s_1, s_2) = \{\mathbf{z}_j(0), \phi_j, \mathbf{c}_j(0) | j = 1, 2\}$ is seed including the initial state vectors, feedback parameters and input signals of $n - \text{NDF}_j$. $F^{T+i}(\cdot)$ means to iterate function F for $T + i$ times. Here, T is the minimal pre-iterations for improving system security. It depends on such facts: According to the definition of Lyapunov exponent, the slight difference between s_1 and s_2 causes great difference between $y_1(T)$ and $y_2(T)$ if T is big enough; also the outputs $\{y_1(i)\}, \{y_2(i)\}$ will be independent on each other after some iterations based on Kolmogorov entropy theory [14].

To mix and hide the dynamic information of underlying systems ($n - \text{NDF}_1$, $n - \text{NDF}_2$), the output function $g(x_1, x_2)$ is defined as:

$$g(x_1, x_2) = q_j \circ \text{mod}(x_1 + x_2) \tag{6}$$

where $\text{mod}(\cdot)$ is a modulo map defined by (2), and $q_j(\cdot)$ is a quantization operation to generate binary bit sequence:

$$q_j(x) = \lceil 2^j x \rceil \bmod 2 , \qquad j \in N, j \geq 1 \tag{7}$$

Then a pseudorandom keystream is generated by

$$k_i = g(y_1(i), y_2(i)) \tag{8}$$

Since the outputs of n-NDF preserve n-dimensional uniform distribution, pairs of output values $(y_j(i), y_j(i + l)), j = 1, 2; l = 1, \ldots, n - 1$ are statistically independent. This advantage makes the pseudorandom keystream generated by (8) be more unpredictable than generated by other 1-D chaotic systems in literature.

Notes and Comments. An alternative quantization operator used in Eq.(7) is the bit extracting method [12, 11, 18]. If x is represented with m-bit binary format, and middle $L = \lfloor m/3 \rfloor$ bits are selected as the keystream, the generation speed of keystream will increase L times, without loss of much security.

3.2   Perturbation Principle

Parameter perturbing has two contributions. One is improving the degrade caused by finite realizing precision to extent signal's period; the other is disturbing the regular chaotic orbit to improve system security.

In subsection2.2, we have proved that the perturbed n-NDF is still chaotic with n-D uniform distribution, if perturbed parameters $\tilde{c}(k)$ satisfies Kelber conditions. Detailedly, the conditions, i.e. $|\tilde{c}_n(i)| \in Z^+ \setminus \{0, 1\}$ and $\tilde{c}_j(i) \neq 0$ for $j = 1, \ldots, n-1$ must be satisfied at any step i. According to this criterion, one can simply set the initial parameters of $\text{NDF}_1, \text{NDF}_2$ satisfy $|c_{1j}(0)| > 2, |c_{2j}(0)| > 2, \text{for} j = 1, \ldots, n - 1$. Then only use a $(n - 1)$-dimensional NDF, named NDF_3 to perturb them as follows:

(a) Get the states of NDF_3, which are denoted by $\mathbf{z}_3(i) = (z_{31}(i), \ldots, z_{3(n-1)}(i))$

(b) Scale $\mathbf{z}_3(i)$ with small factors $\delta_j \in [0.1, 0.9]$ to generate two perturbing vectors, named $\varepsilon_j(i) = \delta_j \cdot \mathbf{z}_3(i)$ for $j = 1, 2$.

(c) Use $\varepsilon_j(i)$ to perturb the first $n - 1$ parameters of original $\mathbf{c}_j(i)$ of $n - \text{NDF}_j, j = 1, 2$, then form two group perturbed parameters $\tilde{c}_j(i)$ as expressed in Eq.(4).

Notes and Comments. Actually, the conditions of choosing δ_j are very loose, only if the perturbed parameters satisfy $\tilde{c}_{ij} = c_{ij} + \delta_i \cdot z_{3j} \in \mathcal{R} \setminus \{0\}$, for $i = 1, 2; j = 1, \ldots, n - 1$ at any instance. In order to obtain good perturbing effects, $\delta_1 \neq \delta_2$ is expected. Obviously, if the perturbing intervals $\triangle_1, \triangle_2$ for $n - \text{NDF}_1$ and $n - \text{NDF}_2$ are not equal, i.e. $\triangle_1 \neq \triangle_2$, then $\delta_1 \neq \delta_2$ is not necessary and the step (b) can be skipped.

4   Cryptographic Analyses of NDF-CKG

For a good keystream generator, some necessary conditions are required, such as 0-1 balance, long period, high linear complexity and proper order of correlation immunity. Detailed discussions are given as follows, with some experimental results.

4.1   Balance Property

Theorem 1. *If both perturbed $n-NDF_1$ and $n-NDF_2$ satisfy Kelber conditions, then pseudorandom keystream $k(i)$ is balanced on $\{0,\ 1\}$.*

Proof. Since Kelber conditions are satisfied, it is ready to get from Eq.(3) that, y_1 and y_2 are identical distribution with pdf $f_1(x) = f_2(x) = 2^{-1}$ when $x \in I = [-1, 1)$. Next, we will prove the signal $y = \mod(y_1 + y_2)$ in Fig.2 be uniform distribution with pdf $f_y(y) = 2^{-1}$ when $y \in I = [-1, 1)$.

   case one: $y_1 = y_2$. This case happens when all the initial conditions of $n-NDF_1$ and $n-NDF_2$ are same, i.e. $s_1 = s_2$, $\delta_1 = \delta_2$ and $\triangle_1 = \triangle_2$. From lemma1, then $y = \mod(y_1 + y_2) = \mod(2y_1)$ is uniform distribution on $I = [-1, 1)$.

   case two: $y_1 \neq y_2$. This case happens even if the initial conditions of NDFs are slight difference. Let H represent the relation information of two chaotic orbits. According to Kolmogorov entropy theory, the measurement of information decreasing rate, H will lose completely after $\eta \approx H/\lambda$ iterations [14], where λ is Lyapunov exponent. When chaotic systems are realized discretely, H will decrease even faster since the quantization errors and perturbing signals make two orbits depart faster. So the chaotic orbits $\{y_1(i)\}$, $\{y_2(i)\}$ with different seeds will be independent after η iterations. That is, y_1 and y_2 are independent and identically distributed(i.i.d). From lemma1, therefore, $y = \mod(y_1 + y_2)$ is uniform distribution on $I = [-1, 1)$.

   Summarizing two above cases, y preserves uniform distribution on $I = [-1, 1)$. Since $k_i = \lceil 2^j y(i) \rceil \mod 2, j \in N$, without loss of generality, assume $j = 1$, then $P\{k_i = 1\} = P\{y(i) \in (-1, -0.5] \cup (0, 0.5]\} = 1/2$ and $P\{k_i = 0\} = P\{y(i) \in (-0.5, 0] \cup (0.5, 1]\} = 1/2$. For other $j > 1$, the derivation process is similar. The proof is completed.

4.2   Correlation Properties

For an pseudorandom sequence, the δ-like autocorrelation and the nearly zero crosscorrelation properties are expected. If any bit in pseudorandom sequence is i.i.d, the perfect correlation properties are satisfied.

Theorem 2. *If keystream $\{k_i\}$ is generated by (6)-(8), then each bit in $\{k_i\}$ is i.i.d, i.e. $\forall(a_1, a_2, \ldots, a_n) \in \{0, 1\}^n$, $P(k_1 = a_1, \ldots, k_n = a_n) = 2^{-n}$.*

Proof. The outputs of $n - NDF_{1,2}$, as mentioned in Sect.2, are n-D uniform distribution. That means, pairs of values $(y_j(i), y_j(i+l))$ for $j = 1, 2; l = 1, \ldots, n-1$ are statistically independent. The coupled signal $y = \mod(y_1 + y_2)$, therefore, are also statistically independent on $(y(i), y(i+l))$ for $l = 1, \ldots, n-1$.

$$P(y(i+l)|y(i)) = P(y(i+l)), \qquad l = 1, \ldots, n-1 \tag{9}$$

Based on the discussions in Sect.4.1, further we can conclude that $\mathbf{y} = (y(i), y(i+1), \ldots, y(i+n-1))$ is n-D uniformly distributed.

Now we can use mathematical induction to prove this theorem. Without loss of generality, assume $j = 1$ in $k_i = q_j(y(i))$. For other $j > 1$, the derivation process is similar.

when $n = 1$, $P(k_i = a_i) = 2^{-1}$ is readily got from theorem 1.

Suppose $n = m$, $P(k_i = a_i, k_{i+1} = a_{i+1}, \ldots, k_{i+m-1} = a_{i+m-1}) = 2^{-m}$ holds, then for $n = m + 1$,

$$
\begin{aligned}
P(k_i = a_i, \ldots, k_{i+m} = a_{i+m}) &= P(k_{i+m} = a_{i+m} | k_i = a_i, \ldots, k_{i+m-1} = a_{i+m-1}) \\
&\quad \cdot P(k_i = a_i, \ldots, k_{i+m-1} = a_{i+m-1}) \\
&= 2^{-m} P(k_{i+m} = a_{i+m} | k_i = a_i, \ldots, k_{i+m-1} = a_{i+m-1})
\end{aligned}
$$

From (9) and the i.i.d assumption of $k_i, k_{i+1}, \ldots, k_{i+m-1}$, we may get

$$
\begin{aligned}
P(k_i = a_i, \ldots, k_{i+m} = a_{i+m}) &= 2^{-m} P(k_{i+m} = a_{i+m} | k_{i+m-1} = a_{i+m-1}) \\
&= 2^{-m} P(k_{i+m} = a_{i+m}) \\
&= 2^{-(m+1)}.
\end{aligned}
$$

The proof is completed.

It is well known that the i.i.d bit sequence has δ-like autocorrelation and near-to-zero cross-correlation, as well as half-length linear complexity [27]. so the binary keystream $\{k_i\}_1^L$ with i.i.d has expected correlation properties and high linear complexity approximating to $L/2$, which are also verified by numeric experiments in Sect.4.5.

4.3   Cycle-Length

The cycle length of $\{k_i\}$ is fully decided by the periods of $n - \text{NDF}_{1,2}$. Under continuous-value implementation, the cycle length of NDF is infinite, however, when it is discretely realized with finite precision, the short cycle length problem will arise.

Assume $n - \text{NDF}$ is realized by integer arithmetic under m-bit wordlength, then the state space I^n is theoretically $P = 2^{mn} - 1$, if and only if the NDFs generate signals with n-D uniform distribution to achieve the maximum length sequences. Nevertheless, there exist several subspaces which are not n-dimensional. This can be explained as follows: In a nth-order linear autoregressive filter(e.g the equivalent linear model of Fig.1), the least significant bit (LSB) of $z(k)$ is only influenced by the LSB's of $z(k-i), i = 1, \ldots, n$. The LSB's of all states can be regarded as binary feedback shift register with the LSB's of the parameters c_i as feedback polynomial. Obviously, the maximal length subspace of a n-th order binary feedback shift register does not include n subsequent zeros. So the state space will be partitioned several subspaces, at least three: a subspace excluding n subsequent even value states, a subspace with even value states only and a zero-value subspace. This disadvantage can be overcome by using an one-to-one nonlinear transition function, i.e. $h(\cdot)$ to jump out from one subspace to another. This way, $h(\cdot)$ concatenates some short-cycle subspaces or all subspaces to a longer or even maximal-cycle state space [29]. In addition, a parameter perturbing method is also utilized to avoid falling into a short period.

It has been turned out that digital realizations using floating-point arithmetic are suitable approximations of the continuous-value model and give very good results as well if the word length of the mantissa is large enough, such as 32 bit floating point arithmetic. Furthermore, with increasing dimension n the wordlength can be decreased. In other words, finite wordlength problem can be partly remedied by increasing n. This may be an advantage of NDF over other chaotic systems to overcome the finite wordlength problem. Though above analyses are half-theoretic, the numeric simulations strongly support the analysis results.

4.4   Key Space

Many chaotic keystream systems are insecure, as mentioned in Sect.1, partly for small key space reason and partly because the undistinguish weak keys result from the irregular attractor of underlying chaotic systems.

For a n-dimensional NDF-CKG, whose secret key consists of the initial states, initial input and the feedback coefficients of two n-NDFs, and denoted by $s = (s_1, s_2) = \{z_j(0), \phi_j, c_j(0) | j = 1, 2\}$. If finite computing precision is m-bits, the key entropy will be $(4n + 2)m$, which is n times larger than that of CCS-PRBG [14]. Also, large amount of numeric experiments show that the attractor of NDF expands evenly over the phase space and the system is sensitive to all components of key under computing precision. In other words, all the keys are approximately equal strength.

It should be noted that there is one defect in coupling keystream family. Assume keystream $\{k_i\}$ is generated when one sets s_1 for $n - \text{NDF}_1$ and s_2 for $n - \text{NDF}_2$. Exchange s_1 and s_2 for the two NDFs, the generated keystream is k'_i. If the two NDFs are perturbed with identical perturbing amplitudes ($\delta_1 = \delta_2$) and perturbing intervals ($\triangle_1 = \triangle_2$), then $\{k_i\} = \{k'_i\}$ because of the nature result of $g(x_1, x_2) = g(x_2, x_1)$. Such an effect will cause the key size of CKGs or CKG-based ciphers decrease $1/2$. To avoid this defect, different perturbing amplitudes, perturbing intervals, or different orders of two NDFs should be used.

4.5   Numeric Experimental Results

In order to verify the theoretical results on cryptographic properties of NDF-CKG with perturbation, some experiments are made. As mentioned in Sect.1, the performances of underlying chaotic systems are important for a good chaos-based cipher. so the properties of NDF, such as n-D uniform distribution, auto/cross-correlation, effects of finite wordlength and effects of order of NDF are evaluated first. After that, the properties of NDF-CKG, such as the 0-1 balance, auto/cross-correlation, linear complexity, key sensitivity, etc., are tested. Without loss of generality, the $h(\cdot)$'s of two n-NDFs are taken from the piecewise linear map:

$$h(x, p) = \begin{cases} (2x + 1 - p)/(1 + p) & x \in (-1, p] \\ (-2x + 1 + p)/(1 - p) & x \in (p, 1) \end{cases} \tag{10}$$

Under 32-bit wordlength, the 2-D densities of 2-NDF and piecewise linear map $h(x,p)$ are depicted in Fig.3. Clearly, the pdf of 2-NDF(Fig.3(a)) coincides well with the theoretical result of (3), while the pdf of $h(x,p)$(Fig.3(b)) is not 2-D uniform distribution, though it is well known with 1-D uniform distribution. So the signals generated by NDF are more random than those generated by usually used PWLCMs.

To check the effects of finite wordlength on NDF, the auto/cross-correlation function (acf/ccf) of 2-NDF with respect to wordlength m is tested. Fig.4(a) shows the normalized acf of a 2-NDF with $c_1 = 1.8, c_2 = 3, z_1 = 0.35, z_2 = -0.68, \phi = 0.23$ under wordlength $m = 5, 6, \ldots, 24$. The results show that the short period will arise if $m < 10$ but if $m > 20$, the period will gradually eliminate. If the computing precision is large enough,e.g m=32bit, the nearly perfect correlation properties will be obtained(see Fig.4(b)-4(d)). Note that in Fig.4(c), the ccf of two output sequences of 2-NDF with identical seeds except slight difference 2^{-m} on c_1 is given. Similarly, Fig.4(d) shows the ccf with slight difference 2^{-m} on z_1. In addition, when the short period arises (Fig.4(e)), the parameter perturbing described in Sect.2.2 can effectively extend the cycle-length as depicted in Fig.4(f).

To investigate the effects of order n on NDF under finite wordlength, Fig.5(a)-5(b) show the acfs of signals generated by 2-NDF and 10-NDF with 10 bit fixed-point arithmetic realization. It is obvious that increasing order n can effectively improve the correlation properties and partly overcome the degradation caused by finite wordlength. In addition, the acf of 2-NDF realized on 32 bit fixed-point arithmetic is evaluated in Fig.5(c). Already the 10 bit system possesses a δ-like acf for many parameter sets. For the 32 bit system the acf is δ-like for almost all parameter sets and is quite similar to what can be expected from a continuous-value system. As can be seen from Fig.4-5, the NDF is sensitive to all parameter sets under realized precision, which guarantees the CKG based on it has large key space with equal key strength.

Next, the cryptographic properties of $\{k_i\}$ generated by NDF-CKG are verified. A third 2-NDF is selected as the perturbing NDF, whose perturbing amplitudes and perturbing intervals are set with $(\delta_1 = 1/10, \delta_2 = 1/5)$ and $(\triangle_1 = 99, \triangle_2 = 101)$, respectively. The pre-iteration T is 32. The seed s satisfying

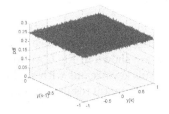

(a) Two-dimensional NDF

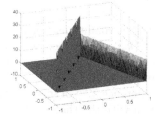

(b) Piecewise linear map h(.)

Fig. 3. Two-dimensional density of $(y(k), y(k-1))$ under wordlength $m = 32bit$

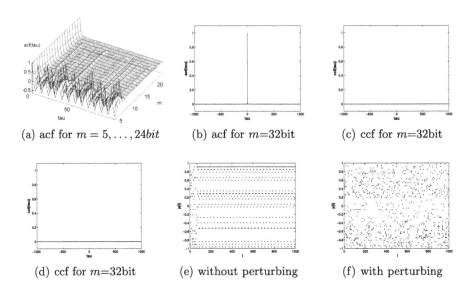

(a) acf for $m = 5, \ldots, 24bit$ (b) acf for m=32bit   (c) ccf for m=32bit

(d) ccf for m=32bit   (e) without perturbing   (f) with perturbing

Fig. 4. Effects of different wordlengths m on 2-NDF.(a)acf for $m = 5, \ldots, 24$, (b)acf for $m = 32$, (c)ccf for $m = 32$ when $|c_1 - c_1'| = 2^{-m}$, (d)ccf for $m = 32$ when $|z_1 - z_1'| = 2^{-m}$, (e)evolution of 2-NDF without perturbing under m=6 and (f) with perturbing under m=6.

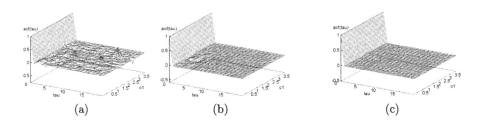

(a)   (b)   (c)

Fig. 5. Acf's of n-NDF with different $n, \mathbf{c}$ under different wordlength m. (a) acf of 2-NDF for $n = 10, m = 10bit, c_2 = 3.0, c_1 \in (0, 4)$, (b) acf of 10-NDF for $n = 10, m = 10, c_{10} = 3.0, c_i = 0.8, i = 2, \ldots, 9, c_1 \in (0, 4)$, (c) acf of 2-NDF for $n = 2, m = 32, c_2 = 3.0, c_1 \in (0, 4)$.

Kelber conditions is generated randomly, and a large number of sub-keystream of $\{k_i\}$ is extracted to test the cryptographic properties. The 0-1 balance, linear complexity and autocorrelation of sub-keystream are shown in Fig.6(a)-6(c) respectively. In Fig.6(d), the cross-correlation of two sub-keystreams with slight difference 2^{-m} of seeds is given. As can be seen, the experimental results coincide well with the theoretical analyses.

Although statistical tests cannot prove that a sequence is really random, they can help to detect certain kinds of weakness a generator may have. The empirical statistic tests of NDF-CKG are performed on the NIST FIPS 142 [37] and the DIEHARD [38] test suits, and the test results pass all test items as expected.

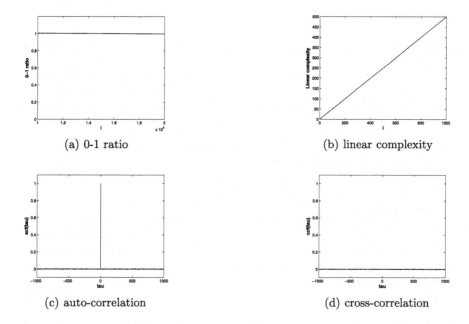

(a) 0-1 ratio

(b) linear complexity

(c) auto-correlation

(d) cross-correlation

Fig. 6. Cryptographic properties of NDF-CKG under wordlength $m = 32bit$

5   Conclusion

Many CKGs are not secure due to the improper construction and the defective chaotic systems used in them. Almost all the existing CKGs work on the chaotic maps with only 1-D uniform distribution, which degrade the randomness of pseudorandom keystreams. Investigating on the NDF with n-D uniform distribution, a coupled NDF-based CKG is proposed to solve these problems. Theoretical analyses and experiments show that the proposed NDF-CKG has perfect cryptographic properties, such as 0-1 balance, good correlation properties, long cycle length, large key space with equal key strength. Because of the inherent parallel structure of filter, moreover, it is very suitable for software realization with parallel algorithm or for digital circuit implementation. All these properties make it suitable for a practical and secure keystream generator.

Acknowledgement

This work is supported by the Program for New Century Excellent Talents in University of China (grant No.NCET-05-0749), by the National Natural Science Foundation of China (grant No.60272096), by the Basic Application research Foundation of Sichuan Province, China (grant No.2006J13-110) and by the Doctor Innovation Fund of Southwest Jiaotong University, 2006.

References

1. Matthews, R.: On the derivation of a chaotic encryption algorithm. Cryptologia,XIII **1** (1989) 29–42.
2. Forré, R.: The Hénon attractor as a keystream generator. In Advances in Cryptology-EuroCrypt'91, LNCS, Berlin Springer-Verlag. **0547** (1991) 76–81.
3. Zhou, H. and Ling,X.: Generating chaotic secure sequence with desired statistical properties and high security. Int.J.Bifurcation and Chaos, bf 7 (1997) 205–213.
4. Habutsu, T., Nishio,Y., Sasase, I., and Mori,S.: A secret key cryptosystem by iterating a chaotic map. In advances in Cryptology-EuroCrypt'91, LNCS, Berlin, Springer-Verlag, **0547** (1991) 127-140.
5. Fridrich, J.: Symmetric ciphers based on two-dimensional chaotic maps. Int.J.Bifurcation and Chaos. **8** (1998) 1259-1284.
6. Protopopescu, V.A., Santoro, R.T., and Tollover, J.S.: Fast and secure encryption-decryption method based on chaotic dynamics. US Patent No.5479513,1995.
7. Zbigniew,K., and Janusz, S.: Application of discrete chaotic dynamical systems in cryptography-dcc method. Int.J.Bifurcation and Chaos, **9** (1999) 1121-1135.
8. Ghobad,H.B. and Clare,D.: A chaotic direct-sequence spread-spectrum communication system. IEEE Trans.Communication, **42** (1994) 1524–1527.
9. Erdmann,D. and Murphy, S.: Hénon stream cipher. Electronics Letters, bf 28 (1992) 893–895.
10. Bruce, S.: Applied Cryptography-Protocols,algorithms,and source code. John Wiley & Sons, Inc., New York, second edition, 1996.
11. Lu, H., Wang, S. and H, G.: Pseudo-random number generator based on coupled map lattices. Int. J. Mod Phys B. **18** (2004) 2409–2414.
12. Kohda, T., Tsuneda,A.: Stream cipher systems based on chaotic binary sequences. In: Proc SCIS96-11C,1996.
13. Kocarev, L., Jakimoski, G. Stojanovski, T., and Parlitz U.: From chaotic maps to encryption schemes. In Proc. IEEE Int. Symposium Circuits and Systems, **4** (1998) 514–517.
14. Li,S., Mou, X., Cai, Y.: Pseudo-Random Bit Generator Based on Couple Chaotic Systems and its Applications in Stream-Cipher Cryptography. INDOCRYPT'2001, LNCS, Springer-Verlag,Berlin, **2247** (2001) 316–329.
15. Chen, G., Mao, Y., and Chui, C.: A symmetric image encryption scheme based on 3D chaotic cat maps. Chaos,Solitons & Fractals, **12** (2004) 749–761.
16. Chua, L.O., Lin, T.: Chaos in digital filters. IEEE Trans. CAS, **35** (1988) 648–658.
17. Lin, T., Chua, L.O.: On chaos of digital filters in the real world. IEEE Trans. CAS, **38** (1991) 557–558.
18. Li,S., Li,Q., Li, W., Mou, X., and Cai, Y.: Statistical properties of digital piecewise linear chaotic maps and their roles in cryptography and pseudo-random coding. In Cryptography and Coding-8th IMA Int.Conf.Proc, LNCS, Berlin, Springer-Verlag, 2001.
19. Kelber, K.: N-Dimensional Uniform Probability Distribution in Nonlinear Autoregressive Filter Structures. IEEE Trans. CAS-I, **47** (2000) 1413–1417.
20. Alvarez, G., Li, S.: Some Basic Cryptographic Requirements for Chaos-based Cryptosystems. I. J. Bifurcation and Chaos, 2005.
21. Wheeler, D.: Problems with chaotic cryptosystems. Cryptologia, XIII **3** (1989) 243–250.
22. Wheeler, D., and Mattews, R.: Supercomputer investigations of a chaotic encryption algorithm. Cryptologic, XV **2** 1991 140–151.

23. Biham, E.: Cryptoanalysis of the chaotic-map cryptosystem suggested at EuroCrypt'91. In Advances in Cryptology-EruoCrypt'91, LNCS, Berlin, Springer-Verlag, **0547** (1991) 532–534.
24. Alvarez, G., Montoya, F., Romera, M., and Pastor, G.: Cryptanalysis of a chaotic encryption system. Physics Letters A, **7** (2000) 191–196.
25. Short, K.M.: Signal extraction from chaotic communications. Int.J.Bifurcation and Chaos, **7** (1997) 1579–1597.
26. Yang, T., Yang, L., and Yang, C.M.: Cryptanalyzing chaotic secure communications using return maps. Physics Letters A, **245** (1998) 495–510.
27. Yang, Y.X., Lin, X.D.: Coding Theory and Cryptology. People's Post and Telecomm. Press, Beijing, China,1992 (In Chinese).
28. Wang, X., Zhang, M., Lai, C., et.al, Error function attack of chaos synchronization based encryption schemes. Chaos **14** (2004) 128–137.
29. Kelber, K., Götz, M., Schwarz, W.: Generation of chaotic signals with n-dimensional uniform probability distribution by digital filter structure. Proc. of the 7th IEEE Digital Signal Processing Workshop (DSPWS'96) Norway: Loen, September,(1996)486–489.
30. Sang, T., Wang, R., and Yan, Y.: Perturbance-based algorithm to expand cycle length of chaotic key stream. Electronics Letters, **34** (1998) 873–874.
31. Sang, T., Wang, R., and Yan, Y.: Clock-controlled chaotic keystream generators. Electronics Letters, **34** (1998) 1932–1934.
32. Bernstein, G. and Lieberman, M.: Secure random number generation using chaotic circuits. IRRR Trans. CAS, bf 37 (1990) 1157–1164.
33. Baptista, M.S.: Cryptography with chaos. Physics Letters A, **240** (1998) 50–54.
34. Alvarez, E., Fernández, A., García, P., etc., New approach to chaotic encryption. Physics Letters A, **263** (1999) 373–375.
35. Rueppel,R.: Analysis and design of stream ciphers. Berlin: Springer, 1986.
36. Frey, D.R.: Chaotic digital encoding: An approach to secure communication. IEEE Trans. CAS-II, **40** (1993) 660–666.
37. Andrew, R., Juan, S., James, N., et al.: A statistical test suite for random and pseudorandom number generators for cryptographic applications. NIST Special Publication 800-22, 2001. http://csrc.nist.gov/rng/.
38. Available Online at: http://stat.fsu.edu/~ geo/diehard.html

Appendix

Lemma 1. *If two signals z and ϕ are statistically independent and the signal z is uniformly distributed on $I = [-1, 1]$, then for all parameters $c \in Z \setminus \{0\}$, the signal $w = \mod(c \cdot z + \phi) \in [-1, 1)$ is uniform distribution on I, and independent on the distribution of ϕ [19].*

Lemma 2. *If $\tilde{c}_n \in Z \setminus \{0\}$ and $h(\cdot)$ preserves uniform distribution, then $y_t = F(\mathbf{z}(t), \phi, \tilde{\mathbf{c}}(t))$ preserves n-D uniform distribution independent on the input signal ϕ [19].*

Lemma 3. *If $|\tilde{c}_{tn}| > 1$ and $|\lambda_i| \neq 1$, then $y_t = F(\mathbf{z}(t), \phi, \tilde{\mathbf{c}}(t))$ preserving n-dimensional uniform distribution is ergodic. That is, for an arbitrary initial* *density $f(\mathbf{z}, 0), \mathbf{z} \in I^n$, with t increasing, the density approaches the invariant pdf given by [19]*

$$\lim_{t \to \infty} f(\mathbf{z}, t) = \lim_{t \to \infty} \mathcal{P}^t f(\mathbf{z}, 0) = \begin{cases} 2^{-n} & \mathbf{z} \in I^n \\ 0 & \mathbf{z} \notin I^n \end{cases} \tag{11}$$

where $\mathcal{P}$ is Perron-Frobenius-Operator(PFO).

For the proofs of above three lemmas please see [19].

Corollary 1. *If the t-th perturbed sub-NDF preserves n-D uniform distribution, then the composite perturbed NDF $(F, \tilde{\mathbf{c}}(t), t = T, 2T, \dots)$ also does.*

Proof. It is a straightforward process to prove it with induction hypothesis. More generally, let $\mathbf{z}(t) = \{y_t, z_{t1}, z_{t2}, \dots, z_{tn}\}$ denote the filter state at t instance. Notice that the perturbed parameters $\tilde{\mathbf{c}}(t)$ are time-varying, while $\mathrm{mod}(\cdot)$ and $h(\cdot)$ keep invariant.

(i) According to Kelber conditions, the output y_t at t instance preserves n-D uniform distribution. From lemma1, the changes of $\tilde{\mathbf{c}}(t)$ do not effect the distributions of $\mathrm{mod}(\cdot)$ and $h(\cdot)$. According to lemma2, the state $\mathbf{z}(t+1) = \{y_{t+1}, y_t, z_{t1}, \dots, z_{t(n-1)}\}$ at $(t+1)$ instance with $\tilde{\mathbf{c}}(t+1)$ also preserves n-D uniform distribution;

(ii) On the assumption that the output y_{t+i} at $(t+i)$ instance preserves n-D uniform distribution, then the output y_{t+i+1} at $(t+i+1)$ instance can also preserve n-D uniform distribution according to step(i).
The proof is completed.

Corollary 2. *If the t-th perturbed sub-NDF is ergodic, then the composite perturbed NDF $(F, \tilde{\mathbf{c}}(t), t = T, 2T, \dots)$ is also ergodic.*

Proof. Let ε_q denote the perturbing point, ε the perturbing space, and $\varepsilon_q \in \varepsilon \subseteq I^{n-1}$. For a statistical approach, we assume the perturbing point to be random. This will be characterized by a probability space $\{\varepsilon, \mathcal{A}, P_q\}$ over the perturbing space ε, where $\mathcal{A}$ is a σ-algebra over ε and P_q is the probability distribution of ε_q over σ.

For convenience, let $\mathbf{z}_i = F(\mathbf{z}_{i-1}, t)$ represent the evolution process of composite perturbed system $(F, \tilde{\mathbf{c}}(t), t = T, 2T, \dots)$ and $I_k \subseteq I^n$ the segment partition of state space. Then for any $\mathbf{z} \subseteq I_k$, we may get

$$P(F(\mathbf{z}, t) \subseteq I_k) = \lim_{r \to \infty} \sum_{q=1}^{r} P(F(\mathbf{z}, t, \tilde{\mathbf{c}}_q(t)) \subseteq I_k, \tilde{\mathbf{c}}_q(t) = c + \varepsilon_q)$$

$$= \lim_{r \to \infty} \sum_{q=1}^{r} P_q \int_{F^{-1}(\mathbf{z}, t, \tilde{\mathbf{c}}_q(t)) \subseteq I_k} f_q(\mathbf{z}, t) \, dz$$

obviously, the pdf of composite perturbed system can be got by

$$f(\mathbf{z}, t) = \frac{d}{d\mathbf{z}} P\left(F(\mathbf{z}, t) \subseteq I_k\right)$$

$$= \lim_{r \to \infty} \sum_{q=1}^{r} P_q \frac{d}{d\mathbf{z}} \int_{F^{-1}(\mathbf{z}, t, \tilde{\mathbf{e}}_q(t)) \subseteq I_k} f_q(\mathbf{z}, t)\, dz$$

$$= \lim_{r \to \infty} \left(P_1 f_1(\mathbf{z}, t) + \cdots + P_r f_r(\mathbf{z}, t)\right) \tag{12}$$

since $\sum_{r=1}^{\infty} P_r = 1$, with Eq.(11) and Eq.(12), we obtain

$$\lim_{t \to \infty} f(\mathbf{z}, t) = \lim_{t \to \infty} \lim_{r \to \infty} \left[P_1 + P_2 + \cdots + P_r\right] f(\mathbf{z}, t)$$

$$= \lim_{t \to \infty} \mathcal{P}^t f(\mathbf{z}, 0) = \begin{cases} 2^{-n} & \mathbf{z} \in I^n \\ 0 & \mathbf{z} \notin I^n \end{cases}.$$

The proof is completed.

Cooperative Intrusion Detection for Web Applications

Nathalie Dagorn

Laboratory of Algorithmics, Cryptology and Security (LACS)
University of Luxembourg
162a Avenue de la Faïencerie, L-1511 Luxembourg, Luxembourg
nathalie.dagorn@uni.lu
http://lacs.uni.lu/

Abstract. This contribution involves cooperative information systems, and more precisely interorganizational systems (IOS). Indeed, experience of real enterprises shows that most IOS interoperate today over the Web. To "ensure" security of these IOS on the Web (in particular, security of the applications they are made of), various hardware and software protection can be employed. Our work falls into the field of intrusion detection, and covers more precisely intrusion detection for Web applications. Several misuse-based intrusion detection systems (IDSs) were developed recently for Web applications, whereas, to our knowledge, only one anomaly-based Web IDS exists and works effectively to date. This one was unfortunately conceived disregarding any kind of cooperation. In previous work, we improved it to gain in sensitivity and specificity. This paper describes a cooperation feature added to the IDS, so that it is able to perform an *alarm correlation* with other detectors, allowing coo-perative intrusion detection, as well as an *event correlation* to detect distributed attacks. The first experiments in real environment show encouraging results.

1 Introduction

In the field of computer security, application level attacks have particularly been increasing for the last years. About 75% of intrusions come today via the Web [26]. The development of intrusion detection systems (IDSs) for Web-based systems is an important topic, which has not been extensively explored yet. Several Web IDSs based on signatures (*misuse* detection) exist and show good results [1,6,13]. Recently, an *anomaly*-based Web IDS was proposed [22], having the advantage to detect unknown attacks. We improved this system over the last months; our work on the subject was described in two previous papers: [9] presents original work, our improvements and our proposal to date, motivated by theoretical and practical examples, whereas [10] focuses on the system's implementation (functional and technical architecture), evaluation and ongoing efforts.

This paper describes a complementary cooperation feature added to the system to allow cooperative intrusion detection (by alarm correlation) and the detection of distributed attacks (by event correlation).

D. Pointcheval, Y. Mu, and K. Chen (Eds.): CANS 2006, LNCS 4301 , pp. 286 – 302, 2006.
© Springer-Verlag Berlin Heidelberg 2006

The paper is organized as follows. Section 2 describes the context and motivation of our research: first, it outlines aspects of IOS, with a particular focus on different cooperation situations, proposing five cooperation levels, a typology and a synthesis table; then, some Web security issues are indicated in this context. Section 3 sums up related work on cooperative IDSs, as well as our previous work on the subject (the development of an anomaly-based IDS for Web applications), in order to provide the reader a good background. Section 4 presents the added cooperation feature: alarms raised in one IDS are propagated to other IDSs to improve detection accuracy and to detect distributed attacks; details on the feature's implementation and a motivating example are also provided. Section 5 describes the complete system's evaluation to date, discusses the preliminary results and outlines ongoing efforts. Section 6 contains some concluding remarks.

2   Context and Motivation

Today, information systems overlap the organizational boundaries. For many organizations, the *intra-organizational integration phase* is complete (or is going well). In order to access new markets or to benefit from synergy effects enabling them to reduce the costs, some of those organizations choose to merge with other powerful actors of their sector, to ally with partners or even competitors. More and more activities of the organization also depend on activities realized outside its boundaries. Organizations thus turn now to an *interorganizational cooperation phase*, for which many benefits in terms of effectiveness are expected.

2.1 Identification of Cooperation Levels

The concepts of integration and interoperability are not restricted to cooperation between organizations. They can apply to various levels or objects, at a large or small scale: organizational units, processes, applications, software, hardware… We propose in [11] to identify five cooperation levels (Fig. 1): the highest level concerns cooperation between organizations, involving technical as well as social concepts like confidence [14,15,27]. Both levels below focus on cooperation between information systems and between applications; they are detailed in the next paragraph. The lowest levels concern cooperation between processes and even components; the more one goes down in the figure, the more the cooperation relates to a very technical level.

2.2 Proposal for an IOS Typology

The levels, which are relevant for us in this paper, are those, which relate to cooperation between information systems and between applications. Several typologies exist, classifying IOS according either to theoretical perspectives [17], or to their functional characteristics [25], or to the type of interdependence existing between the different organizations using the IOS [4]. Essentially based on this last perspective, we tried to find examples of IOS relating to each type of cooperation identified[1].

---

[1] We specify that these groups are only "virtual", so that one IOS could be classified in a group or another according to the circumstances. More details about this topology are available in [11].

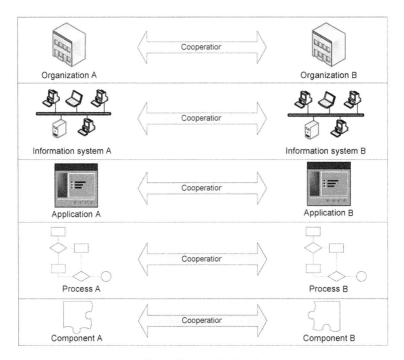

Fig. 1. Cooperation levels

The first group identified is composed of *information sharing IOS*, which enable different organizations to exchange information in a centralized way. This group may contain cooperation situations like a shared extranet, purchase and provisioning platforms, electronic marketplaces or specialized portals.

The second group identified gathers *IOS relating to* the sequence of *provisioning chain activities*. The techniques and technologies used in this context are not mutually exclusive: e.g., transactional Electronic Data Interchange (EDI) systems, XML transactional systems and Web services, proprietary applications.

The third and last group of IOS identified gathers *technologies* initially conceived to be used in an internal context, but which were *extended to support interorganizational cooperation*. These technologies still have a significant development potential; let us quote in particular groupware and workflow systems, Enterprise Resources Planning (ERP) systems or Enterprise Applications Integration (EAI) systems. We add the Internet to these technologies, since it offers services such as e-mail, telnet, ftp, Usenet news, World Wide Web, etc. According to the role the organization attributes to the Internet, this one can be a tool either of contact, or of transaction, or of integration [2].

2.3   Proposal for an IOS Synthesis

A synthesis of the listed IOS is presented in Table 1, summing up their most widespread advantages, limits and risks. More developments regarding each solution can be found in specialized literature. This table might just give the reader some idea on why Web security is an issue in IOS.

One risk mentioned is that of vendor *lock-in*, i.e., the situation in which customers become dependent on a single manufacturer or supplier for some product (good, service), and cannot move to another vendor without substantial costs and/or inconvenience.

But it can especially be noticed that eight out of the fourteen analyzed solutions (i.e., 57%) are right now regularly accessed via the Web, the remaining solutions being able to evolve in this direction in the future or new solutions being likely to be implemented. So, the most frequently mentioned risk shown in the table relates to *Web security*. This issue is confirmed by a study realized in [11].

2.4 Web Security Issues

IOS, which interoperate over the Web, are prone to a variety of Web attacks [30]:

- *Attacks on authentication mechanisms* target a Web site's method of validating the identity of a user, service or application. An attacker may circumvent the authentication process using techniques like brute force, or exploit weaknesses like insufficient authentication or weak password recovery validation.
- *Attacks on authorization mechanisms* target a Web site's method of determining if a user, service or application has the necessary permissions to perform a requested action. Using techniques like credential/session prediction or fixation, or exploiting insufficient authorization or insufficient session expiration, an attacker could increase his privileges to protected areas.
- *Client-side attacks* focus on the abuse or exploitation of a Web site's users. With this intention, an attacker may employ several techniques, among which content spoofing and cross-site scripting.
- *Command execution attacks* execute remote commands on a Web site. Techniques used therefore may be buffer overflow, format string attack, OS commanding, LDAP/SQL/SSI or XPath injection, for instance.
- *Information disclosure attacks* aim to obtain system specific information about a Web site (e.g., software distribution, version numbers, and patch levels). In order to reveal these data, techniques like directory indexing or directory traversal, or the exploitation of information leakage or predictable resource location, can be used.
- *Logical attacks* focus on the abuse or exploitation of a Web application's logic flow. An attacker may be able to circumvent or misuse logic features, using techniques like abuse of functionality, denial of service, or the exploitation of insufficient anti-automation or insufficient process validation.

To prevent or counter these attacks, many hardware and software devices exist and are implemented by the organizations, for instance the use of firewall, DMZ (DeMilitarized Zone), proxy, anti-virus or IDS. Some techniques like cryptography, biometry or steganography, can be employed complementarily[2].

---

[2] Many generic books relating to computer security are available (e.g. [3,7,23]); the reader may refer to them for more details on the listed mechanisms. These solutions are also developed in [11].

Table 1. Synthesis of the presented IOS

	CIS	Pros	Cons	Risks
1	Shared extranet	-Web access -Easy to implement if an intranet exists -Low network cost (Internet)		Web security
	Purchase and provisioning platform	-Web access -Flexibility -Low network cost (Internet)		Web security
	Electronic marketplace	-Web access -Flexibility -Low network cost (Internet)		Web security
	Specialized portal	-Web access -Flexibility -Low network cost (Internet)		Web security
2	EDI	-Well-tested technology -Cheaper if access via the Internet -Universal document format	-Expensive technology if access via a VAN - Not very flexible document format	-Lock-in -Network security
	XML document system	-Web access -Flexible technology -Flexible document format	High costs	Web security
	Integrative Web services (XML-based)	-Web access -Flexible technology -Flexible document format	-Emerging and not yet proven technology -High costs	-Web security -Recent technology
	Proprietary application	Speed	-Development costs -In general, no access via the Internet (restricts the cooperation) -Heavy deployment -Not very flexible -Difficult evolution	-Lock-in -Network security if access via the Internet
3	Internet	Flexibility		Important network security risks
	Groupware	Variety of tools		
	Workflow management system (WfMS)	Enables the integration of different technologies, focusing on the business process	Big initial investment	
	Workflow document system	Web access	Cost of certain products	Web security
	EAI	Possibility of integrating very heterogeneous environments	Development costs	-Lock-in
	ERP	-Web access -Process standardisation	Purchase and implementation costs	-Lock-in -Web security

Obviously, Web security issues cannot be exhaustively covered on one page. The following sections focus on intrusion detection issues and briefly give the reader an overview of what has been done in this area already.

3   Related Work on Cooperative Intrusion Detection

3.1   Related Work in the Field of (Cooperative) Intrusion Detection

In the field of intrusion detection, the detection techniques involved are usually classified into two categories: misuse- and anomaly detection. *Misuse detection* is based on signatures: the IDS analyzes information collected in the traffic for comparison to a database of signatures (i.e., patterns, explicit characteristics) of known attacks, and each matching activity is considered as an attack, with different levels of severity. Misuse detection can unfortunately only accommodate already documented attacks. Unlike this, *anomaly detection* models a system's usual behavior and any significant deviation from the defined baseline is considered as the result of an attack. Anomaly-based systems have the advantage of being able to detect previously unknown attacks; however, they are not as effective as misuse detection systems to detect known attacks. In particular, they suffer from the difficulty of building reliable models of acceptable behavior, may resulting in a high number of (false) alarms caused by unusual activities, which overload their human operators.

In matter of IDS cooperation, recent and relevant references are [21] or [24], for instance. [21] presents IDSs and addresses the problem of managing and correlating the alerts produced. It discusses the role of intrusion detection in the realm of network security with comparisons to traditional methods such as firewalls and cryptography. Finally, it analyzes the challenges in interpreting and combining (i.e., correlating) alerts produced by these systems. Existing academic and commercial systems are classified; their advantage and shortcomings are presented, especially in the case of deployment in large, real-world sites. [24] focuses on discovering novel attack strategies via analysis of security alerts (alert correlation and attack plan recognition). He proposes a framework to help security administrator aggregate redundant alerts, filter out unrelated attacks, correlate security alerts, analyze attack scenarios and take appropriate actions against forthcoming attacks.

3.2   Our Previous Work

Our work falls into the field of anomaly detection. Most academic research in this field relates to network-based anomaly detection. Work relating to the Web application/service level remains rare.

Original approaches. Our work basically combines four approaches.

Kruegel, Vigna and Robertson propose in [22] an approach for Web detection, based on nine *statistical anomaly detection models* (attribute length, attribute character distribution, structural inference, token finder, attribute presence or absence, attribute order, access frequency, inter-request time delay and invocation order[3]), examining http queries and their invocation attributes in Web server logs. To the best of our knowledge, this approach is the first anomaly-detection system specifically tailored to detect Web attacks (which works!). The system has been tested on data gathered at Google, Inc. and two universities in the United States and Europe. In

---

[3] We encourage the reader to refer to [22] for further explanations on these models.

[9,10], we propose an anomaly-based Web IDS, based on Kruegel and al's approach, which we improved with selected work in several research fields.

First, to improve the decision process of the system, we resort to *Bayesian networks*. Indeed, Kruegel, Mutz, Robertson and Valeur [20] propose an event classification scheme based on Bayesian networks to replace the simple, classical threshold-based decision process. In this approach, Bayesian networks improve the aggregation of different model outputs and allow to seamlessly incorporate additional information. Experimental results show that the accuracy of the event classification process is significantly improved using the Bayesian approach rather than a threshold.

To extend this approach, we take advantage of the work of Valdes and Skinner in [29]. Among other interesting properties (for instance, a dynamic adaptation of the system), the major characteristic we make use of is the *specification* at the root node of thirteen final states (five normal states and eight attacks states) relating to network detection; in our proposal, we detail six final states relating to Web detection.

Lastly, to reduce the large number of false alarms generally raised by anomaly detection systems, we use a data mining technique, called *alarm clustering*, developed by Julisch [18,19]: the first step extracts alarm groups, which have similar properties; these alarm groups are then presented to a human expert responsible for identifying the underlying root causes (i.e. the reasons, which the alarms occur for). Afterwards, the second step consists in removing these root causes (respectively, false positives can be filtered out), and thereby reducing the future alarm load. The experiments show that the future alarm load can be reduced by 70%, on the average, using this technique.

Our previous efforts. Let us describe briefly our basic system to help the reader understand the rest of the paper[4].

Data model and working modes. The model analyzes *http requests* as logged by most of the Web servers (e.g., Apache). The analysis process focuses on requests, which contain attributes, more precisely the inputs of the analysis models consist of URI extracted from successful GET requests (URI, which do not contain a query string are irrelevant for the detection process).

The system can operate in training or detection mode. A *training phase* (unsupervised learning) is necessary to determine the characteristics of normal events. During this phase, the system creates profiles for each server-side program and each of its attributes. The task of a model in the *detection phase* is then to return a probability value for a certain query with regards to the established profile. The assumption is that feature values with a sufficient low probability (i.e., anomalous values) potentially indicate an attack. Based on the output probabilities of all the detection models, a query is reported either as normal or as a potential attack by the Bayesian network.

System operation. The global detection process consists of three steps, which we call *analysis, decision* and *refinement of the model*.

---

[4] We encourage the reader to refer to [8,9,10,11] to get more information on the proposed system.

The first step *analyzes* each request received from a monitored Web application. Information specific to the request is captured and serves as input to ten detection models. Nine models are taken over from [22]. We add an *anomaly history model*, which keeps track of anomalies recently seen in the Bayesian network and checks whether an event is one of them. This model also allows to measure the events in time in a weighted manner, in the sense that an event, which has just occurred, has more weight in the system than events, which occurred a long time ago (and which are weighted so as to decrease their importance). Each model issues a real value in the interval [0,1], which reflects the deviation of the event's feature(s) from its profile.

The second step *decides* whether the analyzed request is normal or constitutes an attack. Joining thereby [20], an extended Bayesian network is substituted as a *decision process* to the threshold technique generally used for anomaly detection. The value returned by each model is integrated as evidence into the Bayesian network. According to the model's output, each model node includes either a pair of states (normal, anomalous) or five possible states as defined by [20] (Table 2). Each node is also associated with a *conditional probability table*, whose values are initially established after the training period according to our specific knowledge in the field. To improve the accuracy of the system, we include a *confidence node* for every model in the Bayesian network. The conditional probability tables are adjusted according to the confidence nodes, so that each model output has a weighted influence on the decision according to its confidence level. The model confidence is represented as one of five discrete levels: very high, high, medium, low or none [20]. The root node of the Bayesian network has six possible states (one normal and five attack states): normal, authentication, XSS, command execution, denial of service and other attacks. Fig. 2 shows the structure of the Bayesian network that we propose for the characterization of Web-based attacks. The *anomaly history* node has five states (as described in Table 2); a confidence node is associated with it, including the five levels also described above. Like all the other models, the anomaly history model is connected to the classification node; dotted lines in the figure touching the anomaly history model represent possible links with other probes the system may also be connected to. By preoccupation with readability, the conditional probability tables are not developed in the figure (the largest would count 5 rows x 150 columns). At the end of the decision process, the probabilities of the six states associated with the classification node are calculated. When an event has a "high enough" probability to be anomalous, an alarm is raised. All the anomalous events detected are stored in alarm logs.

Table 2. Anomaly Score Intervals

Anomaly Score Range	Level
[0.00 , 0.50[	Normal
[0.50 , 0.75[	Uncommon
[0.75 , 0.90[	Irregular
[0.90 , 0.95[	Suspicious
[0.95 , 1.00]	Very suspicious

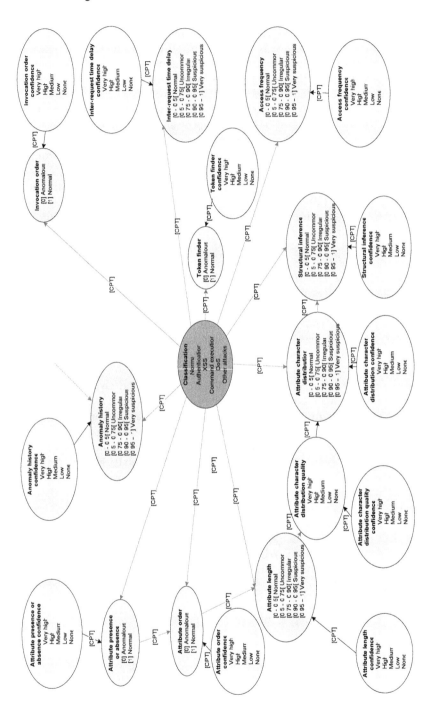

Fig. 2. Bayesian network for the characterization of Web-based attacks

In the third step of the process, the *alarm clustering technique* [18,19] is actively used to group the alarms in clusters, identify their root causes and filter out false positives. After each log analysis, the conditional probability tables are adjusted in the Bayesian network, so that the false positives identified will no more appear in the next sessions. This technique thus helps to *refine* and continuously improve the model.

4   Presentation and Implementation of the Cooperation Feature

Kruegel et al's system [22], described in § 3.2, was unfortunately not designed to consider any kind of cooperation. We are eager to equip our proposed IDS with a cooperation feature. Therefore, some improvements must be made to the previously described system.

4.1   Presentation of the Cooperation Feature

Analysis phase. Two improvements are brought to the analysis phase to enable cooperation.

The anomaly history model we added is now able, through communications, to achieve a *correlation of alarms* coming from one (or several) other source(s), in order to allow the system to cooperate with one (or several) other IDS(s) in the case of a distributed intrusion detection policy. Regarding the content and the amount of history kept, let us specify that the anomaly history is an *alarm* history and not an history of the captured requests. In this sense, the history module just stores the queries, which have been classified as anomalous and not every query come across.

The anomaly history model is also able to achieve a *correlation of events*, in order to detect distributed attack. Two types of distributed attacks are recognized: those where one source IP address targets several destination IP addresses, and those where several source IP addresses target one destination IP address.

Decision process. Two further improvements are brought to the decision process to enable cooperation.

The outputs of the anomaly history model relating to the cooperation feature are directly injected into the anomaly history node of the *Bayesian network*. Thus, the cooperation feature is integrated into the decision process.

The *alarm* rose by an anomalous event in the Bayesian network is also *relayed* to one (or more) other probe(s), and conversely, to enable alarm and event correlation.

Refinement of the model. A last improvement consists in the exchange of *heartbeat messages* between probes. Thereby, each probe can check the presence of the other probes in the correlation network. A probe, which gives no more answer was either voluntarily stopped (normal fact in this case), or suffers from a technical problem (maybe the consequence of an attack?). The goal of this improvement is to detect rapidly the absence of any probe in the network. It can be particularly useful in case of a denial of service attack, for instance.

Fig. 3 gives an idea of how the cooperation feature works. For a better understanding of the involved mechanisms, a motivating example is provided in § 4.3.

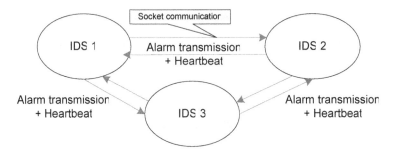

Fig. 3. Overview of the cooperation feature

4.2 Implementation of the Cooperation Feature

The system was implemented using C++ and the SMILE Bayesian statistics library [28]. Its Windows user interface GeNIe has already allowed us to create and test manually the proposed Bayesian network. The latter seems correctly designed; collected data are consistent and meet our expectations.

Common processes. Some processes are common to all models (including the anomaly history model).

In *learning mode*, a file input is preferable with a manual input because it is much faster to constitute the model profiles (stored in configuration files). Once the learning phase initiated, the user selects the file to analyze and the learning process starts. The file is opened and parsed in order to extract the different queries. From each query, the attributes are then extracted. The next treatments vary for each model, for which a specific configuration file is created.

In *detection mode*, a file input is recommended. Once the detection initiated, the user selects the log file to be analyzed and the detection process starts. The file is opened and parsed in order to extract the different queries. From each query, the attributes are then extracted. The models exploit the associated query and its attributes in order to output a numerical value in the interval [0,1]. This value is injected as evidence into the Bayesian network. The corresponding state is propagated in the Bayesian network, the probabilities are recomputed and updated, and the probability for the request to be in a given state is obtained at the classification node. If necessary, an alarm message is raised to the user in the lower window of the system's graphical user interface, indicating the probability for the request to be anomalous, the results of the models and the suspected type of attack.

Specific processes. Only the working process relating to the anomaly history model is detailed in this paragraph (for the nine other models, please see [8,11]).

Exceptionally, there is no *learning mode* for the anomaly history model; the configuration file is elaborated during the detection phase.

In *detection mode*, the model checks for each query if it is already present in the configuration file. If not and if the query is anomalous, the query, the counter of the local occurrences (initially at 1), the local source IP address, the precise date of the local occurrence, a counter of occurrences issued from other probes (alarm correlation feature), the remote source IP address and the precise date of the remote occurrence, are immediately stored in the configuration file. If the (anomalous) query is already present in the configuration file, the date of the last occurrence is updated and the local counter is incremented. According to the values of both counters and the last occurrence date, the model computes a numerical value in [0,1] to generate the observations for the related node in the Bayesian network. It is interesting to note that this computation weights the reoccurrence of attempted queries on remote servers differently from the local server, so that an event is given less importance when it is seen by a remote IDS.

The *alarm correlation feature* is implemented as follows: when a system detects an attack, it sends information about this attack with its occurrence date and source IP address to the other systems, which it communicates with. In the same way, it receives information about detected attacks from the other systems and updates its configuration file for each attack (remote date, remote source IP address and counter of remote alarms). Technically, for each probe, a listener ensures the reception of a socket communication initiated by another probe. Each probe (i) is autonomous and receives the communications from the other probes, (ii) has IP addresses of all the other probes in the correlation network, and (iii) has the possibility of initiating a socket communication to transmit a detected alarm to preset probes. So, the alarm process is completely distributed.

To achieve an *event correlation*, when an alarm is received, the model checks whether its last occurrence was local or remote (by looking for the most recent date on the counters). If it was remote or if it was local but with a different source IP address, then there is good chance that this alarm is the sign of a distributed attack. Indeed, three cases are possible:

- the last alarm was remote, the model checks the source IP address and notices that the source IP address is the same: in this case, one IP source address tries to attack several IP destination addresses;
- the last alarm was remote, the model checks the source IP address and notices that the source IP address is not the same: in this case, several source IP addresses try to attack several IP destination addresses;
- the last alarm was local, the model checks the source IP address and notices that the sources IP address is not the same: in this case, several source IP addresses try to attack one destination IP address.

4.3 Motivating Example

Let us take the example of Fig. 3.

Alarm correlation. Suppose the Web server monitored by IDS 1 receives a request. IDS 1 evaluates it as anomalous. It is thus transmitted via a socket communication on the correlation network to IDS 2 and IDS 3. The latter add this alarm in their anomaly history configuration file and flag it as a remote alarm by incrementing their counter of remote alarms.

Event correlation. Once more, suppose the Web server monitored by IDS 1 receives a request. It is analyzed by the anomaly history model, which notices that the request already exists in its configuration file (i.e., the request is anomalous). By checking the dates on the counters, the model determines that the last alarm occurrence was remote. For the last occurrence and the current request, it checks then the source IP addresses and concludes that they are identical. So, the model assumes that the alarm represents a distributed attack tried by one source IP address over multiple destination IP addresses. This result is displayed in the IDS's graphical user interface.

5 Evaluation, Discussion and Future Work

5.1 Evaluation

We partially evaluated our system in real environment. With this intention, we used a set of data (request logs) issued from a production Web server of a real company, namely a service and consulting company established in Luxembourg (Luxembourg). Consolidated subsidiary of a corporate counting 158000 employees over 35 countries and having revenue of €37 billions[5], the Luxembourg company counts about 90 employees and offers a broad range of IT services and products, in particular for state administrations and the Luxembourg financial sector.

The application to protect is a business application collecting the working times to charge on the company's various projects; it is used by all the employees of the Luxembourg office. This application was developed using Java servlets, running in a JBOSS environment, which is based on an Apache Web server. The same type of server (same architecture, same data) is used for the same purpose in Brussels (Belgium) by the Belgian branch of the company, which counts approximately 250 employees and whose core business is the same.

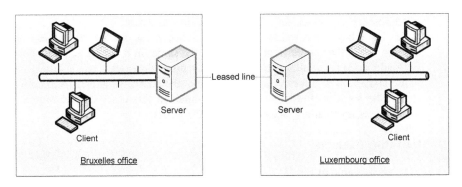

Fig. 4. Architecture of the testing company

The preliminary experiments consist in sending requests containing anomalous events to the implemented analysis models.

For instance, for the *anomaly history model*, one test relates to a request cumulating several anomalous events (reversed attributes, an additional attribute and a too

---

[5] Consolidated financial figures for fiscal year ending March 2006.

long attribute value). This request has already been reported many times, recently, as an attack by the IDS; the anomaly history model stored it in the anomaly file (the remote date is the most recent date of occurrence). When the model receives this request again, it checks if it already exists in its configuration file and returns the result "very suspicious" as well as a probability of only 0,2% for the request to be normal (i.e., a probability of 99,8% to be an attack). The model then determines whether the attack is distributed; in the present case, it displays the message "Distributed attack: one source IP@ to several destination IP@" in the system's log file. Finally, the IDS initiates a socket communication to transmit the detected attack to the other preset probes.

About thirty anomalous events were thus tested (sometimes combined) in normal traffic on the implemented models. Precisely, anomalous requests were injected (which do not constitute attacks inevitably) to check the system's behaviour and its detection capacity. The normal traffic was correctly evaluated; all the attacks were detected by the models and were evaluated as anomalous by the Bayesian network. However, at this stage of development, the Bayesian network did not have sufficient information to specify alarms. This explains why neither false positives nor false negatives were raised. The spectrum of attacks currently covered by those thirty events is only relevant for authentication attacks (because only related models were implemented). Implementation and experiments go on.

```
**********     Anomaly detected     **********
Request:   '159.199.128.202   -   nennoc   [08/May/2006:10:33:49   +0100]
"GET            /secure/timesheet/week/prepare.do?businessDate=2006-05-
01&selectedMenuId=week185467897&tutu=testattack     HTTP/1.1"     200
85860'
Model Attribute presence result: Anomalous
Model Attribute order result: Anomalous
Model Attribute length result: Uncommon
Model Anomaly history result: Very_suspicious
P("Classification" = Normal ) = 0.002053
P("Classification" = Authentification ) = 0.199589
P("Classification" = XSS ) = 0.199589
P("Classification" = Command ) = 0.199589
P("Classification" = DoS ) = 0.199589
P("Classification" = Other ) = 0.199589
Distributed attack: one source IP@ to several destination IP@
```

Fig. 5. Test example for the anomaly history model

5.2 Discussion

The proposed approach, even if shortly described, definitely addresses important security aspects of today's Web infrastructure. However, several points require arguing about.

The evaluation is for the moment the weak part of our work. Especially (i) the evaluation of the added features being in an early stage, the increase in detection performance by the use of the history model hasn't been measured yet; (ii) no numerical comparison to other approaches is possible yet, making impossible to assess the statements that we improve the existing. A baseline to evaluate IDSs is generally given by the false positives and negatives rates, also known as sensitivity and specificity, or precision and recall [5,16]. The basic idea is to measure the number of attacks identified compared to the total number of attacks, and the number of attacks identified compared to the total number of alarms. ROC curves can provide a graphical illustration of the results. The current state of our system does not allow this comparison yet.

A cooperation process is obviously more than the simple exchange of intrusion notifications. At the IDS level, as well as at the enterprise level, there must be a whole framework underlying the cooperation processes; such frameworks exist in the literature, and a new one is also proposed in [11].

There are several issues regarding coordinated attacks as well as attacks on the cooperative IDS, for instance timing issues of event detection. Because time determines the weight of an attack in the anomaly history node, it is obvious that the more the attack will be diluted in time, the more it will be difficult to detect. In the same way, staged distributed attacks will probably not be detected.

What is the real benefit of the cooperation feature compared with a single IDS? First of all, the cooperation feature allows a faster detection, because when an alarm is transmitted, everything is going as if it were detected locally (saving of time). Second, the detection process gains in accuracy since distributed alarms increase for each detected attack its probability of being actually an attack and its criticality. Other benefit is expected, for instance a better reliability for the global system by the transmission of heartbeat messages between IDSs, which allows a faster reaction facing a dysfunction.

Finally, several technical challenges remain to be taken up in the IDS cooperation area. In particular, the interchange format for the cooperation between IDSs has to be improved; in this sense, IDMEF format has been proposed and is intended to be a standard data format, which automated IDSs can use to report alerts about events they deem suspicious [12,31].

5.3 Future Work

Presented work undoubtedly needs further elaboration.

Within the next months, we have the ambition to complete the implementation of the remaining analysis models and to run the system in real environment.

The global validation of the system will consist in really running it on the Web server of the testing company. A three stages validation is planed and should last over eight months, including:

- a training phase on normal events (one full month);
- a phase of evaluation and optimization of the system, including the validation of all the analysis models, of the Bayesian network (already validated manually using GeNIe) and of the alarm clustering process, in particular by simulating various attacks on the system (one month); during this phase, the behaviour of the cooperation feature will also be supervised;
- a detection phase allowing to evaluate the behavior of the optimized system and its long-term performances, including the validation of the cooperation feature over the long-term (six months).

6 Conclusion

The results of our research show that most cooperative activities between information systems take place today via the Web, and that this practice raises major security issues for the concerned Web-based IOS. So, it seemed important to us to contribute to these issues in a research field still little got onto: Web intrusion detection. In this sense, the application layer anomaly detection system proposed in [8,9,10,11] (previous work), able to detect Web-based attacks by examining http requests, shows at this stage of development good results in sensitivity (each step of the detection process reduces the number of false positives to be dealt with) as well as in specificity (if an attack is detected, its type is immediately specified); this allows to handle more efficiently the detection of attacks against Web-based IOS and applications.

To enable the use of the system in a cooperative environment, we were eager to equip it with a cooperation feature. This extension is the central point of the present paper. The addition is twofold: (i) locally as well as globally, by adding a history module to the detection process (feedback), the reoccurrence of malicious queries contributes to future detection decisions and improves the detection delay, (ii) attempts of a single source IP to send malicious queries to different servers, which are being monitored by cooperating IDSs, can be detected by distributing the alarms (i.e., queries, which have been classified as malicious) between these IDSs. The goal of this feature near completion is to achieve effectively alarm correlation as well as event correlation. The alarm process is implemented so as to be totally distributed. Our first experiments on the detection system and on its cooperation feature show encouraging results; implementation and evaluation tasks go on.

References

1. Almgren, M., Debar, H., Dacier, M.: A Lightweight tool for monitoring web server logs. Network and Distributed System Security Symposium (NDSS 2000). San Diego, CA (February 2000)
2. Amami, M., Thévenot, J.: L'Internet marchand: caractérisation et positionnements stratégiques. Systèmes d'Information et Management 5(1) (2000) 5-40
3. Anderson, R.: Security Engineering: A Guide to Building Dependable Distributed Systems. John Wiley & Sons (March 2001). Available at http://www.cl.cam.ac.uk/~rja14/book.html
4. Aubert, B.A., Dussart, A.: Systèmes d'Information Inter-Organisationnels. Rapport Bourgogne. CIRANO (March 2002)
5. Axelsson, S.: The Base-Rate Fallacy and its Implications for the Difficulty of Intrusion Detection. 6th ACM Conference on Computer and Communications Security (1999)
6. Ben Amor, N., Benferhat, S., Elouedi, Z.: Réseaux Bayésiens naïfs et arbres de décision dans les systèmes détection d'intrusions. Technique et Science Informatiques (2006)
7. Cheswick, W.R., Bellovin, S.M., Rubin, A.D.: Firewalls and Internet Security: Repelling the Wily Hacker. Second Edition. Addison-Wesley Professional (February 2003)
8. Dagorn, N.: Détection d'intrusion pour les applications Web. Master's Degree Dissertation in Computer Science. University of Nancy1, France (June 2006)
9. Dagorn, N.: Intrusion Detection for Web Applications (short version). Secrypt International Conference (Secrypt 2006). Setubal, Portugal (August 2006)
10. Dagorn, N.: Intrusion Detection for Web Applications. IADIS International Conference on WWW/Internet (ICWI 2006). Murcia, Spain (October 2006)

11. Dagorn, N.: La sécurité des systèmes d'information coopérants - Proposition d'un système de détection d'anomalie pour les applications Web. Ph.D. dissertation in Management Sciences and Computer Science. Universities of Nancy2 (France) and Luxembourg (Luxembourg) (in progress)

12. Debar, H., Curry, D., Feinstein, B.: The Intrusion Detection Message Exchange Format. Internet Draft IETF (January 27, 2005). http://www.ietf.org/internet-drafts/draft-ietf-idwg-idmef-xml-16.txt (expires: September 17, 2006)

13. Debar, H., Tombini, E.: WebAnalyzer: Détection précise d'attaques contre les serveurs http. 4th Conference on Security and Network Architectures (SAR'05). Batz sur Mer, France (June 2005)

14. Froehlicher, T.: La dynamique de l'organisation relationnelle: conventions et réseaux sociaux au regard de l'enchevêtrement des modes de coordination. Finance Contrôle Stratégie. Economica (2000)

15. Froehlicher, T., Kuhn, A., Schmidt, G. : Compétences relationnelles et métamorphoses des organisations. Eska (2001)

16. Gu, G., Fogla, P., Dagon, D., Lee, W.: Measuring Intrusion Detection Capability: An Information-Theoretic Approach. Symposium on Information, Computer and Communications Security (ASIACCS'06), Taipei, Taiwan. ACM Press (2006) 90-101

17. Ibrahim, M.: Interorganizational Systems From Different Perspectives. Conference of Information Science (Infwet 03). Eindhoven, Niederland (November 2003)

18. Julisch, K.: Clustering Intrusion Detection Alarms to Support Root Cause Analysis. ACM Transactions on Information and System Security 6(4) (November 2003)

19. Julisch, K.: Using Root Cause Analysis to Handle Intrusion Detection Alarms. Ph.D. dissertation. University of Dortmund, Germany (2003)

20. Kruegel, C., Mutz, D., Robertson, W., Valeur, F.: Bayesian Event Classification for Intrusion Detection. 19th Annual Computer Security Applications Conference (ACSAC). IEEE Computer Society Press (December 2003)

21. Kruegel, C., Valeur, F., Vigna, G. : Intrusion Detection and Correlation – Challenges and Solutions. Advances in Information Security 14. Springer Verlag (January 2005)

22. Kruegel, C., Vigna, G., Robertson, W.: A multi-model approach to the detection of web-based attacks. Computer Networks 48(5). Elsevier (August 2005) 717-738

23. Lehtinen, R.: Computer Security Basics. Second Edition. O'Reilly Media (June 2006)

24. Qin, X.: A Probabilistic-Based Framework for INFOSEC Alert Correlation. Ph.D. dissertation. College of Computing, Georgia Institute of Technology, USA (August 2005)

25. Reix, R.: Systèmes d'information et management des organisations. Quatrième édition. Vuibert (June 2002)

26. Scambray, J., Shema, M., Sima, C.: Hacking Exposed Web Applications. Second Edition. Mcgraw-Hill Osborne Media (June 2006)

27. Sharma, P.: The effects of interorganizational systems on process and structure in buyer-seller exchange. Ph.D. dissertation. University of Nebraska–Lincoln, Lincoln, NE (2000)

28. SMILE: Structural Modeling, Inference and Learning Engine. http://genie.sis.pitt.edu/

29. Valdes, A., Skinner, K.: Adaptive, Model-based Monitoring for Cyber Attack Detection. Recent Advances in Intrusion Detection (RAID 2000). Lecture Notes in Computer Science, No. 1907. Edited by H. Debar, L. Me and F. Wu., Springer-Verlag, Toulouse, France (October 2000) 80–92

30. Web Application Security Consortium. http://www.webappsec.org/

31. Wood, M., Erlinger, M.: Intrusion Detection Message Exchange Requirements. Internet-Draft draft-ietf-idwg-requirements-10 (October 2002)

Finding TCP Packet Round-Trip Time for Intrusion Detection: Algorithm and Analysis

Jianhua Yang[1], Byong Lee[1], and Yongzhong Zhang[2]

[1] Department of Mathematics and Computer Science, Bennett College
900 E. Washington Street, Greensboro, NC 27401 USA
{jhyang, blee}@bennett.edu
[2] College of Management, the University of Shanghai for Science and Technology
516 Jungong Rd, Shanghai, 200093 China
yzhang@shtvu.edu.cn

Abstract. Most network intruders launch their attacks through stepping-stones to reduce the risks of being discovered. To uncover such intrusions, one prevalent, challenging, and critical way is to detect a long interactive connection chain. TCP packet round-trip time (RTT) can be used to estimate the length of a connection chain. In this paper, we propose a Standard Deviation-Based Clustering (SDC) Algorithm to find RTTs. SDC takes advantage of the fact that the distribution of RTTs is concentrated on a small range to find RTTs. It outperforms other approaches in terms of packet matching-rate and matching-accuracy. We derive an upper-bound of the probability of making an incorrect selection of RTT through SDC. This paper includes some experimental results to compare SDC with other algorithms and discusses its restrictions as well.

Keywords: Network security, intrusion detection, round-trip time, stepping-stone.

1 Introduction

The use of stepping-stones [1] to attack other computers is gaining popularity on the Internet. One way to prevent this kind of attack is to detect stepping-stones while they are connected. There have been many methods proposed to detect a stepping-stone, such as methods in [1], [2], [11], [12], [13]. The methods proposed in [1], [2] have the problem of not only being vulnerable to an intruder's manipulation, but also having high false positive rate in detecting stepping-stone intrusion. One way to overcome these problems is to examine the whole connection chain to estimate the number of connections (length). There is no good reason to use a connection chain of length three (3) or more to access a host. Yung [3] claims that such a method makes it more difficult for intruders to manipulate connections by delaying or inserting packets.

Estimating the length of a connection chain which starts from a host where a monitor program resides and ends at a victim host has been a focus of research on

D. Pointcheval, Y. Mu, and K. Chen (Eds.): CANS 2006, LNCS 4301, pp. 303–317, 2006.
© Springer-Verlag Berlin Heidelberg 2006

detecting stepping-stone intrusion. Yung [3] proposed to use Ack-delay and Echo-delay comparison to detect an intrusion. His basic idea is to estimate the length of a downstream connection chain by computing the ratio between packet Ack-delay and Echo-delay. To estimate the packet Ack-delay and Echo-delay, Yung proposed to use a statistic method to match TCP send and echo packets. It can result in a correct match only when the echoed packet for one send packet comes back before the next packet is sent. To understand this point well, we here present an example in which we simply assume that each send packet is only echoed by one corresponding packet. For example, it would be trivial to match each send and its corresponding echo in a packet sequence $\{s_1, e_1, s_2, e_2, s_3, e_3, s_4, e_4\}$ in which s_i and e_j represent the timestamps of ith send and j^{th} echo packet respectively. However, if the sequence became $\{s_1, s_2, s_3, e_1, e_2, s_4, e_3, e_4\}$, according to the method in [3], the matching result would be pairs (s_3, e_1), and (s_4, e_3), rather than pairs (s_1, e_1), (s_2, e_2), (s_3, e_3), and (s_4, e_4). Yang and Huang [4] proposed a method to detect stepping-stone intrusion by detecting a long interactive session. Their method is based on the idea that it is highly suspicious to access a host through three or more connections. The method used in [4] to estimate the length of a connection chain from the monitor host to the final destination is to find the RTTs for each level. The number of different levels indicates the chain has different number of connections. Computing the RTTs of TCP packets is essentially to match send and echo packets. Yang and Huang [4] proposed two algorithms to match TCP/IP send and echo packets: the Conservative and the Greedy algorithms. The Conservative algorithm can give accurate packet matching result but with low matching-rate. The Greedy algorithm could 'match' all the send packets but with some incorrect 'matches'. There is a tradeoff for packet matching-rate and matching-accuracy between these two algorithms.

Matching TCP send and echo packets is equivalent to computing TCP packet RTTs. This process is challenging and is significant in detecting stepping-stone intrusion. Whatever method in [3] or [4] is used, only when we have matched send and echo packets precisely can we detect intrusion accurately. In this paper, we propose a novel algorithm SDC to compute the RTTs of TCP packets more accurately than the methods proposed in [4]. We also evaluate the performance of SDC by computing the probability of making a correct selection of RTT through the Chebyshev inequality. SDC can match most of send packets with the same level of correctness as the Conservative algorithm produces, and it produces the same packet matching rate as the Greedy algorithm does, but with a higher matching-accuracy. The experimental results showed that SDC can get both high packet matching-rate and matching-accuracy.

The rest of this paper is arranged as follows. Section 2 discusses the algorithm SDC in details and presents its probabilistic analysis. Section 3 presents some experimental results. In Section 4 we talk about related work. Finally in Section 5 we summarize this paper, discuss the limitations of SDC, and present future work.

2 The Algorithm and Its Probabilistic Analysis

It is easy to match each send packet with its corresponding echo packet when the echo packet of a send is always received before the next packet is sent. This is often the case for a local area network as contrasted to the Internet. On the Internet, overlap of send-echo pair occurs often because of both network delay and host burden. This makes packet matching nontrivial. TCP/IP protocol allows sending the next packet before the previous one is acknowledged [5, 6] for efficiency. As a result, more send packets can be echoed by one packet, and the process makes accurate packet-matching more complicated. First, there is no marker available to identify each packet on the Internet. The available unencrypted information we can use to identify each packet are its size, timestamp, and sequential number. Obviously a packet size cannot provide any information which would be useful in identifying a packet because it depends on an encryption key. The Conservative and Greedy algorithms [4], that use the sequential number to match TCP/IP send and echo packets, have problems in getting both high matching-rate and high matching-accuracy. When there are unmatched send packets followed by some echo packets, there is no way to know which echo packet matches which send packet except for the case that the first send packet always matches the first echo packet, which is the strategy used by the Conservative algorithm. When there is confusion, the strategy used by the Greedy algorithm is to match each send with each echo with FIFO policy which incurs some errors because in some cases they are not one-one map.

The essential problem of the Conservative and Greedy algorithms is they only search for the matched 'candidate' locally when they try to match each send packet. By checking globally, we may have additional information to identify packet-matching even when there exist overlaps of send-echo pair. Through observations over a long period of time, we found that the RTTs of the send packets of a connection chain vary but are bounded within a narrow range. For a sequence of send and echo packets, if we compute all the gaps between each send and each echo packet, organize the gaps into data sets based on each send packet, and combine the data sets to form clusters by taking one element from each data set, then we find that the cluster representing the true RTTs should have the smallest fluctuation among all the clusters.

The strategy of this method is to use the distribution of RTTs to find a packet-matching (or RTTs). We capture $S=\{s_1, s_2, ..., s_n\}$, and $E=\{e_1, e_2, ..., e_m\}$ from one outgoing connection of a host for a period of time. For any send packet s_i, we are not sure which echo packet in E matches s_i, but we do know that the matched packet of s_i must be in E. We assume that each packet in E has possibility to match s_i except for the packets which appear earlier than s_i. We compute the gaps between s_i and each possible packet in E. If we only look at the gaps for s_i, we have no idea which gap represents the true RTT of s_i. But if we look at all the gaps for several send packets in S, it could be clear which gap represents the true RTT of a send packet. Let us demonstrate this point with a real-world example. For the following two sequences S and E that have four send and four echo packets in unit microsecond, respectively,

$S=\{s_1, s_2, s_3, s_4\}=\{1099702684, 1099772525, 1099909440, 1099928524\}$,

$E=\{e_1, e_2, e_3, e_4\}=\{1099828523, 1099898019, 1100036000, 1100058999\}$.

We compute the following data sets based on each send packet s_i in S and echo packet e_i in E:

$S_1=\{\mathit{125839}, 195335, 333316, 356315\}$,
$S_2=\{55998, \mathit{125494}, 263475, 286474\}$,
$S_3=\{-80917, -11421, \mathit{126560}, 149559\}$,
$S_4=\{-100001, -30505, 107476, \mathit{130475}\}$.

By checking the individual data set S_i alone, we have no way to know which element in each data set represents the true RTT. However, if we check all the elements in the four data sets, it is not difficult to recognize that the italicized and bold faced number in each data set represents the true RTT of the corresponding send packet. Even though we do not know exactly which element in each data set represents the true RTT, we know that it must be within each data set. We make a combination by taking one element from each data set, getting 256 combinations from all the elements of the above four data sets. Only the combination with smallest fluctuation has the highest probability to represent the true RTTs with the feature of RTTs distribution considered. In this example, we can verify that the combination consisting of the italicized and bold faced numbers from each data set has the smallest standard deviation among all 256 combinations. Here we use the standard deviation to measure the fluctuation of each combination. Is it always true that the combination with the smallest standard deviation represents the true RTTs? Even though we cannot prove this is true, we can estimate the degree in which it is correct to use the combination with the smallest standard deviation to represent the true RTTs. The SDC Algorithm is proposed based on the above idea.

2.1 The Algorithm SDC

Given two sequences $S=\{s_1, s_2, ..., s_n\}$ and $E=\{e_1, e_2, ..., e_m\}$, if a packet s_i in S is echoed by a packet e_j in E, we denote $s_i \propto e_j$. If all the packets in S and E are captured from an outgoing connection of a host at a period of time, the following conditions must hold:

(1) Any send packet in S must be echoed by one or more packets in E; similarly, any echo packet in E must echo one or more send packets in S;
(2) Packets both in S and E are stored in chronological order; i.e., for any two packets s_i, s_j in S and e_p, e_q in E, if $s_i \propto e_p$, $s_j \propto e_q$, and $i < j$, then $p \leq q$.

Condition (1) indicates that the relationship between a send and its corresponding echo packets may be one-one, many-one, or one-many. The RTT of a send packet can be defined as the gap between the timestamp of a send packet and that of its corresponding echo packet if the relationship between them is one-one. However, if the relationship is many-one or one-many, the gap is not unique. If there are k send packets s_i to s_{i+k-1} echoed by e_j, the RTT of these send packets is defined as the gap between s_{i+k-1} and e_j. Similarly, if a send packet s_i is echoed by k packets e_j to e_{j+k-1}, only s_i and e_j are involved in the RTT definition of s_i. Condition (2) guarantees that send packets must be replied sequentially and a RTT must be a positive value. The above two conditions can be justified by TCP/IP protocol [5], [6].

We compute the gaps between the timestamp of each echo packet in E and that of each send packet in S. It is safe to eliminate the negative values since an RTT must be positive. For the purpose of analysis, we group these gaps in sets according to each echo packet in E, forming data sets E_1, E_2, ..., E_m corresponding to echo packets e_1, e_2, ..., e_m, respectively,

$E_1=\{s_1e_1, s_2e_1,..., s_ne_1\}$,

$E_2=\{s_1e_2, s_2e_2,..., s_ne_2\}$,

...

$E_m=\{s_1e_m, s_2e_m,..., s_ne_m\}$.

An element s_ie_j in E_j represents the gap e_j-s_i between timestamp of jth echo packet in E and that of ith send packet in S, where $1\leq i\leq n$, $1\leq j\leq m$. For the convenience of analysis, we create each data set based on each echo packet in E. These data sets are eventually equivalent to the data sets created based on each send packet in S.

We know that each send packet can be echoed by one or more packets successfully at one time, which indicates that in each data set E_j, there is at most one element that represents the true RTT of the send packet. In the following algorithm, we form a cluster X_u, which is a candidate that may represent the true RTTs, by taking one element from each data set E_j ($1\leq j\leq m$). Each cluster X_u ($1\leq u\leq n^m$) has m elements and some of them may share a same echo or a send packet. We remove all the elements which share the same echo or send packet but keep the one with the smallest gap. Eventually we can get a cluster X_u ($1\leq u\leq n^m$) containing the elements associated with different send and echo packets only. There will be n^m possible clusters, but only one of them can represent the true RTTs. We select the cluster with the smallest standard deviation to represent the true RTTs of the send packets in S among those n^m clusters. The following is the algorithm SDC.

Algorithm SDC(S, E)
Begin:
(1) Generate each data set E_j ($1\leq j\leq m$): $E_j=\{t(i,j) \mid t(i,j) = e_j$-$s_i$, $i=1,...,$ n & $t(i,j)>0\}$;
(2) Combine the elements in each data set E_j ($1\leq j\leq m$) to form a cluster X_u ($1\leq u\leq n^m$): $X_u=\{t(i_j,j)\in E_j \mid \forall 1\leq j\leq m$ & $i_1<i_2...<i_m\}$;
(3) For each cluster X: (a) if $x(i, j)$, $x(i, k) \in X$, $j<k$, then delete $x(i, k)$, and (b) if $x(i, j)$, $x(k, j) \in X$, $i<k$, then delete $x(i, j)$;
(4) Output R = $\{r_1, r_2, ..., r_s\}$ ($1\leq s\leq n$) which is the cluster with the smallest standard deviation among all clusters X_u ($1\leq u\leq n^m$).
End

Let us analyze the time and space complexity of this algorithm. The space complexity is not a serious problem for SDC because it is not necessary to store all the combinations. The time complexity of SDC in the worst case is $O(n^m)$. This will cost much CPU time and make SDC inefficient.. The smaller m and n will have the better time complexity. The parameters m and n can be reduced by dividing a long packet stream of a session into subsections based upon the fact that if an interval between two consecutive send packets, say s_i, and s_{i+1}, is longer than a predefined threshold (usually 1 second), we can assume that all the echo packets after s_{i+1} only reply to the send packets sent after s_{i+1}. This can make m and n smaller but it is difficult to define a proper threshold.

Another factor that can make SDC inefficient is the global computation that looks over all possible Xs to find the RTTs. Instead of generating all the possible Xs, we generate only the clusters which would be candidates of the RTTs. To generate the candidate clusters, we take one element from the first data set E_1 as the first element of candidate X, and then check the second data set E_2 to find one element that can make the smallest standard deviation of X when it is added. In the same way, we can select one element from each of the remaining data sets $E_3 \ldots E_m$ and add them to X so that X has the smallest standard deviation. This process will be repeated for each element in data set E_1. Consequently, we generate n candidates (clusters) upon n elements of data set E_1. Among the n candidates, we select the one with the smallest standard deviation to represent the true RTTs. Using this method, the time complexity of SDC $O(n^m)$ can be reduced to $O(n*(n+n)*(m-1))=O(m*n^2)$.. There is a problem with this method, namely, that we cannot guarantee the correctness of its result because we do not go over all the possible clusters.

2.2 Probabilistic Analysis of SDC

SDC selects the cluster with the smallest standard deviation to represent the true RTTs, but it does not mean that the selected cluster always represents the correct RTTs. It is reasonable to believe, however, that the selected cluster can represent the correct RTTs with a certain probability. In this section, we will compute the probability that the selected cluster R, the cluster with the smallest standard deviation, represents the true RTTs. Each RTT is independent from the others. We only need to compute the probability of making the correct choice of an RTT from R. We first compute the probability of making an incorrect choice of an RTT, say r_j in cluster R. We assume that the distribution of R is Z with mean μ_1 and standard deviation σ_1, and the send packet inter-arrival distribution is Y with mean μ_2 and standard deviation σ_2. According to the SDC Algorithm, the element r_j must be selected from $E_j = \{s_1e_j, s_2e_j, \ldots, s_{k-1}e_j, s_ke_j, s_{k+1}e_j, \ldots, s_ne_j\}$. Let us assume that the correct selection should be s_ke_j, but that other element in E_j is selected. To satisfy the condition that R has the smallest standard deviation, the element in E_j selected incorrectly must be closer to μ_1 than s_ke_j. Only $s_{k-1}e_j$ or $s_{k+1}e_j$ has the highest probability to satisfy this condition because the elements in E_j are in descending order. Here we assume that $s_{k+1}e_j$ is closer to μ_1 than $s_{k-1}e_j$, which means inequality (1) is satisfied,

$$\left| s_{k+1}e_j - \mu_1 \right| < \left| s_ke_j - \mu_1 \right| \tag{1}$$

We assume the smallest inter-arrival of the send packets is L, so that the interval between s_k and s_{k+1} is larger than L while in the worst case is they are equal:

$$s_{k+1} - s_k \geq L = 2q\sigma_1 \tag{2}$$

Here q is a real number that satisfies (2). From the inequality (2), for any echo packet e_j, we have,

$$s_{k+1} - e_j + e_j - s_k \geq 2q\sigma_1$$
$$\left(e_j - s_k \right) - \left(e_j - s_{k+1} \right) \geq 2q\sigma_1$$
$$s_ke_j - s_{k+1}e_j \geq 2q\sigma_1$$
$$s_ke_j - \mu_1 + \mu_1 - s_{k+1}e_j \geq 2q\sigma_1$$
$$\left| s_{k+1}e_j - \mu_1 \right| + \left| s_ke_j - \mu_1 \right| \geq 2q\sigma_1 \tag{3}$$

From equation (1) and (3), we have,

$$\left|s_k e_j - \mu_1\right| > q\sigma_1$$

We compute the probability that r_j is selected incorrectly by using the Chebyshev inequality [7], [8] as the following.

$$P(r_j \text{ is selected incorrectl } y) = P(s_{k+1} e_j \text{ is selected })$$

$$= P(\left|s_{k+1} e_j - \mu_1\right| < \left|s_k e_j - \mu_1\right|)$$

$$\leq P(\left|s_k e_j - \mu_1\right| > q\sigma_1) < \frac{1}{q^2}$$

The probability of making the incorrect selection of a packet RTT is bounded if we select the cluster with smallest standard deviation among all clusters X_u ($1 \leq u \leq n^m$) to represent the true RTTs. So it is easy to compute the probability of making a correct selection of a packet RTT in cluster R by using inequality (4),

$$P(r_j \text{ is selected correctly}) \geq 1 - \frac{1}{q^2} \qquad (4)$$

This demonstrates that the parameter q largely depends on the inter-arrival distribution of the send packets and the distribution of RTTs.

2.3 Estimation of Parameter q

The parameter q is determined by the smallest inter-arrival L of the send packets distribution Y. The probability of making an incorrect selection of a packet RTT is affected by L. If an inter-arrival between two consecutive send packets is the smallest one of Y, we get the highest probability of making a wrong selection of RTT. The chance that an inter-arrival between two consecutive send packets takes the smallest value of Y is very small. Therefore, in practice, to estimate the parameter q, we usually use an inter-arrival L_p which makes the cumulative probability $p(x < L_p)$ in Y be 5% instead, where x represents an inter-arrival between any two consecutive send packets. We estimate L_p based on the assumption that Y is a Gamma distribution with shape parameter β and scale parameter α as shown in (5). The selected L_p must satisfy the following equation.

$$\int_0^{L_p} \frac{(x / \alpha)^{\beta-1} e^{-\frac{x}{\alpha}}}{\alpha \Gamma(\beta)} dx = 0.05 \qquad (5)$$

where $\Gamma(\beta) = \int_0^{\infty} e^{-u} u^{\beta-1} du$.

We can compute L_p from equation (5) if β and α are known. The parameters β and α vary upon the speed of keystrokes and network environment. The most common way to estimate L_p is first to estimate the parameters β and α from a sample of inter-arrivals of send packets using MLE (maximum likelihood estimation) [9], and then to compute the L_p for the distribution Y with the parameters β and α. This method is appropriate for an individual computation, but not for a probabilistic analysis. In this study, instead of estimating a specific value of β and α, we compute ranges of the two parameters, and thus determine a range of values for L_p. The smaller the L_p, the lower probability that an element in data sets E_j ($1 \leq j \leq m$) is selected correctly to represent a true RTT. Therefore, we use the lower bound of L_p to compute the probability for making a correct selection of an element in data sets E_j ($1 \leq j \leq m$) to represent a true RTT using the inequality (4).

We carried out many experiments with different users and different environments on the Internet to build the sample connection chains on different paths at different times. We present some typical examples in Table 1, where the L_p and α are in unit microsecond. We obtained an approximate range of L_p from 32000 to 52000 microseconds from the experimental data. Although the rage of L_p obtained from the experimental data may not represent the exact range of L_p, we can show that it is significant enough for the study with further theoretical analysis. In Section 3, we show how to evaluate the performance of SDC, using the lower bound of L_p to compute the probability of making the correct selection of an RTT.

Table 1. The range of L_p estimated by experiments

Item Sample	Size of each sample	β	α	L_p
1	1297	2.043	137280	51115
2	990	1.956	137480	46448
3	816	1.4434	212600	33733
4	900	1.809	143970	40541
5	176	1.426	280220	43016
6	800	1.629	172720	37617
7	412	1.364	242270	32874

3 Empirical Study

We have proposed that the inter-arrival distribution of TCP send packets of an interactive session can be represented by a Gamma distribution. In this section, we first verify the reasonability of this proposition. It is a very important benchmark to evaluate the performance of SDC in finding the true RTTs of send packets of an interactive TCP session. Second, we compute the probability of making a correct selection of an RTT for some real world examples using the inequality (4). Third, to justify the high performance of SDC in finding true RTTs, we compare SDC with the best existing algorithm used in finding RTTs.

3.1 Verification of Inter-arrival Distribution of TCP Send Packets

We established a TCP interactive session, Acl09→Acl08→H1→H2→H3→H4, in which H1, H2, H3, and H4 are hosts located in the U.S. and Mexico, by using OpenSSH [10]. Acl08 and Acl09 are two local hosts. Host Acl08 is the monitor point where our monitor program resides. We sent packets from the host Acl09 by typing

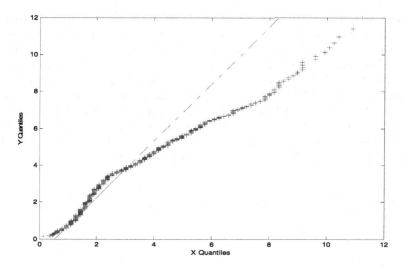

Fig. 1. Verification of send packets inter-arrival distribution

some commands freely and independently. We collected all the send packets on the outgoing connection of Acl08 and computed their inter-arrivals. Then, we fit the distribution of the inter-arrivals using Matlab. Before fitting the distribution, we first drew the histogram of these data to find a distribution they might fit. We found that they are more like a Gamma distribution with a shape parameter larger than one. And then we used the distributing fit function in Matlab to estimate its shape parameter β and scale parameter α.

Once knowing these two parameters, we had a theoretical distribution with shape parameter β and scale parameter α. We used quantile-quantile function in Matlab to verify how well the Gamma distribution agreed with the sample data. Fig.1 shows the verification result of an example, where X and Y axis have scale factor 10^5 in microsecond.

In this example the shape and scale parameters β and α are estimated to be 2.0426, 137280, respectively. From Fig.1, we found that the points with inter-arrival larger than 400,000 microseconds were not well fitted by the Gamma distribution. The dashed line indicates an ideal fitting for the points with inter-arrival larger than 400,000. However the points with inter-arrival less than 400,000 (microseconds) were simulated closely by the Gamma distribution with β=2.0426 and α=137280.

3.2 Probability Estimation

The key idea of the algorithm SDC is to select a cluster with the smallest standard deviation to represent the true RTTs. The best way to justify this point is to compare the RTTs obtained by SDC with the correct RTTs to see if they are consistent. The question is how to compute the correct RTTs. From paper [4] we know that matching each send with its corresponding echo packet is trivial when there is no overlap of send-echo pair. In our first experiment we controlled the speed of keystrokes to generate a scenario without overlap of send-echo pair and this scenario was used to compute the correct RTTs. Then we compared the RTTs obtained from SDC with the correct RTTs to show that SDC can compute the RTTs correctly. In this experiment, the participants were asked to control their keystroke speed. We collected all the send and echo packets in a period of time at Acl08. As a result we established a connection chain similar to the one in Section 3.1. We matched the send and echo packets to compute the correct RTTs, and then used the send and echo packet sequence as the inputs of SDC to find the RTTs. We repeated the experiment many times. One of the comparisons is presented in Fig.2. Here the Y axis represents the RTT value in microseconds and the X axis represents the RTT index number. This experiment result shows that the RTTs from SDC are exactly same as the correct RTTs.

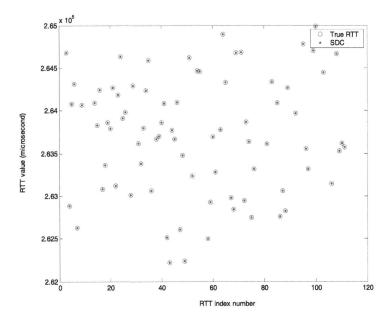

Fig. 2. Verification of SDC under the situation without overlap

This method justified the performance of SDC under a very special situation, i.e., we used correct RTTs to verify with. However, in a real-world situation we do not have correct RTTs due to the overlaps of send-echo pairs. A way to evaluate the performance of SDC is to compute the probability of making a correct selection of RTT.

The second experiment involved evaluating the performance of SDC focusing on the situation when there were overlaps of send-echo pair. We asked the participants to type independently and freely, captured all the send and echo packets in a period of time, and computed the RTTs using SDC. We took L_p=32874 and computed the lower bound of the probability of making a correct selection of RTT by using inequality (4). The results of three examples are presented in Table 2, where μ, σ, q, and p represent average value of the RTTs with unit microsecond, the standard deviation, the q number, and the lower bound of the probability, respectively. The probabilities in these three examples are all higher than 97% and we are confident about the result from SDC. The results show that although we cannot compare the result from SDC with the correct RTTs when there are overlaps of send-echo pair, we still can use SDC to select RTTs to represent correct RTTs with high probability of making a correct selection.

Table 2. The results of probability estimation

Items Examples	μ	σ	q	p
1	264947.0	2810.708	11.695	0.9927
2	265756.3	5514.666	5.9612	0.9719
3	265727.2	5549.605	5.9237	0.9715

3.3 Comparison Between SDC and the Best Algorithm in Finding RTTs

In this section, we compare the performance between SDC and the two best algorithms in finding RTTs. According the literatures, the best algorithm to find RTTs in terms of matching-accuracy is the Conservative algorithm [4] and the Greedy algorithm [4] in terms of packet matching-rate. In addition, there is no algorithm that can obtain both high packet matching-accuracy and high packet matching-rate in finding RTTs. We propose SDC as an algorithm that can achieve both high packet matching-accuracy and high matching-rate in finding RTTs. The test bed is the same as the one in Section 3.1.

First, we compare SDC with the Conservative and Greedy algorithms under the situation that there is no overlap of send-echo pair on the Internet. When we did the experiment we controlled our keystroke speed so that we could make sure there is no overlap of send-echo pair. The three algorithms were run at Acl08 over the same time of period to monitor the same connection chain. The RTTs found by the three algorithms are shown partly in Fig.3, where each point represents the RTT value of one send packet. Fig.3 shows that there is no overlap of send-echo pair and the three algorithms have the same performance in finding the RTTs in terms of matching-accuracy and matching-rate.

Second, we compare the performance of the three algorithms under the situation that there are overlaps of send-echo pair on the Internet. We still used the same test bed as the one described in Section 3.1. In this experiment, instead of controlling the keystroke speed, the participants typed commands at Acl09 freely. We again ran the three algorithms on Acl08 over the same time of period and collected the send and echo packets. The three algorithms gave us three different RTTs. The comparison results are shown partly in Fig.4 and Fig.5.

Fig.4 shows a portion of the RTTs comparison results between the Conservative algorithm and SDC. We collected 169 send packets. Among the 169 send packets, 44 send packets (in Fig.4 only 28 matches are displayed for clarity) are matched by the Conservative algorithm and 169 send packets (in Fig.4 only 71 matches are displayed) are matched by SDC. All the RTTs found by the Conservative algorithm are also found by SDC. Even though we are not sure about the correctness of the other RTTs found by SDC, the results give credence about the correctness of the RTTs computed by SDC from their distribution.

We verify the packet matching-rate of SDC by comparing with the Greedy algorithm. Fig.5 shows a part of the RTTs comparison results between SDC and the Greedy algorithm. It shows that most of the RTTs between the two algorithms are consistent with a few exceptions. Among 169 RTTs found by the SDC, 157 RTTs were also found by the Greedy algorithm. We were not certain about the correctness of the other 12 RTTs (for clarity only 7 of the 12 RTTs are displayed in Fig.5) found by SDC until we compared them with the results of the Conservative algorithm which was supposed to generate the correct results. We found 5 of the 12 RTTs (in Fig.5, the other 7 RTTs are displayed) found by SDC were consistent with the RTTs found by the Conservative algorithm. Even though we cannot judge the correctness of the other 7 of 12 RTTs found by SDC, from their distribution, we could see there existed a possibility that they are correct.

To summarize our comparison results among SDC, the Conservative, and the Greedy algorithms, we found that the algorithm SDC is the only one that can get both high matching-accuracy and high matching-rate in finding RTTs.

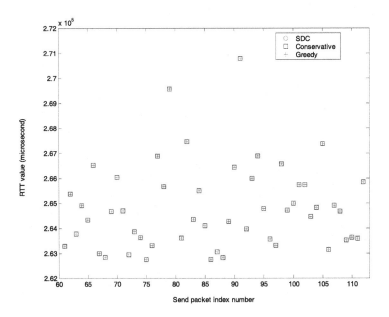

Fig. 3. Packet-matching comparison among the Conservative, Greedy, and SDC without send-echo pair overlaps

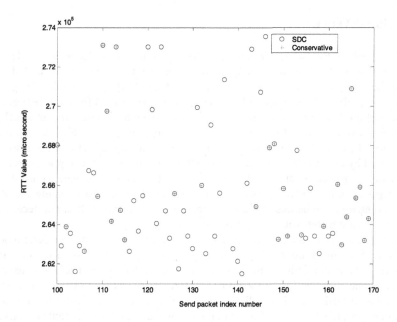

Fig. 4. Comparison between the Conservative and SDC algorithms under overlaps of send-echo pair in finding RTTs

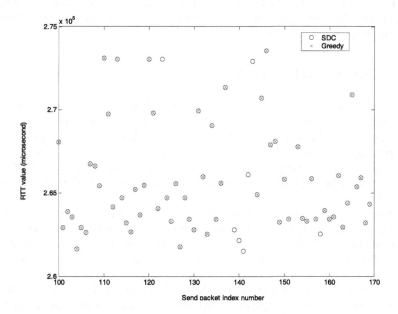

Fig. 5. Comparison between SDC and the Greedy algorithm under overlaps of send-echo pair in finding RTTs

4   Related Work

Work related to this research can be classified into two categories: a) detecting stepping-stones; b) detecting stepping-stone intrusion. Category a) includes the approaches proposed in papers [1], [2], [11], [12], [13], [14]; while Category b) includes the algorithms proposed in papers [3], [4]. The difference between the approaches used in two categories can be characterized as follows: the approaches in category a) can only detect if a host is used as a stepping-stone, while the approaches in category b) can detect not only a host is used as a stepping-stone, but also if the host is used by an intruder. It should be noted that being used as a stepping-stone does not mean being used by an intruder, since some other users also need to use the host as a stepping-stone. In this paper, we propose an algorithm to compute the RTTs, which eventually can be used to detect stepping-stone intrusion. It is not necessary to compare this algorithm with the approaches in category a).

To determine if a host is used as a stepping-stone is easier than to determine if a host is used by an intruder. Most approaches in category a) are used to compare an incoming connection with an outgoing connection to determine if a host is used as a stepping-stone. Content-based method [14], time-based method [1], [2], and packet-number-based method [12], are all classified as the category a). Except for the method given in paper [12], they all suffer from the problems of being vulnerable to intruders' evasion and high false alarm rate in detecting stepping-stone intrusion. The detecting methods based on the RTTs obtained from the clustering algorithm can detect intruders' evasion (time and chaff perturbation), which is not discussed in this paper. It is obvious that the approaches in category b) have no false alarm problem in detecting stepping-stone intrusion.

5   Conclusion and Future Work

Estimating the length of a downstream connection chain is an effective and practical way to detect a stepping-stone intrusion. The core technology of estimating the length of a connection chain is to compute the RTTs by matching each send packet with its corresponding echo packets. We have proposed the algorithm SDC to compute RTTs and a way to evaluate the performance of SDC by probabilistic analysis. SDC takes advantage of the fact that the RTTs of a connection chain obey Gamma distribution to find RTTs.

Empirical studies have shown that SDC can find RTTs with both high packet matching-accuracy and high packet matching-rate. It outperforms the existing best packet-matching algorithm in finding RTTs. Computing results of some real cases showed that the RTT found by SDC can represent the true RTT with a probability higher than 97%.

There are still some problems about the SDC Algorithm. First it is not efficient enough in terms of time complexity. Developing a more efficient one is our future work. We already have discussed briefly a way of reducing the order of the time complexity in Section 2.1. Second, SDC can only compute the packet RTTs for a connection chain on its downstream part. Finding the packet RTTs for the upstream part of a connection chain is more challenging and significant than the present one.

Acknowledgments. We would like to thank Dr. Ray Treadway, and the anonymous reviewers for their helpful feedback and comments on this work.

References

1. Yin Zhang, Vern Paxson: Detecting Stepping-Stones. Proceedings of the 9th USENIX Security Symposium, Denver, CO, August (2000) 67-81.
2. K. Yoda, H. Etoh: Finding Connection Chain for Tracing Intruders. Proc. 6th European Symposium on Research in Computer Security (LNCS 1985), Toulouse, France, September (2000) 31-42.
3. Kwong H. Yung: Detecting Long Connecting Chains of Interactive Terminal Sessions. Proceedings of International Symposium on Recent Advance in Intrusion Detection (RAID), Zurich, Switzerland, October (2002) 1-16.
4. J. Yang, S-H S. Huang: Matching TCP Packets and Its Application to the Detection of Long Connection Chains. Proceedings of 19th IEEE International Conference on Advanced Information Networking and Applications (AINA'05), Taipei, Taiwan, March (2005) 1005-1010.
5. Ylonen, T.: SSH Protocol Architecture. Draft –IETF document, http://www.ietf.org/ internet-drafts/draft-ietf-secsh-architecture-16.txt, June (2004).
6. Ylonen, T.: SSH Transport Layer Protocol. Draft –IETF document, http://www.ietf.org/ internet-drafts/ draft-ietf-secsh-transport-18.txt, June (2004).
7. E. Kao: An Introduction to Stochastic Processes. Duxbury Press, New York, (1996).
8. W. Feller: An Introduction to Probability Theory and Its Applications. Volume I, John Wiley & Sons, Inc., New York, (1968).
9. Normal I. Johnson, Samuel Kotz: Continuous univariate distributions-1. John Wiley & Sons, Inc., New York, (1970) 166-197.
10. T. Ylonen: SSH—Secure Login Connections Over the Internet. 6th USENIX Security Symposium, San Jose, CA, USA, (1996) 37-42.
11. D. L. Donoho (ed.): Detecting Pairs of Jittered Interactive Streams by Exploiting Maximum Tolerable Delay. Proceedings of International Symposium on Recent Advances in Intrusion Detection, Zurich, Switzerland, September (2002) 45-59.
12. A. Blum, D. Song, And S. Venkataraman: Detection of Interactive Stepping-Stones: Algorithms and Confidence Bounds. Proceedings of International Symposium on Recent Advance in Intrusion Detection (RAID), Sophia Antipolis, France, September (2004) 20-35.
13. X. Wang, D.S. Reeves: Robust Correlation of Encrypted Attack Traffic Through Stepping-Stones by Manipulation of Interpacket Delays. Proceedings of the 10th ACM Conference on Computer and Communications Security (CCS 2003), Washington DC, Oct (2003).
14. S. Staniford-Chen, L. Todd Heberlein: Holding Intruders Accountable on the Internet. Proc. IEEE Symposium on Security and Privacy, Oakland, CA, August (1995) 39-49.

Smart Architecture for High-Speed Intrusion Detection and Prevention Systems[*]

Chih-Chiang Wu[1], Sung-Hua Wen[2], and Nen-Fu Huang[2,3]

[1] Computer and Communication Research Center (CCRC), National Tsing Hua University, Taiwan
[2] Institute of Communication Engineering, National Tsing Hua University, Taiwan
[3] Department of Computer Science, National Tsing Hua University, Taiwan
ccwu@cs.nthu.edu.tw

Abstract. The overall performance of an intrusion protection system depends not only on the packet header classification and pattern matching, but also on the post-operative determination of correlative patterns of matched rules. An increasing number of patterns associated with a rule heighten the importance of correlative pattern matching. This work proposes a TCAM-based smart architecture that supports both deep pattern-matching and correlative pattern-matching. The proposed architecture overcomes the difficulties in implementing TCAM when the patterns are very deep and the rules for packet payload involve many patterns whose positions lie within a range. A real case payload is simulated using a Snort 2.3 rule set and simulation results demonstrate the feasibility of the proposed architecture in supporting a high-speed and robust intrusion detection and prevention system.

1 Introduction

Signature matching is the conventional means of detecting the misuse of network protocol behavior in an intrusion detection system and intrusion prevention system (IDS/IPS), and of locating a virus in an anti-virus gateway. Most signature patterns are pre-defined strings, which reveal the presence of worms or viruses. Since various network intrusion methods have been developed, more precise signatures are required to describe the network attacks that cause a rule for packet payload to involve more patterns. We can find in Table 1, the maximum number of patterns in a rule of Snort [1], which is an open-source IDS, is increasing from version to version. In order to match a rule, these patterns should not only be matched by order but they also must be matched by a specified distance or range. Such pattern-matching is called *correlative pattern-matching*. Because the process of correlative patterns is very complicated, the performance of correlative patterns-matching becomes more and more important.

[*] This work was supported by MOE Program for Promoting Academic Excellent of Universities (II) under the grant number NSC-94-2752-E-007-002-PAE, and NSC project under the grant number NSC-94-2213-E007-021.

D. Pointcheval, Y. Mu, and K. Chen (Eds.): CANS 2006, LNCS 4301, pp. 318–328, 2006.

Table 1. The trend of number of patterns in a rule

Versions	Max. number of patterns in a rule
SNORT 2.0	4
SNORT 2.1	6
SNORT 2.2	7
SNORT 2.3	9

Many memory technologies are used for storing the signature database in high-speed IDS/IPS systems. For example, DRAM is usually used for software-based pattern-matching. Although DRAM is a cost-effective solution, when gigabit throughput is required, its refresh characteristic makes it unusable. SRAM is a faster memory device, but it lacks a parallel comparison capability. As the price of Ternary Content Addressable Memory (TCAM) declines, the issue of cost becomes negligible and its parallel comparison capacity makes it more practical for using in gigabit pattern matching. Though TCAM is useful for pattern matching, cascading the TCAM is inefficient for processing deep pattern. In particular, the longest virus pattern announced in ClamAV [2] is far from the width of a single word of TCAM. Additionally, the number of patterns has grown rapidly in the past few years, and the total number of characters has also increased fast. Increasing the length of a pattern reduces the search performance of TCAM as the width of TCAM words is limited. Another problem of using a TCAM device is that only the pattern that has the highest priority is reported. Many patterns with overlapping content cannot be reported simultaneously. Therefore, a new TCAM-based structure is developed herein to overcome these issues.

In this work, a hardware-based pattern matching architecture is presented that not only improves the usage of accompanying FPGA resources when an intrusion detection system is under malicious attack but also increases the processing capacity of pattern-matching and rule-matching. This architecture supports a smart and general matching structure that can solve the problems of matching deep and large patterns and the problem of matching correlative patterns when TCAM is used. With a dedicated FPGA or ASIC, a TCAM-based coprocessor can match correlative patterns and multiple patterns, thus improving the overall performance of Network Intrusion Detection System (NIDS). The open-source Snort IDS will become the attack target of the hacker. Because its open source property, the attacker can obtain the rule database and know how to decrease the throughput of the system.

The rest of this paper is organized as follows. Section 2 reviews related works. Section 3 describes the problem of correlative pattern matching. We describe the proposed architecture in Section 4. Section 5 presents the simulation results. Finally, some conclusions are given in Section 6.

2   Related Work

Two techniques are commonly adopted on a hardware-based pattern matching. One is based on the finite state automata (FSA) [3-6], most of which are implemented by FPGA for flexibility. The other is based on the TCAM or CAM-like circuit [7-9]. Sidhu et al. mapped Non-deterministic Finite Automata (NFA) for regular expression into FPGA to perform fast pattern matching [3] while Moscola et al. translated regular expressions into deterministic finite automata (DFA) [4]. Sourdis mapped a similar design with a deeper pipeline to achieve a bandwidth of 10Gbps [5]. Young et al. also used the chain of byte comparators and ROM to reduce the amount of logic by sorting parts of the data in the memory [6]. Dharmapurikarup et al. proposed an approximate method using bloom filter [10]. Their approach can handle thousands of patterns and detect the patterns at 600Mbps but with number of false positives. Therefore, it needs an additional exact string comparison process to detect the false positive. In all of these works, the compilation time and reconfiguration time required by FPGA design can be in the order of minutes to hours.

In contrast, there are some solutions based on Content Addressable Memory (CAM) device as its seedy parallel comparison ability. Gokhale et al. proposed a fast reprogrammable pattern search system using CAM [7]. Long et al. proposed a keyword match processor using an extension of a standard CAM to handle keys of varying size [8]. Most of these works do not deal with the correlative patterns matching and only handle very few patterns and short pattern length. Our earlier work [13] proposed a high-speed TCAM-based large and deep pattern matching structure that eliminates the problem of cascading TCAM but requires many more FPGA resources to handle continuous virus attack.

In relation to the measurement of the NIDS performance from the input of packets to the reporting of the matched rules, the above-mentioned pattern matching solutions are generally coupled with a host CPU to handle correlative pattern-matching. This method seriously degrades the performance when the rule contains many patterns because correlative patterns matching takes much time than single pattern matching in current software-based solution. Unfortunately, Table 1 presents an increasing number of patterns in a rule. Yu [12] treated such correlative patterns matching as deep pattern matching, based on TCAM and SRAM tables. However, that study had to manage several tables by using a CPU, thus degrading the system when the TCAM hit rate is high. Additionally, that study did not address the "within" option among patterns. So far as we know there is only one article that proposed a hardware-based framework for correlative pattern matching [14]. However, they only checked whether all the patterns in a rule had been matched, without checking the order of and distance among patterns.

3   Correlative Pattern Matching in IDS/IPS

As shown in Fig. 1, a rule may include more than one pattern. We call one bunch of such patterns correlative patterns. These patterns should occur in order and the distance between two consecutive patterns must locate in a pre-defined range.

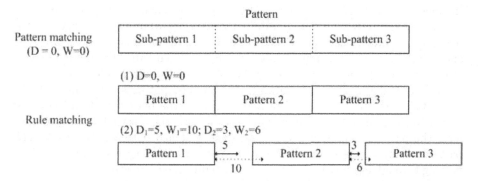

Fig. 1. Examples for patterns and rule for packet payload

Two parameters are used to define the range of distance between two consecutive patterns: distance (D) and Within (W). For example, pattern 2 must occur at 5-10 bytes after pattern 1, while pattern 3 must occur at 3-6 bytes after pattern 2. Note that the negation operator (!) is usually supported in IDS/IPS rule. For example, *content: "USER"; nocase; content: ¡'|0a|"; within: 20*, is used to detect the buffer overflow attack. Therefore, if a pattern does not occur at the expected range, the negation operator should be checked for determining the result.

The D and W in a rule are often not equal to 0. Two consecutive patterns can be treated as one pattern when D and W are equal to 0. Therefore, the case 1 for a rule in Fig. 1 is impossible to exist. However, if TCAM is used to match a pattern, the pattern may be portioned into many sub-patterns due to TCAM's word width limitation. For example, in Fig. 1, a pattern is partitioned into three sub-patterns. If all of these three sub-patterns are matched, the pattern is matched. It is interested that pattern matching can be treated as a case for $D=0$ and $W=0$ by using the same mechanism for matching a rule. Note that pattern 1 is also called as "head pattern", while sub-pattern 1 is called as "head sub-pattern" in this paper. The operation for pattern matching has been described in our previous study [13]. In this paper, we extend the architecture for matching both pattern and rule, which includes correlative patterns.

4   Proposed System Architecture

The whole system architecture is demonstrated in Fig. 2. TCP assembly is performed before the rule matching. Rule matching is a two-stage process: pattern matching stage and correlative pattern matching stage. In the pattern matching stage, the incoming string is shifted one character in one clock cycle and fed into TCAM. If TCAM's word width is w bytes, then each pattern is partitioned into w-byte sub-pattern except the last sub-pattern. If the last sub-pattern is very short, it will be matched frequently. In order to solve this problem, we adopt the method in [12], that some bytes of the previous pattern are appended to let the last sub-pattern fit into w bytes exactly. All the patterns are arranged in descending order and placed in TCAM. For example, the order is "abcde", "abcd*", and "abc**". The "*" means "don't care" byte. When "abcde" is matched, the other two patterns are also matched. We use a multi-output addresses mechanism described in [13] to generate all the matched patterns simultaneously. If sub-patterns or short patterns are matched, then the matched TCAM address is sent to the central control unit (CCU). CCU uses the received address to perform the pattern matching and records each matched pattern's ID (PID) and pattern occurrence position (POP) in the pattern matching result queue. After passing through all the bytes of a packet, we enter the correlative pattern matching stage. In this stage, a PID and POP pair is fed into CCU to match against the rule database. The arbiter is used to switch the stage of CCU and decides the output of CCU is stored into pattern matching result queue or into the rule matched queue.

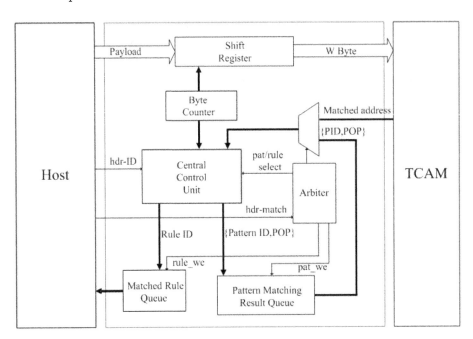

Fig. 2. System architecture

Correlative pattern matching does not always need to be executed. In a high-speed IDS/IPS system, the packet header and packet payload are matched against different rules. The time of header matching is usually shorter than payload matching. Therefore, the "hdr-match" signal in Fig. 2 is used for the arbiter to determine whether the correlative pattern matching should be executed. If the header of a packet matched some header rules, the hdr-ID (HID) is sent to CCU to identify the finally matching result. If HID and correlative patterns are matched with a rule, the matched rule ID (RID) is stored to matched rule queue and the Host is interrupted to retrieve the results. In this stage, the shift register, byte counter and TCAM can be turned off to save power. Pattern and Rule Table is stored in the embedded SRAM for high-speed memory access. Each entry in the pattern table records the PID, a set of TCAM addresses that represent all the related sub-patterns of a pattern, and the number of sub-patterns that is waiting to be matched. Similarly, each entry of the rule table contains the rule ID, the related HID, number of patterns to be matched, all the PIDs that are waiting to be matched, and values of D and W for each pattern.

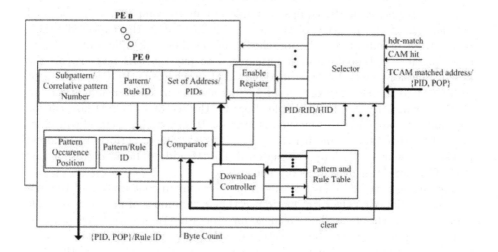

Fig. 3. Central control unit (CCU)

The central control unit (CCU), which is the kernel part of the whole system, is shown in Fig. 3. It consists of four main blocks: Processor Elements (PE), Selector, Pattern and Rule Table, and Download Controller. Several PEs in the CCU can handle the sub-pattern matching results output from TCAM in parallel, while they are also used to handle correlative pattern matching. A PE is enabled when a head sub-pattern is matched in TCAM or a PID for a head pattern enters the CCU. After enabling, the PE downloads the related entry from the pattern and rule table according to the PID or RID it received. Then it waits for following TCAM matched results in pattern matching stage or {PID, POP} pair in the correlative pattern matching stage. In the pattern matching stage, if the comparison result is mismatched with the set of addresses stored in the PE, the PE will release itself and notify the selector that it can be chosen for serving next pattern. However, in the correlative pattern matching stage, PE will check the received PID with its expected PID, and check the received POP with its expected range of pattern's position. No matter the received PID is matched or not matched with its expected PID, if the received POP is less than or in the range of expected pattern's position, the PE has to wait for the next

{PID, POP} pair. If the received POP is larger than its expected range, then PE will check whether the negation option of the pattern is set. If the negation operator of this pattern is not set, the PE will release itself to the Selector. This is because it has no need to check the following {PID, POP} pair. Otherwise, it means the pattern is matched, and the PE will continue to wait for the following {PID, POP} pair. This mechanism guarantees that the correlative patterns are correctly matched by order. While the whole pattern is matched, the PID and POP are stored in the pattern matching result queue and the PE is released. Similarly, if a whole rule (i.e. header rule and correlative patterns) is matched, the matched rule ID is stored to the matched rule queue.

In this paper, each PE equips a simple circuit to compare the position of the pattern. If the position of the pattern is located in the expected range, this pattern is indicated to be matched. This method is simple and fast. Another possible method for range matching is to put the PID and express the range value into several entries in the TCAM. Each {PID, POP} pair is sent to TCAM to match the exact result, and then the matched result is sent to CCU for matching the payload rule. Because the required TCAM size can be determined in advance, this method is feasible. However, this method consumes many TCAM resources, and it needs an additional table to perform the address translation, which translates the matched TCAM address to its corresponding PID. Therefore, this method is not suggested.

Supporting correlative pattern matching is the main contribution of this paper. As mentioned in the introduction section, the number of patterns in a rule is increasing as the trend. The overhead for processing these correlative patterns is increasing accordingly. Many existing IDS/IPS systems use SNORT and only use pure software to implement the system. Because the database and the algorithm for SNORT are all open, attackers can easily attack the weakness of the system. So far as we know many existing software and hardware solutions put all the matched head patterns (i.e. the first pattern of a rule) in a queue. If there are n head patterns in the queue, for each {PID, POP} pair, it requires $O(n)$ time to process the matching. Attackers can use this weakness to slow down the performance of the system. However, in this paper, all the enabled PEs process the matching simultaneously. Therefore, the matching time for each {PID, POP} pair is $O(1)$. The required number of PEs can be determined when the rule set is determined and it only depends on the characteristic of rules.

5   Simulation Results

Some simulations are performed to test the effectiveness of the proposed architecture. After compiling the Snort 2.3 rule set, the partitioned patterns are placed in the TCAM, and pattern table and rule table are placed in the embedded SRAM of the CCU. In these simulations, test packets from DEFCON [11] are fed into the system to evaluate the system performance.

There are two situations that influent the performance of the correlative pattern matching. One is the number of patterns in a rule and the other is

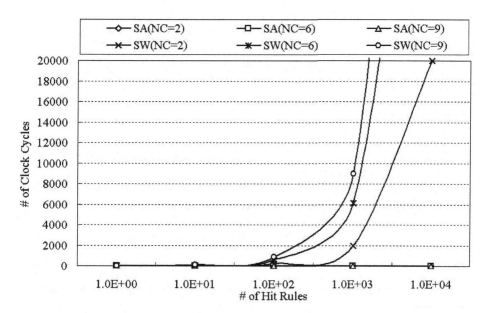

Fig. 4. Correlated patterns match performance comparison in different number of correlated patterns (NC) in a rule and number of matched rules

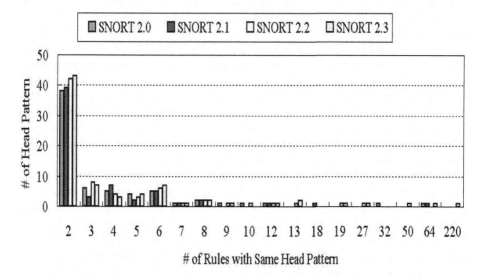

Fig. 5. The trend of the number of the rules with the same head pattern

the number of the rules that have the same head pattern. The first is easy to understand. If there are more patterns to be matched, it will take more time to process the correlative pattern matching. The reason for the second is that in many correlative patterns matching algorithms (e.x. [14] or some pure

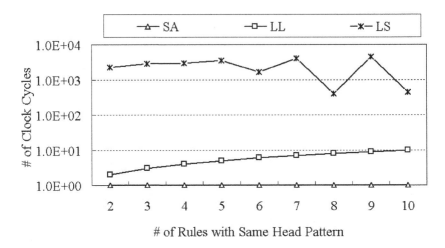

Fig. 6. Performance comparison of different correlative patterns processing methods

software solutions), the more head patterns are matched, the more search time is consumed.

The simulation result shown in Fig. 4 presents the performance comparison between pure software algorithm used in the Snort's algorithm and the proposed smart architecture (SA) with different number of correlative patterns.

It can be seen that the pure software processing takes exponential increasing clock cycles when the number of matched rules is increased. Especially when the number of correlative patterns in a rule (NC) is increased, the number of clock cycles is increased much more, thus decreasing the system performance seriously. On the other hand, SA keeps the processing clock cycles increased little by little as the number of correlative patterns is increased. Such parallel processing ability of SA keeps the system always in high performance. As mentioned before, the required number of PEs can be determined when the rule set is determined and it only depends on the characteristics of rules. Therefore, if the rule set is determined, we can know if the hardware resource is enough to handle the worst-case situation and guarantee the performance.

The second case becomes more serious than before as we can find in Fig. 5, many rules have the same head pattern. We can find in the figure, the number of patterns that are included in many rules is increasing. For example, in Snort 2.0 rule set, there are only 38 head patterns that appear in 2 rules. In Snort 2.3 rule set, 43 head patterns appear in 2 rules. Besides, we can see in this figure, the rule set of Snort 2.3 has 220 rules that have the same head pattern. If attackers use this pattern to attack the IDS/IPS system, some non-well-designed system's performance may be decreased seriously. Therefore, we perform the simulation for different number of the rules with the same head pattern to compare the performance for different approaches.

If we have a matched head pattern, and we want to find the corresponding rule in the rule table. There may have three methods to process the matching. The first one called as LS, is to search all the rules linearly in the rule table. The

Attig [14] proposed another method that is called as LL here to collect all the possible matched rules via linked list. Finally, SA is our proposed architecture. Assuming each accessing memory time is one clock cycle. The simulation result is shown in Fig. 6. It can be concluded that no matter how many rules that have the same head pattern, the SA always needs only a constant time to find out all the possible rules, as there are enough PEs to be triggered when any head pattern is matched. The average time LS will spend to match rule is independent of number of rules with the same head pattern but is much more than the other two methods. As to LL, the clock cycles spent to match rule is proportional to the number of rules.

6 Conclusions

In this paper, a smart architecture is proposed to handle both pattern matching and correlative patterns matching, which is part of the payload rule matching in high-speed intrusion detection and prevention systems. The simulation results show that the proposed architecture is efficient to handle the correlative patterns matching, especially to those rules that have same head pattern (i.e. same first pattern). As the proposed architecture is implemented with parallel processing elements, the system performance can be guaranteed. Even the proposed architecture is the first design that provides the well-consideration correlative patterns matching; we believe the processing cost is relative low due to the reuse of the architecture.

References

[1] SNORT official web site, http://www.snort.org.

[2] ClamAV database, http://www.clamav.net.

[3] R. Sidhu and V. K. Prasanna.: Fast Regular Expression Matching using FPGAs. *Proc. of the 9th annual IEEE Symposium on Field-Progammable Custom Computing Machines (FCCM'01)*, Rohnert Park, California, USA, April 2001, pp. 223-232.

[4] J. Moscola, J. Lockwood, R. P. Loui, and M. Pachos: Implementation of a Content-scanning Module for an Internet Firewall. *Proc. of the 11th annual IEEE Symposium on Field-Progammable Custom Computing Machines (FCCM'03)*, Napa, California, USA, April 2003, pp. 31-38.

[5] Sourdis, et al.: Fast, Large-scale String Match for 10Gbps FPGA-based Network Intrusion Detection System. *Proc. of the 13th Conference on Field Programmable Logic and Applications (FPL'03)*, Lisbon, Portugal, September 2003, pp. 880-889.

[6] Young, et al.: Deep Network Packet Filter Design for Reconfigurable Devices. in *Proc. of the 12th Conference on Field Programmable Logic and Applications (FPL)*, Montpellier, France, September 2002.

[7] M. Gokhale, et. al.: Granidt: Towards Gigabit Rate Network Intrusion Detection Technology. *Proc. of the 12th International Conference on Field Programmable Logic and Applications (FPL'02)*, Montpellier, France, September 2002, pp. 404-413.

[8] Long Bu and John A. Chandy: FPGA Based Network Intrusion Detection using Content Addressable Memories. *Proc. of the 12th annual IEEE Symposium on Field-Progammable Custom Computing Machines (FCCM'04)*, Napa, California, USA, April 2004. pp 316-317.

[9] M. Silberstein, et al.: Designing a CAM-based Coprocessor for Boosting Performance of Antivirus Software. *Technion technique report*, March 2004.

[10] Sarang Dharmapurikarup, et al.: Deep Packet Inspection using Parallel Bloom Filters. *IEEE Micro*, Vol. 24, No.1, January 2004. pp. 52-61.

[11] DEFCON web site, http://www.defcon.org.

[12] Fang Yu, Randy H. Katz and T. V. Lakshman: Gigabit Rate Packet Pattern-Matching Using TCAM. *Proc. of the 12th IEEE International Conference on Network Protocols(ICNP'04)*, Berlin Germany, October 2004. pp. 147-183.

[13] C. -C. Wu, S. -H. Wen, N. -F. Huang, and C. N. Kao: A Pattern Matching Coprocessor for Deep and Large Signature Set in Network Security System. *IEEE Globecom 2005*, St. Louis, USA, November 2005.

[14] Michael E. Attig and John Lockwood: A Framework for Rule Processing in Reconfigurable Network Systems. *Proc. of the 13th annual IEEE Symposium on Field-Progammable Custom Computing Machines (FCCM'05)*, Napa, California, USA, April 2005.

A Multi-agent Cooperative Model and System for Integrated Security Monitoring*

Xianxian Li and Lijun Liu

School of Computer Science and Engineering, Beihang University, Beijing, China
{lixx, liulijun}@buaa.edu.cn

Abstract. The increasing complexity of various network threats has made the integration and cooperation of multiple security monitoring technologies necessary in network security defense. However, most existing works have focused on certain special monitoring technologies such as intrusion detection, and studies on integrated security monitoring system are quite insufficient. In this paper, a novel formal model called MCSM (Multi-agent Cooperation model for Security Monitoring based on knowledge) is proposed. In MCSM, the integrated security monitoring is modeled as a FSA (Finite State Automata) with multiple agents, and a general knowledge structure for multiple agents is constructed. We have successfully developed an IMS (Integrated Monitoring System) called ACT-BroSA (Broad-spectrum security Scan and Analysis system) based on MCSM. Results of experiments show that the integrated monitoring capability is significantly improved.

Keywords: Network security, Security monitoring, Multi-agent cooperation, Knowledge Management.

1 Introduction

With the increasing complexity of different network threats, relying on any single technology is not enough to meet the secure defense requirements. Then it brings about an important area: how to integrate multiple security monitoring technologies in network defense? In some cases, integrating multiple detection technologies can improve the integral monitoring effect significantly. For example, we can check the vulnerable situation of the object host and eliminate false alarms by integrating IDS (Intrusion Detection System) and vulnerability scan system [1, 2, 3], and the combination of IDS and security audit system may be used to automatically extract intrusion evidences.

To integrate multiple security monitoring systems, we face two basic challenges: cooperating and uniformly managing the knowledge for different systems, because various security systems are heterogeneous in architectures and working mechanisms. Unfortunately, to the best of our knowledge, there is no efficient solution available to construct a compact integrated security monitoring system up to now.

---

* This work is supported by Program for New Century Excellent Talents in University.

D. Pointcheval, Y. Mu, and K. Chen (Eds.): CANS 2006, LNCS 4301, pp. 329–341, 2006.

In this paper we propose a novel formal model called MCSM (Multi-agent Cooperation model for Security Monitoring based on knowledge) for constructing the IMS. In MCSM, every monitoring system is modeled as an agent and multi-agent technology is used to model the integration and cooperation of multiple monitoring technologies. The model consists of two levels: the KAM (Knowledge Action Model) and the CDM (Cooperation Detection Model). In the KAM, we build a general knowledge structure for multi-type monitoring systems based on predicate logic. This structure can support efficient scan algorithms and provide the unified knowledge management for integrating multiple systems. In CDM, we further describe how the knowledge structure can affect their cooperation. Then the cooperating and scheduling mechanisms of multi-agents are modeled with the FSA (Finite State Automata).

Based on MCSM, we have proposed a novel method for constructing IMS which includes a new architecture and the supporting technologies, and successfully developed the ACT-BroSA (Broad-spectrum security Scan and Analysis system). In ACT-BroSA, we implemented the integration and cooperation of multiple security monitoring systems. We also evaluated the efficiency of the scan algorithm and the effect of the cooperative monitoring, which are the most important aspects of MCSM.

In the field of modeling security system using multi-agent, most existing works focused on certain technologies such as firewall [6, 7, 10] and IDS [8, 9]. Research works on the integration and cooperation of multi-type systems are still quite few. In the system development field, the existing solutions [4, 5] provided by the industry community focused too much on the integration of special security products through extern interfaces, but the general cooperation mechanism and the theoretical model study were neglected. Our work mainly focuses on the modeling and constructing of integrated security system, and we believe it is an important complement to current works.

2 Related Work

Many efforts have been made on the modeling of security system based on multi-agent technology [8-15, 18]. A multi-agent based model for distributed intrusion detection and response is proposed in [8, 10]. [9] and [12] explore the implementation of intrusion detection and firewall framework based on the mobility of agent. They all focus on special security technology, but the integration and cooperation of multi-type security technologies are not discussed.

In [14], an intelligent network security management model based on multi-agents is proposed. It refers to the decision making and the cooperation of agents based on interactions, but the detailed cooperation and decision mechanisms are not described. [15] constructs a model for the network security management and proposes a new multi-agent architecture. The main focus is the agents' function and the model architecture rather than the cooperation mechanism.

The works in [16] and [17] focus on the cooperation mechanism of multi-agents. In [16], the knowledge is defined as a character of agent and the knowledge structure is discussed. [17] describes the cooperation mechanism between agents and proposes a new layered topology of the multi-agent system. The formal model about the knowledge and the cooperation activity is not considered in both of them.

Our work described in this paper differs from them because it focuses on the integration and cooperation of multi-type security technologies. In our model, the knowledge structure and its impact on the cooperative activities of multi-agents are described in detail.

3 Knowledge Action Model (KAM)

An IMS needs to process different types of threats (such as network intrusion, virus, vulnerability probe, audit event, etc.), so a unified description for them is very helpful for the IMS. Existing work mainly focus on characterizing behaviors of intruders. But it is difficult to build a unified model for describing intrusion actions since they are different in thousands ways. In our studies, we concentrate on the data structure that expresses these threats, instead of semantic characterization of intrusion behaviors. Our purpose here is to build the unified knowledge management for multiple monitoring systems and support an efficient scan algorithm.

3.1 Scan Model

We find that the data expressing various security threats are made up of some basic elements with certain characters, and we call each element "knowledge particle". Based on this, we can describe various threats as structured data and construct the unified knowledge management model for IMS from the viewpoint of data analysis. To describe the knowledge, we'll give some notions formally.

Definition 1. The set consisting of all knowledge particles is called a Knowledge Domain.

Knowledge Domain A is a finite set. It may grow dynamically with the accumulation of knowledge.

Definition 2. A finite sequence $a_1a_2,...,a_n$ $(n{\geq}1)$ on knowledge domain A is called Knowledge Snippet. The set of all knowledge snippets is denoted by A^*.

The basic function of a security monitoring system is to perform scan actions on the source data and check whether the source data match the security knowledge. We use predicate logic to model this process.

Let S be the set of source data that are scanned by the monitoring systems, and S can be considered as countable and infinite.

For every knowledge particle a, an analysis algorithm f_a is a mapping from S to $\{0,1\}$, that is, $f_a(s){\in}\{0, 1\}$ for $\forall s{\in} S$.

Now we can describe the **Scan Model** as follows:

Syntax: Constant set S is a countable infinite set, X a set of variants, and Knowledge domain A is a finite set of unitary predicates.

Semantics: The element of S is explained as the source data, and is denoted by s. Variant x is explained as a mapping from X to S. For $\forall a{\in}A$, $a(x)|_{x=s}=f_a(s)$, where f_a is the analysis algorithm defined above.

Semantics of Knowledge Snippet: For $a_1a_2,...,a_n \in A^*$, we define $a_1a_2,...,a_n(x) = a_1(x) \wedge a_2(x) \wedge,...,\wedge a_n(x)$.

Hence, knowledge snippet may also be explained as a predicate.

3.2 Knowledge Structure Model

Definition 3. If $a, b \in A$, $a(s) \wedge b(s) = 0$ for $\forall s \in S$, then we say that a and b are Mutually Exclusive.

Definition 4. A Knowledge Tree is a tree consisting of knowledge particles, as shown in Fig.1.

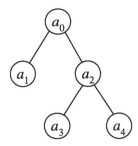

Fig. 1. Knowledge tree structure

In a knowledge tree, the path from every node to the root node forms a knowledge snippet (e.g., the knowledge snippet from a_3 to a_0 is $a_0a_2a_3$ in Fig.1).

Definition 5. Let T be a knowledge tree. If all the brother nodes of T (except the root node) are pairwise mutually exclusive, then we say that T is Well-Structured.

Definition 6. Let F be a forest consisting of multiple well-structured knowledge trees. If the root nodes of all trees are pairwise mutually exclusive, then we call F an Orthonormal Knowledge Base.

Definition 7. Given a knowledge tree T, a knowledge snippet from a leaf node to the root node is called an Integral Knowledge (IK for short) for T, and is denoted by P. The set of all the IKs of T is called the Knowledge Base of T, and then the knowledge base of a forest is the union of all the knowledge bases of its member trees.

For example, the knowledge base of the tree in Fig.1 is the set $\{a_0a_1, a_0a_2a_3, a_0a_2a_4\}$.

Let T be a knowledge tree (or forest), and let $\{P_1, P_2,...,P_n\}$ be the knowledge base of T. We define

$$T(s) = P_1(s) \vee P_2(s) \vee,...,\vee P_n(s), \text{ for } \forall s \in S.$$

Then a knowledge tree (or forest) may also be explained as a predicate in BSM model.

Lemma 1. Let $\{P_1, P_2,...,P_n\}$ be the knowledge base of a well-structured know-ledge tree T. If $P_i \neq P_j$, then $P_i(s) \wedge P_j(s) = 0$ for all $s \in S$.

Proof: We assume that $P_i = a_0a_1,...,a_n$, $P_j = a_0b_1,...,b_m$, where a_0 is the root node, a_n and b_m are leaf nodes, and $a_n \neq b_m$ (otherwise $P_i = P_j$). There exists a k ($1 \leq k \leq \min\{n,m\}$)

such that $a_k \neq b_k$ and $a_{k-1} = b_{k-1}$. This implies that a_k and b_k are brother nodes of T, thus $a_k(s) \wedge b_k(s) = 0$ since T is well-structured. Hence, $P_i(s) \wedge P_j(s) = a_0(s) \wedge a_1(s) \wedge, \dots, \wedge a_n(s) \wedge b_1(s) \wedge, \dots, \wedge b_m(s) = 0$.

Theorem 1. Let $\{P_1, P_2, \dots, P_n\}$ be the knowledge base of a well-structured knowledge tree T. For $\forall\ s \in S$, $T(s) = 1$ **iff** there exists a unique $P_i \in \{P_1, P_2, \dots, P_n\}$ such that $P_i(s) = 1$.

Proof: The existence can be concluded from the definition of $T(s)$, and the uniqueness can be known from Lemma 1.

Corollary 1. Let K be an orthonormal knowledge base. $\{P_1, P_2, \dots, P_n\}$ is K's knowledge set. For $\forall\ s \in S$, $K(s) = 1$ **iff** there exists a unique $P_i \in \{P_1, P_2, \dots, P_n\}$ such that $P_i(s) = 1$.

3.3 An Scan Algorithm for the Orthonormal Knowledge Base

Let K be an orthonormal knowledge base, and F_K is the scan algorithm on K. The function of F_K is to check whether $K(s) = 1$ holds for $\forall s \in S$. It is described as follows:

```
The root node of the first knowledge tree of K is
denoted by a_0
   Begin
         a=a_0
         While(a≠ Null)
         {
                 if a(s)= True then
                     if isLeaf(a)=True then
                         return 1;
                     else
                         a=leftChild(a);
                     end if
                 else
                     a=rightNode(a);
                 end if
         }
         return 0;
   End
```

Let a be a node of K. If a is a root node of a tree in K, then we use $N_K(a)$ to denote the number of trees in K. If a is not a root node, then $N_K(a)$ denotes the number of a's brother nodes (including a). Let $P = a_1 a_2, \dots, a_n$ be an knowledge of K, we define

$$N_K(P) = \sum_{i=1}^{n} N_K(a_i).$$

Complexity Analysis of the algorithm. Let ω be the time cost of scanning a knowledge particle. The computing complexity of F_K is:

$$o(F_K) \leq \omega \cdot \text{Max}\{\ N_K(P)|\ P \text{ is a knowledge of } K\ \}.$$

Note that the complexity of an algorithm that scans a knowledge base M without well-structured form is $\omega \cdot l \cdot |M|$, where l is the average number of the particles in a knowledge. In security monitoring, $|M|$ can be very large, but $N_K(P)$ in an orthonormal knowledge base is very small, then $o(F_K)$ is much less than $\omega \cdot l \cdot |M|$. So the efficiency of scan algorithm can be improved largely by constructing the knowledge base in the well-structured way.

4 Cooperation Detection Model (CDM)

In CDM, every security monitoring system is modeled as an agent and the IMS is modeled as a multi-agent system.

4.1 Multi-agent State Space Model

Let $Syn = \{A_1, A_2, ..., A_N\}$ be an IMS which consists of N subsystems (agents). Let *Action* be the set of actions that all agents may take, which includes actions like alert, log, run a program, activate cooperation, etc. We use Θ to denote null action and define $\Theta \in Action$.

Definition 8. Let *Syn* and *Action* be the sets defined above. $(A, C) \in Syn \times Action$ is called a State of A. The set $\{(A, C) | C \in Action\}$ is called a State Space of A, and is denoted by $STATE_A$. The Cartesian Product $\Pi_{A \in Syn} STATE_A = STATE_{A_1} \times ... \times STATE_{A_N}$ is called a Global State Space of *Syn*, and is denoted by $STATE_{Syn}$. For a non-empty subset $\Phi \subset Syn$, $\Pi_{A \in \Phi} STATE_A$ is called a Local State Space, and is denoted by $STATE_\Phi$.

Definition 9. An element of $STATE_{Syn}$ is called a Global State, and an element of $STATE_\Phi$ is called a Local State.

Definition 10. A mapping on $STATE_A$ is called a State Function of A, a mapping on $STATE_{Syn}$ is called a Global State Function, and a mapping on **$STATE_\Phi$** is called a Local State Function.

The state function of identity mapping is denoted by ε. The set of all state functions of A is denoted by TF_A, and the set of all local state functions on $STATE_\Phi$ is denoted by TF_Φ.

Let TF_{Syn} be the set of all state functions (including local state functions). We define two operations on TF_{Syn} as follows:

Combination operation "$\cdot$": $\sigma_1 \cdot \sigma_2(\alpha) = \sigma_1(\sigma_2(\alpha))$, where α is a state.

Union operation "$\oplus$": For $\sigma_1 \in TF_\Phi$, $\sigma_2 \in TF_\Psi$, and $\Phi \cap \Psi = \varnothing$, $(\sigma_1 \oplus \sigma_2)(\alpha) = \sigma_1(\alpha_1) \cup \sigma_2(\alpha_2)$, where $\alpha \in STATE_{\Phi \cup \Psi}$, $\alpha_1 \in STATE_\Phi$, $\alpha_2 \in STATE_\Psi$.

For the operation "$\cdot$", there is a unit function ε, such that $\varepsilon \cdot \sigma = \sigma \cdot \varepsilon = \sigma$.

We define a special state function symbol θ as follows:

For any state function σ, we have $\theta \cdot \sigma = \sigma \cdot \theta = \theta$ and $\theta \oplus \sigma = \sigma \oplus \theta = \sigma$. We call θ a zero function. Let $B = \{\varepsilon, \theta\}$, then B and the two operations defined above have formed a simple algebraic structure. We will use it to describe the knowledge semantics of multi-agents.

4.2 Cooperation Model

A rule that controls the agent's activity consists of two parts: the precondition and the action that will be taken when the precondition is satisfied. The latter is just a state transition of the agent, which is corresponding to a state function.

We first assume that an agent have only one orthonormal knowledge base. Let A be an agent. K_A is the knowledge base of A, P is an integrated knowledge in K_A, TF_A is the set of all state functions of A, and S is the set of source data.

Definition 11. An Activity Rule R of agent A is a mapping from $K_A \times S$ to TF_A defined by the following

$$R(P, s) = \begin{cases} \sigma_P, & \text{if } P(s) = 1 \\ \varepsilon, & \text{if } P(s) = 0 \end{cases}, \quad \text{where } \sigma_P \in TF_A.$$

The state of A will be transferred by σ_P when the precondition P is satisfied. If P is fixed, a mapping from S to TF_A is also defined by the above formula, then $R(P, s)$ may be written as $R_P(s)$. We call R_P a Concomitant Knowledge Rule of P.

Let K be the knowledge base of A. We can also define a mapping from S to TF_A:

$$R_K(s) = \begin{cases} R_P(s), & \text{if there is a } P \in K \text{ such that } K(s) = P(s) = 1 \\ \varepsilon, & K(s) = 0 \end{cases}$$

We call R_K a Concomitant Knowledge Rule of K.

$B = \{\varepsilon, \theta\}$ is the algebraic structure defined above. We define a mapping from $K \times S$ to B:

$$f(P, s) = \begin{cases} \varepsilon, & \text{if } P(s) = 1 \\ \theta, & \text{else} \end{cases} \quad \text{where } P \in K, s \in S$$

We call f a Standard Projection Function.

Theorem 2. Let K be an orthonormal knowledge base. For $\forall s \in S$, if $K(s)=1$, then

$$R_K(s) = \oplus_{P \in K} f(P, s) \cdot R_P(s) \tag{1}$$

Proof: From theorem 3.1, since $K(s)=1$, there is a $P_0 \in K$ such that $P_0(s)=1$, and $P(s)=0$ for $\forall P \in K \backslash \{P_0\}$. Thus $f(P, s) = \theta$ and $f(P_0, s) = \varepsilon$. Then it follows that

$$\oplus_{P \in K} f(P, s) \cdot R_P(s) = R_{P_0}(s) \oplus (\oplus_{P \in K \backslash \{P_0\}} \theta \cdot R_P(s)) = R_{P_0}(s) \oplus \theta = R_{P_0}(s) \tag{2}$$

We know $R_K(s) = R_{P_0}(s)$ from the definition of $R_K(s)$. So we have $R_K(s) = \oplus_{P \in K} f(P, s) \cdot R_P(s)$.

We can see that R_K is a "linear composition" of all the R_P. And the knowledge rules of a knowledge base are similar to a set of "orthonormal basis" in the linear space. This is just the reason why we call the knowledge base to be "orthonormal".

Now we give the formal model for monitoring activities of single agent.

Definition 12. The Single-agent Detection Model for an agent A is a quadruple: SDM $= <S, STATE_A, R_K, ST_0 >$, where

(1) S is the set of source data.
(2) $STATE_A$ is the state space of A.
(3) R_K is the function from $S \times STATE_A$ to $STATE_A$ defined above.
(4) $ST_0 \in STATE_A$ is the initial state of A.

The cooperation rules that control the cooperative activities of multiple agents are different from the knowledge rules which only control the activities of single agent, because multiple agents' knowledge bases may be used in the cooperative activities.

Definition 13. Let P_1, P_2, ..., P_m $(m \geq 2)$ be some *Knowledge*s of different agents. We define a mapping from S to TF_{Syn} by

$$R_{P_1 P_2 \ldots P_m}(s) = \begin{cases} \sigma, \text{if } P_1(s) \wedge P_2(s) \wedge \cdots P_m(s) = 1 \\ \varepsilon, \text{else} \end{cases}, \quad \text{where } s \in S, \ \sigma \in TF_{Syn}.$$

We call $R_{P_1 P_2 \ldots P_m}$ a Concomitant Cooperation Rule with knowledge sequence $P_1 P_2 \ldots P_m$ and call $P_1 P_2 \ldots P_m$ the Concomitant Knowledge Sequence of $R_{P_1 P_2 \ldots P_m}$.

Definition 14. The set of all the cooperation rules is called the Cooperation Rule Base, denoted by R_{Coop}.

If $P_1 P_2 \ldots P_m$ is a concomitant knowledge sequence of one rule in R_{Coop}, then $P_1 P_2 \ldots P_m$ is said to belong to R_{Coop}, denoted by $P_1 P_2 \ldots P_m \in R_{Coop}$. We define $P_1 P_2 \ldots P_m(s) = P_1(s) \wedge P_2(s) \wedge \ldots \wedge P_m(s)$.

An agent may have multiple knowledge bases. If knowledge bases K and H belong to an agent, then K and H are said to be homogeneous, denoted by $K \approx H$. Although an agent may have multiple knowledge bases, only one can be activated on running.

Definition 15. Let C be the set of configuration parameters, K_{Syn} is the set of all the orthonormal knowledge bases, $B = \{\varepsilon, \theta\}$. ϕ is a mapping from $C \times (R_{Coop} \cup K_{Syn}) \times S$ to B. We call ϕ a Scheduling Function if it satisfies the following properties:

(1) For $\forall c \in C, r \in R_{Coop}$ and $s \in S$,

$$\phi(c, r, s) = \begin{cases} \varepsilon, \text{if } Q(s) = 1 \\ \theta, \text{else} \end{cases}, \quad \text{where } Q \text{ is the concomitant knowledge sequence of } r.$$

(2) For $\forall c \in C, K_1, K_2 \in K_{Syn}$ and $s \in S$, if $K_1 \approx K_2$ and $K_1 \neq K_2$ then

$$\phi(c, K_1, s) \cdot \phi(c, K_2, s) = \theta$$

(3) Let $P_1 P_2 \ldots P_m$ $(P_i \in K_i)$ be a concomitant knowledge sequence of a rule in R_{Coop}. For $\forall c \in C, s \in S$, if $P_1 P_2 \ldots P_m(s) = 1$, then $\phi(c, K_i, s) = \theta$, $i = 1, \ldots, m$.

Based on scheduling function, for $c \in C$ and $s \in S$, we further define

$$\phi R(c, s) = (\oplus_{r \in R_{Coop}} \phi(c, r, s) \cdot r) \oplus (\oplus_{K \in K_{Syn}} \phi(c, K, s) \cdot R_K(s)) \tag{3}$$

Then $\phi R(c, s)$ is a state function on $STATE_{Syn}$. Hence ϕR has defined a function from $C \times S \times STATE_{Syn}$ to $STATE_{Syn}$: $\phi R(c, s, \alpha) = \phi R(c, s)(\alpha)$.

Now we can describe the MCSM model as follows.

Definition 16. The Multi-agent Cooperation model for Security Monitoring is a quadruple: **MCSM** $= < C \times S, STATE_{Syn}, \phi R, ST_0 >$, where

(1) S is the set of source data, C is the set of configuration parameters.
(2) $STATE_{Syn}$ is the global state space of Syn.
(3) ϕR is the function from $C \times S \times STATE_{Syn}$ to $STATE_{Syn}$ defined above. We call it the Scheduling Engine of Syn.
(4) $ST_0 \in STATE_{Syn}$ is the initial state of Syn.

MCSM is a FSA model with $C \times S$ as its input set. It clearly describes the cooperating and scheduling mechanism of multi-agents, and provides a theoretical basis for the designing and constructing of an IMS.

5 System Design and Implementation

In the MCSM model, we characterize the principles of an IMS by the FSA, which includes a new architecture. Then we successfully design and develop the ACT-BroSA system, and realize the integration of multiple security monitoring systems (including the IDS, virus detection, security audit, content monitoring and the vulnerability scan system in current version). ACT-BroSA has been deployed in several important networks and has played a promising role in distributed security monitoring.

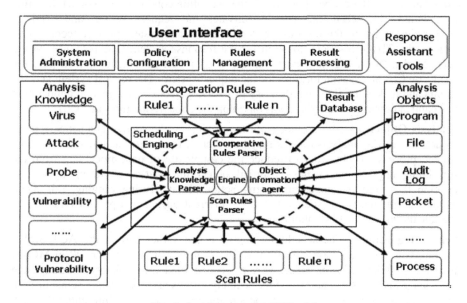

Fig. 2. Architecture of ACT-BroSA

The IMS architecture is shown in Fig.2. We outline the design and supporting technologies of the most important parts as follows.

Analysis Knowledge. Based on the orthonormal knowledge structure in KAM, we designed a general description language and storage mechanism for different monitoring systems. Knowledge of different security threats such as the virus, intrusions and probes is under unified management. When the system starts running, certain knowledge bases are activated by the scheduling engine according to the configuration parameters. Every instance of ACT-BroSA becomes a special security monitoring system with its own knowledge base after instantiation.

Scan Rules. During implementation, we find that the scan mechanisms are very similar when the corresponding particles' data types are same. Hence we can implement eight kinds of scan algorithms and use scan rules to describe the mapping relations between the particles and scan algorithms. During running, the scheduling engine activates the proper algorithm according to the particle and the scan rules and performs the scan actions. So we can share scan algorithms among the different monitoring systems in ACT-BroSA. Meanwhile, we extract the scan algorithms out of the kernel engine and make them configurable using the scan rules. This changes the traditional implementation mechanism that hard-coding the analysis algorithms in the system engine, and improves the scalability of the system.

Cooperation Rules. In CDM model, we formally describe the cooperative monitoring when a cooperation rule is activated. In implementation, we describe the cooperation rule as a quadruple: *CooperRule=<ActivatingCondition, RequestSystem, ResponseSystem, CooperateData>*, and use a simple script to describe it. We also propose a technique called "Cooperation Information Bus (CIB)" to support the data exchange during the cooperation. When the activating condition of a cooperation rule is satisfied, the scheduling engine activates the request system and sends a cooperation signal to the response system. The request system puts the cooperation data on the CIB at a special location for the response system. The response system gets the data from CIB and performs the cooperation scan actions, then puts the results on CIB at a special location for the request system. The request system gets the results and makes the final decision. By this way, we construct a general cooperation mechanism between security systems based on the cooperation rules and CIB.

Analysis Objects. Analysis objects are the carriers of the source data set S in BSM model. In an IMS, analysis objects may be different forms such as program, file, log, packet, process, etc. In order to reduce the complexity of data processing from the scheduling engine, we design a unified object information capturing agent and envelop the complex object processing actions in it. During running, this agent extracts all the necessary source data from different objects and provides the data to the scheduling engine for monitoring.

Scheduling Engine. The scheduling engine is the kernel part of the ACT-BroSA system. It is the implementation form of the state transition function ϕR in MCSM model. In implementation, since we introduce unified mechanisms to manage the knowledge and objects, and extract the scan algorithms and cooperation semantics out of the engine using scan rules and cooperation rules, the scheduling engine is very small and scalable. This makes it flexible to easily integrate new monitoring systems.

6 Experiment and Analysis

6.1 Efficiency of the Scan Algorithm

In our first experiment, the scan algorithm F_K and $F_{K'}$ introduced in Section 3.3 are realized in our content monitoring system as an example, and their performances are compared. The function of the content monitoring system is to monitor the content of the WWW and Mail application traffic on the network in real-time based on monitoring policies (i.e. security knowledge).

The monitoring system is deployed on a Linux PC with Pentium IV 1.8Ghz CPU and 1G memory in our lab, running on a 100M local network with about 20 hosts.

We run the content monitoring system based on the two algorithms respectively, and measure the processing time per packet needed in the two situations. To better evaluate them, we vary the number of knowledge rules and the length of the packet payloads in both cases.

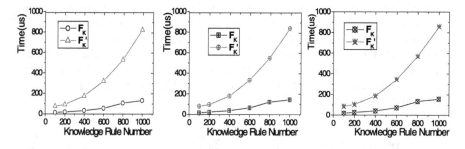

Fig. 3. Process time/packet with 300 Bytes payload

Fig. 4. Process time/packet with 600 Bytes payload

Fig. 5. Process time/packet with 900 Bytes payload

We plot the curves of the processing time per packet when the packet payload length is 300, 600, 900 bytes in Fig.3, 4 and 5 respectively. Clearly, with the same amount of knowledge rules and payload length, the time F_K needs to process a packet is much less than that of $F_{K'}$. The difference is enlarged with the increase of knowledge numbers. For example, with 600 bytes packet payload length (as shown in Fig.4), the difference is 79.75-17.21 = 62.54 *(um)* when the knowledge rules number is 100, and it becomes 836.15-143.76 = 692.39 *(um)* when rules number is 1000. The reason can be found from the analysis in Section3.3, the efficiency of $F_{K'}$ is greatly dependent on the rule numbers of the knowledge base, but the F_K is much better. Also, with the changing of the payload length in all figures, we can see F_K is much steadier than $F_{K'}$.

6.2   Effect of the Cooperative Monitoring

In the ACT-BroSA system, we designed a general cooperation mechanism between security systems and implement multiple cooperation functions. In this experiment, we take the cooperation between the IDS and the vulnerability scan system (VSS) as an example to evaluate the effect of cooperative monitoring.

When an attack feature is detected by IDS, there may be two cases: one is that the object host is vulnerable to the attack, and the other is that the object is not vulnerable. In the first case, the alert of the IDS is real and effective, but in the later case IDS makes a false alarm. The cooperation process is: when IDS detects an attack, it activates the VSS in real-time to check whether the object is vulnerable. Then IDS can make a right decision based on the cooperation result.

We conduct the test on our 100M local network with about 20 hosts. The ACT-BroSA instances of IDS and VSS run on two Linux hosts respectively. Both hosts have Pentium IV 1.8Ghz CPU and 1G memory.

During the test, we perform 20 attacks toward 10 object hosts using attack tools developed ourselves. Among the 20 attacks, there are 5 real intrusions, and other 15 are false attacks (i.e. object hosts are not vulnerable). We measure the detection accuracy rate of IDS with and without the cooperation function on respectively. We also measure the time delay introduced by the cooperation in order to evaluate its impact on the real-time monitoring.

We plot the histograms of the cooperation function test data in Fig.6. In the case of without cooperation function, there are 20 alerts total, but only 5 alerts are effective and the accuracy rate is only 25%. In the case of with cooperation function, IDS cooperates with VSS successfully and eliminates all the 15 false alarms.

Fig.7 plots the time delay values of the 20 times cooperation. The average time delay introduced by the cooperation is 0.78 second (as shown by the dashed in Fig.7) and the longest delay is less than 1 second. It should be worthy in practice to gain a high monitoring accuracy at such a small cost.

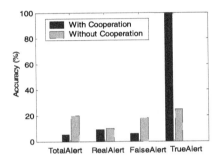

Fig. 6. Alert statistics

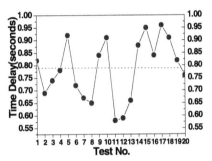

Fig. 7. Cooperation time delay

7   Conclusion

We have successfully applied a novel approach in the constructing of integrated security monitoring system. We first proposed a formal model called MCSM and formally described the integrated management and cooperation mechanism of multiple security technologies. Based on MCSM, we design and developed an IMS called the ACT-BroSA. The implementation and experiment further validated the effectiveness of the MCSM model and our design method. We believe our work is helpful to the current field of integrated network security management.

References

1. Allen J., Christie A., Fithen W., McHugh J., Pickel J., Stoner E. State of the Practice of Intrusion Detection Technologies. Technical Report CMU/SEI-99-TR-028, Carnegie Mellon University, Software Engineering Institute, 2000
2. Debar H., Dacier M., Wespi A. Towards a taxonomy of intrusion-detection systems[J]. Computer Nertworks, 1999, V31(8):805-822
3. S. Axelsson. The base-rate fallacy and its implications for the difficulty of intrusion detection. In Proceedings of the 6th ACM Conference on Computer and Communications Security,1999

4. Check Point. Build Your Security Infrastructure With Best-of-Breed Products From OPSEC. Check Point Software Technologies Ltd, 2004
5. Symantec. Symantec Enterprise Security Architecture (SESA™). Symantec Enterprise Security, 2002
6. Sotiris Ioannidis, Angelos D. Keromytis, Steve M. Bellovin and Jonathan M. Smith. Implementing a Distributed Firewall. In Proceedings of the 7th ACM conference on Computer and communications security(2000) 190~199
7. Al-Shaer, E.S., Hamed, H.H.. Discovery of policy anomalies in distributed firewalls. In Proceedings of twenty-third Annual Joint Conference of the IEEE Computer and Communications Societies Vol.4 (INFOCOM 2004): 26055~2616
8. Du Yue, Wang Hui-qiang, Pang Yong-gang. Design of A Distributed Intrusion Detection System Based on Independent Agents. In Proceedings of International Conference on Intelligent Sensing and Information Processing(2004) 254~257
9. Noria Foukia. IDReAM: Intrusion Detection and Response Executed with Agent Mobility. The 3rd International Joint Conference on Autonomous Agents and Multi-agent Systems (AAMAS 2004), August 2004
10. M. Zaki, Tarek S. Sobh. A cooperative agent-based model for active security systems. Journal of Network and Computer Applications,November 2004
11. Gustavo A. Santana Torrellas, Luis A. Villa Vargas. Modelling a flexible network security systems using multi-agents systems: security assessment considerations. In Proceedings of the 1st international symposium on Information and communication technologies, September 2003
12. Muralidaran Gangadharan, Kai Hwang. Intranet Security with Micro-Firewalls and Mobile Agents for Proactive Intrusion Response. the 2001 IEEE International conference on Computer Networks and Mobile Computing, October 2001
13. Z. Fu, H. Huang, T. Wu, S. F. Wu, F. Gong, C. Xu, and I. Baldine. ISCP: Design and Implementation of An Inter-Domain Security Management Agent (SMA) Coordination Protocol. In Proceedings of the 2000 IEEE/IFIP Network Operations and Management Symposium(2000) 565~578
14. Karima Boudaoud, Charles McCathieNevile. An Intelligent Agent-based Model for Security Management. In Proceedings of the Seventh International Symposium on Computers and Communications(2002):877~882
15. K. Boudaoud, H. Lubiod, R. Boutaba and Z. Guessoum. Network Security Management with Intelligent Agents. In Proceedings of the 2000 IEEE/IFIP Network Operations and Management Symposium, April 2000, p579~592
16. David S., Christophe L., Noureddine Z. Distributed Cooperation Modeling for Maintenance Using Petri Nets and Multi-Agents Systems. In Proceedings of 2003 IEEE International Symposium on Computational Intelligence in Robotics and Automation, July 2003, vol.1:366~371
17. Qiuming Zhu, Plamen V. Petrov, Jeffrey D. Hicks and Alexander D. Stoycn. The Topologies of Cooperation in Knowledge Intensive Multi-Agent System. In Proceedings of 2003 International Conference on Integration of Knowledge Intensive Multi-Agent Systems, Oct 2003, p741~746
18. V. Gorodetski, I. Kotenko. The Multi-agent Systems for Computer Network Security Assurance: Frameworks and Case Studies. In Proceedings of the 2002 IEEE International Conference on Artificial Intelligence Systems, September 2002

Detecting DDoS Attacks Based on Multi-stream Fused HMM in Source-End Network

Jian Kang, Yuan Zhang, and Jiu-bin Ju

Department of Computer Science & Technology, Jilin University,
Changchun, 130012, China
kj885788@gmail.com

Abstract. DDoS (Distributed Denial-of-Service) attacks detection system deployed in source-end network is superior in detection and prevention than that in victim network, because it can perceive and throttle attacks before data flow to Internet. However, the current existed works in source-end network lead to a high false-positive rate and false-negative rate for the reason that they are based on single-feature, and they couldn't synthesize multi-features simultaneously. This paper proposes a novel approach using Multi-stream Fused Hidden Markov Model (MF-HMM) on source-end DDoS detection for integrating multi-features simultaneously. The multi-features include the S-D-P feature, TCP header Flags, and IP header ID field. Through experiments, we compared our original approach based on multiple detection feature with other main algorithms (such as CUSUM and HMM) based on single-feature. The results present that our approach effectively reduces false-positive rate and false-negative rate, and improve the precision of detection.

1 Introduction

Comparing with DDoS detection system in victim network, source-end DDoS detection not only can perceive and prevent from attacks early, but also enhance security and QoS of the whole network. However, the attack flow in source-end network is so dispersive that the traditional detecting algorithm troubled in distinguishing attack flows and normal flows, and led to high false-positive rate and false-negative rate. Thus, the key problem is how to raise precision and sensitivity of source-end DDoS detection.

The existed detection sysytems are based on single-feature extracted from source-end network, so they could not synthesize multiple factors. Although the single-feature detection algorithm has been improved, it limited in precision rising—it cannot describe complex diversification in source-end network.

Therefore, this paper proposes a novel approach using Multi-stream Fused Hidden Markov Model (MF-HMM) on source-end DDoS detecting for integrating multi-features simultaneously. The multiple factors include the S-D-P feature, the Flags and the ID field contained in TCP/IP header. Experiments can help us compare MF-HMM with other models like CUSUM algorithm and HMM based on single observing feature. The results present that MF-HMM

D. Pointcheval, Y. Mu, and K. Chen (Eds.): CANS 2006, LNCS 4301, pp. 342–353, 2006.
© Springer-Verlag Berlin Heidelberg 2006

effectively reduce the false-positive rate and false-negative rate. The MF-HMM proposed in this paper can adapt to diversified network and raise the precision of detection.

2   Related Work

Mirkovic et al. proposed D-WARD as a representative source-end DDoS detection system in [1]. In a normal TCP session, the flow from source to destination (which is defined as TCP_sent_to) is controlled by the reverse acknowledge flow (TCP_received_from). Under DDoS attacking, TCP_sent_to is far greater than TCP_received_from. D-WARD defines max_tcprto as the max possible rate for TCP_sent_to/TCP_received_from under normal network environments. If the observed rate is higher than max_tcprto in real time, it is determined as an attack. However, the false-positive rate and false-negative rate in D-WARD is high.

Paper [2] extracted the same ratio with that in D-WORD as observing feature. But because of introducing a nonparametric change point detection method in statistics and improving D-WARD by nonparametric recursive CUSUM algorithm, the improved system is more advanced in detecting precision than D-WARD.

Peng et al. in [3] considered the number of new source IP addresses appeared in data flow in unit time as observing feature. The abnormal increase of this number determines if attacks appeared. They used CUSUM algorithm to detect source-end DDoS attacks. However, high false-positive rate is led because they took only one feature into account.

Zhou et al. in [4] used HMM to detect DDoS attacks. They use TCP Header Flags to describe TCP package as observing feature. They constructed the observing sequence with the weight sum of each bit of TCP Header Flags, and trained HMM by data packages under normal network. The trained HMM can be seen as criterion to judge if there are attacks.

Therefore, existing researches on source-end DDoS detecting system are based on single-feature. Although there are improvements to the algorithms themselves, the insufficient detection information contained in single-feature constrains the enhancement of the detecting precision.

3   Multi-features Extraction

Moore et al. in [5] presented a famous result: most DDoS attacks use TCP package (over 94%), then UDP package (2%) and ICMP package (2%). From the result, we can see the importance of detecting TCP packages in DDoS attacks. Thus, in this paper, extracting and detecting multi-features of TCP Flooding attacks are to be discussed. Analyzed characteristics and mechanisms of representative DDoS attacks, we defined the conception of S-D-P feature. Preparing for MF-HMM represented in Sect.4, we constructed multi-features including S-D-P feature, TCP Header Flags and ID field in IP Header.

3.1   TCP Header Flags

We choose TCP Header Flags as one of the features describing TCP package in source-end network. In order to represent this feature in numerical value, we define different weights to different flags as [4]. Figure 1 presents the weights. Equation (1) is to calculate the observing feature value of TCP Header Flags.

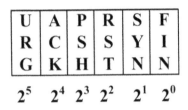

Fig. 1. Weights of different TCP header Flags

$$O_i = 2^5 \times \mathrm{URG} + 2^4 \times \mathrm{ACK} + 2^3 \times \mathrm{PSH} + 2^2 \times \mathrm{RST} + 2^1 \times \mathrm{SYN} + 2^0 \times \mathrm{FIN} \ . \quad (1)$$

Calculated through (1), we could get observation symbol set $V = \{1, 2, \ldots, 63\}$.

3.2   IP Header Identification Field

In DDoS detecting, ID field in IP header is significant for detection. In general, ID field is written by operating system (OS). Main DDoS attacks use IP Spoof strategy, and they fill in ID fields in different random algorithms. Those random algorithms can be learned in [6]. Thus, it is obvious the distinction between ID field written by spoof strategy and ID field written by OS.

In IP header, the length of ID field is 16 bits, and the corresponding value range is $0 \sim 65535$. In order to reduce this large set and assure light computation, mapping is needed. Our experiments show that ID fields distributed averagely, and Table.1 presents the way we mapped the values.

Table 1. Mapping Rule of ID Fields

ID range	0	1~999	1000~1999	......	64000~64999	65000~65535
Mapped value	1	2	3	......	66	67

According to Table.1, the observation symbol set $V = \{1, 2, \ldots, 67\}$.

3.3   S-D-P Feature

When attacks appear in source-end work, IP addresses and port numbers will change obviously. Because attackers spoof source IP addresses to avoid detecting and tracing back. And in order to deplete victim's resources in a short time, they send large numbers of spoofed packages to one or more ports of the victim. Thus, research on IP addresses and port numbers is necessary to DDoS detection.

We use three-tuple (IP_source, $IP\_destination$, $PORT\_destination$) to specify S-D-P feature of TCP/IP header. Here, IP_source presents source IP addresses; $IP\_destination$ presents destination IP addresses; $PORT\_destination$ presents destination port number. If S-D-P feature is modeled by HMM, the observation symbol set would contain $2^{32} \times 2^{32} \times 2^{16}$ elements. That set is so huge that we reduce it through mapping.

In general, IP addresses are divided into five classes:A, B, C, D, and E. Class D and Class E are so scarcely appeared that can be overlooked. We map IP Address Class A, Class B, and Class C to hexadecimal identifiers according to their binary codes in the first byte. In the same way, port number range can be divided into three parts: well-known port, registered port, and dynamic (private or ephemeral) port. We map them to hexadecimal identifiers. Table 2 presents the mapping.

Table 2. Mapping of IP addresses and ports

IP Address class	First byte(binary)	Identifier(hex)
Class A	0	0X1
Class B	10	0X2
Class C	110	0X3
Port type	**Port range(decimal)**	**Identifier(hex)**
Well-known port	0~1023	0X1
Registered port	1024~49151	0X2
Dynamic/Private/Ephemeral ports	49152~65535	0X3

Through the mapping above, there are $3 \times 3 \times 3$ elements in the new observation symbol set. So, the new observation symbol set $V = \{1, 2, \ldots\ldots, 27\}$.

4   MF-HMM

We use the Multi-stream Fused (MF-HMM) proposed by Zeng et al. in [7] to synthesize multi-features effective to precision of detecting. According to the maximum entropy principle and the maximum mutual information (MMI) criterion, MF-HMM constructs a new structure linking multiple HMMs. MF-HMM is the generalization of Two-stream Fused HMM [8]. It is suitable for the recognition and detection with multiple features problem. Paper [7] pointed out the advantages of MF-HMM:

1. Every observing feature can be modeled by a component HMM, so the performance of every feature can be analyzed individually. And the analysis could be used for feature selection.
2. Compared with other existing models (for example, CHMM [9] and MHMM [10] e.g.), MF-HMM reaches a better balance between model complexity and performance.
3. Reliabilities of component HMM can be used to adjust the corresponding weights in final fusion. And if one component HMM fails due to some reason, the other HMM can still work. Thus, the final fusion performance can be robust.

In our source-end network DDoS detection system, we use Multi-stream Fused HMM with three features which described in sect. 3.

4.1   MF-HMM Overview

HMM is the basis of MF-HMM. And paper [11] discussed HMM in detail.

Let $\{O^{(i)}, i = 1, ..., n\}$ represents n tightly coupled observing sequences. Assume that $\{O^{(i)}, i = 1, ..., n\}$ can be modeled by n corresponding HMMs with hidden states $\{Q^{(i)}, i = 1, ..., n\}$. In MF-HMM, an optimal solution for $p(O^{(1)}; O^{(2)}; ...; O^{(n)})$ is given by $\hat{p}(O^{(1)}; O^{(2)}; ...; O^{(n)})$ according to the maximum entropy principle and the maximum mutual information criterion.

There are two steps in calculating $\hat{p}(O^{(1)}; O^{(2)}; ...; O^{(n)})$. First, the i-th $\hat{p}^{(i)}(O^{(1)}; O^{(2)}; ...; O^{(n)})$ can be given through (2).

$$\hat{p}^{(i)}(O^{(1)}; O^{(2)}; \ldots; O^{(n)})$$
$$= p(O^{(1)})p(O^{(2)}) \ldots p(O^{(n)}) \times \frac{p(Q^{(i)}, O^{(1)}, \ldots, O^{(i-1)}, O^{(i+1)}, \ldots, O^{(n)})}{p(Q^{(i)})p(O^{(1)}) \cdots p(O^{(i-1)})p(O^{(i+1)}) \cdots p(O^{(n)})}$$
$$= p(Q^{(i)} \times p(O^{(1)}, \ldots, O^{(i-1)}, O^{(i+1)}, \ldots, O^{(n)} | Q^{(i)})$$

$$(2)$$

And assuming

$$p(O^{(1)}, ..., O^{(i-1)}, O^{(i+1)}, ..., O^{(n)} | Q^{(i)}) = \prod_{j \neq i, j=1}^{n} p(O^{(j)} | Q^{(i)}) \qquad (3)$$

It has a good record in recognizing and detecting DDoS attacks, though the conditional independence assumption is always violated in practice. The success is because of the small number of parameters to be estimated in assumption. Without this assumption, some complicated algorithms need more training data, and are more susceptible to local maximum during parameter estimation.

So, the estimate of $\hat{p}^{(i)}(O^{(1)}; O^{(2)}; ...; O^{(n)})$ can be given by (4).

$$\hat{p}^{(i)}(O^{(1)}; O^{(2)}; ...; O^{(n)}) = p(O^{(i)}) \prod_{j \neq i, j=1}^{n} p(O^{(j)} | Q^{(i)}) \qquad (4)$$

There are different expressions to different i. To our Multi-stream Fused HMM, Equation (4) corresponds to (5), (6), (7).

$$\hat{p}^{(1)}(O^{(1)}; O^{(2)}; O^{(3)}) = p(O^{(1)})p(O^{(2)}|Q^{(1)})p(O^{(3)}|Q^{(1)}) \qquad (5)$$
$$\hat{p}^{(2)}(O^{(1)}; O^{(2)}; O^{(3)}) = p(O^{(2)})p(O^{(1)}|Q^{(2)})p(O^{(3)}|Q^{(2)}) \qquad (6)$$
$$\hat{p}^{(3)}(O^{(1)}; O^{(2)}; O^{(3)}) = p(O^{(3)})p(O^{(1)}|Q^{(3)})p(O^{(2)}|Q^{(3)}) \qquad (7)$$

Thus, the estimate of $\hat{p}(O^{(1)}; O^{(2)}; ...; O^{(n)})$ can be calculated by (8). In practice, if those n component HMMs have different reliabilities, they may be combined by different weights for a better result. In our experiment, the weights of ID field, S-D-P feature, and TCP header flags in turn are 0.3, 0.33, and 0.37.

$$\hat{p}(O^{(1)}; O^{(2)}; ...; O^{(n)}) = \sum_{i=1}^{n} \lambda^{(i)} \hat{p}^{(i)}(O^{(1)}; O^{(2)}; ...; O^{(n)}) \qquad (8)$$

Here, $\sum_{i=1}^{n} \lambda^{(i)} = 1$.

4.2   Learning Algorithm of MF-HMM

There are three main steps in the learning algorithm of MF-HMM:

1. n component HMMs are trained independently by representative algorithm (Baum Welch Algorithm, Segmented K-Means Algorithm, or Hybrid Method EM Algorithm [11])
2. The best hidden state sequences of the component HMMs are estimated by the Viterbi algorithm [11].
3. Calculate the coupling parameters between the n HMMs, viz.

$$\hat{B}^{(i,j)} = \arg\max_{B^{(i,j)}} p(O^{(j)}|\hat{Q}^{(i)}) \quad i, j = 1, 2, ..., n, i \neq j \ . \qquad (9)$$

To our Multi-stream Fused HMM, step one is to do:

$$\hat{\Pi}^{(1)}, \hat{A}^{(1)}, \hat{B}^{(1)} = \arg\max_{\Pi^{(1)}, A^{(1)}, B^{(1)}} (\log p(O^{(1)})) \qquad (10)$$

$$\hat{\Pi}^{(2)}, \hat{A}^{(2)}, \hat{B}^{(2)} = \arg\max_{\Pi^{(2)}, A^{(2)}, B^{(2)}} (\log p(O^{(2)})) \qquad (11)$$

$$\hat{\Pi}^{(3)}, \hat{A}^{(3)}, \hat{B}^{(3)} = \arg\max_{\Pi^{(3)}, A^{(3)}, B^{(3)}} (\log p(O^{(3)})) \qquad (12)$$

And then step two:

$$\hat{Q}^{(1)} = \arg\max_{Q^{(1)}} (\log p(O^{(1)}, Q^{(1)}) \qquad (13)$$

$$\hat{Q}^{(2)} = \arg\max_{Q^{(2)}}(\log p(O^{(2)}, Q^{(2)})) \tag{14}$$

$$\hat{Q}^{(3)} = \arg\max_{Q^{(3)}}(\log p(O^{(3)}, Q^{(3)})) \tag{15}$$

At last, step three is to estimate the coupling parameters between HMM1, HMM2, and HMM3:

$$\hat{B}^{(1,2)} = \arg\max_{B^{(1,2)}} p(O^{(2)}|\hat{Q}^{(1)}) \tag{16}$$

$$\hat{B}^{(1,3)} = \arg\max_{B^{(1,3)}} p(O^{(3)}|\hat{Q}^{(1)}) \tag{17}$$

$$\hat{B}^{(2,1)} = \arg\max_{B^{(2,1)}} p(O^{(1)}|\hat{Q}^{(2)}) \tag{18}$$

$$\hat{B}^{(2,3)} = \arg\max_{B^{(2,3)}} p(O^{(3)}|\hat{Q}^{(2)}) \tag{19}$$

$$\hat{B}^{(3,1)} = \arg\max_{B^{(3,1)}} p(O^{(1)}|\hat{Q}^{(3)}) \tag{20}$$

$$\hat{B}^{(3,2)} = \arg\max_{B^{(3,2)}} p(O^{(2)}|\hat{Q}^{(3)}) \tag{21}$$

5   DDoS Detection and Estimation

5.1   Assumption Based on MF-HMM Detection

The distinction is obviously between the data package in normal state and that under attacking. That is to say, to MF-HMM trained with normal data stream, the output probability of normal data package sequences is more than that of data package sequences with attacks. Thus, we determine whether attacks or normal depended on output probability of MF-HMM.

5.2   Pretreatment to Detected Sequence

In experiment, we construct detected sequence with the three features mentioned in sect.3 from detected data stream. Let the length of the detected sequence is L. Split the detected sequence with a k length splitting window, and the sequence can be divided into L/k subsequences. So the set of these subsequences is $\{X_i\}$, here $1 \le i \le L/k$.

5.3 Attack Determination Algorithm

Input each subsequence X_i to MF-HMM, calculate the output probability $\log \hat{p}(O^{(1)}; O^{(2)}; O^{(3)})$. If that probability is smaller than the threshold of the output: ε, mark X_i as "questionable subsequence". Calculated and marked all of the subsequences, we get the ratio δ through (22).

$$\delta = \frac{numbers\ of\ questionable\ subsequences}{numbers\ of\ all\ subsequences} \tag{22}$$

At last, compare δ with the attack $Threshold$: if $\delta > Threshold$, it is determined that DDoS attacks are taking place; else, there is no attack. Figure 2 shows the process of attack detection and determination.

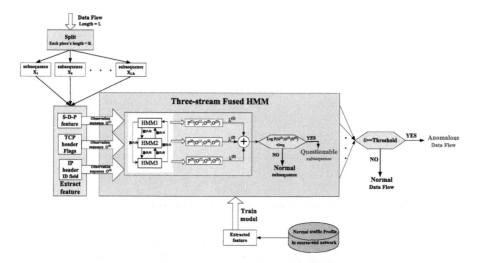

Fig. 2. DDoS detection process based on MF-HMM with three features

6 Experiment

In order to build MF-HMM based on normal source-end network and confirm ε and δ, we collected data for three months—10 times per day, and 1,000,000 data packages per time. To attack data stream, we used representative DDoS attack tool—TFN2K, which deployed in several hosts. S-D-P feature, TCP header flags, and ID fields are used when building Multi-stream Fused HMM. We compared MF-HMM based on multiple features with other four detection algorithms based on single-feature:

1. MF-HMM based on three features is called TF-HMM;
2. HMM use S-D-P feature only is called SDP;
3. HMM use TCP header flags only is called TCP-flag;
4. HMM use ID field only is called ID-segment;
5. Detection based on nonparametric recursive CUSUM algorithm is called CUSUM.

6.1 Output Probabilities of TF-HMM in Normal State and Attacking State

In experiment 1, we observe TF-HMM's output probability. To both the normal state and attacking state, sampling last for 300 seconds, and overlap the two into one time axis as presented in Fig.3.

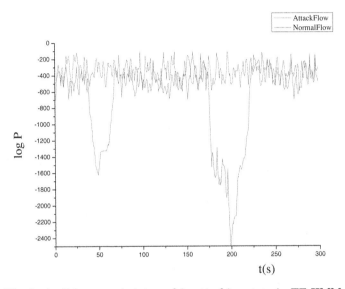

Fig. 3. logP in normal state and in attacking state in TF-HMM

In Fig.3, the abscissa **t** represents time, with the unit of second. The ordinate $logP$ represents the output probability $\log \hat{p}(O^{(1)}; O^{(2)}; O^{(3)})$. We can see the obvious difference of $logP$ in TF-HMM between normal state and attacking state. In normal state, the value of logP fluctuated in the range of $-102 \sim -610$; while under the attacks, the peak value could reach to eight times of the normal value, even larger. Attacks were launched two times in Fig.3: the first time near 42 second lasted for about 30 seconds; the second time near 175 second lasted for about 50 seconds.

6.2 False-Positive Rate and False-Negative Rate Experiment

In experiment 2, we compared the false-positive rate and the false-negative rate of 5 detection algorithms in different network environments. It means that there are data from 10 different groups—the first 5 groups are captured from different network services and mutative stream intensity, without attacks; while the last 5 groups are experiments under attacking. These data were inputted into detection system, and the results were presented by table.3.

From table.3, all of the first 5 groups showed us the false-positive. Especially, the 3rd group used CUSUM algorithm led a high false-positive rate to 65 times. The result from TF-HMM is closer to REAL than other algorithms

Table 3. False-positive and false-negative of 5 detection algorithms

	No.1	No.2	No.3	No.4	No.5	No.6	No.7	No.8	No.9	No.10
SDP	29	8	18	6	8	204	79	43	0	965
TCP-flag	20	12	15	3	2	222	85	39	0	798
ID-segment	22	8	35	5	5	195	78	34	0	845
CUSUM	45	21	65	12	37	105	34	52	0	1042
TF-HMM	5	1	2	2	1	290	92	23	2	511
REAL	0	0	0	0	0	300	100	20	2	500

based on single-feature. In the 6th group, we launched attacks intensely, and all algorithms result to false-negative reports. The false-negative rate of CUSUM was the highest, while TF-HMM performed better than other algorithms. In the 10th group, we increased both of the attack intension and normal data stream: false-positive rate of TF-HMM was lower than other algorithms. In addition, it is valuable to mention that, in the 9th group, under the large normal data stream, we launched attacks for two times separately. The results showed us: TF-HMM could recognize attack accurately; in contrast, other algorithms could not. Thus, TF-HMM is sensitive in source-end detection, and adapt to the new DDoS attacks with high distribution and low attack intension.

To sum up, in this 5 detection algorithms, CUSUM algorithm cannot learn the normal network state, so leads to high false-positive rate and false-negative rate. The other algorithms based on single-feature cannot reflect real condition of source-end network actually because of the limitation of single-feature, though they improved detection systems. TF-HMM based on three features synthesizes more detection information, enhances the precision of detection, and is better than the other.

6.3   Average Detection Rate Experiment

We definite Detection Rate (DR) is the ratio of the number of attacks detected and the number of attacks real existed, viz. the percentage of the recognized attacks in the whole real attacks. In experiment 3, we varied attack intension, normal data stream intension, and sampling time. Thus, there are obvious differences between every two groups. From the 100 groups of data gained, we calculated their average DRs as presented in Table.4.

Table 4. Average DRs of 5 Detection Algorithms

CUSUM	ID-segment	S-D-P	TCP-flag	TF-HMM
48.64%	60.78%	68.93%	70.27%	91.12%

The average DRs of the three algorithms based on single-feature are higher than CUSUM algorithm, so learning algorithm–HMM can reflect the variety in source-end network better. However, using fewer detection information, these three algorithms have handicaps in increasing the precision of detection. In contrast, TF-HMM based on three features, with the average DR of 91.12% which is 1.87 times of CUSUM algorithm, utilizes more detection information, and increases the precision of detection to a satisfied result.

7 Conclusion

DDoS detection attacks in source-end network could perceive attacks before it enter to Internet. Comparing with DDoS detection in victim, source-end DDoS detection is superior in recognizing DDoS attacks and tracing back the attack sources. However, because attack stream is thin in source-end network, a sensitive and accurate algorithm is needed. The existing works are based on single-feature, so could not synthesize multiple information. Although there is improvement on single-feature detection algorithm, it is hard to depict the subtle varieties in source-end network, and so leads to the limitation on improving detection precision.

To the problems above, this paper proposes a novel DDoS detection algorithm synthesizing multiple features. The multi-features include S-D-P feature, TCP header Flags and IP header ID field, and MF-HMM is used in this algorithm. Experiments show us the results that MF-HMM perform better than other 4 algorithms based on single-feature, and effectively reduce the false-positive rate and false-negative rate. The MF-HMM proposed in this paper is effective to detect the new DDoS attacks with high distribution and low attack intension in source-end network.

References

1. Jelena, Mirkovic.: D-WARD. Source-End Defense Against Distributed Denial-of-Service Attacks, (2003), CSD of UCLA, 101–125
2. Jian Kang, Zhe Zhang, Jiu-bin Ju: Protect e-commerce against DDoS attacks with improved D-WARD detection system. IEEE International Conference on e-Technology, e-Commerce and e-Service, Hong Kong, April 2005
3. Tao Peng, Christopher Leckie, Kotagiri Ramamohanarao: Detecting Distributed Denial of Service Attacks Using Source IP Address Monitoring. Networking 2004, Athens, Greece, May 2004
4. Dongqing Zhou, Haifeng Zhang: A DDoS Attack Detection Method Based on Hidden Markov Model. Journal of Computer Research and Development, Vol.**42**, (2005) 1594-1599
5. D.Moore, G.Voelker, S.Savage: Inferring internet denial-of-service activity. The 10th USENIX Security Symposium, Washington, 2001
6. Chang-Han Jong, Shiuh-Pyng Shieh: Detecting Distributed DoS/Scanning by Anomaly Distribution of Packet Fields. International Computer Symposium, 2002

7. Zeng Z, Tu J, Pianfetti: Audio-visual affect recognition through multi-stream fused HMM for HCI. IEEE Computer Society Conference on Computer Vision and Pattern Recognition, June 2005

8. Pan, H., Levinson, S., Huang, T.S., and Liang, Z.P.: A fused Hidden Markov Model With Application to Bimodal Speech Processing. IEEE Transaction on Signal Processing, Vol.**52**, No.3, (2004) 573-581

9. Brand, M., Oliver, N.: Coupled hidden Markov models for complex action recognition. Computer Vision Pattern Recognition, (1997)201-206

10. Saul, L.k., Jordan, M.I.: Mixed memory Markov model: Decomposing complex stochastic processes as mixture of simpler ones. Machine Learning, Vol.**37**, (1999) 75-88

11. Rabiner, L.R.: A Tutorial on Hidden Markov Models and Selected Applications in Speech Recognition. Proceedings of IEEE, Vol.**77**, No.2, February 1989

An Immune-Based Model for Service Survivability

Jinquan Zeng, Xiaojie Liu, Tao Li, Feixian Sun, Lingxi Peng, and Caiming Liu

Department of Computer Science, Sichuan University, Chengdu 610065, China
liuxiaojie@cs.scu.edu.cn, zengjq@371.net

Abstract. In order to enhance service survivability, an immune-based model for service survivability, referred to as ISSM, is presented. In the model, the concepts and formal definitions of self, nonself, immunocyte, diversity system, and etc., are given; the antibody concentration and the dynamic change process of host status are described. Building on the relationship between the antibody concentration and the state of an illness in the human immune system, the systemic service capability and the service risk are calculated quantitatively. Based on the differences of the immune system among individuals, a service survivability algorithm, dynamic service migration algorithm, is put forth. Simulation results show that the model is real-time and adaptive, thus providing an effective solution for service survivability.

Keywords: artificial immune system, service survivability, risk evaluation.

1 Introduction

In the long course of human being fighting against antigens, a unique defense system is formed in our body to safeguard us [1]. In the human immune system, the first defense is the skin, saliva, sweat, and etc., which obstruct antigens from intrusion. The second is phagocytes or macrophages that surveil and kill them once antigens invade. In spite of the two kinds of defenses, some antigens still can break through and invade our body. Then the last defense, Adaptive Immune System, plays a vital role in the human immune system. Through the adaptive immune response, the system can adaptively recognize antigens and protect our body. Meanwhile, each individual has different immune system. The virus or bacteria causing one ill does not necessarily do the same to another. It is just the differences that enable some of us to survive some severe illnesses (e.g. plague) and enhance survivability of the whole human being.

Amazingly similar to the human immune system, the development of the network security technology mainly witnesses the three phases. The first phase studies how to prevent intrusion, such as firewall, encryption, and etc. The second phase studies how to detect intrusion involving intrusion detection, integrality verification, and etc. As not all unknown attacks are predictable and not all security holes are prohibited, some attacks will succeed in intrusion. So it is necessary to study how the system, after attacked, can fulfill its services while 'being sick'. The study of the third phase

D. Pointcheval, Y. Mu, and K. Chen (Eds.): CANS 2006, LNCS 4301, pp. 354–363, 2006.

emphasizes the system's capability in fulfilling essential services in the present of attacks, failures, or accidents, which is a new direction of network security technology development.

Currently, the studies of survivability mainly include the definition [2], requirement analysis method [3], the design model [4], and etc. Westmark summarized the studies of network survivability and finds that most studies focus on the definition and significance of survivability, but the realizable method is little studied [5]. Zhang et al. gave a realizable method, emergency algorithm [6], which is only a simply idea without concrete realization. Chen et al. gave a model based mobile agent for service survivability by delivering essential services [15], but which lacks risk evaluation and active response strategies. Real-time risk evaluation and response are vital in the survivability system, where the system can actively adjust its defense strategies to fulfill essential services and decrease damages. However, most current methods of risk evaluation lack real time [9] and adaptability [10], and can not evaluate service risk [11].

The paper proposes a realizable model for service survivability, called ISSM. According to the relationship in the human immune system between the antibody concentration and the state of an illness, the 'health status' and service capability are evaluated real-timely by calculating the antibody concentration, and based on the differences of the immune system among individuals, an active-defense method, dynamic service migration algorithm, is presented. Fast migration and different defense capabilities in the diversity system hope to transfer attacking target in real time to reduce attacking damages and fulfill essential services.

The rest of the paper is organized as follows. In Section 2, we establish an immune-based model for service survivability. In Section 3, simulations and experimental results are provided. Finally, Section 4 contains our summary and conclusions.

2 Model Theories

2.1 Lifecycle Model

Compared to the conventional network security technology, survivability emphasizes the system's capability in fulfilling essential services while 'being sick'. Every one suffers illness at times, and he can keep working when it is not serious. If it is too serious to fulfill his work, then he needs treatment to recover and his job will be transferred to another healthy person to do. This process is a cycle: healthy, ill, treated, recovered.

Similarly, the information system also confronts various attacks. Fig. 1 shows the lifecycle of the system status. If a serving host suffers attacks, when the risk reaches a certain degree, the host will send the alarm signal and transform into the alarm status. If the attacks lessens or the host resumes to the normal status through self-adjustment, then the alarm will be removed, but if the host suffers the continuous attacks at the alarm status, it shows that the risk is serious and the host needs recovery, then the host transforms into the failure status. Meanwhile, other hosts will be triggered to compete for the service and the failed host transforms into the recovery status. When the failed host recovers, it will join the candidate hosts.

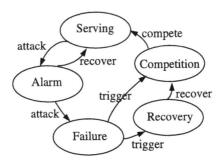

Fig. 1. Lifecycle of system status

2.2 Risk Evaluation

As the antibody concentration varies with the state of an illness, the 'health status' and service capability of the system can be evaluated by calculating the antibody concentration.

2.2.1 Antigen Presentation

Antigens $(Ag, Ag \subset U, U=\{0,1\}^l)$ in our approach are binary strings with fixed length l, which are extracted from the Internet Protocol (IP) packets transferred in the network. The string includes source/destination IP addresses, port number, protocol type, protocol status, and etc. Define the normal behaviors set in network: *Self*, illegitimate behaviors set: *Nonself*, such that $Self \cup Nonself = U$ and $Self \cap Nonself = \Phi$.

2.2.2 Immunocyte

Let B denote the set of immunocytes given by $B=\{<ab,age,count,con>|ab \in U, age \in N, count \in N, con \in R\}$, where ab is the antibody (antibody gene), age is the age of the immunocyte, $count$ is the antigen number matched by the antibody ab, con is the antibody concentration, N is the set of natural numbers and R is the set of real numbers.

B contains two subsets: the mature immunocyte B_{mature} given by $B_{mature}=\{b|b \in B, b.count<\alpha\}$ and the memory cell B_{memory} given by $B_{memory}=\{b|b \in B, b.count \geq \alpha\}$, such that $B_{mature} \cup B_{memory}=B$ and $B_{mature} \cap B_{memory}= \Phi$. A mature immunocyte evolves from an immature immunocyte after self tolerance (see equation (1)), and a memory immunocyte evolves from a mature immunocyte which matches enough antigens($\geq \alpha$) in its lifecycle.

2.2.3 Self Tolerance

In order to avoid matching self, immature immunocytes newly-produced given by $NB=\{<ab,age>|ab\in U, age\in N\}$ in antibody gene library shall undergo self tolerance before they evolve into mature immunocytes.

$$f_{tolerance}(nb) = \begin{cases} 0 & iff\ \exists x\in Self\ \wedge\ f_{match}(nb.ab,x)=1\wedge nb.age\leq\beta \\ 1 & otherwise \end{cases} \tag{1}$$

Equation (1) depicts that, within a certain tolerance period β, immunocytes not matching self evolve into mature immunocytes, while those matching will be eliminated. $f_{match}(x,y)$ is the affinity computing formula between x and y.

2.2.4 Consanguinity

Define the consanguinity [7] of the immunocyte B: $Consanguinity=\{<x,y>|x,y\in B\wedge f_{match}(x.ab,y.ab)=1\}$. Let set $X\subseteq B$, for random $x,y\in X$ and $<x,y>\in Consanguinity$, X is called a *consanguinity class* generated by *Consanguinity*. If any element among B-X has no *Consanguinity* with the elements in X, then X is a *maximal consanguinity class*. If $<x,y>\in Consanguinity$, then x,y have the same gene and can detect the same type attack.

2.2.5 Host Risk

After the primary response (see equation (2)) by the mature immunocyte and the secondary response (see equation (3)) by the memory cell, clone selection takes place and the antibody is produced. Meanwhile, the mature immunocyte evolves into the memory cell. When not matching successfully, the antibody concentration of the memory cell will be restrained (see equation (4)), where η is the antibody concentration holding cycle.

$$B'_{memory} = \{x|\forall b\in B_{mature}\wedge b.count\geq a, (x.ab=b.ab, x.age=0,$$
$$x.count=b.count, x.con=\lambda_1)\} \tag{2}$$

$$B''_{memory} = \{x|x\in B_{memory}\wedge\exists ag\in Nonself\wedge f_{match}(x.ab,ag)=1, (x.age=0,$$
$$x.count=x.count+1, x.con=\lambda_1+\lambda_2\times x.con)\} \tag{3}$$

$$B'''_{memory} = \left\{x\middle|\forall ag\in Nonself\wedge x\in B_{memory}\wedge f_{match}(x.ab,ag)=0,\right.$$
$$\left.\left(x.age=x.age+1, x.con=\begin{cases} x.con\left(1-\dfrac{1}{\eta-x.age}\right), & x.age<\eta \\ 0, & x.age\geq\eta \end{cases}\right)\right\} \tag{4}$$

According to the antibody concentration of memory cells, the host risk can be evaluated real-timely. Suppose at time t, the maximal consanguinity class of memory cells set $B_{memory}(t)$ of the host is $\{C_1, \cdots, C_n\}$, then the number of attack types suffered at time t is n. Equation (5) depicts the risk of the attack type i, and Equation (6) depicts the total risk of the host, where μ_i is the risk coefficient.

$$R_i(t) = \frac{2}{1 + e^{-\mu_i \sum_{b \in C_i} b.con}} - 1 \tag{5}$$

$$R_h(t) = \frac{2}{1 + e^{-\sum_{i=1}^{n} \mu_i \sum_{b \in C_i} b.con}} - 1 \tag{6}$$

2.2.6 Service Risk

In the process of service operation, there are different attacks that not all aim at the service. The service enemy is the attack aiming at the service. The service enemy changes frequently, because there're new attacks imposed by attackers. Meantime, immunocytes are produced continuously and mutated to adapt and detect the new attacks.

$$En(t) = \begin{cases} \Phi & t = 0 \\ En(t-1) \cup En_{new}(t) & t \geq 1 \end{cases} \tag{7}$$

$$En_{new}(t) = \left\{ ag \,\middle|\, ag \in Ag(t) \wedge \exists b \in B_{memory}(t) \wedge f_{match}(ag, b) = 1 \wedge \right.$$

$$\left. \frac{2}{1 + e^{-\mu_i \sum_{b \in C_i} b.con}} - 1 > \theta \wedge f_{costimulation}(ag) = 1 \right\} \tag{8}$$

$$f_{costimulation}(ag) = \begin{cases} 1 & C_i \text{ is the service enemy confirmed} \\ & \text{by external signal} \\ 0 & otherwise \end{cases} \tag{9}$$

Equation (7) depicts the dynamic change process of the service enemy, where $En_{new}(t)$ is the new enemies at time t. The new enemies at time t are the attacks that have risk value bigger than θ and a co-stimulation value 1, where θ is risk threshold. $f_{costimulation}(ag)(ag \in Ag)$ simulates the co-stimulation in the human immune system and further confirms whether the attack is the service enemy.

Let the set of service enemies at time t $En(t)$, and the maximal consanguinity class set corresponding to $En(t)$ is $\{C_1, \cdots, C_m\}$, then the service risk at time t is depicted by equation (10), Where ω_i is the damage coefficient.

$$R_s(t) = \frac{2}{1 + e^{-\sum_{i=1}^{m} \omega_i \sum_{b \in C_i} b.con}} - 1 \tag{10}$$

2.3 Dynamic Service Migration Algorithm

2.3.1 Diversity System
Define the hosts set: H. The maximal consanguinity class set of immunocytes of the host j $(j \in H)$ is given by $Cons_j = \{C_{j1}, \cdots, C_{jn}\}$, and the maximal consanguinity class set of immunocytes of the host $k (k \in H)$ is given by $Cons_k = \{C_{k1}, \cdots, C_{km}\}$.

$$dis(j,k) = \sum_{C_{jp} \in Cons_j, C_{kq} \in Cons_k} f_{same}(C_{jp}, C_{kq}) \tag{11}$$

$$f_{same}(C_x, C_y) = \begin{cases} 1 & iff \quad \exists z \in C_x \wedge z \notin C_y \\ 0 & otherwise \end{cases} \tag{12}$$

Equation (11) depicts the diversity distance of immunocytes of host j and host k, and the capability of the two hosts that detect different attacks. The bigger the value is, and the stronger the capability of detecting different attacks is. $f_{same}(C_x, C_y)$ is used to judge whether C_x and C_y can detect different attacks: if C_x and C_y can detect different attacks, then 1 is returned; if C_x and C_y can detect same attacks, then 0 is returned.

Define the diversity System: $\forall i, j \in Host \wedge dis(i,j) \geq 1$. According to the definition of the diversity system, each host can defend at least one specific attack.

2.3.2 Algorithm Description
The service capability of the host is obtained through calculating host risk, and the different defense capability against the service enemies determines the service competition among hosts.

Algorithm 1: dynamic service migration algorithm
    Begin
        calculates the risk r_i of the serving host i;
        updates the set of service enemies;
        If the serving time terminates or $r_i \geq \theta_1$ Then
        //θ_1 is the migration threshold of service risk
        Begin
            triggers the rest hosts to compete for the service;
            selects host k with the least enemies as the service migration target;
            calculates the service time T_k; //see equation (13)
            service migrates;

      host *i* transforms into the recovery status;
    End
  Else
   If $\theta_2 \leq r_i < \theta_1$ Then
     //θ_2 is the alarm threshold of service risk
    Begin
      sends the alarm signal;
      host *i* transforms into the alarm status;
    End
    Else
    Begin
      removes the alarm signal;
      host *i* transforms into the serving status;
    End
  End.

$$T_k = \frac{c_1}{c_2 r_k} \tag{13}$$

Where r_k is the risk of the host k and c_1, c_2 are the coefficients.

Theorem 1. Diversity system is survivable.

Proof. According to the definition of diversity system, lifecycle model of the system and service migration algorithm, if a host is attacked and the host risk becomes higher, the host will transform into the recovery status, where the host will be recovered. After recovery is finished, the host will defend the attack and join the candidate hosts. So diversity system is survivable.

Theorem 2. With the increase of service migration frequencies, the service will migrate to the host with the least risk.

Proof. According to the definition of diversity system and service migration algorithm, with the increase of migration frequencies, the set of service enemies will become larger and more complete. But the service migration target is the host with the least service enemies. So the service will migrate to the host with the least risk along with the increase of service migration frequencies.

3   Simulations and Experimental Results

In our experiment, 6 hosts provided WWW service. Another 10 hosts imposed over 20 types of network attacks such as syn flood, land, smurf, teardrop, and etc. The antigen consisted of the source/destination IP address, port number, protocol type, IP flags, IP overall packet length, TCP/ UDP/ICMP fields, and etc. The antibody concentration coefficient λ_1 was 0.001 and λ_2 was 0.9998; the holding cycle η was 10; the service cycle coefficient c_1 and c_2 was 560 and 2, respectively. The r-contiguous bits matching rule was used to calculate the affinity. During our experiment, we found that WWW service responded faster and performed better, when the attack risk value was around 0.3. When the attack risk value was around 0.7, WWW service responded much slower and performed worse. So the service risk alarm threshold θ_2 was 0.3; the service risk migration threshold θ_1 was 0.72; the attack risk threshold θ was 0.3.

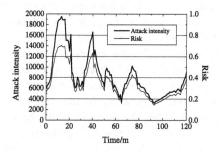

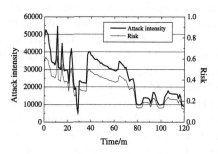

Fig. 2. Attack intensity curve and risk change curve of host A suffered from syn flood attack

Fig. 3. Attack intensity curve and risk change curve of host A suffered from many network attacks

Fig. 2 illustrates the attack intensity curve (i.e. the number of the attack packet) of host A suffered syn flood attack and the risk change curve detected. Fig. 3 shows the attack intensity curve of host A suffered many network attacks and the total risk change curve detected. The attack intensity change is fully reflected by the antibody concentration change illustrated in Fig. 2 and Fig. 3. In Fig. 3, for instance, at time 10 the attack intensity is 35965 IP packets, and the risk value is 0.45; at time 11 the attack intensity abruptly increases to 54692 IP packets. With the increase of the antibody concentration through clone selection, the risk value rapidly increases to 0.63.

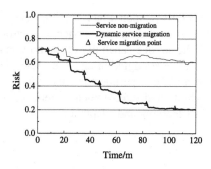

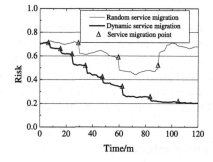

Fig. 4. Risk change curves of non-migration service and dynamic service migration

Fig. 5. Risk change curves of random migration service and dynamic service migration

Fig. 4 and Fig.5 illustrate the risk change curves of WWW service. Fig. 4 illustrates the risk comparison curves between non-migration service and dynamic service migration. Fig. 5 shows the risk comparison curves between random migration service at a fixed service time and dynamic service migration. In Fig. 4, non-migration service enables attackers to easily analyze and carry out attacks, so the risk value is higher. In Fig. 5, because the migration target is randomly selected, the risk value is random. But when the total risk of the migration target is higher, the fixed-time method will leave much time for attackers to take actions and augment the potential risk of the service. When the dynamic service migration is adopted, according to the real-time risk evaluation of the host and service, the set of service enemies is added and the service risk is reduced gradually. For example, at time 24 the service risk is 0.62; after service migration, at time 28 the risk value is decreased to 0.52. If the total risk of the host is higher, the service time will become shorter, and the host will be less exposed to attackers. After service migration, the attacking target is transferred real-timely and damages are reduced. When the total risk of the host is lower, the service time will become longer, and it is useful in practical application. In our experiment, non-migration WWW service responds slowest and is poorest survivability. For WWW service that randomly selects the migration target at a fixed service time, the response is unstable and the survivability is poorer. For WWW service with dynamic migration, the service response is faster and better and has stronger survivability.

Currently, the studies of network survivability lack realizable methods [2-6], risk evaluation and active response strategies [15]. Risk evaluation methods lack real time [9] and adaptability [10], and can not evaluate service risk [11]. However, our proposed model, ISSM, selects the migration target and adjusts the service time based on real-time detection results of host risk and service risk, transfers attacking target in real time to reduce attack damages and fulfills essential services, and is an active-defense method.

4   Conclusion

ISSM is presented to the study of service survivability, upon which the lifecycle of the system is described in the paper. Furthermore, a dynamic service migration algorithm for service survivability is put forth. The service capability of the host and the service risk are calculated quantitatively and service migration target are selected adaptively in the model. The theoretical analysis and the experiment results show that ISSM is an efficient solution for service survivability and offers the characteristics of real-time calculation, quantitative description, self-learning and adaptation.

Acknowledgement

This work is supported by the National Natural Science Foundation of China under Grant No.60373110, No.60573130 and 60502011, the National Research Foundation for the Doctoral Program of Higher Education of China under Grant

No.20030610003, the New Century Excellent Expert Program of Ministry of Education of China under Grant No.NCET-04-0870, and the Innovation Foundation of Sichuan University under Grant No.2004CF10.

References

1. Li, T.: Computer Immunology. Publishing House of Electronics Industry Beijing (2004)
2. Knight, J. C., Strunk, E. A., Sullivan, K. J.: Towards a Rigorous Definition of Information System Survivability. In Proc. of DISCEX (2003) 78-89
3. Linger, E. C., Lipson, H. F.: Requirements Definition for Survivable Network Systems. In Proc. of ICRE (1998)
4. Richard, C. L., Howard, F. L., et al.: Life-Cycle Models for Survivable Systems. TECHNICAL REPORT CMU/SEI-2002-TR-026
5. Westmark, V. R.: A Definition for Information System Survivability. In Proc. of HICSS (2004) 303-312
6. Zhang, Y. Q.□Zhang, H. Z.: Analysis on characters of survivability and emergent algorithms. Journal on Communications, vol. 26(1) (2005) 124-128
7. Li, T.: An immunity based network security risk estimation. Science in China Ser. F Information Sciences, vol. 48(5) (2005) 798-816
8. Tedesco, G., Aickelin, U.: Data Reduction in Intrusion Alert Correlation. WSEAS Transactions on Computers, vol. 1(5) (2006) 186-193
9. Madan, B. B., Goševa-Popstojanova, K., Vaidyanathan, K., et al.: Modeling and quantification of security attributes of software systems. In Proc. of the International Conference on Dependable Systems and Networks, Washington, (2002) 505-514
10. Li, H, Cai, Zhong. M, Han, C. Z, Guan, X. H.: An Intrusion Detect ion Framework Based on Information Fusion. MINI-MICRO SYSTEMS, vol. 24(9) (2003) 1602-1606
11. Wang, Y. F., Li, T., et al.: A Real Time Method of Risk Evaluation Based on Artificial Immune System for Network Security. ACTA ELECTRONICA SINICA, vol. 33(5) (2005) 945-949
12. Kim, J., Bentley, P. J.: Towards an artificial immune system for network intrusion detection: an investigation of dynamic clonal selection. In Proc. of the Congress on Evolutionary Computation (2002) 1015-1020
13. Twycross, J., Aickelin, U.: Experimenting with innate immunity. In Proc. of the Workshop on Artificial Immune Systems and Immune System Modelling, Bristol (2006) 18-19
14. Harmer, P. K., Williams, P. D., Gunsch, G. H., et al.: An artificial immune system architecture for computer security applications. IEEE Transaction on Evolutionary Computation, Vol. 6 (2002) 252-280
15. Chen, X. Q., Zhang, J. H., Fu, L., et al.: Model for the Deliver of Essential Services in the Survivability Network System Based on Mobile Agent. Journal of Chongqing University, vol. 27(10) (2004) 37-39
16. Li, T.: An immune based dynamic intrusion detection model. Chinese Science Bulletin, vol. 50(17) (2005) 1912-1919

X^{2BT} Trusted Reputation System: A Robust Mechanism for P2P Networks

Lan Yu, Willy Susilo, and Rei Safavi-Naini

Center for Information Security
School of Information Technology and Computer Science
University of Wollongong
Wollongong 2522, Australia
{ly85, wsusilo, rei}@uow.edu.au

Abstract. Over the past few years, Peer-to-Peer (P2P) networks have grown extensively and dramatically changed large-scale file transfer. One of the most popular P2P network is the *BitTorrent* system. BitTorrent can efficiently distribute large files by optimizing the use of network bandwidth and providing scalability. Due to the open and anonymous nature of P2P systems BitTorrent also provides an ideal environment for distribution of malicious, low quality, or doctored information. A number of reputation systems, including P2PRep with its successors XRep and X^{2}Rep, had been proposed to address security weaknesses of Gnutella P2P file sharing networks. Although it has been claimed that these methods are also applicable to the other file sharing networks, it is not clear how to achieve this task. Moreover, some of the shortcomings of these reputation systems such as online-polling only and cold-start may be exploited by malicious attackers. In this paper, we propose a reputation system, called X^{2BT}Rep, which is an extension of the X^{2}Rep and for BitTorrent network. We show that the proposed system improves the security and the quality of information distributed over P2P networks.

Keyword: P2P, Reputation System, XRep, X^{2}Rep, and X^{2BT}Rep.

1 Introduction

Peer-to-peer (P2P) file sharing is one of the most significant technical models of the internet. Rather than traditional client-server architecture, P2P networks equip each node with an equivalent capability or responsibility and they can share computer resources and services via direct connections. Over the last few years, a series of P2P networks and channels, such as Napster [18], Gnutella [24], Kazaa [16], eDonkey [10] and BitTorrent [27], have been developed. Among them, BitTorrent is the most influential and innovative protocol [17,21], designed to be a large-scale file distribution tool. Studies in the most recent research [20, 25, 23] indicate that BitTorrent has consumed more than a third of the internet's bandwidth and is rapidly emerging as the preferred means of many

D. Pointcheval, Y. Mu, and K. Chen (Eds.): CANS 2006, LNCS 4301, pp. 364–380, 2006.

content providers to distribute legitimate content, such as the free computer operating system, Linux.

One of the primary advantages of BitTorrent is the fact that resources and services can be easily contributed, searched and obtained. Also, it utilizes unused the upload capacity of downloaders, which overcomes the problem of *free-riding* (i.e. users prefer to download but refuse to upload [2]) that occurs in other P2P networks. As a result, network bandwidth can be used as efficiently as possible. Moreover, several other significant features, such as scalability, fault tolerance and diversity in service, provide BitTorrent with sufficient potential for future growth.

Along with the aforementioned advantages, inherent risks and threats with BitTorrent have become a stumbling block against further progress. First, due to anonymity, misbehaving users can arbitrarily distribute low-quality, even malicious content over the network without witnesses, such as Trojan horses and viruses. Second, it provides a good environment for malicious attackers to subvert systems in hiding, because of no enforcement rule of joining, leaving and staying in the system. Third, in a BitTorrent network, users can easily expose their private information when joining the system, such as users' IP address and port, and hence, users' privacy can be violated by adversaries.

Previous evidence and studies [1, 3, 22] show that reputation systems are a robust solution to protect P2P networks from malicious attacks. In a reputation system, the quality of a given resource/peer is determined by a user, based on historical information from other users [26]. The main advantage of such reputation systems is to protect against most known attacks and vulnerabilities, and simultaneously retain the characteristic of anonymity as well as maintaining minimal overheads. During the past few years, research has been conducted to develop several protocols of reputation systems to protect P2P networks, such as P2PRep, XRep, and X^{2}Rep. Unfortunately, these protocols are *only* designed for Gnutella-like P2P networks, which have a different architecture from BitTorrent. Therefore, none of them can be integrated into the BitTorrent protocol even though some proposals claim that they can be adjusted to any P2P systems. Moreover, they have shortcomings like online-polling only, cold-start and performance bottleneck problems.

1.1   Our Contribution

In this paper, we propose the *first* robust reputation system, X^{2BT}Rep, devoted to BitTorrent networks. It is an extension of the X^{2}Rep trust semantics algorithm. The outstanding advantage of X^{2BT}Rep is that it prevents all known attacks on BitTorrent-like networks. Other major contributions of X^{2BT}Rep are *credibility award* and *credibility chain exchange* algorithms. *Credibility award* is a method to overcome the cold-start problem, so that newcomers can participate in the system as quickly as possible. The method of *credibility chain exchange* improves trusted ratings sharing among all the peers, which avoids the limits of ratings sharing between peers with few interests in previous reputation systems.

Moreover, our approach can be implemented on other centralized P2P networks as well, such as Napster.

1.2 Notations

We use PK_i and SK_i to denote a pair of public and private keys belonging to the owner i. We denote public key encryption with curly brackets, preceded by the key with which something was encrypted, as in $\{M\}_{PK_i}$, which means message M encrypted with public key PK_i. Signing is denoted as square brackets, with the symbol of the key subscripting the closed bracket, as in $[M]_{SK_i}$. Cryptographic certificate is denoted with combination of the signing and the public key, as in $([M]_{SK_i}, PK_i)$. Notations used in this paper are summarized as follows.

- Let (PK_i, SK_i) denote peer i's public and private key, respectively.
- Let $\{M\}_{PK_i}$ be a message M *encrypted* with a public key PK_i.
- Let $([M]_{SK_i}, PK_i)$ denote a message M *signed* by a private key SK_i, associated with a public key PK_i.

1.3 Paper Organization

The rest of this paper is structured as follows: Section 2 presents a literature review. Section 3 analyzes two reputation systems including predecessors to ours such as XRep and X^2Rep, and discusses their weaknesses. Section 4 gives a detailed overview of the BitTorrent network and demonstrates its advantages and disadvantages. Section 5 proposes our protocol X^{2BT}Rep by describing its assumptions, several enhanced approaches and the protocol. Section 6 evaluates the security issues of our proposal. Finally, Section 7 concludes the paper.

2 Related Works

The internet has produced vast new opportunities to interact with strangers. These interactions can be fun, informative and even profitable [26]. Along with the benefits, however, they also involve risks. Data from a provider may be different from the description. Products may be low quality or be shipped with inappropriate packaging.

In real life, similar risks of interaction with strangers can be reduced through reputations. A stranger's reliability can be traced through an authority, such as bank or government, or can be judged via past personal experience. Also, people can make friends with strangers through the introduction of their trusted friends.

In the same way, reputation systems play an important role in the internet service, helping to foster trust and elicit cooperation among loosely connected and geographically dispersed economic agents [9]. In reputation systems, the quality of a given resource or peer can be determined by a user based on historical information from other users. These systems encourage good behaviors and deter dishonest participation.

The model of eBay relies on a binary reputation system mechanism for quality signalling and quality control. Buyers and sellers can report feedback at the end of transactions. The format of the solicited feedback can be a designation of "positive", "negative" or "neutral", together with a short text comment. eBay publishes the sum of positive, negative and neutral ratings plus all comments to all its users. The binary reputation system mechanism exploited by eBay is able to build trusted relationships between strangers. First, buyers and sellers can determine the other parties' abilities and manners via historical information on past interactions. Second, the hope of positive feedback or anxiety of gaining a negative reputation for the future leads to a trustworthy behavior in both parties.

3   Previous Studies of Reputation Systems

In the following sections, we present more detailed analyzes of our predecessors, including XRep, and X^{2}Rep.

3.1   XRep

XRep [7] reputation system is a distributed polling algorithm designed for the Gnutella P2P sharing protocol, where each peer keeps track of reputation ratings and shares them with other peers. The reputation ratings are based on the experience of both resources and peers, and are used to minimize the potential downloading risks of a resource offered by a peer.

To be able to identify resources and peers, XRep makes two assumptions. Each servent keeps a consistent pair of public (PK_i) and private keys (SK_i) for multiple use. There is a peer_id (P_i) associated with the peer which is the digest of the public key obtained using a secure hash function. On the other hand, each resource is related to an identifier $(Resource_{id})$ computed from the hash of the resource's content.

There are two types of votes in the XRep protocol. One is the resource vote, which is a binary value describing whether the resource is good(1) or bad(0). Another is the servent vote which can be generated as an ordinal scale (e.g. from A to D or from $\star$ to $\star\star\star\star\star$) or a continuous one (e.g. 80%).

Before deciding to download, an initiator asks other peers' opinions on either satisfied resources or offerers. These peers feedback a list of votes to the initiator. Then three mechanisms are utilized by the initiator to assess votes. First, votes are all encrypted with the initiator's public key. This allows the initiator to detect tampered votes after decryption. Second, in order to prevent a clique of dummy or controlled votes, the initiator calculates votes from the same network Id in an average value, or only selects a single vote as the final value. Third, the initiator randomly chooses several peers in the voting list and sends messages requesting confirmation on votes to ensure the existence of the peers. The peers who receive the request must return a response message; otherwise their votes will be discarded.

We nevertheless find the mechanisms provided by XRep cannot evaluate votes and remove those from suspicious attackers effectively; furthermore, they may have negative impacts. First of all, XRep requires that PollReply messages include not only votes but also peers' IP and port. This enables attackers to track the IP addresses of other peers and launch a massive attack against those peers. Second, XRep employs a simple cluster computation to evaluate votes, so that the votes are either entirely accepted or blindly discarded. Hence, the download decision may be based on an inadequate evaluation. Finally, requesting confirmation can generate much additional overhead if a large number of peers have been chosen.

3.2 X^2Rep

X^2Rep [6] extends XRep and is designed to protect against the weaknesses of XRep. As in XRep, a distributed polling algorithm is employed in X^2Rep to manage the reputations based on resources and servents. However, it is an improvement on XRep and has the ability to compute the weight of a peer based on past voting experiences.

The weight of a peer introduced by the X^2Rep protocol is the most critical part of the voting evaluation process. It is measured in terms of *credibility rating*. Each peer builds and maintains a table of credibility ratings. The table contains peer_ids and the credibility values of other peers who have previously submitted votes. The credibility value c_{ij} given by a peer P_i for another peer P_j is a real number in the interval [0, 1]. For an unknown peers or recognized malicious attackers, its credibility value is set to zero.

To evaluate votes from peers, X^2Rep employs a different algorithm: the evaluation computation allows only votes from peers whose credibility values are more than zero to be involved. The computation uses the credibility values of the peers to multiply their vote value and the final results are given to the user to determine the download, whilst those votes from unknown peers or recognized malicious attackers are temporarily stored. After download completion, the user updates their opinions on the resource and the offerer. And then, the credibility ratings of the peers who have submitted votes are refreshed. If the votes are the same as P_i's opinions, the corresponding submitters' credibility ratings increase by 0.05. Otherwise, the credibility ratings are reduced to zero.

X^2Rep effectively improves on XRep is security shortcomings. Credibility rating provides a more reliable assessment of the resources and the offerer before initiating a download. The protocol replaces the IP and port of a peer with a self-signed certificate within PollReply messages, which avoids the exposure of personal privacy. Furthermore, it reduces additional overheads because of discarding several unnecessary XRep network communication phases.

Nonetheless, there are several shortcomings of X^2Rep reputation systems as follows:

- **Online polling only** – both XRep and X^2Rep protocols require peers to be online during the polling process. However, it is impractical for peers to run the reputation systems around the clock simply in order to distribute votes.

- **Cold-start** – in X^{2}Rep, newcomers with inadequate credibility ratings may take a risk to download resources. They also have to struggle for credibility ratings in other peers so as to continuously participate in polling distribution. However, establishing sufficient credibility ratings in either newcomers' or in other peers' repositories takes a long time for newcomers.
- **Performance bottlenecks** – X^{2}Rep suffers from a problem in that peers can only generate a limited number of credibility ratings. Final adjusted trust values presented to users will be restricted to the limited number of credibility ratings. Hence, users may make download selections based on inadequate reputation values.

4   A Robust P2P System – BitTorrent

BitTorrent is a P2P file-sharing protocol [5], the brainchild of Bram Cohen, designed to distribute large resources by utilizing the unused upload capacity of downloaders. The philosophy of BitTorrent is that peers should upload while they are downloading. In conventional client/server downloading, a high demand by clients leads to degradation of the server performance. On the other hand, there is a significant number of selfish clients in traditional P2P networks, such as Gnutella. With BitTorrent, high bandwidth utilization can be achieved and free-riding can be prevented. Recently, several studies and surveys [11,13] have indicated that BitTorrent has become a "king" of P2P internet traffic and has grown into an option for content providers to efficiently distribute data (e.g. BitTorrent helped *Redhat* to distribute 1.77GB Linux Redhat 9 to more than 180,000 clients in the first five months [12]).

4.1   Basic Description of BitTorrent

The basic idea of BitTorrent is to split a file into several equal-sized *pieces* (except for the last piece, which may be smaller). The downloaders of the file are reciprocated with pieces from multiple peers by uploading pieces which they possess. Once the download finishes, the downloaders can reassemble all the pieces into the original file.

Since BitTorrent does not provide a search mechanism, it employs search engines in *Web Server*. The web server maintains a list of *torrent files*. Each torrent file refers to a resource with a common *tracker* entry. The file also includes the number of pieces and the SHA1 hash digest of each piece, which will be used to verify its integrity. The tracker is the central point in the BitTorrent network, and keeps track of all the active peers in the process of uploading/downloading the corresponding resource. Peers in the network are either *seeder* (peers with a complete copy of the resource) or *leecher* (peers with a partial resource).

1) Before initializing the download, the initiator ($Peer_0$) needs to obtain a torrent file from the web server. 2) After fetching the torrent file, $Peer_0$ then contacts the tracker using a simple protocol layered on top of HTTP and sends information about its IP address and the file currently downloading. The tracker responds with a random list of other peers' information, including IP address/Port. 3)

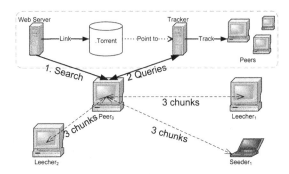

Fig. 1. BitTorrent Architecture

From this point onwards, $Peer_0$ establishes connections with other peers and begins to download. Figure 1 shows a basic architecture of BitTorrent.

4.2 Security Threat to BitTorrent

The main concern[1] with BitTorrent is the **distribution of false information**. A peer may publish a torrent file claiming to be something it is not. (I.e., "LinuxKernel.torrent" actually contains the Sasser worm.) This is caused by the lack of a way of verifying either resources or peers.

Since torrent files are published on the web, some web sites provide a way to authenticate the content of files by associating web forum entries with each published file, where users can post feedback and indicate invalid files. However, this solution is a faulty reputation system. First, the format of the feedback reported by users is undefined, which can be a symbol, a word, a sentence or something else. Second, the feedback that may includes ads, nonsense, even fraudulent messages is published in raw format to all the users. Third, it is inconvenient for users to give feedback since new torrent files are always being published on the web forum and it is difficult to recover the web page associated the old torrent files. Therefore, we propose our new first reputation system designed for BitTorrent networks.

5 X^{2BT}Rep Reputation Management System

X^{2BT}Rep is designed to overcome the distribution of false contents, of BitTorrent networks. It can be seamlessly integrated into the current BitTorrent protocol, whilst at the same time retaining the protocol's characteristics of openness,

---

[1] BitTorrent infrastructure suffers from the distributed denial-of-service (DDoS) attack [15], as it puts too much reliance on the tracker. A DDoS attack is a common online assault that aims to overwhelm network bandwidth using a flood of data, to prevent access to servers. Since avoiding this type of attack requires an overhaul of the BitTorrent protocol itself, it is outside the scope of the paper.

scalability and minimum additional overheads. Moreover, our proposal addresses the shortcomings of other reputation systems including, XRep and X^{2}Rep. In this chapter, we discuss the basic requirements of X^{2BT}Rep, describe its advanced functionalities and demonstrate the protocol.

5.1   Basic Requirements

Assumptions. Our solution is a system that combines both resources' and peers' reputations. We make the following two assumptions with respect to resources and peers. First, each peer i keeps a consistent pair of public (PK_i) and private keys (SK_i) for multiple use. Also, there is a peer_id (P_i) associated with the peer, which is the digest of the public key obtained using a secure hash function. Second, each torrent file is associated with an identifier $(info\_hash)$, which is the SHA1 hash of the torrent file.

Additionally, a centralized tracker manages the reputations of both torrent files and the provider of the torrent files along with a list of active peers. In response to a query queried by a peer, the tracker sends back the reputation system and the IP addresses of current download users. After downloading the resource, peers evaluates the resource and provides their votes to the centralized tracker.

Offerer. Each torrent file has a creator with a copy of the corresponding resource shared for downloading. In this paper, we denote the creators of the torrent files as *offerers*. A offerer is same as ordinary peers and has a public and private key pair with an unique ID. In our proposal, a torrent file is required to contain the ID of its offerer. And the identifier $(info\_hash)$ for a torrent file is the hash of the information in the torrent file, including piece length, hashes of each piece, the ID of the offerer and the created time.

Local Repositories. Each peer records its own experiences on torrent files, the offerers of each torrent file and the pollers who provide votes on either torrent files or offerers. Each peer is required to store data about its experiences in three **local experience repositories**:

- a *torrent repository*, which stores a pair $(info\_hash, value)$, where a *value* describes whether an *info_hash* that the peer has experienced is good (1) or poor (0) in the peer's opinion.
- an *offerer repository*, which stores a vector $(offerer\_id, v_1, v_2, \ldots v_k, m)$ that presents the most recent k times and the total number m of experiences where a peer has interacted with an offerer whose identifier is *offerer_id* (*offerer_id* is the same as *peer_id*). $v_1, v_2, \ldots v_k$ are values that are either good (1) or poor (0). During the initialization for a new offerer, all the values are set to zero. If a new experience is added in, the oldest one will be removed and the value m will be increased by one.
- a *credibility repository*, which is a pair $(peer\_id, value)$. The credibility parameter is a weight that describes the reliability of other peers and measures

the trustworthiness of votes from other peers in the voting system. The real *value*, with an interval from 0 to 1, is set to zero during the initialization for a new poller.

Voting. There are two types of votes: the *torrent vote* and the *offerer vote*. In order to generate a vote on either a torrent file or an offerer, each peer checks its local torrent or offerer repositories and uses the following calculation:

- *Torrent Vote* – the vote for a torrent file is a Boolean value 0 or 1 associated with *info_hash*, which is denoted as $v_H = 0/1$;
- *Offerer Vote* – the vote from a peer P_i for an offerer P_o is calculated as follows:

$$v_{oi} = (\sum_{x=1}^{k} v_x/k, m) \qquad (1)$$

It should be noted that votes for an offerer not only contains a continuous scale expressing the recent behavior of P_o, but also a sum of experiences with P_o.

To protect authenticity and integrity, each poller generates a self-signed certificate called a *vote certificate*, which contains an identifier of a torrent, an offerer's id, a poller's id, opinions on either the torrent or the offerer and a time stamp, and then combines its public key for verification before submitting it to a tracker. The format is shown as follows:

$$([info\_hash, ID_o, ID_i, v_H/v_{oi}, TS]_{SK_i}, PK_i) \qquad (2)$$

Secure Sockets Layer. SSL is an encryption protocol invoked on a secure Web Server to provide a reliable, encrypted and integrity-protected stream to the application. One of the best-known BitTorrent clients, *Azureus* [4], provides SSL to support tracker security. In our solution, we recommend that *HTTPs* is used in order to protect the tracker/peer communication. HTTPs is an http protocol using a Secure Socket Layer (SSL) which can be easily integrated into existing BitTorrent architecture. The HTTPs protocol offers several advantages including protection of the confidentiality of messages as well as authentication of a secure server.

5.2   Further Discussion of Two Novel Algorithms

In order to improve the shortcomings in XRep and X^2Rep, we introduce two algorithms: *Credibility Award Algorithm* and *Credibility Chain Exchange*.

Credibility Award Algorithm. This is an algorithm to enable newcomers to be involved in the system as soon as possible by means of encouraging them to participate actively. It is designed to counteract the cold-start problem of X^2Rep.

To implement the credibility award algorithm, a client first needs to have a full copy of the downloaded file and to have submitted a vote notifying other peers that the file is genuine. It is also required that the client keeps uploading for the benefit of other downloaders. Suppose that a downloader receives a vote and several pieces from the client, and finds that the file is genuine after downloading is complete. The downloader will then give some bonus credibility values according to the client's uploading contribution.

This algorithm can help newcomers to increase their credibility ratings with other peers. Moreover, it is an incentive mechanism to promote each peer's contribution to the community.

Credibility Chain Exchange. This aims to establish information in a confidence exchange system based on a reliability parameter, i.e. the credibility rating. The goal of this algorithm is to break the weakness of the performance bottleneck in the X^{2}Rep protocol.

A credibility chain exchange algorithm can effectively help a peer to establish a relationship of trust with an unknown peer via an intermediary node. In our proposal, credibility is regarded as an indication of trust. If the credibility of peer B given by peer A is reliable (it can be expressed as the credibility value c_{AB}, which is higher than a threshold), it means that peer B has provided accurate votes in the past and can be trusted by A. If A happens to meet peer C, and C is a friend of B, then B can introduce C to A. In the end, A quickly establishes a relationship with C. The relationship, denoted as c_{AC}, is calculated by multiplying c_{AB} and c_{BC}.

However, malicious peers may pretend to be trustworthy and then attempt to introduce a clique of dummy or controlled "friends" to honest users (e.g. referral attacks, cf. Section 6). In order to repulse this kind of attack and establish reliable relationships with peers, users may make a selection by themselves instead of readily accepting referrals from other peers. Furthermore, users can maintain a database to keep track of the reliability of friends introduced by other peers and adjust the credibility ratings of those introducers accordingly. For instance, the credibility ratings of a peer will be punished by being decreased when the user disagrees with votes from friends introduced by that peer.

With the help of a credibility chain exchange algorithm, peers can build up a comprehensive and reliable database of credibility ratings for pollers. As a result, peers have greater capability to assess resources and offerers, and hence, the likelihood of content pollution can be reduced.

5.3 Protocol Designs

The X^{2BT}Rep protocol consists of several phases 1: *(1) torrent search, (2) exchange of votes, (3) evaluation of votes, (4) tracker queries, (5) pieces and credibility chain exchange,* and *(6) updating and voting reputation value.*

Phase 1: Torrent Search. As with the original BitTorrent protocol, an initiator P_i first searches for a torrent file from a web site W before downloading resources. The torrent file must contain the offerer's ID and created time.

Phase 2: Exchange of Votes. P_i establishes an SSL connection with the centralized tracker via the entry point in the torrent file. Then it checks the identification of PK_T in the torrent certificate and the one from the SSL connection. If they are the same, P_i begins to exchange votes on either the torrent or the offerer between the tracker via Poll and PollReply messages.

The Poll message contains the *vote certificate* relating to the offerer. The vote certificate includes *info_hash*, P_o, P_i, vote v_{oi} on the offerer and *Time Stamp*. Upon receiving the Poll message, the centralized tracker checks its centralized repositories and responds with a group of votes corresponding to the *info_hash* and the *offerer* via PollReply messages. The PollReply messages, signed with SK_T then combined with PK_i, allow P_i to preserve the confidentiality and integrity of votes.

As observed in [12], 90% of the leechers remain in the network for less than 10,000 seconds during the beginning of the torrent usage. It can be observed that the number of votes on the torrent given by seeders is very low at the beginning of downloading. Moreover, the tracker log illustrated in Figure 2 (a) and (b) traces the torrent of the 1.77GB Linux Redhat 9 over a period of five months from April to August 2003. This figure clearly demonstrates that seeds reach their peak more than 12 hours after the peak of leechers is achieved. In order to avoid a lack of information, each downloader is supposed to provide its opinion on the offerer for other peers' reference before initiating downloading, if possible.

Phase 3: Votes Evaluation. To make a decision on a possible transaction, P_i needs to convert the votes from the previous phase into evaluation values. However, a received vote may be spoofed or generated by a group of colluding peers. In order to reduce these malicious activities, an additional factor called the *credibility rating*, introduced in the X^2Rep protocol [6], is used to remove malicious votes and produce adjusted values on the resource and the offerer.

To present trust values to the user for decision-making regarding downloading, two formulas are introduced below to evaluate the trustworthiness of the torrent and the offerer. It is recommended that the number of valid votes be combined with the trust values to make the decision.

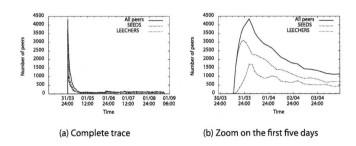

(a) Complete trace   (b) Zoom on the first five days

Fig. 2. Number of active peers over time (sourced from [12])

Table 1. Sequence of messages and operations inX^{2BT}Rep protocol

Phase	Description
1 Torrent Search	*Initiator to Web Server: (keyword)*
	Web Server to Initiator: (torrent file)
2 Exchange of Votes	*Initiator to Tracker: Poll(Vote$_i$)*
	Tracker to Initiator: PollReply($\{[info\_hash, P_o, Votes]_{SK_T}\}_{PK_i}$)
3 Votes Evaluation	*- Initiator evaluates valid votes and makes a download decision.*
	- Tracker may removes the suspicious Vote$_i$ and adds true one
	into the vote group.
4 Tracker Queries	*Initiator to Tracker: TrackerGet(info_hash, P$_i$, my IP/Port)*
	Tracker to Initiator: TrackerResponse(interval, peers/failure)
5 Pieces and Credibility	*- Initiator & Peers: Pieces exchange*
Chain Exchange	*- Initiator implements two additional advanced algorithms*
6 Updating and Voting	*- After download, check the resource's quality*
Reputation Value	*- Update repositories and credibility ratings*
	- Initiator to Tracker: new Poll(Vote$_i$)

– Adjusted torrent trust value:

$$V_H = (\sum v_H * c_{ij})/\sum c_{ij} \ (where \ c_{ij} \neq 0);$$

– Adjusted offerer trust value:

$$V_o = (\sum v_{oj} * c_{ij})/\sum c_{ij} \ (where \ c_{ij} \neq 0);$$

After this evaluation process, P_i can trust its assessment of either the resource or the offerer, and can therefore make a decision whether or not to download the resource. If the evidence on the reputation is not sufficient, downloading may be made by accepting a level of risk.

On the tracker side, the new vote from P_i is added into the vote group after being checked and simplified by the tracker T. A suspicious vote, such as a duplicate or invalid vote, will be removed by the tracker.

Phase 4: Tracker Queries. After deciding to download a resource, the peer P_i queries the tracker in order to obtain a list of peers in the process of downloading, and at the same time submits its IP address and port. The tracker returns a random list of the keys containing: *peer_id, IP* and *port*, which can be used to establish connections with peers in the next phase.

Phase 5: Pieces and Credibility Chain Exchange. In this phase, P_i contacts peers in the list one by one and then exchanges pieces of the file by index as described in the torrent file. Furthermore, the two algorithms, including the credibility award algorithm and the credibility chain exchange, are implemented in this phase.

In the implementation of the credibility award algorithm, the peer P_i needs to maintain a temporary parameter μ_j, which indicates how many pieces have been successfully downloaded from a seeder P_j during the process of downloading. After completing a download, a *credibility award rate* Δ is calculated as shown below for pieces provided by the seeder P_j. In phase 6, the *rate* will be used to calculate a bonus for the seeder according to its contribution.

$$\Delta = \mu_j/n \ (n \text{ is the total number of Pieces.})$$

The following section describes the credibility chain exchange algorithm. If the credibility C_{ik} given by the peer P_i for peer P_k passes beyond a threshold value δ, P_i then sends a request message CredRequest to peer P_k. The request message includes ID_i, ID_k, IDs and $flag$, which map the P_i's ID, peer P_k's ID, a collection of peer_ids whose credibility values P_i intends to receive from peer P_k, and the tag assigned to distinguish the request message from pieces exchange messages. Peer P_k checks its credibility repository and returns the credibility values of peer_ids with matching IDs. The message, signed with P_k's private key and combined with its public key, is encrypted with the PK_i of P_i before being sent back. After P_i receives the returned message CredResponse, it calculates a new credibility value for each peer_id in the IDs (if duplicate credibilities are found, the peer with the highest credibility C_{ik} is chosen), and inserts it into the credibility repository.

Phase 6: Updating and Voting Reputation Value. After completing resource downloading, peer P_i assesses the quality of the resource, updates local repositories and submits a new vote on both the torrent and the offerer to the centralized tracker.

Updating the state on a Peer

1. The torrent repository: if the quality of the resource is good, the value in the torrent repository is 1, otherwise it is 0.
2. The offerer repository: the content value of the above resource as above, is added into the table, and the oldest one is removed from the table. However, if a malicious offerer generates the torrent, it does not upload at all. This value will be zero. For example, after the common life cycle of a torrent file (for example, 20 days), if no peer finishes the download, it will set the reputation value to 0 at this time.
3. The credibility repository: for each peer which provided a vote:
   - If the voting peer P_j provides an accurate vote on either the torrent and the offerer.
     - For seeder $C_{ij} = C_{ij} + 0.05(1 + \Delta)$, only if the quality of the resource is good.
     - For others, $C_{ij} = C_{ij} + 0.05$
   - If the voting peer P_j provides an inaccurate vote on the torrent: $C_{ij} = 0$.

Submitting a final vote to the Tracker

   - After updating the state on local repositories, the peer P_i recalculates a new *vote certificate* on both the torrent and the offerer, then submits the vote via a FinalPoll message to the centralized tracker. After receiving the vote, the tracker deletes the old vote and updates the new vote $(P_i, v_H/v_{oi})$ on the corresponding torrent and offerer groups.

6   Security Considerations

Along with the distribution of good resources and services to peers in P2P networks, malicious peers can propagate inauthentic data or virus. Also, several research studies [8, 19, 14] indicate possible attacks based on reputation-based systems. In this section, we assert that our solution can prevent these attacks upon both BitTorrent networks and reputation-based systems.

6.1   Distribution on Fake Information

This attack exploits the fact that there is no way of verifying resources or peers in a BitTorrent network. In our solution, if a malicious user generates a torrent file to distribute a false resource, the offerer_id of the user and the info_hash of the torrent file will be associated with a bad reputation, and, its subsequent downloading therefore will be prevented.

6.2   Pseudospoofing

The simplest attack is undertaken by exploiting "cheap pseudonyms" in the reputation system. A malicious user registers a pseudonym, behaves in a corrupt manner for a while and then turns into a new pseudonym after earning a bad reputation. Our solution makes this attack ineffective because the behavior of a newcomer is limited with respect to influencing the voting process system.

However, we also provide several mechanisms to help newcomers to participate in the system. First, newcomers can acquire a high reputation value by actively sharing genuine resources and polling accurate votes. Second, newcomers can help to distribute genuine resources among peers to be granted greater credibility values. More uploading time gives more credibility. Third, newcomers can generate a large reliable credibility repository for themselves using the credibility chain exchange algorithm.

6.3   Reputation Spoofing

In this attack, malicious users try to find some vulnerability in the reputation algorithm and spoof the reputation scores. In our solution, the credibility parameter is the key that affects the performance of the system. The credibility value from A to B increases only if the votes from B are same as A's opinion. In our solution, attackers may take advantage of the *credibility award algorithm* or the *credibility chain exchange* to increase credibility as soon as possible. Fortunately, our reputation algorithms prevent this type of attack. The formula of the *credibility award algorithm* itself makes malicious attacks expensive to keep uploading over a long period and the increment of the award is limited rather than infinite. Also, the equation of the *credibility chain exchange* can protect against this attack by doing a multiplication of the sender's credibility.

6.4   Whitewashing Attack

This is a common attack in the eBay online transaction system. It refers to an attacker that actively participates in the system by providing genuine items, but occasionally dumps a small number of inferior goods to be sold to others. In our scheme, an attacker may distribute bona fide resources most of the times, while spreading malicious resources sometimes; or an attacker polls accurately on most offerers and torrent files, but gives a small number of incorrect votes to others. In the first case, although it is difficult to identify the attacker, our torrent reputation-based system can block the distribution of malicious resources by associating the torrent files with a bad reputation. For the second scenario, the occasional malicious-behavior still makes the credibility of the attacker to other peers drop sharply. This was proven in our experiments, which are demonstrated in the appendix section.

6.5   Reputation Attack by Collectives

When malicious users know each other, they may try to harm the system by acting as a group. Shilling is an attack of this kind. Instead of creating multiple phony identities as in a pseudospoofing attack, this attack maintains several 'real' identities in order to influence the voting process on a doctored resource and a malicious peer. It can be effectively guarded against through our solution, due to the existence of the credibility parameter. Although malicious attackers may submit false votes to gain high credibility values for each peer in the same group, the false votes may have a negative effect on other well-behavior users. Our mechanism deals with shilling by trying to ensure there is a great number of well-behaved users, making it expensive for malicious users to create and maintain a sufficient number of shills. Also, once shills provide a false vote, their credibility values will be set to zero.

6.6   Referral Attack

Referral attack takes advantage of the opportunity to discovering potential relationships with peers by introduction. It is a new attack, where a malicious attacker may forge a group of dummy and controlled peers, try to introduce them to other peers and then utilize the forged peers to influence the judgment of other peers. A malicious attacker will always behave well in the polling process to acquire high credibility ratings with other peers. The high ratings help the attacker to have the capability to introduce false peers to other peers. Using a digest-based mechanism to build cliques of false peers is easy in most reputation systems. Once the false peers have been accepted by other peers, the malicious peer can generate spoofed votes by using false Ids, and after that the decision of other peers may be influenced by those votes. Even though the credibility ratings of false peers may become zero due to negative votes, the malicious attacker is able to continuously introduce new forged peers.

In our protocol the self friend selection method that those malicious attackers are incapable of unconstrained introduction of peers. Also, users can establish a simple table to keep track of the reliability of friends introduced by other peers. If a malicious attacker introduces a false peer and utilizes the false Id to behave badly, his behavior can be witnessed in the table and he will be punished by the credibility ratings. These two solutions can be easily implemented and effectively prevent this kind of attack.

Furthermore, we have evaluated our system and shown that it is *reliable* and *effective*. We have conducted experiments on a large number of peers with multiplex characteristics in terms of varying numbers of resources, the introduction of polluted resources, noise on voting and different malicious strategies. An analysis of the results of these experiments has demonstrated a good understanding of our reputation system. However, due to the page limitation, we omit the detail in this paper and we refer the reader to the full version of this paper.

7 Conclusion

In this paper, we introduce a robust new reputation system called X^{2BT}Rep, which is designed on and easily integrated into the BitTorrent file sharing protocol. It is an extension of X^{2}Rep. However, we improve X^{2}Rep and outline two significant algorithms, *Credibility Award* and *Credibility Chain Exchange*, so that our solution guards against not only known attacks in P2P networks but also several shortcomings identified in other reputation systems. Furthermore, it retains certain the characteristics of anonymity and openness, in key P2P networks.

References

1. K. Aberer and Z. Despotovic. Managing trust in a peer-2-peer information system. Technical report, 2001.
2. E. Adar and B. Huberman. Free-riding on gnutella. *First Monday*, (5(10)), October 2000.
3. V. V. Bhat. Reputation management in peer-to-peer systems. Technical report, Department of Computer Sciences, University of Texas at Austin, December 2004, Available at http://www.cs.utexas.edu/ vishwas/documents/Reputation.pdf.
4. A.-J. B. Client. Available at http://azureus.sourceforge.net/.
5. B. Cohen. Incentives build robustness in bittorrent. *In Workshop on Economics of Peer-to-Peer Systems, Berkeley, CA, USA*, May 2003.
6. N. Curtis, R. Safavi-Naini, and W. Susilo. X^{2}rep: Enhanced trust semantics for the xrep protocol. *Applied Crypotgraphy and Network Security. Second International Conference ACNS2004 . Proceedings. LNCS3089*, pages 205–219, 2004.
7. E. Damiani, S. D. C. di Vimercati, S. Paraboschi, P. Samarati, and F. Violante. A reputation-based approach for choosing reliable resources in peer-to-peer networks. *Proceedings of the 9th ACM conference on Computer and Communications Security*, pages 207–216, November 2002.
8. C. Dellarocas. Immunizing outline reputation reporting system against unfair rating and discriminatory behavior. *2nd ACM Conference on Electronic Commerce*, pages 150–157, 2000.
9. C. Dellarocas. The digitization of word-of-mouth: Promise and challenges of online feedback mechanisms. *Management Science 49 (10)*, pages 1407–1424, 2003.

10. eDonkey protocol description. [Online]. http://kent.dl.sourceforge.net/pdonkey/eDonkey-protocol-0.6.2.html.

11. N. D. Eubanks. Bittorrent: Digital river of the hacker culture. *School of Information and Library Science, University of North Carolina at Chapel Hill*, April, 2005.

12. M. Izal, G. Urvoy-Keller, E. W. Biersack, P. A. Felber, A. A. Amra, and L. Garces-Erice. Dissecting bittorrent: five months in a torrent's lifetime. *PAM'2004, 5th Annual Passive & Active Measurement Workshop, April 19-20, 2004, Antibes Juan-les-Pins, France*, April 2004.

13. T. Karagiannis, A. Broido, N. Brownlee, K. Claffy, and M. Faloutsos. Is p2p dying or just hiding? *Presented at Globecom 2004, Dallas, TX*, November/December, 2004.

14. J. Kong. Formal notations of anonymity for peer-to-peer networks. Technical report, UCLA Computer Science Technical Report CSD-TR050016, May 2005.

15. R. Lemos. Bittorrent servers under attack. Available at http://news.com.com/BitTorrent+servers+under+attack/2100-7349_3-5473754.html?part=rss&tag=5473754&subj=news.7349.5.

16. K. media desktop. [Online]. Available at http://www.kazaa.com/.

17. T. Mennecke. Bittorrent remains powerhouse network. *Slyck News*, Available at http://www.slyck.com/news.php?story=649, January 31, 2005.

18. Napster. [Online]. Available at http://www.Napster.com/.

19. A. Oram. *Peer-to-Peer: Harnessing the Power of Disruptive Technologies*. O'Reilly & Associates, Inc., March 2001.

20. A. Parker. The true picture of peer-to-peer filesharing. [Online]. Available at http://www.cachelogic.com, 2004.

21. A. Pasick. Livewire - file-sharing network thrives beneath the radar. *Yahoo Technology News*, Available at http://in.tech.yahoo.com/041103/137/2ho4i.html.

22. J. O. Patterson. A matter of trust: Reputation management in peer-to-peer networks. Technical report, 2003, Available at http://csci.mrs.umn.edu/Personal/pub/Patterson/SeminarIIPaperDevelopment/sem2_draft.doc.

23. J. Pouwelse, P. Garbacki, D. Epema, and H. Sips. A measurement study of the bittorrent peer-to-peer file-sharing system. *Elsevier Science*, May 2004.

24. G. protocol development. [Online]. Available at http://rfc-gnutella.sf.net/.

25. D. Qiu and R. Shrikant. Modeling and performance analysis of bittorrent-like peer-to-peer networks. *SIGCOMM*, September 2004.

26. P. Resnick, R. Zeckhauser, E. Friedman, and K. Kuwabara. Reputation systems: Facilitating trust in internet interactions. *Communications of the ACM 43(12)*, 2000.

27. O. B. website. [Online]. Available at http://www.BitTorrent.com/.

Author Index

Lecture Notes in Computer Science

For information about Vols. 1–4231

please contact your bookseller or Springer

Vol. 4271: F.V. Fomin (Ed.), Graph-Theoretic Concepts in Computer Science. XIII, 358 pages. 2006.

Vol. 4270: H. Zha, Z. Pan, H. Thwaites, A.C. Addison, M. Forte (Eds.), Interactive Technologies and Sociotechnical Systems. XVI, 547 pages. 2006.

Vol. 4269: R. State, S. van der Meer, D. O'Sullivan, T. Pfeifer (Eds.), Large Scale Management of Distributed Systems. XIII, 282 pages. 2006.

Vol. 4268: G. Parr, D. Malone, M. Ó Foghlú (Eds.), Autonomic Principles of IP Operations and Management. XIII, 237 pages. 2006.

Vol. 4267: A. Helmy, B. Jennings, L. Murphy, T. Pfeifer (Eds.), Autonomic Management of Mobile Multimedia Services. XIII, 257 pages. 2006.

Vol. 4266: H. Yoshiura, K. Sakurai, K. Rannenberg, Y. Murayama, S. Kawamura (Eds.), Advances in Information and Computer Security. XIII, 438 pages. 2006.

Vol. 4265: L. Todorovski, N. Lavrač, K.P. Jantke (Eds.), Discovery Science. XIV, 384 pages. 2006. (Sublibrary LNAI).

Vol. 4264: J.L. Balcázar, P.M. Long, F. Stephan (Eds.), Algorithmic Learning Theory. XIII, 393 pages. 2006. (Sublibrary LNAI).

Vol. 4263: A. Levi, E. Savas, H. Yenigün, S. Balcisoy, Y. Saygin (Eds.), Computer and Information Sciences – ISCIS 2006. XXIII, 1084 pages. 2006.

Vol. 4262: K. Havelund, M. N\'u\~nez, G. Ro\csu, B. Wolff (Eds.), Formal Approaches to Software Testing and Runtime Verification. XXXXXX, 24555555 pages. 2006.

Vol. 4261: Y. Zhuang, S. Yang, Y. Rui, Q. He (Eds.), Advances in Multimedia Information Processing - PCM 2006. XXII, 1040 pages. 2006.

Vol. 4260: Z. Liu, J. He (Eds.), Formal Methods and Software Engineering. XII, 778 pages. 2006.

Vol. 4259: S. Greco, Y. Hata, S. Hirano, M. Inuiguchi, S. Miyamoto, H.S. Nguyen, R. Słowiński (Eds.), Rough Sets and Current Trends in Computing. XXII, 951 pages. 2006. (Sublibrary LNAI).

Vol. 4257: I. Richardson, P. Runeson, R. Messnarz (Eds.), Software Process Improvement. XI, 219 pages. 2006.

Vol. 4256: L. Feng, G. Wang, C. Zeng, R. Huang (Eds.), Web Information Systems – WISE 2006 Workshops. XIV, 320 pages. 2006.

Vol. 4255: K. Aberer, Z. Peng, E.A. Rundensteiner, Y. Zhang, X. Li (Eds.), Web Information Systems – WISE 2006. XIV, 563 pages. 2006.

Vol. 4254: T. Grust, H. Höpfner, A. Illarramendi, S. Jablonski, M. Mesiti, S. Müller, P.-L. Patranjan, K.-U. Sattler, M. Spiliopoulou, J. Wijsen (Eds.), Current Trends in Database Technology – EDBT 2006. XXXI, 932 pages. 2006.

Vol. 4253: B. Gabrys, R.J. Howlett, L.C. Jain (Eds.), Knowledge-Based Intelligent Information and Engineering Systems, Part III. XXXII, 1301 pages. 2006. (Sublibrary LNAI).

Vol. 4252: B. Gabrys, R.J. Howlett, L.C. Jain (Eds.), Knowledge-Based Intelligent Information and Engineering Systems, Part II. XXXIII, 1335 pages. 2006. (Sublibrary LNAI).

Vol. 4251: B. Gabrys, R.J. Howlett, L.C. Jain (Eds.), Knowledge-Based Intelligent Information and Engineering Systems, Part I. LXVI, 1297 pages. 2006. (Sublibrary LNAI).

Vol. 4250: H.J. van den Herik, S.-C. Hsu, T.-s. Hsu, H.H.L.M. Donkers (Eds.), Advances in Computer Games. XIV, 273 pages. 2006.

Vol. 4249: L. Goubin, M. Matsui (Eds.), Cryptographic Hardware and Embedded Systems - CHES 2006. XII, 462 pages. 2006.

Vol. 4248: S. Staab, V. Svátek (Eds.), Managing Knowledge in a World of Networks. XIV, 400 pages. 2006. (Sublibrary LNAI).

Vol. 4247: T.-D. Wang, X. Li, S.-H. Chen, X. Wang, H. Abbass, H. Iba, G. Chen, X. Yao (Eds.), Simulated Evolution and Learning. XXI, 940 pages. 2006.

Vol. 4246: M. Hermann, A. Voronkov (Eds.), Logic for Programming, Artificial Intelligence, and Reasoning. XIII, 588 pages. 2006. (Sublibrary LNAI).

Vol. 4245: A. Kuba, L.G. Nyúl, K. Palágyi (Eds.), Discrete Geometry for Computer Imagery. XIII, 688 pages. 2006.

Vol. 4244: S. Spaccapietra (Ed.), Journal on Data Semantics VII. XI, 267 pages. 2006.

Vol. 4243: T. Yakhno, E.J. Neuhold (Eds.), Advances in Information Systems. XIII, 420 pages. 2006.

Vol. 4242: A. Rashid, M. Aksit (Eds.), Transactions on Aspect-Oriented Software Development II. IX, 289 pages. 2006.

Vol. 4241: R.R. Beichel, M. Sonka (Eds.), Computer Vision Approaches to Medical Image Analysis. XI, 262 pages. 2006.

Vol. 4239: H.Y. Youn, M. Kim, H. Morikawa (Eds.), Ubiquitous Computing Systems. XVI, 548 pages. 2006.

Vol. 4238: Y.-T. Kim, M. Takano (Eds.), Management of Convergence Networks and Services. XVIII, 605 pages. 2006.

Vol. 4237: H. Leitold, E. Markatos (Eds.), Communications and Multimedia Security. XII, 253 pages. 2006.

Vol. 4236: L. Breveglieri, I. Koren, D. Naccache, J.-P. Seifert (Eds.), Fault Diagnosis and Tolerance in Cryptography. XIII, 253 pages. 2006.

Vol. 4234: I. King, J. Wang, L. Chan, D. Wang (Eds.), Neural Information Processing, Part III. XXII, 1227 pages. 2006.

Vol. 4233: I. King, J. Wang, L. Chan, D. Wang (Eds.), Neural Information Processing, Part II. XXII, 1203 pages. 2006.

Vol. 4232: I. King, J. Wang, L. Chan, D. Wang (Eds.), Neural Information Processing, Part I. XLVI, 1153 pages. 2006.